FIFTH EDITION **Understanding Industrial Relations**

FIFTH EDITION # Understanding Industrial Relations

**DAVID FARNHAM**
*Professor of Employment Relations*
*University of Portsmouth*

**JOHN PIMLOTT**
*Lecturer in Industrial Relations*
*University of Southampton*

CASSELL

Cassell
Villiers House
41/47 Strand
London WC2N 5JE

387 Park Avenue South
New York
NY 10016-8810

First edition 1979
Second edition 1983
Third edition 1986
Fourth edition 1990
Fifth edition 1995

**British Library Cataloguing-in-Publication Data**
A catalogue record for this book is available from the British Library

ISBN 0-304-33155-4 (hardback)
      0-304-33083-3 (paperback)

Typeset by Colset Private Limited, Singapore
Printed and bound in Great Britain by The Bath Press

# Contents

# Preface to Fifth Edition

In this edition, we have extensively updated the empirical data to bring our book into line with what has happened in industrial relations since 1990, when the previous edition appeared. This edition takes into account recent changes in the labour market, employment practices, the law and Europe, insofar as these impinge on contemporary British industrial relations. We would like to thank all those colleagues who contributed to getting this edition to the publishers on time, especially Sylvia Horton, without whose assistance we would have been unable to update Chapter 7.

David Farnham
John Pimlott

*October 1994*

# Preface to First Edition

The purpose of this book is to provide a comprehensive introduction to British industrial relations in its wider contexts. Whilst it is aimed primarily at students of industrial relations whether they are managers or trade unionists, this book can be used by practitioners of industrial relations, by those reading for degrees and professional qualifications, and by anyone who wants an understanding of the principles and practices of contemporary industrial relations. This text should also be useful to the lay public and specialist groups, such as the teaching profession, who would like a broad appreciation of how those involved in industrial relations regulate and conduct their business together. In this way, we hope, our readers will obtain a better knowledge and awareness of the multiplicity of factors influencing employment practices and the ways in which industrial relations decisions are made in Britain today.

We have written this book for three main reasons. First, our experience as teachers of industrial relations over a number of years has made us increasingly aware that there is a need for an introductory book in this field. In it, we seek not only to explain British industrial relations practices and to put them into their wider social perspectives, but also to examine them through explicit descriptive, analytical and conceptual frameworks. Second, with the increasing volume of labour law, the debate about worker participation in managerial decision making, and the variety of industrial relations changes which have taken place in Britain since the early 1970s, we consider that the time is now right to attempt a synthesis of some of the recent literature and principal research findings in the field. Third, in undertaking this task, we believe that our complementary academic and teaching backgrounds – in addition to our previous industrial experiences – give some degree of balance to our study of industrial relations.

David Farnham
John Pimlott

*July 1979*

# Introduction

This book provides a comprehensive introduction to British industrial relations. Its aim is to put British industrial relations practices, and the contexts in which they take place, into satisfactory descriptive and analytical frameworks. It is an approach, we hope, which not only is rigorous in its method but also relates the realities of British industrial relations to a sound conceptual base. Our purpose throughout is to describe and outline those empirical findings and analytical tools which help to explain the complex nature of industrial relations between employers and employees in their many contrasting, often contradictory, and sometimes confusing aspects. We hope that in using this book, our readers will gain some insights into the rich diversity and yet underlying coherence of British industrial relations.

Because of this complexity, our objective is to achieve some degree of balance between being comprehensive in our coverage and selective in the use of material; between considering common practices and theoretical principles; between providing concrete examples and abstract concepts; and between discussing past experience and present controversy. We are not seeking to produce an industrial relations handbook or an instant kit of industrial relations tools which can be mechanically applied to solve industrial relations problems, even if this were possible. We seek, rather, to provide a book which is informative, thought-provoking and balanced in its views, but which demonstrates the uniqueness of British industrial relations and encourages its readers to be sceptical about simplistic explanations of industrial relations phenomena and behaviour.

We start from three basic assumptions about the nature of industrial relations in Britain. The first is that the focus of industrial relations is how individuals and groups, the organizations representing their interests and wider institutional forces determine decisions affecting employment relationships. These include the contractual relationships between employers and employees and the power relationships between employers and trade unions. Implicit in our approach is the view that employers, managers, employees, trade unions and government all have interests in industrial relations decision making in our sort of society. Industrial relations is not the sole prerogative of management or the trade unions: it is an activity in which all these groups are vitally concerned.

Our second assumption is that industrial relations practices are indivisible from their concepts, principles and theories. What happens in industrial relations and how it happens are its *practices*. They are essentially empirical phenomena and are best identified by the descriptive method. Arising out of such practices is a language of industrial relations. These are its *concepts*. Although these concepts are abstract and analytic, they are useful in describing and classifying industrial relations phenomena. Closely related to the concepts of industrial relations are its *principles*. They centre on the patterns of order, systematization and regularity which are discernible within industrial relations practices and situations. They identify and separate out the essential characteristics and general conventions of industrial relations. They have to be understood by students of industrial relations and applied by industrial relations practitioners.

At a higher level of abstraction still, why certain practices happen in industrial relations are its *theories*. These are explanatory in nature although if they are used prescriptively theories can have a 'normative' character. When used normatively, industrial relations theories depend on an individual's value judgments and perception of the world, suggesting what 'ought to be' in given social situations. Compared with the practices, concepts and principles of industrial relations, its theories are more likely to be the subject of greater speculation, whether by academics, practitioners or others. Nevertheless, theories are essential since without theories of behaviour, people can neither act out their own social roles nor understand the roles of others and their social environments. Ultimately a social theory is a way of perceiving, understanding and predicting people's actions in practical, real-life situations. Those 'practical' people who insist that they are immune from abstract 'theory' are usually unaware of the preconceptions or prejudices which determine their own views of the world in which they live. As John Maynard Keynes commented many years ago: 'practical men, who believe themselves to be quite exempt from any intellectual influences, are usually the slaves of some defunct economist'.[1]

Collective bargaining, for example, is a common industrial relations practice. What it is, how it operates and its results can be observed and described in specific cases. In general terms, collective bargaining is also an industrial relations concept and it can be described and analysed as such. Its basic principles, such as the conditions necessary for its existence, its main elements, its structure, and its strengths and weaknesses, for instance, can then be abstracted and compared with other industrial relations practices and so on. Ultimately, through the processes of reasoning, observation and empirical investigation, the essential nature of collective bargaining, its fundamental purposes and why it exists can be examined and discussed in their theoretic contexts. Some commentators, for example, explain collective bargaining in economic terms, some as a political process, and others as a reflection of class relations in capitalist economies. In short, by using the appropriate conceptual, analytic and theoretic tools, we are better able to describe, analyse and understand the practices of collective bargaining or of any other industrial relations activity.

Our third assumption derives from the second. It is that different people perceive industrial relations in different ways and from different theoretical positions. This is one of the problems in teaching and in learning about industrial relations: there is no single approach to the subject which satisfies everyone. Some people view industrial relations in terms of class conflict between the owners of private capital and the working class with wage labour to sell. Others see it in terms of industrial conflict between employers and employees and their representative organizations. Others see conflict of any kind at work as being abnormal, unnecessary and anti-social. For these reasons, industrial relations becomes both an academic and a political arena where the opposing ideologies and different value systems of individuals and groups compete against one another and for the minds and actions of the uncommitted.

These three fundamental assumptions are the cornerstones upon which this book is based. Our method and the descriptive and explanatory frameworks which we have arrived at and use stem from these assumptions. It is an approach, we believe, which describes, analyses and explains the complex nature of industrial relations in advanced market economies like that of Britain.

Our approach is essentially an *institutional* one which we believe to be useful for students new to the subject. This does not deny the validity of other approaches deriving from behavioural, systems or Marxist assumptions. However, our starting point in trying to understand industrial relations is that it comprises a *network of institutions* or a 'patterned set of social relationships directed towards a definable set of social objectives'.[2] Institutions of all kinds, whether they are political, economic, social or industrial relations ones, have an existence beyond the particular persons involved in them at any one time and, within certain limits, they establish the patterns of social behaviour amongst their participants by institutionalizing them. In other words, the behaviour of people within an institution is constrained within certain expected social norms and parameters. Individual and group behaviour which is institutionalized is largely conditioned by the expectations both of others within the institution and of society generally as to how its participants *should* behave. It seems to be tautological but trade unionists, for example, behave as trade unionists precisely because they are members of trade unions. It is unions as organizations and trade unionists as people, bound together by a set of common norms and common values, which make up the 'institution' of trade unionism.

In addition to trade unionism, there are other major industrial relations institutions considered in this book. These include collective bargaining, employers, the law, management and the state's role in industrial relations. A knowledge of these institutions and their individual participants is important if we are to understand everyday industrial relations situations. It is these institutions which largely predetermine the broad limits within which industrial relations practitioners and participants, such as managers, trade unionists and third-party representatives, act in practical situations. We repeat, because of their involvement in industrial relations, the behaviour of the participants becomes institu-tionalized within certain expected norms and parameters. Although industrial relations institutions are broadly compatible with one another, there are nevertheless conflicts between and within them. The norms and values associated with an institution like trade unionism, for example, may be directly con-trary to some of those associated with the institution of management, the principles of shop steward organization or those of the state.

The institutions of industrial relations subsume four subsidiary social networks. These are a *network of organizations*; a *network of participants*; a *net-work of processes*; and a *network of decisions*: all of which interact and interrelate together within the industrial relations environment and beyond it. The main industrial relations organizations existing in Britain include, for example, the Advisory Concilia-tion and Arbitration Service; the Central Arbitration Committee; employers' associations, firms and other work enterprises acting as employers; industrial tribunals; shop stewards committees; and trade unions. In turn, the industrial relations participants operating within and among these organizations include arbitrators, conciliators and mediators; union branch officers; full-time trade union officers; personnel officers; managers; officials of employers' associations; union stewards; trade union members; and employees who are either members or not members of trade unions.

Similarly, there are a number of industrial relations processes through which industrial decisions are made and implemented. These include: conciliation; dispute settlement; grievance handling; industrial tribunals; negotiation; joint consultation; managerial prerogatives; trade union policy making; strikes; lock-outs; conflict avoidance procedures and so on. Finally, industrial relations decisions can be found in a variety of sources, including: arbitration awards; case law; collective agreements; courts of inquiry; custom and practice at the workplace; the findings of industrial tribunals; parliamentary statutes; union rule books; works rules and so on. It is this network of institutions, with their subsidiary networks of organizations, participants, processes and decisions, which provides the core of industrial relations and the main elements of this book.

The book is divided into four parts. Part One gives the general background to industrial relations. First we identify and describe the labour market and economic context within which industrial relations

take place (Chapter 1). Second, we examine and compare the main theories of industrial relations to provide a framework for analysing industrial rela-tions institutions, practices and activities throughout the text (Chapter 2).

Part Two focuses on the main institutional and organizational features of British industrial relations. Initially we analyse the nature of employers and management and the ways in which they manage industrial relations with unions, employees and their representatives (Chapter 3). We then consider the roles of employers' associations as representatives and agents of employer interests (Chapter 4). This leads on to an examination of trade unions as bargaining agencies, their structures and internal organization, and how they conduct their internal and interunion affairs (Chapter 5). This is followed by an outline of the nature, structure and results of collective bargaining in both the private and public sectors (Chapter 6).

Part Three is concerned with the state and indus-trial relations. First we describe and analyse the relationships between employers and the Conser-vative Party, the unions and the Labour Party and the roles of the Confederation of British Industry and the Trades Union Congress (Chapter 7). We then discuss the principles underlying state intervention in indus-trial relations, including its traditional role and its emerging one, as well as the activities of state agencies in industrial relations (Chapter 8). Next the elements of individual employment law and trade union law are outlined. We look at, for example, the contract of employment, the job protection rights of employees, trade unions and the law, and the law regulating union ballots, picketing and trade disputes (Chapters 9 and 10).

In Part Four, we examine industrial relations practices at workplace and establishment level. The right to manage and employment practices are explored, as well as the non-union firm (Chapter 11). We then turn to the personnel management function within enterprises outlining its scope, activities, tasks and relationship to line management, and examining the debate about personnel and human resources management (Chapter 12). The importance of union stewards and workgroup representation is also considered, with the workplace relationships between stewards and managers outlined and accounted for (Chapter 13). In the next chapter, we examine the central part which negotiating and con-sultative machinery and employee involvement practices play in regulating relations between employers and employees and employers and trade unions at enterprise level (Chapter 14). Finally, we focus on the changing balance of power in industrial relations and draw some tentative conclusions about the emerging patterns of industrial relations in the 1990s (Chapter 15).

References

1. J. M. Keynes, *The General Theory of Employment, Interest and Money*, Macmillan, London, 1936, p. 383.
2. D. Martin (ed.), *50 Key Words: Sociology*, Lutterworth Press, Guildford, 1970, p. 35.

# PART ONE

## The Background to Industrial Relations

# 1

# Labour Markets and the Economic Context

The labour market influences a variety of industrial relations institutions and practices. These include: working practices; personnel management; collective bargaining; wage levels and structures; terms and conditions of employment; and the recruitment, selection and retention policies of employers. When the labour market changes, all these aspects of employment and employment relations begin the painful process of adjustment. In turn, the labour market is affected by the general level of economic activity, changes in the level of unemployment and technological change. Other factors influencing the labour market include: the birth-rate; the number of men and women willing to work and seeking work; and the output of educational and training establishments.

The British labour market is an extremely complex and varied institution, with a multiplicity of specialized sub-markets. In these markets, those offering their abilities, knowledge and specialist skills sell them to those wishing to buy them in order to meet the human resource needs of their enterprises. This chapter outlines the major characteristics of the labour market and shows how changes in its composition affect industrial relations in many ways. It also shows that the free play of labour market forces is moderated to varying degrees by a number of factors. These include: the economic policies of governments; the collective bargaining power of trade unions; taxation policies; income thresholds provided by social security payments; social changes, such as the role played by women in modern society; technological change; the legal regulation of employment; social and cultural attitudes to work; and, more recently, the laws and social policies of the European Union (Figure 1.1).

## 1.1 The Importance of Labour Markets

The labour market is of considerable importance to those seeking work, as well as to those already in employment. It affects employers recruiting and selecting new employees and trade unions seeking to protect their members' terms and conditions of employment. How and where to obtain labour with the qualities and in the quantities required by the needs of an organization is a major task of personnel or human resources management. If the labour market is slack, usually meaning that the level of unemployment is relatively high, the employer is able to pick and choose and obtain labour at wage rates advantageous to itself. Yet it is not uncommon for employers to discover, despite a high overall rate of unemployment, that it is still very difficult to find people with appropriate skills, knowledge and abilities. If the labour market is tight, usually meaning a low level of unemployment, employers can also find it difficult to obtain the labour they want. Consequently, they often have to raise the level of pay offered and improve the terms of employment of those working for them.

Where employers are situated in one of the more prosperous areas of Britain, they might find it almost impossible to secure the labour they need on the open market. They therefore resort to the expensive and inflationary device of raising pay levels sufficiently to attract employees away from other firms. If they are unable to obtain additional employees, they might decide to recruit in the less prosperous regions and offer assistance with relocation and other expenses. They might even decide to expand their businesses into those areas. Alternatively, they might decide to change their approach to the labour market and use employment agencies, recruit unskilled people and train them, or recruit older people. Increasingly, they seek to attract married women into the labour force by offering training and convenient hours of employment.

Another strategy is for the employing organization to decide not to accept more contracts or orders than it can effectively handle, given its present labour capacity. This is a dangerous option as the organization could eventually lose its place in its product

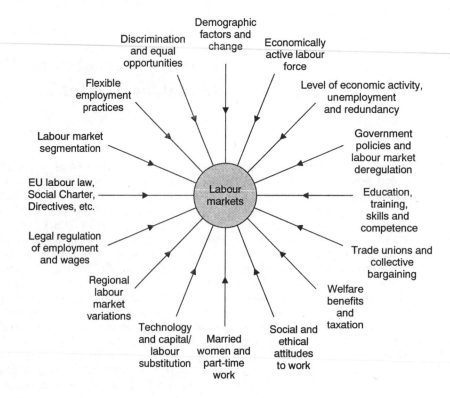

*Figure 1.1* Factors influencing and shaping labour markets.

market and be unable to compete with those firms choosing expansion. Any individual employing organization can develop many methods and practices in relation to the labour markets with which it interfaces. But it is generally agreed that, apart from a few minor adjustments, it cannot influence the long-term supply of labour available to it.

The importance of the labour market to unemployed people seeking jobs, and to those with jobs but looking for better ones, lies in the market's ability to provide them with the information which allows them to make advantageous choices. If any labour market is to work efficiently and fairly, participants must possess considerable knowledge of the forces operating within and upon the market, as well as detailed understanding of what it can provide and at what prices. There is considerable evidence to suggest that many employers and employees possess at best an imperfect knowledge of labour market conditions and pay rates. Employers are often at a loss in estimating what pay and conditions they should offer in order to secure certain types of labour, as well as where and how to find it. Similarly, many employees

have only a vague idea of what wage and salary levels are paid elsewhere for their types of skills, educational qualifications and experience. Even when they are aware that higher wages could be obtained elsewhere they often do not act upon it:

> when people change jobs or decide not to move, a complex of social and psychological factors affect their choice much more than differences in pay . . . the knowledge that workers have of alternative employment opportunities, and their ability to respond to them by moving house, or travelling longer distances to work, are severely limited. In all these ways the labour market differs from what is supposed to happen in the product market, or the market for money.[1]

Obviously, despite the vital role they play in allocating and deploying labour amongst different employers, labour markets are hedged about with all sorts of practical limitations and restrictions.

For trade unions the structure of the labour market is important, since increases or decreases in the supply of labour or demand for it affect membership numbers and union bargaining power. Much of the history of the growth and decline in union membership is related to changes, over relatively long periods, in the labour market. The labour market is, in turn, affected by economic factors such as the growth rate of the economy, the decline in certain industries and the emergence and expansion of others. Technological change also affects demand and supply in the labour market, as old skills become obsolete and new ones emerge. Trade unions have little choice but to adjust in the long term to these economic and labour market movements. In the past they sought to slow down the impact of labour market changes by the use of strict apprenticeship controls, by closed-shop agreements, by imposing strict job demarcation rules and by refusing to accept new technologies. But these devices rarely, if ever, stem the forces of labour market change in the long term, and are hardly used at all now.

Trade unions also seek to mitigate labour market forces through collective bargaining. They do this by seeking to establish higher rates of pay, and better conditions of employment, than might otherwise prevail if free market forces were left to operate. How successful collective bargaining has been in moderating labour market forces has been the subject of a great deal of research and debate among labour market economists. The consensus of opinion appears to be that in the short term trade unions might be successful, through collective bargaining, in establishing better pay rates than market forces suggest should be the case. They at least prevent a relative fall in real pay. But in the long run, it seems, market forces prevail, moderated to some extent by traditional expectations of what constitutes the right social and customary differentials between occupations.

## 1.2  The Working Population

The British working population, or the civilian labour force, when measured as a proportion of the total population gives an important insight into the country's level of social and economic development. In pre-industrial Britain, without compulsory schooling, and where the means of support in retirement and in sickness were extremely unevenly distributed, almost all but the very young and the very old were in some form of active work. In late twentieth-century Britain, with a high proportion of elderly people and large numbers of young people continuing their education after the age of 16 years, with few people working beyond the contractual age of

retirement and many taking early retirement, plus a relatively high rate of unemployment, only a relatively small proportion of the population is in the active labour force. But for the considerable number of married women entering the labour market (over 3 million since 1971), the fall would be substantial. The trend, therefore, is for the labour force to constitute a smaller proportion of the total population. This has developed along with rising living standards. It has been made possible by long-term improvements in the gross national product per capita, productivity increases and the development and application of new technologies and working methods.

### The labour force and participation rates

The civilian labour force in Britain consists of people aged 16 or over with jobs, excluding those in the armed forces, together with those in that age group seeking work. In 1991, the labour force numbered about 28 million people, comprising 15.8 million men and 12.2 million women, of whom 2.4 million were unemployed (Figure 1.2).

Between 1971 and 1991, the active labour force grew by 3.2 million, with the years between 1983 and 1991 accounting for over two million of that figure. Official projections, however, suggest that between 1991 and 2001, the labour force will grow by only 0.8 million. Most of the growth in the labour force between 1971 and 1991 came from women, other than female school and college leavers, entering the labour market. Furthermore, between 1991 and 2001, while the growth of men in the labour force will be less than 1 per cent, there will be 5.4 per cent more women. Women, by 2001, are expected to make up to 45 per cent of the labour force (Figure 1.3 and Table 1.1). The overall size of the labour force is, therefore, determined by two fundamental factors. First, there is the *population effect*; that is, the number in the population in each age group. Second, there is the *activity rate effect*; that is, the proportion of the population in different age and sex groups in the labour force.

Between 1979 and 1993, the labour force increased in size each year except for the years 1982, 1983 and 1991. The increases are almost entirely owing to women, mainly married women, entering the labour force: over three million between 1971 and 1991. By comparison, during the same period the number of men only increased by some 300 000 or 10 per cent of the female rate of increase.

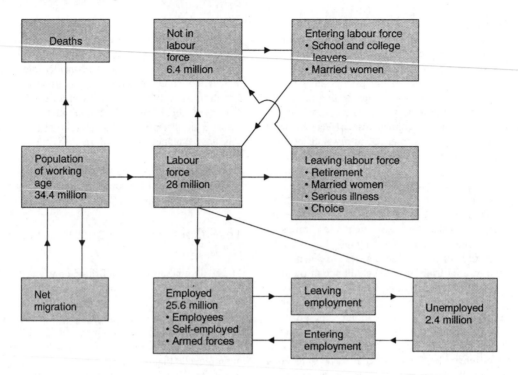

*Figure 1.2* Labour force movements in Britain 1991.

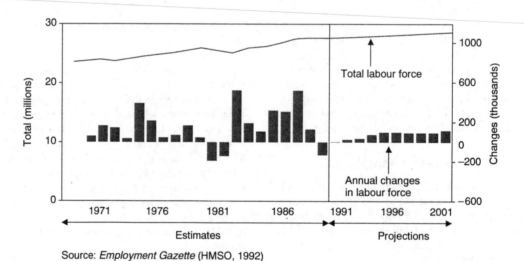

Source: *Employment Gazette* (HMSO, 1992)

*Figure 1.3* Estimates and projections of the total and annual changes in the civilian labour force in Great Britain 1971–2001.

*Table 1.1* Estimates and projections of the civilian labour force by age and sex in Great Britain, 1971, 1992 and 2001.

| Age | 1971 (thousands) | | | 1991 (thousands) | | | 2001 (thousands) | | | Percentage change 1991–2001 | | |
|---|---|---|---|---|---|---|---|---|---|---|---|---|
| | Men | Women | Total | Men | Women | Total | Men | Women | Total | Men | Women | Total |
| 16–19 | 1 054 | 947 | 2 001 | 1 113 | 1 015 | 2 128 | 1 086 | 935 | 2 021 | −2.4 | −7.9 | −5.0 |
| 20–24 | 1 839 | 1 241 | 3 080 | 1 903 | 1 559 | 3 462 | 1 439 | 1 239 | 2 678 | −24.4 | −20.5 | −22.6 |
| 25–34 | 3 249 | 1 523 | 4 772 | 4 130 | 3 012 | 7 142 | 3 755 | 2 967 | 6 722 | −9.0 | −1.5 | −5.9 |
| 35–44 | 3 067 | 1 883 | 4 950 | 3 658 | 2 957 | 6 615 | 4 101 | 3 493 | 7 594 | 112.1 | 18.1 | 14.8 |
| 45–54 | 3 132 | 2 104 | 5 236 | 2 929 | 2 343 | 5 272 | 3 397 | 2 789 | 6 186 | 16.0 | 19.0 | 17.3 |
| 55–59(f)/64(m) | 2 688 | 869 | 3 557 | 1 865 | 786 | 2 651 | 1 993 | 907 | 2 900 | 6.9 | 15.4 | 9.4 |
| Over 60(f)/65(m) | 534 | 764 | 1 298 | 298 | 513 | 811 | 229 | 516 | 745 | 23.1 | 0.6 | 8.1 |
| All ages | 15 563 | 9 331 | 24 894 | 15 896 | 12 185 | 28 081 | 16 000 | 12 846 | 28 846 | 0.7 | 5.4 | 2.7 |

*Source: Labour Market Quarterly Review* (May 1992) and *Employment Gazette* (HMSO, 1992)

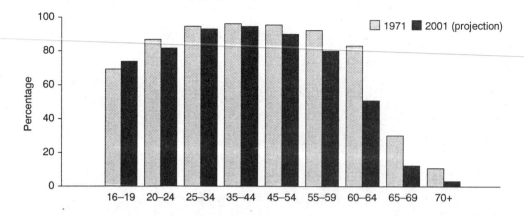

Source: *Employment Gazette* (HMSO, 1992)

*Figure 1.4* Labour force activity rates by age, men.

The labour force is projected to grow only slightly up to 2001, at a rate appreciably slower than for the decade 1981–91. The composition of the projected labour force up to 2001 reveals a rise in the 35–59 age group and a fall in the 20–34 group. In short, the age profile of the labour force will rise, with many fewer young people being represented. However, these official projections of only slight growth in the overall size of the labour force up to 2001, with women accounting for 90 per cent of the increase, assume stable economic activity and stable demand for labour. Should either a sharp increase or a sharp decrease in the level of national economic activity take place, these labour force projections will need revision.

The main cause of the projected slow and slight growth in the labour force up to 2001 is the low birth rate years of the 1970s. The number of young people of 16 plus in the labour force has fallen markedly compared with the 1970s and 1980s. The impact of this so-called 'demographic timebomb', has, however, been obscured by the economic recession of the early 1990s, but should rapid economic growth take place its consequences will quickly become apparent, with far fewer people in their twenties being available for work by the late 1990s.

The diverging activity rates of males and females in the labour force will, as previously stated, bring about fundamental shifts in the pattern of employment by 2001. Figures 1.4 and 1.5 compare the estimated activity rates for men and women in 1971, by age groups, with projected activity rates for 2001. For women the activity rate will have increased sharply in all age groups, except for those over 60; while for men it will have fallen for all but the 16–19 group. The most striking change will be the increased activity rates for females aged between 25 and 44.

This reflects a number of economic and social factors, such as the availability of part-time work and child-care facilities, and changes in social attitudes which have meant that women born later in the century have tended to have a greater underlying attachment to the labour force.[2]

Other trends revealed by Figure 1.3 and Table 1.1 include:

- the activity rate for males between 25 and 44 declined slightly during the 1980s and is projected to continue to do so to 2001;
- most of the decline in the male activity rate for the 55-plus group took place during the 1980s, and while this decline will continue up to 2001 it will be at a much slower rate;
- for both males and females the activity rate for the 60 plus group will continue to fall, though the fall will be sharper for males.

These projections concerning the labour force to 2001 rest on two important assumptions. First, while the population projections are safe, because changes in the birth and death rates will have little effect on the labour force by 2001, the assumptions concerning emigration and immigration could prove incorrect if unexpected population movements result, for example, from the Single European Market, and development in Eastern Europe, Hong Kong and elsewhere.

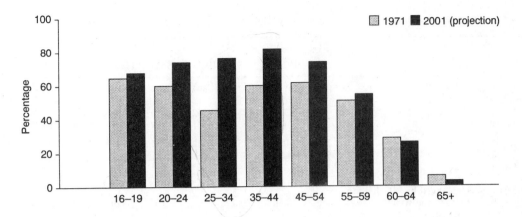

Source: *Employment Gazette* (HMSO, 1992)

*Figure 1.5* Labour force activity rates by age, women.

Second, unemployment levels could move unexpectedly either up or down. For example, a rise or fall of half a million on the unemployment figure could, by 2001, decrease or increase the labour force by some 200 000.

## Employment by industry and occupation

The main trends in employment in major economic sectors have been apparent for many years. As shown in Table 1.2, employment has shifted substantially from the manufacturing sector to the services sector during the past 20 years. Employment changes by industry group, as demonstrated by Table 1.2, show substantial reductions in employment in agriculture, forestry and fishing; energy and water supply; coalmining and quarrying; steel making; heavy engineering and vehicles; manufacturing industry; and construction. All these industries provided long-term, full-time employment for large numbers of skilled and semi-skilled men.

The long, slow decline in the relative size of Britain's manufacturing base can be traced back to before the Second World War. But since 1979, the decline has clearly accelerated. This decline in manufacturing capacity has been accompanied by a rise in the importation of manufactured goods and a transfer of employment to the public sector and especially private sector service industries, including distribution and financial services.

The changing pattern of occupational employment is illustrated by Table 1.3, which compares broad occupational groupings in 1984 and 1991. Unskilled manual occupations have seen the sharpest reductions, alongside considerable growth in white-collar work, including substantial increases in professional, administrative, managerial, technical, caring and clerical occupations. Noticeable growth has also taken place in self-employment and those on government work-schemes and in training.

Along with these industrial and occupational changes has come a shift in the pattern of regional employment. The manufacturing and industrial areas of Britain, such as the North West, South Wales, Scotland and the North East, have lost employment and the South East, East Anglia and the South West have gained employment, especially in private sector services and new technology industries. The sharp decline in Britain's manufacturing base to around one-quarter of total output has been made possible without severe drops in living standards by the contribution of North Sea oil and gas revenues. It has also been facilitated by the growth of private sector services in areas such as banking, insurance, finance, hotels, catering and tourism. The new industries associated with computers and microelectronics have also contributed to employment and national income growth.

The impact on industrial relations during the 1980s of these changes in the overall regional, occupational and industrial pattern of employment has been significant. The importance of the long-established structure of national collective bargaining based upon whole industries such as engineering, coal, steel, docks and railways has declined, along with employment and trade union membership. A new

*Table 1.2* Employees in employment: by sex and industry, United Kingdom (thousands).

| | SIC*<br>(1980) | 1971 | 1979 | 1981 | 1983 | 1986 | 1990 | 1991 | 1992 |
|---|---|---|---|---|---|---|---|---|---|
| **All industries** | 0–9 | 22 139 | 23 173 | 21 892 | 21 067 | 21 387 | 22 899 | 22 229 | 21 758 |
| of which | | | | | | | | | |
| Males | | 13 726 | 13 487 | 12 562 | 11 940 | 11 744 | 12 069 | 11 592 | 11 253 |
| Females | | 8 413 | 9 686 | 9 331 | 9 127 | 9 644 | 10 830 | 10 637 | 10 504 |
| Manufacturing | 2–4 | 8 065 | 7 253 | 6 222 | 5 525 | 5 227 | 5 138 | 4 793 | 4 589 |
| Services | 6–9 | 11 627 | 13 580 | 13 468 | 13 501 | 14 297 | 15 945 | 15 744 | 15 644 |
| Other | 0,1,5 | 2 447 | 2 340 | 2 203 | 2 042 | 1 863 | 1 817 | 1 692 | 1 524 |
| **Employees in employment by SIC division** | | | | | | | | | |
| Agriculture, forestry and fishing | 0 | 450 | 380 | 363 | 350 | 329 | 298 | 291 | 283 |
| Energy and water supply | 1 | 798 | 722 | 710 | 648 | 545 | 449 | 439 | 403 |
| Other minerals and ore extraction etc | 2 | 1 282 | 1 147 | 939 | 817 | 729 | 721 | 657 | 635 |
| Metal goods, engineering and vehicles | 3 | 3 709 | 3 374 | 2 923 | 2 548 | 2 372 | 2 310 | 2 139 | 2 030 |
| Other manufacturing industries | 4 | 3 074 | 2 732 | 2 360 | 2 159 | 2 126 | 2 106 | 1 997 | 1 924 |
| Construction | 5 | 1 198 | 1 239 | 1 130 | 1 044 | 989 | 1 070 | 962 | 839 |
| Distribution, catering and repairs | 6 | 3 686 | 4 257 | 4 172 | 4 118 | 4 298 | 4 822 | 4 686 | 4 605 |
| Transport and communication | 7 | 1 556 | 1 479 | 1 425 | 1 345 | 1 298 | 1 382 | 1 349 | 1 324 |
| Banking, finance, insurance, etc | 8 | 1 336 | 1 647 | 1 739 | 1 875 | 2 166 | 2 744 | 2 687 | 2 639 |
| Other services | 9 | 5 049 | 6 197 | 6 132 | 6 163 | 6 536 | 6 996 | 7 022 | 7 076 |

*Source*: *Social Trends* (HMSO, 1993)
*Standard Industrial Classification.

*Table 1.3* Occupational analysis of persons in employment 1984 and 1991.

| | | | Estimated changes 1984–91 | |
|---|---|---|---|---|
| Employees and self-employed | 1984 | 1991 | Thousands | Per cent |
| Broad grouping | | | | |
| Managerial and professional | 6 868 | 8 571 | 1 703 | 24.8 |
| Clerical and related | 3 546 | 3 936 | 390 | 11.0 |
| Other non-manual occupations | 1 779 | 2 004 | 225 | 12.6 |
| Craft and similar occupations including foremen in processing, production, repairing etc. | 3 993 | 3 861 | −132 | −3.3 |
| General labourers | 302 | 150 | −152 | −50.3 |
| Other manual occupations | 6 584 | 6 671 | 87 | 1.3 |
| All occupations (employees and self-employed) | 23 072 | 25 193 | 2 121 | 9.2 |
| On government employment and training programmes | 315 | 408 | 93 | 29.5 |
| All in employment | 23 072 | 25 601 | 2 529 | 11.0 |

*Source*: *Employment Gazette* (HMSO, 1992)

style of collective bargaining has risen in some sectors to meet the needs of the new growth areas of employment. This new-style bargaining, though still small in numerical terms when compared with that prevailing in older but declining industries, has established new approaches to industrial relations. They have, on occasions, sharply divided the trade union movement.

The major features of these new-style agreements reflect the characteristics of the new industries in which they are located. They focus on medium-sized companies and plants rather than on large employers and the massive factories of the past, or 'Fordism' as it was. They involve developments on green-field sites, often unconnected with the traditional industrial

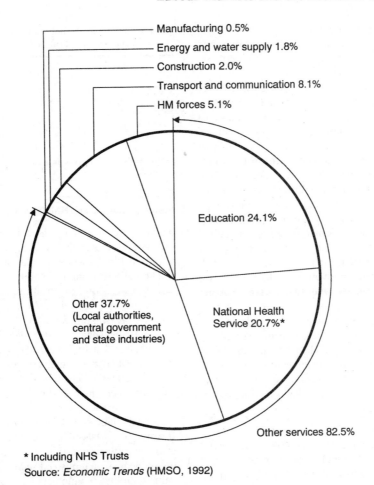

Manufacturing 0.5%

Energy and water supply 1.8%

Construction 2.0%

Transport and communication 8.1%

HM forces 5.1%

Education 24.1%

Other 37.7%
(Local authorities,
central government
and state industries)

National Health
Service 20.7%*

Other services 82.5%

\* Including NHS Trusts

Source: *Economic Trends* (HMSO, 1992)

*Figure 1.6* Analysis of public sector employment by industry group, mid-1991.

regions. In some cases, a new style of management, which seeks to limit or decrease the appeal of trade unionism to the workforce, has emerged and stresses new forms of employee relations. These include employee involvement and commitment, informal team relationships, labour flexibility, employee training, effective employer–employee communications, single status employment and job security for its favoured core workers. These new-style collective agreements often involve the recognition of a single union for all employees and some form of arbitration to replace resort to strike action. Many of these agreements have been concluded with organizations owned and managed by Japanese or American companies, which regard a break with the past style of British industrial relations and management practices as essential for their commercial success. It is difficult to determine, however, whether this new-style

bargaining represents a permanent adjustment, by both employers and trade unions, to the changes in Britain's industrial structure and patterns of employment, or whether it is merely symbolic and transient.

Comparison of employment numbers between the private and public sectors shows that in 1991 out of an estimated employed labour force of about 26 million, some 20 million were in the private sector and 6 million in the public sector, with the remainder being on some form of government training scheme. Most of the decrease in public sector employment since 1981 can be accounted for by the fall in employment in public corporations largely because of privatization. Figure 1.6 breaks down public sector employment by industry groups, showing that education and the National Health Service comprise 45 per cent of public sector employment. Although the public sector employed about one-quarter of all employees by the mid-1990s further privatization programmes could well reduce both absolutely and relatively those employed in public sector enterprises in the future.

This decline in public sector employment, where trade union membership is traditionally very high, could be further exacerbated by the determination of the government to introduce private sector management systems into the public sector. These include: performance-related pay; strict cost-control accounting; contracting out; market force competition; and decentralized pay bargaining. With the election of a fourth successive Conservative government in 1992 it is reasonable to expect that the anti-public sector stance, which was so obvious throughout the 1980s, will continue, though perhaps at a lower level of intensity. It is likely that the privatization of British Rail, British Coal and perhaps even the Post Office and the Prison Service will take place. Further pressures are also likely to be brought to bear across the whole of the public sector for the contracting-out of many functions and services presently carried out by public sector employees. The trade unions will be faced not only with possible membership losses in the public sector, but also with a loss of collective bargaining strength as the industrial relations system is fundamentally changed.

> 'privatisation or the hiving-off of services' was the second most important (employee relations) issue according to the public sector managers in the three years up to 1990. ... Only 'pay levels' eclipsed it as the employee relations issue of most widespread concern to public sector managers.[3]

There are three residual influences reshaping the labour force. First, the number and proportion of self-employed persons has grown during the 1980s from 1.9 million or 8 per cent of the workforce in 1979 to 3.3 million or 12 per cent in 1990. Government measures and grants undoubtedly encouraged this growth in self-employment, with marked increases in building, construction, transport, catering, retailing, engineering, financial services and consultancy. Over the same period, the proportion of self-employed females rose from 19 per cent in 1979 to a remarkable 47 per cent in 1990. It is anticipated that the self-employed sector will continue to expand in the 1990s, with females continuing to grow as a proportion. Second, those on work-related government training schemes, excluding those on youth training programmes, rose from almost zero in 1979 to 16 000 in 1983 and 424 000 in 1990. Third, the economic

Table 1.4 Economic activity rates in Great Britain by age, sex and ethnic origin, spring 1992 (percentages).

|  | All of working age | |
| --- | --- | --- |
|  | Male | Female |
| Ethnic origin |  |  |
| White | 87.1 | 64.0 |
| Black | 75.7 | 29.0 |
| Indian | 78.7 | 36.9 |
| Pakistani or Bangladeshi | 67.3 | 31.4 |
| Other | 77.8 | 40.0 |
| All | 86.5 | 61.8 |

Source: *Social Trends* (HMSO, 1993)

activity rate of ethnic minorities in the population (Table 1.4), especially females, is, in general, lower than that for the white population.

The collective impact of these projected occupational changes on industrial relations and collective bargaining is extremely difficult to estimate. It is, however, reasonable to expect, given the experience of the 1980s, that a further decline in trade union membership density is very likely, though not of the severity experienced in the 1980s. If, however, the unions reshape their structure and improve their appeal to meet the needs of the occupational groups which are expanding, this would obviously affect the industrial relations and collective bargaining climate. It would be misleading to see the changes anticipated in the workforce and the labour market as evidence of the demise of industrial relations, collective bargaining and trade unionism. As the TUC puts it:

> in a period of adversity, unions and the TUC need to concentrate on certain basic tasks such as representing existing members, organising new members, building stable and mutually productive relations with employers, and providing good services.[4]

It is, however, difficult to detect any clear signs that the unions and the TUC, in the five years since this statement was made, are able to point to clear indications of success in achieving these objectives.

In summary, since 1979, the labour market has been subjected to a variety of forces, including the two most serious economic recessions since 1945, considerable industrial and occupational restructuring, high unemployment and demographic changes. The major characteristics of the labour force in the 1990s, and the employment trends which appear to be emerging, are likely to be as follows. There will be:

- a growing labour force, but only slowly, for the rest of the 1990s;

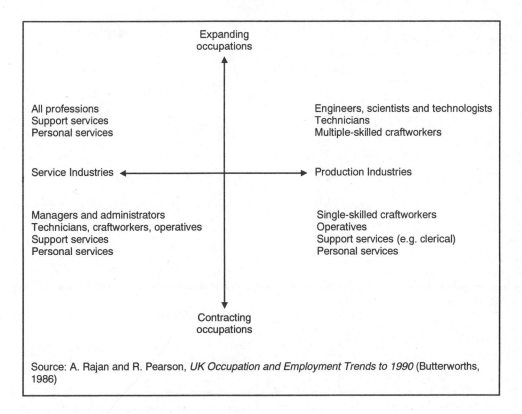

Figure 1.7 represented by the diagram:

```
                        Expanding
                        occupations
                            ↑
All professions                          Engineers, scientists and technologists
Support services                         Technicians
Personal services                        Multiple-skilled craftworkers


Service Industries  ←───────────────────→  Production Industries


Managers and administrators              Single-skilled craftworkers
Technicians, craftworkers, operatives    Operatives
Support services                         Support services (e.g. clerical)
Personal services                        Personal services

                            ↓
                        Contracting
                        occupations
```

Source: A. Rajan and R. Pearson, *UK Occupation and Employment Trends to 1990* (Butterworths, 1986)

*Figure 1.7* The changing occupational balance in the UK.

- a continued high proportion of the population, compared to most other European countries, seeking to be economically active;
- a continued decline in full-time male and female manual occupations;
- a continued expansion of non-manual occupations, both full-time and part-time, for both sexes;
- a higher proportion of jobs being part-time, of fixed term duration or casual;
- a continued rise in female participation rates, with more married women entering employment;
- by the end of the 1990s, females should constitute 45 per cent of the labour force;
- a decline in the proportion of males in the labour force;
- an ageing labour force, with a fall in those people aged 35 and under;
- distinct regional differences in employment, but with the situation probably becoming more stable than in the past;
- a continued decline of employment in the primary and manufacturing sectors, with the services sectors continuing to expand;
- an expansion of employment in the private sector

services;
- a contraction of public sector employment;
- a continued increase in self-employment, especially for women, but at a slower rate;
- an increase in the employment of professionals, managers, technicians and clerical/administrative personnel;
- after rapid growth since 1984, a growing number of people on work-related government training and employment schemes;
- in general, ethnic minority participation rates will remain lower than average for the rest of the population.

Figure 1.7 illustrates the changing occupational structure of the British labour force up to the early 1990s. It is reasonable to assume, given the forecast data available, that the expansions and contractions indicated in the diagram will continue into the next century.

## Unemployment

Table 1.5 and Figure 1.8 indicate that in the 30 years following the end of the Second World War,

*Table 1.5* Percentage rate of unemployment in the UK for selected years 1921–1992.

| Year | Percentage unemployed |
|------|----------------------|
| 1921 | 11.3 |
| 1931 | 15.1 |
| 1941 | 1.2 |
| 1951 | 1.1 |
| 1961 | 1.4 |
| 1971 | 3.2 |
| 1981 | 11.4 |
| 1982 | 12.1 |
| 1983 | 12.9 |
| 1984 | 13.1 |
| 1985 | 11.8 |
| 1986 | 11.8 |
| 1987 | 10.6 |
| 1988 | 8.1 |
| 1989 | 6.3 |
| 1990 | 5.8 |
| 1991 | 8.1 |
| 1992 | 9.6 (June) |

*Source*: A. H. Halsey, *British Social Trends since 1990* (Macmillan, 1988) and *Employment Gazette* (HMSO, 1993)

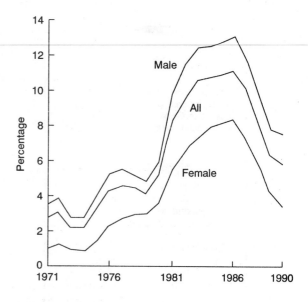

Source: *Social Trends* (HMSO, 1992)

*Figure 1.8* Unemployment rate: annual averages by sex, United Kingdom.

Keynesian full employment policies were successful in holding down unemployment in Britain. Since 1979, when Keynesian economic management policies were largely abandoned, unemployment has risen and has apparently proved intractable to non-Keynesian solutions. Some economists argue, however, that full employment was only obtained at the cost of relatively low growth, increasing inflation, unwillingness to accept industrial and occupational changes by employers, trade unions, managers and work people, and low levels of capital investment.

The national economic policies pursued during the 1980s and with decreasing enthusiasm in the early 1990s, were aimed, according to the government, at enabling Britain to become more competitive, controlling inflation, lowering public expenditure and taxation, increasing capital investment, restructuring industry, raising productivity and encouraging the use of new technology in organizations. An unavoidable and regrettable consequence, it was argued, was a period of transition during which unemployment was relatively high and persistent. This would, the government said, fall rapidly, once a modernized and market-led economy moved into its expansionary phase. Considerable difference of opinion was expressed, especially after 1985, as to whether Britain had entered this expansionary phase. In terms

of unemployment, however, there was a small but progressive fall, month by month, in the overall level, but it rose again in 1991, 1992 and 1993. Those who were unconvinced by this trend claimed it was owing largely to the many technical changes which the government had made to the statistical methods of compiling the unemployment figures. These were modified 24 times in the ten years after 1979. Since 1984, however, an alternative system of measuring unemployment, designed by the International Labour Organisation (ILO) and the Organisation for Economic Co-operation and Development (OECD) has been available (ILO/OECD measure of unemployment). While the ILO/OECD measure uses a more liberal interpretation of unemployment than the government, one of counting benefit claimants only, the difference between the two outcomes, while significant, is not considerable in either economic or political terms.

Unemployment can be categorized and measured in a number of different ways. These include sex, age, occupation, industry, region and duration. Generally, the unemployment rate for men is higher than that for women, while manual workers and older people are likely to be unemployed for a longer period before finding a job than are non-manual workers and younger people. Table 1.6 illustrates the considerable

Table 1.6 Regional unemployment in Britain, 1974, 1984, 1988 and 1991.

| Region | Percentage unemployed | | | |
|---|---|---|---|---|
| | 1974 | 1984 | 1988 | 1991 |
| South East | 1.5 | 9.5 | 5.2 | 7.0 |
| East Anglia | 1.9 | 10.1 | 4.7 | 5.8 |
| South West | 2.6 | 11.4 | 6.1 | 7.1 |
| West Midlands | 2.1 | 15.3 | 8.8 | 8.6 |
| East Midlands | 2.2 | 12.2 | 7.3 | 7.2 |
| Yorkshire and Humberside | 2.6 | 14.4 | 9.6 | 8.7 |
| North West | 3.4 | 15.9 | 10.8 | 9.4 |
| North | 4.4 | 18.3 | 11.9 | 10.4 |
| Wales | 3.6 | 16.3 | 10.4 | 8.7 |
| Scotland | 3.9 | 15.1 | 11.5 | 8.7 |

Source: Employment Gazette (various)

differences in regional unemployment which have persisted for many decades. This is despite government measures designed to remedy the worst aspects of regional unemployment.

The characteristics of the unemployed are revealed by the Annual Labour Force Survey conducted by the Department of Employment. The 1991 Survey estimated the number of unemployed on the internationally agreed ILO definition to be 2.3 million, compared with the claimant count for the same period of 2.1 million. Some 200 000 benefit claimants were for many reasons either not seeking work or were unable to seek it. This was because of illness or domestic circumstances, or because they believed no work was available. Clearly, an appreciable proportion of the unemployed would not or could not have taken employment even if a suitable job was available. The survey also showed that many women registered as unemployed, but not actively seeking work, gave their reason for not doing so as looking after dependants or their families. Most women seeking employment were looking for part-time work. It would appear that for many women, with domestic commitments, part-time employment is the most attractive proposition. By comparison, very few men were seeking part-time employment.

The 1990 survey showed, like previous surveys, that there are three major categories explaining the reasons why people came to be unemployed. The first category, which covered more than half the unemployed, included those who had previously been in work, but had been dismissed, been made redundant or resigned, or whose temporary job ended. The second category, about a quarter of the unemployed, were those returning to the labour market - mainly

married women seeking work. The third and smallest category were new entrants to the labour market, who had not previously had a job, such as those leaving full-time education or immigrants. For those leaving work:

There were considerable differences in the reasons [given for leaving their job] quoted by the unemployed men and unemployed women who provided information. The reason most frequently given by men for leaving their last job was that they were made redundant or dismissed ... and ... the ending of a temporary job was another common reason. ... For women, there were also frequently stated reasons for leaving their previous work, but the main one ... was that they had left for family or personal reasons.[5]

Despite the statistical and definitional problems involved, the 1990 Labour Force Survey clearly shows that unemployment rates are lower in non-manual occupations and higher in manual, particularly unskilled manual occupations. Fewer than 3 per cent of those whose last job had been in managerial or professional categories were unemployed. This compared with 16 per cent among general labourers. Not surprisingly, the unemployment rate is higher for people with low or no educational qualifications and low among well-qualified people. In the spring of 1990, only 2.5 per cent of those with higher qualifications (i.e. above A level) were unemployed, compared with 11 per cent of those without qualifications. Unemployment was particularly high among unqualified young people, with 20 per cent of the unemployed age group 16–24 years possessing no qualifications.

About one-third of the unemployed, according to the 1990 survey, had been out of work for less than three months, with a further third having been unemployed for between three and 12 months. Young unemployed people find new jobs more quickly than older people. About 80 per cent of 16–24-year-olds had been unemployed in the spring of 1990, for under one year, compared with 46 per cent of those aged between 45 and retirement age. Of those who had been unemployed for over three years, only 6 per cent were aged between 16 and 24 years, compared with 35 per cent over 45 years. In general, women tend to be out of work for shorter periods than do men, 77 per cent for less than one year and only 8 per cent for over three years. This compares with 57 per cent and 23 per cent respectively for men.

The methods used by the unemployed in finding work vary. The two most frequent approaches are visits to a Job Centre (30 per cent in 1990) or newspaper job vacancy advertisements (33 per cent). Others use private employment agencies, personal contacts or direct approaches to employers. Manual workers are more likely to use Job Centres or personal contacts or make direct approaches to employers than non-manuals. Non-manual workers are more likely to use private employment agencies and newspaper vacancy columns. The profile of the type of persons most likely to be unemployed in the 1990s emerges, then, as a male unskilled manual worker over 45 years of age, in poor health, living in the North, made redundant from a declining industry and without any formal educational qualifications; or a 20-year-old unskilled person, without any qualifications, living in the West Midlands. Both are likely to have been unemployed for more than one year.

## Labour market theories/explanations

Labour economists and others have, since the nineteenth century, grappled with the complexities of the labour market and attempted to develop explanatory models or theories. Figure 1.9 summarizes, in general terms, the main theories and their characteristics.

The *classical theory* developed during the nineteenth century largely followed the work of Adam Smith, Thomas Malthus, David Ricardo and others. The classical theory argues that the level of employment will depend upon the supply of and demand for labour, with the level of wages bringing the two into equilibrium. Population growth will have the effect of depressing wages towards the level of mere subsistence. Unemployment, it is argued, is either 'frictional' as people move between jobs, or voluntary where they make the choice not to work for whatever reasons. The theory assumes no or very little government interference in the economy and a large homogeneous labour force. A basic assumption of this classical theory is that the labour market is self-regulatory and will tend towards low unemployment.

The classical theory was unable, however, to explain the high and persistent unemployment of the 1920s and 1930s. John Maynard Keynes, a Cambridge economist, in one of the most influential books of the twentieth century, *The General Theory of Employment, Interest and Money* (published in 1936), rejected the classical theory, arguing that unemployment was largely the result of inadequate demand in the economy and structural changes, and not because the level of wages was too high to clear the labour market. Keynes also rejected the view that unemployment was voluntary. The *Keynesian analysis* dominated British economic policy from the early 1940s to the early 1970s. During that period the level of unemployment was kept to a small fraction of that in the inter-war period, by government manipulation of the level of aggregate demand in the economy through budget, taxation and public expenditure policies.

The *neoclassical/monetarist theory* of unemployment emerged in the 1970s in Britain as a result of the growing influence of the ideas of Milton Friedman and the Chicago school of monetarist economists. The monetarists rejected Keynesian economics, claiming that it created inflation, high taxation, low economic growth and steadily rising unemployment. They reintroduced many of the ideas of the early classical theorists and argued that inflation, excessive growth in the money supply, trade union power, high wages, high unemployment benefits and malfunctions in the supply side of the economy caused high and rising unemployment. They postulated a 'natural rate' of unemployment that was dependent upon wages being at a level which would clear the labour market, except for those in transition between jobs and those voluntarily rejecting jobs at the current wage level. High unemployment would, therefore, be 'natural' if wages and social security benefits were too high, trade unions too powerful and government borrowing and spending too high.

The *hysteresis theory of unemployment*, developed in the 1980s, suggests that unemployment causes unemployment, and that there is no such thing as a 'natural rate'. If high unemployment persists over

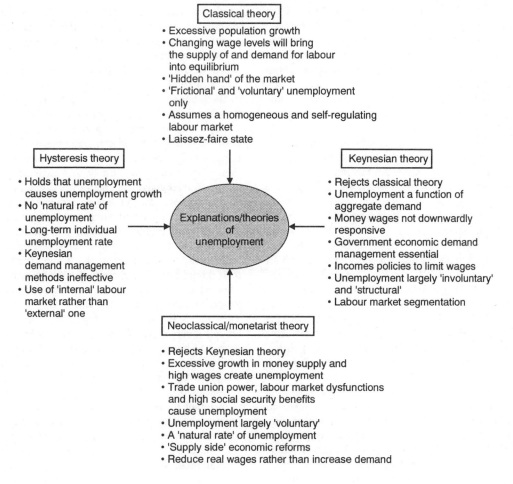

*Figure 1.9* Explanations/theories of unemployment.

time it will create a higher level. Where the unemployed total contains a high proportion of long-term unemployment, the hysteresis effect will be strong. And where employers make use of their own 'internal' employees as a labour market when seeking to fill new positions, the hysteresis effect is strengthened. Furthermore, the hysteresis theory proposes that future unemployment levels are largely dependent on the mean duration of current unemployment. If, as in the USA, duration is much shorter on average, then unemployment will fall faster or grow more slowly than is the case in the UK, where duration is higher.

These four theories of unemployment have all been subjected to severe criticism and many of their shortcomings and inconsistencies have been exposed. It is clear, however, that government attempts to reduce

unemployment during the twentieth century have rested heavily on the theories which held most political appeal for them at the time.

## 1.3 Labour Market Analysis

A broad understanding of the British labour market is essential for an understanding of industrial relations. Labour markets, and the changes continuously taking place within them, affect: trade union membership levels; trade union organization and power; the relative strength of the parties engaged in collective bargaining; payment levels and conditions of employment; management policies on recruitment and retention of employees; and decisions involving the substitution of capital and technology for labour. Where labour is cheap and plentiful, and unemployment high, the employer is inclined to drive a hard bargain and employees have to accept the employer's terms until conditions change. Where labour is hard to obtain, employers have to compete with each other for scarce labour resources. The unemployed and those seeking better jobs can then take advantage of the situation and trade unions can increase their collective bargaining demands.

At some stage in this reflationary process, the national economy usually shows signs of overheating. This manifests itself as monthly increases in inflation, wage rises in excess of productivity increases and balance of payments deficits. The government of the day is then forced to act. It does so either by making an agreement with employers and trade unions to limit price and wage increases, as in the 1960s and 1970s, or by deflating the economy. This latter policy raises unemployment, reduces consumer demand, delays capital investment decisions, reduces the bargaining power of trade unions and attempts to correct the balance of payments situation by choking off import penetration. This method of reducing inflationary pressure, through deflationary policies, fits more closely the free market monetarist approach adopted by governments since 1979.

The labour market is therefore a vital part of both the national economy and the industrial relations system in Britain. In this section the two major components of the labour market – supply and demand – are described and analysed, not as distinct, separate and independent parts of the labour market, which they are not, but as closely interlocked components. Most attention is focused on the changes which have taken place in the labour market since 1979 and the changes likely to take place in the 1990s. This requires examining the segmentation of the labour market, its apparent divisions into 'internal' and 'external' sectors, the increasing importance of women as a source of labour and the consequences of changes in labour law. Attempts by government to free the lower end of the labour market are also important. These have been designed to reduce the floor of social benefits for the unemployed, especially those unwilling to take jobs at current pay levels, and to remove low pay protection for those in employment.

Other labour market characteristics which require examination include the rigidities of supply caused by structural unemployment, worker immobility and regional economic differences. There is also a growing tendency for firms to employ a highly skilled and flexible 'core' of valued, permanent and well-paid employees, alongside a less skilled and less valued 'disposable' sector. The disposable or 'peripheral' workforce can be taken on and laid off according to economic circumstances. This gives rise to the so-called 'flexible firm'. It results in a weakening of the power of trade unions to modify the adverse effects of the labour market by imposing closed shops, job demarcation and hiring restrictions.

The study of labour markets has traditionally been carried out by labour economists who, not unnaturally, have described and analysed the operation of the forces of supply and demand in the terms and language of their own discipline. The labour market, however, unlike product and service markets, is comprised of women and men as parts of families, communities and society. Labour market behaviour is, therefore, also a subject of interest to sociologists, who use the methods and language of their discipline to interpret events. The contributions of both the economist and the sociologist are essential to any understanding of the British labour market. This makes the subject matter comprehensive but renders it very detailed and complex. It is beyond the scope of a book of this nature to describe the working and tendencies of the labour market in all its multiple complexities. As a broad guide, however, to the various theories or models which have been advanced at different times to explain how the labour market functions, Figure 1.10 illustrates schematically some of the major theories. In the remainder of this chapter the component elements of these various theories will be examined.

## Labour supply

As described in Section 1.2, the supply of labour is dependent upon two factors: the age and sex structure of the total population and the rate at which those of working age participate in work. The first is known as the population effect and the second as the participation rate or activity rate. The total population of working age as a proportion of the total population of Britain has declined during the century, largely owing to the raising of the school-leaving age and the greater number of people living beyond retirement age. Thus a smaller proportion of the population has been available for work. For example, the labour force, as a proportion of the total population over school age, was 63 per cent in 1911, 62 per cent in 1961 and 60 per cent in 1981. While this trend will probably continue into the twenty-first century, the decline in the labour force as a proportion of the

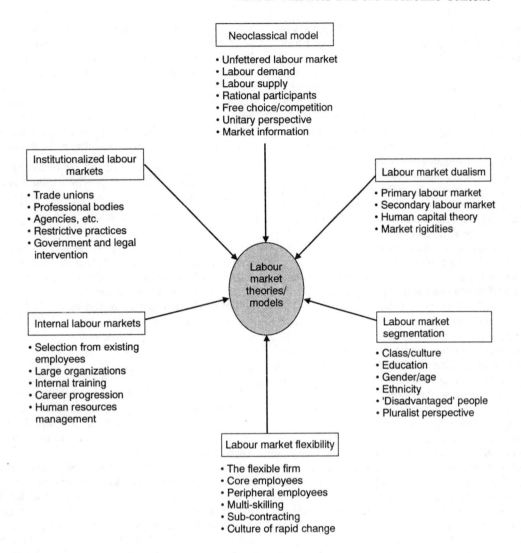

*Figure 1.10* Labour market theories/models.

total population of working age is unlikely to be of the same magnitude as in the past.

The fall in the participation rate for males has been much sharper than the rate for both sexes: it was 93 per cent in 1911, 86 per cent in 1961, 77 per cent in 1981 and 75 per cent in 1991. Conversely, the participation rate for females has risen markedly from 35 per cent in 1911, to 37 per cent in 1961, to 45 per cent in 1981 and to 53 per cent in 1991. While the fall in the male participation rate is expected to continue, but probably at a slower rate, the participation rate for females, mainly married women in part-time jobs, is likely to go on rising. The labour force could,

at some time in the future, become almost evenly balanced between males and females. The consequences of this change for trade union membership and policies, for management practices and for the conduct of industrial relations could be fundamental.

The reasons people enter the labour force are both economic and social. Most people seek work in order to make a living and to establish some sort of occupational career. The alternative is to live on state benefits and, unless they have a private source of income, remain at the bottom of the socio-economic pyramid. For the vast majority of adults of working age, this is no choice at all. It is those who live in depressed regions, and are unemployed, those who have been made redundant in their forties or fifties, those without skills and attributes which attract employers, and those whose health makes work impossible, who often give up the uneven struggle to find employment and drop out of the workforce. Obviously, in all but a few cases, the economic reasons for working predominate but social reasons for entering the labour force are not insignificant. For example, many married women work in order to obtain some independence and a social role outside the family. Some women, on the other hand, see part-time employment as a means of supplementing the family income and improving their standard of living. The social factors which increase workforce activity rates include the attitude of society towards women taking paid work, as well as the attitude of women themselves towards financial independence and social equality with men. The degree to which the work ethic is held by individuals, families, communities and the nation is still considered to be an important motivating force in seeking employment.

The supply of labour is also influenced by the social class structure. Some families, for example, seek to transfer their occupational status between generations, by providing appropriate educational opportunities and by inculcating the appropriate social values and behavioural patterns in their children. These social patterns are evident in the way that most but not all children of professional and business parents themselves enter careers or occupations of similar status. Similarly, the families of skilled manual and clerical parents encourage their children to achieve at least their level of occupational status. Many children, however, do not enter the labour force at the level of their parents. This is because social mobility, largely determined by educational achievement, ensures that many do better than their parents, while a few do worse in terms of occupational status. Thus the labour market opportunities of individuals depend:

> on the one hand, on qualifications, aspirations and information which are determined by upbringing and by education and, on the other hand, the occupational structure which is determined by the interplay of technical and social factors and which determines the level and range of skills and of earning opportunities.[6]

The supply of labour is, therefore, to some degree determined in terms of its quality, aptitudes and attainments by many complex social and economic factors. The short-term labour needs and shortages of employers cannot necessarily be satisfied by increasing educational and training opportunities, though without these little can be achieved in the long run. The ability of individuals to achieve qualifications, skills and the necessary attitudes to achieve better paid employment is often hampered by the division of society into class, racial, gender, national, religious and other social and cultural differences.

> These divisions are created and reinforced by discrimination, differential access to education and training, professional associations, trade unions, employers and ratified by social beliefs and conventions.[7]

If this social analysis of labour supply is valid, it would appear that radical changes are needed not only in the educational and training system, but also in the attitudes of people in society to different class cultures, behavioural patterns and beliefs. In a highly class-conscious country like Britain, this is an extremely difficult task to achieve.

## Making labour markets work

Governments in Britain have, since the Labour Exchanges Act 1909, sought to improve the efficiency of the labour market, by seeking to ensure that the buyers and sellers of labour are aware of each other's needs. They have also provided state-assisted training and allowances, so that unemployed school-leavers unable to find work, and those seeking to secure a marketable skill, can obtain the necessary training. In the 1970s and the 1980s, this task was increasingly state subsidized. The professional efficiency of training was improved through the Manpower Services Commission, which became the Training Agency in 1988. In 1990, the responsibility for training was largely devolved to 82 newly created Training and Enterprise Councils (TECs) on a geographical basis. Job Centres, as the labour exchanges became known, and government training schemes were aimed at matching the needs of those seeking employment with the needs of those offering employment. They also sought to change the skill and occupational profile of the labour force in line with modern needs. The major training schemes now available are the Youth Training Scheme, which has largely replaced the apprenticeship system, and the Employment Training scheme. This was introduced in 1988 and is largely intended for the adult unemployed. A major and controversial element in both these schemes is that failure to take part in them can lead to the loss of state benefits for the unemployed.

During the 1980s, governments took measures which, they believed, would improve labour supply and would ensure, at the lower end of the market, that the unemployed would see the advantage in taking comparatively low-paid jobs, rather than remaining unemployed. At the same time, governments changed trade union and employment legislation so that the ability of organized labour to resist the market forces, which might encourage people to take lower-paid jobs, was minimized. A lowering of the floor of social welfare rights for the unemployed and the poorest in Britain was achieved by allowing the real value of social security benefits to decline relative to earnings. Other measures included: progressively excluding certain groups from the official definition of unemployment; more rigid definition of the criteria covering those genuinely seeking work; subjecting the long-term unemployed to searching enquiries to ascertain why they had not found work; and laying down more formal rules for granting benefit and limiting local discretion in their compilation. Trade union power was weakened by narrowing the definition of lawful disputes and lawful picketing, by legally abolishing the closed shop and by reducing the ability of industrial tribunals to hear cases of alleged unfair dismissal. Protections for the low paid were removed by rescinding the Fair Wages Resolutions of the House of Commons and abolishing the Wages Councils in 1993. Furthermore, the government in 1992 successfully persuaded the European Community to allow Britain to opt out of the Social Chapter of the Maastricht Treaty, which is intended to provide a floor of workers' rights, and to allow workers in general to share in the social and economic gains of the single European market.

This twin strategy, which appeared not only harsh but also inhumane to many people, was defended on the grounds that, at the same time that employers were greatly in need of people for low-paid and relatively unskilled work, there was a ready pool of unemployed unskilled labour. If these jobs could be filled, it was argued, the level of economic activity would increase and, after a time lag, living standards would rise. Output, in turn, would increase and the burden of taxation to provide unemployment pay and social benefits would be reduced. Whether these measures would have the economic effects hoped for, by the 'freeing up' of the lower end of the labour market, was controversial and unproven.

Other, though probably marginal, changes which continue to take place in the supply of labour include: the growth in home working; job sharing; measures allowing the early return of women to work after childbirth; early retirement options; the sharp growth in overtime working as economic activity increases; the growth in temporary employment opportunities; and the increased number of people moonlighting or taking second jobs. It is also believed that the so-called 'black economy', where people do paid work which cannot be traced by social security departments or the Inland Revenue, is expanding, though hard evidence to prove this is difficult to come by.

## Impact on trade unions

The characteristics of labour supply indicated above have greatly reduced the ability of trade unions to protect their members' jobs and conditions of work. The power of the closed shop agreement has been all but eliminated by legal changes and the actions of employers. The ending, for all practical purposes, of formal apprenticeships has ended craft union control over entry to certain trades. Job demarcation practices, designed to maintain employment levels and traditional skills, have given way to the use of multiskilled flexible employees. The growth of women in employment, particularly in part-time employment, many of whom do not join trade unions, has presented full-time male workers, with a greater inclination to join unions, with strong market competition and the threat of substitution in the job market. Similarly, the government strategy of freeing the bottom end of the labour market, by reducing trade union powers at the same time as lowering the floor of social benefits for the unemployed and the poor, has created conditions where more people, particularly women, are taking relatively low-paid, mainly part-time work to supplement family income. As trade unions are not and never have been able to organize the low paid effectively, they have been unable to stem what, for them, are adverse labour market forces. In addition to all these radically changed labour market conditions, the trade unions have had to face historically high levels of unemployment, massive job losses in manufacturing and a reduction in the size of the public sector, where they have traditionally been strongly organized.

## Labour demand

The analysis of the demand for labour has been traditionally separated by economists from the analysis of the supply of labour, not because the two processes are distinct and discrete, but because the sheer complexity of the labour market makes it necessary. Demand for labour, unlike the supply of labour, is an area of academic study where the role of the economist is clearly evident and that of the sociologist less so. Yet the demand for labour cannot wholly be understood in economic terms, as it involves political explanations of the nature of capitalist production and the ideological differences held by employer and labour collectivities. However, the importance of these ideological differences has declined greatly since the late 1980s.

In neoclassical labour market theory, the industry's or firm's demand for labour depends upon the demand for its product, with labour being employed up to the point where a profit is no longer being made. In conditions of perfect competition – a completely unrealistic assumption in practice – the price paid both for the product and for labour reaches its natural level on the open market. Production, claimed the classical economists, reaches the point where demand is satisfied and equilibrium is achieved, both in terms of product output and the labour required. The demand for labour remains constant until new economic forces bring the necessity for readjustments and a new level of equilibrium is eventually achieved. The forces bringing about change in the so-called equilibrium position include: price or cost changes; new and better products; the substitution of capital for labour; new technologies; foreign competition; and cheaper or dearer labour. This somewhat simplistic theory of perfect competition views labour as merely one of the elements in the production process. As the product market changes, so demand for labour changes and in the long run, with some important exceptions, the volume of labour needed is dependent upon the overall demand for products. When all the complex empirical data concerning labour demand are considered, the neoclassical theory of the demand for labour, albeit in a more detailed and mathematical form, appears to be upheld, 'perhaps the most important conclusion is that empirical research of labour demand has, on the whole, supported the conclusion of economic theory in this area'.[8]

This conclusion is of vital importance, as it would appear to support the view that labour demand is determined by market forces in the product services market. It follows that whilst trade union activity and collective bargaining can exercise some influence over labour demand, and the price

of labour, it is more likely to be short term and transitory.

> In a private enterprise economy, the labour market, like other factor markets, is a dependent one. It depends on the supply and demand position in the product market. Given a supply of labour that is fixed in the short run, demand for labour, and therefore its price, depends on the demand, supply, and prices established . . . in the product markets.[9]

From the viewpoint of industrial relations and human resources management, a practical and empirical description of the demand for labour is probably more rewarding than the approach taken by the neoclassical economists. In the long term, and for macroeconomic understanding of labour market demand, however, their conclusions are vital, especially if politicians and governments rely upon economic theories when choosing policies to manage the national economy.

Developments in the labour market since the 1970s suggest that four major trends now characterize the demand for labour by employers. First, labour markets are becoming more distinct, differentiated or segmented. Second, employing organizations are distinguishing between their internal market, made up of their own employees, and the external market when creating new posts or filling vacant ones. Third, employing organizations can be divided into primary ones, or those seeking highly skilled and able people, and secondary ones, recruiting relatively unskilled and low-paid people. Fourth, there is a trend, no more than that, towards firms dividing their need for employees into two categories: highly valued 'core' workers and less valued 'peripheral' ones. The latter can be taken on and laid off as required by the business cycle.

Labour market segmentation theory suggests that the national labour market is not highly competitive but is constituted of many different and separate labour markets, with little real competition among them. There is, however, usually considerable competition inside each market. Segmentation takes place not only between highly specialized skills, but also between industries and services which mainly recruit those with experience of working within them. Furthermore, labour market segmentation begins before people actually enter the labour market, since they seek qualifications, knowledge and skills which will ensure entry to a clearly defined occupation or industry. This in turn is largely determined by social class, family background and access to educational opportunities. Another factor is the cultural attitudes within society about the suitability of certain occupations for one gender rather than for the other. Thus labour market segmentation is deeply entrenched, not only in the labour market itself but also in the social and educational structure of society generally.

Labour market segmentation analysis is also used to distinguish between broad groups in the labour market, such as women, ethnic minorities, school leavers and young people. These terms, for many labour economists, have replaced the more general terms of working class and middle class. Group segmentation and occupational segmentation converge at many points, particularly in terms of non-competitiveness and the social factors underpinning and perpetuating them. Implicit in labour market segmentation theory is the rejection of the neo-classical theory that competitiveness between individuals comprising the labour market is its most important feature. The neoclassical theory of the labour market sees it as a unitary whole, while the segmentation theory sees it as pluralistic.

Segmentation analysis also rejects human capital theory. This theory views the labour market as a place where individuals display their inherent characteristics, personal qualities and cultural attributes, which are seen as largely independent of social conditioning or social advantage. The essence of labour market segmentation theory lies in its emphasis on the social forces creating labour market, occupational and group rigidities. It also considers the ways that discriminatory cultures and practices prevent education and training from completely overcoming these rigidities.

> The market cannot be blamed for inequality, low pay and the like – it merely reproduces the inequality which is brought to it, without being in any way part of its creation . . . By rewarding people not solely in accord with their prospective productivities, a segmented market acquires an active role in the generation of inequality and low pay.[10]

Figure 1.11 illustrates how labour market segmentation affects both the supply of and the demand for labour in the modern economy. Primary and secondary employing organizations have different labour demands. Primary sector high-technology employers, for example, require highly skilled core employees. They tend to recruit core employees through their internal market, and the cosmopolitan employees in the external labour market. Secondary sector employers, usually working with lower-level technologies, tend to recruit semi-skilled, or first-peripheral, workers and unskilled, or second-peripheral, workers, by using internal labour markets. But they also recruit extensively from the lower end of the external labour market.

The concept of internal and external labour market behaviour is based upon the evidence that many large primary sector organizations prefer to recruit labour by selecting people with the desired personal characteristics and training them for a succession of more exacting and often highly specialized tasks. This process implies that in looking for people to fill new positions, or vacant ones, they first look internally rather than towards the external labour market. Such organizations develop recruitment, selection and promotion policies which ensure their choice of employees on the basis of personal characteristics, such as intelligence, attitudes, aptitudes, education and emotional stability. They then train them for life-long careers within their organization. During this time, these employees can expect to progress to ever more exacting work and better pay. Not all jobs are filled internally, as some external recruitment is necessary for highly specialized and professional positions at the top end of the organization's work-force and for unskilled tasks at the other end. For the development of an efficient internal labour market, organizations have to deploy sophisticated recruitment and selection methods, and a highly professional approach to internal staff training, development and career growth. Moreover, all employees have to accept that a flexible attitude to work is essential. Such organizations tend to develop a human resources management approach to the managing of people.

The internal labour market, however, has its limitations. For example, during a period of very low unemployment, organizations might fail to recruit sufficient internal people of the right calibre. Alternatively, the best employees might leave for higher pay elsewhere. Organizations might expand rapidly and establish greenfield plants where they can only secure labour by resorting to the external market. Loss of employees can be limited by progressive personnel policies ensuring that a clearly defined career path is available, offering ever more rewarding work, promotion and better pay and conditions of employment.

Organizations in the secondary sector tend to rely for their labour needs on the external market. They

| PRIMARY SECTOR ORGANIZATIONS | |
|---|---|
| CORE EMPLOYEES | COSMOPOLITAN EMPLOYEES |
| Functional flexibility<br>Job security<br>Lifetime commitment to firm<br>High rewards<br>Regular retraining<br>Skills specific to the firm | Highly specific tasks<br>High demand in labour market<br>Commitment to occupation<br>High rewards<br>High responsibility<br>No retraining by firm<br>Skills not specific to firm |
| INTERNAL<br>LABOUR MARKET | EXTERNAL<br>LABOUR MARKET |
| Numerical flexibility<br>Little security<br>Low material rewards<br>Little responsibility<br>Lack of career prospects<br>Little skill requirement | Numerical flexibility<br>No job security<br>Low material rewards<br>Little responsibility<br>No training |
| FIRST-PERIPHERAL EMPLOYEES | SECOND-PERIPHERAL EMPLOYEES |
| SECONDARY SECTOR ORGANIZATIONS | |

Source: R. Loveridge and A. Mok, *Theories of Labour Market Segmentation* (Academic Press, 1981)

*Figure 1.11* Labour market segmentation.

are normally unwilling to face the costs of expensive training programmes and rely largely on government-funded training programmes to provide a constant supply of suitable labour. Secondary sector organizations recruiting their labour on the external market come closest to the supply and demand model postulated by the classical economists. Since successful primary sector organizations, through high-technology domination, market leadership and high profits, are able to support a higher level of labour costs, they can attract the most able people. This is something which their competitors cannot match. Their market domination relies on the quality of their employees. This, in turn, relies upon the quality of their internal personnel policies and practices, hence the importance of human resources management approaches for them. In terms of industrial relations and trade union membership, core and cosmopolitan employees in the primary sector are increasingly less likely to join trade unions and seek advancement through collective bargaining. Their loyalty towards their employer, rather than towards a trade union, largely depends upon the employer's ability to ensure

steady advancement in job status and financial rewards.

Peripheral employees working in the secondary sector are likely to retain many of the traditional characteristics of trade union solidarity. But as many of the workers in this sector are unskilled and part-time, they are unlikely to place much loyalty or reliance on either the employer or a trade union to fundamentally improve their economic position. They expect to enter and leave employment, as the level of economic activity changes, and to receive the pay and conditions which the labour market determines. Furthermore, their opportunities of being recruited into the internal labour market of a primary sector employer are limited by the social forces which underpin and reinforce labour market segmentation.

Since the 1980s, the quest for a flexible labour force has become a major policy objective for many employing organizations. The search for flexible employees, with the skills and aptitudes to undertake a variety of reasonably related tasks, and the development of multiskilled craft workers, obviously affected labour demand. Historically, the process of industrialization was marked by the tendency to divide labour into ever more specialized functions. As long as labour was plentiful and relatively cheap, the low productivity and workforce rigidities, which this division of labour encouraged, was supportable. Under the competitive economic pressures created since the early 1980s, and the weakened abilities of trade unions to defend labour demarcation practices, managers have increasingly required employees to accept task flexibility and to work in other locations and on other processes at the workplace. Furthermore, the long-held distinction between non-manual and manual employment has given way to harmonization or single-status employment. This establishes broadly similar working conditions and conditions of employment, with the obvious exception of pay, for all employees regardless of job status.

This search for labour flexibility, as a means of securing lower unit labour costs and raising overall productivity, has resulted in the division of some organizations' workforces into core and peripheral employees, thereby creating the so-called flexible firm. Core employees are highly valued, skilled, permanent and well paid. Peripheral employees are unskilled, often part-timers, with poorer employment conditions, and are regarded as disposable, according to market circumstances. Core employees come from the organization's internal labour market and peripheral employees are obtained on the external market. This process reinforces labour market segmentation by selecting core employees from those sectors of the population which are relatively socially advantaged. Peripheral employees, in contrast, are largely selected from the socially disadvantaged – the poor, ethnic minorities, the least educated and the large pool of unskilled females.

A further characteristic of the flexible firm is the use it makes of temporary or seasonal labour and the self-employed. This is to meet cyclical demands for its products or services. Such labour is recruited either on a temporary basis or on short-term contracts. Sometimes use is made of agency labour so that the firm does not become the direct employer. As pay is relatively low for both the peripheral and the temporary employees of the flexible firm, the importance of government measures aimed at freeing the lower end of the labour market, by reducing the value of the floor of social benefits and by the abolition of wages councils, can be clearly seen. Any long-term development of the flexible firm is likely to bring fundamental changes in the labour market. It could also create a significant new division between core and peripheral employees, replacing the older division between staff and hourly paid or 'works' employees.

> At one extreme, it is becoming easier to play the labour market for some types of work, obtaining relatively cheap and easily disposable employees of the required competence, and allowing the anxiety about job loss to sustain acceptable effort levels. At the other extreme, it is also becoming easier to build up a package of employment, training and payment practices that elicit high labour efficiency through the very different route of cultivated commitment . . . It is increased choice in employment packages that is making many employers think in terms of the peripheral and core components of their workforces.[11]

## Occupational pay

It has long been contended by some politicians, as well as by labour market economists, that pay levels are largely determined in the long term by movements in the demand for labour and its supply, the level and duration of unemployment, by trade union bargaining strength and, to a lesser degree, by the provision of state unemployment and other benefits. It is improbable that changes in any one of these four factors have an immediate effect upon the price paid for labour in general. In highly specific areas of the labour market, however, for computer specialists say, rapid changes in labour demand which cannot be matched by supply in the short term can lead to higher pay increases. In the labour market, therefore, it is probable that changes in any of these factors are likely to take some time to work through the market. For example, there is no clear evidence what effect the substantial increase in unemployment since the late 1970s has had upon pay levels in general. During the 1980s and 1990s, against a background of the worst recessions since 1945, high unemployment, large-scale redundancy, greatly weakened trade unionism and strong government resistance to pay increases, the average earnings of men almost doubled and those for women rose by 220 per cent. As prices during the same period rose by 'only' 130 per cent, there was a substantial increase in real earnings for those in employment. This evidence would not, therefore, appear to support the view that adverse economic circumstances and high unemployment necessarily place a brake on either money wages or real wages.

Historical evidence suggests that new economic circumstances have to persist for some time before

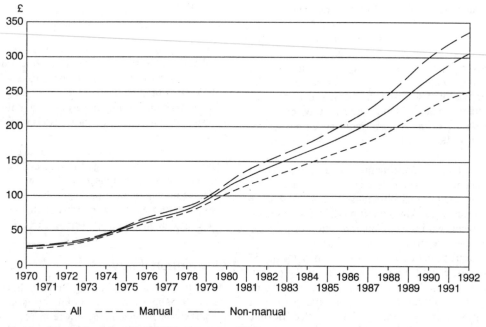

Source: *Employment Gazette* (HMSO, November 1992)

*Figure 1.12* Average gross weekly earnings, full-time employees on adult rates.

long-established attitudes and behaviour change, and before institutions, such as trade unions and employers' associations, adjust their bargaining policies and practices. For example, during the period from 1945 to the early 1960s, average pay increased comparatively slowly, despite low unemployment and the existence of powerful trade unions. It is not unreasonable to believe that the attitudes and practices concerning pay increases, ingrained by the inter-war years, still held sway. Similarly, the cultural attitudes and behaviour of employers, employees and trade unions formed during the high wage and price inflation of the 1970s and 1980s might only now, in the 1990s, be undergoing a fundamental change.

> Unions cause unemployment to be higher than it needs be when they cause the real union wage to be above its 'full employment level' and encourage government to set rates of unemployment compensation at relatively high levels . . . it is the taxpayer, the consumer and the economically inactive who finance the excessive real wages of employed union labour.[12]

Those who oppose such views insist that trade unions possess relatively little power compared with the power possessed by the owners and managers of com-

panies and capital. They point to the fact that, compared with progressive taxation, the unions have had little influence over the redistribution of national income from wealth and profits to pay and state benefits. Trade union strength is largely confined, they argue, to preventing downward movements in pay, to securing job control and to preventing dismissals. In short, trade unions are too weak rather than too strong.

> An analysis of economic power reveals a very different state of affairs to the frequently expressed opinion that unions are too powerful. Such an opinion focuses upon symptoms and ignores causes. In reality, unions are weaker than employers, whose possession of the means of production enables them to command decision-making procedures. . . . For the most part unions remain insecure bodies reacting to, rather than initiating, labour market developments and possessing little ability to influence wider economic events.[13]

The annual earnings survey conducted by the Department of Employment each April reveals a wide distribution of adult earnings from those who earn less than £100 per week to those earning more than

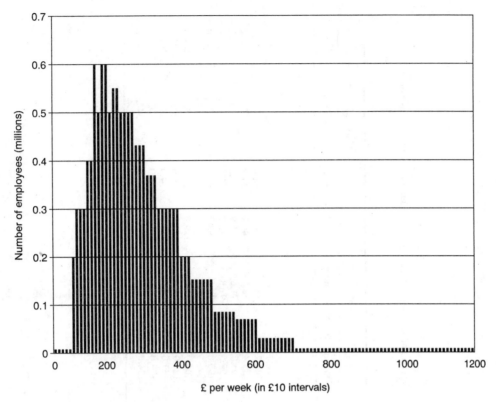

Source: *Employment Gazette* (HMSO, 1992)

*Figure 1.13* Distribution of gross weekly earnings, full-time employees on adult rates.

£600 per week. Most adult workers, however, as Figure 1.13 and Table 1.7 illustrate, earn between £200 and £400 per week. The average, or mean, gross weekly pay of all full-time employees in April 1992 was £305, with 'median' earnings, that is, the earning of a person exactly half-way up the earnings distribution scale, being £265 per week; 10 per cent of employees earned less than £148 per week; while 10 per cent earned more than £490. Women employees received pay which on average was 71 per cent of that received by men. Between April 1991 and April 1992, average earnings, despite a recession and rising unemployment, rose by 7 per cent, while over the same period the Retail Prices Index rose by 4.3 per cent. Those in employment, therefore, enjoyed a rise in real earnings as well as money earnings.

The increase in average earnings from one year to the next is the result of three main factors: first, the level of pay settlements; second, changes in the amounts earned in addition to basic pay levels, such as overtime and bonus payments; third, the effects of structural changes in the pattern of employment, with movements taking place between lower- and higher-paid occupations and industries.

Earnings of employees also vary between industrial and service sectors of the economy and between occupations. The variations in average earnings in April 1992 between industrial sectors ranged from £391 per week in energy and water supply to £220 in agriculture. The range of average weekly earnings between the major sectors of the economy, such as manufacturing (£300), construction (£306) and services (£304), was only slight, however. The distribution of average weekly earnings between occupations, as Figure 1.14 illustrates, was more pronounced. While changes in occupational earnings do take

Table 1.7 Distributions and dispersions of pay in April 1992 (full-time employees on adult rates, whose pay for the survey pay-period was not affected by absence)..

| Gross weekly earnings: | Men | | | Women | | | Men and women | | |
|---|---|---|---|---|---|---|---|---|---|
| percentage earning less than | Manual | Non-manual | All | Manual | Non-manual | All | Manual | Non-manual | All |
| £100 | 0.6 | 0.4 | 0.5 | 6.7 | 1.1 | 2.1 | 11.7 | 0.8 | 1.1 |
| £150 | 7.8 | 3.9 | 5.6 | 44.7 | 13.7 | 19.2 | 14.4 | 8.3 | 10.5 |
| £200 | 26.1 | 12.4 | 18.7 | 75.4 | 38.6 | 45.2 | 34.9 | 24.4 | 28.2 |
| £300 | 69.8 | 35.7 | 51.3 | 95.7 | 71.6 | 75.9 | 74.5 | 52.1 | 60.1 |
| £420 | 92.3 | 65.6 | 77.8 | 99.5 | 91.8 | 93.2 | 93.6 | 77.6 | 83.3 |
| £600 | 98.7 | 87.9 | 92.8 | 100.0 | 98.6 | 98.9 | 98.9 | 92.8 | 95.0 |
| 10 per cent earned less than (£) | 158.0 | 188.0 | 170.0 | 106.0 | 141.0 | 129.0 | 137.0 | 156.0 | 148.0 |
| 25 per cent earned less than (£) | 197.0 | 258.0 | 219.0 | 127.0 | 174.0 | 161.0 | 178.0 | 201.0 | 192.0 |
| 50 per cent earned less than (£) | 251.0 | 353.0 | 296.0 | 157.0 | 228.0 | 211.0 | 234.0 | 291.0 | 265.0 |
| 25 per cent earned more than (£) | 317.0 | 473.0 | 402.0 | 199.0 | 306.0 | 296.0 | 302.0 | 402.0 | 366.0 |
| 10 per cent earned more than (£) | 397.0 | 641.0 | 544.0 | 254.0 | 402.0 | 387.0 | 381.0 | 544.0 | 490.0 |

Source: Employment Gazette (HMSO, 1992)

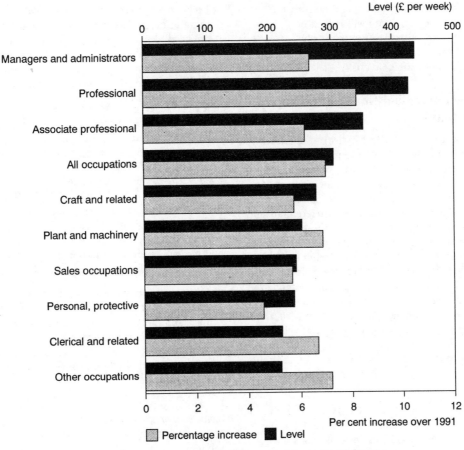

Level (£ per week)

Full-time employees on adult rates

Source: *Employment Gazette* (HMSO, November 1992)

*Figure 1.14* Average gross weekly earnings by occupational major group, April 1992.

place, the time scale is often measured in decades rather than in a few years. For example, the top three occupational earnings groups in Figure 1.14 were also in the top five groups in 1979. At the bottom of the scale, however, there had been some movement since 1979, with personal, protective and sales occupations having fallen from a higher occupational earnings rating in 1979.

Labour economists have debated for most of this century the impact that trade unions and collective bargaining have on long-term movements in earnings. One school of thought believes that the power of trade unions to raise earnings beyond the level which labour market forces, if left to operate naturally, would result in, is considerable.

Trade unions play a relatively minor role in wage setting in the United States and, indeed, in

Japan, but in many European countries they are the principal actors. . . . The empirical evidence suggests that unions [in Britain] have an important impact on earnings. Union workers enjoy substantial wage premiums although the magnitude of the union wage gap has varied over the years.[14]

Another school of thought suggests that while trade unions might in the short term be able to influence upwards the level of wages, in the long term the market rate will be re-established, though only through upheavals in the wider economy.

It may be tempting to conclude . . . that unions cannot do much to influence the general level of wages in the long run; that we need not worry – the going rate is still set by the market.

Such a signal for inaction would be truly disastrous: the going rate will indeed be re-established, but only after a terrible retribution by inflation and unemployment, with political if not economic crisis.[15]

## 1.4  Technological Change and the Labour Market

Changes in technology affect industrial relations by creating new products, new materials and new production systems, and by changing the occupational structure of the labour market. All these forces compel employers, employees and trade unions to alter working methods, job content, pay differentials and skill protection practices. When technological change is fundamental, for example the introduction of steam power or of electricity, whole industries and many occupations eventually disappear, taking with them long-standing working practices and even whole trade unions. The process, however, is usually extended over comparatively long periods of time, allowing people and institutions to adjust to changing circumstances slowly.

The history of industrialization and of capitalist development is largely the history of technological change.

> The fundamental impulse that sets and keeps the capitalist engine in motion comes from the new consumers' goods, the new methods of production or transportation, the new markets, the new form of industrial organisation that capitalist enterprise creates.[16]

This process of innovation is continuous and involves acceptance of change by people and institutions. In order to create greater wealth, it is often necessary for individuals and occupational groups not only to accept change but also to foster and encourage it, regardless of its attendant insecurities and social upheavals. Those individuals, companies and nations which do not embrace and foster technological change are left behind, unable to compete in producer and consumer markets, and destined to lower standards of living. If they stick to outdated technologies, they eventually lose either their jobs, or markets or both on massive scales. For industrial exporting nations, such as Britain, the choice is either to pursue and accept new technologies or to suffer absolute decline as an industrial nation. The technological imperative imposes itself upon employers and trade unions alike. As one union puts it:

Technology of course has always been changing. In an economy like ours which is dominated by the need to make profits, every manufacturer must continually improve methods of production in order to stay ahead of the competition. If this doesn't happen, the goods don't sell.[17]

It is, however, dangerous to believe in a crude form of technological determinism, since whilst technology is a powerful force it is not an overwhelming one. New technologies can be rejected or ignored but the consequences of doing so have to be accepted and lived with. Changes can be left entirely to market forces for their implementation or their effects can be planned for and people protected. Trade unions can blindly oppose the use of new technologies, or consider the long-term advantages associated with them and bargain to ensure that they are introduced with proper concern for everyone involved.

> The real problem is not whether technological development by itself is good or bad. That is a misleading way of looking at it. The important issue is the control of technological development . . . the way to ensure that scientific knowledge can benefit the workforce is by careful but firm negotiation through the union machinery.[18]

In short, organized workers often oppose new technologies unfeelingly imposed by employers and harsh market forces, since these can result in heavy job losses, loss of occupational status and skill, and deterioration in terms and conditions of employment for those remaining in work. Conversely, they usually accept them where their introduction is negotiated and their worst social consequences eliminated or ameliorated.

The economic history of Britain since the early nineteenth century has been largely the history of the exploitation of new technologies on which whole new industries and products were subsequently based. These industries then gave rise to a long upward cycle of economic activity before going into decline and being replaced by new technologies which repeated the process. The Russian economist, Kondratiev, writing in the early years of this century, believed that long business cycles of expansion, boom and decline were related to fundamentally new technologies. Schumpeter, the American economist, argued that the capitalist system was dependent for its dynamism and prosperity upon the 'creative destruction' of new technologies. Renewed interest in these ideas were expressed in the 1980s by writers such as Toffler, who seek to understand the consequences of the micro-electronics revolution or the 'third wave' of rapid economic, social and technological change.

Briefly, there have been three fundamental technological revolutions which have shaped human civilization. The first was the agrarian revolution which produced food and clothing by crop growing and animal husbandry and led to permanent human settlements. This basic economic system, while undergoing considerable development and refinement, remained essentially unchanged for several thousand years. Then the second agrarian revolution and the first industrial revolution, based on the steam engine, took place in England in the late eighteenth and early nineteenth centuries. Subsequent technological developments fed the momentum of the industrial revolution. These included the development of electricity, gas, the internal combustion engine, motor vehicles, chemicals, petroleum, aeroplanes, synthetic fabrics, plastics, radio, television and many other inventions. The third great phase of economic and social development effectively started in the 1970s with computers and the advent of microelectronics, biotechnology, robotics and information technology. It is believed that the electronics revolution which we are now experiencing is as fundamental and as all-pervasive as the previous agrarian and industrial revolutions. It is already transforming social, cultural, economic and political life. It is argued, for example, that the microelectronics revolution will:

> profoundly affect the industrial structure, performance and attitudes of the developed countries. These are not just marginal effects . . . they are deep and widespread and collectively signal a fundamental and irreversible change in the way the industrialised societies will live.[19]

The practical uses and applications of microelectronics, computers, information technology and robotics are almost limitless, though their use has been much greater in modernizing old processes of production and in developing new processes, than in developing new products. Table 1.8 indicates the rapid assimilation of computing facilities, the main component of new technology, into British industry and commerce.

New technology is being introduced into manufacturing, office systems, financial services and retailing. In manufacturing, new technology is used in computer-aided design, in computer-aided manufacturing, in flexible manufacturing systems and in robotics. The integration of these systems could

eventually make fully automated manufacturing processes commonplace. While care must be taken not to exaggerate the impact of these new technologies, it is certainly feasible that a range of products, such as consumer durables and even automobiles, could eventually be designed by computers, with components manufactured by computer-controlled machine tools and products assembled by robots. Whether or not this happens on a large scale depends more upon economic and political factors than upon technological ones.

In the office, the impact of the new technologies is already very evident in the form of the word processor. Its flexibility, storage capacity and instant recall make it ideal for the storage of vast quantities of information and its immediate replication in paper form. Optical character recognition equipment is capable of reading and storing documents on its own. Bulky paper storage systems involving costly office space are eliminated. Advanced information systems and satellite communications make possible the fully integrated technological office.

In retailing, bar code sales control systems and electronic checkout systems, or electronic point-of-sale systems, have already revolutionized selling and merchandizing in large chain stores. These systems permit greater control over stock levels and the labour intensive task of pricing individual items is eliminated. The future of large-scale retailing probably involves little money handling as cashless sales systems become commonplace. The use by mail-order firms of tele-shopping systems could revolutionize the sale of consumer durables, furnishings and clothing, though the response of consumers to these changes is still uncertain.

In financial services, the application of new technologies has met little resistance. Banks, insurance companies and building societies have rapidly introduced computer-controlled accounts systems, direct data transmission between branches and head offices, and word processors to standardize customer communications. Computer-linked automatic call machines enable 24-hour customer access, though it is unlikely that counter services will ever be totally eliminated. These changes do not appear to have reduced the number of people working in financial services. On the contrary, their numbers have grown as financial service systems have expanded, as more and more people make cashless purchases and use personal bank accounts.

In the late 1970s, when the awesome potential of microelectronics or the silicon chip revolution was

Table 1.8 Computing facilities by size of establishment, 1984 and 1990 (percentages).

| | All establishments | | Number of employees at establishments | | | | | | | |
| | | | 25–99 | | 100–499 | | 500–999 | | 1000 or more | |
| | 1984 | 1990 | 1984 | 1990 | 1984 | 1990 | 1984 | 1990 | 1984 | 1990 |
|---|---|---|---|---|---|---|---|---|---|---|
| **Types of computing facilities in use:** | | | | | | | | | | |
| On-site facilities: | | | | | | | | | | |
| Main-frame computer | 9 | 18 | 5 | 13 | 18 | 34 | 36 | 37 | 54 | 62 |
| Mini computer | 23 | 39 | 19 | 33 | 34 | 60 | 54 | 69 | 72 | 80 |
| Isolated micro-computer(s) | – | 59 | – | 54 | – | 76 | – | 83 | – | 95 |
| Networked micro-computers | 27 | 29 | 22 | 22 | 40 | 49 | 61 | 62 | 74 | 73 |
| Computer linked to employee working at home | – | 4 | – | 3 | – | 8 | – | 12 | – | 20 |
| Any on-site facilities | **47** | **75** | **40** | **70** | **64** | **90** | **82** | **90** | **93** | **98** |
| Off-site facilities: | | | | | | | | | | |
| Link to computer elsewhere in same organization | 26 | 50 | 20 | 44 | 40 | 67 | 54 | 77 | 69 | 87 |
| Link to computer in another organization | 6 | 15 | 5 | 12 | 9 | 22 | 20 | 27 | 22 | 42 |
| Any computing facilities | **61** | **84** | **54** | **81** | **82** | **95** | **93** | **93** | **98** | **99** |

Source: Millward et al., Workplace Industrial Relations in Transition (Dartmouth, 1992), p. 14

being slowly understood, many pessimistic projections were made predicting the demise of whole industries and occupations, with unemployment of massive proportions reaching a possible 5 million people by 1990. As Jenkins and Sherman wrote at the time:

It is impossible to over dramatize the forthcoming crisis as it potentially strikes a blow at the very core of industrialized societies – the whole work ethic. We have based our social structures on this ethic and now it would appear that it is to become redundant along with millions of people.[20]

Clearly, making social and economic predictions is very hazardous, for while the official unemployment total in early 1993 stood at around 3 million, it was the result of recession and deflation rather than the introduction of new technologies, with the work ethic being held in probably higher esteem than at any time during the post-war period, by both government and the general population. Furthermore, a detailed and extensive survey of technical changes at the workplace in the 1980s found little evidence of any sense of crisis or trade union opposition created by the introduction of the new technologies. The researchers found:

that British workers generally experience and accept a very high level of major change. Major change affecting manual workers is common, and change affecting office workers is even more so. We found no evidence in our study of 2 000 workplaces that the rate or form of change affecting either category of employee was inhibited by trade union organisation. Technical change was generally popular among the workers affected.[21]

It was popularly predicted in the late 1970s that worker and trade union opposition, or even Luddism, would delay or even prevent the introduction of new technologies into British industries and services. With the exception of a few dramatic disputes in newspapers, the printing industry and the railways, the reverse has tended to be the case. Indeed, the evidence of the largest research survey carried out into the problems associated with the introduction of new technology found that:

So great has been the support of workers and trade union representatives for technical change that management have not had to use consultation, participation or negotiation to win

their consent to change. Even major changes have been introduced with surprisingly little consultation.[22]

Unless it is argued that the willing acceptance of technical change by workers and trade unions is the result of their deep sense of insecurity and fear generated by high unemployment, or the unchallengeable dominance of macho managers, the empirical evidence suggests that the introduction of technical change is inhibited by the attitudes and concerns of companies and their managers.

The most common obstacles to change that have consistently emerged from managers' accounts have been lack of qualified or skilled manpower, lack of management confidence owing to the economic climate, lack of finance to fund investment and lack of management awareness of new developments.[23]

It was also apparent, by the late 1980s, that the introduction of new technology had been more widespread in the private sector than in the public sector. In the private sector, manufacturing industry was more likely to have made use of new technologies than services. Overseas-owned private sector establishments were also found to be using new technology to a greater degree than their British-owned counterparts. By the 1990s, however, the public sector had caught up with the private sector.

New technology agreements, which were seen by the TUC and the major unions to be an extremely important area of collective bargaining in the 1980s, appear after a brief period of activity to have been relatively little used. Most surveys of new technology agreements negotiated between employers and trade unions strongly indicate that they are only used in a minority of situations where new technology is to be introduced. Research again indicates that:

In sum, then, the record of collective bargaining on information technology is not an impressive one. Unions have been unable to challenge management effectively on the strategy of technological change at all . . . The unions have concentrated their efforts on negotiating over the effects of information technology, for the most part on a reactive and narrow basis.[24]

If the incidence of negotiated new technology agreements is remarkably low even in cases where trade unions are relatively strong, the low incidence of consultation is perhaps even more surprising.

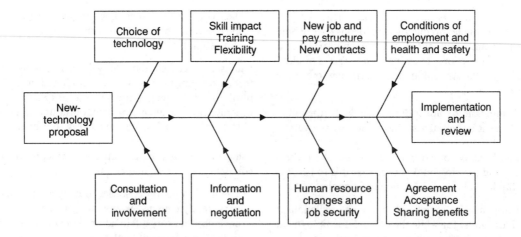

*Figure 1.15* New technology: consultation and negotiation.

Even according to the accounts of managers, shop stewards were consulted about any stage of the introduction of advanced technical change affecting manual workers in only 39 per cent of cases.[25]

It is extremely difficult not to draw the conclusion, from the research evidence available, that the introduction of new technology is a matter of far less concern to the average worker and trade union representative than negotiations concerning pay and conditions of employment. A survey of some 2 000 workplaces found substantial evidence that management proposals for organizational changes were much more resented and resisted by workers and union representatives than was the introduction of new technology. These organizational changes involved: new working practices; multiskilling; task, hours and workplace flexibility; and reduced manning levels.

Works managers reported that manual workers were in favour from the start of three-quarters of advanced technical changes in manufacturing industry. In contrast, they also reported that in three-quarters of the organisational changes in that sector, workers were initially opposed to the proposals.[26]

Turning to the impact of new technology on employment, and the number of jobs lost and gained by it, it appears that the projections of the late 1970s were almost certainly unduly pessimistic. Historically, there is little doubt that the major technical changes of the past have initially resulted in

job losses but, in the long term, they have created many new jobs. The displacement of handcraft textile production by steam-powered machinery in mills in the early nineteenth century, for example, certainly had that effect. Job losses also occurred in horse-based transportation with the introduction first of steam power and then of the internal combustion engine. Both these inventions became the basis of very substantial new industries. There is little reason to doubt that the 'new' industries of computers, microelectronics and information technology, which are already substantial employers in their own right, will eventually become even larger employers of people. This view, of course, is of little comfort to those who lose their jobs during the period of transition from one technology to another. Nevertheless, future generations might well have good reason to be grateful for the jobs, work and higher living standards which these technologies bring them.

## 1.5 National Economic Management

The economic framework within which industrial relations has operated since 1979 can best be described, like the political framework, as neo-*laissez-faire* capitalism. During the 1980s a determined attempt was made by government to reduce state intervention in the economy. This was done by leaving prices, incomes and employment to be determined largely by market forces, by reducing the public sector through expenditure cuts and privatization, and by cutting public expenditure and taxation in real terms. Trade union power was also undermined by legislation passed after 1980, though compared with the loss of membership and high unemployment, its effects were probably marginal at the collective bargaining table. The protagonists of the new spirit of private enterprise and market capitalism argued that only by breaking free from state intervention in the economy, and trade union monopoly bargaining power in the labour market, could the British economy become more efficient, competitive, innovative and resourceful. But many feared at the time the social and political strains that might be imposed by such a regime:

> The circumstances bearing upon the nation now may prove too severe a test on its ability to preserve its familiar shape. It may fail either to break through to dynamic growth or to resume its halting liberal movement towards a less divided society. It may become embedded instead in a texture of politics and industrial relations more harsh, vengeful and embittered than any it has known before.[27]

The question which needs to be asked is: why did it become necessary in the late 1970s for a popularly elected government to embark upon such painful and divisive economic and social policies? The straightforward and simple answer to this question is because of the persistent and seemingly irreversible decline of the British economy by comparison with its major industrial competitors. Equally, increases in living standards expected by the majority of the people had not been fulfilled. Neither had their expectations for improved public services, national health provision and welfare state benefits been generally satisfied. Between 1945 and the late 1970s, a succession of different governments tried to plan, stimulate or cajole the economy and its major decision makers into greater output, but with little lasting effect. The radical right-wing economic policies pursued with apparent popular support since the election of the first Thatcher government in 1979 were a clear break with all previous postwar policies which had been based largely upon political consensus and powerful government economic intervention.

> For more than thirty years every British Government has had a different answer to the question of economic and industrial decline. The Thatcher administration has adopted a novel approach. It has tried to change the question. Instead of the Government being regarded as primarily responsible for solving Britain's

problems, the onus has shifted to the people. In the process the post-war consensus about economic management has been challenged. . . . [But] has the Government created sufficient widespread consent, as opposed to acquiescence, to promote a new 'settlement' about how the economy and society should be run to match that of the previous thirty years?[28]

In order to understand the consensus economic policies which dominated economics for 30 years up to 1979, it is necessary to outline briefly the forces which shaped the British economy before 1945.

## Classical laissez-faire capitalism

Britain was the first country to pass through the industrial revolution. That revolution was based upon steam power, machine manufacturing and an increasingly sophisticated banking and financial system. The overriding economic philosophy was to leave economic decisions to entrepreneurs, capitalists and bankers – a *laissez-faire* philosophy. The 'hidden hand' of the market, it was believed, would determine prices and costs as well as reward enterprise and efficiency and punish sloth and inefficiency. The role of government was to be residual: confined to ensuring a sound money system based upon the gold standard and the Bank of England. The courts were to play their part by upholding the common law doctrine of 'restraint of trade'. The problems resulting from movements in the trade cycle and the resultant fluctuations in unemployment were not seen to be in any way the responsibility of government. The adherents of the new capitalist economic order believed that left to its own devices the market system would prove to be self-correcting through the price mechanism and the flow of gold reserves. It was against this economic background and set of beliefs that the British trade unions emerged and matured. Their main concerns were membership growth, legal protection, organizational consolidation, collective bargaining and institutional adaptation – albeit in piecemeal fashion – to this confident and dynamic economic order.

The British economy, whilst it began to lose its impetus and to be challenged by the United States and imperial Germany in the late nineteenth century, did not begin to reveal its deep-seated weaknesses until the great depression of the 1920s and 1930s. In those decades, the basic industries of coal, iron and steel, textiles, agriculture and railways contracted severely. Unprecedentedly high levels of unemployment ensued, which did not begin to fall substantially until the beginning of the Second World War. During the 1930s, serious challenges were made to *laissez-faire* political economy, free trade and the self-correcting forces of free market capitalism. The most **persuasive** analysis came from the Cambridge economist, John Maynard Keynes, whose seminal book *The General Theory of Employment, Interest and Money*, published in 1936, was to become the economic orthodoxy for almost 30 years after 1945.

## Keynesian demand management

Keynes argued that the economy could well persist at high levels of unemployment for long periods and that the self-correcting mechanism of the market was largely a delusion. If the existing economic order was to be preserved, as well as the political democracy it supported, he argued, it would be necessary for governments to stimulate aggregate demand through budgetary and public works measures. In this way, the level of economic activity would be raised which, by a multiplier effect, would increase business transactions and lower levels of unemployment. The white paper on full employment supported by the wartime coalition government in 1944 was heavily influenced by Keynesian ideas and became politically and morally binding upon successive British governments for the next three decades. This gave rise to a political consensus on managing the economy, with both Labour and Conservative governments manipulating aggregate demand, public spending and budget deficits in order to achieve full employment. During this period both the Trades Union Congress and the Confederation of British Industry were fully consulted on economic policy, were continually involved in national economic bodies and played an important role in national economic management.

In simple terms, it became the task of governments, regardless of the political party they represented, to use budgetary measures to stimulate or deflate the economy, as circumstances required, and to keep the level of unemployment as low as possible without causing wage-led inflation. If the level of unemployment began to rise, and economic activity declined, the Keynesian orthodoxy required government to stimulate consumer demand and reduce unemployment by reducing taxation or by increasing public expenditure. If such measures resulted in a budget deficit, seen as the road to economic and financial disaster before 1939, the government would borrow in order to balance the public accounts. Deficit budgeting became an acceptable method of ensuring relative prosperity, steady economic growth and very low levels of unemployment.

The only economic forces which limited the use of demand management techniques for managing the national economy were external. These included the balance of payments and the exchange rate of sterling against the dollar, which had been fixed by international agreement after 1945. If the balance of payments moved into deficit, or the sterling exchange rate came under pressure, the government of the day would deflate the economy by taking measures which would reduce economic activity and increase unemployment. The net result of the Keynesian revolution in government management of the national economy was almost 30 years of unprecedented prosperity and steadily rising living standards for the mass of British people.

During this same period, it soon became apparent that Britain was being rapidly outstripped by its economic competitors. Countries like West Germany, France and Japan, which had been devastated at the end of the Second World War, were soon to develop economies which were able to provide their populations with much higher living standards than those enjoyed by the majority of British people. Britain's share of total world trade and world manufacturing output declined rapidly, productivity lagged behind most other advanced industrial countries and unit wage costs rose more rapidly. Above all, and what was perhaps the most damaging aspect of the British economy, was the persistently high and rising level of inflation of the 1960s and 1970s.

By the mid-1970s, the relative decline in the UK's position as a major economic power was painfully apparent. Its manifestations were: declining manufacturing capacity and a falling share in world trade; high and persistent inflation; low investment; low profitability; stagnant living standards; sterling crises; and balance of payments deficits. It was also a high-taxation economy, with rising public expenditure, and increasing trade union power. This resulted in a lack of competitiveness, an outdated economic structure and a persistent underlying growth in the level of unemployment. Serious doubts grew in elements of all political parties about the ability of Keynesian demand management methods to solve the UK's deep-seated economic problems. Doubts about Keynesianism became an outright rejection in many major industrial and financial institutions but especially in the Conservative Party.

Keynesian demand management was challenged as a workable system of national economic management. It was also seen as the root cause of almost all of the UK's economic problems of the postwar era.

Doubts about the continuing efficiency of Keynesian policies first penetrated the Labour government, led by James Callaghan, who spoke on monetarist economics to the Labour Party Conference in 1976.

> We used to think that you could just spend your way out of recession, and increase employment, by cutting taxes and boosting Government spending. I tell you in all candour that that option no longer exists, and that in so far as it ever did exist, it worked by injecting inflation into the economy. And each time that happened, the average level of unemployment has risen. Higher inflation followed by higher unemployment. That is the history of the last twenty years.[29]

By the late 1970s, the 30-year consensus on Keynesian economic management was nearing its end. Many politicians and economists denigrated it without acknowledging its profound contribution to the development of British capitalism. First, it was instrumental in facilitating the longest and most sustained period of full employment, economic growth and prosperity experienced in Britain and in many other countries. Second, it is claimed, Keynesianism contributed to the stability of liberal democracy and the foundation of a welfare state, within a capitalist economic framework.

The abandonment of Keynesian economic management, however, could not take place until an alternative economic theory, and an accompanying set of policy tools, had been fashioned. It also required a radical government to implement them. The former was provided by the new monetarist school of economic theory led by Milton Friedman of the University of Chicago and the latter by the Conservative government led by Margaret Thatcher, after the general election of 1979.

> Breaking decisively with past Conservative policy, the new government proceeded to 'roll back the frontiers of the state' by abandoning the commitment to full employment (arguing that government attempts to raise employment simply caused inflation), abolishing controls on exchange, incomes and prices, cutting public expenditure and taxation, raising interest rates and cutting the money supply with the aim of

reducing inflation . . . It introduced legislation designed to curb union power [and] . . . it set about introducing market forces to the public sector.[30]

Economic collectivism and the welfare state were to give way to economic individualism and the growth of an 'enterprise culture'. At the same time, socialism was to be eliminated and the role of government in economic and social affairs to be reduced. Market mechanisms and market forces would be left to determine not only supply and demand but also economic prosperity and the level of employment. The major and central task of government was seen to be the control of the monetary system. Its duty was to determine both the money supply, and its rate of increase, and to reduce central government expenditure and public debt. Within a well-regulated and controlled monetary system, the rest of the economy, it was argued, could be left to self-regulating market forces. Prosperity would follow after a difficult period of adjustment from the Keynesian past. Government, it was believed, could assist the speed of adjustment by taking measures to ensure that the supply side of the economy – long neglected by Keynesian demand side economics – worked more efficiently.

## Monetarism and supply side economics

The monetarist economists, of whom Milton Friedman is one of the best known, were mainly concerned with explaining the origins and causes of inflation, the chief economic problem of governments since the 1960s. This contrasts with Keynesians, who focused on the problems of unemployment and economic depression which characterized the 1920s and 1930s. In simple terms, monetarists believe that the origins of inflation lie in excessively high levels of government expenditure which lead to rapid growth in the money supply. They argue that the quantity of money, if expanded more rapidly than the growth of goods and services, results in inflation. This in turn results in higher unemployment.

One of the chief causes of excessive monetary growth, monetarists believe, is government borrowing, or the public sector borrowing requirement (PSBR), with the PSBR being used to finance budget deficits. Monetarists argue that if inflation is to be controlled, then government must control public expenditure and balance its budget, or at least greatly reduce its budget deficit and therefore its borrowing requirements. Deficit budgeting, and the expansion of consumer demand in order to reduce unemployment, monetarists argue, only results in a spiral of higher inflation and higher unemployment. Monetarists claim that the use of income policies and of social contracts to obtain the agreement of trade unions to reduce wage demands in order to achieve lower unemployment levels does not work. This is because government expansion of the money supply is the cause of the inflation, whilst union wage demands are only a consequence of price inflation.

One of the practical difficulties in using monetarist theory as a government policy tool, which rapidly emerged after 1979, was the problem of defining and measuring money and the money supply. It was also difficult to devise methods for controlling it. Independent economists and the Treasury, in the late 1970s and the early 1980s, devised a number of ways of defining and measuring the money supply and its growth rate. All of them were controversial, and there was little agreement among academic economists. Furthermore, they were usually technically very complex. Nevertheless, after the publication of the government's medium-term financial strategy in 1980, which was an almost pure statement of Friedmanite orthodoxy, Keynesian demand management was officially abandoned and has never been resuscitated. It was substituted by monetary policy in which the control of the money supply, and the reduction of public expenditure and the PSBR, became the crucial means by which the economy would be handled and inflation defeated. Money growth targets were proclaimed and their achievement was seen as vital to the government's economic policy success. The government firmly stated that it would not deviate from its monetary targets or revert to prices and incomes policies even if unemployment rose sharply, as indeed it did.

Interest rates were used as the chief weapon for controlling the money supply, reaching a record level of 17 per cent in November 1979. Despite such high interest rates, money supply continued to grow above the target set. The economy moved sharply into recession and unemployment rose to over three million. In the 1984 budget, the government introduced a new method of measuring the money supply but by 1986 it had clearly abandoned its narrow reliance on monetary policy and money targets. By the late 1980s, strict monetary policy had been quietly dropped and the government instead relied heavily upon interest rates to control the level of economic activity. With the government's budget substantially in surplus by the second half of the 1980s, taxes were reduced,

and the economy expanded and unemployment fell to about two million early in 1989. The monetarist experiment was over.

During the 1980s, there was considerable controversy about what became known as the natural rate of unemployment or the 'non-accelerating inflation rate of unemployment'. It was argued by monetarists that the 'natural' rate of unemployment was the rate resulting from the economic conditions prevailing at any given time. Where the economy was uncompetitive, the structure of industry outdated, the labour market inefficient and inflexible, trade union controls at the workplace strong, and productivity low, then the natural rate of unemployment would be high. If unemployment was to be reduced, these adverse factors had to be removed. If the unemployment level was at its natural level, and expansionist Keynesian demand management methods were used to lower it, then inflation would result. There would not be a permanent drop in unemployment. It is believed that where reflationary measures are persevered with, both high unemployment and high inflation will result. This would appear to be the same analysis offered by James Callaghan to the Labour Party Conference in 1976.

Supply side economics, like monetarism, originated largely in the United States. It is closely linked to monetarism and its policies can, its adherents argue, reduce the natural level of unemployment. Supply siders advocate: measures to improve the efficiency of product and labour markets; legislation to reduce trade union bargaining power, means of controlling working practices and labour costs; increased competition between producers; better education and training of the labour force; the introduction of new technologies; the privatization of allegedly inefficient state monopolies; and the abolition of wages councils.

The most controversial supply side policy is the reduction of personal taxation levels, particularly for higher income earners. This is advocated in the belief that high direct taxation reduces the motivation to work, with lower taxes increasing personal work motivation. Furthermore, it is argued, in the long run higher earnings, lower unemployment and greater output will result and total tax yields rise. It has been argued that:

> Lower tax rates encourage saving, investing, working and risk taking. As people switch into these activities out of leisure, consumption, tax shelters and working nontaxable income, the incentive effects cause an increase in the market

supply of goods and services – thus the name 'supply side economics'. As people respond to the higher after-tax income and wealth, or greater profitability, incomes rise and the tax base grows.[31]

The three Thatcher administrations after 1979 used supply side economic policies as an adjunct to their monetarist policies. The first step was the abolition of exchange controls in 1979, thus allowing sterling to find its market level in the world's foreign exchanges and exposing British exports to competition. Privatization and public sector competitive tendering were also used in an attempt to increase market competitiveness. Other measures included: deregulating the Stock Exchange to improve the efficiency of financial markets; permitting building societies to compete with banks; introducing measures aimed at improving the workings of labour markets; and the introduction of new technologies. Even the professions of law, medicine and education were not exempt from this process.

The most important supply side measure was the reduction in personal income tax. The first cuts were made in 1979 when the basic rate was reduced to 30 per cent and the top rate to 60 per cent. Further cuts were made in subsequent budgets. These tax cuts were made possible by substantial budget surpluses. Yet whether they increased the incentive to work and save has yet to be demonstrated. By general agreement, it would appear that these cuts in personal taxation increased consumer expenditure and house buying sufficiently to cause the underlying rate of inflation to rise. Moreover, during the late 1980s, the balance of payments moved heavily into deficit. The government used the single tool left at its disposal, namely interest rate increases, in an attempt to suppress inflation and reduce imports.

After the resignation of Mrs Thatcher as Prime Minister in November 1990, brought about by a backbench revolt in the Conservative parliamentary party, official government economic policy under Prime Minister John Major followed a pragmatic path involving the use of neo-monetarist and neo-Keynesian policies. With the onset of a worldwide recession in 1990 the government resorted to neither Keynesian demand stimulation policies nor rigid monetarism. As a consequence, national economic policy since 1990 appeared to lack clear purpose, direction and political will. Meanwhile, unemployment reached 3 million, economic growth was stagnant, the balance of payments was heavily in

deficit, the PSBR was set to exceed £50 billion and sterling had been forced out of the EC exchange rate mechanism.

The four major historical phases, or periods, of economic thinking and the related strategies used by governments to justify their economic policies are illustrated schematically in Figure 1.16.

## 1.6    The European Union Labour Market

The Single European Act, passed by the British Parliament in 1986, came into force in 1992. It created for Britain, as it does for the other 11 member countries of the European Union (EU) a single internal market of over 300 million people requiring the free movement of labour, capital, goods and services.

In terms of the single labour market, the Single European Act means that nationals of the EU member countries are free, at least in a legal sense, to seek employment without hindrance in any EU country. This means, in theory, that employers in the EU have access to a labour force of some 150 million people of working age. As Table 1.9 demonstrates, however, the total labour forces of member countries as a percentage of the population of working age varies appreciably. Moreover, the female labour force as a percentage of the female population of working age varies considerably between countries. If, for example, the participation rate in the labour force, of both men and women, in all but one of the other eleven member countries of the EU were to reach the British level, the labour force of the EU would expand greatly.

Most of the increases in the participation rate of men, and particularly women, in the labour forces of many of the countries indicated in Table 1.9 have been the result of fundamental changes in economic, social and cultural attitudes. It is reasonable to assume that participation rates will continue along the same upward path. It is, however, more problematic how much movement of labour will take place between EU member states. There is already substantial evidence to show that the movement of labour between the regions of countries, such as Britain for example, is limited by cultural, kinship and linguistic allegiances, and by housing problems, skill inadequacies and educational shortcomings. How much more difficult it is, then, for labour to move between member states where those factors are compounded by problems of language, social security

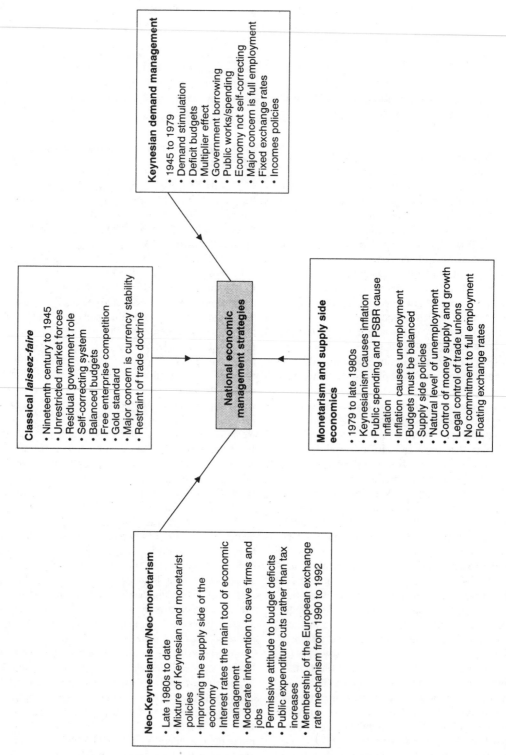

**Classical *laissez-faire***
- Nineteenth century to 1945
- Unrestricted market forces
- Residual government role
- Self-correcting system
- Balanced budgets
- Free enterprise competition
- Gold standard
- Major concern is currency stability
- Restraint of trade doctrine

**Keynesian demand management**
- 1945 to 1979
- Demand stimulation
- Deficit budgets
- Multiplier effect
- Government borrowing
- Public works/spending
- Economy not self-correcting
- Major concern is full employment
- Fixed exchange rates
- Incomes policies

**National economic management strategies**

**Monetarism and supply side economics**
- 1979 to late 1980s
- Keynesianism causes inflation
- Public spending and PSBR cause inflation
- Inflation causes unemployment
- Budgets must be balanced
- Supply side policies
- 'Natural level' of unemployment
- Control of money supply and growth
- Legal control of trade unions
- No commitment to full employment
- Floating exchange rates

**Neo-Keynesianism/Neo-monetarism**
- Late 1980s to date
- Mixture of Keynesian and monetarist policies
- Improving the supply side of the economy
- Interest rates the main tool of economic management
- Moderate intervention to save firms and jobs
- Permissive attitude to budget deficits
- Public expenditure cuts rather than tax increases
- Membership of the European exchange rate mechanism from 1990 to 1992

*Figure 1.16* National economic management strategies.

*Table 1.9* Total labour force in EU countries as a percentage of the population aged 15–64; and female labour force as a percentage of the female population aged 15–64 (in parentheses) for 1960–1989.

| Country | 1960 | 1980 | 1985 | 1989 |
|---|---|---|---|---|
| Belgium | 60.7 (36.4) | 63.0 (47.0) | 62.0 (48.3) | 62.1 (51.6) |
| Denmark | 71.2 (43.5) | 80.3 (71.4) | 81.0 (74.5) | 83.4 (77.3) |
| France | 70.4 (46.6) | 68.1 (54.4) | 65.8 (54.9) | 65.7 (56.2) |
| Germany | 70.3 (49.2) | 68.5 (51.4) | 67.6 (52.3) | 68.6 (54.7) |
| Greece | 65.8 (41.6) | 55.9 (33.0) | 59.6 (41.8) | 59.2 (43.4) |
| Ireland | 67.3 (34.8) | 62.3 (36.3) | 61.3 (36.6) | 60.3 (37.5) |
| Italy | 66.6 (39.6) | 60.8 (39.6) | 59.8 (41.0) | 61.2 (44.3) |
| Luxembourg | 61.8 (32.6) | 64.4 (39.9) | 63.9 (48.3) | 70.3 (49.8) |
| Netherlands | 61.7 (26.2) | 57.7 (35.5) | 58.6 (40.9) | 65.5 (51.0) |
| Portugal | 59.4 (19.9) | 73.9 (57.0) | 71.9 (58.0) | 71.9 (59.6) |
| Spain | 61.6 (26.0) | 57.1 (32.2) | 55.9 (33.3) | 58.6 (39.9) |
| United Kingdom | 72.0 (46.1) | 74.4 (58.3) | 74.6 (60.5) | 76.1 (65.4) |

*Source*: A. Ferner and R. Hyman, *Industrial Relations in the New Europe* (Blackwell, 1992)

benefits, pensions and health care. If the aim of a free and mobile EU-wide labour market is to become a reality, then not only will the social and cultural attitudes of large numbers of indigenous people need to change, but social benefits, housing and health care provisions will have to become harmonized.

Even if large wage differentials emerged between rich and poor areas, non-market obstacles inhibit workers from responding to these price signals. Social and personal circumstances as well as cultural traditions are powerful forces tying people to specific areas. . . . Thus the role of the market mechanism in encouraging the free movement of labour may not be so fluid and smooth as laid down in the text-books.[32]

The labour market of the EU is, however, changing rapidly. As a whole, the EU is experiencing a decline in the proportion of the labour force employed in agriculture, mining and manufacturing industry, and an increase in employment in the services sector. Women are a rising proportion of the EU labour force and the female participation rate is rising rapidly in countries where social attitudes to women working are changing markedly, such as Spain, Italy and Ireland. There is a growing demand from employers for part-timers and those willing to accept short-term and fixed-term contracts and temporary employment. There is also a discernible trend away from large-scale production, or the 'Fordism' of the past, and a growth in medium-sized manufacturing companies capable of responding rapidly to changes in product design, technology, consumer choice and market movements.

In order to achieve these corporate characteristics, 'flexibility' has become the dominant necessity required of both the organization and its employees.

Four major forces appear to be shaping the EU labour market as it responds to the Single European Act (Figure 1.17). First, there is the movement towards European integration and economic convergence required by the indicative timetable laid down for the achievement of a single European currency, fixed exchange rates and a central bank. Such movements are seen to be compatible with the development of a more homogeneous labour market with pay levels and labour costs which reflect competitive efficiency.

Second, there are the conditions contained in the 1989 agreement on a Social Charter of Fundamental Workers' Rights and the Social Action Programme to implement it. Neither of these currently applies to Britain. The eventual impact of the Social Charter on the EU labour market could be considerable as it intends to establish a wide range of benefits for employees, including hours of work, holidays, a living wage, sickness pay and many other matters relating to the employment of EU employees, with the exception of British employees.

The third force shaping the EU labour market is to be found in the body of law relating to employment, the many judgements concerning the rights of employees handed down by the European Court of Justice and the legally enforceable Directives and Regulations concerning workers issued by the European Commission. Examples of EU labour law are those relating to employee rights on the Transfer

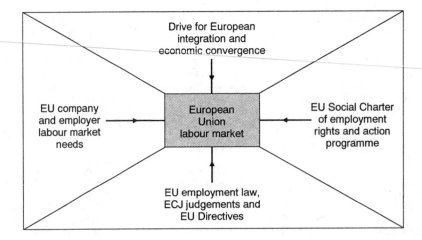

*Figure 1.17* Forces shaping the EU labour market.

of Undertakings and redundancy. Decisions of the European Court of Justice have been mainly concerned with equal pay for women and equality of opportunity in employment. EU directives deal with, for example, health and safety at work, part-time employment, hours of work and maternity rights.

Finally, the demand for labour at the level of the EU labour market is heavily influenced by the needs of European companies and employers. Generally speaking, while employers and their representative bodies have been vigorous supporters of the single market, they have strongly opposed the Social Charter on the grounds not only that it will increase unit labour costs, but also that it introduces even more rigidities into the present EU labour market. Furthermore, EU employers and companies believe that the Social Charter will hinder their ability and right to locate their operations in low labour cost regions and countries of the EU. Employers have pressed successfully for the formal recognition of professional, educational and technical qualifications across the EU, and support the use of the EU Social Fund to provide financial assistance for training and to encourage workers to move from one member state to another in order to find work or change jobs. Employers and their representative organizations have consistently recognized, however, that while the economic objectives of the EU are vital, they are probably subordinate to its long-term mission of political integration and unity.

Free movement of labour is a touchstone of the European integration project. Economically it is regarded as desirable for at once it helps resolve the unemployment problem in labour surplus regions and ease labour market tightening in labour deficit areas. Politically, it is seen as important for through mobility workers from different nations can assimilate, thereby contributing to the removal of historic antagonisms in the region and to the formation of a 'socio-psychological' foundation for European institutions.[33]

## 1.7   Summary Points

- An understanding of the British labour market and the demographic, economic, legal, social and other forces which shape it is an essential prerequisite for the understanding of British industrial relations.
- Because of the sheer complexity of the labour market, descriptions of its component parts provide a better understanding of how it works, rather than theory or model building. Some labour market theories, however, have been influential in determining the policies of some governments.
- Reports and analyses of the labour market and the labour force are carried out from year to year by various departments of government. Careful study of these reports is essential for any understanding of how the labour market is changing.
- The most important trends in the British labour market concern: the decline in manufacturing employment; the increase in service sector

employment; the increase in the proportion of female workers; the higher age profile of the work force and the decline in male manual employment.

- Unemployment has increased since the late 1970s and remains persistently high. The ability, and perhaps the willingness, of governments to bring about 'full employment' appears to be in doubt.
- Since 1979, government policy has sought to improve the efficiency of the labour market and the supply side of the economy, in order that more people might be 'priced back into work'.
- There is little conclusive evidence to show that, in general, trade unions are able, other than in the short term, to raise wage levels above what the market is able or willing to sustain in the long run.
- The introduction of new technologies since the 1970s has taken place with little trade union opposition.
- National management of the economy using Keynesian demand management policies to secure and sustain 'full employment' was abandoned in the 1980s in favour of monetarist methods and higher levels of unemployment. Monetarist policies were, in turn, quietly dropped in the late 1980s. It is now difficult to define or describe how the national economy is being managed.
- The creation of the single European market in 1992 has, at least in theory, brought into existence an EU-wide labour market. How workers, employers, governments and trade unions will respond to and use this vast labour market is uncertain.

## 1.8   References

1. W. E. J. McCarthy (ed.), Introduction, in *Trade Unions*, Penguin, Harmondsworth, 1985, p. 15.
2. *Employment Gazette*, April 1992, p. 179.
3. Neil Millward *et al.*, *Workplace Industrial Relations in Transition*, Dartmouth, Aldershot, 1992, p. 360.
4. Trades Union Congress, *Meeting the Challenge*, TUC, London, 1988, p. 1.
5. *Employment Gazette*, May 1991, p. 292.
6. B. Roberts *et al.* (eds), *New Approaches to Economic Life*, Manchester University Press, 1985, p. 113.
7. *Ibid.*, p. 113.
8. P. Fallon, *The Economics of Labour Markets*, Philip Allan, Oxford, 1988, p. 133.
9. G. Thomason, *A Textbook of Human Resource Management*, Institute of Personnel Management, London, 1988, p. 167.
10. P. Ryan in F. Wilkinson (ed.), *The Dynamics of Labour Market Segmentation*, Academic Press, London, 1981, p. 6.
11. W. Brown, The changing role of trade unions, *British Journal of Industrial Relations*, July 1988, p. 163.
12. C. Mulvey, *The Economic Analysis of Trade Unions*, Martin Robertson, Oxford, 1978, p. 147.
13. B. Burkitt, Excessive trade union powers: existing reality or contemporary myth? in McCarthy, *op. cit.*, pp. 386-7.
14. Robert F. Elliott, *Labour Economics*, McGraw-Hill, Maidenhead, 1990, pp. 461-2.
15. Peter Mathias, Economists, trade unions and wages, in McCarthy, *op. cit.*, pp. 320-1.
16. J. A. Schumpeter, *Capitalism, Socialism and Democracy*, Unwin University Books, London, 1943, p. 83.
17. Transport and General Workers Union, *Microelectronics: New Technology, Old Problems, New Opportunities*, TGWU, London, 1979, p. 2.
18. *Ibid.*, pp. 3-4.
19. I. Maddock, Beyond the Protestant ethic, *New Scientist*, November 1978, p. 594.
20. C. Jenkins and B. Sherman, *The Collapse of Work*, Eyre Methuen, London, 1979, p. 182.
21. W. W. Daniel, *Workplace Industrial Relations and Technical Change*, Frances Pinter, Shaftesbury, 1987, p. 260.
22. *Ibid.*, p. 260.
23. *Ibid.*, p. 272.
24. OECD, *New Directions in Work Organisation*, OECD, Paris, 1992, p. 188.
25. W. W. Daniel, *op. cit.*, p. 282.
26. *Ibid.*, p. 268.
27. A. Fox, *History and Heritage*, Allen and Unwin, London, 1985, p. 451.
28. P. Riddell, *The Thatcher Government*, Blackwell, Oxford, 1985, pp. 1-2.
29. James Callaghan quoted in S. Brittan, *The Role and Limits of Government: Essays in Political Economy*, Maurice Temple Smith, London, 1983, p. 105.
30. J. MacInnes, *Thatcherism at Work*, Open University Press, Milton Keynes, 1987, p. 3.
31. P. C. Robers, Supply side economics: an assessment of American experience in the 1980s, *National Westminster Bank Quarterly Review*, February 1989, p. 63.
32. Paul Teague and John Grahl, *Industrial Relations and European Integration*, Lawrence and Wishart, London, 1992, p. 143.
33. *Ibid.*, p. 142.

# 2

## Theories of Industrial Relations

The social sciences examine, explain and try to predict the behaviour of individuals and groups in those personal, interpersonal and institutionalized activities which are not biologically determined. There are, however, a number of difficulties in studying humans in their social situations. One is the inherent complexity of the task. For example, to what extent is it possible to separate out the psychological, economic, social and political aspects of people's behaviour in organizations and society? Second, there is the difficulty of constructing abstract concepts, models and theories of human actions from observed behaviour and then to articulate these images, whether verbally or in writing, in language which is rigorous to the specialist on the one hand, but comprehensible to the interested non-specialist on the other. The ultimate problem for the student of the social sciences is how to be objective about essentially subjective social phenomena. Indeed, some social philosophers argue that there is no such thing as a truly objective social science. Social reality at any given time, by this view, is dependent upon the particular paradigm being used by the social scientist or human actor.

What is true for the social sciences generally is true for the study of industrial relations particularly. We do not intend to evade these and other related issues in this book. Our purpose in this chapter is to outline and to compare the main academic theories by which industrial relations institutions, structures and processes are analysed by different social theorists. We also suggest a set of frameworks by which the complex phenomena of industrial relations institutions and activities may be conceptualized and categorized. A theory of industrial relations is not an arid academic exercise for its own sake, nor unrelated to the real world. All social actions in life and all the decisions preceding them are based on people's theoretical appraisals of particular social situations, even if they are not manifestly aware of them. This applies, in particular, to the emotive and political area of industrial relations. Every social act people make is a combination of theory, experience, social condition-

ing and practice. In other words, the theories which individuals develop about industrial relations are attempts to construct logically consistent ways of understanding and explaining social behaviour and real-life activities in this complex field of human interest.

It soon becomes clear in real-life situations, however, that people can examine the same industrial relations issue from quite different viewpoints. Consequently each of them behaves as if he or she were in different social situations. An example of this would be the contrasting perceptions which a personnel manager and a shop steward might have of a pay dispute in the company in which they work. One of them might perceive the issue in managerial, corporate and middle-class terms, the other in union and working-class terms and each will act in accordance with his or her beliefs about the situation but in different ways. In this chapter, we examine phenomena such as these and what we consider to be the major theories of industrial relations.

### 2.1 Unitary Theory

The following quotation is taken from the evidence submitted to the Donovan Commission in 1966 by the then chairman and managing director of the Rugby Portland Cement Company, Halford Reddish, who, without realizing it, was putting forward an essentially unitary and human relations view of industrial organization and industrial relations to the Commissioners:

1. I am asked 'how good relations are achieved in a company which does not negotiate with trade unions'.
2. Our thinking proceeds as follows . . .
   Modern industrial organization is in effect a partnership between the labour of yesterday (which we call capital) and the labour of today (all of us who work for wages and salaries) . . .
4. We deplore the use of the terms 'industrial rela-

tions' and 'labour relations'. We prefer 'human relations', by which we mean a recognition of the essential human dignity of the individual . . .

5. An employee, at whatever level, must be made to feel that he is not merely a number on a pay-roll but a recognized member of a team . . .
6. We reject the idea that amongst the employees of a company there are 'two sides' meaning the executive directors and managers on the one hand and the weekly-paid employees on the other. Executive directors are just as much employees of the company as anyone else. We are all on the same side, members of the same team . . .
8. We recognize that the tone of any organization depends primarily on one man, on the executive head of it: on his philosophy, on his outlook, on the standards which he sets, on his example: in short, on his leadership.
9. Leadership is surely the key to good human relations – leadership at all levels. It must embrace, *inter alia*: . . . Maintenance of strict discipline, as firm as it is fair . . . A conviction that loyalty must be a two-way traffic. I expect every employee to be loyal to the company and to me as the temporary captain of the team: he has an equal right to expect loyalty from me . . . Communication – in the widest sense of the term . . .[1]

The essence of the unitary theory of industrial relations, held by Halford Reddish and others, is that every work organization is an integrated and harmonious whole existing for a common purpose. They assume that each employee identifies unreservedly with the aims of the enterprise and with its methods of operating. By this view, there is no conflict of interest between those supplying financial capital to the enterprise and their managerial representatives, and those contributing their labour and job skills. By definition the owners of capital and labour are joint partners to the common aims of efficient production, high profits and good pay in which everyone in the organization has a stake. It follows that there cannot be 'two sides' in industry. Indeed managers and managed alike are merely parts of the same 'team'. This team, however, is expected to be provided with strong leadership from the top to keep it working and to ensure commitment to the tasks to be done and to its managerial office holders.

This requires, on the part of management, at the minimum a paternalistic approach towards subordinate employees or, at the other extreme, a more authoritarian one, together with a suitable com-

munication structure to keep employees informed of managerial and enterprise decisions. Conversely, employees are expected to remain loyal to the organization and to its management in deference to the common problems facing managers and subordinates alike. Thus the unitary theory of industrial relations emerges from a belief that work enterprises, whether privately or publicly owned, are very much like a professional football team: 'Team spirit and undivided management authority co-exist to the benefit of all.'[2] Work organizations, in short, are viewed as unitary in their structure and unitary in their purposes, and as having a single source of authority and a cohesive set of participants motivated by common goals. Consequently industrial relations is assumed to be based on mutual co-operation and harmony of interest between management and managed within the enterprise.

One implication of unitarism is that factionalism within the enterprise, or in a part of it, is seen as a pathological social condition. Subordinate employees are not expected to challenge managerial decisions or the right to manage, while trade unionism is viewed as an illegitimate intrusion into the unified and co-operative structure of the workplace. More than this, it is suggested, trade unionism competes almost malevolently with management for the loyalty and commitment of employees to their employer. In other words, unitary theory in its traditional or classical form denies the validity of conflict at work whether between management and employees, between management and unions, or even between the organization and its customers. The concepts of common purpose and harmony of interests further imply:

> that apparent conflict is either (a) merely frictional, e.g. due to incompatible personalities or 'things going wrong', or (b) caused by faulty 'communications', e.g. 'misunderstanding' about aims or methods, or (c) the result of stupidity in the form of failure to grasp the communality of interest, or (d) the work of agitators inciting the supine majority who would otherwise be content.[3]

Collective bargaining and trade unions are therefore perceived as being anti-social, anti-managerial mechanisms, since acceptance of two opposed and competing interest groups within the enterprise, in the persons of management and union representatives, only precipitates and crystallizes unnecessary and destructive industrial conflict between what in effect are viewed as two non-competing, co-operative parties.

It soon becomes evident that the unitary theory of industrial relations is predominantly managerially oriented in its inception, in its emphasis and in its application. Indeed it is a theoretical perspective with which many managers and employers identify because it reassures them in their roles as organizational decision makers and legitimizes the acceptance of their authority by subordinate employees. A number of American-based companies in Britain, for example, are unitary organizations and carry over this perspective in one form or another from the United States, as illustrated by their preference neither to deal with nor to negotiate with trade unions. Even where such companies have been forced into conceding trade union recognition to their manual employees, they are often very reluctant to extend equivalent rights to their non-manual counterparts. However, it would be wrong to associate unitarism with American firms alone. Many British companies, large and small, are also directed by boards and managed by executives with basically unitary views. Some of these organizations, while reluctantly negotiating with trade unions, nevertheless continue to direct their industrial relations policies along unitary lines by limiting, for example, the subject matter about which they are prepared to bargain with trade union representatives to a narrow range of issues.

Some employees also hold unitary theories of work and of industrial relations. It seems likely, for example, that the churches and the armed services have traditionally tended towards unitary structures and consensus values which have generally been accepted by their managerial cadres and their subordinates alike. Whether these circumstances will continue, however, has to be seen in the light of European developments. The growth of unionization has already substantially proceeded within some of the armed forces in western Europe, for example, whilst both the Anglican and Catholic churches have become internally factionalized and pluralized in recent years.

In summary, traditional unitary theory in its purest form stresses the harmonious nature of work enterprises and of industrial relations within them. To what extent it represents consistent and compatible viewpoints amongst different status groups within particular organizations depends upon two main factors: first, the social structure of the organization; and, second, whether the unitary value system is accepted by subordinate personnel within it. The latter is, perhaps, the linchpin around which unitary theory of industrial relations is accepted or rejected.

A variant of unitary theory, 'neo-unitary' theory,

appears to have emerged in some organizations since the 1980s. It builds on existing unitary concepts but is more sophisticated in the ways it is articulated and applied within enterprises. Its main aim seems to be to integrate employees, as individuals, into the companies in which they work. Its orientation is distinctly market centred, managerialist and individualist. By gaining employee commitment to quality production, customer needs and job flexibility, employers embracing this frame of reference have expectations of employee loyalty, customer satisfaction and product security in increasingly competitive market conditions. Companies adopting a neo-unitary approach to managing people share a number of ways in which they do this: they try to create a sense of common purpose and shared corporate culture; they emphasize to all employees the primacy of customer service; they set explicit work targets for employees; they invest heavily in training and management development; and they sometimes provide employment security for their workers.

The personnel management techniques used to facilitate employee commitment, quality output and worker flexibility include: performance-related pay; profit sharing; harmonization of terms and conditions; employee involvement; and a 'human resources' management function, rather than a personnel management function. The emphasis of neo-unitary approaches to industrial relations – or what some of its protagonists describe as 'employee relations' – is that committed, motivated and well-trained people are the key to corporate success. Neo-unitary theory can be summed up in the words of a leading industrialist, speaking to a conference of senior personnel managers in 1987:

> Increasingly . . . businesses are having to tailor everything they do towards creating and servicing a sustained customer need . . . Something more is called for in getting a competitive edge: that 'something more' is the commitment, capability and contribution of the people working in an organisation. The sheer quality of the people – in particular the quality of the managers – is what makes the difference . . . It is my contention that the people employed are the major determinant of corporate competitiveness and success. Managerial vision is the key to change – vision to create ambitions . . . goals for the organisation and vision to win the commitment of employees to those goals and to draw from them their maximum contribution to achieving them.[4]

## 2.2 Conflict Theory

Conflict theory is based on two interrelated views of society and of industrial relations between employers and employees. The first is that although Britain and western industrialized societies are still class based, they are essentially 'post-capitalist' in the sense that political and industrial conflict are increasingly institutionally separated within them and that industrial conflict has become less violent because its existence has been accepted and its manifestations have been socially regulated through agreed constitutional arrangements. The second view is that work organizations are microcosms of society. Since society comprises a variety of individuals and of social groups, each having their own social values and each pursuing their own self-interests and objectives, it is argued, those controlling and managing work enterprises similarly have to accommodate the differing values and competing interests within them. It is only by doing this that private or public enterprises can function effectively. Industrial relations between employers and unions and between managers and trade unionists, by this view, are an expression of the conflict and the power relations between organized groups in society generally. As such, it is claimed, industrial conflict between managers and their subordinates has to be recognized as an endemic feature of work relationships and managed accordingly.

### Post-capitalism

A major element in post-capitalist theories of contemporary society and industrial relations is the proposition that the nature of class conflict has substantially changed from that suggested by Marx in his nineteenth-century analysis. In Marxist theory class conflict is perceived as being synonymous with industrial conflict and political conflict. Under market capitalism, Marxists argue, the capitalists or the owners of the means of production are identical with the ruling class in industry and politics, while wage-earners, owning only their labour resources, are relatively powerless in industrial relations and in politics. Capitalists are the social elite and the proletariat are the socially weak. What, then, has changed according to post-capitalist analysis? First, it is argued, we now live in a more open and socially mobile society compared with the class-based social divisions associated with nineteenth-century and early twentieth-century capitalism. The widening of educational opportunity, the democratization of

politics, and the growth of public sector industry, for instance, have opened up recruitment to a whole range of sought-after roles in society, including those within industry, politics, education, the professions, the arts and so on, which would have been inconceivable a hundred years ago. Moreover, the creation of the welfare state, it is suggested, mitigated the worst effects of social deprivation, economic inequality and abject poverty.

Second, the post-capitalists argue, the distribution of authority, property and social status in society is more widely diffused than in the past. The positions which individuals occupy in the authority structure of industry, for example, do not necessarily correlate with their positions in the political structure or with their social standing in the community. The village postal worker can become the local councillor, the schoolteacher a Member of Parliament and the trade unionist a Justice of the Peace. Similarly the union convener within the workplace might have potentially more industrial power than the senior management with which he or she negotiates. Such individuals may also have had more political power if they were on the selection panel of the local constituency Labour Party responsible for selecting the prospective parliamentary candidate in a safe Labour seat. In other words, post-capitalists take the view that the dominant and subordinate classes within industry need no longer necessarily correspond with the political or social divisions of society generally.

Above all, these theorists believe, the institutionalization of conflict in industry not only has decreased in intensity but also has changed its form. Several changes seem to be of particular importance in this respect:

(1) the organization of conflicting interest groups itself; (2) the establishment of 'parliamentary' negotiating bodies in which these groups meet; (3) the institutions of mediation and arbitration; (4) formal representations of labor within the individual enterprise; and (5) tendencies towards and institutionalization of workers' participation in industrial management.[5]

Thus, it is argued, the emergence of trade unionism, employers' organizations and collective bargaining, together with union representation at enterprise and workplace level, now effectively regulate the inevitable social conflicts arising between management and subordinates at work. Even where these conflicts seem irresolvable, third-party intervention, usually through state agencies providing conciliation and arbitration services, is now available to provide workable remedies. By this analysis, extending worker participation in managerial decision making, as happens in board level worker representation in countries like Denmark, the Netherlands and Germany, is seen as a logical progression in institutionalizing the power relations between managers and subordinates at work. Post-capitalist society, in short, is viewed as an open society in which political, economic and social power is increasingly dispersed and in which the regulation of industrial and political conflict are of necessity dissociated.

## Pluralism

A second theoretical concept closely related to that of post-capitalism, and of central importance in the conflict theory of industrial relations, is 'pluralism'. According to Clegg, one of its major apologists:

> Pluralism emerged as a criticism of the political doctrine of sovereignty – that somewhere in an independent political system there must be a final authority whose decisions are definitive. Not so, said the pluralist. Within any political system there are groups with their own interests and beliefs, and the government itself . . . depends on their consent and co-operation. There are no definitive decisions by final authorities: only continuous compromises.[6]

A plural society, in other words, is a relatively stable one but not static. It has to accommodate to different and divergent pressure groups to enable social and political changes to take place constitutionally. This is achieved through negotiation, concession and compromise between pressure groups, and between many of them and government.

It is from this analysis of political pluralism that industrial relations pluralism is derived. Just as society is perceived as comprising a number of interest groups held together in some sort of loose balance by the agency of the state, so work organizations are viewed as being held in balance by the agency of management. The pluralist concepts of political sovereignty and of managerial prerogative have much in common. Trade unions are viewed as the legitimate representatives of employee interests at work with the right to challenge the right to manage. There are also, it is suggested, similarities between the processes of political concession and compromise, on the one hand, and of collective bargaining on the other. Above all, the pluralist argues, 'greater stability

and adaptability is given to industrial relations by collective bargaining than by shackling and outlawing trade unions'.[7] According to pluralist theory, the central feature of industrial relations is the potential conflict existing between employer and employed and between management and managed within work enterprises. Unlike in unitary theory, however, trade unionism is accepted by pluralists as having both a representative function and an important part in regulating this conflict, rather than in causing it. Similarly, collective bargaining is recognized as being the institutional means by which conflict between employers and employees over the wage – work bargain, and its adaptation, is regularized and resolved. Industrial conflict, therefore, is accepted by pluralists not only as being inevitable but also as requiring containment within the social mechanisms of collective bargaining, conciliation and arbitration.

There is little doubt that the pluralist and post-capitalist analyses of industrial relations, with their emphasis on the twin virtues of collective bargaining and parliamentary democracy as separate but conflict-resolving and rule-making processes, were the predominant academic orthodoxy in Britain during the 1960s and 1970s. Initially they were strongly associated with the thinking of a small group of University of Oxford academics. Their individual and collective views, for example, had an important impact on the deliberations and findings of the Royal Commission, chaired by Lord Donovan between 1965 and 1968, and on its final Report. The so-called 'Oxford' approach to industrial relations influenced not only public policy and a generation of scholars in the field but also industrial relations practitioners. During the 1980s and 1990s, however, neo-unitary theory enjoyed a partial renaissance amongst some managers and students of industrial relations, as shifts to the right in British politics, to market economics and the weakening of union bargaining power in segments of the labour market, occurred.

Criticism of industrial relations pluralism also comes from other quarters. The latter believe, for instance, that those working within the pluralist framework implicitly accept the institutions, principles and assumptions of the social and political *status quo* as unproblematic.

> In doing so they add their professional status, personal prestige, and influential involvement in public policy making to the forces and influences which lead subordinate groups to continue seeing the *status quo* as legitimate, inevitable,

unchangeable, 'only to be expected', subject only to changes at the margin.[8]

Others, such as Goldthorpe, have argued that the liberal pluralist approach to industrial relations is fundamentally conservative. Indeed:

> the changes which it seeks to promote are ones designed to bring about the more effective integration of labour into the existing structure of economic and social relations, in industry and the wider society, rather than ones intended to produce any basic alteration in this structure.[9]

Nevertheless, despite its critics and a renascent neo-unitarism, industrial conflict theory remains a major theoretical approach to industrial relations in Britain. Yet whilst collective bargaining fits easily into pluralist theory, consultation or joint problem solving does so to a lesser extent. For this reason it is useful to distinguish between 'hard' pluralism and collective bargaining, which are conflict centred, and 'soft' pluralism and joint consultation, which are problem centred.

## 2.3   Social Action Theory

Social action theory in industrial relations emphasizes the individual responses of the social actors, such as managers, employees and union representatives, to given situations. It contrasts with systems theory which suggests that behaviour in an industrial relations system is explicable in terms of its structural features. Social action theory is pre-eminently associated with the studies of Max Weber. According to Weber, action is social 'by virtue of the subjective meaning attached to it by the acting individual . . . it takes account of the behaviour of others and is thereby oriented in its course'.[10] He insists that in order for social actions to be explained they must be interpreted in terms of their subjectively intended meanings, not their objectively valid ones. If only observable behaviour is examined, it is argued, the significance and value which individual actors place upon their behaviour are likely to be misinterpreted.

Social action, then, is behaviour having subjective meaning for individual actors, with social action theory focusing on understanding particular actions in industrial relations situations rather than on just observing explicit industrial relations behaviour. This contrasts with systems theory which regards behaviour in industrial relations as reflecting the impersonal processes external to the system's social

actors over which they have little or no control. In emphasizing that social action derives from the personal meanings which individuals attach to their own and other people's actions, social action theorists are suggesting that social actors are constrained by the ways in which they construct their own social reality. 'On the one hand, it seems, Society makes man, on the other, Man makes society'.[11] Individual actors, however, do not share the same value systems which 'means that individuals attach different meanings to their interaction'.[12] Managers and union representatives, for example, do not come together because they have the same goals and values 'but because, for a while at least, their differing ends may be served by the same means'.[13]

Figure 2.1 indicates the main influences affecting individual choice and social action in given situations. The fundamental point is that social action emerges out of the meanings and circumstances attributed by individuals to particular social situations, thereby defining their social reality. Through interaction between actors, such as that between personnel managers and union officers, line managers and personnel specialists and union representatives and their members, individuals as well as having an element of choice in interpreting their own roles, and in acting out their intentions, also modify, change and transform social meanings for themselves and for others. The major difference between a social action approach in examining behaviour in industrial relations and a systems approach is this: action theory assumes an existing system where action occurs, but cannot explain the nature of the system, 'while the Systems approach is unable to explain satisfactorily why particular actors act as they do'.[14] The first views the industrial relations system as a product of the actions of its parts, the other aims to explain the actions of its parts in terms of the nature of the system as a whole.

Social action theory also has its critics. Marxists argue, for example, that those supporting the action frame of reference neglect the 'structural influences of which the actors themselves may be unconscious'. Whilst the consciousness of individual actors in the industrial relations system towards its politico-economic structures can be to some extent autonomous, it is limited in practice. This is because: 'Definitions of reality are themselves socially generated and sustained, and the ability of men to achieve their goals is constrained by the objective characteristics of their situation.'[15] Perhaps the most useful feature of social action theory in industrial

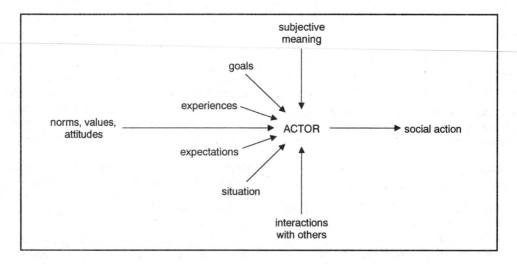

*Figure 2.1* The main influences on individual social action.

relations is the 'way in which it stresses that the individual retains at least some freedom of action and ability to influence events'.[16] Although the structures of the industrial relations system may influence the actions of its actors, these in turn also influence the system as a whole, including its outputs.

## 2.4  Systems Theory

If conflict theory has dominated much British thinking in the field, then so-called 'systems theory' has been the major American contribution to industrial relations theorizing. Systems theory has also influenced British and European students of industrial relations, including those supporting conflict theory. Systems theory was first articulated by John Dunlop in his seminal book *Industrial Relations Systems*, published in the United States in 1958. Its purpose is to present a general theory of industrial relations and 'to provide tools of analysis to interpret and to gain understanding of the widest possible range of industrial-relations facts and practice'.[17] An industrial relations system is not, for Dunlop, part of a society's economic system but a separate and distinctive subsystem of its own, partially overlapping the economic and political decision-making systems with which it interacts. In his view, systems theory provides the analytical tools and the theoretical basis to make industrial relations an academic discipline in its own right.

According to Dunlop:

An industrial-relations system at any one time in its development is regarded as comprised of

certain actors, certain contexts, an ideology which binds the industrial-relations system together, and a body of rules created to govern the actors at the work place and work community.[18]

It is this network or web of rules, consisting of procedures for establishing the rules, the substantive rules themselves, and the procedures for deciding their application to particular situations, which are the products of the system. 'The establishment and administration of these rules is the major concern or output of the industrial-relations subsystem of industrial society.'[19] These rules are of various kinds and may be written, oral or custom and practice. They include managerial decisions, trade union regulations, laws of the state, awards by governmental agencies, collective agreements, and workplace traditions. Furthermore, they cover not only pay and conditions but also disciplinary matters, methods of working, the rights and duties of employers and employees and so on. It is the 'rules' of industrial relations which have to be explained by the 'independent' variables of an industrial relations system.

As can be seen in Figure 2.2, there are three sets of independent variables or factors in an industrial relations system: the 'actors', the 'contexts' and the 'ideology' of the system. The actors or active participants comprise: first, a hierarchy of managers and their representatives; second, a hierarchy of non-managerial employees and their representatives; and third, specialized third-party agencies whether

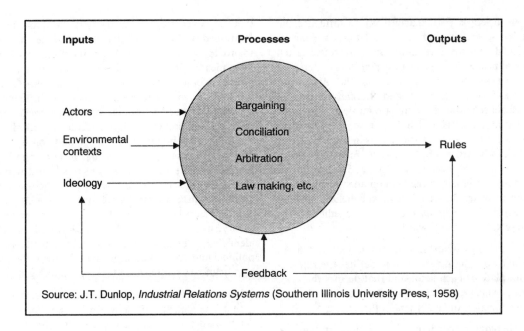

| Inputs | Processes | Outputs |
|--------|-----------|---------|

Actors ————→

Environmental contexts ————→

Ideology ————→

Bargaining

Conciliation

Arbitration

Law making, etc.

————→ Rules

———— Feedback ————

Source: J.T. Dunlop, *Industrial Relations Systems* (Southern Illinois University Press, 1958)

*Figure 2.2* A simple model of an industrial relations system.

governmental or private ones. Dunlop argues that managerial hierarchies need not own the capital assets of production and may be located in either private or public enterprises. He also suggests that although employees may not necessarily be formally organized, they often are. Indeed, they may be organized into a number of competing or complementary employee organizations. In his view, however, totalitarian societies normally have governmental agencies which are so powerful that they override managers and employees on almost all matters.

Dunlop also describes three environmental contexts that play a decisive part in shaping the rules of an industrial relations system and with which these actors interact. These are:

(1) the technological characteristics of the work place and work community, (2) the market or budgetary constraints which impinge on the actors, and (3) the locus and distribution of power in the larger society.[20]

He regards particular technologies as having far-reaching consequences in determining industrial relations rule making. Technology, for example, affects the size of the workforce, its concentration or dispersion, its location and proximity to the employees' places of residence, and the duration of employment.

It also influences the proportions of skills in the workforce, the ratio of male to female workers, and health and safety at the place of work. An industrial relations system also has to adapt to the product markets or to the budgetary constraints of the enterprise. Although these impinge on management initially, they ultimately concern all the actors in a particular system. Such constraints may be local, national or international. Dunlop considers, for example, the balance of payments to be a form of market constraint for national systems of industrial relations. Furthermore, in Britain, for example, voluntary organizations like charitable trusts and public enterprises are no less constrained by budgetary forces, for example, than are private businesses. These constraints are no less operative in planned economies than in market economies.

By the locus and distribution of power in the larger society, Dunlop means the distribution of power *outside* the industrial relations system which is given to that system. This is important because the relative distribution of power in society tends to be reflected within the industrial relations system itself. Yet it need not necessarily determine the behaviour of the actors in industrial relations. It is, rather, a context which helps to structure the industrial relations system itself. The distribution of power within the larger society is particularly likely to influence the state's specialist industrial relations agencies. National industrial relations systems reflect such societal power. This helps to explain the differences which exist, he argues, between the American, British, Spanish, Swedish and Russian systems of industrial relations. Equally, a plant-level system of industrial relations which is part of a more centralized, industry-wide structure, as in Britain, differs significantly from one which is formally decentralized to plant level as in the United States.

The final element in the Dunlopian systems theory is the ideology or set of ideas and beliefs held by the actors which binds the system together. More precisely, in Dunlop's words:

> The ideology of the industrial-relations system is a body of common ideas that defines the role and place of each actor and that defines the ideas which each actor holds towards the place and function of the others in the system.[21]

The ideology of an industrial relations system, he says, must be distinguished from that of the wider society. Nevertheless, they would be expected to be similar or at least compatible with each other. Each of the main sets of actors in an industrial relations system might even have its own ideology. But the hallmark of a mature industrial relations system is that its constituent ideologies are sufficiently congruent to allow the emergence of a common set of ideas which recognize an acceptable role for each in the system. In this respect, Dunlop quotes the ideology of voluntarism, or legal abstentionism, as being the traditionally accepted one by the parties in the British system of industrial relations at the time he was writing.

These, then, are the main concepts described by Dunlop in his systems theory of industrial relations. The ideas have been refined and developed by other writers but they have not radically changed Dunlop's model. As Wood and his colleagues argue the 'rules' approach to industrial relations does not and need not focus upon rules *per se* 'but also on both rule-making and application, and their links with behaviour'.[22] Systems theory, however, has its critics. On the one hand, supporters of the systems approach have criticized its lack of analytical rigour and its static view of industrial relations. They have suggested that the model requires refinement and development. For example, they have argued that Dunlop's systems theory uses the term 'system' in a too loose and undefined manner. They also consider

that in concentrating on the structural or static features of industrial relations, Dunlop has omitted to provide a framework for analysing the processes or dynamics of industrial relations decision making. There are other criticisms of systems theory: first, its inability to give sufficient weight to 'influenced action, and actors' definitions' of industrial relations; second, its notion of a unifying ideology; and, third, the difficulties in analysing change and conflict. Its major weakness, however, is that little emphasis is placed upon the actor's definitions of social structure 'and how the interaction between structure and definition influence [social] action'.[23]

Marxist critics, on the other hand, view systems theory, like pluralist theory with which it is closely identified, as being too concerned with defending the political and economic *status quo*. For them the real significance of pluralism and systems thinking is that:

> It provides a plausible explanation of reality in that it recognizes conflicts which are visibly apparent yet it is as protective of the *status quo*, and as unquestioning about existing relationships, as the purely static unitary approach.[24]

Notwithstanding these points, systems theory like conflict theory has had a major impact on industrial relations theorizing and research work among non-Marxist thinkers in the field since the 1960s. As such, it needs to be understood by students and practitioners of industrial relations so that they can assess its relative strengths and weaknesses for themselves.

## 2.5  Marxist Theory

Marxist interpretations of industrial relations are not strictly theories of industrial relations *per se*. Marxism is, rather, a general theory of society and of social change with implications for the analysis of industrial relations within capitalist societies. Marxist analysis, in other words, is essentially a method of social inquiry into the power relationships of society and a way of interpreting social reality. It is not a definitive political creed. Indeed there are a number of different schools of Marxist scholarship, social thought and political action. This means that Marxist thinking is neither necessarily dogmatic nor monolithic, although it can be sectarian. Hence it is not strictly accurate to refer to *a* Marxist theory of industrial relations. To understand the relevance of Marxist theory to industrial relations it is necessary to separate out those main features of general Marxist analysis which contribute to its special character as a means of interpreting relations between the capitalist and wage earning classes. Further, Marx himself wrote comparatively little about trade unionism and collective bargaining, basically because neither of these institutions was firmly established in Britain when he was studying nineteenth-century capitalist development. Thus the application of Marxian theory as it relates to industrial relations derives indirectly from later Marxist scholars rather than directly from the works of Marx himself.

The starting points for the Marxist analysis of society are the assumptions that: social change is universal; class conflict is the catalytic source of such change; and these conflicts, which arise out of differences in economic power between competing social groups, are rooted in the structures and institutions of society itself. Relations between social groups, in other words, are perceived as being not only dominated by pressures for change but also encompassed by inevitable internal contradictions which must eventually transform the class-based nature of pre-capitalist and capitalist societies. The conceptual method by which Marxists examine the dynamic character of social relations is described as 'dialectical materialism'.

> When reality is viewed dialectically it is seen as a process involving interdependent parts which interact on each other. When reality is also viewed materialistically it is seen as phenomena predominantly influenced by economic factors. The dialectical relationship between economic factors, therefore, provides the prime motivation for change. This briefly is what Marxism in the first instance is about.[25]

Dialectical materialism, in other words, assumes that a society's social and political institutions grow out of its economic infrastructure or power base, and that it is from the dialectical conflict between social classes with opposed economic interests that social change takes place.

For Marxists, as can be seen from Figure 2.3, the capitalist or bourgeois state is only one stage in the evolution of human society. The first stage is primitive communism. Feudalism emerges out of this and from feudalism capitalism develops. The significance of capitalism, in the Marxist view, is that it too is a changing phenomenon which has not done away with class antagonisms but has given rise to new social conflicts within society, those between the 'bourgeoisie' and the 'proletariat'.

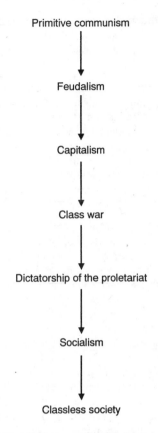

Figure 2.3 Marxist theory and social change.

> By bourgeoisie is meant the class of modern Capitalists, owners of the means of social production and employers of wage labour. By proletariat, the class of modern wage-labourers who, having no means of production of their own, are reduced to selling their labour power in order to live.[26]

The contradictions which persist between those who privately own the means of production in the pursuit of profit, on the one hand, and those who have to sell their labour for wages to survive, on the other, are thus perceived as being irreconcilable in the context of a class-based bourgeois society.

For Marxists moreover, unlike pluralists and unitarists, political and class conflict are synonymous with industrial conflict since 'the capitalist structure of industry and of wage-labour is closely connected with the pattern of class division in society'.[27] Thus the conflict taking place in industrial relations between those who buy labour and those who sell it is seen as a permanent feature of capitalism, merely reflecting the predominant power base of the bourgeoisie and the class relations of capitalist society generally. By this view:

> Class conflict permeates the whole of society and is not just an industrial phenomenon. In the same way trade unionism is a social as well as industrial phenomenon. Trade unions are, by implication, challenging the property relations whenever they challenge the distribution of the national product. They are challenging all the prerogatives which go with the ownership of the means of production, not simply the exercise of control over labour power in industry.[28]

There are both short-term and long-term implications in the Marxist analysis of bourgeois society and of the class-based structure of capitalist industrial relations. Within society, for example, the class struggle between capital and labour is regarded as being continuous – even where trade unions are absent. It takes place, it is argued, because capitalists and proletarians seek to maintain and to extend their relative positions in the economic power structure enabling 'surplus value' to be distributed between them. Such conflict is seen to be unremitting and unavoidable. Neither employees individually nor trade unions collectively can be divorced from the realities of these power relations, either by disregarding them or by succumbing to the manipulative techniques of employer persuasion.

Trade union organization is viewed as the inevitable consequence of the capitalist exploitation of wage labour. The vulnerability of employees as individuals invariably leads them to form collectivities or unions in order to protect their own class interests, although many Marxists do not believe that trade unions in themselves provide the basis for revolutionary action. Collective bargaining and militant trade unionism, however, cannot resolve the problems of industrial relations in capitalist society. They merely accommodate temporarily the contradictions inherent within the capitalist mode of production and social relations. Indeed the continuous relationship of conflict, whether open or concealed, 'stems from a conflict of interests in industry and society which is closely linked with the operation of contradictory tendencies in the capitalist economic system'.[29]

More significantly, industrial relations become not ends in themselves, but a means to an end – the furtherance of the class war between capital and labour, for by Marxist analysis, bourgeois society inevitably gives rise to political revolution by the proletariat. Out of this emerges a dictatorship of the proletariat, then socialism and ultimately the communism of the classless society. Trade unionism and industrial relations conflict are merely symptoms of the inherent class divisions within capitalism. They are, Marxists contend, a main element in the working-class struggle against capitalist exploitation, and in the eventual emergence of a socialist economy, followed by utopian communism. It is out of trade union consciousness and industrial conflict, they suggest, that working class consciousness and political revolution can be precipitated. As such, these conflicts are instrumental in the 'formation of the proletariat into a class, overthrow of bourgeois supremacy, conquest of political power by the proletariat'[30] and in acting out the materialist conception of history. To Marxists, industrial relations are essentially politicized and part of the class struggle. They become overtly political when either class seeks to influence the state to intervene on its behalf. They become potentially revolutionary when working-class organizations, including trade unions, seek to abolish the power base of the bourgeois class within capitalism and to establish a socialist society.

## 2.6   Collectivism and Individualism in Industrial Relations

What, therefore, are industrial relations? What sense can be made of this complex area of human activity which appears to have at least five theoretical perspectives – the unitary and its neo-unitary variant; the conflict-pluralist; the social action; the systems; and the Marxist – each of which is based on its own assumptions about human behaviour and none of which seems to relate substantially to the others. Is there, indeed, any *one* valid theory of industrial relations or any combination of theories which put contemporary industrial relations in Britain into appropriate analytical and descriptive frameworks?

In the first place, traditional unitary theory provides an image of an ideal world in which there is industrial relations stability and an absence of any industrial conflict. Its interpretation of the nature of society emphasizes orderly and stable work organizations, imbued with senses of common purpose and a value consensus which are shared and supported by all working members of the enterprise, and it focuses on individualist or personal relations between each employer and each of the employees. It does not accept that there is overt and covert competition and conflict between those seeking the control and allocation of limited and scarce resources in work enterprises and in society. Those holding a unitary perspective of industrial relations in a market economy like that of Britain believe that the purpose of industrial relations arrangements is to advance what are perceived to be the common goals of management and subordinate employees through mutual co-operation at work. At the same time, this allows management exclusive or predominant decision-making authority within work organizations and a legitimation of virtually unchallenged managerial prerogative in the working environment. Whilst stressing the commonality of interests between management and subordinates at work, unitary theory simultaneously justifies the considerable differentials and inequalities in income, status and power which exist between managers and non-managerial employees in our sort of society. Unitary theory, therefore, provides a major source of support and authority for many managers. It also provides a sense of security for those subordinate employees who identify with its underlying assumptions of enlightened managerialism and conflict-free industrial relations. Further, as conceded earlier, more sophisticated neo-unitary approaches to managing industrial relations, or more properly 'employee relations', have emerged among some British employers during the 1980s and 1990s. This was in response to competitive product market pressures, weakened unions and increased employer and managerial confidence in the workplace and the labour market.

An alternative view of industrial relations is that deriving from conflict theory and pluralist theory, in both their hard and soft versions. The basic argument is that diverse pressure groups, pursuing their own self-interest through intergroup negotiation and compromise, are a basic feature of our society. In this context, the main purpose of society's industrial relations institutions is to resolve conflict within and between different organizational and employment interest groups. In this model, industrial relations focus on collective and representative relations between employers and employee organizations. This is not to deny the class-based structure of British society. But it suggests that the Marxist stress on the inevitable and polarized class struggle in industry and society between capitalists and proletariat, whilst probably a valid interpretation of nineteenth-century Victorian capitalism, does little to explain the complex political, economic and social conflicts in late twentieth-century Britain and other advanced societies. In our view, the existence of the mixed economy, the welfare state, political democracy, advancing prosperity and contemporary trade unionism have radically transformed the lives of ordinary citizens, at home, at work and politically, compared with their position in the heyday of the old market capitalism which ceased to exist, in effect, after 1939.

Despite its critics, pluralism neither inherently views social relations statically, nor morally justifies the political, economic and social *status quo*. Indeed a pluralist theory is just as useful a method of perceiving social behaviour and industrial relations practices in dynamic terms, as is the Marxist analysis. It is a pragmatic interpretation of society and of its power relations but it does not necessarily justify them. A pluralist can also accept that 'within the existing form of society . . . a disordered state of industrial relations may best be understood not as a pathological, but as a normal condition'.[31] Perhaps the weakest and strongest element in the industrial conflict and pluralist position is, somewhat paradoxically, its attempt to avoid absolute moral value judgments. On the other hand, both unitary theory and Marxist theory are essentially value laden – but from diametrically opposed political and moral viewpoints.

The key contribution which social action theory provides in industrial relations is the importance attached to individual meanings and actions in work relationships. These include inter-managerial relationships, relationships between managers and union representatives, amongst union representatives, and between union representatives and their members. It is the industrial relations actors' own definitions of their work situations which are taken as the basis for explaining their behaviour and relationships. The obverse to systems theory, it emphasizes the relevance of individual actors in perceiving the nature of their work, in making personal choices, in interacting with others, and in taking industrial relations decisions. The actions of industrial relations participants, in other words, are not viewed as being determined solely by the structural constraints within which they operate, but by the expectations and values of the individual actors and the meanings *they* assign to particular industrial relations situations.

Systems theory also has something to offer the student of industrial relations. Its emphasis on the diverse forms of industrial relations rules which exist, the different rule-making methods, and the ways in which rules are applied is a useful contribution to industrial relations theorizing, and to understanding industrial relations practices. One of the most valuable insights which systems theory provides is its identification of the variety of industrial relations variables and the complex ways in which they interact. By focusing on the 'outputs' or rules of industrial relations systems, on their 'processes' such as collective bargaining and other types of rule making, and on their 'inputs' such as the actors involved in rule making, systems theory provides a useful framework for classifying and describing the elements within any industrial relations structure. For example, it can be used to compare different industrial relations systems at workplace, enterprise, national or international levels.

The major disadvantage of systems theory as an analytical tool is its concentration on the structural features of industrial relations at particular points in time. In other words, it is a static theory from which it is difficult to explain industrial relations change. Its harsher critics argue that by concentrating on the structure of social order and on highlighting the mechanisms of social control within industrial relations, systems theory – like that of conflict theory – is politically biased towards the *status quo*. In our view, however, although systems theory focuses upon structure rather than upon change, it does not necessarily justify the existing social order when it is used as a tool to analyse and describe an industrial relations structure.

One of the strongest features of Marxist theory is its dynamic approach to industrial relations and its explanations of its 'inner logic' and of social change. With its strong moral condemnation of capitalist values and its rejection of the ethics of liberal political economy, Marxist theory is overtly subjective and critical about industrial relations in what it describes as capitalist societies. In practical terms the strength of Marxism as a means of interpreting industrial relations is that it provides a theoretical perspective which not only analyses what is perceived as social reality, but also rejects it on moral grounds and suggests means for changing it. Is there, then, anything in Marxist theory which can be utilized in an attempt to understand industrial relations in contemporary society?

An essential element, in our view, is the endemic nature of social conflict in liberal democracies which is highlighted by Marxist theory. This is not to argue that social conflict and industrial conflict are necessarily identical. They clearly overlap but they are not always synonymous. Experience in Britain suggests that the institutional means for resolving

political and industrial conflict arising from social class differences have become largely, but not always, separated. Moreover, the 'capitalist class' and 'working class' dichotomy appears to be too simplistic an explanation of the class structure in contemporary Britain. There is neither an integrated capitalist class nor an integrated working class. The so-called capitalist and working classes have never been either homogeneous or exclusive. In the 1980s and 1990s, there has been a growth in the relative size of the middle class, a shrinkage of the working class and the emergence of a growing 'underclass' which is unemployed and generally at the margins of society. Social stratification, in short, is multidimensional. It incorporates both individual and collective differentials in income, wealth, status, education, occupation, power, quality of life and social values. However, in so far as Marxist theory focuses on the inherent class nature of liberal democracies – which is partially reflected in their industrial relations institutions – it provides a useful analytical tool for understanding those conflicts in industrial relations deriving from competing class and power interests at work and in society.

Having examined the main theoretical approaches to analysing industrial relations, we would conclude that the dominant industrial relations orthodoxy, or paradigm, during the 1960s and 1970s was conflict theory and pluralism. It was, in fact, the consensus model of industrial relations broadly accepted by many managements, especially in the large corporate and public sectors, by the trade unions and by successive governments as a matter of public policy. Although classical unitarism was strongly entrenched in most small-scale private businesses, it was a residual and enfeebled model of industrial relations, largely on the periphery of practical and academic debate. Neo-unitary approaches to industrial relations were virtually limited (but scarcely recognized) to a small minority of large North American and Japanese companies, operating what were in effect, at that time, idiosyncratic but progressive personnel and employee relations policies.

Since the early 1980s, however, pluralist and collectivist perceptions of industrial relations have not been as secure among some employers and members of the public as they were previously. Nor has pluralism any longer been the preferred frame of reference in the determination of government policy on industrial relations. During the 1980s and 1990s, in short, conflict theory and pluralism in industrial relations were challenged, first, by softer forms of modified

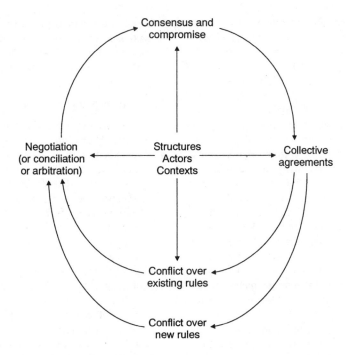

*Figure 2.4* Conflict and consensus in collective bargaining.

pluralism, embodying such ideas as 'no-strike' agreements and single union recognition. Second, they were also faced by renascent unitary and individualist ideas, of both the classical and more sophisticated neo-unitary varieties. This is not to suggest that pluralist theories of industrial relations have been totally supplanted by unitary analyses of employee relations but that pluralist ideas are not as dominant now as they were in the period 1945–79. In fact, there appears to be an increasing dichotomy and intellectual division between those holding and practising pluralist views of industrial relations and those holding and practising unitary ones on employee relations.

Pluralist theory, for example, accounts for two apparently irreconcilable elements in industrial relations. There seems to exist, at one and the same time, a degree of order, stability and moral legitimacy within and between industrial relations institutions, on the one hand, and considerable impetus for change, coercion and ideological conflict within and between them, on the other. In short, consensus and equilibrium in industrial relations appear to coexist with conflict, instability and power relations. Yet this should not be surprising since consensus and agreement, whether between unions and management, or

between union and union, or even between a union and its membership, are only complementary processes to conflict and dissent between them. Clearly, consensus and accommodation between the competing parties and their representatives in industrial relations can only emerge, by a process of negotiation and compromise, out of initial conflict between them. Similarly, industrial relations conflict usually results from a breakdown in industrial relations consensus.

As can be seen in Figure 2.4, a set of agreed industrial relations rules, such as collective agreements between an employer and a union for example, only arises from a consensus and compromise between the parties. This temporarily resolves the conflict between them. Such a consensus only continues until one of the parties attempts to move away from the established rules, either by breaching them or by trying to create new rules. This results in industrial conflict and in the use of power by one of the parties against the other, so as to achieve its own goals by force. A new consensus only obtains after a period of bargaining, concession and compromise between them. If a new consensus does not emerge through negotiation, conciliation or arbitration this induces either a breakdown in relations between the parties or a unilateral enforcement of the stronger party's rules on the other. Such decisions are of course affected by the industrial relations structures and contexts within which the actors operate.

Unitary perceptions of industrial relations, by contrast, are distinctly managerial in orientation and emphasis. They reinforce managerial values and organizational norms in the work situation. They are therefore aimed at legitimizing the right to manage and the freedom to manage within organizations, without the intervention and intrusion of unions and their representatives in the processes of industrial relations. According to these values and theoretic framework, one way in which management handles subordinate employees is by unilaterally enforcing corporate rules upon them, using authoritarian or paternalist styles of management. Alternatively, neo-unitary or sophisticated approaches to manpower management, or 'human resources management', result in the application of manipulative or reward-centred styles of managing employees. These seek to incorporate employees as individuals within the enterprises in which they work, by getting their commitment to organizational goals and objectives, whilst aiming at a homogeneous corporate culture with which all employees can identify.

It would appear that the major contrasts in industrial relations theory at the present time are between pluralist theory and unitary theory. Whilst pluralist theory was the dominant intellectual and policy emphasis in industrial relations in the period up to the mid-1980s, unitary theory has seemed to enjoy some degree of renaissance during the late 1980s and early 1990s, at least amongst certain employers and their workforces. In essence, where pluralism is intellectually and practically in the ascendant, it is closely allied with systems theory and conflict theory and is traditionally associated with a number of specific features of political economy. These include: consensus politics; demand-management economic policies; bipartisan public policy on industrial relations; tripartite relations amongst government, employers and unions; and collectivism in industrial relations. Unitarism, in contrast, is more closely allied with social action theory and 'human relations' management theory. It is more likely to emerge under other features of political economy. These are: conviction politics; supply-side economic policies; partisan public policy on industrial relations; collective bargaining, market-led wage determination and a market economy; and employee relations individualism. The 1990s are likely to see a new balance being determined between the forces of pluralism and collectivism, on the one side, and of unitarism and individualism on the other. Where the exact balance is likely to be determined is uncertain at this time.

## 2.7   Summary Points

- There are a number of different theories of industrial relations.
- Students need to be aware of them and to realize that individuals perceive the realities and practices of industrial relations in different ways. These perceptions derive from the views that individuals have of society, from their own personal experiences and from their beliefs and values about the purposes of industrial relations institutions and practices.
- Classical unitary theory emphasizes the co-operative nature of work and work relations, its stable structure and its rejection of industrial relations conflict between employers and workers.
- Neo-unitary theory is more sophisticated than traditional unitarism and emphasizes the integration of employee, customer and managerial needs in conditions of change.
- Industrial conflict and pluralist theory sees the institutions of industrial relations as conflict identification and conflict resolving mechanisms, though soft pluralism emphasizes the use of joint problem-solving techniques between employer and employee representatives.
- Social action theory emphasizes the importance of individual responses to industrial relations situations, as mediated by the ways people assign meanings to the structures within which they operate and the ways they perceive the actions of others.
- Systems theory focuses on industrial relations 'systems' as the institutional means by which the rules of employment are established and administered in industrial societies.
- Marxist theory, in contrast, highlights the class nature of the employment contract and the continuous class and power struggles between those representing capital and labour in market economies.
- Until recently, the dominant industrial relations paradigm in Britain was conflict theory and pluralism. Whilst this remains a major theoretical approach to industrial relations by scholars, and to industrial relations practice by participants, there have been challenges to its dominance since the early 1980s.

- These challenges have derived from a resurgence of classical unitary and the emergence of neo-unitary theory, which are employer-led ideas and management approaches to industrial relations.
- These circumstances reflect the changed economic and political circumstances since 1980. To what extent the balance between negotiated, pluralist collectivism and employer-led, unitary individualism is modified in the next few years is a key issue in industrial theory and practice.

## 2.8 References

1. H. Reddish, Written memorandum of evidence to the Royal Commission on trade unions and employers' associations, in B. Barrett, E. Rhodes, and J. Beishon (eds.), *Industrial Relations and the Wider Society*, Collier Macmillan, London, 1975, p. 298f.
2. A. Fox, *Royal Commission on Trade Unions and Employers' Associations Research Papers. 3. Industrial Sociology and Industrial Relations*, HMSO, London, 1966, p. 2.
3. *Ibid.*, p. 12.
4. G. Armstrong, Commitment through employee relations, Presentation made to Institute of Personnel Management National Conference, Harrogate, October 1987.
5. R. Dahrendorf, *Class and Class Conflict in Industrial Society*, Routledge and Kegan Paul, London, 1959, p. 257.
6. H. A. Clegg, Pluralism in industrial relations, *British Journal of Industrial Relations*, November 1975, p. 309.
7. *Ibid.*, p. 311.
8. A. Fox, Industrial relations: a social critique of pluralist ideology, in J. Child (ed.), *Man and Organization*, Allen and Unwin, London, 1973, p. 219f.
9. J. H. Goldthorpe, Industrial relations in Great Britain: a critique of reformism, *Politics and Society*, 1974, vol. 4(4).
10. M. Weber, *Economy and Society*, vol. 1, Bedminster Press, New York, 1896, p. 4.
11. D. Silverman, *The Theory of Organizations*, Heinemann, London, 1970, p. 141.
12. P. Kirkbride, Industrial relations theory and research, *Management Decision*, vol. 17(4), 1977, p. 333.
13. Silverman, *op. cit.*, p. 137.
14. *Ibid.*, p. 142.
15. R. Hyman, *Strikes*, 2nd edn, Fontana, London, 1977, p. 72.
16. M. P. Jackson, *Industrial Relations*, 2nd edn, Croom Helm, London, 1982, p. 27.
17. J. T. Dunlop, *Industrial Relations Systems*, Southern Illinois University Press, Carbondale, 1958, p. vii.
18. *Ibid.*, p. 7.
19. *Ibid.*, p. 13.
20. *Ibid.*, p. 9.
21. *Ibid.*, p. 16f.
22. S. J. Wood, A. Wagner, E. G. A. Armstrong, J. F .B. Goodman and J. E. Davis, The 'industrial relations system' concept as a basis for theory in industrial relations, *British Journal of Industrial Relations*, 13(3), 1975, p. 305.
23. D. Fatchett and W. M. Whittingham, Trends and developments in industrial relations theory, *Industrial Relations Journal*, 1976, p. 51f.
24. V. L. Allen, Marxism and the personnel manager, *Personnel Management*, December 1976, p. 21.
25. Allen, *op. cit.*, p. 22.
26. K. Marx and F. Engels, *The Communist Manifesto*, Penguin, Harmondsworth, 1967, p. 79.
27. R. Hyman, *Industrial Relations*, Macmillan, London, 1975, p. 21.
28. V. L. Allen, *The Sociology of Industrial Relations*, Longmans, London, 1971, p. 40.
29. Hyman (1975), *op. cit.*, p. 31.
30. Marx and Engels, *op. cit.*, p. 95.
31. Goldthorpe, *op. cit.*, p. 452.

# PART TWO

## The Institutional Framework

# 3

# Employers and Management

There are many thousands of producer and service enterprises in Britain. They vary in size, type of ownership, method of finance, what they produce, who works in them and how they are internally structured but all of them – other than the relatively small number of one-person businesses and working partnerships – have two main institutional features in common. Each of them is an employer of people and each of them has to be managed by specialist managerial employees to achieve its objectives. It is the role of organizations as employers, and the function of management within them, which provide the connecting themes of this chapter.

## 3.1  Employing Organizations

Organizations produce those goods and services demanded by individuals or corporate consumers who are prepared to pay for them either directly in the market-place or indirectly through taxation and public funding. A wide variety of producer or service organizations exist in Britain today. They are found in the extractive, manufacturing, distributive, financial, educational and welfare sectors and incorporate a diverse range of enterprises and establishments including farms, factories, offices, schools, universities, hospitals, banks, insurance companies and so on. Some are large organizations, others are small; some are privately owned, others are public bodies.

A useful way of classifying organizations is by their orientation and ownership, as can be seen in Figure 3.1. An organization's orientation reflects the primary goals it seeks to achieve. The basic goals of private businesses are to satisfy consumer demand in the market-place, whilst those of the public services are to satisfy citizens' needs within the community 'regardless of whether the citizen can translate that need into effective demand or of whether any means can be found of charging directly for the service.' Private and public organizations are distinguishable

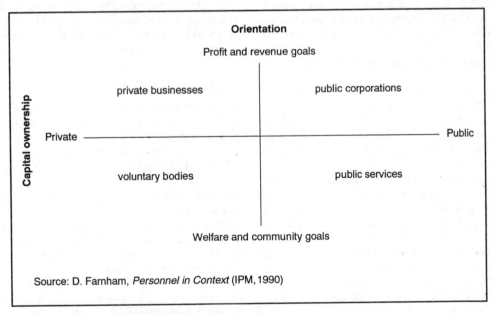

Source: D. Farnham, *Personnel in Context* (IPM, 1990)

*Figure 3.1* Organization typology by orientation and ownership.

*Table 3.1* Number of registered companies on British registers 1984–92.

| | 1984 | 1985 | 1986 | 1987 | 1988 | 1989 | 1990 | 1991 | 1992 |
|---|---|---|---|---|---|---|---|---|---|
| | | | | | (thousands) | | | | |
| Public companies | 3.7 | 4.3 | 5.1 | 5.2 | 6.6 | 9.8 | 11.1 | 11.7 | 11.6 |
| Private companies | 891.2 | 863.8 | 848.8 | 871.4 | 914.0 | 963.1 | 998.7 | 1 020.2 | 1 968.2 |
| Total | 894.9 | 868.1 | 853.9 | 876.6 | 920.6 | 972.9 | 1 009.8 | 1 031.9 | 1 079.8 |

*Source*: Department of Trade, *Companies in 1987–88* (HMSO, 1988) and *Companies in 1991–93* (HMSO, 1993)

'by the terms demand and need and their derivative objectives are characterized differently'.[1]

## Private businesses

Private businesses employ over 19 million people, about half of these in the large market sector, the rest in the small market sector. Although large numbers of small, unincorporated businesses exist – often employing very few or only temporary or part-time staff – the most common form of business organization is the registered company. There were over a million registered companies in Britain in 1992.

As can be seen from Table 3.1, there are two main types of business corporation, the private limited company and the public limited company. Private companies are required to have at least two shareholders and a maximum of 50 and are precluded from issuing shares to the general public. A public limited company (PLC) is required to have a minimum of seven shareholders but there is no upper limit on either the number of shareholders or its share transactions; its shares are bought and sold on the Stock Exchange.

A major feature of the corporate sector is its concentration into a small number of very large PLCs, including multinationals, and a substantial but expanding number of much smaller private firms. One reason for the concentrated size of PLCs is the amalgamations and mergers which have taken place among large and medium-sized firms in recent years. Another feature of PLCs is their pattern of share ownership. Table 3.2 shows that institutional holdings, such as those of banks, pension funds and insurance companies, are proportionally increasing whilst individual shareholdings are decreasing. These changes reflect the continued divorce of corporate ownership and managerial control in PLCs and the consolidation of a professional managerial elite within them, responsible for their financial profitability, corporate effectiveness and control of

*Table 3.2* Percentage distribution of shareholdings in British PLCs 1963–92.

| | 1963 | 1969 | 1975 | 1981 | 1992 |
|---|---|---|---|---|---|
| Individuals | 54.0 | 47.3 | 37.5 | 28.2 | 20.0 |
| Charities | 2.1 | 2.1 | 2.3 | 2.2 | 2.2 |
| Institutions | 30.3 | 36.1 | 48.0 | 57.9 | 60.5 |
| Companies | 5.1 | 5.4 | 3.0 | 5.1 | 3.3 |
| Public sector | 1.5 | 2.5 | 3.6 | 3.0 | 1.2 |
| Overseas | 7.0 | 6.6 | 5.6 | 3.6 | 12.8 |
| Total | 100.0 | 100.0 | 100.0 | 100.0 | 100.0 |

*Source*: *The Observer* (13 October 1983) and *Stock Exchange Quarterly* (January to March 1993)

resources, including people. Research shows that in late twentieth-century Britain, 'the owners of the largest modern enterprises are other enterprises, which are, in turn, owned by other enterprises'. These organizations are linked to one another, not by individuals and families, but 'by interweaving chains of intercorporate relations'.[2]

## Public corporations

Public corporations employ about 900 000 people in Britain and are defined as public trading bodies having a substantial degree of financial independence of the public authority which created them. They include nationalized industries such as coal, the post office, and the railways, and other public bodies such as the Bank of England, British Broadcasting Corporation, Royal Mint and UK Atomic Energy Authority. In 1985 there were some 17 nationalized industries and about 30 other public corporations. By 1992 only 10 nationalized industries remained and 29 public corporations.

Public corporations have five main features. First, their capital is publicly owned and they are managed by government appointed executives. Second, they are not subject to company law and have a different legal status from private businesses. Third, they obtain their current revenue, or part of it, from selling their goods or services; their capital expenditure is raised by borrowing from the Treasury or the general public. Fourth, they are exempt from the normal parliamentary financial scrutiny exercised over government departments. Fifth, their boards are usually appointed by a secretary of state and their employees are not civil servants.

Over 30 important public corporations were privatized in the 1980s and 1990s, with their assets being sold off to private shareholders. These included former nationalized industries such as British Telecom, British Gas and the Electricity Council. Other privatized bodies included British Petroleum, the water authorities, the British Airports Authority and organizations such as British Aerospace, British Ports and Cable and Wireless. This programme of privatization not only transferred large public assets into private ownership but also had significant implications for the structure and practices of industrial relations of these enterprises. The total number of employees transferred from public corporations to private employment amounted to over 700 000 between 1982 and 1992.

## Public services

The major public services are the civil service, including government agencies, the National Health Service (NHS) and the local authority services, including the police. They employ about five million people, who provide a wide range of services to individuals, their families, the community and private businesses. Funds are provided collectively through national insurance, taxation and local property taxes. The civil service, which is the administrative arm of central government, comprises government departments and a number of departmental and non-departmental agencies. It employs two main categories of civil servants – industrial civil servants and non-industrial civil servants – but over two-thirds of these are employed in agencies such as the Benefits Agency, Property Services Agency and Her Majesty's Stationery Office.

The NHS is based on the principle that medical and health care should be readily available, largely free of charge at the point of use, by anyone normally resident in Britain. It uses the services of a wide range of staff, including doctors and nurses, administrative and clerical groups, and ancillary staff such as porters, domestics, gardeners and cooks. The local authorities provide both strategic services over wide geographical areas and essentially local services. They employ a wide range of personnel in manual and non-manual grades, including skilled and less skilled trades as well as technical and professional staff such as engineers, surveyors, accountants, lawyers, architects and teachers. One feature of public service employment in recent years has been 'market testing' and 'compulsory competitive tendering' (CCT). This requires public employers to put certain services out to tender. Successful tenders may come from either 'in-house' or private contractors, which may result in changes in employment and/or terms and conditions of employment.

## Voluntary bodies

Voluntary bodies are usually small, privately owned organizations providing specialized services to their own members or special interest groups. Examples include professional bodies, trade unions, employers' associations and political pressure groups. Being small-scale organizations, and as they often have social rather than economic objectives, voluntary bodies do not usually have major industrial relations problems. Nevertheless, they employ people, their managers manage employees, and where trade unions are recognized their managerial representatives negotiate with union representatives. An emerging element in the voluntary sector is worker or producer cooperatives where the enterprises are owned and managed by their members. Larger co-operatives are more likely to employ professional managers, though, responsible for implementing the policies determined by their memberships and management boards.

## 3.2 The Employer–Employee Relationship

For centuries the common law referred to the two parties to the employment relationship as that of 'master' and 'servant'. Freedom of contract between the parties became the predominant legal doctrine in the early and mid-nineteenth century, in theory at least. In practice this was not the case. Until 1875, for example, manual workers were in certain circumstances liable to criminal prosecution for breaching their contracts of service. The social gap between master and servant was even greater than the differences between them contractually, and the economic balance of power was severely weighted in favour of the masters.

During the last hundred years, the legal, social and economic contexts of the employment relationship have altered. For example, although the contract of employment is still commonly referred to as a contract of service, modern legal usage has slowly replaced the terms 'master' and 'servant' with the more egalitarian terms 'employer' and 'employee'. Further, employees now have a number of significant statutory employment protection and trade union membership rights. The social and economic circumstances of the workplace have also generally improved to the advantage of employees through, in the main, more enlightened employment policies, trade union organization, improved working conditions and the welfare state. On the other hand, however, there is evidence in the 1980s and 1990s of some employers – especially those in the small corporate sector – taking advantage of their labour market power in conditions of high unemployment, weakened trade unions and employment legislation favouring employer interests.

In the days of the master and servant relationship and a free labour market, the master was invariably an individual person contracting other individuals, his servants, to render personal services to him in return for some consideration either in cash or in kind. Even with the emergence of the first factories, the master who owned the capital of the business was a 'natural person' whom all could see and physically identify. Slowly, small family firms replaced individual proprietors as employing authorities and these, in turn, gave way to the modern corporate employer of today.

Apart from very small businesses, the typical employer is now a private or public corporate body: PLCs, private companies, the Crown, health authorities, local authorities, public utilities, public corporations and so on. Such organizations are not only large scale but also abstract, legal entities. They have been created by Parliament and the law to provide, amongst other things, a convenient identity to one side of the employment contract. 'Furthermore, when that person is a legal fiction, the rights and duties of the employer are assumed by a variety of managers who act as the agent of the employer'.[3] The archetypal employer today is, in other words, an organization whose 'corporate personality' is a legal creation, determined largely by what the law prescribes.

The concept of the employer, then, has evolved from that of the master as an identifiable natural person in the early days of the industrial revolution to that of a legal entity today. The principle of incorporation in one form or another:

makes the employer a corporate body or a corporation, which means in the eyes of the law the employer has a legal, if fictional or artificial personality or existence, which is separate and distinct from the personality and existence of anyone who happens to be a member of the organization at the time.[4]

Although work organizations are tangible and real enough for those working in them, they are also legal and fictional bodies which employ people, own property and enter into commercial contracts. The contract of employment between an employer and an employee, for example, is now usually drawn up by the managerial agents of the employer, acting on behalf of the principal or legal entity which they represent, rather than by the employer as a person.

The legal duties of employers, like those of employees, depend upon the terms of the contract between them, although in the absence of any specific agreement certain common law duties apply. These include, for example, the duty of the employer to pay its employees for their services, although remuneration is only payable where it has been agreed, whether expressly or implied. If the contract provides for payment, but the amount has not been specified, the employer has to pay a 'reasonable' amount or 'the customary rate' for the job. Frequently, the remuneration payable is determined by the collective agreement negotiated between employer and union representatives whose terms become incorporated into the personal contracts of employment of individual employees. In other cases, employment contracts are largely employer regulated through the use of so-called 'personal' contracts, unilaterally determined by the employer. Other common law duties of the employer include: providing the opportunity to earn remuneration; taking reasonable care of the employee's safety; indemnifying employees for any loss sustained in performing their duties; and not exposing employees to grave danger of health or person.

In turn, the major common law duties of employees include: being ready and willing to work; rendering personal service to their employer; respecting the employer's trade secrets; and taking reasonable care of the employer's property. More importantly, employees also have the common law duties of obeying all reasonable and legitimate instructions given to them by their employers and their managerial agents, and of avoiding wilful disruption of the employer's undertaking. The duty of reasonable obedience, for example, requires that employees, once employed, agree to submit to the reasonable authority of an employer in all those matters falling within the scope of the work to be done. This means in practice that the contractual relationship between the parties is a dependent and a subordinate one for the employees, not a coequal one with the employer. Also encompassed within the duty of obeying lawful and reasonable employer commands, there is the common law right of employers to discipline employees who are unsatisfactory in the performance of their job tasks. Finally, by requiring employees to co-operate with their employers, and not to disrupt their businesses wilfully, the common law upholds the power to manage of employers and of their managerial agents. The duty to co-operate also means there is little provision for common law legal protection for those employees engaging in industrial action against their employers in a trade dispute.

In retrospect, the history of the employer-employee relationship is embodied in the development of the employment contract. In practice there has been a progressive liberalization of the relationship, especially in the period 1960–79, with a steady restriction of the employer's absolute freedoms and prerogatives at work. These were effectively constrained by the growth of trade unionism and collective bargaining, and by state interventionism in industrial relations, although the specific impact of these factors on particular employers varied by sector, industry, enterprise and establishment. Since 1979, the balance of bargaining power between employers and employees has generally shifted in the employers' favour. This is largely the result of continuously high levels of unemployment and weakened trade union power. Changes in the balance of power between employer and employees therefore should not be exaggerated, especially during periods of high unemployment. As Jack Jones, former general secretary of the Transport and General Workers Union put it:

> There is no doubt about it: power lies with the employer, but with the growth of the unions, there is a more balanced relationship, with give and take on both sides. And that is how it should be.[5]

## 3.3 The Role of Management in Enterprises

All three major sectors of the economy, the large corporate sector, the small corporate sector and the public sector, employ large numbers of managers. It is estimated, for example, that there are at least 2.5 million managers in Britain, comprising over 10 per cent of the labour force.[6] These professional managers, most of them employees themselves, are not a homogeneous group. But it is their responsibility to ensure the efficient and effective managing of the organizational resources for which they are accountable, including subordinate employees. It is their task 'to organize the use of resources (including the work of others) towards the objectives of an enterprise'.[7] Managers are, in short, accountable to those owning the organization's capital assets for its economic viability or success. They are agents of organizational efficiency and custodians of employer interests.

### Managerial work

Classical management theorists, such as Fayol, view managers as rational decision makers whose main activities are planning, organizing, directing, co-ordinating and controlling organizational resources. Other theorists believe managers to be neutral intermediaries in the decision making process who take into account in their decision making role the competing needs of employees, consumers or customers, the community, government and, in the case of private industry, shareholders. More recent studies of the managerial role, however, present a somewhat different picture. Mintzberg, for example, classifies managerial behaviour into three sets of roles, common to all levels of management.[8] He describes these as 'interpersonal', 'informational' and 'decisional' roles. In their interpersonal roles managers act as figureheads, leaders and liaison persons; in their informational roles as monitors, disseminators and spokespersons; in their decisional roles as entrepreneurs, disturbance handlers, resource allocators and negotiators. The importance of Mintzberg's work is that it highlights the uncertainty within which most managers operate. Managers are not normally reflective thinkers, they are 'doers' coping with unexpected events and unforeseen circumstances.

Other research shows that managers typically switch every few minutes 'from one subject or person to another, rarely completing one task before being involved in another'.[9] In this sense managing is a responsive rather than an analytical activity. Other documented features of managerial work include: its verbal nature, managers are talkers and listeners rather than readers and writers; its dependence upon other people, involving reciprocal relationships based on trading and exchange; its political nature; and its uncertainty. In short, managerial work 'is one of fragmented activity, incomplete tasks, interruptions, variety and unpredictable events'.[10]

## Management, ownership and control

In the private sector, with the expansion in size and influence of the joint stock company, some writers argue that the control function of ownership is replaced by that of top management, with shareholders becoming less influential in corporate affairs. The logic behind the argument of the 'managerialists' is that if the largest shareholder or group of shareholders in large companies do not have a sufficient proportion of votes in company affairs 'then those companies are managerially rather than owner controlled'.[11] Managerialism is not an homogeneous theory, however, and some authors suggest that since the modern managerial elite has a different relationship to private property than did the old capitalist class, it pursues significantly different business policies than did its predecessors. Hence, they claim, conflicts between management and subordinate employees no longer exist. Other managerialists such as Dahrendorf do not accept this view, believing that what separates management from non-managerial employees is not property but the authority to make distributional decisions within industrial, commercial and other enterprises.

Non-managerialists either do not accept that a divorce of ownership from control exists, or at least minimize its effects. They argue that ownership is still sufficiently concentrated to ensure owner control. It is further reinforced, they suggest, by interlocking directorates and by the identification of top management with the property owning class. Recent research, however, indicates that in terms of shareholdings there has been a divorce of ownership from control in larger private enterprises. And for managers generally 'the interests of owners are seen to take precedence over other groups who have claims on the resources of the enterprise'.[12] Management as a group, it seems, must of necessity co-operate in corporate policy making with those representing shareholder interests at board level. Also, if management is collectively responsible for business efficiency and corporate effectiveness, 'then it cannot be neutral in its contractual relationships with employees'.[13] Ultimately business enterprises are evaluated by the economic criteria of the market-place. It is

management's collective responsibility to ensure that these market criteria are satisfied on behalf of owner interests. This requires, amongst other things, the effective managing of the enterprise's capital, physical and human resources.

In the 'old' public sector the functions of managing, owning and controlling enterprises were generally more clearly delineated than in the private sector. Those managing public enterprises and establishments were appointed to run them in ways likely to achieve the objectives and purposes for which they were created. Ownership rested with the appropriate public authorities, with ultimate control vested in government or other decision taking bodies. Clearly, policy differences did emerge between the political controllers such as secretaries of state, local councillors, or governing bodies and professional managers such as chief executives, heads of institutions and directors of services. But conflicts of these sorts were usually avoided.

## Management structures

The term 'management' is used in two main senses. First, it is used to describe managers as a group within enterprises: 'the management'. Second, it is used to describe in general terms what managers do, that is managing organizational resources or 'management' as a set of activities. In the group sense, management may be viewed: as an economic resource, performing a series of technical functions including organizing and administering human and other resources within enterprises; as a system of authority through which corporate policies are translated into activities and tasks by subordinate managers and employees; and as a social elite. Management as a group, in other words, is a technical function, a political activity and a social cadre.

In undertaking its technical and political functions, management is stratified vertically by power and status and horizontally by task and specialism, especially as organizations increase in size. Vertically, there is a separation of decision taking from action taking 'so that vertical jobs are distinguished on the basis of the amount of discretion to decide',[14] with management operating within its own structure and hierarchy of power and authority. According to a study by Chandler and Daems, one in five industrial workers in Europe and the United States was employed by companies with hierarchies of at least six vertical levels by the mid-1970s. Similar managerial hierarchies existed in public sector enterprises.

In both cases 'the invisible hand of market mechanisms' in co-ordinating flows and allocating resources in major industries has been replaced by 'the visible hand of managerial direction'.[15]

Vertical managerial roles may be classified into three main levels of power and influence: corporate, administrative and executive or policy making, programming and interpretive. More simply, the terms corporate or senior management, middle or executive management and first line or supervisory management are often used. Senior management is the relatively small managerial group whose main task is developing and reviewing corporate objectives and policies. Middle management implements corporate objectives and policies and manages subordinate managers. First line management supervises the activities and tasks of non-managerial employees, with relatively little job or role discretion. In recent years there has been some evidence of organizational and managerial 'de-layering', however, with the middle layers of management being squeezed out of organizations. This is owing partly to the introduction of information technologies into organizations and partly to more decentralized and devolved systems of management.

Horizontally, managerial jobs and work roles are differentiated according to their operational, functional or departmental responsibilities, with individual managers heading specific subunits. The main managerial functional groupings are production (or operations), marketing, finance, research and development, administration and personnel. In small enterprises the horizontal division of managerial work is frequently minimal, with generalist management skills often more important than specialist ones. In larger enterprises, by contrast, general management is mainly a senior managerial task, necessitating the coordination and integration of functional specialisms towards stated corporate goals and objectives.

## The personnel function

A standard definition of personnel management is that it is 'that part of management concerned with people at work and with their relationships within an enterprise'. According to the Institute of Personnel Management, the professional personnel management association in Britain, it is the aim of personnel management to bring together and to develop into effective organizations those men and women working in them, having regard to the well-being of individuals and of working groups 'to enable them to make their best contribution to [organizational] success'.[16] From a managerial viewpoint the major personnel management problem in any organization is how the efforts of workpeople can be organized and co-ordinated 'in order to attain the highest levels of efficiency, adaptability and productivity'.[17] The underlying issue is how organizational and managerial objectives can be integrated with individual and workgroup aspirations, without generating destabilizing intraorganizational conflict. It is a difficult balance to achieve in practice.

The personnel management function within enterprises is an ambiguous and complex one. First, personnel management is the responsibility of both line managers and personnel specialists. Line managers are responsible for 'managing people', their subordinates. Personnel managers do not normally manage people, except within their own functional specialism, but are responsible for 'managing the people systems' within enterprises. There is therefore some degree of uncertainty regarding which aspects of personnel management should be left to line managers and what should be the responsibilities of personnel specialists. 'Ambiguities in definition generate confusion at the operational level about the nature and locus of personnel management responsibilities'.[18]

Second, the personnel management function within organizations incorporates, to varying degrees, both a management-centred control role and an employee-centred welfare role. The management control role is rooted in managerial concern for efficiency and effectiveness at work and puts managing people firmly into the mainstream of managerial activity. The welfare role, in contrast, is concerned with the well-being of individual employees or workgroups and how they are treated by the organizations employing them. It derives from the activities of the 'welfare movement' which was introduced into some factories by a few altruistic and humane employers at the beginning of the century. Clearly, conflicts of accountabilities can emerge within the personnel function between personnel's concern with efficiency and organizational effectiveness, on the one side, and its aims to seek justice, fair terms and satisfying work conditions for employees on the other. The one assumes pluralistic work enterprises, whilst the other emphasizes their more unitary features. Also, in furthering corporate and enterprise goals, personnel is clearly identified with employer objectives. In concerning itself with employee equity and fairness, however, personnel is seeking a more independent professional role, midway between employer and employee interests.

Third, there are degrees of role specialization within the specialist personnel function itself. For example, personnel professionals in charge of personnel departments and personnel units normally undertake a large number of tasks ranging across personnel work. They are more properly described as 'personnel generalists'. In this capacity they are more likely to be involved in personnel policy determination and industrial relations than are their subordinates. Personnel subordinates, on the other hand, are sometimes described as 'personnel specialists' to distinguish their role from the roles performed by personnel generalists or personnel managers. This is because, directed by personnel managers, they normally undertake a much narrower range of personnel tasks and activities. Principal areas where personnel subordinates have duties include recruitment and selection, payment administration and personnel information and record keeping.

The specialized personnel management function in enterprises, therefore, and the personnel management function of line managers, play key roles in enabling organizations to achieve their corporate objectives through the people working in them. Co-operation and mutual understanding between professional personnel managers and hard-pressed line managers are necessary to this end, even if in practice the relationship can be problematic. In addition to how personnel activities and tasks might be allocated between personnel managers and line managers, there is the extent to which the work of personnel managers has line or staff authority. There is also the problem of co-ordinating personnel management activities across enterprises. There is no general agreement as to how these issues are best resolved. A contingency approach dependent upon organizational and contextual circumstances is the most appropriate personnel strategy.

A new model of personnel management emerged among some employers, especially in the private sector, in the early 1980s, and in the public sector since the mid-1980s. Although it has a variety of meanings, it is generally known as 'human resources management' (HRM). Whilst mainline personnel management is directed mainly at an organization's employees, without necessarily being totally identified with managerial interests, HRM's orientation is different. It is aimed at satisfying managerial needs for human resources within enterprises, with an emphasis on human resources planning, monitoring

and control. It is less concerned than traditional personnel management with personnel problem solving and the mediatory role of the personnel function. HRM seeks to get the right quantity of human resource skills within organizations, at the right price, without taking a patronizing interest in employees' personal affairs. It is a business-centred approach to the personnel function, fitting in closely with the company's corporate strategy and corporate planning activities. HRM reflects a market ethic of the personnel function and is supported by a personnel philosophy emphasizing employer–employee mutuality, common corporate culture, employee commitment and employee involvement. It is underpinned by a neo-unitary approach to managing people individually and to co-operative employee relations. Although not a general model of the personnel function, it closely identifies with larger successful companies, with sophisticated personnel policies.

Research on the personnel function, derived from the 1990 Workplace Industrial Relations Survey (WIRS), shows that during the 1980s there was no drop, across the economy, in the proportion of establishments with designated personnel specialists. Indeed, there may have been a slight increase. However, whilst over a half of the establishments surveyed in 1990 had at least one manager spending a substantial part of his or her time on personnel work, only a third of this group were designated personnel specialists. The factors positively associated with having designated personnel staff in organizations were: being foreign owned establishments in the market sector; having recognized trade unions for collective bargaining purposes; and using advanced technology in the workplace.

Two main conclusions of the survey related to the personnel function. First, personnel and related matters were being given somewhat greater attention within organizations over the second half of the 1980s than was the case previously. This included managers, with titles other than that of 'personnel manager', who were also apparently giving more of their time to personnel and related work than they had in earlier years. A second conclusion is that 'any picture of personnel management in Britain in 1990 would be seriously incomplete if it were to concentrate on designated personnel managers alone'.[19] Establishment size was one factor likely to indicate that there was at least one designated personnel specialist present. As in the 1984 WIRS, however, establishments with fewer than 200 employees were relatively unlikely to employ personnel specialists, whilst 60 per cent of those above this level did.

## 3.4 Managing Industrial Relations

How managements handle the complex organizational and human resources problems arising in industrial relations is a debatable and contentious issue. On the one side, in small scale enterprises for example, a relatively unstructured and *ad hoc* approach may be adopted. On the other hand, there is a tendency for industrial relations and employment matters to be standardized and administered bureaucratically in larger private and public enterprises even if, as one early study concludes, strike incidence appears to be linked with standardization and formalization of management practices, especially with 'both "formalisation in industrial relations" and "facilities for shop stewards"'. It also seems possible, according to another study, that 'if personnel managers foster steward organisation and centralise decisions, then they may well stimulate industrial action'.[20]

Whatever the evidence relating to the organizational impact of professionalizing the industrial relations function, and it would appear to point in both directions, there is little doubt that senior managements in some larger enterprises now view the managing of industrial relations with their employees and representative bodies as both a necessary and a vital managerial task. It has not always been the case. Indeed, the Donovan Commission claimed unofficial strikes at that time to be the result of the inadequate conduct of industrial relations at company and plant level between managements and unions. The Commission believed that this would persist so long as companies paid 'inadequate attention to their pay structures and personnel policies' and workplace negotiations remained 'in their chaotic state'.[21] The Commission implied that the prime responsibility for this chaos rested with management generally and top management in particular. Accordingly, it strongly recommended that in order to promote the orderly and effective regulation of industrial relations within firms and factories 'the boards of companies [should] review industrial relations within their undertakings'.[22]

In the Commission's view, this required appropriate corporate strategies and policies on industrial relations, with management negotiating comprehensive procedural agreements with trade union representatives at company and plant level regulating their collective bargaining arrangements, methods of grievance handling, disciplinary practices, redundancy schemes, facilities for shop stewards, and health and safety at work. The Royal Commission's prognosis was that company boards and senior management needed to initiate the reconstruction of workplace industrial relations by the promotion of positive personnel policies, by the creation of orderly collective bargaining machinery, by the formalization of industrial relations procedures and, in conjunction with the trade unions, by the regularization of the role of shop stewards in the negotiating process.

These themes were subsequently taken up in the industrial relations code of practice, published by the Department of Employment in 1972. It maintained, for instance, that good industrial relations are the joint responsibility of management, employees and the trade unions representing them. 'But the primary responsibility for their promotion rests with management. It should therefore take the initiative in creating and developing them.' It recommended that managers at the highest level should give, 'and show that they give, just as much attention to industrial relations as to such functions as finance, marketing, production or administration'.[23]

The traditional approach of management has been to accord a low priority to the managing of industrial relations. Because of this, and its consequences, the Donovan Commission and other industrial relations reformists have advocated that managerial initiative in the formalization of effective policies, procedures and practices in industrial relations is a necessary condition for improving the quality and the effectiveness of industrial relations decision making, and in reducing the incidence of industrial conflict at work. In the past especially, the classical response to the trade union presence and to the exigencies of collective bargaining by the boards of many enterprises was at its best reactive and, at its worst, defensive. It was rarely predictive. As one piece of research concluded:

> where the directors' role in industrial relations was concerned ... What was found was purposive inaction, influential non-participation, a very active form of unconcern ... and instrumental inconsistency.

In short, 'directors literally do not want to know about industrial relations'.[24]

The reasons for this are not hard to identify. First, even today many managements, especially in the private sector, continue to view the prospect of power sharing with trade unions as threatening their decision-making authority and organizational legitimacy. Even where trade unions are recognized, much managerial time is spent in attempting to preserve management's traditional prerogatives rather than in developing new areas of joint regulation with the trade unions with which it negotiates. By this view, trade unionism is seen as an unwarranted challenge to the right to manage. Second, industrial relations is only part of the overall management function. Most managements can probably never be totally expert in the field of industrial relations since, unlike the trade unions, it is not the very essence of their organizational role. For these reasons, even today there continues to be considerable difficulty in obtaining total commitment and attention to the managing of industrial relations at board or top management level in some enterprises. 'First, industrial relations matters are not readily quantifiable';[25] second, until recently it was relatively rare for boards to appoint, as a consistent practice, directors of personnel or industrial relations. Even now, board and senior managerial appointments continue to be dominated by accountants, lawyers and other of the more traditional professional groups. Such persons, whether by training, experience or inclination, are rarely imbued in the nuances, subtleties and culture of industrial relations decision-making and problem solving.

A third factor giving rise to reluctance by many managers to become deeply involved in industrial relations derives from the continued practice of concluding industry-wide or national collective agreements in a few industries. Although these multiemployer agreements are declining in importance, where they operate there is little incentive for line managers to be involved in day-to-day industrial relations. In other instances, especially where large personnel departments have become established, line managers often prefer to delegate their industrial relations role to personnel managers rather than cope with it themselves. This is often encouraged by the personnel and industrial relations specialists themselves, since it provides added status, power and prestige to their own roles within their employing organizations. For these reasons, therefore, industrial relations – certainly until recently – has had a fairly low priority within the overall corporate strategy of many enterprises, especially in small and medium-sized private sector ones. Industrial relations have also been poorly managed because many managements have often lacked the skills, confidence and commitment for dealing with the trade unions effectively at plant or operational levels.

It is very difficult in practice to determine by objective criteria whether an organization's industrial relations activities and outputs are 'good' or 'bad', 'effective' or 'ineffective', 'satisfactory' or 'unsatisfactory'. Much depends on how these terms are defined and measured and by what criteria they are evaluated. However, partly because of the Donovan Commission's influence, the impact of public policy in the 1970s, the extension of employment legislation and more democratic trade unions, many managements, especially in large scale private corporations, have adopted a more structured and strategic approach to managing industrial relations in recent years. In manufacturing industry, at least, few major multiplant companies employing more than 5 000 employees 'are now likely to be without a main board director with head office responsibility for employee relations'.[26]

In a survey of manufacturing firms conducted for the Confederation of British Industry in 1980, Arthur Marsh found that a 'substantial proportion' of single establishment firms and a 'preponderance' of multiplant firms saw their employee relations 'as having become more formal, either institutionally, procedurally or in relation to the setting down of rules',[27] thus narrowing the gap between public sector and private sector practices. He, nevertheless, concludes that although the boards of these companies believe it proper to have a general philosophy enshrining their managerial style, they often continue to prefer an informal '"action" frame for their employee relations rather than a more structured approach'.[28] As one writer comments, many managements in Britain have abandoned the old 'formal system' of industrial relations embodying national bargaining. 'But they do not as yet appear to have found an adequate model to replace it.'[29]

More recently, further evidence examining the industrial relations approaches of large multiplant companies in the private sector indicates that managerial approaches to industrial relations and personnel management have become more sophisticated than previously. They tend to vary according to the business strategies and organizational structures of enterprises. Indeed, moves to decentralize collective bargaining are often linked with the development of elaborate corporate systems to monitor the financial performance of operating units and to constrain their financial autonomy. Marginson and his colleagues, for example, found two major aspects of structure associated with collective bargaining decentralization. First, enterprises which are more diversified across industrial sectors are more likely to give their establishments some industrial relations autonomy, whilst those whose activities are concentrated in a single business are more likely to instruct their establishments and limit their autonomy. Second, enterprises which are more financially devolved, as establishment profit centres or as profit centres retaining funds for strategic investment purposes, give their establishments more autonomy, with financially centralized enterprises, on the other hand, being 'very likely to instruct establishments over personnel and industrial relations decisions'.[30]

Marginson concludes that whilst pay bargaining structures give the impression that the industrial relations decisions of many enterprises are decentralized, the existence of enterprise structures on other issues, including payment systems, qualifies this. The majority of such enterprises also claim to have an overall policy on the management of their employees. Finally, any differences in the managing of industrial relations are associated with the business structure of the enterprise, and the extent of its financial decentralization and product diversification, rather than with other factors.

There is also some evidence that public service employers are adopting more proactive approaches to industrial relations and personnel management. Since the 1980s particularly, there has been a significant shift in industrial relations and personnel management values, policies and practices in the remaining public services. To some extent, these changes are epitomized by the increased use of the terms 'employee relations' and 'human resources management' in public service organizations, terms which originated in the private sector. Public service employers can no longer universally claim to be 'model' or 'good practice' employers, as they did in the past. Like their private sector counterparts, they are now far more likely to be concerned with efficient human resource utilization, effective employee performance, flexible working arrangements and widening pay and benefits differentials among different employee groups. Again, like some leading-edge private employers, more public service employers appear to be adopting: more sophisticated and systematic recruitment practices; staff appraisal procedures; performance related and individualized reward systems; structured management and staff development programmes; direct communications between line managers and their subordinates; and some decentralized negotiation and consultation arrangements with staff unions. 'Public service and

private sector employment practices, in short, are increasingly converging, but with the private sector providing the dominant model to be followed.'[31]

## 3.5  Managerial Approaches to Industrial Relations

Managerial approaches to industrial relations have traditionally been characterized by inconsistency, informality, and lack of structure. Managers have also tended to be reactive in industrial relations situations rather than proactive. As indicated above, there is some evidence to suggest, however, that many more employers are beginning to think of themselves as adopting a more participative and consultative style of management than was once the case, with a proportion considering that they are more proactive than reactive. In analysing the ways in which management approach industrial relations we need to examine three key concepts: managerial styles, strategies and policies.

### Managerial styles

Managerial style in industrial relations is related to a number of organizational and managerial variables and different classificatory systems have been used to analyse them. Fox, for example, puts forward six patterns of industrial relations between management and employees varying according to the degree of legitimacy afforded by each side to the other. He describes these as: the 'traditional', 'classical conflict', 'sophisticated modern', 'standard modern', 'continuous challenge' and 'sophisticated paternal' patterns.

The approach of traditionalist employers is to oppose trade unions and not to recognize them. This is normally characterized by unitary frames of reference by both management and employees, with management often adopting an authoritarian style of dealing with employees. In the classical conflict pattern, unions exist to challenge managerial control and are normally recognized but management is likely to impose decisions unilaterally upon its workforce, either without prior discussion or by forcing decisions through the negotiating and consultative machinery to its own advantage. The sophisticated modern style is where management legitimizes the union role in defined areas of joint decision making because it sees this role 'as conducive to its own interests as measured by stability, promotion of

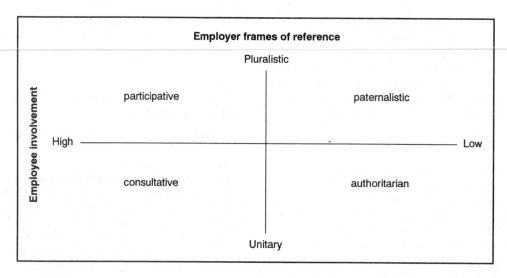

*Figure 3.2* Managerial styles.

consent, bureaucratic regulation, effective communication or the handling of change'.[32]

In seeking union collaboration and support for corporate goals and objectives, a management using the sophisticated modern approach considers a number of key elements. According to Purcell, these are:

1. the encouragement of union membership and support for the closed shop where appropriate.
2. the encouragement of membership participation in trade unions;
3. the encouragement of inter-union co-operation and the development of shop steward committees;
4. the institutionalization of irreducible conflict;
5. the minimization of areas of avoidable conflict;
6. the maximization of areas of common interest;
7. the reduction of the power of strategic groups;
8. the development of effective control systems.[33]

In short, by institutionalizing industrial conflict and by legitimizing trade union power, managements adopting the sophisticated modern style aim to achieve managerial control within the workplace through appropriate collective bargaining strategies.

The standard modern style, which is the dominant approach, is essentially pragmatic, with employers changing and modifying their industrial relations styles in response to internal and external changes. These include managerial preferences, market forces and government policies. Oscillations between different approaches to industrial relations, however, 'undermine stability and continuity and more especially place major limitations on the extent to which

trust can be generated and maintained'.[34] This can result in confusion and uncertainty caused by a mixture of unitary and pluralistic perspectives.

Where employees, workgroups and unions refuse to legitimate management's right to manage, we have the continuous challenge pattern, with 'periods of uneasy truce as each side licks its wounds and watches the enemy for signs of a weak spot in its defences'.[35] Sophisticated paternalist employers, by contrast, do not normally recognize trade unions and management is able to pursue its organizational policies without internal challenges. Further, most sophisticated paternalists put a great deal of time and energy into managing their employees in professional and skilled ways. For example, they pay a lot of attention to progressive personnel policies, stressing the importance of individual employee contributions within the enterprise. They often have sensitive recruitment and selection procedures, ensuring that only employees with 'correct' attitudes are employed, high pay and attractive fringe benefits, and appropriately designed and implemented management training programmes. They also have relatively high ratios of personnel specialists working for them, providing key services and advice to line management.

Another typology of managerial styles relates employer frames of reference to levels of employee involvement, as shown in Figure 3.2. This provides four major managerial styles in industrial relations: 'participative', 'paternalistic', 'consultative' and 'authoritarian'. The participative style, for instance, incorporates pluralistic employer frames of reference and relatively high levels of employee involvement. Authoritarian managerial styles, on the other hand, are related to unitary frames of reference and low employee involvement. Consultative and paternalistic styles, in turn, are connected with unitary frames of reference and high employee involvement, and pluralistic frames of reference and low employee involvement respectively. As in all typological classifications these are 'pure' or 'ideal' types. In practice, managerial styles in industrial relations can vary within enterprises between different operational areas, locations or time. Each has specific implications for the ways employers manage industrial relations.

Purcell has proposed four 'generic types of industrial relations' within organizations 'combining the two scales of formalisation and trust together.' The four patterns he identifies are 'cooperative constitutionalism', 'adaptive cooperation', 'antagonistic constitutionalism' and 'uninhibited antagonism'. Co-operative constitutionalism combines high formalization of industrial relations and high trust between the parties; adaptive co-operation low formalization and high trust; antagonistic constitutionalism high formalization and low trust; and uninhibited antagonism low formalization and low trust. Each pattern is, again, an 'ideal' type and patterns can vary over time. Each pattern results in differences in behaviour of the parties and in the industrial relations structures within which they operate. These include 'bargaining, consultation and communication, the operation of procedures, union organisation and attitudes, and management organisation and attitudes'.[36]

A more recent analysis by Purcell identifies two dimensions of management style. He describes these as 'individualism' and 'collectivism'. Individualism is the extent to which personnel policies are focused on the rights and capabilities of individual workers, whilst collectivism is the extent to which management policy is directed towards 'inhibiting or encouraging the development of collective representation by employees and allowing [them] a collective voice in management decision making'. These two dimensions of management style, which Purcell defines as the 'originating philosophies and policies which influence [managerial] action', are not necessarily mutually incompatible, although most employers prefer to operate within one or other of these prescriptive styles. Further, there are variants of individualism and collectivism. High levels of individualism, for example, are associated with 'employee development', and low levels with 'labour control'. Similarly,

high levels of collectivism are associated with extensive structures for employee representation and participation, where management willingly cooperates with and supports such bodies, while low levels of collectivism are associated with predominantly unitary managerial attitudes and beliefs.[37]

Purcell claims that once it is recognized that 'modern companies are capable of making strategic business choices we must allow for preferences to exist in the way employees are managed'. Where they do, however, style is closely related with business policy. Although not all firms appear to have long-run business policies, this appears to be changing. In his view, the fact that certain 'excellent companies' are reported as having distinctive management styles, which are linked with competitive advantage in the market place, is encouraging other companies to search for distinctive styles of management, appropriate to their circumstances. In his view, this is demonstrated by:

> The 'new industrial relations', the growth of interest in human resource management, the move to decentralize and emphasize the role of line management and new approaches to personnel management [and] are all indicative of this search for a management style linked to business policy.[38]

## Strategies

Industrial relations strategies are defined as long-term goals developed by management 'to preserve or change the procedures, practice or results of industrial relations activities over time'. That some organizations have such strategies is based on a number of assumptions, for example: that corporate management usually determine overall strategies to achieve their corporate goals; that strategic thinking is necessary for corporate success; that corporate leaders have some choice in the matter; and 'that choosing their industrial relations policies rationally implies they be linked to other objectives and policies'.[39]

In practice, of course, this may not always be the case. As Marsh concludes in his study of British manufacturing industry, there is considerable evidence indicating that boards of directors and top management prefer to react to industrial relations issues rather than producing explicit guidelines serving as 'a guide to day-to-day decision making both for themselves and for other levels of management'. What these managements appear to be doing is following the long-established tradition of *ad hoc* decision-making after prior consultation, finding this preferable to more bureaucratic methods of determining and modifying employee relations policy at main board level and elsewhere in their companies'.[40] In contrast, when he was director of personnel at British Leyland in the early 1980s, Pat Lowry is reported as being a firm supporter of tackling industrial relations issues by means of a long-term rational approach:

> the important thing is always to work to plan, always know your objectives. You have to plan your way out of the industrial relations mire. Then you have to accept that the unions are in business for their own ends. They are not necessarily yours.[41]

Opinion is divided therefore between those arguing that employers do not generally have industrial relations strategies, those arguing that 'they can and should have such strategies and those who believe that, even if their managers do not recognize it, all organizations do have strategies'.[42]

Those managements developing strategic approaches to industrial relations appear to be influenced by a number of factors. These include: union strength; price competitiveness of their products; ratios of labour to capital costs; labour market trends; technology; and union policy and organization. It is argued, moreover, that strategic thinking in industrial relations is only credible:

- if the industrial relations strategy is justifiable by its relationship to a clear and acceptable business strategy;
- if there exists an effective organizational capacity for study and analysis of conditions, monitoring of effects of actions and explaining the rationality of the strategy in question;
- if there is considerable acceptance of the legitimacy of management and its control systems by employees;
- if top management have the educational training to allow them to attack problems in a systematic, detached, 'rational' fashion.

Given the structure of many large-scale British organizations, however, these writers believe that it is difficult to develop strategic approaches within such enterprises. It is much easier doing it successfully, they argue, 'in a "green-field site" situation'.[43]

One potentially important indicator of the way in which industrial relations and personnel issues are managed strategically is the extent to which responsibility for them rests at the top of organizations, at board or governing body level. Representation of the personnel function at board level may indicate a positive corporate commitment to the managing of human resources, whilst any increase in the incidence of board membership could demonstrate a growth in the personnel function's influence strategically, with a fall indicating the reverse. The WIRS evidence in fact records that there was 'no significant change in the incidence of board-level personnel management representation between 1980 and 1990'.[44] In 1980, 71 per cent of the establishments in the WIRS reported any personnel representation at board level, compared with 73 per cent in 1984 and 69 per cent in 1990, whilst specialist board-level representation for each of these years was 42 per cent, 43 per cent and 40 per cent respectively. However, turning to the views of personnel and other managers regarding their perceptions of the influence of personnel departments, we observe that, in 1990, seven out of ten personnel specialists claimed the influence of their department had increased over the three previous years, with only 20 per cent saying that it had decreased. Even among non-personnel specialists, two out of five managers took a similar view. It was managers 'in foreign-owned, smaller and non-unionized establishments and with substantial concentrations of white-collar employees [who] were more likely to suggest that their influence had increased', whilst it was managers in private manufacturing and construction who indicated that personnel's influence had remained unchanged.[45]

## Policies

One of the first formal definitions of industrial relations policy was provided by the Commission on Industrial Relations (CIR). The CIR argued that a corporate industrial relations policy should form an integral part of the total strategy through which enterprises pursue their corporate objectives.

> In this way it will define the company's course of action with regard to particular industrial relations issues; it will also reflect the interaction of industrial relations with policies in other areas, such as production, marketing or finance.[46]

The CIR believed that since industrial relations takes account of all aspects of the relationship between employer and employees, a corporate policy on industrial relations should be conceived in the broadest possible way. Accordingly it recommended that such policies should cover trade union recognition, collective bargaining, grievance procedures and consultative arrangements 'and the broad range of employment policies all of which impinge on industrial relations'.[47]

Another definition of industrial relations policy is provided by Brewster, Gill and Richbell. They define it as:

a set of proposals and actions which establishes the organization's approach to its employees and acts as a reference point for management. These proposals and actions are selected, either consciously or unconsciously, by those with formal authority in the organization.[48]

They distinguish between 'espoused policy' and 'operational policy'. Espoused policy incorporates the proposals, objectives and standards that top management state that they hold for dealing with employees and employment matters. Operational policy is the way senior management are seen to order industrial relations policies *vis à vis* other policies 'through the mechanisms of restrictions, control and direction' which they impose on line management. Operational policy, they claim, is the way that senior management control the organization 'and, crucially through the control, reward and punishment of line management'.[49]

Espoused policy and operational policy can differ. Espoused policy, for example, is narrower and more dynamic than operational policy. Moreover, where they differ, it is argued, 'line management will in effect follow the operational policy'. This means in practice that it is operational policy which is experienced by the workforce 'and it is that and their response to it that determines industrial relations, not the espoused policy.' It is operational policy which has the 'greater long-term effect on the quality of industrial relations, while the espoused policy tends to have less effect'.[50]

Brewster and his colleagues also distinguish between the roles performed by different managerial groups in creating and executing industrial relations policies. The 'instigators' determine industrial relations policy and are normally a small core of senior managers which may or may not include personnel specialists. They determine not only espoused policy but also operational policy, though they are rarely aware of doing the latter. It is their values which are indicated to those down the managerial hierarchy 'by

the control systems, the areas which are monitored and the kinds of performances that are rewarded or punished'. In practice, lower managers 'adapt their behaviour to conform with their perception of the operational policy, rather than the espoused policies'.[51]

The 'implementers' are the main body of the managerial hierarchy 'and it is their actions, or lack of action, which reflect the operational policy'. Operational policy, it is claimed, develops largely in response to line management's assessments of the wishes of their superiors. Line managers gain an understanding of operational policy as they are 'rewarded, punished, well thought of, or reprimanded'.

There is a third group, the 'facilitators', who are industrial relations specialists. They advise and assist in the implementation of industrial relations policy but are also members of one or other of the two main groups. Where the instigators are involved in decisions implementing major change in industrial relations policy, 'the facilitators may become more visible and active as a small group'. Also differences between their functions and those of the people who will implement the policy 'may become more visible and obvious'[52] in relation to it.

## 3.6 Employee Motivation, Involvement and Commitment

Managers have continuously sought a legitimation of their work role from subordinate employees and a degree of employee commitment to the processes of work, consistent with high output, low costs and the absence of industrial conflict.

At various times and places they have asserted that compliance was owed to the superior social status of masters, the absolute rights of property ownership, the inherent prerogatives of the managerial function, or to the businessman's special skills and initiative in the production of goods and services.[53]

To secure such compliance by their subordinates, management has adopted a variety of strategies. These range from coercion and force, on the one hand, to more subtle and manipulative methods of work control on the other.

The latter include, for example, scientific management techniques, the development of social skills associated with the so-called 'human relations' movement and the 'industrial welfare' school. The welfare

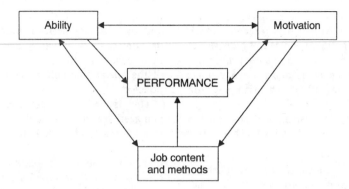

*Figure 3.3* Factors influencing performance improvement.

approach for example, although not extensively used today except by sophisticated paternalist employers, is concerned with the comfort and attractiveness of working conditions, canteen facilities, employee counselling, sports and social clubs, low-cost housing and so on. In the 1960s and early 1970s, a few managements were influenced by the ideas and methods of the behavioural sciences, for instance in the use of participative styles of management and in the application of job enlargement and job enrichment techniques, many of which were imported from the United States. In the 1980s and 1990s, in contrast, leading-edge employers, especially in the private sector, have had more interest in 'involving' employees in those decisions affecting their jobs and working lives directly, in order to get them 'committed' to the goals, values and policies of their employers' organizations. Motivating, involving and committing subordinate employees, however, remain major problems for management today.

## Motivating employees

A central feature of all managers' jobs is to improve the work performance of their subordinates. The objective of improving work performance lies in the goals of the department, the work location or the organization. These goals may include reducing labour costs, improving a service, or increasing the quantity or quality of work output. Although the problem of improving work performance is mainly a line management task, the personnel specialist usually has the training and the background to guide the line manager in this complex area. As shown in Figure 3.3, this concern with performance improvement may be viewed from three linked but relatively

discrete vantage points. First, work performance may be improved by developing the ability of employees to do their jobs better. This necessitates, in the first instance, finding and allocating the most suitable people to do the work. It is the purpose of an organization's recruitment, selection and personnel allocation procedures to do these tasks. Improving the knowledge and skills of those already employed is the purpose of its training and development programmes.

Second, work performance may also be improved by altering the content of the job, the methods employed to do it, or the immediate work environment in which the job is done. The techniques of job design associated with work simplification, ergonomics and human factors engineering, for example, are directed towards these ends.

The third major factor affecting work performance is the motivation or commitment of employees towards their job tasks. The essence of the problem from the employer's and the manager's viewpoint is how to identify and manage those factors which cause individuals and workgroups to increase or decrease the effort put into their work.

Early theories of employee motivation viewed the problem in uni-dimensional terms. The scientific management movement, for example, saw motivation in essentially economic terms: select the most efficient work methods, its supporters claimed, and this will secure the maximum economic prosperity for employer and employees alike. Scientific management had at its very foundation the firm conviction 'that it is possible to give the workman what he most wants – high wages – and the employer what he wants – a low labor cost – for his manufactures'.[54] The human relations school, on the other hand, believed social factors within the workgroup to be the major determinants of employee motivation.

> The study of the bank wiremen showed that their behavior at work could not be understood without considering the informal organization of the group and the relation of this informal organization to the total social organization of the company.[55]

One result of the human relations approach was the concentration of organizational research upon the social dynamics of small group behaviour at work. Because of this, it tended to neglect the effects of technology, pay structures and the interaction of organizations with their external environments on employee motivation and work performance.

It was not until the 1940s and 1950s that it became widely recognized that the problems of human motivation generally, and of employee motivation specifically, were more complex than those which earlier theorists had believed. Abraham Maslow, an American psychologist, for example, argues that people's behaviour is centred around a series of psychological needs arranged in a hierarchy of intensity. 'There are at least five sets of goals, which we may call basic needs. These are briefly physiological, safety, love, esteem, and self-actualization.'[56] The satisfaction of one set of needs at a given level, he argues, leads to attempts to satisfy additional needs at the next higher level and so on. Once a need is attained, it no longer remains a major motivating force, although if it ceases to be satisfied it re-emerges. In the workplace, for example, 'safety' or 'security' needs are concerned with security of employment, a fair level of payment and freedom from arbitrary action from management.

Once such safety needs have been adequately satisfied, Maslow suggests, an individual's 'love' or 'social' needs are released and these need to be satisfied too. These are based on the need to affiliate with others, to communicate with them and to interact at a personal level with one's fellows. 'Esteem' needs are those based on the desire for an acceptable self-image, whilst 'self-actualization', at the apex of the needs hierarchy, is related to a person's concern for emotional self-fulfilment and individual creativity. These are satisfied, it is argued, where the individual is allowed to perform at a level of personal excellence which brings his or her creative skills and abilities into play. In short, by the Maslovian hierarchy of needs, human beings are viewed as perpetually wanting animals, both generally and in their work roles.

Any thwarting or possibility of thwarting of these basic human goals, or danger to the defenses which protect them, or to the conditions upon which they rest, is considered to be a psychological threat.[57]

The theory of a hierarchy of needs forms the basis of the motivation–hygiene analysis of Herzberg. The latter's research found the motivating factors or 'satisfiers' in a job to be those elements deriving from the job content and offering intrinsic rewards at work. The factors which are extrinsic and do not motivate employees, he suggests, derive from the job context. These are the hygiene factors which he sees as potential 'dissatisfiers'. Whilst their absence causes dissatisfaction, he argues, their presence does not act as a positive motivating force on individual workers. In further developing the ideas of Maslow, Herzberg not only gives emphasis to the personal, egotistical and self-actualization needs of people at work, but also views work as a means of individual fulfilment, personal growth and goal achievement for employees.

By the 1960s, the behavioural sciences had become established as important sources of managerial thinking on the problems of motivation and of employee commitment to work, especially in the United States. Douglas McGregor, for example, in line with the views of human behaviour developed by social scientists like Maslow, found it difficult to accept the traditional assumptions held by management about employee orientation to work. He believes that it is managerial assumptions about controlling labour resources which determine the climate of organizational relationships. He argues that the traditional concept of management is based on the assumption that the direction and control of an organization and its employees should be determined by management alone. This approach reflects a set of assumptions about human motivation which McGregor calls 'Theory X'. These include, he says, assumptions that the average human being dislikes work, will avoid it if he or she can, prefers to be directed rather than self-directed at work and has relatively little occupational ambition. Theory X also assumes:

> Because of this human characteristic of dislike of work, most people must be coerced, controlled, directed, threatened with punishment to get them to put forth adequate effort towards the achievement of organizational objectives.[58]

McGregor proposes an alternative theory, 'Theory Y'. This is based on quite different assumptions about human behaviour which he feels are more in accord with behavioural science knowledge about human activity. These assumptions are that people do not inherently dislike work and that they welcome self-direction and self-control in the service of work objectives to which they are committed, providing that there are adequate rewards associated with their achievement. The most significant of these rewards, he believes, is the satisfaction of ego and self-actualization needs. Theory Y further assumes that the average human being not only accepts but also, in the right conditions, seeks job responsibility and that the capacity to exercise ingenuity and creativity in solving organizational problems is widely distributed throughout the working population. Unfortunately, 'the conditions of modern industrial life give only limited opportunity for these relatively dormant human needs to find expression'.[59]

In McGregor's analysis, the central principle of management and motivation deriving from the assumption of Theory X is that the direction and control of employees and of their work situations should be exercised through managerial authority alone. The assumptions of Theory Y, on the other hand, point to the principle of integrating individual and organizational needs at work. This suggests that individuals can best achieve their own goals within an organization by directing their work efforts towards the achievement of organizational objectives. In postulating Theories X and Y, however, McGregor is merely identifying a range of ideas about people and motivation at work and appropriate managerial styles for handling them. He does not see these theories as managerial strategies in themselves, but as underlying beliefs about the nature of humankind which influence managers in adopting a particular strategy when managing subordinates.

Another American behavioural scientist who has taken up the theme of integrating individual and organizational needs at work is Chris Argyris. His main focus has been on the effect of the work environment on the personal development of the individual. In his view, most organizations are run in ways which inhibit the realization of the individual's full potential at work. He sees the importance of developing individuals to their highest levels of psychological maturity. In this way, the total potential of their psychological energies can be released to the benefit of the organization and the individual's self-image. Unfortunately interpersonal incompetence amongst individuals in work organizations, together with certain organizational charac-

teristics, he argues, prevent people becoming mature in outlook. Argyris insists that effective management must aim at the full development of the individual and at authentic interpersonal relationships and coherent organization. He advocates, for example, organizational structures which are flexible and project based and where managerial relationships are between peers rather than hierarchical.

It is apparent from what has been said about the motivational theories described so far that at least two common themes seem to run through them. The first is that if management wants to achieve a realistic balance between meeting the needs of the individual and those of the organization which it manages, it is necessary to develop an appropriate organizational climate. This implies the necessity of structuring organizations so that employees can develop and mature as individuals, and as members of work-groups, whilst at the same time working for the success of the enterprise itself. Related to this theme is another: although a number of factors determine the climate within an organization, the prevailing influence is the way in which people behave individually and in groups, as leaders and as followers. An example of this is to be found, for instance, in the writings of the American social psychologist, Rensis Likert. In his view, the behavioural patterns of managers and their approach to their relationships with the employees whom they control are fundamental to job performance and job satisfaction. In other words, the motivation of people at work is directly related to leadership styles and to the organizational environment.

Likert's researches have sought to establish the nature of the relationship between management styles, work performance and job satisfaction in the managed group. His findings show that departments which are low in efficiency tend to be run by managers who are 'job centred' and exert constant pressure on subordinates to achieve high output. Departments which attain high performance levels, on the other hand, tend to be run by managers who are 'employee centred'. These managers concentrate on building effective workgroups which are set high achievement goals. Such managers are more concerned with work targets rather than with work methods. They also allow maximum participation to their subordinates in the decision-making process. In his researches, Likert identified four main styles or 'systems' of management. Of these, he suggests, 'System 4' – 'Participative Group Management' – generally produces higher productivity, greater involvement of individuals and better labour–management relations than the other three systems. He maintains that this leadership style should provide the following: adequate economic rewards for employees; decision-making through group processes; open communication channels; and close personal understanding between superiors and subordinates. To facilitate this, Likert argues, organizations should be structured as a series of overlapping groups linked by people who are members of more than one group.

Having outlined some of the principal 'psychologically universalistic' or neo-human relations theories of work, we should point out that these behavioural interpretations of work and employee motivation are to a large extent managerially and employer orientated in their analyses. However, from the industrial relations viewpoint, and from the sociological perspective, they are somewhat limited in their explanations of certain types of employee behaviour and some aspects of employer-employee relations. First, human relations theorists take a relatively narrow view of the nature of industrial conflict. Although contemporary theorists adopt a more realistic view of industrial conflict compared with the early human relations writers like Mayo and his colleagues, they continue to emphasize that conflict should be dealt with on a problem-solving pattern within enterprises rather than on a distributive bargaining basis. By this analysis, conflict resolution at work between management and employees is still viewed in terms of improving interpersonal relations and the importance of collective bargaining is rarely acknowledged; neo-human relations is very unitary in its emphases.

Second, most of the behavioural theories which have been described are prone to underplay the importance of organizational variables, like workplace culture, trade union organization and social class differences which are not directly amenable to change by management.

As a consequence they tend to underrate the intractability of industrial conflict and take a correspondingly optimistic view of the prospects for achieving intra-organizational harmony and unity of purpose.[60]

In short, behavioural science theories fail to consider power and ideology in industrial relations.

Third, the prescriptions of the neo-human relations approach also underestimate the role of technology as a determinant of workplace behaviour. The general conclusions of behavioural research suggest that employees seek greater involvement in their work tasks and good relations among themselves and with management, irrespective of the technology involved. Among other things, the Luton studies by Goldthorpe and his colleagues conclude that certain types of technology preclude the possibility of job enrichment and increased participation in the job. Accordingly, such workers have a purely calculative and instrumental attitude towards their jobs and become preoccupied with high financial rewards and pay incentives at work. The growing recognition amongst other social scientists of the importance of technology on workplace behaviour has far reaching implications for managerial industrial relations policies. Production line technologies, for instance, may give little scope for enriching jobs or improving the quality of human relations at plant level.

The human relations approach to improving industrial behaviour and efficiency also 'makes a series of assumptions about motivation which cannot objectively be either proved or disproved'.[61] Such phrases as 'good communications', 'job enrichment', 'participative management', 'sensitivity training' and 'team leadership' have become an integral part of the vocabulary of influential areas of British management at various times. But their long-term beneficial effects in reducing industrial conflict, improving employee morale, and raising organizational productivity have yet to be proved.

If these theories are taken in isolation, they are unlikely to contribute to our understanding of employee motivation. In focusing on the job context and on the intrinsic rewards of work, they ignore the bargaining context between management and unions and the role of extrinsic rewards at work. Some British research indicates that human relations theories and the instrumental orientation approach of the 'action theorists' like Goldthorpe and his colleagues can contribute to a better understanding *both* of the complexities of employee behaviour *and* of job motivation within the workplace. By this view, it is suggested, it is only when attention is focused on both the job contexts and the bargaining contexts at work, together with the different priorities and attitudes characteristic of each, that workgroup behaviour can be adequately analysed. Although the contexts vary according to managerial styles, organizational structures, payment systems and different technologies, for instance, it is claimed that there is a spectrum of attitudes towards management and job motivation. Certain employees are in the middle of that spectrum and seek both extrinsic and intrinsic rewards from work, 'with the one becoming salient in one context and the other in another. Equally they see both areas of common and conflicting interests with management in different contexts'.[62] Whether in these circumstances a rise in demand for greater intrinsic rewards in their work by employees can abate the demand for higher material rewards for their work or for more power-sharing with management has yet to be demonstrated.

Such findings accord with the view that the strength and intensity of employee motivation at work is strongly related to the rewards which people expect from attaining desired goals in their jobs. Obviously the choice of these goals and the value placed on a particular set of rewards are highly individual. Furthermore, they are not always amenable to employee control. They depend upon the nature of the work tasks, the organizational structure and the technology involved. But the important point which 'expectancy theory' makes is that any movement towards improved performance by employees is influenced by two main factors. The first is the probability that work rewards depend on effort and that effective performance by employees will result in given rewards. The second is the value of the rewards perceived by individual workers. A job's intrinsic rewards are seen to be those stemming from the performance of the job or from its tasks by individual employees, whilst its extrinsic rewards are regarded as those external to individuals and are found in the job situation. These are often determined collectively, such as pay, payments systems, working conditions and so on.

Effort and improved performance at work are viewed by 'expectancy' theorists, then, as being related to the rewards in work, the rewards for working, and the likelihood that these rewards derive from contributing a certain level of effort by the employees concerned. Such an approach is compatible with the possibility that some employees will seek collective means to maximize their extrinsic rewards in performing their job tasks, and will contribute a certain level of work effort to achieve these. But there is no reason to expect that these employees will not seek to optimize their job satisfaction at work, through also demanding appropriately structured working methods where this is possible.

## Developments in motivational theory

Recent research indicates that there is no single solution to the problems facing managers in their attempts at motivating their subordinate staff in organizations. It also suggests that 'following fashion' may well be the only explanation why some organizations modify or change their approaches to employee motivation. The Work Research Unit (WRU) concludes that practitioners, when seeking to design motivational systems within their establishments, need to have regard to both current thinking and established practice and to distil, from these, the ideas and methods best suited to the particular requirements of their own organizations. If motivated behaviour is goal-directed, where individuals engage in activities leading to the attainment of goals and rewards valued by themselves, then the implications for those designing motivational and reward systems are simple but two-fold. First, they must be aware of what it is that individuals in their organisations value and, second, 'they need to ensure that the reward follows from the delivery of the act or acts the organisation wants individuals to carry out'.[63]

Traditional motivation theory is founded on the belief that motivation is a response, on the part of individuals, to satisfy their needs for economic well-being, social relationships, personal growth and so on. An alternative view is that motivation involves a more evaluative, cognitive process. Equity theory, for example, seeks to explain motivation in terms of mental processes, the basic tenet being that individuals act to keep their effort–reward ratio in line with those of other individuals or referent groups. Another cognitive theory is attribution theory, which suggests that current motivation depends on how individuals have rationalized success or failure in the past. Typically, individuals use attributions based on ability, effort, difficulty or luck. For example, where success is attributed to ability or effort by an individual, that individual will be motivated to repeat that success. Managers therefore can do a lot to influence employee attributions through feedback, communications, appraisal and guidance.

In practice, it is currently argued that motivating and rewarding employees can involve a variety of psychological approaches and personnel systems. These include: job evaluation, for providing a systematic way for sorting out internal pay relativities; payment for skills; performance appraisal and goal setting; individual incentives and merit pay; gainsharing; and profit sharing and share ownership.

According to the WRU, all these different approaches to motivating and rewarding employees have their advantages and disadvantages. 'What is needed, in designing reward systems, is a careful analysis of the make-up, needs and wishes of the organisation and its employees'. This includes taking account of corporate culture, management style and related factors. The WRU therefore identifies a number of pointers which managements need to bear in mind in doing this. It claims that:

- Immediate line managers and supervisors have an important role to play in motivating staff, and their selection and training need to reflect this.
- Job evaluation best suits large, stable organizations where there are few pressures for change.
- Payment for skills is a way of overcoming some of the difficulties associated with job evaluation, and helps foster a developmental culture.
- Performance appraisal, as generally practised, has little motivational value. Objectivity and consistency of application are difficult to achieve and call for skills on the part of appraisers that are not commonly found in the organizational setting.
- Goal setting, if carried out in a supportive climate, can be an acceptable and stimulating way of improving performance.
- For some people, individual financial incentives and merit pay can be highly motivational, but certain conditions need to be fulfilled for them to operate successfully.
- Gainsharing suffers from the dilution of the incentive effect, which all groups suffer from, but it can create an environment where productivity issues can be examined in a co-operative way.
- Profit sharing and share ownership can provide managers and workers with a sense of common purpose, and improve communication and understanding. Profit-related pay would seem to offer an attractive way of allowing all employed by an organization to share in its success.[64]

Each organization, in short, is unique and, to varying degrees, requires solutions to employee motivation and reward which, in turn, are enterprise-specific.

## Employee involvement

Another managerial approach aimed at developing the work commitment of employees is the device of 'employee involvement'. This is defined as the various means used 'to harness the talents and co-operation of the work-force in the common interests they share with management'.[65] Employee involvement, which is unitary, must be distinguished from 'industrial democracy' and 'worker participation', which are pluralist. The aim of industrial democracy, for example, is normally the extension of managerial power-sharing in enterprises by a strengthening of trade union organization and by widening the scope of collective bargaining. Employee participation goes still further. It aims at changing the basic authority structures of enterprises, especially private ones, by legislating for employee representation on company boards as practised in some parts of western Europe.

In outline, employee involvement, industrial democracy and worker participation provide contrasting perspectives on the nature of work enterprises and their systems of managerial control and employee commitment. Together they provide the interface between three areas of enterprise authority and decision making. These are: those where employers and management are prepared to share decisions with or devolve them to employees or their representatives; those where employees expect to influence or share decisions with employers; and those where the law gives rights to employees or places restrictions on managerial power and authority. Employee involvement, by aiming to get the support and commitment of all employees in an organization to managerial objectives and goals, thereby reinforcing a sense of common purpose between management and employees, is essentially unitary in its purposes and its methods. It is defensive of the right to manage and the organizational *status quo*. It is, however, a set of industrial relations practices which some managements turned to in the 1980s and 1990s, in response to economic recession, the relative weakness of trade unionism and certain labour and skills shortages.

There are a number of employee involvement practices. The main ones are: financial involvement, job involvement and employee communication and information. Financial involvement, for example, though not widespread in Britain, but more common in western Europe, is limited to the private sector. It takes the form of profit sharing or share options, aiming to give employees a capital stake in the enterprises in which they work. With profit sharing, distribution of surpluses is in cash or in shares, normally cash. With share option schemes, employees are authorized to buy shares at a fixed price, at some future period, or can allow their option to lapse.

One of the more common forms of employee involvement is job involvement. The main aim of job involvement is to enable subordinate employees to contribute to the ways in which their job tasks are organized and performed. In this way the job satisfaction of individual employees is raised and organizational effectiveness is enhanced. Various job involvement techniques are used. These include suggestion schemes, attitude surveys, job enlargement, job enrichment, job rotation, quality circles and autonomous workgroups. In practice, no single method of job involvement guarantees employee commitment or increased efficiency. Further, in implementing appropriate job involvement techniques, management needs to take account of a number of factors. These include:

> managerial style, the effectiveness of the communications system, the adequacy of industrial relations procedures, the quality of supervision, the quality of the working environment and so on.[66]

Effective systems of employee communication and information are crucial to any scheme of employee involvement in order to increase trust between management and subordinates and improve industrial relations. Employees cannot be genuinely involved in any enterprise where communication and information channels are weak or non-existent. As the code of industrial relations practice states: 'management needs both to give information to employees and to receive information from them. Effective arrangements should be made to facilitate this two-way flow'.[67] An effective communication and information strategy normally requires a positive lead being given by top management. A wide variety of information can be communicated. The most basic information relates to the employee's immediate job, since a number of surveys show that information affecting the job tasks of employees is usually considered to be their most important priority. A comprehensive and integrated communication and information strategy, however, requires other corporate information to be made available to all employees, including supervisory and managerial staff. This includes general, marketing and financial information, whilst the Confederation of British Industry stresses the importance of information relating to 'progress, profitability, plans, policies and people'. Further, whatever the form of communication used, it is recommended that it is 'provided regularly and systematically in a readily understandable form'.[68]

In the past few years, the Department of Employment has conducted four surveys of employee involvement practices within the corporate sector (in 1985, 1986, 1988 and 1991). These arose from the requirement of Section 1 of the Employment Act 1982 for companies with more than 250 employees to include in their annual reports statements of actions taken to promote employee involvement arrangements. The law requires each statement to describe action taken to introduce, maintain or develop arrangements aimed at: providing employees with information; consulting employees or their representatives; encouraging the involvement of employees in the company's performance; and achieving a common awareness by employees of the financial factors affecting corporate performance.

The Department of Employment's 1991 survey, covering 377 companies, was based on a statistically random sample of organizations, each with over 250 employees. The survey illustrates the extent and forms of employee involvement arrangements chosen by a variety of firms and, in comparison with the 1988 survey, highlights recent trends. Table 3.3 shows the range of employee involvement practices, by company size, for 1991 and 1988. The 1991 survey concludes that 'employee involvement arrangements have been consolidated and developed over recent years to suit individual companies, and that they are now, even more than previously, an established part of working life'.[69]

The main conclusions of the 1991 survey are as follows. First, the employee involvement practices reported have increased further, compared with the relatively high levels already found in the 1988 survey. Virtually all companies to which the legislation applies now report at least one employee involvement practice in their annual reports. Second, employee involvement reporting increases with company size but the largest increase between 1988 and 1991 was in smaller companies. Third, reported financial participation arrangements, such as employee share schemes and bonus payments, have risen substantially, from 53 per cent in 1988 to 77 per cent in 1991. Over half of all the companies surveyed have a share scheme which all employees can join. Fourth, the types of practices reported showed a shift towards more informal structures for employee involvement, away from formal, committee-based arrangements. Fifth, there is also more emphasis being placed on involving employees in improving quality at work and on business and corporate performance.

When employees enter into consultative and negotiating arrangements with management through their representatives, employee involvement shifts imper-

*Table 3.3* Employee involvement practices, by company size (percentage of companies, 1991 and 1988).

| | 251–1 000 employees | | 1 001–5 000 employees | | Over 5 000 employees | | Total | |
|---|---|---|---|---|---|---|---|---|
| | 1991 *n* = 267 | 1988 *n* = 200 | 1991 *n* = 88 | 1988 *n* = 66 | 1991 *n* = 22 | 1988 *n* = 16 | 1991 *n* = 377 | 1988 *n* = 282 |
| **Information passing** | | | | | | | | |
| Publications | 37.8 | 25.0 | 45.5 | 51.0 | 59.1 | 68.0 | 40.8 | 33.5 |
| Employee report/accounts | 16.9 | 15.9 | 17.0 | 42.9 | 31.8 | 38.1 | 17.8 | 23.5 |
| Presentations/seminars | 10.9 | 5.7 | 23.9 | 11.2 | 36.4 | 30.9 | 15.4 | 8.4 |
| Noticeboards | 4.9 | 3.4 | 9.1 | 14.3 | 4.5 | 4.1 | 5.8 | 6.0 |
| Total (information passing) | 47.9 | 38.6 | 55.7 | 66.3 | 68.2 | 76.3 | 50.9 | 47.2 |
| **Interactive practices** | | | | | | | | |
| Meetings/management line communications | 50.6 | 55.7 | 59.1 | 69.4 | 54.5 | 84.5 | 52.8 | 60.5 |
| Briefing or discussion groups | 22.5 | 13.6 | 29.5 | 27.6 | 27.3 | 46.4 | 24.4 | 18.7 |
| Access to senior management | 13.1 | 10.2 | 25.0 | 9.2 | 22.7 | 17.5 | 16.4 | 10.4 |
| Consultative councils/groups (incl. local) | 43.1 | 55.7 | 43.2 | 68.4 | 50.0 | 80.4 | 43.5 | 60.0 |
| TU and staff association channels | 30.3 | 31.8 | 28.4 | 35.7 | 36.4 | 49.5 | 30.2 | 33.7 |
| Quality circles and suggestion schemes | 14.6 | 8.0 | 21.6 | 12.2 | 9.1 | 12.4 | 15.9 | 9.2 |
| Training | 35.6 | 22.7 | 45.5 | 21.4 | 63.6 | 43.3 | 39.5 | 23.6 |
| Health and safety committees/Welfare committees | 29.6 | 13.6 | 35.2 | 23.5 | 40.9 | 26.8 | 31.6 | 16.7 |
| Pension scheme involvement | 8.2 | 10.2 | 12.5 | 15.3 | 13.6 | 22.7 | 9.5 | 12.1 |
| Total (interactive practices) | 77.9 | 69.3 | 83.0 | 82.7 | 95.5 | 89.7 | 80.1 | 73.6 |
| **Financial Participation** | | | | | | | | |
| Employee share schemes | 71.2 | 44.3 | 76.1 | 62.2 | 81.8 | 78.4 | 72.9 | 50.4 |
| Incentive and bonus payments | 24.7 | 15.9 | 30.7 | 23.5 | 27.3 | 27.8 | 26.3 | 18.3 |
| Total (financial participation) | 75.7 | 47.7 | 79.5 | 63.3 | 81.8 | 81.4 | 76.9 | 53.2 |
| **Other** | | | | | | | | |
| Career development, TQM, Attitude surveys, Monthly management accounts, Board level participation, Study groups | 15.7 | 13.6 | 20.5 | 19.4 | 18.2 | 47.4 | 17.0 | 16.8 |
| Total companies reporting any practice (per cent) | 92.9 | 85.2 | 97.7 | 93.9 | 100.0 | 97.9 | 94.4 | 88.0 |

*Source: Employment Gazette* (HMSO, 1991)

ceptibly into employee representation. Although employee representation is a separate and different process from employee involvement in style and in content they are nevertheless related and are not necessarily incompatible with each other. Whereas employee involvement is unitary in its purposes and is normally centred on the interests and activities of individual employees or small work-groups, the major characteristics of consultation and negotiation are their pluralistic and collective nature. They normally take place at higher levels of enterprise decision-making than do employee involvement practices.

Where management introduces or changes methods of employee involvement and employee representation in an enterprise, it needs to take a number of organizational factors into consideration. These include its history, managerial style, enterprise culture, technologies, size and type of workforce, union membership, market position, ownership, geographical location and so on. In general, involvement practices are largely directed towards maximizing consensus, trust and employee commitment to organizational goals. Whilst this can be true of consultative practices also, employee representation usually has different purposes and its impact on enterprises varies. Normally it aims at reconciling differences of interest between employers, employees and their representatives and is distributive, power-based and pluralist. Employee involvement, by contrast, is integrative, task-centred and unitary.

## Employee commitment

Increasing interest has been shown in recent years, by some managements, in the concept of 'employee commitment'. Indeed, employee commitment, as well as the employer's reciprocal obligations to its employees, is sometimes regarded as a special feature of Japanese-managed companies. It is a characteristic to which is attributed enhanced quality and performance in such organizations. Employee commitment is not to be confused with employee involvement, though the terms are used interchangeably by some writers and practitioners. In general, employee involvement denotes the processes set up by managements in organizations to incorporate employees, normally individually but sometimes collectively, in decisions of various kinds, particularly affecting the ways in which work is done.

In contrast to employee involvement, employee commitment is normally used to denote the kinds of feelings or behavioural patterns which workers have towards the organization which employs them. They are normally grouped into three categories:

- belief in, and acceptance of, the organization itself and/or its goals and values;
- willingness to exert effort on behalf of the organization beyond what is contracted for. This might include giving private time to work, postponing a holiday, or making some personal sacrifice for the organization without the expectation of personal gain;
- desire to maintain membership of the organization.[70]

Employee commitment may or may not arise from employee involvement practices but it does not presuppose any active participation in organizational decision-making. In essence, employee commitment is always voluntary and personal, cannot be imposed and cannot be initiated by others. And since it is given voluntarily by employees, it can also be withdrawn by them. Like employee involvement, employee commitment programmes are closely linked with HRM styles of personnel management.

The reason why some employers try to promote feelings of commitment among employees, or to win high levels of staff commitment to employing organizations and to their jobs, is based on several assumptions. First, committed employees will be prepared to devote most of their energies to their work or to the employer rather than to their private affairs. Second, employees will favour the organization in which they work rather than others, even if this involves some financial loss. Third, employees will give additional time and effort to the organization when these are needed. Fourth, employees will give priority to the employer when its values and interests seem to be in conflict with those, for example, of the trade union or professional body of which they are also members. Nevertheless, employee commitment has its limitations, for it can turn into fanaticism or unquestioning compliance, with undesirable consequences for the employer.

Employee commitment always has an objective for both the employers and individuals concerned. For example, it might be centred on work in general, a specific job, the employing organization, a section or a department within it, or on a specific product or service. Alternatively, commitment may be towards a type of work, a functional role, a trade or profession, a trade union or professional association, or career development. The existence of these different objectives of commitment makes it evident that a managerial policy to facilitate employee commitment, without defining which level or dimension of commitment it is aimed at, is bound to fail. 'The degree of commitment as well as the priority given to any object will depend on a number of factors, which sometimes in turn affect or are affected by the strength of commitment to different objects'.[71] Thus for some people, the most important aspect of their working life is that they belong to a trade or a profession. They acquire skills, knowledge and experience, as well as standards of conduct and other attributes of their trade or profession. Where employing organizations make demands that are at variance with an individual's occupational code of conduct, for example, that individual can experience conflict and incongruence between the two, which may not be easy to resolve.

Employer assumptions underlying proposals to increase employee commitment are that corporate performance can be improved or the costs of production reduced. Commitment relates to performance, it is claimed, in three ways. First, strong commitment to work in general is likely to result in conscientious and self-directed application to work, regular attendance, minimal disciplinary supervision and a high level of effort. Second, strong commitment to a specific job also results in a high level of effort, since effective performance is related to self-esteem, including personal ambition and career plans. Third, strong commitment to the organization facilitates performance by reducing the costs of high labour turnover. Constant staff leakages from organizations add to production costs, since these necessitate additional recruitment, training and employee supervision.

From the foregoing analysis, it is clear that employee commitment is a complex and varied concept, with a number of meanings attached to it. Further, the link between commitment, effort and performance is not straightforward.

> In general, commitment can affect absenteeism, turnover, effort and quality of performance. It will also have a bearing on employees' concern for the future of the organization. All this has a number of implications for personnel and organizational policies.[72]

First, it is useful to know about the strength of employee commitment with respect to work in general, to the organization and to individual jobs and tasks. Differences in commitment between departments and levels of staff, for example, raise important questions about the way work is organized and about the attitudes of staff. Second, commitment at work also depends upon other things which are happening in the work context. Hence a perceived balance between the rewards provided and the contribution made has to be maintained, and to be seen as equitable, if commitment is regarded as important for the organization. Reciprocity between rewards and commitment is affected by a number of factors. These include: corporate policy; organizational climate; managerial style; and work characteristics. The characteristics which have been shown to be important are: the degree of job autonomy; the sense of work purpose and achievement; and the treatment experienced. Where these factors are perceived negatively by employees, alienation can develop.

All these aspects can be influenced by company policies but elements of commitment have been identified which are affected by different corporate strategies. The first is the instrumental/calculative element. This depends on the employees' perceptions of the equity of the rewards and treatment obtained and develops in relation to status, training and salary level. It also relates to factors such as job characteristics and the sense of being valued by the organization. A multiple strategy for increasing commitment is more likely to succeed than a single measure such as profit sharing or performance related pay. Second, commitment to the values and objectives of the organization is derived from the actions of people within it. This is best done when employees first start work and are most open to being influenced, whether through the information they are given or the experiences they undergo. Third, it is claimed that 'a company policy aimed at generating commitment among relatively new employees is particularly worthwhile'. This can ensure that the early influences, induction and training processes are positive and that they will normally result in increased employee commitment and performance.[73]

Fourth, reducing labour turnover by increasing commitment involves assessing the costs and benefits, taking into account the availability of people with appropriate skills, the costs of recruitment and the value to the company of retaining existing employees. 'It may be important for the organization to be seen as providing opportunities for exercising and developing professional competence, a stimulating environment and the resources on which innovatory work depends.'[74] Fifth, employee commitment is particularly at risk where employees are engaged in work which is extensively automated. This calls for sound training and experience, with work design incorporating a degree of control, discretion and challenge. Commitment and individual effort are further enhanced where employees are included in the planning and development of new work processes. Finally, where takeovers, mergers or other structural changes are likely, everyone's job is going to be affected. Career planning and employee counselling are crucial as bases for decisions about retraining, moves to other jobs, and decisions about leaving the employer.

The shift by some employers from a 'labour control' strategy, based on managerial aims to establish order, exercise control and achieve efficiency in managing the workforce, to an employee commitment one has been heavily influenced by North American and Japanese practice. In the commitment strategy, jobs are designed to be broader than before and to combine planning and implementation. Individual responsibilities are expected to change as conditions change and teams, rather than individuals, are often the organizational units accountable for performance. With a commitment strategy, performance expectations are high, emphasize 'continuous improvement' and reflect the requirements of the market-place. Reward and compensation policies take account of the increased importance of both group achievement, through profit and gain sharing, and the expanded scope of individual contribution, through performance pay. Equally important is the challenge to management of giving employees some assurance of employment security, in conditions of change, by offering them priority in training and in retraining as old jobs are replaced by new ones. However, as one distinguished American commentator has concluded:

> Underlying all these policies is a management philosophy, often embodied in a published statement, that acknowledges the legitimate claims of a company's multiple stakeholders – owners, employees, customers, and the public. At the center of this philosophy is a belief that eliciting employee commitment will lead to enhanced performance.[75]

## 3.7  Summary Points

- There is a wide variety of employing organizations in Britain, some with profit and revenue goals, others with welfare and community ones.

- There is a tendency for large-scale enterprises to develop, which employ considerable numbers of employees whose relationships with the employer are generally impersonal and bureaucratically controlled.

- The employment relationship, between employer and employee, is more liberalized than that between master and servant was, but it remains, ultimately, one of power and subordination.

- Increasingly employers are abstract legal entities and corporate bodies providing one party to the employment contract, which remains rooted in common law, even though employees have a series of employment protection rights provided by Parliament and, increasingly, European legislation.

- The responsibility for the effective and efficient managing of modern complex enterprises lies with managers, who are themselves normally employees. Although managerial work is viewed as rational, planned and value-free, research suggests that managerial tasks and activities are fragmented and reactive rather than cohesive and proactive.

- It is senior managers who direct and control organizations, not enterprise shareholders, as firms become larger and as capital ownership is diffused. Similar patterns of management control and direction are apparent in the public sector, although the 'political paymasters' have considerable influence in determining overall employment strategy in public organizations.

- Managerial roles are differentiated by vertical status and horizontal specialism. Vertically there is a hierarchical separation of decision taking and action taking, whilst horizontal tasks and activities are segmented by a managerial division of labour-based functional expertise and skills. General management is a senior managerial task which co-ordinates and integrates functional specialisms within enterprises, whether private or public.

- One of management's key functions is personnel management, whose central objective is to incorporate labour or human resources into the enterprise. The personnel function is, however, problematic: it is split between line management and specialist staff; it incorporates both a control and a welfare role; it has senior generalists, with strategic tasks, and junior generalists, with routine ones; it is being challenged by a new 'human resources management' (HRM) approach to managing people, aimed at integrating employee and corporate objectives within organizations.

- The managing of industrial relations has become increasingly standardized in larger private and public organizations, with many managements adopting more proactive approaches to managing industrial relations.

- Managerial styles of industrial relations are categorized in a number of ways: traditional; classical conflict; sophisticated modern; standard modern; continuous challenge; and sophisticated paternalist. The individualist and collectivist dimensions of industrial relations policies are also apparent in each employing organization.

- Managerial industrial relations strategies are long-term plans aimed at influencing employee and/or union activities over time. More companies are accepting the importance of linking corporate strategy with industrial relations planning. Short-term industrial relations policies have been distinguished as espoused policy and operational policy. Espoused policy states managerial intentions in dealing with employees and employment matters. Operational policy, which can differ from espoused policy, is the way that senior management control the organization and reward and punish line management when they implement policy decisions.

- A distinction is made between policy instigators, implementers and facilitators. Instigators determine espoused and operational policy, implementers are the main body of the managerial hierarchy whose actions reflect operational policy, whilst the facilitators or industrial relations specialists advise and assist in implementing policy but are also members of one or other of the two main groups.

- A major problem for management in large organizations is how to motivate its employees towards greater effort and commitment to managerial objectives. Early theories of motivation were simplistic and reductionist. More recently, a series of complex behavioural theories have been proposed. They argue: the need to integrate individual and organizational goals at the workplace; the importance of participative styles of leadership; and the necessity of gearing job rewards to the efforts and expectations of employees.

- Behavioural scientists tend to take a narrow view of industrial conflict and to underestimate the impact of technology and of collective bargaining

on employee and workgroup behaviour. There is some evidence, however, suggesting that certain employees seek both high job satisfaction and high extrinsic rewards in performing their job tasks.

- In the 1980s and 1990s employment strategies of employee involvement and employee commitment have come to the fore, largely influenced by American and Japanese practice. Employee involvement aims to solicit the maximum support of employees to managerial goals and objectives and to reinforce a sense of common purpose between employers and employees. It includes: financial involvement; job involvement; employee communication; and employee information. These employment relation practices shade into employee representative systems but have different aims and objectives from them.

- Employee involvement is integrative, unitary and task-based, whilst employee representation tends to be distributive, pluralist and power-based. Employee commitment is also unitary and task-based and denotes the feelings, either positive or negative, that individuals have towards the organization employing them. Like employee involvement, employee commitment strategies are linked to HRM styles of personnel management.

## 3.8 References

1. G. Thomason, *A Textbook of Personnel Management*, 4th edn, Institute of Personnel Management, London, 1981, p. 9.
2. J. Scott, *Capitalist Property and Financial Power*, Wheatsheaf, Brighton, 1986, p. 1.
3. G. Thomason, *A Textbook of Personnel Management*, Institute of Personnel Management, London, 1975, p. 75.
4. *Ibid.*, p. 87.
5. J. Jones, The Dimbleby lecture 1977, The human face of labour, *The Listener*, 8 December 1977, p. 742.
6. Office of Population Censuses and Surveys, *Census 1981. National Report. Great Britain Part 2*, HMSO, London, 1983, p. 6.
7. A. Crichton, *Personnel Management in Context*, Batsford, London, 1968, p. 49.
8. H. Mintzberg, *The Nature of Managerial Work*, Prentice-Hall, Englewood Cliffs, New Jersey, 1973.
9. R. Stewart, The nature of management? A problem for management education, *Journal of Management Studies*, vol. 21(3), 1984, p. 326.
10. J. Hunt, *Managing People at Work*, Pan, London, 1981, p. 173.

11. D. Farnham, *Personnel in Context*, Institute of Personnel Management, London, 1990, p. 16.
12. R. Mansfield, M. Poole, P. Blyton and P. Frost, *The British Manager in Profile*, British Institute of Management, London, 1981, p. 116.
13. Farnham, *op. cit.*, p. 17.
14. Thomason (1981), *op. cit.*, p. 17.
15. A. D. Chandler and H. Daems (eds), *Management Hierarchies*, Harvard University Press, London, 1980, p. 1.
16. Institute of Personnel Management, *The Institute of Personnel Management*, IPM, London, 1980, p. 1.
17. D. Barber, *The Practice of Personnel Management*, Institute of Personnel Management, London, 1982, p. 8.
18. K. Legge, *Power, Innovation and Problem Solving in Personnel Management*, McGraw-Hill, London, 1978, p. 26.
19. N. Millward, M. Stevens, D. Smart and W. Hawes, *Workplace Industrial Relations in Transition*, Dartmouth, Basingstoke, 1992, p. 31.
20. H. A. Turner, G. Roberts and D. Roberts, *Management Characteristics and Labour Conflict*, Cambridge University Press, Cambridge, 1977, p. 71; E. Batstone, What have personnel managers done for industrial relations? *Personnel Management*, June 1980, p. 39.
21. Royal Commission on Trade Unions and Employers' Associations, *Report*, HMSO, London, 1968, p. 120.
22. *Ibid.*, p. 45.
23. Department of Employment, *Industrial Relations Code of Practice*, HMSO, London, 1977, p. 4.
24. J. T. Winkler, The ghost at the bargaining table: directors and industrial relations, *British Journal of Industrial Relations*, July 1974, pp. 193 and 201.
25. A. Marsh, *Managers and Shop Stewards*, Institute of Personnel Management, London, 1973, p. 172.
26. A. Marsh, *Employee Relations Policy and Decision Making*, CBI, London, 1982, p. 62.
27. *Ibid.*, p. 187.
28. *Ibid.*, p. 219.
29. K. Sisson, Changing strategies in industrial relations, *Personnel Management*, May 1984, p. 27.
30. P. Marginson, How centralized is the management of industrial relations? *Personnel Management*, October 1986, p. 57.
31. D. Farnham, Human resources management and employee relations, in D. Farnham and S. Horton (eds), *Managing the New Public Services*, Macmillan, Basingstoke, 1993, p. 124.
32. A. Fox, *Beyond Contract: Work, Power and Trust Relations*, Faber and Faber, London, 1974, pp. 297–310.
33. J. Purcell, management control through collective bargaining: a future strategy, in K. Thurley and S. Wood (eds), *Industrial Relations and Management Strategy*, Cambridge University Press, Cambridge, 1983, p. 53.
34. J. Purcell, *Good Industrial Relations*, Macmillan, London, 1981, p. 82.
35. Fox, *op. cit.*, p. 311.
36. Purcell (1981), *op. cit.*, pp. 61 and 68.
37. J. Purcell, Mapping management styles in employee relations, *Journal of Management Studies*, 24(5), September 1987, pp. 534–54.
38. *Ibid.*, p. 547.
39. K. Thurley and S. Wood, Business strategy and industrial relations strategy, in K. Thurley and S. Wood (eds), *op. cit.*, pp. 198ff.
40. Marsh (1982), *op. cit.*, p. 219.
41. Quoted in *The Guardian*, 10 July 1980.
42. K. Thurley and S. Wood, Introduction, in K. Thurley and S. Wood (eds), *op. cit.*, p. 2.
43. *Ibid.*, p. 223.
44. Millward *et al.* (1992), *op. cit.*, p. 49.
45. *Ibid.*, p. 52.
46. Commission on Industrial Relations, *Report No. 34. The Role of Management in Industrial Relations*, HMSO, London, 1973, p. 4.
47. *Ibid.*, p. 5.
48. C. J. Brewster, C. S. Gill and S. Richbell, Industrial relations and policy: a framework for analysis, in K. Thurley and S. Wood (eds), *op. cit.*, p. 62.
49. *Ibid.*, p. 64.
50. *Ibid.*, p. 71.
51. *Ibid.*, p. 70.
52. *Ibid.*, p. 70.
53. A. Fox, *Man Mismanagement*, Hutchinson, London, 1974, p. 35.
54. F. W. Taylor, *Scientific Management*, Harper and Row, London, 1964, p. 10.
55. F. J. Rothlisberger and W. J. Dickson, *Management and the Worker*, Harvard University Press, Cambridge, Mass., 1939, p. 551.
56. A. H. Maslow, A theory of human motivation, *Psychological Review*, May 1943, p. 394.
57. *Ibid.*, p. 395.
58. D. McGregor, *The Human Side of Enterprise*, McGraw-Hill, New York, 1960, p. 34.
59. *Ibid.*, p. 39.
60. T. Kempner, K. MacMillan and K. Hawkins, *Business and Society*, Allen Lane, London, 1974, p. 73.
61. K. Hawkins, *Conflict and Change*, Holt, Rinehart and Winston, London, 1972, p. 38.
62. W. W. Daniel, Understanding employee behaviour in its context: illustrations from productivity bargaining, in J. Child (ed.), *Man and Organization*, Allen and Unwin, London, 1973, p. 61.
63. T. M. Ridley, *Motivating and Rewarding Employees: Some Aspects of Theory and Practice*, ACAS, London, 1992, p. 7.
64. *Ibid.*, p. 23.
65. Granada Guildhall lectures, *The Role of Trade Unions*, Granada, London, 1980, p. 28.
66. Institute of Personnel Management, *Practical Participa-*

*tion and Involvement. 3. The Individual and the Job*, IPM, London, 1982, p. 189.

67. Department of Employment, *op. cit.*, p. 14.

68. Confederation of British Industry, *Communication with People at Work*, CBI, London, 1977, pp. 12 and 22.

69. Employee involvement: a recent survey, *Employment Gazette*, December 1991, p. 664.

70. G. White, *Employee Commitment*, ACAS, London, 1987, p. 5.

71. *Ibid.*, p. 8.

72. *Ibid.*, p. 14.

73. *Ibid.*, p. 15.

74. *Ibid.*, p. 16.

75. R. E. Walton, From control to commitment in the workplace, *Harvard Business Review*, March–April 1985, p. 8.

# 4

# Employers' Associations

Just as employees join trade unions to protect their collective interests against employers and management, so employers have formed and join their own organizations to defend their collective interests, not only against trade unions but also for more general purposes. These bodies, being collectivities of organizations rather than of people, are often described as employers' associations. Like trade unions they are diverse institutions. A few are concerned solely with industrial relations issues, whilst others engage only in trading and commercial matters. Some of them participate in both industrial relations and trading activities to varying degrees. The Trade Union and Labour Relations (Consolidation) Act 1992 defines employers' associations as any body which:

> consists wholly or mainly of employers or individual owners of undertakings of one or more descriptions and whose principal purposes include the regulation of relations between employers of that description or those descriptions and workers or trade unions . . .

Employers' associations also consist of 'constituent or affiliated' organizations or their representatives, where their purposes include regulating relations between employers and their workers or trade unions.[1]

## 4.1 Origins and Growth

Employers' associations, like trade unions, have a long history. Although it is difficult to specify the first informal groupings of employers which were created, there is some evidence to indicate that formal organizations of employers, or 'masters' as they were then described, were established in certain trades as early as the eighteenth century. There were some early associations or combinations among master printers, master shipwrights and cotton employers, for example. Other examples of early organization among employers include the London Master Builders in the 1830s, the Mining Association of Great Britain, formed in 1854, the North of England Ironmasters of

the 1860s, and the Amalgamated Weavers Association in the cotton industry after 1884. These employers' associations, certainly until the last years of the nineteenth century, had two main characteristics. First, they were invariably small-scale local bodies limiting their activities to particular regions or towns. Second, they were frequently unstable organizations which emerged to deal with a specific industrial relations problems facing their members, such as an industrial dispute, and then lay dormant again when this had been resolved.

It was not until the growth of the 'new unionism' after 1889, and the impact which this had on the activities of certain trade unions, that the first national employers' associations were formed. These included the Shipbuilding Employers Federation in 1889, the Shipping Federation in 1890, the Federated Association of Boot and Shoe Manufacturers in 1891, the Federation of Master Cotton Spinners Associations, also in 1891, and the Employers Federation of Engineering Associations in 1896. This last named association, after enforcing a national lock-out which started over a union claim for an eight-hour day in London during 1897, became the Engineering Employers Federation (EEF) in 1899. These national associations had similar goals to those of the earlier local associations. Their main object was to 'keep a common line and help one another in resisting the unions, particularly to help one of their number who was singled out for union attack'.[2] The shipowners, for example, were particularly active against the closed shop.

These national associations were more securely based and more permanently established than their earlier, locally based predecessors. On the other hand, their emergence was somewhat surprising, for British employers combined only reluctantly with one another, and under pressure, and were uneasy in co-operating with their trading competitors. By 1914, however, a number of important associations in the staple trades had become firmly established, their main purpose being to constitute the employers' side of joint boards. The bargaining unit for wages and hours was 'generally delimited by district and occupation, but on grievance procedure and working practices there were some near industry-wide agreements'.[3]

By 1936, with the growth and extension of national collective bargaining in a number of key industries such as engineering, shipbuilding and building construction, it is estimated that there were about 270 national employers' associations dealing with employment matters and 'approximately 1 550 other employers' organizations consisting for the most part of local or regional branches of the national federations'.[4] In other words, there were over 1 800 associations dealing with industrial relations issues between employers and unions at that time. By the late 1950s, the Ministry of Labour concluded that there were some 1 600 employers' associations in Britain, although it could not say precisely what proportion of these were national as distinct from local bodies. It did not believe, however, that the proportion had changed significantly since the mid 1930s.[5]

When the Donovan Commission reported in 1968, the Department of Employment and Productivity listed some 1 350 employers' associations, ranging from the EEF covering 4 600 establishments and over two million employees to some very small associations in a section of an industry, in one locality. All of them were concerned directly or indirectly with negotiating wages and conditions of employment and many of them had trade association activities too. At that time, according to the Confederation of British Industry, in many major industries federated firms employed some 80 per cent of the labour force, though in some industries the proportion was less than 50 per cent.[6]

From what has been described so far, it is clear that industrial action by trade unions has been a major factor persuading employers to create their own collective associations. Certainly in the late nineteenth century, employers' associations were established to protect the right of employers to manage and to organize production in their enterprises without interference from the unions. Since then, they aimed, amongst other things, at preventing wage cutting in the labour market among competing employers. For some employers, multiemployer bargaining through employers' associations was a protection against leap-frogging negotiating tactics by militant trade unions. In some relatively compact and uniform industries like footwear and furniture, for example, 'homogeneity in respect of technology, location, product

market and labour market [was] very important'[7] in determining collective organization amongst employers. In short, a variety of historical, structural, institutional and economic factors has given rise to the need for employers' associations in different industries and at different times.

## 4.2   Types of Employers' Associations

Table 4.1 shows that employers' associations are found in a variety of manufacturing and service industries throughout Britain. In 1987 there were 300 known employers' organizations, compared with 340 in 1979, with a total membership of 308 027 employers or local associations of employers during the early 1980s. By 1991, this had fallen to 258 associations, with a total organizational membership of about 293 000.

Some guide to the density of organization amongst employers is provided by the 1980 workplace industrial relations survey. This study of some 2 000 private and public establishments employing 25 or more employees showed that 27 per cent of all the establishments surveyed, including those in the public sector, were members of employers' associations at that time. This comprised 56 per cent of all manufacturing establishments and 65 per cent of those in the construction industry. Membership in distributive and service sector establishments was much lower, varying between 11 and 33 per cent.[8]

The relatively high density of organization amongst manufacturing employers and establishments during the late 1970s and early 1980s was confirmed by the University of Warwick's survey of manufacturing establishments in the winter of 1977–8 (The Warwick Survey 1977–8). This investigation, covering 970 establishments with 50 or more employees, showed that 75 per cent of the establishments surveyed were members of employers' associations. This varied between 71 per cent for mechanical and electrical engineering establishments to 82 per cent for textile establishments. Foreign ownership appeared to have only a slightly inhibiting effect, with '69 per cent of foreign-owned establishments being, in employers' organisations compared with 75 per cent of the British'.[9] In the private sector, at least, establishments and employers were substantially more likely to be members of employers' associations where trade unions were recognized for manual employees than where they were not recognized.

With the move away from industry-wide collective bargaining over the second half of the 1980s, there

Table 4.1 Major employers' associations: number of members for selected years 1979-91.

| Association | 1979 | 1981 | 1983 | 1985 | 1987 | 1991 |
|---|---|---|---|---|---|---|
| Engineering Employers Federation West Midland | 18 | 18 | 19 | 17 | 17 | 15 |
| Engineering Employers London Association | 1 210 | 1 125 | 886 | 939 | 902 | 1 122 |
| Engineering Employers West of England Association | 850 | 1 147 | 911 | * | 666 | 507 |
| Other Engineering Employers Associations | 454 | 409 | 361 | * | * | 350 |
| National Farmers Union | 3 369 | 3 013 | 2 808 | 3 762 | 2 910 | 2 382 |
| Building Employers Confederation | 125 856[u] | 125 102[u] | 121 494[u] | 117 778[u] | 114 375[u] | 100 004[u] |
| General Council of British Shipping/British Shipping Federation | 10 146 | 10 000 | 9 465 | 9 357 | 9 251 | 7 871 |
| Freight Transport Association | 229 | 213 | 177[u] | 154 | d | d |
| Test and County Cricket Board | 15 890[u] | 15 038[u] | 13 566[u] | 13 463[u] | 13 588[u] | 12 869[u] |
| Electrical Contractors Association | 19 | 19 | 19 | 19 | 19 | 19 |
| Chemical Industries Association | 2 193 | 2 232 | 2 162 | 2 179 | 2 296 | 2 412 |
| British Printing Industries Federation | 339[u] | 339[u] | 164[u] | 155[u] | 154[u] | 159[u] |
| Newspaper Society | 3 178 | 2 650 | 2 606 | 2 669 | 3 117 | 3 154 |
| Retail Motor Federation | 293 | 282 | 277 | 267 | 251 | 266 |
| National Federation of Retail Newsagents | * | 15 444 | 14 264 | 13 377 | 13 672 | 12 169 |
| Road Haulage Association | 28 367 | 28 669 | 29 636 | 30 081 | 31 765 | 29 000 |
| | 15 045[u] | 12 732[u] | 11 277[u] | 10 025[u] | 10 407[u] | 10 535[u] |

*Table 4.1* (continued)

| Association | 1979 | 1981 | 1983 | 1985 | 1987 | 1991 |
|---|---|---|---|---|---|---|
| Heating and Ventilating Contractors Association | 1 185 | 1 193 | 1 192 | 1 180 | 1 176 | 1 237 |
| British Paper and Board Industry Federation | 109 | 84 | 69 | 68 | 66 | 66 |
| Federation of Civil Engineering Contractors | 518 | 481 | 444 | 400 | 376 | 319 |
| Federation of Master Builders | 20 328 | 20 118 | 20 059 | 19 804 | 19 651 | 20 491 |
| National Pharmaceutical Association | * | * | 6 977 | 7 103 | 7 114 | 6 848 |
| National Association of British and Irish Millers | 46[u] | 48[u] | 50[u] | 52[u] | 50[u] | 37[u] |
| Dairy Trade Federation | 4 400[u] | 4 500[u] | 4 100[u] | 4 100[u] | *[u] | 3 300[u] |
| Newspaper Publishers Association | 10 | 12 | 11 | 10 | d | d |
| Publishers Association | 257 | 289 | 243 | 550 | 238 | 178 |
| British Jewellery and Giftware Federation | 2 035[u] | 1 951[u] | 1 661[u] | *[u] | *[u] | 1 825 |
| Total of above associations | [25] 236 344 | [26] 248 679 | [26] 265 665 | [24] 238 109 | [21] 232 061 | [24] 216 957 |
| Total of other associations | [315] 56 759 | [303] 105 095 | [286] 73 207 | [290] 82 380 | [278] 75 886 | [233] 76 000 |

*Figures not available. [u]Unlisted employers' association. d Disbanded.
*Source: Annual Report of the Certification Officer* (HMSO 1980–88)

*Table 4.2* Membership of employers' associations 1990 (per cent).

|  | All establishments | Manufacturing | Private services |
|---|---|---|---|
| Members | 13 | 20 | 10 |
| Non-members | 82 | 74 | 82 |
| Don't know | 4 | 6 | 5 |

*Source*: WIRS 1992

has been a steady leakage of employer association membership since then. Some indication of the density of employer association membership in the early 1990s can be observed from the 1990 Workplace Industrial Relations Survey, as outlined in Table 4.2. About 25 per cent of the enterprises sampled in the 1980 workplace survey were members of employers' associations but 'by 1990 the figure had fallen by half to just 13 per cent'. In 1990, membership was highest in engineering, textiles and construction, with densities of 32 per cent, 32 per cent and 75 per cent respectively. In the service sector, where membership has never been high, density was highest in retail distribution, with one in eight managers reporting it. In all sectors, employer association membership was not necessarily confined to the smallest establishments. Nor were there differences in the incidence of membership between foreign-owned and indigenous establishments. Overall, however, according to the 1990 Workplace Industrial Relations Survey, 'four times as many establishments abandoned employers' associations membership between 1984 and 1990 than the numbers which took it up'.[10]

Employers' associations differ widely in their structure and organization in different industries. A useful classification is to categorize them into three main types. First, there are national federations to which local employers' associations, based on geographical areas, are affiliated. The Engineering Employers Federation, for example, consists of 15 local associations, each with its own member firms, covering up to a million manual and staff employees in many thousands of establishments. The largest local associations in the Federation are the London district, with about 500 member firms; the West Midlands, with over 1 000; and the West of England Association, with some 350. Similarly, the Building Employers Confederation, with about 8 000 member firms, is organized into local associations and regions.

The second type of association is that having a single national body, like the Electrical Contractors Association, with local branches throughout the country. The Electrical Contractors Association has over 2 000 member firms, representing about 80 per cent of the companies and employees in the industry. These companies are organized into a number of branches and regions in England, Wales and Ireland. The third type of employers' association is the single association with a national coverage. These include the Co-operative Employers Association, the Multiple Shoe Retailers Association, and the Multiple Food Retailers Employers Association. Other examples include the British Brush Manufacturers Association, the Vehicle Builders and Repairers Association and the Association of Metropolitan Authorities.

Until its merger with the Local Government Training Board, to form the Local Government Management Board, the Local Authorities Conditions of Service Advisory Board (LACSAB) was probably the most outstanding example of an employers' association operating in public industry. It was both a servicing agency and a negotiating agency, working on a variety of personnel and industrial relations issues on behalf of local government employers, and was funded mainly through the rate support grant and the local authority provincial councils. In practice, its work and activities also extended to a number of other public organizations and charitable bodies outside local government. It was a somewhat unusual organization since other public sector industries tended to rely heavily on small industrial relations secretariats to service their employer representatives rather than on a specialized employers' association like LACSAB. It was formed at the end of the Second World War as a company limited by guarantee.

As a relatively 'new' employers' association, the Local Government Management Board (LGMB) has inherited a diverse range of responsibilities from LACSAB and the Local Government Training Board. It is funded through the revenue support grant and by direct subscriptions from the local authorities. The Board claims to bring together a crucial set of interests which have a direct impact on the way local government works. The Board concentrates its resources on activities where: it can add value through work which local authorities cannot do effectively for themselves; there are no other agencies better placed to provide advice and assistance; and it has the skills and expertise to make positive contributions to the managing of local government. One area in which the LGMB is involved is general personnel management and training. The services provided here include: local government research; information services; management practice and development; national vocational qualifications; recruitment and retention; advice on training and development and the provision of training materials; and examinations and awards.

The other main area of the LGMB's activities is industrial relations. This covers national negotiations, advice on pay, gradings and pensions, and employment advice generally. The main pay and conditions which are negotiated through the Board cover some 3 million employees in local government, in some 30 separate bargaining units, as well as the provision of help to local authorities in resolving local disputes. Further, in addition to giving advice on pay and conditions of service, the LGMB makes information available to local authority employers on a wide range of employment issues. These include employment law, human resources policies and equality programmes. The core activity of the Negotiations Directorate is to operate the national negotiating machinery for the employers. This involves not only negotiating on a variety of pay and non-pay issues but also dealing with disputes and appeals which are not settled locally, together with a variety of casework advice on pay and conditions.

The industrial activities of the LGMB are never static. Recently, the Board has examined the possibility of merging some of the main national negotiating bodies, in the context of single table bargaining. It has negotiated within a new framework for the police services, following the publication of the Sheehy Report. And it has extended the non-local government base for some of its services, such as in the schools information service. Its other interests have included: providing a support service for local authorities determining pay locally; preparing new grading structures for specialist groups of staff, such as those of the magistrates courts; and developing appropriate training and briefing material for authorities contemplating local pay determination.

## 4.3 Activities

Employers' associations undertake three main activities on behalf of their members. First, they represent employers in their dealings with trade unions. Second, they give specialist assistance to their members by providing advisory and other services to their constituent enterprises and establishments.

Third, employers' associations act as political and economic pressure groups *vis-à-vis* government, departments of state and the general public.

### Industrial relations functions

Traditionally, in representing employer interests in their relations with trade unions, employers' associations undertook two main activities: negotiating terms and conditions of employment with trade union representatives and the processing of disputes between employers and trade unions. This function is generally declining, although it is clearly set out, for example, in the objects of the Building Employers Confederation. It seeks, amongst other things:

To promote the formation of regularized methods of procedure in regard to:

i. The negotiation and conclusion of agreements relating to wages, hours and other conditions of employment.
ii. The adjustment of any differences arising out of the operation of such agreements.
iii. The prevention of cessations of work pending such adjustment.
iv. The adjustment of differences involving demarcation of work.

To settle any question arising with trade unions or other labour organizations in connection with building works.[11]

Before 1914 collective bargaining, where it existed, took place mainly at district or regional level between local employers' associations and district union committees. During the First World War bargaining shifted to industry level, with some workplace bargaining. During the interwar period, industry-wide or multiemployer collective bargaining between national employers' associations and national trade unions became normal practice. In the period since 1945, initially workplace bargaining and more recently single employer bargaining have become common practices in parts of private industry, especially in manufacturing. This has weakened the traditional bargaining role of some employers' associations, as has the decline of trade union power and the individualizing of industrial relations during the 1980s. However, substantive agreements on pay and conditions and procedural agreements on negotiating arrangements between employers and trade unions continue to be concluded in some cases on an industry-wide basis in the first instance.

Employers' associations continue to play a part in these activities. These substantive agreements largely determine minimum rates of pay rather than actual earnings. Individual employers, therefore, negotiate additional payments at company or workplace level with union officials, although even some elements of enterprise or workplace earnings – such as shift allowances, holiday payments, overtime premiums and so on – are calculated on the basic rates laid down in national agreements. It is mainly non-pay conditions such as the length of the working week and holiday entitlements which are still standard elements, and it is these which are determined by national agreements between employers' associations and trade unions, with district agreements of virtually no importance.

National agreements on pay may be classified into three categories. First, there are minimum agreements where employers' associations and trade unions determine a decreasing proportion of enterprise or workplace earnings. In these industries, the gap or 'drift' between national agreements and local earnings is high. The second category is the comprehensive agreement. These agreements provide relatively little opportunity for earnings drift to occur. They also enable employers' associations and trade union officers – rather than managers and workplace representatives – to play a substantial part in pay determination. Third, there are partial agreements. These are intermediate between minimum and comprehensive agreements, where nationally determined basic rates still have an important influence on employee earnings and on additional payments made at company or workplace level.

A leading industry where minimum multiemployer agreements apply is chemicals, where the Chemical Industries Association (CIA), which has a membership of over 100 companies, is involved in negotiating three national agreements with the trade unions. These are: the Chemical and Allied Industries' Joint Industrial Council (JIC), established in 1918; the CIA/craft union agreement, established in 1945; and the Pharmaceutical and Fine Chemical Group Joint Industrial Council, established in 1918. The terms of the national agreements on basic pay, shift pay and call-out pay tend to be regarded as the minimum to be paid at company level, although with regard to working hours, holiday entitlements, overtime premiums and holiday pay, the national agreements are closely adhered to. For example, the national agreements tend to impose rigid standards for hours of work, with most companies operating a 38-hour

week and only a few moving towards 37.5 hours. Actual pay rates in member companies, however, tend to be well above the national minima, with many companies enhancing the industry minima by incorporating regular bonuses or other allowances into their basic rates. In recent years, the JICs have attempted to bring total earnings into line and to make national wage rates more relevant to employers locally by consolidating an element of their 'superstructure' payments – which include all payments other than those agreed by the JIC – into the minimum rates. The CIA claims that the two-tier bargaining system has many benefits for employers. By setting a floor of wages, and providing a solid framework for company agreements, two-tier bargaining has a great influence as a trend setter throughout the industry. It also provides access to national trade union officers and allows constructive relations to be maintained between employers and the unions in the areas of health and safety, training and productivity improvements.

In contrast, employers' associations continue to play a major part in the negotiation of comprehensive agreements in electrical contracting, the flax and hemp industry and the imported timber sawmilling industry. For many years, the joint industry board (JIB) in electrical contracting, comprising the Electrical Contractors Association (ECA) and the Electrical, Electronic, Telecommunication and Plumbing Union, now incorporated in the Amalgamated Engineering and Electrical Union (AEEU), has graded the industry's manual workforce and determined standard wage rates across the industry. It also lays down conditions of employment, including welfare benefit schemes, which are applied far beyond the confines of the electrical contracting industry. Another feature of the JIB agreement is that its disputes procedure exempts firms from being taken to industrial tribunals in all cases of unfair dismissal, with the final decisions of the Board being binding on the parties. The ECA has over 2 000 member firms, throughout the British Isles, ranging from those with international scope employing thousands of operatives, skilled and 'master' craft workers to those with a few skilled employees only.

The reasons for these tightly controlled and centralized collective agreements in the electrical contracting industry include: the labour intensive nature of the industry; the need for the fixed labour costs of its members firms to be known in advance; the practice of having long-term, fixed price contracts in the trade; and the large number of small firms in the industry which, without such agreements, might be subject to leap-frog pay bargaining by the AEEU. Because of these factors, the ECA needs to have fairly strict control over its members' pay negotiations and predicted labour costs. The traditional links between JIB rates and electricians' pay in related industries, however, appear to be weakening as unemployment amongst electricians has reduced pay pressures on individual employers and increased the influence of economic and market factors on earnings and settlements.

Another set of comprehensive collective agreements has been recently established in the flax and hemp industry. The Flax and Hemp Joint Industrial Council was created in 1987 and consists of representatives of the Flax and Linen Association, the Transport and General Workers Union and the Scottish Council of Textile Trade Unions. The employers and unions now negotiate multiemployer, voluntary agreements which set national pay rates throughout the industry, in place of those formerly determined by the Flax and Hemp Wages Council. Similarly, the industry-wide agreement of the National Joint Council for the Imported Timber Sawmilling Industry covers virtually 100 per cent of the hourly paid employees in the industry, with no company of any size withdrawing from its scope in recent years.

A good example of an industry having a partial national agreement, which is neither as limited as a minimum agreement nor as tight as a comprehensive one, is footwear manufacturing. Footwear manufacture is often cited as a classic example of multiemployer bargaining and is claimed to provide a model illustration of the benefits of national-level negotiations for both employers and unions. The British footwear industry is the third largest in Europe, is concentrated in rural areas and small towns and consists of a large number of small to medium-sized, family-owned businesses. It is also a relatively labour-intensive industry, using small batch production methods, and has few economies of scale. The demand for its products fluctuates seasonally and the industry is faced with intense foreign competition. The principal employers' association is the British Footwear Manufacturers' Federation (BFMF) and the main union is the National Union of Footwear, Leather and Allied Trades. About 70 per cent of firms in the industry, employing about three-quarters of the total labour force, are members of the BFMF and union density is around 90 per cent of the workforce.

The cornerstone of collective bargaining in the footwear manufacturing industry is the National Conference Agreement (NCA). It is a wide-ranging agreement, which is traditionally renegotiated every two years, and applies to both federated and non-federated firms. Established over a hundred years ago, the NCA sets minimum wage rates and piecework standards, hours of work and holiday entitlements. This ensures that employers, and employees, do not face unfair competition from low-paying 'sweat shops'. Nor do they have to deal with deliberate wage cutting by unscrupulous firms in the industry. The NCA also includes a special agreement on guaranteed weekly wages and, by custom, has provided for some form of wage indexation linked with the retail prices index. Although the NCA sets minimum wage rates, actual shopfloor earnings generally increase pro rata with the rise in rates negotiated within the National Conference. Supplementary bargaining at company level covers items such as sick pay, shiftwork payments and pensions.

There are also partial national collective agreements in the paper and board industry. These are negotiated between the British Paper and Board Industry Federation and the process and craft unions respectively. For the employers, the two national agreements facilitate an understanding of the industry, its opportunities and its problems with the unions. They also create a climate in which a constructive atmosphere of local bargaining can be achieved between employers and unions.

The ways in which employers' associations handle disputes on behalf of their members vary between industries and associations. Cases fall into two categories, 'namely those disputes which concern the interpretation of a national agreement and those which arise out of domestic negotiations in the individual firm'.[12] From their earliest days, district and national procedures for avoiding disputes and resolving conflicts between employers and unions were negotiated in order to provide a framework of rules aimed at regulating relations between the parties. They were an attempt at resolving industrial conflict between employers and unions through conciliatory methods although, by the end of the nineteenth century, some procedures contained a quasi-judicial element too.

As they have developed, there are now usually three main levels in most national disputes procedures. First, there is the domestic level which often has a number of preliminary stages. The second level is the initial external stage, either through local or district machinery, although this too may have some substages. At this level, the employer is more likely to be represented by officers of its employers' association than by internal management. Finally, there is the highly formalized national level of the procedure, or the 'court' of last resort, where senior officers of the employers' association and the unions represent the parties. In some industries, there may be final recourse to external and binding arbitration if the dispute is not resolved at national level. In the paper and board industry, for example, the British Paper and Board Industry Federation regards the operation of the industry's external disputes procedure as so important to its member firms that it devotes much of its time to maintaining the procedure on their behalf. Indeed, the industry has an almost strike-free record.

## Advisory and other services

In their research for the Donovan Commission, Munns and McCarthy claimed:

> Although the major effort of employers' associations' staff in their industrial relations activities is directed towards the negotiation of agreements and the settling of disputes in conjunction with trade union officials, there is present in all . . . an element in their service to members in which they act as consultants about individual problems.[13]

Since then, the function of providing industrial relations advice to members is an aspect of employers' association activity which initially expanded but recently has declined. One reason for the expansion was the development of enterprise and plant bargaining which has detracted from the traditional role of employers' associations as multiemployer negotiators at industry level. Another factor was the growing impact of employment legislation, especially since the 1970s. In these circumstances, and with their officers' specialist knowledge of industrial relations generally and of their own industries particularly, employers' associations were ideally placed to service their members' industrial relations requirements at employer and workplace level. This was particularly the case for smaller employers without the resources to employ their own personnel and industrial relations specialists, and even for larger enterprises which had personnel specialists.

The services provided by employers' associations to their members fall into two main categories: general and diagnostic. Most of their activities relate to requests by member firms for immediate help in

their routine industrial relations problems or 'fire-fighting' activities. But some associations such as the Engineering Employers Federation and the Newspaper Society, for example, have specialist 'fire prevention' services for their members. The general services provided are wide ranging. They include interpreting agreements, introducing new payment systems, applying work study techniques, and setting up job evaluation schemes. Many associations also provide comprehensive statistics on earnings and labour resources in their industries, although, because of market pressures, some employers are reluctant to share statistical information with their trading competitors. Other services provided by employers' associations include supervisory, management and industrial relations training, especially for small and medium-sized employers. Advice on health and safety at work is also important. Most employers' associations are obviously well placed to collect accident figures, disseminate safety information, and provide training for safety officers. Finally, answering legal inquiries and providing legal advice in employment matters are also a major activity of most employers' associations. In some industries, representation of their members before industrial tribunals is an important facility provided to member firms too.

Some useful evidence of the relative importance to private manufacturing establishments of the advisory services provided by employers' associations is included in the Warwick Survey in the late 1970s. This suggested that the most common services obtained from these associations were legal advice and information on local pay levels. The next grouping centred around education and training and redundancy policy, with advice on recruitment, work study or bonus schemes, and job evaluation constituting a third cluster. It is also significant that most services were used more by large establishments than by small ones.

The most recent evidence about the role of employers' associations in providing advice to managers is provided by the workplace industrial relations survey 1990. As indicated in Table 4.3, this shows that in 1990 a wide variety of sources of advice on personnel and industrial relations issues, other than employers' associations, were available to managers. This shows a remarkable change of behaviour by managers between 1980 and 1990. In 1980, almost two-thirds of all the establishments surveyed had consulted an external body, including employers' associations, but by 1990 that proportion had fallen to a third. According to the survey evidence, 'not sur-

*Table 4.3* Managers' sources of advice 1980 and 1990 (per cent).

|  | Body consulted | |
|---|---|---|
|  | 1980 | 1990 |
| Any outside body | 38 | 33 |
| Employers' association | 12 | 7 |
| Full time trade union officers | 12 | 8 |
| Outside lawyers | 10 | 19 |
| ACAS | 9 | 15 |
| Management consultants | 4 | 8 |
| Outside accountants | 3 | 2 |
| Outside personnel managers | 10 | 8 |

*Source*: WIRS 1990

prisingly, in view of the fall in their membership, employers' associations were consulted much less frequently than before'.[14] On the other hand, other external sources of advice, such as the Advisory Conciliation and Arbitration Service and outside lawyers, were in much higher demand than before, in comparison with employers' associations.

## Representation

Employers' associations also fulfil representative functions. The National Farmers Union, for example, is possibly one of the most effective representative lobbies in Britain; it has representation in Parliament and the European Parliament and maintains strong links with agricultural policy makers in Whitehall and the European Union. In general, employers' associations aim to influence the creation and application of social and economic policy affecting their members' interests at local, industry and central levels. Central government and local government are obvious targets, but so too are trade unions especially in issues opposing employer interests and influencing public opinion. Representing employer interests collectively takes a variety of forms including telephoning and corresponding with government officials and other public servants, political lobbying, fund raising and political campaigns.

Employers' associations were also important sources of recruitment for individuals serving as employer representatives on various tripartite bodies created by governments in the immediate postwar period. These included industrial tribunals, wages councils and the National Economic Development Council. Apart from industrial tribunals, these other

corporatist bodies no longer exist, so the requirements for employer representation are considerably less than they were in the 1960s and 1970s.

## 4.4   Internal Structures and Administration

Employers' associations are, like trade unions, diverse in their structure but, at the same time, have certain common features. One thing which they share is their low-key approach in carrying out their functions. Employers' associations and their officers rarely seek publicity for their organizations or for themselves when working for their member organizations. With few exceptions, they engage in their day-to-day activities as negotiators, conciliators, advisers and representatives, without courting public attention or attracting the media. In this way, they maintain their members' private interests without allowing them to become public issues. It is not always possible to do this as, for example, when their members are in a well publicized dispute with the unions with which they negotiate. But nevertheless their preference is to run their internal affairs and to advance the interests of their members privately rather than publicly and confidentially rather than openly. For these reasons, it is suggested that there is a certain 'clubbishness' surrounding the activities of employers' associations and their internal operations. In that this is derived from an identity of interest based on common goals and shared values among their members, together with an often narrow network of stable personal relationships with one another, this is probably true.

In their internal affairs, the structure of employers' associations is influenced by a number of factors, such as the geographical dispersion of the industry, the size distribution of member firms, and their product markets. Many employers' associations originated as district and regional bodies among local employers. The employers' associations in building construction, engineering and printing are typical examples of this. Their present organizational structures, like those of the unions with which they deal, are considerably influenced by their historical antecedents and local roots. Indeed some 75 per cent of present-day employers' associations are local associations. Although national policies are formulated, agreed and implemented by members, there is also scope for local associations to deal with specific problems facing them and to take local initiatives in matters particularly affecting their members. In practice, the commitment of individual employers to 'association' or 'federation' policy is far less forcibly applied than it is in the trade unions. If one of the larger associations in the Engineering Employers Federation has the resources to develop a specialist advisory service to management, for example, it does so without an agreement that all affiliated associations in the Federation should take the same action. Similarly, because of the relatively high levels of trade union organization and of local labour market pressures in certain of its areas, some regions of the Building Employers Confederation are more autonomous than others.

In other cases, the geographical location of an industry has a major influence on employer association structure and administration. In geographically concentrated industries like cotton textiles and furniture manufacturing, for example, the structural features of employers' associations differ widely from those found in more geographically dispersed industries like building construction and engineering. Similarly where an industry consists of a relatively small number of medium-sized and large firms, employer co-operation in industrial relations is better organized nationally rather than locally, as in potteries through the China Clay Association and in rubber manufacturing. In other words, the relative importance of local and national associations, and the ways in which they are organized, vary considerably between industries. The autonomy of local associations varies greatly too, with local bodies affiliated to national federations having greater freedom and autonomy than the local branches of national associations. Finally, some employers' associations are organized on product lines which makes them, in effect, confederations of associations. An example of this is the Federation of Medium and Small Employers which comprises a number of small specialist associations covering a wide variety of trades, although its industrial relations functions are virtually negligible.

Employers' associations, then, are diversely structured. Each varies in the number of establishments it covers, the number of employees in member firms, and the ways in which it runs its affairs. Whilst it is likely that many employers are organized in those industries which have employers' associations, there are some important exceptions. It seems likely, for example, that employers which do not become members are usually very large or very small firms. Very large firms, like the car manufacturers in the engineering industry, often do not affiliate or federate because they have sufficient resources of

their own to develop industrial relations expertise. In other cases, they either do not wish to be constrained by national agreements or they prefer to develop their own industrial relations policies. In the past, for example Austin-Rover, Philips, the General Electric Company and the Rank Group all left the EEF in order to withdraw from direct involvement in national bargaining. Very small firms, on the other hand, frequently do not federate because they are non-unionized, or because they feel that they do not require the services provided by an employers' association. In other cases they do not join because they claim that they cannot afford the membership subscriptions involved.

Employers' associations usually obtain their main income from membership subscriptions rather than from investments. There is usually a small initial membership fee and subsequent annual subscriptions. A few have a flat rate subscription, with others basing subscriptions on the number of workers employed, the size of their wage bill or, in rare cases, capital employed. Rarely do subscriptions exceed 0.5 per cent of corporate wage bills. The main costs are staff and administration. Like trade unions, subscription income varies with the size and activities of an association, although it is probable that federations have the highest income. In some cases, as in engineering, electrical contracting and road haulage, employers' associations maintain special indemnity or strike funds out of which payments can be made to member organizations involved in industrial action. These are rarely used nowadays.

The structure of decision making within employers' associations is analogous to that within trade unions, although representing a firm is clearly different from representing trade unionists. 'It is a representative structure in which power to act is delegated to elected individuals from the ranks of the membership.'[15] In the larger associations, ultimate power is vested in the annual general meeting of members. However, a national council is often elected to determine policy, an executive committee or management board to support the main office holders – such as the association president and treasurer – and a number of standing committees concerned with particular aspects of the association's business. The individuals on these bodies are usually company directors or senior members of management within their firms. Employers' associations generally differ from trade unions, however, in the way in which decisions are taken within their meetings or committees. The preferred method is to arrive at a decision by consensus rather than by voting. It is considered that if policies have to be generally acceptable, majority voting can result in a substantial minority being dissatisfied. But there are exceptions to consensus taking, and membership voting is sometimes used to obtain a direct expression of views on crucial issues like the decision to lock-out, for example. On these occasions when votes are taken, voting power is related to a member firm's wages and salary bill – as in engineering – not to the number of employees, or to its volume of output. But the general aim is to obtain a consensus of opinion within associations rather than to take a vote. Such decisions often serve as policy recommendations rather than being mandatory for all the employers in membership.

All the larger employers' associations employ full-time officers with varying titles. Some of them mainly service internal committees and their elected office holders, whilst others principally act as professional representatives in dealings with member firms, the trade unions or public authorities. The number of full-time officers employed by different associations depends on the range of activities and services provided by the organization. Many smaller associations do not employ full-time staff at all; they rely instead on the services of local firms of chartered accountants or solicitors to run them. Similarly, a number of locally based clothing, footwear and provincial newspaper associations are serviced by their member firms, sometimes on a voluntary basis.

In the larger local and national associations, the executive staff is usually organized into specialist departments under the ultimate control of a Director or Director-General. There might be, for example, an industrial relations division, a legal section, an establishment department, an education and training department, and an economics division, with the association being headed by a Director and/or Secretary. Apart from specialized professional staff such as solicitors, accountants, economists and statisticians, large associations also employ specialist industrial relations officers. They come from a wide variety of backgrounds including management, the civil service and local authority administration.

In general, experience and qualifications are regarded as desirable rather than essential attributes of an applicant for employment; the essential thing is that he should be 'the right man for the job' in terms of personal qualities and mental, physical and intellectual capacity.[16]

## 4.5 Summary Points

- Some employers' associations have a long history, and emerged on a district by district basis in response to union pressure in the nineteenth century.
- Most have been created in reaction to trade union growth, to protect the right to manage, to prevent wage cutting among employers or to stop leap frog pay bargaining by the unions.
- National and local associations exist across a wide spectrum of industries, including some in the public sector.
- National associations may be classified as national federations, national associations with branches and single national bodies.
- Their activities include negotiating collectively for employers on pay, conditions and in dispute settlement.
- They provide a range of specialist industrial relations advice and services to their members, although in some cases this aspect of their work is declining.
- The employer association role in multiemployer bargaining has declined in recent years too, with many associations concentrating on establishing minimum agreements on pay and standard agreements on conditions.
- In other cases, either comprehensive or partial national collective agreements are negotiated.
- Employers' associations can be involved in the resolution of disputes between employers and unions. Disputes arising out of the interpretation of existing agreements are 'disputes of right' and those in relation to new agreements are 'disputes of interest'.
- Once a dispute is external to a firm, employers' associations have an important role in processing it on behalf of their members. This process contains conciliatory, judicial and power elements.
- With the decline of multiemployer bargaining, the advisory function of employer associations is becoming somewhat less important than it was previously.
- Associations continue to play an important role in political lobbying and in representing employer interests in Whitehall and in Europe. Their role in this is a low key one.
- Their internal structures vary considerably according to their industry, geography, size of establishment and products.

- Very large and very small firms tend not to join employers' associations.
- Employers' associations prefer to take decisions by consensus rather than by majority voting. Where voting occurs, it is normally related to the members' pay bills rather than the number of workers employed.
- Employer association policies tend to be guidelines for action by members, unlike the more rigidly applied policies determined by trade unions.

## 4.6    References

1. Trade Union and Labour Relations (Consolidation) Act 1992, c. 52, s. 122.
2. E. H. Phelps Brown, *The Growth of British Industrial Relations*, Macmillan, London, 1965, p. xxvi.
3. *Ibid.*
4. Department of Employment and Productivity, *Industrial Relations Handbook*, revised edition, HMSO, London, 1970, p. 14.
5. *Ibid.*
6. Royal Commission on Trade Unions and Employers' Associations 1965–1968, *Report* (Chairman Lord Donovan), HMSO, London, 1968, pp. 7 and 21.
7. Commission on Industrial Relations, *CIR Study 1. Employers' Organizations in Industrial Relations*, HMSO, London, 1972, p. 8.
8. W. W. Daniel and N. Millward, *Workplace Industrial Relations in Britain*, Heinemann, London, 1983, p. 120.
9. W. Brown (ed.), *The Changing Contours of British Industrial Relations: a Survey of Manufacturing Industry*, Blackwell, Oxford, 1981, p. 18.
10. N. Millward, M. Stevens, D. Smart and W. Hawes, *Workplace Industrial Relations in Transition*, Aldershot, Dartmouth, 1992, pp. 46–7.
11. Quoted in CIR, *op. cit.*, p. 5.
12. V. G. Munns and W. E. J. McCarthy, *Royal Commission on Trade Unions and Employers' Associations Research Papers 7. Employers' Associations*, HMSO, London, 1967, p. 9.
13. *Ibid.*, p. 51.
14. Millward *et al.*, *op. cit.*, p. 48.
15. Munns and McCarthy, *op. cit.*, p. 64.
16. *Ibid.*, p. 70.

# 5

# Trade Unions

Trade unions are still an important institution in British industrial relations. They play a major role in representing employee interests in regulating labour market relations and managerial relations with employers. Although trade unions vary individually in their structures, types and activities, they also demonstrate certain similarities as organizations and institutions. Many trade unions also have deep historical roots. It is difficult to understand contemporary trade unionism, and the ways in which it reacts to current issues, without some appreciation of the major developments in trade union history. This is one of the paradoxes of modern trade unions. On the one hand, they seek to protect their members' employment interests in the contemporary world, using methods most appropriate to these purposes. Yet on the other hand, they are essentially conservative and reactive bodies, strongly influenced by the experiences and traditions of their early leaders and members.

## 5.1 The Characteristics of Trade Unionism

According to the Webbs, a trade union 'is a continuous association of wage earners for the purpose of maintaining or improving the conditions of their working lives.'[1] This classical definition of trade unionism remains true in substance, since it is the status of a person's work as an employee which determines his or her potential eligibility for trade union membership. It needs to be recognized, however, that:

> Trade Unionism is not an 'all or nothing' quality, but one which can exist in varying degree. The 'amount' of unionization can therefore be measured along a continuum, though not a simple one. The position is complicated by the fact that any given level of unionization can be represented by varying proportions of unionateness and completeness.[2]

By this view, the degree of 'unionization' amongst any group of employees is a compound of a union's levels of 'unionateness' and 'completeness'. Unionateness is a qualitative concept, while completeness is a quantitative measurement. Completeness is more usually referred to as 'union density' or 'density of union membership' and it expresses the actual union membership of an employee group, divided by its potential union membership, as a percentage. It is thus a numeric expression of trade union membership amongst a given group of employees.

The concept of unionateness, on the other hand, is a useful tool for analysing trade union behaviour and it suggests that unions have a number of characteristics which vary according to their policies and activities as organizations. Unionateness is used as a measure of the commitment of a body to the general principles and ideology of trade unionism. It has seven elements:

1. Whether a given body declares itself a trade union.
2. Whether it is registered as a trade union.
3. Whether it is affiliated to the TUC.
4. Whether it is affiliated to the Labour Party.
5. Whether it is independent of employers for purposes of negotiation.
6. Whether it regards collective bargaining and the protection of the interests of its members, as employees, as a major function.
7. Whether it is prepared to be militant, using all forms of industrial actions which may be effective.[3]

The above can, in effect, be reduced to five criteria, relating to: collective bargaining; independence; militancy; affiliation to the Trades Union Congress (TUC); and Labour Party affiliation. In essence, a trade union may be conceptually defined as any organization of employees which, first, has as one of its main objectives negotiating with employers in order to regulate the pay and conditions of its members and, second, is independent of the employers with which it negotiates or seeks to negotiate. Whether it is prepared to be militant, whether it is a TUC affiliate, and whether it is a Labour Party affiliate are merely additional measures of unionateness. The fact that some organizations of employees continue to call themselves 'Associations', 'Guilds' or 'Institutions' is not a major determinant of unionateness nowadays. For example, even though it describes itself as an 'association', the Transport Salaried Staffs Association has most of the characteristics of unionateness. It can hardly be described as being non-unionate. The National Association of Headteachers, the Association of First Division Civil Servants, and the Banking Insurance and Finance Union, for example, whilst not affiliated to the Labour Party, are highly unionate in most other respects.

The criteria of 'registration' as a trade union and of 'independence' as separate determinants of unionateness are no longer strictly tenable. Under the Employment Protection Act 1975, the functions of the former Chief Registrar of Friendly Societies and the Registrar of Trade Unions and Employers' Associations, established under the Industrial Relations Act 1971, were taken over by the Certification Officer. The Officer's main duty is to determine whether a trade union is 'independent' as defined by the Trade Union and Labour Relations (Consolidation) Act 1992. Certification as an independent trade union, with the legal rights provided under labour law, is only granted to those organizations of employees not under the domination or control of an employer and not liable to interference in their activities by an employer. A number of staff associations in the financial sector, such as the Sun Life Staff Association, have been certified as independent trade unions, but other 'company unions' have not obtained certificates from the Certification Officer. In other words, in order to be 'registered' or issued with a certificate of independence as a trade union under current legislation, a union must by definition be independent of the employers with which it either negotiates or seeks negotiating rights.

By these criteria it is possible to categorize trade unions according to their degrees of unionateness. Thus unions like the National Union of Mineworkers, the National Union of Rail, Maritime and Transport Workers and the Transport and General Workers Union, like most well-known trade unions, would be considered as highly unionate bodies since they satisfy all five main criteria of unionateness. However, at the other end of the spectrum, there are a number of organizations of employees which, while partially satisfying the collective bargaining criterion, have a fairly low level of unionateness on the four other criteria. These include bodies like the Balfour Beatty Group Staff Association, the Britannic Field Staff Association, the Gallaher Sales Staff Association and so on. These organizations of employees, or staff associations as they are more generally described, are not *bona fide* trade unions in the accepted sense of the term.

In some cases, staff associations develop into embryonic trade unions, either by becoming more unionate bodies by amalgamation and merger, or by opening up their membership base later. A number of unionate organizations, such as the National Union of Teachers, the National and Local Government Officers Association (which became part of UNISON in 1993), the Banking Insurance and Finance Union, and the Engineers and Managers Association, originated as staff associations and evolved into *bona fide* unions. It is arguable that for any union to survive and to grow as an organization over time, it has to become increasingly unionate. It took many years, for example, for the school teachers, local government officers, professional engineers and managers, and even the Association of University Teachers, to accept the logic and necessity of affiliation to the Trades Union Congress.

Between the slightly unionate staff associations and the highly unionate bodies, there is a range of unions exhibiting intermediate levels of unionateness. These include, for example, the Secondary Heads Association, the Prison Governors Association and the National Association of Probation Officers. The Royal College of Nursing, the Royal College of Midwives and other such bodies in the National Health Service, all of which have negotiating rights on appropriate Whitley Councils, are also trade unions in that they independently represent employee interests through collective bargaining, as do bodies like the British Medical Association and British Dental Association. Nevertheless, they are dual-purpose organizations because they also have functions as professional associations.

The major purposes of professional bodies are the education and certification of practitioners and the maintenance of professional standards amongst members. These aims derive from the traditional model of the independent fee-paid practitioner contracting his or her services to personal clients in the private sector. It is only with the growth of employee status amongst professional groups in the economy, especially in the public sector, that such organizations have had to take on a trade union and collective bargaining role in addition to their professional one. This has frequently led to conflicts within such bodies between those supporting the professional conscious image of their organization and those coming to terms with the reality of a trade union consciousness brought about by the nature of their employment.

It is clear in practice that different unions exhibit contrasting degrees of commitment to the principles of trade unionism and to the ideological implications of collective representation, joint negotiation and industrial relations. Traditional craft-type unionism differs from non-craft unionism. Similarly, the social and industrial solidarity associated with trade unionists like mineworkers and shipbuilders, who used to live and work in closely knit working class communities, contrasts vividly with the more instrumental trade unionism of most white collar employees who commute to their employment from more diffuse middle class suburbs. These comments, however, do not modify the views, first, that the essence of independent trade unionism is collective bargaining for its members; second, that the concept of unionateness is a useful tool for analysing the basic characteristics of trade unionism; and third, that trade unions exhibit differing degrees of unionateness amongst each other and within themselves at particular points in time.

## 5.2   The Origins and Growth Of Trade Unions

The British trade union movement can only be understood as it is today if its history since the early nineteenth century is understood. The forces of history and tradition, whilst being generally strong in such British institutions as the law, the armed forces and Parliament, are particularly strong in the trade unions. As Alan Flanders observed:

> no one who knows trade unionism from the inside would possibly doubt that the appeal to tradition is a very telling argument and that these are grounds for concluding that trade unions are especially prone to take tradition as their principal guide on industrial and social behaviour.[4]

It is beyond the scope of this book to examine in detail the long complex history of British trade unions. There already exists a considerable body of trade union history so only a brief outline is given

here. It should be clearly recognized, however, that whilst sometimes appearing to be radical and militant, the trade unions are intensely conservative bodies in that they are proud of their long history and of their many achievements in the face of powerful opposition and, at times, political persecution. This conservatism makes them slow to acknowledge the need for change and helps to explain their determination to keep faith with their forebears who founded and fashioned the unions. As Phelps Brown has written:

> There is another way in which the past makes the present intelligible. It enables us to understand attitudes which are incongruous with the needs of the present day, for it shows how they have been inherited and preserved. We encounter the living past, the power of myth. A movement such as trade unionism . . . needs the unifying and galvanizing force of tradition . . . events of the past instill attitudes which institutions pass on to successive generations of entrants, who come to behave as if those events had happened to them. Their perception of the world about them is historically conditioned.[5]

The early trade unions, which slowly and painfully emerged during the first half of the nineteenth century, were created in response to the working conditions imposed by the private enterprise system which developed out of the industrial capitalism of the industrial revolution. In the face of great adversity created by employers, Parliament and the law, the first effective and durable unions were formed by skilled workers who enjoyed relatively high wages and continuity of employment, such as printers, shoemakers, weavers, engineers and carpenters. Such unions as the Amalgamated Society of Engineers (formed in 1851), and the Amalgamated Society of Carpenters and Joiners (1860), possessed a national organization, permanent membership, regular subscriptions, full-time officers, formal rule books and a range of membership benefits. Sidney and Beatrice Webb dubbed this durable and cautious form of organization the 'New Model Unionism'. They pointed out its exclusive nature, in strictly confining membership to the highly skilled and relatively prosperous section of the working class of the period.

By the end of the nineteenth century, the New Model Unions had been accepted as necessary and even desirable by many employers, by liberal middle-class public opinion and by Parliament. The cautious, constitutional, respectable and, at times, deferential nature of these new unions had won acceptance within the framework of Victorian society and politics.

> What is also remarkable is the extent to which the unions gained acceptance and approval in the course of the nineteenth century, and became integrated in the economic and political structure of the country.[6]

It is important to recognize, however, that the total membership of the New Model Unions was very small as a proportion of the labour force of the day. The great mass of unskilled and badly paid workers could not join these unions, neither was their structure one which they could emulate. Nevertheless, a vital bridgehead had been established by the Victorian working classes. Perhaps a different form of trade unionism could be fashioned which would meet the needs of the relatively unskilled.

By the closing decades of the nineteenth century, the industrial revolution had transformed the face of Britain. It had created large new industrial cities in which factories, docks, railways, shipyards, gasworks and steelworks were located, and where large numbers of non-craft or general workers were concentrated. With a sharp trade depression, the new legal status of trade unions, growing working-class consciousness and nascent socialism, the scene was set for the emergence of another form of unionism with very different characteristics from either the New Model variety or that of the coalminers and textile workers. The Webbs described the unions created by the relatively unskilled general workers in the closing years of the nineteenth century as the 'New Unionism'. This was because their characteristics of low membership subscriptions, strike benefits, relatively simple rule books, open and transitory membership, socialist principles, hostility to employers and profits, and a willingness to take strike action distinguished them from the New Model unions.

> The symbol of the new unionism was the 'Great Dock Strike' of 1889 . . . The next nine years were to see eleven more substantial stoppages, the greatest of which, the miners' lockout of 1893, lasted nearly four times as long as the 'Great Dock Strike' and cost thirty times as many working days.[7]

New unions, or 'General Unions' as they came to be

called, were formed, for example, among dockers, seafarers, gasworkers and general labourers, and they soon displayed a militant attitude towards obtaining higher wages and shorter working hours for their members. It is not true, however, that the new unionism was strongly representative of the lowest social levels of the working class: 'the General Unions, at any rate between 1892 and 1911, depended far more for their foothold on certain industries and large works, than on their ability to recruit indiscriminately'.[8] This was certainly true of the gasworkers and the dockers. Because of the absence of reliable membership statistics for many of the new 'General Unions', it is not possible to ascertain the exact growth of membership. However, it is beyond doubt they accounted for a considerable expansion of total trade union membership between the late 1880s and the outbreak of the First World War in 1914.

Trade union membership grew rapidly before, during and after the First World War and by 1920 almost half the British labour force was in trade unions. But during those years no major change took place in trade union structure comparable to the rise of the new model unions in the middle of the nineteenth century and the new unions during its closing decades. During the 1920s, however, structural changes took place which largely determined the shape of British trade unionism up to the present time. A small number of large, powerful unions were formed in the 1920s through a series of amalgamations and mergers. They included the Transport and General Workers Union, the Amalgamated Engineering Union and the General and Municipal Workers Union (later the General Municipal Boilermakers and Allied Trades Union). These unions were to largely dominate the Trades Union Congress (TUC) and the Labour Party through their block votes for the next 60 years.

Under the impact of the trade depression between the two world wars, trade union membership, power and influence was greatly reduced. By 1933 trade union membership, measured as a percentage or density of the workforce, had fallen from its peak of 48 per cent in 1920 to 23 per cent. Helped by the gradual expansion of the economy in the late 1930s, the war economy of 1940–45, and the full-employment policies pursued after 1945, union density rose to 45 per cent in 1948 and remained broadly at that level until the late 1960s. During the early 1970s, union membership rose again and reached the density high-point of 50 per cent in 1974, with 11.75 million members. By 1979 there were 13.3

million union members in Britain, giving a union density of some 55 per cent.

By the late 1970s trade union power measured by its ability to raise wages, improve working conditions and influence the decisions and legislation of governments had reached its peak. In a little over a century the trade unions had risen from relative obscurity and political impotence to a degree of power and influence which many believed rivalled that of the state itself. The exercise of that power became a major political issue in the 1970s. How to reduce trade union power became a major electoral issue in the general election of 1979. The Conservative government elected in that year, and re-elected in 1983, 1987 and 1992, made the reduction of trade union power a principal objective which, with the help of high unemployment, new trade union laws and the defeat of the miners' strike in 1985, was largely achieved by the mid-1980s. By the late 1980s, union density had fallen to about 40 per cent of the employed labour force, or the level at which it was in the 1960s. It would be a mistake, however, to see the loss of trade union membership, power, influence and public support as evidence that the British trade union movement is in terminal decline. The problem facing the unions today is how to adapt to the changes which have taken place since 1979 in the workplace, in the national economy, in the trade union legal framework and in the way the electorate perceives its political role. How successful they have been, even after more than a decade of searching for a new identity, remains uncertain.

> During the 1980s unions made considerable efforts to re-orient their policies and methods . . . yet there is little consensus on the responses to be adopted, and the effectiveness of new policy initiatives remains unclear. . . . Unions have survived, but they have not created a new identity, and the idea of a labour 'movement' is perhaps more distant than ever.[9]

## 5.3 Developments in Trade Unionism

It is commonly claimed that there are too may trade unions in Britain, and that many industrial relations problems are seriously exacerbated by multiunionism and interunion conflicts. Envious eyes are cast at the small number of industrial unions in West Germany and in some other countries. A closer examination of British unions, however, reveals that there is a very high proportion of union membership concentrated

in a comparatively small number of trade unions, as Table 5.1 shows. In 1900, there were 1 323 trade unions, which had been reduced to 287 at the end of 1990. Until 1976 the Department of Employment recorded all organizations of employees which were known to include in their objectives that of negotiating with employers. The effect of this definition was to record many small professional organizations which had very limited industrial relations functions. The figure of 287 certificated unions at the end of 1990 differs from the higher return of 323 unions listed by the Certification Officer for that year, which includes not only unions granted certification, but also organizations which seek legal recognition as a preliminary to securing certification status or for tax relief purposes. The higher figure given by the Certification Officer also includes the various sections of federations of trade unions, for example, the National Union of Mineworkers. Trade union membership statistics are now effectively limited to those organizations appearing to satisfy the statutory definition of a trade union under Section 28 of the Trade Union and Labour Relations (Consolidation) Act 1992.

Further reductions in the number of trade unions have been largely accomplished by amalgamations, which have concentrated large memberships into a small number of unions. This is a trend which is likely to continue. In 1960, for example, as shown in Table 5.1, some 17 unions with 100 000 members or more accounted for 67 per cent of total union membership. By 1990 there were 23 unions of this size, with a membership accounting for 80 per cent of all trade union members in Britain. Similarly, whilst TUC affiliates accounted for fewer than one-quarter of the total number of unions in the early 1990s, the combined membership of TUC unions amounted to 80 per cent of overall union membership at that time. Despite the persistence of multiunionism in British industry, the trend in the postwar period has been one of rapid reduction in the number of small unions, with the substantial majority of members belonging to a relatively small number of unions affiliated to the TUC.

Trade union membership is often measured in terms of total membership size. Absolute membership figures, however, indicate very little unless expressed as a percentage or 'density' of potential trade union membership, either of the overall labour force or of total employment in particular sectors of the economy, industries or occupations. Density figures relating to the sex composition of trade union

*Table 5.1* Size and number of British trade unions in 1960, 1976 and 1990.

| Number of members | 1960 | | | 1976 | | | 1990 | | |
|---|---|---|---|---|---|---|---|---|---|
| | Number of unions | Total all membership (in 000s) | % of all membership | Number of unions | Total membership (in 000s) | % of all membership | Number of unions | Total membership (in 000s) | % of all membership |
| Under 500 | 308 | 51 | 0.5 | 203 | 38 | 0.3 | 109 | 19 | 0.2 |
| 500–9 999 | 249 | 661 | 6.7 | 180 | 480 | 3.9 | 107 | 289 | 2.9 |
| 10 000–24 999 | 44 | 718 | 7.3 | 23 | 396 | 3.2 | 15 | 238 | 2.4 |
| 25 000–99 999 | 32 | 1 782 | 18.2 | 31 | 1 618 | 13.1 | 32 | 1 382 | 13.9 |
| 100 000–249 999 | 10 | 1 742 | 17.8 | 14 | 2 053 | 16.6 | 14 | 2 233 | 22.4 |
| 250 000 and above | 7 | 4 848 | 49.5 | 11 | 7 790 | 62.9 | 9 | 5 785 | 58.2 |
| Total | 650 | 9 802 | 100.0 | 462 | 12 375 | 100.0 | 287 | 9 947 | 100.0 |

*Source: Employment Gazette* (various)

*Table 5.2* Aggregate union membership, density and unemployment in Great Britain: selected years 1948-87.

| Year | Union membership number (000s) | Potential union membership A (000s) | Density A | Potential union membership B (000s) | Density B | Unemployment level in Great Britain (%) |
|---|---|---|---|---|---|---|
| 1948 | 9 102 | 20 270 | 44.9 | 19 994 | 45.5 | 1.5 |
| 1960 | 9 437 | 21 755 | 43.4 | 21 450 | 44.0 | 1.6 |
| 1968 | 9 739 | 22 703 | 42.9 | 22 186 | 43.9 | 2.4 |
| 1972 | 10 738 | 22 452 | 47.8 | 21 650 | 49.6 | 3.6 |
| 1976 | 11 905 | 23 326 | 51.0 | 22 048 | 54.0 | 5.4 |
| 1980 | 12 239 | 23 452 | 52.2 | 22 458 | 54.5 | 6.7 |
| 1984 | 10 336 | 23 611 | 43.8 | 20 741 | 49.8 | 11.5 |
| 1987 | 9 874 | 24 105 | 41.0 | 21 325 | 46.3 | 10.4 |

*Source*: Waddington, *British Journal of Industrial Relations*, June 1992
Potential union membership A is the labour force including the registered unemployed but excluding employers, the self-employed and members of the armed forces. Potential membership B is the labour force excluding the registered unemployed, the self-employed, the armed forces and employers.

membership and employment patterns also reveal important trends.

Table 5.2 illustrates the changes in overall trade union density for selected years between 1948 and 1987. (In order to demonstrate the impact of changing levels of unemployment on trade union membership and density, density percentages are given which (A) include the unemployed in the labour force and (B) exclude them.) The growing divergence between density A and B percentages since the late 1970s, along with the marked reduction in both trade union membership and density, corresponds with a sharp upward trend in unemployment in the same period. Under adverse economic conditions between 1979 and 1990, the unions lost 3 million members and overall density (A) fell to 38 per cent.

Table 5.3 illustrates the trends in trade union membership and density in the five major employment sectors of the British economy between 1948 and 1987. The table shows that union density is highest in the public sector and manufacturing, and lowest in private sector services, agriculture, forestry and fishing, and construction. Between 1969 and 1979, growth in union membership and density in

*Table 5.3* Union membership and density by sector in Great Britain 1948-87.

| | 1948 | | 1968 | | 1979 | | 1987 | |
|---|---|---|---|---|---|---|---|---|
| | Union membership (000s) | Union density (%) | Union membership (000s) | Union density (%) | Union membership (000s) | Union density (%) | Union membership (000s) | Union density (%) |
| Public sector | 3 284.7 | 71.4 | 3 716.7 | 68.0 | 5 130.3 | 83.7 | 4 871.4 | 81.7 |
| Utilities * | 218.2 | 67.9 | 305.5 | 73.8 | 326.5 | 94.9 | 275.4 | 96.4 |
| Public services † | 1 464.3 | 59.9 | 2 248.5 | 59.7 | 5 758.5 | 79.6 | 3 801.1 | 78.9 |
| Manufacturing | 3 722.0 | 51.8 | 4 125.3 | 50.7 | 5 152.6 | 72.9 | 3 042.9 | 60.1 |
| Manual | 3 549.6 | 58.8 | 3 790.5 | 62.8 | 4 209.5 | 83.4 | 2 437.4 | 65.5 |
| White collar | 172.4 | 15.0 | 334.8 | 15.9 | 943.1 | 46.7 | 605.5 | 45.3 |
| Construction | 611.2 | 47.4 | 472.0 | 32.0 | 519.7 | 41.4 | 306.4 | 29.8 |
| Agriculture, forestry and fishing | 224.5 | 22.9 | 131.1 | 25.9 | 85.9 | 24.1 | 42.0 | 13.9 |
| Private services | 665.2 | 14.7 | 771.3 | 12.8 | 1 267.4 | 18.1 | 1 250.6 | 14.4 |

*Source*: Waddington, *British Journal of Industrial Relations*, June 1992
*Note*: union density is calculated from potential union membership by sector, which excludes the unemployed, the self-employed, the armed forces and employers.
* Utilities comprise the gas, water and electricity industries.
† Public services comprise national and local government, education and health services.

*Table 5.4* Union membership and density by sex in Great Britain: selected years 1948–87.

| Year | Men | | Women | |
|------|-----|-----|-------|-----|
| | Union membership (000s) | Union density (%) | Union membership (000s) | Union density (%) |
| 1948 | 7 454 | 56.2 | 1 648 | 24.5 |
| 1960 | 7 558 | 53.9 | 1 879 | 25.3 |
| 1968 | 7 518 | 53.7 | 2 221 | 27.2 |
| 1972 | 8 041 | 60.4 | 2 697 | 32.4 |
| 1976 | 8 477 | 64.7 | 3 428 | 38.3 |
| 1980 | 8 468 | 65.0 | 3 771 | 39.9 |
| 1984 | 6 866 | 59.1 | 3 470 | 38.0 |
| 1987 | 6 415 | 55.2 | 3 459 | 35.7 |

*Source*: Waddington, *British Journal of Industrial Relations*, June 1992
*Note*: Union density is calculated from potential union membership which excludes the unemployed, the self-employed, employers and the armed forces.

both the manufacturing and public sectors was very strong. But between 1979 and 1987 union density in manufacturing fell sharply while in the public sector it remained comparatively unchanged. In agriculture, forestry and fishing, construction and private sector services, union membership and density fell sharply between 1979 and 1987. It would also appear that the trends illustrated in Table 5.3 have continued in the period 1987 to 1992.

Table 5.4 shows union membership and density by sex. Since the Second World War, the growth in the proportion of females in the trade unions has been a principal feature of the period. While male membership has declined by a million since 1948, female membership has increased by 2 million or over 100 per cent, though a high proportion of this increase has been amongst part-time female workers. Since 1979 male union membership and density, as well as male employment levels, have declined markedly. Female union membership, density and employment levels also declined, but much less severely than for men. The evidence available since 1987 suggests that male union membership and density has continued to decline while for females it has remained static.

Trade union density by occupational group, sex and employment status in 1991 is illustrated in Table 5.5. The table demonstrates a close link between high union density and public sector employment in occupations such as health and associated professions and teaching, with a high density for both men and

women. By comparison, union density is lowest in occupations such as agriculture, skilled construction trades, marketing and private sector services in general. Overall, union density is higher among men than among women; but where density is high or low for men the same pattern is reflected in female density. A clear difference in union density between the sexes appears, however, when full-time males are compared with part-time females in the same occupations.

Table 5.5 also demonstrates that trade union membership is still concentrated in male manual employment, in basic industries, the public sector and manufacturing, all of which are, in aggregate, contracting in employment terms. On the other hand, union density is relatively weak in the expanding areas of employment, such as private sector services employing a growing number of females, for example, hotels and catering, business services, distribution and retailing.

> The decline of trade union membership and density during the 1980s wiped out the membership gains of the preceding decade. The effect of this decline was particularly pronounced among male and manual workers. While union membership remained concentrated in manufacturing and public sector industries, employment in those sectors continued to contract. . . . Currently the 7.4 million unorganised workers in private services represent the largest potential for union growth. Furthermore, employment in this sector is predicted to expand substantially by 2000.[10]

Figure 5.1 brings together in diagrammatic form the salient factors of trade union membership, density, growth and decline. It also highlights some of the main factors which influence and shape trade union membership and density, which are more fully explored in the next section.

## 5.4  Factors Influencing Union Membership

The factors influencing the level and density of trade union membership are many, varied and complex. They are also extremely difficult to measure, quantify or rank in order of importance. Figure 5.2 attempts to list the more important factors, dividing them into positive and negative categories.

Most of the factors influencing trade union membership growth and decline listed in Figure 5.2

Table 5.5 Percentage of union density by occupational group, sex and employment status, Great Britain, spring 1991.

| | All persons | | | | Men | | | | Women | | | |
|---|---|---|---|---|---|---|---|---|---|---|---|---|
| | Employees | | Self-employed | All in employment | Employees | | Self-employed | All in employment | Employees | | Self-employed | All in employment |
| | Full-time | Part-time | | | Full-time | Part-time | | | Full-time | Part-time | | |
| All occupations | 42 | 22 | 10 | 33 | 43 | 13 | 11 | 36 | 39 | 23 | 9 | 30 |
| Corporate managers and administrators | 29 | 16 | * | 27 | 29 | * | * | 28 | 29 | 15 | * | 25 |
| Managers/proprietors in agriculture and services | 17 | * | 11 | 14 | 16 | * | 13 | 15 | 18 | * | 6 | 12 |
| Science and engineering professionals | 34 | * | * | 31 | 35 | * | * | 31 | 31 | * | * | 27 |
| Health professionals | 49 | * | 45 | 47 | 53 | * | 46 | 50 | 42 | * | * | 43 |
| Teaching professionals | 82 | 39 | * | 70 | 82 | 39 | * | 75 | 82 | 38 | * | 66 |
| Other professional occupations | 36 | 34 | 11 | 30 | 31 | * | 11 | 26 | 45 | 36 | * | 40 |
| Science and engineering associated professionals | 36 | * | * | 34 | 36 | * | * | 34 | 37 | * | – | 32 |
| Health associated professionals | 81 | 70 | * | 74 | 76 | * | * | 70 | 82 | 70 | * | 74 |
| Other associated professionals | 43 | 20 | 23 | 35 | 43 | * | 25 | 37 | 44 | 21 | 19 | 33 |
| Clerical occupations | 41 | 22 | * | 35 | 44 | * | * | 41 | 38 | 23 | * | 32 |
| Secretarial occupations | 21 | 11 | * | 17 | 41 | * | – | 38 | 20 | 11 | * | 16 |
| Skilled construction trades | 35 | – | 3 | 14 | 35 | – | 3 | 14 | * | – | – | * |
| Skilled engineering trades | 57 | * | 14 | 51 | 57 | * | 14 | 52 | 47 | * | – | 40 |
| Other skilled trades | 41 | 19 | 5 | 31 | 41 | * | 6 | 31 | 41 | 21 | – | 31 |
| Protective service occupations | 54 | * | * | 51 | 53 | * | * | 52 | 58 | * | * | 43 |
| Personal service occupations | 35 | 19 | 10 | 25 | 36 | * | * | 29 | 34 | 20 | – | 24 |
| Buyers, brokers and sales representatives | 20 | * | * | 16 | 20 | * | * | 17 | 18 | * | 11 | 15 |
| Other sales occupations | 16 | 13 | * | 14 | 17 | * | * | 12 | 16 | 14 | * | 14 |
| Industrial plant and machinery operatives/assemblers | 53 | 29 | * | 48 | 56 | * | * | 52 | 44 | 32 | * | 40 |
| Drivers and mobile crane operatives | 52 | * | 14 | 44 | 52 | * | 14 | 44 | 44 | * | * | 31 |
| Other occupations in agriculture, forestry and fishing | 13 | * | * | 11 | 14 | * | * | 12 | * | * | * | * |
| Other elementary occupations | 55 | 24 | * | 36 | 58 | 11 | * | 45 | 43 | 26 | * | 28 |

Source: Employment Gazette (HMSO, 1993)

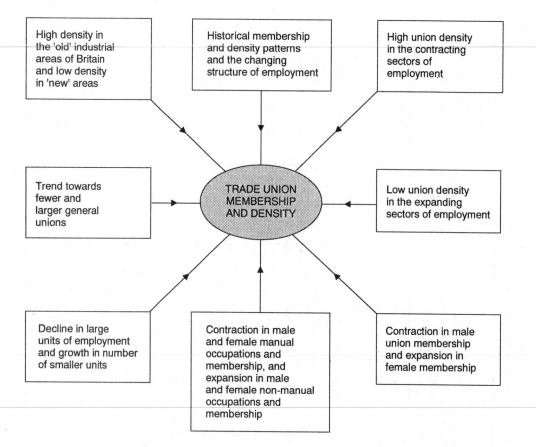

*Figure 5.1* Trade union membership, density and distribution.

can, for analytical purposes, be grouped into four categories: first, structural changes in the pattern of national employment; second, growth and decline in the national economy; third, the political, legal and social climate of industrial relations; fourth, trade union image, appeal and leadership. While it is helpful in terms of clarity and presentation to keep these four categories separate, in reality they overlap and interact. Each of these four major elements affecting trade union membership will be considered in turn.

## Structural changes in the pattern of national employment

One common explanation of changes in the level and density of trade union membership focuses on the constantly changing pattern of national employment as old industries and occupations decline and new ones emerge. Evidence of the importance of such changes are to be found in the large numbers of trade

unions which have disappeared or declined as the occupations, skills and industries they drew their membership from declined or became extinct. Likewise, as whole sectors of the economy decline or expand, trade union membership, after time lags, also changes. This can be illustrated by the substantial growth in public sector employment after 1945, which led to the rapid growth of trade unions, strongly encouraged by national government, in that sector. Similarly, during the 1980s, manufacturing industry, coalmining and steelmaking contracted sharply and so did trade union membership in those industries. In the same period growth took place, for example, in private sector services, banking and finance, and electronics, and while trade union membership also grew in those industries it did not grow as fast as employment, so density remained low.

One explanation of the decline in union density during the 1980s focuses on secular changes in the composition of employment . . . by 1979

| POSITIVE FACTORS | NEGATIVE FACTORS |
|---|---|
| • Low unemployment | • Economic recession |
| • Stable composition of employment and industrial structure | • Rapidly changing composition of employment and industrial structure |
| • Large employing organizations and workplaces | • Small employing organizations and workplaces |
| • Size of the public sector | |
| • High inflation requiring defensive wage increases | • Expansion in geographical areas with little trade union tradition |
| • Willingness of managements to recognize and negotiate with unions | • Anti-union employers and managers |
| • Positive appeal of trade unions – image, leadership, etc. | • Unfavourable trade union image |
| • High levels of male full-time employment | • High levels of female and part-time employment |
| • Positive and favourable attitude by government to trade union membership and collective bargaining | • Negative attitude of government to trade union membership and collective bargaining |
| • Long-established 'brown-field' places of employment | • Expansion of 'green-field' sites |
| • Low levels of product/service market competition | • High levels of product/service market competition |
| • Terms of employment determined by collective bargaining | • Growth in private sector service employment and decline in manufacturing and public sector employment |
| • A favourable political climate | • Unfavourable political climate |

*Figure 5.2* Factors influencing union membership.

union membership was concentrated in manufacturing and the public sector, yet was relatively sparse in private-sector services. Employment growth in the latter and contraction in the former during the 1980s is seen as adversely influencing density levels. Compounding sectoral shifts in employment are increases in the number of women, white-collar and part-time employees, groups exhibiting historically lower unionisation rates than their male manual and full-time counterparts.[11]

The adverse effects of structural shifts in the composition of employment on trade union membership and density in the 1980s and 1990s were exacerbated not only by the growth in female, part-time and white collar employment, but also by a geographical shift in employment to southern and eastern England where tradition and culture were, in general, less receptive to trade unionism. In general, the southernmost

regions of Britain have a lower trade union membership density than elsewhere.

Structural change in industry and the pattern of employment also affects the size of workplaces and establishments. Generally speaking, the larger the workplace and the more people employed the higher will be union membership and density. While workplace size grew between 1945 and 1979, during the 1980s it declined markedly with the percentage of employees in workplaces with 500 and more falling from 54 to 42 per cent; and for workplaces with 1000 and more employees from 41 to 29 per cent. 'In other words the 1980s trend in workplace size has been strongly against unionisation'.[12]

## Growth and decline in the national economy

Historical evidence strongly suggests that fluctuations in national economic activity, or the business cycle, are closely associated with fluctuations in the level of union membership and density. When the economy is in the growth upswing with falling unemployment, trade union membership rises; conversely, when the economy is in recession with high unemployment, union membership falls. It is important to distinguish movements in the level of economic activity from structural changes in employment patterns, for it is possible for changes in the level of economic activity to take place with little initial change in the general pattern of employment, though it is not unusual for the one to be closely associated with the other.

Inflation, as distinct from the level of unemployment, because it usually constitutes a threat to employees' standards of living, may encourage them to join trade unions in order to defend the purchasing power of their incomes. It is therefore argued:

> that prices generally have a positive impact upon union growth because of the 'threat effect' – the tendency of workers to unionise in an attempt to defend their standard of living against the threat posed by rising prices – and that wage rises will have a similar impact because of the 'credit effect' – the tendency of workers to credit wage rises to unions and to support them in the hope of doing as well or even better in the future.[13]

While the historical evidence linking recession with falling trade union membership appears very strong, the evidence linking economic prosperity with rising union membership is not convincing. Obviously, the relationships between union membership and density on the one hand, and unemployment, wage levels, inflation, taxation and job insecurity on the other hand, is complex and problematic.

## The political, legal and social climate

The attitude of governments towards trade unions and the degree of public approval they enjoy is obviously important to their membership appeal. Favourable government attitudes in the nineteenth century towards responsible and constitutionally minded trade unions were essential for their early survival and growth. The approval of the Victorian middle classes of their sober and earnest endeavours to 'improve' their members' lives was also essential. Similarly, the Whitley reports after the First World War favoured trade union growth, as did the nationalization and welfare state legislation after the Second World War. This greatly expanded the public sector, bringing with

it recognition and approval for the unions. Conversely, the strikes and the social upheaval they seemed to espouse between 1910 and 1913 and the year-long miners' strike in 1984–85 were all turned to electoral advantage by governments or oppositions not naturally sympathetic towards trade unionism and its goals.

Since 1979 the role of the trade unions and the TUC in relation to government has been severely curtailed. Between the end of the Second World War and the election of the first Thatcher Conservative government in 1979, the trade unions, mainly acting through the TUC, exercised ever greater power at national level. They were respectfully consulted by both Labour and Conservative governments on matters related to the national economy, public expenditure, taxation, the welfare state, industrial policy, inflation and perhaps above all on the form and operation of successive prices and incomes policies. The unions and the TUC were an indispensable element in the tripartite consensus politics, often described as corporatism, which in varying forms existed between 1945 and 1979. After 1979, the unions were deliberately, ostentatiously and determinedly excluded from all the major processes of government; they were not consulted, and their leaders were not appointed to prominent public bodies. They were never invited to 10 Downing Street, no matter how dire a strike situation or unemployment became. The abrupt change in the public's perception of the national role of the TUC, plus the undoubted disapproval of a majority of the British people of the unions' conduct during the Winter of Discontent in 1978-9, led to a sharp decline in trade union popularity and moral standing. How much this contributed, however, to the rapid loss of union membership after 1979 is debatable.

There were two other important factors which during the 1980s changed the climate for trade unionism and industrial relations: first, the emergence of more confident managers determined to exercise greater authority over the workplace; second, the extensive and comprehensive range of legislation relating to trade unions and employment enacted during the 1980s. These two factors are now considered.

The economic and political climate of the 1980s encouraged many organizations and their managers to establish a greater degree of influence over their employees in both unionized and non-unionized workplaces. Certain common features of this 'new' style of management soon became apparent: changes in working practices including staffing levels, hours of work, multiple skilling and labour flexibility; team working led by hands-on managers; performance appraisal and performance related pay; and the rapid introduction of new technology. The scope and depth of collective bargaining were restricted. Attempts were made to weaken the collective appeal of trade unionism by individualizing the relationship between manager and employee, and by encouraging the employee to identify closely with the objectives, or 'mission', of the organization.

During the 1980s, management operated in an environment of increased competition in product markets and greatly reduced bargaining power on the part of the unions has been able to take the initiative in industrial relations. It has sought greater control over the work process and has in many areas asserted managerial authority.[14]

The 1980s also saw a profound change in the legislative climate with the passing of the Employment Acts 1980, 1982, 1988, 1989 and 1990, and the Trade Union Act 1984 (now largely consolidated into the TULRCA 1992). By the mid-1980s a radically new legal climate relating, *inter alia*, to industrial action, closed shops, picketing, trade union ballots, the political levy and union membership rights had been established. This legislation was clearly intended to weaken trade unionism and collective bargaining, abolish the closed shop, give 'moderate' trade unionists a voice through the secret ballot and make taking industrial action difficult, protracted and expensive.

The employment and trade union legislation of the 1980s marked a clear departure from the tradition of 'voluntarism' which had prevailed from the late nineteenth century. The voluntary approach, which characterized the attitude of the state to industrial relations up to the 1960s, required minimum legal regulation of trade unions, employers, collective bargaining, wages and industrial action. The state and the law merely guided the participants to resolve through negotiation their differences. This system, it can be argued, broke down in the 1960s and 1970s with the growth of highly disruptive and damaging strikes, the abuse of individual rights by the closed shop, the inflationary impact of high wage settlements, the power of the unions and the TUC to determine the policies and legislation of democratically elected governments, and the brake placed on economic growth, productivity and efficiency by trade union imposed working practices.

This view of trade union activity in the 1960s and 1970s can legitimately be criticized as over-simplified, distorted and one-sided. But the purpose here is not to discuss the necessity or wisdom of abandoning the voluntary system of industrial relations, but to assess the impact of the labour legislation of the 1980s and 1990s on trade union membership.

By the late 1970s and after more than a decade of damaging and increasingly unpopular industrial action and intense political controversy over the power of the trade unions, public opinion, including a majority of trade unionists themselves, moved firmly in favour of limiting union power. The first of four successive Conservative governments in 1979 pledged to curtail the unions by the enactment of legal constraints, which enjoyed a large degree of popular support. It is against this background of public opinion, the doubts of trade unionists themselves and the election of successive Conservative governments with substantial majorities that trade union membership began a long decline. Though it cannot be empirically proved, it is not improbable that this general climate of disapproval of current trade unionism, when also coupled to the clear helplessness of trade unions to prevent massive job losses, discouraged employees from joining trade unions and possibly led to many dropping out of membership. Moreover, where management took advantage of this new political, economic and legal climate to discourage trade union membership, to re-assert managerial controls and to reduce the role of collective bargaining, many employers undoubtedly found trade union membership less than appealing. The impact of the legislative changes of the 1980s on trade union membership, while being of some, if marginal, significance, were not as causative as other factors.

It is unlikely, therefore, that legislative change caused the decline in membership during the 1980s. This is not to argue that legislation had no influence, but to suggest that the structural and economic context of legislative enactment conditions its effect.[15]

Social and sociological factors, though extremely difficult to quantify, also help to explain why trade union membership and density fluctuates geographically and over time. It appears that employees are more likely to be union members if they live in the North of England, Scotland and Wales or in those regions with heavy industry and a high concentration of manual workers. In aggregate men are more likely to join unions than women. This is particularly true of male white-collar workers. There is little evidence to suggest, however, that factors such as marital status and family responsibilities influence unionization among either men or women. Empirical research shows that the widespread belief that married women employees are less likely to join unions than other women is unfounded.

In general, those whose education extends beyond the minimum school-leaving age and those who obtain formal qualifications are less likely to join trade unions than those who leave school at the legal minimum age without any formal educational qualification. The main exceptions are teachers and nurses, who belong to highly unionized professions. Not surprisingly, research evidence shows that white collar employees, and those in higher status occupations, are significantly less likely to join trade unions than are manual employees. The most important exceptions are the civil service, the health service, education and other areas of white collar employment in the public sector. Research in both Britain and America also indicates a positive relationship between the age of the individual, the length of work experience and trade union membership. The longer an individual has been at work the more likely it is that he or she has been exposed to work situations encouraging them to join unions. This again is more true for manual workers than for white collar employees.

## Trade union image and leadership

The study of trade union history suggests that the image of an individual union, or of unions collectively, can influence membership levels by attracting new members and retaining existing ones. The chief components of trade union image appear to be: leadership; perceived power; size; ability to secure significant wage increases; improvements in working conditions and job security; collective bargaining scope; success in imposing job regulation on management; successful industrial action; a high public and media profile; and the ability to influence national politics and governments.

For the individual employee, recognizing his or her relative individual powerlessness in relation to management at the workplace, the employing organization and government policies, the opportunities offered by being a member of a manifestly powerful trade union cannot be insignificant. This 'power' appeal is just as likely to be as persuasive in a period of recession as in a period of prosperity, if the union is able to prevent redundancies, the imposition of onerous changes in working practices and wage cuts. If, however, trade unions appear to be helpless in the face of recession, management assertiveness and government hostility, then the 'power' appeal of trade

unionism may suffer and membership will perhaps be adversely affected.

During the 1960s and 1970s, with relatively low levels of unemployment and modest but steady economic growth, and with successive Labour and Conservative governments seeking to involve the trade unions in national economic policy making, the unions were perceived to possess considerable power. During the same two decades union membership and density also increased substantially. It is not unreasonable to see the two as not unrelated.

Conversely, during the 1980s and 1990s unemployment reached and remained at unprecedentedly high levels for the period since 1945, and the actions and policies of government were unashamedly anti-trade union. The TUC was ruthlessly excluded from almost all the processes of government and the power of the unions rapidly declined. Trade union membership also fell heavily. It is, however, very uncertain how causally connected these two trends were, for as already argued the major cause of union membership loss in the 1980s and 1990s was structural changes in the composition of employment. It is not, however, unreasonable to believe that the undeniable diminution in the power of trade union leaders to influence government policies or deter their actions, or to prevent plant closures, mass redundancy and the imposition of changes in working practices, was not unconnected with the loss of union membership.

This brief examination of the major factors influencing the level and density of trade union membership in Britain suggests great causal complexity and that categorical assertions are unwise. It would appear, however, that increases and decreases in trade union membership can be closely linked with structural changes in the composition of employment, the level of unemployment, the state of the national economy, occupational change, industrial restucturing and labour market movements. The influence of other factors, such as the size of the employing organization, size of workplace and size of the public sector, is also clearly important. It is less obvious what public opinion, the attitude of government, management policies, trade union leadership and personal and job-related characteristics have upon the level of trade union membership.

## 5.5  Classification and Structural Determinants

The classical analytical tool for probing the structure of British trade unions has been to divide them into three traditional types derived from their historical

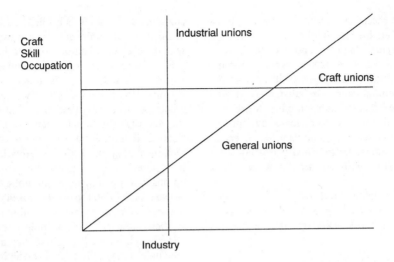

*Figure 5.3* Traditional trade union classification.

antecedents. In this approach it is suggested that first 'craft' unions emerged, whose membership was strictly confined to those craft workers who had served a recognized appenticeship. Second, a number of 'industrial' unions were formed in coalmining, docks, railways and gas, which aimed recruitment exclusively at workers in these industries. Finally, the 'general' unions were established by amalgamation amongst existing trade unions. These enrolled almost all types of employee regardless of their occupation or industry. Thus we have three seemingly useful categories of union type: 'craft', 'industrial' and 'general' (Figure 5.3).

With this traditional classification, we can look at every trade union and ask what features each possesses enabling it to be placed into one of three categories. Such an approach depends upon there being a pure set of characteristics which enables the classifier to approximate each union to the pure type, and then to label it craft, industrial or general.

The problems of this particular structural analysis of trade unions quickly emerge when the classifier attempts to isolate a pure type. If a craft union is defined as one only enrolling specific workers who have served apprenticeships, while refusing membership to all other workers, it soon becomes apparent that only a few small unions qualify as such. These include, for example, those catering for musicians, airline pilots, shuttlemakers, coopers, journalists and power loom overlookers. Similarly, if attempts are made to find examples of industrial unions, similar problems of definition are encountered. It cannot be claimed that either the National Union

of Mineworkers or the National Union of Rail, Maritime and Transport Workers, for instance, are industrial unions. In both mining and transport, several other unions have substantial memberships, such as the Union of Democratic Mineworkers and the National Association of Colliery Overmen, Deputies and Shotfirers in the former, and the Transport and General Workers Union, Transport Salaried Staffs Association and United Road Transport Union and many others in the latter. Furthermore, there is the problem of defining an industry. For example, can the railways be defined as an 'industry' or are they merely a part of the transport industry?

The third category, 'general' unions, may be perceived as merely a residual category, covering all the other unions which cannot be easily defined as either craft or industrial organizations. It is not surprising therefore that, lacking even the doubtful definitional rigour of the first two categories, we have least trouble in describing two of the largest British unions, the Transport and General Workers Union and the GMB (formally known as the General Municipal and Boilermakers Union) as general unions. These two unions, which were originally formed out of amalgamations after the First World War, have members drawn from almost every occupation and industry in Britain.

The essential weakness of the craft, industrial and general structural analysis is that it confuses rather than clarifies the problems of definition. It forces each union into a single category, when in fact the overwhelming majority of unions have features common to all three categories. The Amalgamated

Engineering and Electrical Union, for example, has a large number of engineering workers in membership. But is also recruits foundry and electrical, electronic and telecommunications workers, construction employees and relatively unskilled workers. Clearly, such a union cannot be adequately located within a simple three-category model. Moreover, such a structural analysis does not allow for the development of white collar unionism: either exclusive white collar unions or so called craft, industrial and general unions with substantial white collar sections.

One observer of British trade union structure, in a pioneering study, rejected the classical categories of classification some thirty years ago, on the grounds that:

> Since certain important classifications of union types have their origin in the slogans of dead ideological debate, rather than in objective description, they neither explain the present morphology of trade unionism nor illuminate its likely behaviour.[16]

He suggested a more fruitful analysis which categorized unions into those with 'open' and those with 'closed' membership recruitment policies. Although there are few traditional craft unions left, they usually restrict or 'close' their membership to those men and women working at a clearly definable trade, normally involving a formal period of training. The unions of this type which remain operate a closed recruitment policy in line with their fundamental purpose of representing their members' interests to the exclusion of all other related employees.

Similarly, small, skilled cotton textile unions restrict their membership by admitting only a limited number of recruits to their ranks through promotion and time-serving at their jobs. Equivalent policies used to be pursued by the train drivers, who would only admit members into the Associated Society of Locomotive Engineers and Firemen after many years of service in other railway grades. Similar restrictions on membership, albeit in a modern context, are now applied, for example, by the British Air Line Pilots Association. Unions with closed policies do not seek growth in numbers but, in the past, aimed at security in closed shop situations and strong, if small, organization. Other unions, such as the mineworkers', which might be regarded as a typical industrial union, also follow closed membership policies because they do not recruit members from outside their immediate spheres of influence. In consequence their memberships expand or contract largely according to the changing staffing levels in their industries.

Open membership policies are usually associated with the big general unions, such as the Transport and General Workers Union, Amalgamated Engineering and Electrical Union, Manufacturing Science and Finance Union, and GMB. They seek membership growth almost regardless of their members' jobs or the industry in which they work. Such unions organize their internal structures to cope with diverse membership needs. Yet union growth patterns over a long period of time suggest that whilst, in general, unions with open membership policies grew rapidly, at least until 1979, those with closed policies have, in the main, remained relatively static in size, declined as their industry's labour force has diminished, or disappeared altogether. These include the unions in the coalmining, railway and textile industries.

> This distinction between 'open' and 'closed' unionism is seen as most significant when unions are viewed dynamically – i.e. in relation to membership growth and decline. . . . The main growth pattern in evidence is thus one of 'open' unions, with boundaries that are increasingly difficult to define.[17]

Factors other than their relative open or closed nature also influence union growth, structure and organization. These can be divided into external economic and environmental factors, and internal union decisions and policies. The first group of factors assumes that unions can do little but adjust to external forces over which they have little control. The second category suggests that the unions which are most successful seek, through leadership policy initiatives and deliberate internal change, to convince existing and potential members that they can effectively challenge and overcome adverse economic and environmental circumstances by adapting proactively to them. Both these views of union growth and structure are far more complicated and problematic than are either the 'craft–industrial–general' or the 'open–closed' theories.

The external economic and environmental factors influencing union growth and structure are: the business cycle; the level and rate of change of unemployment; the relationship between pay and changes in the general price level; and the attitudes and policies of employees and government towards union recognition, collective bargaining and trade unionism. The most influential long-term external forces bringing about fundamental change in trade union growth and organization are those structural economic movements causing the decline of certain industries and occupations and the growth and birth of others. Unions are forced to accept the consequences of these forces in the long term, though they may seek to resist or mitigate them in the short term. If a union's membership is based in a declining industry, it can do little more than fight a rearguard action. According to this view, no amount of strong perceptive leadership or changes in internal structures can prevent a steady leakage of membership and bargaining power. Examples in recent decades include unions in the steel industry, railways, the docks and coalmining.

Conversely, whilst declining industries and occupations usually result in falling union membership, expanding industries and occupations may present other unions with opportunities for membership recruitment, employer recognition and collective bargaining. In these circumstances the view that dynamic and imaginative union leadership can achieve union growth and reshape the union map has obvious validity. Much, it is argued, depends upon the ability of these unions to exploit opportunities for membership growth by highlighting the fears, discontents and insecurities of employees. Examples are to be found in the growth of the Manufacturing Science and Finance Union, the public sector union UNISON and the Banking Insurance and Finance Union.

A detailed analysis of change in trade unions argues that the external agents of change have been overstated and that the ability of unions to change within themselves has been understated. Whilst accepting that external economic and environmental factors play a powerful role in shaping trade unions, this study argues that internal factors, such as dynamic union leadership, the mobilization of membership opinion, worker militancy, rank-and-file policy participation, the vertical dispersal of union power and new methods of job regulation can, in many cases, offset adverse external forces. It would appear that the process of change in trade unions emerges as the result of the interaction of a wide variety of external and internal factors:

significant and lasting change depends on the existence of two critical pre-conditions: first, a more or less united leadership committed to change; second, a decision making structure that is sufficiently receptive to change to enable the leaders to get their way.[18]

A further explanation of how trade union structure is determined concerns the influence of collective bar-gaining on the character, structure, internal government and membership of trade unions. Because collective bargaining is central to the purposes and objectives of trade unions, it is concluded that it must be the predominant force shaping and changing them. A change in collective bargaining structure, it is argued, is followed by changes in the internal structure and organization of the unions involved.

Collective bargaining is put forward not only as an influence on other aspects of union behaviour, not just as an important influence, but as the 'main', 'major', 'foremost', or 'principal' influence. These adjectives imply that, where collective bargaining is the predominant method of regulation, its dimensions account for union behaviour more adequately than any other set of explanatory variables can do.[19]

Furthermore, collective bargaining is heavily influenced by the attitudes of employers and the structure of employers' associations, which in turn, according to this view, determine union membership, structure and internal organization. This explanation of trade union structure and change depends heavily upon the many external economic and institutional factors determining the various types of collective bargaining.

A further explanation of how trade union structure is determined has involved analysis of unions' membership characteristics to see if they recruit either vertically or horizontally. According to Coates and Topham:

A horizontal union recruits from a grade or grades of workers spread across industrial boundaries – all clerks in the clerks' union, all supervisors in the supervisors' union, and so on. This principle corresponds closely to, and therefore includes, the craft organizations – all fitters in the fitters' union, all plumbers in the plumbers' union, and so on. The vertical union, on the other hand, aims to recruit all workers, whatever their grade or occupation, with a common industrial background and thus corresponds to the industrial classification. These categories are useful, in that they draw attention to recognizable tendencies in union organization and recruitment strategies.[20]

This method of analysis of union structure is a clear improvement upon the 'craft', 'industrial' and 'general' union categories. However, it suffers from the same weakness: it is only possible to approximate

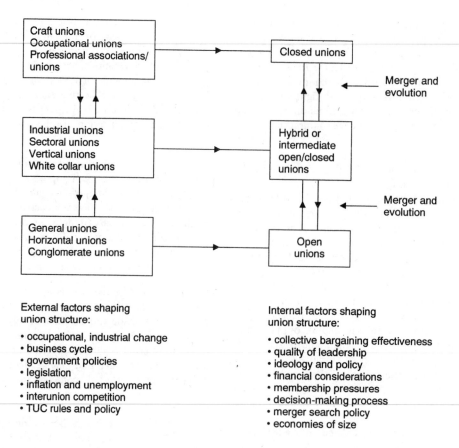

*Figure 5.4* Trade union structure.

unions into either the vertical or the horizontal categories, with the general unions possessing both characteristics. Figure 5.4 attempts to bring together some of the major characteristics of trade union structure, the explanatory categories used, and the internal and external factors shaping and changing union structure.

The dramatic fall in union membership during the 1980s has seen a trend towards a few large unions with open recruitment policies. This, in practice, has made them regard almost all employees as potential members, regardless of their skill, occupation, service or industry. Furthermore, these unions seek to grow by amalgamations or mergers wherever and whenever they can. Examples are to be found in the Manufacturing Science and Finance Union, the Amalgamated Engineering and Electrical Union, GMB and UNISON (the result of a merger between NALGO, NUPE

and COHSE in 1993). Such 'super unions' appear to resemble the very large private corporations or conglomerates which have emerged through growth and takeovers and produce a multiple range of products and services. If this market strategy has produced powerful and successful companies, it might do the same for certain union groupings.

## 5.6 Multiunionism and Union Membership

Table 5.6 shows the major trade unions with over 100 000 members each, that were affiliated to the TUC in 1960, 1979 and 1991. In 1960 there were 17 TUC affiliates with more than 100 000 members each, including three unions no longer existing in their own right due to amalgamations and mergers. By the early 1990s there were over 20 TUC affiliates with over

*Table 5.6* TUC affiliated unions with over 100 000 members in 1960, 1979 and 1991*

| Union[†] | 1960 | 1979 | 1991 |
|---|---|---|---|
| Transport and General Workers Union | 1 302 000 | 2 086 000 | 1 224 000 |
| GMB | 796 000 | 967 000 | 933 000 |
| National and Local Government Officers Association (d) | 274 000 | 753 000 | 744 000 |
| Amalgamated Engineering Union (AEU) (a) | 937 000 | 1 298 000 | 702 000 |
| Manufacturing Science and Finance Union | – | – | 653 000 |
| National Union of Public Employees (d) | 200 000 | 692 000 | 579 000 |
| Union of Shop Distributive and Allied Workers | 355 000 | 470 000 | 362 000 |
| Union of Construction Allied Trades and Technicians | 192 000 | 348 000 | 207 000 |
| Confederation of Health Service Employees (d) | – | 213 000 | 203 000 |
| Union of Communication Workers | 160 000 | 203 000 | 201 000 |
| Banking Insurance and Finance Union | – | 132 000 | 171 000 |
| National Union of Teachers | 245 000 | 249 000 | 169 000 |
| Society of Graphical and Allied Trades (b) | 158 000 | 206 000 | 166 000 |
| National Communications Union | – | 126 000 | 155 000 |
| Civil and Public Services Association | 140 000 | 224 000 | 123 000 |
| National Graphical Association (b) | – | 111 000 | 123 000 |
| National Association of School Masters and Union of Women Teachers | – | 122 000 | 120 000 |
| National Union of Railwaymen (c) | 334 000 | 180 000 | 118 000 |
| National Union of Mineworkers | 586 000 | 260 000 | 116 000 |
| National Union of Civil and Public Servants | – | – | 113 000 |

*Sources*: TUC Annual Reports and Annual Reports of the Certification Officer
* Non-TUC unions with more than 100 000 members in 1991 were (1) Royal College of Nursing of the United Kingdom (289 000) and (2) Electrical Electronic Telecommunications and Plumbing Union (EETPU) (367 000), which was expelled from the TUC in 1988.
[†] Some of these unions had different titles in 1960 and 1979.
(a)   The AEU and EEPTU merged in 1993 to form the Amalgamated Engineering Electrical Union (AEEU).
(b)   These two unions merged in 1991 to form the Graphical, Paper and Media Union.
(c)   Merged with National Union of Seamen in 1990 to become National Union of Railway, Maritime and Transport Workers.
(d)   These three unions merged in 1993 to form UNISON (the name of this union is not an acronym).

100 000 members each. The only large union not now affiliated to the TUC is the Royal College of Nursing of the United Kingdom, with something approaching 300 000 members. With the exceptions of the National Union of Mineworkers and the National Union of Railwaymen, all the unions in Table 5.6 experienced membership growth between 1960 and 1979. For some unions, such as the National and Local Government Officers Association (NALGO) and the National Union of Public Employees (NUPE), their growth was very substantial indeed. Between 1979 and 1991 all but two of the unions in Table 5.6 lost members, with some, such as the Transport and General Workers Union (TGWU), the Amalgamated Engineering Union (AEU), the Union of Construction Allied Trades and Technicians (UCATT) and the National Union of Mineworkers (NUM), suffering substantial membership losses. Those unions with memberships in the traditional industries were most severely

affected by rising plant closures and unemployment after 1979, whilst those with members in the public sector, financial services and the new technology industries suffered least. Some unions avoided the worst consequences by amalgamating or merging with other unions.

Union structure in Britain has been criticized on the grounds that there are too many unions whose structures lead to competitive recruitment and to demarcation conflicts. Even at the turn of the century, the Webbs observed that 'to competition between overlapping unions is to be attributed nine-tenths of the ineffectiveness of the trade union world'.[21] Some 60 years later the Royal Commission on Trade Unions and Employers' Associations asked, 'What can be done to reduce multiunionism?'[22] The TUC in 1918, 1927 and 1964 produced reports suggesting ways to reform the structure of British trade unions and to reduce their number. Although substantial reductions have been made in the number of trade unions – from over 1 000 in 1900 to under 300 in the early 1990s – Britain retains a multiplicity of trade unions, with overlapping memberships and sometimes conflicting policies within the same industry and firms.

Many of the proposals for trade union structural reform, coming from both within and without the trade union movement, focus on the case for large industrial unions. Yet the original trade union impetus for industrial unions was mainly political, since it was rooted in the syndicalist theory that workers should first create industrial unions and then, through a general strike, take over their industries and establish a socialist society. By such means, it was envisaged, trade unionism would become a revolutionary force, thus avoiding all the alleged weaknesses of the parliamentary road to socialism. Prior to the First World War, for example, the coalminers proposed: 'That our objective be, to build up an organization that will ultimately take over the mining industry, and carry it on in the interests of the workers'.[23] Most trade unions, however, ignored this political motive, and those which accepted the advantages of industrial unionism did so mainly because it was an obviously tidy form of trade unionism. In practice, union structure closely followed the emerging structure of industry and the developing pattern of national collective bargaining within it.

Many years later, the report of the Donovan Commission (1968) concluded 'there is no sign of any general evolution towards industrial unionism'.[24] The reasons for this are, first, the preference of British trade unionists has been to form organizations representative of specific occupations or related groups of occupations. This tendency has been reinforced by the inclination of employees to identify themselves with occupational interests, and with the skills necessary to do their job, rather than with an industry. Second, there is the problem of defining an industry: where, for example, does the engineering industry begin and end? Third, at the beginning of the century, when the call for industrial unionism was at its strongest, industry was characterized by large numbers of small and medium-sized firms, operating within single industries. Today giant firms, including multinational corporations, straddle several industries and deal with more than one industrial union. Finally, even if the theoretical objections could be overcome, the practical problems associated with industrial unionism are probably insuperable.

However defined, industrial unionism would involve a drastic upheaval in the structure of almost every major union in the country and virtually all expanding unions. It would, for example, mean the dismemberment of craft unions and . . . the giant general unions.[25]

The most obvious way of reducing the number of trade unions is through amalgamation or merger. Since the law was changed in 1964, amalgamations are now possible with a simple majority of the votes cast by the members of each union involved. On this basis, a number of significant amalgamations have taken place between various trade unions, such as between the Amalgamated Society of Boilermakers Shipwrights Blacksmiths and Structural Workers and the General and Municipal Workers Union in 1982 to form the General Municipal and Boilermakers (GMB). There has also been a strong tendency for open unions to amalgamate, and this has led to the growth of a small number of very large unions. Not all these amalgamations have been for the better, however. Many have taken place for political, financial and organizational reasons, with little hope of improving the overall structure of British trade unionism or collective bargaining and industrial relations. Furthermore, the growth of large unions through amalgamation has often only transferred the conflict between unions into conflict within the new union.

Trade union mergers or amalgamations do not follow a single definable pattern. It is useful to distinguish between the objectives of different mergers by using a three-fold classification. 'Thus we refer to *defensive, consolidating* or *expansionist* mergers, and seek to apply those terms to both the major and minor unions involved in a given merger'.[26] A defensive merger, for example, enables the minor union to escape irreversible decline as its membership contracts and its falling finances prevent it from effectively servicing its members. For the major union, the same merger could be an expansionist one, since it seeks to expand its membership and activities into new areas of employment. In certain cases, even the major union in a merger could be seeking to protect its position defensively. A good example of a defensive merger took place in 1971 when the Union of Construction Allied Trades and Technicians (UCATT) was formed by the amalgamation of four building trade unions: the Amalgamated Society of Painters and Decorators; the Amalgamated Union of Building Trade Workers; the Association of Building

Technicians; and the Amalgamated Society of Wood-workers. Before the creation of UCATT, union membership in the construction industry had been falling rapidly and it was hoped that one large general union would reverse this trend. The formation of UCATT, in fact, stabilized membership within the industry, since union membership at amalgamation in 1971 was 260 000, rose to 348 000 in 1979, but fell to 207 000 in 1991.

A consolidating merger between trade unions usually takes place 'where the aim of those involved [is] to consolidate a shared position in a given industry or occupational area'.[27] An example of a consolidating merger arose in the engineering industry in 1971, when the Amalgamated Engineering Union (AEU) and the Amalgamated Union of Foundry Workers merged with the Draughtsmen and Allied Technicians Association (DATA) and the much smaller Construction Engineering Union to form the Amalgamated Union of Engineering Workers. This merger consolidated the AEU's membership and bargaining power in the engineering industry. It was not defensive because the two largest unions, the AEU and DATA, had steadily rising memberships between 1961 and 1971, and none of the merging unions was in serious financial difficulties. Subsequently, however, the union broke up, with the white-collar technicians forming their own union, the Technical Administrative and Supervisory Section (TASS).

An expansionist merger takes place when the major union seeks 'the basis for further expansion and development, sometimes into quite new job territories'.[28] Much of the growth and expansion of the Transport and General Workers Union (TGWU) and the former Association of Scientific Technical and Managerial Staff (ASTMS) took place by merging with many smaller unions over a long period. Between 1969 and 1976, for example, ASTMS was involved as the major union in 17 successful mergers with minor unions or professional associations in many diverse fields of white-collar employment. The TGWU, which was itself formed by the merger in 1922 of 18 unions, grew considerably by continually seeking mergers with smaller unions. Between 1968 and 1974, for example, the TGWU absorbed into its membership no less than 15 small unions catering mainly for manual workers. In 1981 the National Union of Agricultural and Allied Workers (NUAAW) merged with the TGWU in a purely defensive decision by the NUAAW. This can hardly be said to have improved the rationale of British union structure.

The minor unions in all these cases were concerned with achieving defensive mergers with the TGWU, whose trade group structure they found attractive. For its part the TGWU saw the mergers as an effective way of expanding its membership and penetrating into new job territories.

The late 1980s and early 1990s have seen the beginning of what could become the most important wave of trade union mergers since the 1920s (Table 5.7). In 1988 TASS (with 250 000 members) and ASTMS (with 390 000 members) merged, after a successful membership ballot, to form the Manufacturing Science and Finance Union (MSF), with a claimed membership of 653 000. Both ASTMS and TASS had taken into membership, prior to their own merger, several small trade unions. This expansionist merger, as the name of the union suggests, is intended to create a union seeking members in those occupations, industries and services which are growing. In early 1989 the Association of Professional Executive Clerical and Computer Staff, after a membership ballot, merged its 83 000 members with the General Municipal and Boilermakers (GMB) to form a union of about 900 000 members, making it the second largest in the TUC. This union straddles a very wide range of industries, such as chemicals, oil, engineering, electronics, textiles, footwear and tobacco, as well as services such as the health service, local government, education and finance. There is hardly a major industry or service in which it does not have some members and is seeking to recruit more.

The pace and size of union mergers increased in the early 1990s with the creation of the Amalgamated Engineering and Electrical Union (AEEU), the Graphical Paper and Media Union, the National Union of Railway Maritime and Transport Workers (RMT), and the giant public sector union UNISON, formed in 1993 by the merger of the National Association of Local Government Officers (NALGO), the National Union of Public Employees (NUPE) and the Confederation of Health Service Employees (COHSE). With a membership of 1.4 million, UNISON is the largest trade union in Britain and in the TUC.

Further union mergers are likely as falling membership, intense competition for members, membership demands for consumer services and the financial advantages of size continue to press on many unions. Just as in the past, it is difficult to detect the rationale of these recent mergers in terms of collective bargaining or industrial relations. The largest unions now appear willing to take members regardless of their industry, service or occupation, and even the

*Table 5.7* Principal union mergers since 1980.

| Trade union created | Merging unions | Type of merger |
| --- | --- | --- |
| GMB (formally, General Municipal Boilermakers and Allied Trade Union, GMBATU) | • Amalgamated Society of Boilermakers, Shipwrights, Blacksmiths and Structural Workers (1982)<br>• Association of Professional Executive Clerical and Computer Staff (1988) | Defensive<br><br>Defensive |
| Amalgamated Engineering and Electrical Union (AEEU) (formerly the Amalgamated Engineering Union, AEU) | • Union of Foundry Workers (1984)<br>• Constructional Engineering Union (1984)<br>• Electrical Electronic Plumbing and Telecommunications Union (1993) | Consolidating<br>Consolidating<br>Expansionist |
| Electrical Electronic Plumbing and Telecommunications Union (EETPU) | • During 1989 and 1990 twelve unions transferred engagements to EETPU | Defensive |
| Manufacturing Science and Finance Union (MSF) | • Technical and Supervisory Section (TASS) (1987)<br>• Association of Scientific Technical and Managerial Staffs (1987) | Expansionist<br><br>Expansionist |
| National Communication Union (NCU) | • Post Office Engineering Union (1985)<br>• Civil and Public Servants Association (Post Group) (1985) | Defensive<br>Defensive |
| National Union of Civil and Public Servants (NUCAPS) | • Civil Service Union (1988)<br>• Society of Civil and Public Servants (1988) | Consolidating<br>Defensive |
| Graphical Paper and Media Union (GPMU) | • Society of Graphical and Allied Trades (1962) (in 1991)<br>• National Graphical Association (1962) (in 1991) | Defensive<br><br>Defensive |
| UNISON (this is the name of the union, not an acronym) | • National and Local Government Officers Association (1993)<br>• National Union of Public Employees (1993)<br>• Confederation of Health Service Employees (1993) | Consolidating<br><br>Consolidating<br><br>Consolidating |
| National Union of Railway Maritime and Transport Workers (RMT) | • National Union of Railwaymen (1990)<br>• National Union of Seamen (1990) | Defensive<br>Defensive |

*Source*: Annual reports of Certification Officers and TUC
Year of merger given in parentheses

boundary line between the public and private sectors is being increasingly ignored. They are 'open' unions in almost every respect. A TUC review of union mergers (1991) observed that:

the underlying motives of most contemporary mergers are defensive or consolidatory, rather than expansionist. The merger partners wish to recover lost membership or improve their bargaining position in established areas; many are experiencing financial problems . . . the merger process will continue and grow over the next ten years. It should at least halve the number of TUC unions before the turn of the

century [but] from the outside according to traditional classifications, British unions will look as illogical and unplanned as before.[28]

## 5.7 Democracy and Internal Affairs

Trade unions emerged in Britain at a time when only a minority of the population was enfranchised, and when representative political democracy was in its infancy. Almost invariably as they were formed, trade unions adopted democratic constitutions giving their members, in theory at least, ultimate control over the policy decisions and the organization of their own union. Trade unionists were therefore familiar with democratic political principles, and many of the problems associated with them, whilst Parliament was almost completely unrepresentative of substantial sections of the population. Thus the value of trade union democracy has always extended far beyond that of the individual union.

> In large measure, the chance that the collectivist society which is developing in most countries will be democratic rests on the possibility that trade unions, although supporters of socialist objectives, will maintain their independence of the state, and will act to protect their members and the citizenry in general against the tremendous state power inherent in a collective society.[30]

Equally, as a long and detailed comparative study of union democracy in America and Britain concluded: 'the future of unionism is inseparable from the future of organized society'.[31] The experience of trade unionists in Poland in the 1980s suggests that this statement holds good for both capitalist and the former communist societies. By these views, the retention of individual freedoms and collective rights within a pluralist democracy like Britain is inescapably bound up with the problem of trade union internal democracy. The unions are seen to be one of the most influential collectivist institutions outside the agencies of the state. This perhaps idealistic view of the contribution of trade unions to democracy is, however, firmly rejected by others:

> [The] legalised powers of the unions have become the biggest obstacle to raising the living standards of the working class as a whole. They are the chief cause of the unnecessarily big differences between the best and the worst paid workers. They are the prime source of unemployment. They are the main reason for the decline of the British economy in general.[32]

Union democracy is not merely an exercise in democratic self-government for its own sake. After all, as organizations, unions are largely concerned with protecting their members' incomes and working conditions. It is arguable that what constitutes their interests should be decided by the members themselves. Union democracy, therefore, has a very instrumental objective requiring practical representative organization to achieve it. Most union constitutions and rule books emphasize the right of members at local level to debate motions and to advance resolutions which can then be processed through all levels of trade union government up to the highest policy

making bodies. Figure 5.5 illustrates in schematic form the structure and processes of trade union government and democracy.

The local union branch, often based on a geographical area rather than the place of work, is seen, in theory at least, as the basic and most vital element in the democratic organizational chain. The next level of trade union organization is the 'district', 'division' or 'region', with the national headquarters, often in London, being the apex of the union's formal authority structure. The geographical and functional levels between the branches and the national office usually possess powerful rights and some degree of autonomy too, as in the mineworkers' and the engineering workers' unions. The transport workers' union, for example, is divided not only into geographical regions but also into different 'trade groups'. These are largely autonomous groupings, providing an internal structure which helps to ensure that the interests of individual members are not lost within an organization which has some 1.2 million members.

A majority of unions also hold annual conferences, whilst others hold biennial or even triennial conferences, at which local resolutions processed through the branch and regional levels are debated. Branches send delegates to their conferences according to membership distribution, with the delegates often mandated to vote on major policy issues in accordance with the majority view of local members. National executive committees are charged with the efficient and effective running of their unions between conferences and with carrying out conference policy decisions. Some unions, such as the TGWU, hold very large conferences, with hundreds of official delegates. Others elect a comparatively small National Committee or Executive which has the power to determine union policy on a broad range of collective bargaining and other issues.

Trade union democracy became, after 1979, a matter of political concern to central government. It was argued that the system of union democracy, undoubtedly enshrined in union rule books, did not function in practice. Because the members of many, but not all, unions were required to attend branch meetings if they wished to vote on policy issues or to elect their general secretary, unions, it was claimed, were controlled by unrepresentative minorities of extreme and committed left-wing members. The vast majority of members were not willing or able to attend branch meetings or to take part in policy debates and elections. The solution was seen to lie in introducing legislation which would

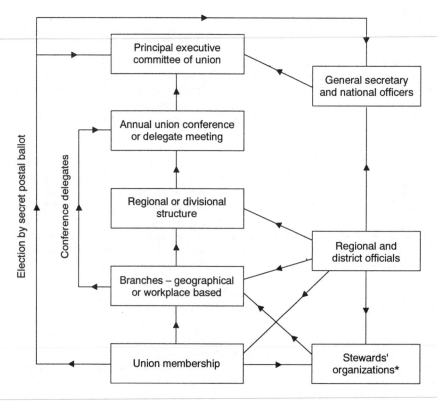

* Stewards' organizations are often not acknowledged as a formal or
official part of union government

*Figure 5.5* Schematic structure of trade union government.

make it compulsory for unions to involve members through government-funded and secret postal ballots. This would, it was believed, take power away from the allegedly unrepresentative minority of politically motivated activists and 'give the unions back to their members' (Trade Union Act 1984 and Employment Act 1988 – now embodied in the Trade Union and Labour Relations (Consolidation) Act 1992). Union members, voting from home, and using a secret postal ballot, now have the legal right to elect union executive members and general secretaries, decide if the union should have a political fund and vote on whether industrial action should be sanctioned. It will be some years before the impact of secret union ballots can be evaluated. But in the case of the ballots already conducted under the legislation requiring, for example, union members to decide if they wish to retain union political levies and funds, the result has been overwhelmingly in favour of retention. This is hardly the result for which the government had

hoped. The impact of secret ballots on the political complexion of trade union leaders and executive committees is much more difficult to assess.

With varying degrees of reluctance, unions have been forced to comply with the new legal requirements. The consequences have probably been less marked than the government anticipated. In few unions have the new election methods brought radical changes in the political disposition of the executive.[33]

## Membership participation

It is generally accepted by students of politics that the writing of formal democratic constitutions by no means ensures that democratic principles will be followed by those responsible for administering them. Union democracy cannot flourish when branch meetings are only attended by a tiny fraction of the membership, or if a politically determined and cohesive minority seeks to impose its politics upon an apathetic majority. Neither can it do so where a small number of powerful national officers manipulate union conferences for their own ends in order to retain their own power and authority. Similarly, democracy becomes discredited if union rules are used to prevent the emergence of an effective opposition within a union; for example, by prohibiting particular groups from disseminating their views in written form. Democracy is also threatened when powerful general secretaries change their union's policies a short time after a union conference on the dubious grounds that the circumstances facing the union have substantially changed.

Some trade unionists, on the other hand, argue that union democracy has little real purpose because it hinders the efficient operation of trade unions in the narrow pursuit of the economic self-interest of their members. Put another way:

> business unionism, as a set of ideas, justifying
> the narrowest definitions of a union's role in
> society, also helps to legitimate one-party
> oligarchy, for it implies that union leadership is
> simply the administration of an organization
> with defined, undebatable goals: the
> maximization of the member's income and
> general welfare.[34]

Attention must therefore be given to those factors either enhancing or inhibiting the development and maintenance of internal union democracy.

Full-time union officers enjoy considerable security of tenure in their jobs. Because of their knowledge of union affairs, continuity in office, bargaining experience and political skills, they usually exercise a very considerable influence over the determination of union policies, resources and organization. 'No king on earth is as safe in his job as a Trade Union official', claims one of Shaw's characters in *The Apple Cart*.[35] Whilst this can be regarded as a typical Shavian exaggeration, very few union officers are dismissed or removed from office. The methods of appointing full-time union officers, who do not serve on the union's national executive body, have some bearing upon the influence they wield within their unions. A few unions elect their officers in the belief that the process ensures members will pick the persons best suited for the job, as well as helping to encourage democratic control of the union. Elected officers, it is argued, are usually more responsive to the hopes and aspirations of their members than selected

officers. Moreover, if they are subject to periodic re-election, they are conscious that they can be removed from office if they do not satisfy membership needs.

Yet election often reduces the job security of officials and can prevent them from persuading their members to follow necessary but unpopular policies. Evidence also suggests that elected officers usually have to serve for a long period as voluntary officeholders before they can expect election to a full-time post. Consequently, they may be middle-aged before commencing their professional trade union career. This has obvious implications for their training and their role in policy and organizational matters. An alternative method of appointing full-time officers, and one favoured by some three-quarters of unions, is by an internal selection process. This, it is argued, avoids the defects of elections and enables the union to secure the services of younger, vigorous and educated professionals. These, it is said, if provided with a clear career structure in the union, will work hard in the interests of the union and of themselves. Job security is improved and vocational training made easier. On the other hand, non-elected officers, who are usually selected by other and more senior full-time officers, are more likely to be answerable to them than to the ordinary union membership to whom they are nominally accountable.

> Most officers found little in the election/
> re-election system to recommend it – strongly
> pointing out that may of the assumed
> inadequacies of the appointment system could
> be, and were, overcome by unions favouring this
> process.[36]

The law now requires all trade unions to elect their general secretary; this usually involves a considerable political campaign and a power struggle among various factions in individual unions. Elections, if they are to have meaning and relevance for union members – and thereby break through the apathy barrier – have to involve real choice between competing candidates offering different policies, ideologies and styles of leadership. Such candidates, in turn, are supported by party factions, each fighting to gain support and votes for its candidate. Such a 'party system', it is argued, brings corresponding benefits because 'democracy is strengthened when members are not only related to the larger organization but are also affiliated with or loyal to subgroups within the organization'.[37] Mutually warring factions, on the other hand, are 'a luxury most unions cannot afford'.[38] In recent times, the elections of the general secretaries of many of the largest unions have been marked by distinct political differences between the major candidates, and vigorous campaigns which were closely covered by the mass media.

Despite the opportunities provided for democratic participation, membership involvement in union affairs has never been high and much attention has been focused upon the small attendances at branch meetings and low polls in union elections, which the introduction of compulsory legal secret ballots appears not to have improved. However, little equivalent comment is made about poorly attended and often perfunctory annual meetings of shareholders, ostensibly responsible for controlling very large public companies. Nevertheless, attempts have been made by some unions to improve interest in branch meetings by moving them from geographical to workplace or industrial branches, where meetings are sometimes held during working hours. Although such arrangements allow stewards to take an active part in union activities, there is a continued reluctance by ordinary trade unionists to become involved in union policy making. For most of them the steward, rather than the formal union structure, is the union. Unions with memberships which are scattered across wide areas of industry or are working in small isolated units, such as the shopworkers and seafarers, for instance, find it particularly difficult to develop effective branch activities. Here the co-ordinating role of the full-time officers is crucial.

A further factor inhibiting membership participation in union affairs is union size. Relatively small, compact and often closed unions, with elected officers well known to members and with high membership identification with the union and its policies, usually have effective membership involvement. But some large, open unions with selected officers, who are increasingly without personal practical experience of their members' occupations, suffer from poor branch involvement. Yet general observation can be misleading, as much depends upon the structure of the union under examination.

> It is not by itself the size of the major unions that prevents a vigorous and coherent internal process of democratic participation. It is the miscellaneity of so much of the membership composition . . . The problems of external structure and strategy and of internal organisation and democracy meet here.[39]

One of the unsolved problems of trade union democracy concerns the self-perceived needs of union members. Why do employees join trade unions? Is it for protection and advancement of their terms and conditions of employment by those with the experience and professionalism to carry out the task? Or do they themselves wish to determine, through democratic procedures, what is seen to be to their advantage and how it should be advanced? Few union members value democratic procedures merely as an exercise in self-government. If professional officers can achieve their ends, participative democracy can be seen by many members as a meaningless procedure. The very considerable power, however, which trade unions can possess, and the large number of people in them, strongly suggest that they need to be democratically accountable to their members. Effective union democracy through the use of suitable forms of membership ballots is increasingly accepted.

## Membership ballots

A great deal of media and political attention has been paid to the fact that in many unions there is considerable divergence between the views and attitudes of the leadership and those of rank-and-file members. In most, but not all cases, a situation develops where the union leadership – which usually means the general secretary and national executive committee – holds political opinions and attitudes to industrial action which do not appear to be held by the majority of their members. Many reasons have been advanced to explain this divergence. A commonly held view is that the vast majority of union members have little interest in their union's internal democratic processes, in elections to office or in debating and shaping policy. In the face of such mass apathy, it is argued, a highly motivated political minority can be dominant and use, for their own ends, the union's formal democratic processes. They usually act strictly within the confines of the union rule book and obtain office, position and policy control legitimately. A few unions have apparently been functioning efficiently for many years with a left-wing leadership and right-wing membership.

The usual response to this divergence of opinion and attitude between union leaders and members is to urge the apathetic members to attend their branch meetings, to take part in union elections and to debate and shape union policy. Such exhortations are rarely if ever effective. Considerable political and media attention has been paid to important union elections, such as those for the posts of general secretary or president of the largest unions, with the media and politicians drawing attention to the main candidates' political and ideological convictions. Although media campaigns have created more interest in union elections, the common system of voting at branch meetings or at the workplace, which was the usual method of voting until the postal ballot legislation of the 1980s, inhibits high turnouts for voting.

One answer to the reluctance of many union members to take part in branch voting is to provide them with a postal ballot. This requires unions to post ballot forms to each member and provide them with a stamped addressed envelope for their voting return. The member can then make up his or her own mind at home, vote and post the ballot form to an independent counting agency, such as the Electoral Reform Society or the Advisory Conciliation and Arbitration Service. The same balloting system can also be used for other important decisions, such as whether to accept or reject pay offers, change union rules or take industrial action.

Objectors to postal ballots argue that they further reduce the importance of branch meetings, isolate each member when voting, reduce the opportunity for debate before voting, give considerable influence to the media over how individual members vote and place an unacceptable financial burden on the unions. Above all, they claim, it is an intolerable interference with the right of individual unions to determine their own internal affairs, rules and democratic procedures. The TUC, largely in response to media pressure and the threat of legislation after 1979, encouraged affiliated unions to review their democratic procedures and balloting systems. By decision of Congress, TUC affiliates were initially forbidden to accept government finance to cover the cost of secret postal and workplace ballots when it became available. This policy was subsequently reviewed, and it was left to individual unions to decide whether or not to claim for the cost of their ballots. By the late 1980s many unions were claiming under the 1980 and 1988 Employment Acts for reimbursement of the costs of postal ballots. In 1991, for example, 78 unions, including many TUC affiliates, made application in respect of 716 ballots, of which the Certification Officer granted payment for 550 costing a total of four million pounds.

The Trade Union Act 1984 (now largely incorporated along with the Employment Act 1988 into the Trade Union and Labour Relations (Consolidation) Act 1992 (TULRCA 1992)), which, it was claimed,

would return the unions to their members, requires trade unions to conduct secret postal ballots, at least once every five years, for the election by all members to their principal policy making executive bodies. This legal requirement brought to an end the practice in some unions of electing their principal executive committees at their annual conference or at branch meetings, sometimes by a show of hands. Where the general secretary or president of the union is a voting member of the union's principal executive committee, he or she must be elected by secret postal ballot at least once every five years. Some unions sought to avoid this legal obligation after 1984 by changing their rules and making their general secretaries nonvoting members of their national executives. The 1988 Employment Act closed this legislative loophole by making it a legal requirement for both voting and non-voting members of union national executives to be elected by secret ballot. The same legislation makes it the right of every candidate at national executive elections to have an election address sent out to all voting members along with the voting papers, at no cost to themselves.

The 1984 Act also regulated the internal democratic procedures of trade unions by requiring them to hold properly conducted secret ballots before taking official industrial action. Only those members who would be involved in taking industrial action can vote, and a majority of those voting must make it clear that they wish to take part in the action. These requirements have made it necessary for unions to make alterations in their rule books regarding the calling and endorsement of industrial action. The 1984 Act also required trade unions to hold secret ballots of all their members, at least once every ten years, on whether they wish the union to have a political fund and to spend it on political objects. Further, the Act closely defined political objects and made it unlawful for a union which had not successfully balloted its members on a political fund to spend money on these political objects.

This legislation, however, did not achieve the objective the Conservative government believed it would, namely of producing ballot majorities for the abolition of union political funds, thereby removing from the Labour Party its major source of financial support. All the largest unions affiliated to the TUC achieved substantial votes for the continuation of political funds. Several big unions, including the white-collar unions NALGO and CPSA, took the opportunity offered by the legislation to hold successful ballots to establish political funds. In the case of CPSA, it is also affiliated to the Labour Party.

The 1988 Employment Act established two further important rights for individual trade union members which could have a considerable impact upon the way unions are internally governed. The first ensures that where union members take a grievance against their union to court, the court cannot refuse to hear the case. The court is not able to dismiss or suspend proceedings, providing members have made a formal complaint to the union about their grievance. This legal change makes it much easier for a union member to challenge a union's interpretation of its rules, or challenge the imposition of a disciplinary penalty on its members, before the courts. The 1988 Act also established a Commissioner for the Rights of Trade Union Members, known as 'the Commissioner'. The Commissioner has the power to grant assistance to union members seeking to bring their grievances before the courts. The Commissioner's assistance ensures that union members can pursue legal cases without involving them in any significant personal financial costs.

The Trade Union Reform and Employment Rights Act 1993 now further requires the scrutineers of union elections to inspect, if appropriate, the union's register of member's names and addresses for accuracy; to appoint an independent person to store and distribute the voting papers and count the votes cast; and to ensure that all candidates are treated equally. The legislation controlling the election of members of a union's principal executive committee is now complex, detailed and legally enforceable.

## 5.8  Relations between Unions

In Britain, many different unions represent identical grades or closely related grades of employees in the same industries and services and even in the same firm. This is an inevitable consequence of the multi-union nature of British trade unionism. Where several trade unions operate in the same industry or service, such as in engineering, car manufacturing or the National Health Service, it is not surprising that there are often conflicts of interest amongst them which have to be resolved.

### Interunion conflict

The problems of multiunionism and interunion conflict are not new. The Donovan Commission recommended, for example, that:

the TUC should intensify its effort to encourage the unions concerned to adopt closer working arrangements. The TUC should also consider adopting the principle of 'one union for one grade of work within one factory' as a guide for the future development of structure.[40]

Clearly the complex structure of British trade unionism and interunion conflict are inextricably linked. Yet there are many causes of interunion conflict. The most frequent include: first, competition between unions for new members; second, the accusation that one union is poaching another union's members or potential members in its 'sphere of influence'; third, the desire of a union not to lose promoted members to another union; fourth, problems of job demarcation at the workplace; fifth, disagreement over which union should have recognition and negotiating rights with particular employers; and sixth, differing policies on pay and conditions of employment towards the employers with which they negotiate.

Most, if not all, trade unions value membership growth as a vital element in their strength in relation to the employers with which they negotiate, and in terms of their influence within the labour movement generally. Large memberships also bring valuable financial economies of scale in providing services to members. The recruitment of members is therefore an important internal union objective. Similarly, there is evidence to suggest that potential and existing trade unionists are strongly attracted by the protection offered by large, expanding and vigorous unions. Competition amongst unions to recruit members within the same industries and enterprises is therefore inescapable. Only some form of agreed external regulation can effectively limit conflict and disorder between competing trade unions.

Unions can find that they lose members to other unions when those members are promoted. In response to this, many open manual unions have developed white-collar, technician and supervisory sections to recruit in the expanding area of white-collar employment and to avoid membership loss by promotion. In the recent past, some white collar unions or unions with white collar sections have come increasingly into conflict with each other on membership recruitment issues. Job demarcation has also long been a source of interunion disagreement. This can sometimes express itself in bitter strikes, such as have occurred in printing, newspaper publishing and shipbuilding in the past. Unions, particularly those catering for skilled employees, regard certain work, closely related to their members' skills, as 'theirs'. If management, other unions or competing groups of employees attempt to perform 'their' work, they resist this by imposing industrial sanctions against employers and employees alike. The problem is made even more intractable by the tendency for new technology to blur the traditional distinctions amongst craft workers and between them and other employees. Another major cause of interunion conflict arises out of different policies to pay negotiations and other conditions of employment among trade unions in the same industry. One union, for example, might be willing to accept an offer from an employer which other unions with a similar membership wish to reject. Federations of trade unions and the TUC industrial committees have become accepted means of bringing about compromise solutions to such issues.

The TUC has long recognized its responsibility for regulating interunion conflicts amongst those unions affiliated to it. Its 1920 constitution, for example, provided for the establishment of dispute committees for dealing with interunion disputes. In 1924 these disputes had reached such serious proportions that Congress adopted Rule 12, which gave the General Council powers to intervene in interunion disputes involving the alleged poaching of members by rival unions. At the 1939 Congress held at Bridlington the TUC established a further set of rules, and an accepted code of behaviour for member unions to regulate interunion competition was agreed. These rules, the TUC Disputes Principles and Procedures, are commonly referred to as the 'Bridlington Principles'. Later Congresses have amended and expanded these principles. For example, in 1976 the TUC revised 'Rules 10, 11, 12 and 13 and the regulations governing procedure in regard to disputes to bring them into line with recent practice', adding that they 'constitute a code of conduct accepted as morally binding by affiliated organisations. They are not intended . . . to be a legally enforceable contract'.[41] This was done because the TUC was understandably anxious to ensure, wherever possible, that interunion disputes are settled by the trade union movement itself rather than by the courts or by other external agencies.

The Bridlington Principles embody the following guidelines. First, they are aimed at encouraging closely related unions and federations of unions to develop specific and general working agreements on 'spheres of influence' amongst themselves. These include, for example: transfer of members between unions, including transfer of union benefits where appropriate; 'recognition of cards'; fully agreed and clearly understood demarcation arrangements; and recognized procedures for settling disagreements and misinterpretations among themselves. The TUC suggests that, when practicable, closely associated unions should examine the case for mergers or amalgamations among themselves. Second, where employees apply for membership to a union, they are normally expected to be asked which unions they have previously been members of, if they have correctly resigned from their former unions, and whether they are involved in either a union disciplinary matter or an industrial dispute. It also has to be established that they do not owe unpaid membership subscriptions to other unions. Third, the TUC recommends a model application form for trade unions when recruiting new members. In this way the union and the applicant's former union can normally exchange the requisite information within 21 days of a membership application, thereby ensuring full knowledge of the applicant's previous membership history. Fourth, unions are not expected to commence organizing and recruiting at any place of employment until they have confirmed that other unions are not already involved there. Agreements on 'spheres of influence' are of considerable use in avoiding interunion conflicts. Fifth, it is recommended that unions should consider the possibility of dual union membership arrangements where appropriate. Such arrangements enable management temporarily to transfer workers between jobs without provoking a demarcation dispute. Sixth, in the event of demarcation disputes between unions, industrial action is not expected to take place until the unions have referred the matter to the TUC.

Where unions cannot regulate their own relationships with each other, they can refer the matter, under TUC Rule 12, to a TUC disputes committee established by the General Council. In a majority of cases referred to the TUC, settlement is reached without resort to a disputes committee. When a case is put to a disputes committee – made up of three members of the General Council – hearings are held, investigations carried out and either an award or a recommendation is made. An award is usually made in a demarcation issue not involving an employer, which could of course ignore it. A recommendation is usually made in those cases involving employers only. Awards and recommendations are binding upon all affiliated unions and they are reported to Congress in its annual report. If a union refuses to accept the verdict of the disputes committee, it can, in the first instance, be suspended by the General Council. It can then be subsequently disaffiliated at the next Congress, although there is a right of appeal to Congress by the union concerned. Very few unions have actually been disaffiliated by Congress under the Bridlington Principles. The most notable in recent years took place in 1988 when the EETPU was expelled. In essence, interunion conflicts stem largely from overlapping union membership, competing recruitment activities and closely related spheres of influence. The TUC Bridlington Principles do not remove the causes of interunion conflict but only deal with their symptoms. The need for the TUC, however, to possess the power to regulate interunion conflicts continues to be essential. As the TUC's General Secretary said at its Annual Congress in 1988, in response to a government proposal to change the law so as to define narrowly the grounds on which a union could refuse membership or expel a member:

> Without the cohesion that comes from ultimate power to deal with interunion relationships, the TUC is weakened in all its dealings with government and public bodies; its credibility with employers is undermined . . . and its credibility with trade union members would be minimal.[42]

The Trade Union Reform and Employment Rights Act 1993 has established the legal grounds on which a union can refuse membership to an applicant or expel an existing member. These grounds are:

(a) that the applicant for membership does not fulfil the requirements for membership laid down in the union's rule book relating to trade, profession, qualifications or other occupational description;

(b) that the union only represents members in a defined geographical area or areas;

(c) that the union only represents members working for a particular employer or employers;

(d) that the conduct of the person expelled or excluded is unacceptable in relation to the rule book and that the conduct in question does not give rise to a complaint regarding unjustifiable discipline under the TULRC Act (1992).

The effect of these changes in the law relating to trade union membership will be to render the recommendations of the TUC Disputes Committee unenforceable. This will allow unions to poach each other's members, or to recruit outside their recognized 'sphere of influence' without fear of reprisal. The TUC will, therefore, not only lose one of its vital functions, but also clearly lose status and influence in the eyes of affiliated unions and their members.

Where individuals feel they have been unreasonably refused membership of the union of their choice or expelled from a union, they will be able to apply to an industrial tribunal for a hearing. If the tribunal finds in their favour, they will, after an interval, be able to seek compensation from the union concerned.

## Single union recognition

In 1987 the TUC established a special review body to report, *inter alia*, on the problems presented by the increasing number of single union, 'no-strike' agreements being negotiated by some unions with employers. The body was also to determine how the interunion conflicts caused by these agreements would be resolved. The union showing the greatest interest in signing such agreements was the EETPU, though similar agreements had been negotiated by the GMB, AEU and TGWU. These 'new-style' agreements, as they became known, are distinguished by the following characteristics:

- the recognition by the employing organization of only one union with sole bargaining rights;
- single status employment conditions for all staff;
- a communications and consultation system based on a company council or advisory board;
- union support for employee commitment to the aims and objectives of the company;
- employee acceptance of team-working, performance appraisal, quality awareness and other management methods;
- flexibility in terms of skill, task, place of work, hours of work, etc.;
- all staff to accept regular training, retraining and redeployment;
- 'no-strike' provisions coupled with compulsory arbitration, often involving 'pendulum' arbitration;
- most single union agreements have been signed with foreign owned high-technology companies on so-called greenfield sites since the early 1980s.

The advantages to the employer of single union agreements would appear to be substantial, particularly on greenfield sites where management wish to avoid all the complexities and rigidities associated with multiunionism. Single union agreements to date have been concentrated in high-technology companies facing intense product market competition, where conventional collective bargaining would inhibit rapid market adjustment and flexibility. The successful implementation of single union agreements depends, however, upon the quality of management.

> However success does not depend on the wording of an agreement. It depends on the underlying management philosophies and working practices which that philosophy generates. No matter how good the agreement might be a poor management will fail. Conversely, a good management will succeed against the odds.[43]

The publicity surrounding these new-style agreements has far outweighed their numerical significance, both in the number of agreements and in the union members covered by them. The TUC review body in 1988 listed only 26 such agreements; only a handful of the largest TUC-affiliated unions have been involved with them. By 1992, however, it is probable that some 150 such agreements had been concluded. Nevertheless, by comparison with conventional collective agreements between trade unions and employers, new-style agreements are a marginal activity.

The importance of such agreements, however, does not lie in their number but in their breach with long-established trade union beliefs about the freedom to strike and the exclusion of the right of other unions to seek recognition arrangements with the same employer. In practice, the other elements of new-style agreements, with the exception of single union recognition, are not uncommon in the more conventional collective agreements between unions and employers. The problem created by these new-style agreements is that all unions except the single union signing the recognition agreement are denied negotiating rights with the employer. The situation becomes critical for the TUC when the employer recognizes other unions in its other plants, and where single union agreements cut across the existing rights of other unions to recognition. At its 1985 Congress, the TUC clearly acknowledged this danger in single union agreements and tightened its Bridlington Rules, enabling it to instruct unions which had negotiated such agreements to renegotiate them so that other unions could be recognized. This change in the rules had the effect of restricting single union agreements to greenfield site developments.

Between the Congresses of 1985 and 1988, the TUC disputes committee instructed a number of unions to withdraw from single union agreements which cut across the recognition rights of other unions. In 1987 the EETPU, on TUC instructions, withdrew from single union deals with Yuasa, the Japanese battery manufacturer, and at a Thorn-EMI plant. The EETPU, however, refused to withdraw from single union deals with Orion Electric and Christian Salvesen, and was suspended from the TUC in July 1988. At the Congress of that year the EETPU was expelled from membership of the TUC after its case had been heard. In both Orion Electric and Christian Salvesen other unions, notably the TGWU, GMB and USDAW, had members yet the EETPU allegedly signed single union agreements without consulting these unions. This alleged refusal by the EETPU to acknowledge the legitimate interests of other unions was the reason given by the TUC for their expulsion.

> The issues . . . at stake do not amount to a choice between modern trade unions and an outdated approach to industrial relations. Nor are single unions or 'no strike' deals the issue. The TUC's rules do not preclude single union agreements – only agreements that ignore the reasonable interests of other unions. And in the two cases concerned whether or not the agreement was 'no strike' was totally immaterial.[44]

At the 1988 Congress, the TUC's Special Review Body recommended a new code of practice designed to prevent the signing of single union agreements not taking into account the legitimate interests of other affiliated unions. The code, which was intended to work in conjunction with the TUC's existing Bridlington Rules, was approved by Congress. In essence, the code requires unions considering negotiating single union agreements to inform the TUC of their intention and to do so at the initial stage. The TUC then issues guidance to the union on whether or not their intentions meet with the requirements of the Bridlington Rules and the new code. If another union or unions have a significant number of members at the site in question, say 10 per cent of the workforce, or are recognized by the same employer at other establishments, the TUC recommends that the union making the agreement consults with them.

The conflict within the TUC over this new-style bargaining goes much deeper, however, than disagreements over which union should be recognized by an employer. To some extent the conflict centres around two distinctly different views of the future of British trade unionism. One group, exemplified by the TGWU, believes that the 'traditional' attitudes of the unions towards employers, collective bargaining and politics should remain fundamentally unchanged. The other group of unions, led by the EETPU, believe that a 'new realism' is necessary so that the trade union movement can adjust to the profound economic, political and social changes through which Britain has passed since 1979, as well as the even more fundamental changes facing Britain and its work-force in the 1990s. The conflict over single union, no-strike agreements is perhaps no more than a surface manifestation of the ideological divisions amongst themselves which the 1980s have highlighted for the unions. These divisions do not constitute an insoluble crisis for the TUC. Yet the task of consolidating the union movement, and giving it a clear set of goals for the 1990s, could prove to be one of the greatest challenges the TUC has faced during its long history.

## 5.9   The European Community and European Union

Until 1988, the attitude of the TUC and the majority of British trade unions to the European Community was at the best lukewarm and at the worst hostile and dismissive. The prevailing view was, however, prag-matic and cautious, for the TUC strongly believed that Britain was capable of solving its own economic problems without resort to EC membership.

In 1972 the TUC opposed the signing of the Treaty of Accession which made Britain a full member of the EC. In the June 1975 referendum on Britain's membership of the EC the TUC split, as did the Labour Party, into pro and anti camps, with a clear majority of unions urging a 'No' vote. After the 1975 referendum, which supported continued membership of the EC, the TUC softened its attitude to Europe and took up its places on various EC councils and other bodies. The arrival of the TUC in Brussels also gave fresh impetus and authority to the European Trade Union Confederation (ETUC).

In 1980 the TUC, disappointed at its lack of progress with employment and economic issues in Brussels, called on a future Labour government to hold a second referendum. In 1981, the TUC urged a future Labour government to take Britain out of the European Community. By the mid-1980s, with the Prime Minister, Margaret Thatcher, increasingly hostile to the EC, the TUC's opposition began to wane. And after the defeat of the Labour Party at three successive general elections and the passing of trade union and employment legislation hostile to trade union interests, the TUC reversed its policy on the EC to one of commitment and even enthusiasm. At the 1988 Congress, a policy for a Social Europe was warmly embraced, with Jacques Delors, the EC President, receiving a standing ovation for a speech largely devoted to the 'social dimensions' of the rapidly developing EC. The TUC's conversion was complete. This conversion, however, probably owed more to the TUC's frustration and weakness in the face of three successive Thatcher governments than to genuine enthusiasm for the ideals of European integration.

> In particular it seems at times that the TUC may be expecting too much from European integration, especially with regard to the social and labour market regulation they want implemented by the Community. If the Community cannot deliver these statutes it is possible that the TUC may retreat into 'naive Keynesian' policy once again. The European question is far from over for the TUC.[45]

The policies and relationships developed by the TUC and British trade unions in relation to the EC since the late 1980s can, for the sake of analysis, be separated into several categories or areas, as demonstrated by Figure 5.6.

### Community trade union structures

The TUC has always prided itself on its international trade union and labour links. Individual British trade unions, as well as the TUC, have a long history of co-operation with such bodies as the International Confederation of Free Trade Unions (1949), various international trade union secretariats such as the International Chemical Workers' Federation (ICF), and the International Labour Organization (ILO), established in 1919.

At the European level, the TUC is affiliated to the European Trade Union Confederation (ETUC 1973), along with 35 other national trade union organi-zations, representing some 40 million workers. While the ETUC plays a valuable role in building links with various official councils, committees and other EC bodies centred on Brussels, it has so far not developed a clear industrial relations or collective bargaining role in relation to European companies and employing bodies. It is, however, developing an important function *vis-à-vis* the implementation

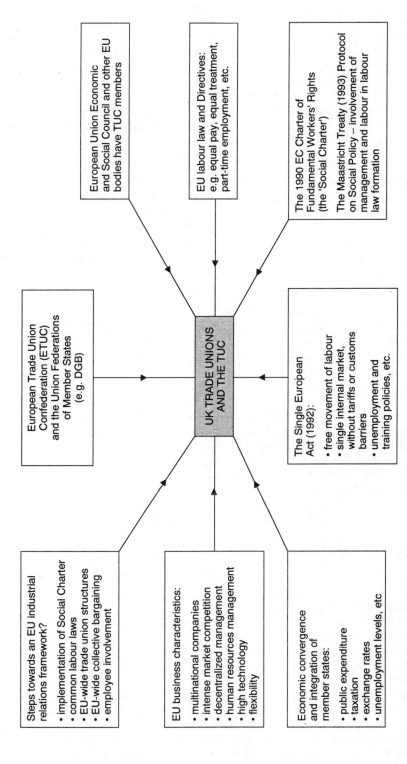

*Figure 5.6* UK trade unions, the TUC and the European Union.

of the embryonic Social Charter (1989), and the development of a common system of labour law for the EC, now the European Union (EU).

If, or when, the European trade unions begin to develop an EU-wide industrial relations system and collective bargaining structures, the ETUC could well become the prime initiator and coordinator. The role which could be played by linkages between the trade union federations of EU countries, such as the British TUC, the German DGB or the French CGT, is more problematic.

The most striking example of the potential effectiveness of the ETUC is to be found in the joint draft accord on labour law submitted by the ETUC and the European employers' organizations UNICE/CEEP in 1991, which eventually became Articles 118, 118A and 118B of the modified Treaty of Rome and the basis of future European labour law.

## EU labour law and Council Directives

EU labour law largely stems from three sources: first, the provisions of the Treaty of Rome, such as Article 119 on equal pay for equal work; second, the harmonization Directives of the 1980s in the area of collective labour relations and equality at work; third, attempts to implement EU labour law through the conditional granting of community funds for regional aid. Furthermore, many EU member states have been obliged to conform with EU labour law after employees had taken cases to the European Court complaining that their country of origin was not complying with EU labour law. In Britain, this led to changes in the law relating to equal pay, sex discrimination, health and safety, employer insolvency, redundancy and the rights of part-time employees.

## The Social Charter and the Maastricht Protocol

The 1989 EC Community Charter of Fundamental Social Rights of Workers (the 'Social Charter') was approved by 11 of the 12 EC member states, with Britain refusing to adhere. The rights listed in the Charter include: the right of unions to organize and to be recognized; employees to be consulted and provided with information; employee participation; improvements in working conditions; fair levels of remuneration; and the right of unions to negotiate with employers and to take industrial action. The TUC has urged the British government to accept the Charter and to commence implementation of the

rights for workers covered by it. The government has refused on the grounds that to do so would damage the competitiveness of the UK economy. The British government also believes that the contents of the Charter are best left for member states to determine voluntarily and for unions and employers to establish if they so wish by negotiation.

The Maastricht Treaty on European Union (1992), following which the EC became the European Union, or EU, contains a Protocol on Social Policy which is intended to continue the work on social rights started by the Social Charter. Britain did not sign the Protocol. The Social Charter, the Maastricht Protocol and any related EU acts or directives agreed by the Council will not, therefore, apply directly to British employees.

The European Union Treaty (1992) extends and deepens EU labour law in the following areas:

- health and safety at work;
- working conditions;
- social security provisions for workers;
- protection against termination of employment;
- EU financial support for the promotion of employment and job creation.

Furthermore, the Maastricht Treaty permits member states to entrust 'management and labour' at their joint request with the implementation of directives relating to the Social Charter. This means that EU labour law can be implemented through collective bargaining between trade unions and employers' organizations, known as the 'social partners', in all member states but Britain.

> The future of European labour law lies with the instruments agreed by the Member States at Maastricht: directives and EC level collective agreements, to be implemented within Member States, and enforced, *inter alia*, using the techniques developed to enforce Community law.[46]

## Other factors influencing the development of an EU industrial relations framework

The Single European Act, which is intended to create a unified mass market, might also encourage EU trade unions to form closer relationships to establish, through collective bargaining, common terms and conditions of employment across Europe. This process, if it happens at all, will doubtless face formidable obstacles in terms of the diversity of economic, political, cultural and business structures in member countries. However, the Single European Act, by creating a huge internal market without tariffs or customs barriers, where the free movement of labour is possible, could eventually provide sufficiently homogeneous conditions for an EU-wide industrial relations system to emerge.

The process of economic convergence across Europe will also be helped by existing EU policies designed to bring the public expenditure, taxation and exchange rates policies of member states closer together. Should a single currency controlled by an EU Central Bank also eventually come into existence, the convergence of member state economies might reach the point where EU-wide collective bargaining could become a reality.

> The immediate enactment of a fully fledged European industrial relations area does not appear on the agenda, but it is conceivable that it may emerge incrementally over a period of time.[47]

It is reasonable to conclude cautiously that the TUC and many individual British trade unions will increasingly come to recognize that it is in their long-term interest to support Britain's full involvement in the process of European integration. It is also possible that the TUC will provide the leadership and imagination in building an EU-wide industrial relations framework, though progress will undoubtedly be slow, uncertain and politically hazardous.

## 5.10 Trade Union Responses and Emerging Strategies

By the early 1990s, after some 14 years of adverse circumstances for British trade unions, two very different views as to their present condition and future prospects have emerged. One view, in an exaggerated form, perceives the unions to be: crippled by irredeemable membership losses; politically impotent and deliberately ignored by a hostile government; despairing of ever seeing a Labour government elected; scorned at the workplace by 'macho' managers; bewildered by the speed and breadth of industrial restructuring; unable to grapple with the consequences of new technologies; subject to internal conflict; and unable or unwilling to come to terms with the economic reality of free-market forces, and the political realities facing Britain in the closing decade of the twentieth century. Furthermore, similar

things are happening to trade unions in other countries, such as the United States, Japan and a number of European countries. Evidence that this pessimistic view of the precipitate decline in trade union power, influence and authority has some foundation is supplied by the empirical findings of the 1990 national survey of workplace industrial relations:

> contrary to what some have claimed, there were major changes in employee relations during the 1980s. Perhaps the most important of these were the decline in the representation of workers by trade unions and decline in the coverage of collective bargaining. . . . Indeed, so great were the changes that it is not unreasonable to conclude that the traditional, distinctive 'system' of British industrial relations no longer characterised the economy as a whole.[48]

The second, and contrary, view of the state of the trade unions by the early 1990s holds that this description of terminal decline is not only patently untrue but also the creation of a politically antagonistic media. Of course, it is argued, the trade unions have lost members and are suffering structurally from the consequences of economic change and labour market upheavals. Yet this has happened many times before in the history of trade unionism and they have recovered. As discussed earlier, trade union density stood at 48 per cent in 1920 and, largely owing to depression and economic change, had fallen to about 20 per cent by the mid-1930s, recovering again to over 50 per cent by the 1970s. Surviving hostile employers, severely adverse economic circumstances, restrictive labour laws and belligerent governments are not a new experience for trade unions. On the contrary, it is an essential element in their historical experience. After a period of reaction and painful adjustment to new economic and political circumstances, it is argued, they re-emerge, stronger and more united, to prove their durability and adaptability.

> Despite eight years of recession, the British trade union movement and many of its European counterparts are in remarkably good shape. The British movement clearly faces some big problems but these are not sufficiently widespread, serious or novel to warrant talk of a crisis or watershed.[49]

> It seems likely that the weakening of unions at the point of production in Britain and elsewhere is in large part a reflection of recession and may hence be reversed in the economic upturn.[50]

How the unions will respond to their undeniably severe problems will depend upon many factors. There appear to be three broad strategies they could follow. One choice is to refuse to yield before the economic and social changes created by the severity of market forces and the ideologies and policies of Britain's 'New Right' governments since 1979. By this view, they should seek to defend their position by asserting the moral and social undesirability of an economic philosophy which, it is claimed, is based upon greed and individual self-interest, with the old, the young and the weak going to the wall. Consequently, union leaders need to urge their members to await a change in the political climate and the return of a Labour government. By this 'traditional' or 'Labourist' view the unions will stay faithful to their long-held social beliefs and political hopes, even if it is a high-risk strategy to take.

The second possible strategy rests upon the belief that economically, politically and socially Britain has, since 1979, gone through a period of fundamental and irreversible historical change. The unions must adjust to it or be marginalized from power and influence. By this view, unions need to accept the changes as permanent and shape their organizations and policies to them. This approach can be called the 'new realism' or the 'new industrial relations' and sees unions becoming more business-like, hard-headed and efficient in representing the interests of their members and in seeking new ones. They are seen as not concerning themselves with the wider social injustices and the great political issues of the day, nor promising their members and supporters that a future Labour government will transform their lives.

The 'new realists' accept the need to adjust to the requirements of employers, for example, by negotiating single-union, no-strike agreements and by recruiting workers in comparatively well-paid, skilled and secure occupations and by providing them with a range of individual services. This will leave the unskilled, part-timers, women, ethnic minorities and the unemployed to be recruited and protected by the 'traditionalist' unions. The new realists argue that if the unions are to survive they have little real choice but to adapt to the world in which they have to live. The new realists' approach means, for some trade unions, the need to accept dominant employer ideologies and the inevitability of the 'ratchet effect' on the patterns of industrial relations at the start of the 1990s. According to Brown:

Perhaps more than at any time this century [the union] role depends upon the use the employers choose to make of them in the management of labour. It depends, to put it another way, on the conduct of collective bargaining. . . . It is hard to avoid the conclusion that the structure of trade-unionism, originally developed for the needs of employee solidarity, is increasingly being shaped to the needs of employers.[51]

The dangers of business unionism, or the new realism, are seen to lie in the loss of identity for some unions, as they adjust ever closer to the ideological needs of free-market economics and the labour needs of employers. Yet this could be seen as a small price to pay in return for a large and satisfied membership and the exclusion by employers of other unions.

The third possible strategic alternative for trade unions lies in the pragmatic and largely ideologically neutral creation of a handful of very large and powerful super trade unions, straddling all sectors of the economy. These would embrace every type of employee and negotiate from a position of numerical, financial and organizational power with employers. They would also express a willingness to discuss with the government of the day, in politically neutral terms, matters of direct practical and financial concern to their members. This process is, in an unplanned way, already taking place and can be seen in recent union amalgamations and mergers. The process would appear to be continuing as more and more unions, both small and large, perceive the advantages to be gained from being part of a larger and more powerful organization. A small number of very large unions could, arguably, reduce the growing incidence of interunion disputes related to new-style single union bargaining. On the other hand, however, such powerful unions could well be in direct competition with each other for members and employer recognition.

One trend of major importance is towards the creation of more general unions (i.e. multi-industry, multi-occupational) prepared to organise in many sectors of the economy. It has to be recognised that one effect of the creation of, in effect, more general unions, is likely to be even sharper competition.[52]

The TUC, although obviously aware of and deeply concerned at the dangers inherent in each of the three possible strategies outlined above, has urged affiliated unions to adopt a much more practical set of policies for the future. At its 1988 Congress, the TUC urged the adoption of six key proposals for strengthening the unions in the 1990s. First, it advocated the improvement of industrial relations with employers and employers' organizations, and of communications with professional organizations such as the Institute of Personnel Management. Discussion with employers should revolve around practical issues such as new technology, national and local bargaining options, the training of employees, productivity improvements and bargaining structures at company and plant level. Second, the unions should greatly improve their labour market intelligence. This would enable them to understand better what is happening in terms of how and where jobs are being lost and created, including greater regional knowledge about the expansion and contraction of employment. Third, the TUC recommended the improvement of services to members, especially financial services, including personal pension arrangements, loans, mortgages and insurance. Fourth, measures to promote trade unionism are recommended, such as the influencing of government thinking as it affects union members and their families. This includes, for example, the improvement of the health service, state education, youth training and social security. Fifth, the TUC wants to see ways of improving the unions' public image by using the media more persistently and professionally in persuading the public of the legitimate concerns of the unions on matters of great public issue. It also wants the unions to convince the public that the unions intend to resolve differences and conflicts amongst themselves and not to initiate or exacerbate them, as well as showing that unions are highly relevant to modern society. Sixth, to facilitate union growth, the TUC wants affiliates to target union recruitment more carefully, sensitively and expertly upon women workers and young people.

The TUC, at its annual conference in 1992, decided on further strategies to enable the trade unions to come to terms with the problems of the 1990s. These included: a campaign for a return by all governments to the commitment to full employment policies; the promotion of an employees' charter which would establish rights for all employees analogous to those being established in citizens' charters; the development of services in relation to trade union education, health and safety and equal rights; and the development of policies for the improvement of interunion relations. The TUC also launched a 'Network Europe' aimed at: pressing for an EU strategy for growth and employment; strengthening union links in multinational companies; lobbying for European social and economic legislation which will benefit UK employees and their families; and making use of qualified majority voting provided by the Maastricht Treaty, thereby trying to by-pass the British government's refusal to accept the provisions of the EU Social Charter.

## 5.11  Summary Points

- Trade union power and influence are largely determined by their size in terms of membership and density; size is most effectively achieved and maintained by union mergers.
- The major determinants of union membership levels are changes in the structure of employment, the level of unemployment, the industrial relations and legislative policies of government, and the attitudes of employers.
- Since 1979, trade union power has declined substantially in terms of membership, density, recognition, collective bargaining and political influence; whether this decline is permanent or temporary, only time will tell.
- Attempts to classify trade unions into structural types have had only limited success; the most successful structure appears to be that of the 'open' union willing to enrol and organize members regardless of their occupation, industry or service.
- The future success of the unions will depend upon their ability to expand membership into the low density sectors of the economy: to recruit women and part-timers and achieve recognition from non-union employers.
- Interunion conflicts largely result from membership disputes which it is the duty of the TUC to resolve; during the 1980s, single-union recognition agreements have exacerbated the problem.
- During the 1980s, the internal affairs and government of trade unions were strongly affected by legislation enforcing secret postal ballots and the rights of union members.
- After decades of opposition to British membership of the European Community, the TUC in 1988 became committed supporters; its main concern has been for the implementation of the 1989 Social Charter. It is as yet unclear how enthusiastic the TUC is for EU-wide collective bargaining and a common industrial relations framework.

## 5.12    References

1. S. and B. Webb, *The History of Trade Unionism* (1894), reprinted by Augustus Kelly, New York, 1965, p. 1.

2. R. M. Blackburn and K. Prandy, White collar unionisation: a conceptual framework, *British Journal of Sociology*, June 1965, p. 119.

3. *Ibid.*, p. 112.

4. A. Flanders, *Trade Unions*, Hutchinson, London, 1968, p. 10.

5. H. Phelps Brown, *The Origins of Trade Union Power*, Oxford University Press, Oxford, 1986, p. 16.

6. *Ibid.*, p. 23.

7. H. A. Clegg, Alan Fox and A. F. Thompson, *A History of British Trade Unions since 1889*, Oxford University Press, Oxford, 1964, p. 87.

8. E. J. Hobsbawm quoted in Clegg, Fox and Thompson, *ibid.*, p. 87.

9. Anthony Ferner and Richard Hyman, *Industrial Relations In The New Europe*, Blackwell, Oxford, 1992, p. 47.

10. Jeremy Waddington, Trade Union Membership in Britain, 1980–1987: Unemployment and Restructuring, *British Journal of Industrial Relations*, June 1992, pp. 311–13.

11. *Ibid.*, p. 302.

12. *Ibid.*, p. 305.

13. R. Price and G. S. Bain, Union growth in Britain: retrospect and prospect, *British Journal of Industrial Relations*, Vol. 19, 1983, p. 56.

14. Sid Kessler and Fred Bayliss, *Contemporary British Industrial Relations*, Macmillan, Basingstoke, 1992, pp. 107–8.

15. Jeremy Waddington, *op. cit.*, p. 311.

16. H. A. Turner, *Trade Union Growth, Structure and Policy*, Allen and Unwin, London, 1962, p. 241.

17. J. Hughes, *Royal Commission on Trade Unions and Employers' Associations, Research Paper 5 (Part I) Trade Union Structure and Government*, HMSO, London, 1967, p. 1.

18. R. Undy, V. Ellis, W. E. J. McCarthy and A. M. Halmos, *Change in Trade Unions: The Development of UK Unions since the 1960s*, Hutchinson, London, 1981, p. 330.

19. H. A. Clegg, *Trade Unionism under Collective Bargaining*, Blackwell, Oxford, 1976, p. 11.

20. K. Coates and T. Topham, *Trade Unions in Britain*, Fontana Press, London, 1988, p. 51.

21. S. and B. Webb quoted in H. A. Turner, *op. cit.*, p. 241.

22. Royal Commission on Trade Unions and Employers' Associations *Report*, HMSO, London, 1968, p. 179.

23. *The Miners' Next Step*, quoted in Will Paynter, *British Trade Unions*, Allen and Unwin, London, 1970, p. 95.

24. Royal Commission, *op. cit.*, p. 181.

25. *Ibid.*, p. 180.

26. Undy *et al.*, *op. cit.*, p. 22.

27. *Ibid.*, p. 167.

28. *Ibid.*

29. Trades Union Congress, *Towards 2000*, TUC, London, 1991, p. 20.

30. S. M. Lipset, M. A. Trow and J. S. Coleman, *Union Democracy: The Internal Politics of the International Typographical Union*, The Free Press, Illinois, 1956, p. 411.

31. J. D. Edelstein and M. Warner, *Comparative Union Democracy*, Allen and Unwin, London, 1975, p. 339.

32. F. A. Hayek, The trade unions and Britain's economic decline, in W. E. J. McCarthy (ed.), *Trade Unions*, Penguin Books, Harmondsworth, 1985, p. 358.

33. Anthony Ferner and Richard Hyman, *op. cit.*, p. 43.

34. Lipset, Trow and Coleman, *op. cit.*, p. 406.

35. G. B. Shaw, *The Apple Cart*, Penguin, Harmondsworth, 1956, p. 47.

36. Diane Watson, *Managers of Discontent*, Routledge, London, 1988, p. 77.

37. Lipset *et al.*, *op. cit.*, p. 15.

38. P. Taft quoted in J. Hughes, *Royal Commission on Trade Unions and Employers' Associations, Research Paper 5 (Part 2) Membership Participation and Trade Union Government*, HMSO, London, 1967, p. 67.

39. *Ibid.*, p. 79.

40. Royal Commission, *op cit.*, p. 271.

41. Trades Union Congress, *TUC Disputes, Principles and Procedures*, TUC, London (nd).

42. N. Willis, General Secretary TUC, speaking at the 1988 TUC Congress, quoted in *Personnel Management*, October 1988, p. 17.

43. Brian Towers (ed.), *A Handbook of Industrial Relations Practice*, Kogan Page, London, 1989, p. 259.

44. TUC Information Note, *The EETPU Suspension*, TUC, London, 1988.

45. Paul Teague and John Grahl, *Industrial Relations and European Integration*, Lawrence and Wishart, London, 1992, p. 209.

46. Brian Bercusson, Maastricht: a fundamental change in European labour law, *Industrial Relations Journal*, Autumn 1992, p. 188.

47. Paul Teague and John Grahl, *op. cit.*, p. 91.

48. Neil Millward *et al.*, *Workplace Industrial Relations in Transition*, Dartmouth, Aldershot, 1992, p. 350.

49. J. Kelly, *Trade Unions and Socialist Politics*, Verso, London, 1988, p. 268.

50. Ferner and Hyman, *op. cit.*, p. xxiii.

51. W. Brown, The changing roles of trade unions in the management of labour, *British Journal of Industrial Relations*, July 1986, pp. 164–5.

52. TUC, *Meeting the Challenge: First Report of the Special Review Body*, TUC, London, 1988, p. 13.

# 6

# Collective Bargaining

Collective bargaining is that method of determining working conditions and terms of employment through negotiations 'between an employer, a group of employers or one or more employers' organisations, on the one hand, and one or more representative workers' organisations on the other, with a view to reaching an agreement'.[1] For many years collective bargaining was the institutional centrepiece and focal point of British industrial relations. Indeed the Donovan Commission categorically stated 'that collective bargaining is the best method of conducting industrial relations'. It therefore saw wide scope in Britain for extending both the 'subject matter of collective bargaining and the number of employees covered by it'.[2] In the 1980 workplace industrial relations survey (WIRS), it was calculated that trade unions were recognized for collective bargaining purposes in 64 per cent of all establishments employing 25 or more employees. The corresponding figure for establishments in the public sector was 94 per cent. In the private sector, unions were recognized for manual workers in 65 per cent of private manufacturing establishments and for non-manual workers in 27 per cent of establishments. The corresponding figures for private services were 33 per cent and 28 per cent respectively. It was size of establishments especially 'and, to a lesser extent, the size of enterprises [which] were strongly associated with the extent of recognition'.[3]

In the 1984 WIRS, union recognition as a proportion of all establishments had marginally increased to 66 per cent. It had also increased to 99 per cent in all public sector establishments, consisting of 91 per cent for manual workers and 98 per cent for non-manuals. By 1984, union recognition in the private services had also increased, from 33 per cent to 38 per cent for manual workers and from 28 per cent to 30 per cent for non-manuals. In private manufacturing, however, union recognition had fallen to 55 per cent and 26 per cent for manual and non-manual workers respectively.[4]

Further changes took place in trade union recogni-

tion by employers for collective bargaining purposes, over pay and conditions of service, in Britain during the late 1980s, as shown by the 1990 WIRS. In 1990, overall union recognition, in establishments with recognized unions for any workers, had fallen to 53 per cent. This consisted of 44 per cent of the establishments in private manufacturing, 36 per cent in the private services and 87 per cent in the public sector. For establishments with recognized unions for manual workers, union recognition had also fallen, from 62 per cent in 1984 to 48 per cent or, on a sectoral basis, to 44 per cent in private manufacturing, 31 per cent in the private services and 78 per cent in the public sector. For non-manual workers, union recognition was also down from 54 per cent in 1984 to 43 per cent, consisting of 23 per cent, 26 per cent and 84 per cent for private manufacturing, the private services and the public sector respectively. As the 1990 WIRS concludes: 'the clear picture is one of substantial decline in the extent of [union] recognition since 1984. . . . Thus by 1990 only just over half the workplaces were ones where the employer recognized one or more unions for collective bargaining over basic pay for some of the employees present.'[5]

## 6.1   The Nature of Collective Bargaining

The term 'collective bargaining', like 'industrial democracy', was first used by the Webbs. Its precise nature, however, is subject to much academic debate. Put briefly, the Webbs described collective bargaining as an economic institution, with trade unionism acting as a labour cartel by controlling entry into the trade. Allan Flanders has argued, on the other hand, that collective bargaining is primarily a political rather than an economic process and 'that the value of a union to its members lies less in its economic achievements than in its capacity to protect their dignity'.[6] More recently, the Webbs' classical analysis of collective bargaining and trade unionism has been defended against Flanders' criticisms and reappraisal of it on the grounds that it is 'as a bargaining agent' that the union finds its major 'justification in the eyes of its members and that the issues relating to financial reward are still, whether for material or symbolic reasons or both, among its major bargaining preoccupations'.[7] Marxists, by contrast, contend that collective bargaining is merely a means of social control within industry and an institutionalized expression of the class struggle between those owning capital and those selling labour in capitalist societies. By this view, 'an unceasing *power struggle* is therefore a central feature of industrial relations'.[8]

In practice we do not consider the theoretical distinction between collective bargaining as an economic process and collective bargaining as a political process to be conceptually or empirically valid. Indeed collective bargaining can be viewed from at least three perspectives, none of which necessarily conflicts with the others and each of which represents different stages in the development of the collective bargaining process. 'These viewpoints are that collective bargaining is (1) a means of contracting for the sale of labor, (2) a form of industrial government, and (3) simply a system of industrial relations.'[9] These three viewpoints have been described as the 'marketing' concept of collective bargaining, the 'governmental' concept, and the 'industrial relations' or 'managerial relations' concept respectively. The marketing concept, for example, views collective bargaining as the means by which labour is bought and sold in the market place. In this context, collective bargaining is perceived primarily as an economic and exchange relationship. In other words, it is the method of conducting industrial relations which determines the standard terms and conditions of employment by which labour is supplied to an employer either by its present employees or by newly hired workers. This concept of collective bargaining focuses on the substantive content of collective agreements, on the pay, hours of work, and fringe benefits which are mutually agreed between employers and trade union representatives.

The marketing concept of collective bargaining is nearest to the Webbs' analysis. It assumes, correctly in our view, that industrial relations begins in the labour market. This view of collective bargaining is based on the belief that it provides the means to remedy the fundamental bargaining inequalities existing between the strong position of the corporate employer, on the one hand, and the weak position of the individual employee, on the other, in the buying and selling of labour. The individual pay-work

bargain between employer and employee, in short, is not regarded as being between equals. Nor is it made voluntarily by an individual worker with the employer but is negotiated out of economic necessity, since most people have to work in order to live. It is this fundamental imbalance of power which collective bargaining is designed to remedy. By using the device of the 'common rule', it is argued, employees can insist collectively that if an employer hires any of their number, it must offer them not only the standard rate of pay but also the standard conditions of employment for the job.

To what extent collective bargaining establishes an equality of advantage between managements and employees is subject to debate. It is even debatable whether collective bargaining has the power in the long term to redistribute real income between pay and profits. However, since a collective agreement may be necessary to both an employer and its employees, whereas under individual bargaining an agreement is of greater concern to the individual employee, then the imbalance of power against employees in the labour market is to some degree mitigated by collective bargaining. This is also a factor which reinforces the very determined defence of collective bargaining by trade unions when it is proposed to restrict or legally control 'free collective bargaining'.

The governmental concept of collective bargaining views the process as a constitutional system or rule making institution determining relations between management and trade union representatives. In this case, collective bargaining is seen as a political and power relationship. Trade unions in other words are regarded as sharing industrial sovereignty with management and, as the representatives of employees collectively, they use that power to advance their members' aspirations and employment interests at work. This view of collective bargaining stresses both the continuity of the management–union relationship and the continuous process of rule making which takes place between management and unions. In this way, the negotiation of substantive collective agreements on pay and conditions is not an end in itself. The disputes procedure for resolving differences between employers and unions provides the means of modifying the terms of an agreement when necessary. Hence in mature collective bargaining, the distinction between disputes arising out of existing collective agreements and those deriving from matters not covered by collective agreements becomes blurred. Similarly, when collective bargaining procedures are agreed so that employment rules can be continually made and applied between employers and trade unions and 'when labor and management deal with labor relations analytically and systematically after such a fashion, it is proper to refer to the system as "industrial jurisprudence"'.[10]

The industrial relations or managerial relations concept of collective bargaining proceeds from the governmental concept. It views collective bargaining as a system of 'industrial governance', since through it trade unions join with employers in reaching decisions on matters in which both parties have equal rather than competing interests. The presence of the union in enterprise decision making, in other words, allows representative participation by employees in the determination of those policies most affecting their working lives. In this way collective bargaining involves trade union representatives, whether they like it or not, in organizational and managerial decision making in those areas covered by collective agreement. As the area of joint regulation expands, so too does the participation of trade unions in the management of the enterprise. Defining authority within the enterprise, for example, involves specifying areas of joint concern within which industrial relations decisions are made by mutual agreement. Underlying the concept of collective bargaining as a process of industrial governance is the principle that those who are integral to the running of an enterprise should have some voice in determining the decisions of most concern to them. This 'principle of mutuality', it is suggested, correlates with the concept of political democracy, so that collective bargaining becomes a means for establishing its equivalent – industrial democracy – at the workplace.

We do not believe that these three perspectives of collective bargaining are contradictory, incompatible or exhaustive.

> All three aspects of collective bargaining can thus be simultaneously maintained, but each provides a different emphasis, stresses a different guiding principle, and can influence the nature of the actions taken by the parties.[11]

The important thing to understand is that the nature and depth of collective bargaining differs not only between separate negotiating groups but also within any particular negotiating group at different times. As collective bargaining matures between an employer and a particular negotiating group, it can logically progress through the marketing stage, to the governmental stage and ultimately the managerial stage if the parties wish. Similarly, it can regress from

the managerial stage, to the governmental, to the marketing stage. Clearly, the essence of the collective bargaining process is its representative nature, its power basis, its adaptability and its flexibility to particular circumstances.

What, briefly, are the conditions necessary for collective bargaining to emerge and to survive as an effective means for regulating relations between employers and trade unions? First, the parties must be sufficiently organized. This means, in practice, that freedom of association and of organization amongst employees into independent trade unions are indispensable conditions for the establishment of viable collective bargaining. Unless employees have the freedom to form themselves into stable organizations independent of both employer and state control, unions do not have the power base from which to negotiate effective collective agreements on behalf of their members. Whether employers are collectively organized depends on the levels at which collective bargaining takes place, the strength of the trade unions, and the structure of industrial relations within the industry. Organization on the part of the employers, therefore, is not a necessary but an enabling condition for collective bargaining to take place.

The second and fundamental condition for collective bargaining to emerge is that employers recognize trade unions for bargaining purposes. Yet the history of trade union recognition in Britain has been a long and frequently bitter struggle. In view of the obstacles which trade unions have often had to overcome in the early stages of their growth, including employer opposition, hostile decisions from the courts, and restrictive legislation, it is not surprising that progress in obtaining trade union recognition has been a slow and conflict ridden process. In Britain, which led the way in the nineteenth century in trade union organization, the struggle to win recognition from employers lasted many decades and continues even today. This was epitomized, perhaps, by the bitter dispute over trade union recognition between Grunwick Processing Laboratories and the Association of Professional Clerical and Computer Staffs in the late 1970s and at Times Newspapers, at Wapping, in the mid-1980s.

After union organization and recognition from an employer have been achieved, and for collective bargaining to be successful, it is also necessary that the parties negotiate in good faith and accept the agreements entered into as binding upon each other. But either side, of course, is free at some later date to use the relevant procedural agreement to terminate or to modify existing agreements and to enter into new negotiations.

There are two methods by which the conditions necessary for effective collective bargaining can develop. One is by legal means, the other is voluntarily. In Britain the preference has been for trade union organization, trade union recognition, bargaining in good faith and the mutual observation of collective agreements to be achieved in accordance with the voluntary or abstentionist principle. The legal standing of collective agreements between the parties continues to be that they are 'binding in honour only'. They only become legally enforceable contracts if the parties mutually agree to do this. Collective bargaining, in short, has not only been the major method of conducting industrial relations in Britain. It has also been the method in which the parties to it have preferred to build a framework of voluntary rather than compulsory procedural agreements governing their formal relations. These have enabled them to create a flexible body of substantive rules on pay and conditions which regulate their mutual rights and obligations in the labour market and the workplace. They also regulate day-to-day managerial relations between management, employees and unions at enterprise and establishment level.

## 6.2    Developments in Collective Bargaining

The extent and scope of collective bargaining reform have been a major policy issue in British industrial relations since the 1960s, especially after the publication of the Donovan report in 1968. In essence, three main problems have stood out in the debate. The first has concerned the private sector pay bargaining system. The central issue here has been how company or plant bargaining can be reconciled to industry-wide, multiemployer bargaining and, when they exist, to the exigencies of national incomes policies. The second issue has concerned public sector pay bargaining. The main issue here has been the extent to which the constraints imposed by government financed industry-wide agreements are compatible with the devolution of negotiating machinery in this sector, on the one hand, and with non-intervention by government in the bargaining process within them, on the other. The third issue, since the late 1980s, has been the future of collective bargaining, especially in the private sector, and its role as an industrial relations institution, where employers are increasingly likely to

resist union recognition, to derecognize them or to limit the bargaining agenda.

These three problems, two associated with the private sector and the other with the public sector, although interrelated, are in practice separate issues. But the suggested solutions to collective bargaining and industrial relations reform in Britain, such as the Donovan Commission's recommendations, have sometimes been proposed as all-purpose panaceas rather than as specific prescriptions for particular cases.

## The Donovan Commission

The first and one of the most influential analyses of collective bargaining in Britain in the postwar period was that of the Donovan Commission which was set up in 1965 and published its report in June 1968. The central diagnosis of the Royal Commission was that Britain had 'two systems' of industrial relations. One was the 'formal system' embodied in the official institutions of collective bargaining at national level. The other was the 'informal system' based on the actual behaviour of managers, shop stewards, and workgroups at the place of work. In the words of the Commission:

The formal system assumes industry-wide organisations capable of imposing their decisions on their members. The informal system rests on the wide autonomy of managers in individual companies and the power of industrial work groups.

According to the Royal Commission, these two systems of collective bargaining were in conflict, with the informal system continuously undermining the regulative effect of industry-wide agreements on pay and conditions of employment. Symptomatic of this conflict, the Commission believed, was the increasing gap or 'wage drift' between nationally agreed rates of pay and actual earnings at the workplace; the failure of national disputes procedures to contain unofficial and unconstitutional strikes at factory level; the absence of company personnel policies; and the persistence of restrictive labour practices and low productivity within firms.

To remedy this, effective and orderly collective bargaining is required over such issues as the control of incentive schemes, the regulation of hours actually worked, the use of job evaluation, work practices and the linking of pay to changes in performance, facilities for shop stewards and disciplinary rules and appeals.[12]

The Commission did not consider, however, that such matters could be dealt with effectively by national agreements. It recommended instead that whilst industry-level agreements should be limited to those matters which they could effectively determine, comprehensive company agreements could provide 'the remedy'. These could regulate pay within firms, deal with grievances, discipline, and redundancy, and provide facilities for shop stewards at the workplace. Donovan envisaged, in other words, the formalization of a two-tier structure of national and company collective bargaining, but not the abolition of national negotiations as such.

The Royal Commission took the view that top managements should initiate the reform of collective bargaining within their own companies. They should do this, the report recommended, by developing authoritative collective bargaining machinery, comprehensive procedural agreements and the joint discussion of measures to promote health and safety within their firms. Within such a framework, it was argued, management and unions would then be able to negotiate productivity agreements relating pay to output, thereby lowering unit costs of production, raising the pay of employees, stabilizing prices to consumers, and improving company profitability. The Royal Commission, however, was not entirely convinced that corporate management would be generally committed to undertake these policy initiatives. It further recommended, therefore, that an Industrial Relations Act should be passed requiring larger companies, the nationalized industries, and the public services to register their procedural agreements with the Department of Employment and Productivity (DEP). An Industrial Relations Commission (CIR) was also to be established by this Act and, on reference from the DEP, it would investigate and report on cases arising out of the registration of these agreements. It would also consider problems referred to it by the DEP either concerning companies not large enough to be covered by the obligation to register their collective agreements, or disputes over trade union recognition between employers and trade unions. There were, however, to be no penalties for non-compliance by employers to the CIR's recommendations.

The prognosis for collective bargaining change embodied in the majority report of the Donovan Commission was to be voluntary procedural reform between employers and unions at company level. The law, however, was only to be used to prod reluctant companies in the direction of collective bargaining initiatives, rather than to coerce them into it. Through such measures, it was anticipated, collective bargaining structures would be reformed, the principle of joint negotiation would be extended, productivity agreements could be negotiated, and any conflicts between management and unions within firms would be resolved. Donovan, therefore, was 'mini-reformist' in its purposes, aiming at a common approach to collective bargaining change across most industries. As such, it did not really threaten existing industrial relations. However, it failed to distinguish between the collective bargaining problems inherent in some private sector industries, such as in engineering and large-scale manufacturing at that time, and those in the rest of private industry and the public sector. It also made very scant and superficial references to the problems of simultaneously devolving collective bargaining from multiemployer to company level, and of managing incomes policy centrally.

In the event, the Labour government published its White Paper, *In Place of Strife*, in January 1969. Whilst embracing most of the recommendations made by the Donovan Commission, it also contained several paragraphs relating to proposed 'cooling-off' periods in the case of unconstitutional strikes and to the holding of strike ballots in certain other instances. These proposals were totally unacceptable to the trade union movement and a general election was called in 1970 before the Labour government had time to reconsider its proposals for industrial relations legislation.

## The 1970s

The in-coming Conservative government's approach to the reform of collective bargaining was very different in its emphasis. Indeed it is doubtful whether the reform of collective bargaining was in any sense its major policy objective for industrial relations. Its aim was, rather, to reform and to change trade unionism, not collective bargaining *per se*. While the Donovan Commission had in effect concluded that trade unions were too weak and needed strengthening in order to perform their collective bargaining functions adequately, the Conservative Party had already drawn quite contrary conclusions in its pamphlet *Fair Deal at Work*, published in April 1968. It felt that the unions were too strong and that if the Conservative Party's industrial relations objectives were to be achieved to the benefit of the country at large, then trade union power needed weakening by changes in the law on industrial relations.

The Conservatives' stated objectives were aimed at:

1. More responsible collective bargaining to improve the content of agreements and to ensure that, once made, they are kept.
2. The removal of barriers to industrial efficiency, higher productivity and higher real earnings.
3. The achievement of greater co-operation between management, employees and trade unions in securing industrial peace and progress.
4. Providing fair and reasonable protection for the basic rights of individuals – including the right to work in the occupation of their choice and for which they are best qualified.

In contrast to Donovan, and despite its earlier claim that 'collective bargaining by independent trade unions and employers free of State control is one of the hallmarks of liberty in an industrial society', the Conservative government enacted the Industrial Relations Act 1971. This legislation epitomized the approach of many critics of British collective bargaining at that time. It reflected the view that direct statutory intervention in industrial relations, especially in trade union affairs and in industrial disputes, through 'a fair, relevant and sensible framework of law, while providing no panaceas, can exert stabilising pressures and help to raise general standards in the way men do business together'.[13] Whatever the merits of the new legislation in advancing individual rights at work, the 1971 Act ultimately proved unworkable and had little direct impact on reforming collective bargaining or in integrating it with a viable incomes policy. It is arguable that the enactment of the Industrial Relations Act to some extent hindered the voluntary reform of collective bargaining by employers and trade unions in the 1970s.

Other proposals for the reform of Britain's collective bargaining structure came a few years later. They included those of the Confederation of British Industry (CBI) in 1977. It believed that:

The present system of bargaining has failed. It is one major reason why we have not achieved high employment, high growth, high productivity, and high real earnings; it has hindered good industrial relations; and it has made it harder for the UK to compete and earn her way in the world.

There was little doubt in the CBI's view that one of the major problems facing private industry at that time was the fundamental shift in the balance of bargaining power to the advantage of organized labour. In its opinion, this was compounded by poor productivity, low profitability, inadequate cash flow, the high cost of borrowing and an 'imbalance in the public sector' which 'has had serious repercussions in the private sector, particularly in the last few years'.[14] For these reasons, there had been, in the CBI's view, uneconomic levels of pay bargaining which were not only inflationary but also against the public interest.

To remedy such instability in the collective bargaining structure, and to improve Britain's economic performance, the CBI saw three broad courses of action to be possible: permanent controls by government on pay bargaining; reliance on market forces together with strict control of the money supply; or free collective bargaining within the constraints of monetary discipline and some central influence on the overall level of wage and salary settlements. Having compared these different approaches, the CBI concluded that the most suitable direction of change would be a combination of the second and third choices before us – a system based on market forces and monetary discipline, but one in which central guidance influences pay claims and settlements. In order to achieve bargaining reform, and to create the conditions necessary for high economic growth and greater material prosperity, the CBI went on to suggest that any changes in collective bargaining and pay determination would need to be concentrated on four related fronts: first, action by Government as the country's financial controller and as a pay bargainer in its own right; second, the creation of wider understanding of the nation's economic circumstances; third, the reconstruction of collective bargaining arrangements to reduce competitive bargaining between different pay groups; and fourth, the restoration of greater balance in bargaining power between employers and trade unions.

Like other analyses of British industrial relations at that time, the CBI could see no established pattern or discernible order within the collective bargaining arrangements covering that three-quarters of the full-time employed labour force subject to collective agreements in the late 1970s.

Although in the public sector bargaining on pay is predominantly at national level, in private industry company or plant bargaining plays a significant part. There are thousands of distinct agreements, often with separate settlement dates, and with a large number of agreements operated within a single company.[15]

To remedy these structural deficiencies within which pay was negotiated, and to contain what it regarded as 'inherently inflationary' and 'competitive bargaining', the CBI maintained that the principal initiative for change rested with the employers.

Amongst its proposals, the CBI suggested that there should be a restructuring of bargaining arrangements within individual plants or companies and across industries. It saw no reason, for example, why multi-tier bargaining should not take place at more than one level, say at industry or national, company or employer and plant or workplace level. It thought it desirable, however, that there should normally be a clear separation of those items of the employment package negotiated at different bargaining levels. There should, for instance, be no item bargained at more than one level, and only those items for which flexibility was required should be bargained at the lower levels. Moreover, strict application of the guidelines would be likely to rule out most bargaining at departmental level, because expertise will not be generally sufficiently high to ensure control. The CBI also considered that there should be a minimum number of bargaining units or negotiating groups consistent with the structure and organization of the industry or company in question.

This move towards fewer and larger bargaining units within plants, companies, or industries, it was felt, should be accompanied, secondly, by collective action amongst employers to synchronize pay settlement dates. There could thus be a compression of the annual pay round into a much shorter period of time within, say, three months or so. It was suggested, too, that within the shorter pay round, there would be some advantage if those groups with the greatest bargaining power negotiated first. Finally, the CBI argued, more attention should be focused within companies on the development of rational and easily understood pay structures than had previously been the case. In its view, inadequate internal pay structures not only reflected the disorder of Britain's collective bargaining arrangements, but also generated inflationary pressures within the economy. The overriding principles in pay structures should be that adequate control can be maintained and that there should be accepted differentials related to skill, effort and responsibility. The approach of the CBI,

then, was to advocate reform of private sector collective bargaining through employer initiative, tighter monetary discipline and freer market forces, with the latter acting to constrain inflationary pay negotiations between what it regarded as weak employers and strong trade unions.

Another plea for collective bargaining reform at that time came from within a section of the Trades Union Congress (TUC). Its main concern was with the problems and inadequacies of pay determination within the public services, excluding the nationalized industries. The dissatisfactions amongst unions representing civil service, health service, and local authority employees were, by the late 1970s, twofold. First, they felt that decisions on the pay of public sector employees had become too much a matter for political debate and public discussion rather than of responsible collective bargaining. Implicit in this view was the belief that incomes policies had always operated with far greater rigidity towards public sector employees than towards their private sector counterparts. Second, they also considered that public sector pay problems had been made worse by the centralized nature of the negotiating machinery within their industries.

Towards the end of 1977, David Basnett, then general secretary of the National Union of General and Municipal Workers and chair of the TUC, suggested that a new approach towards public service pay bargaining was required and that the impetus for the change must come from the trade union side. It would involve establishing a more comprehensive machinery to bring together 'unions in local government and the health service, and the industrial and non-industrial civil services, to form a new TUC Public Services Committee'. Once established, he argued, this Committee would convene a regular conference of its member unions. There were common objectives which this Committee would seek. These could include: first, establishing more regular contact with government ministers to discuss economic policy; second, making further moves towards synchronization of the principal pay settlement dates within the public services; third, replacing one-off emergency inquiries with permanent pay review bodies. Such bodies could thereby establish genuine pay comparisons between public sector and private sector employees and their findings would be made available to negotiators; fourth, the undertaking of regular reviews of pay structures. Then finally, a review of pay negotiating machinery in the public services could be attempted. 'This would give more authority to lower levels of management and local union officials. The more problems that can be solved at local level, the better.'[16] In 1979, a TUC Public Services Committee was formally established but, as outlined below, the change in the political and economic climate after 1980 seriously frustrated most of its objectives.

## The 1980s and 1990s

During the 1980s and the early 1990s patterns of collective bargaining and industrial relations in Britain changed radically. The changes were in response to three main influences and their impact on employers, employees and the unions. These influences were: government economic policy; government labour market and industrial relations policy; and employer-led initiatives in restructuring and managing employment relations and personnel management within both private sector and public sector organizations. The net result was 'the rediscovery of the management prerogative', with the resulting changes being 'reflected in the collapse of multi-employer bargaining, the development of single employer bargaining and, within that, the concentration on decentralized unit-specific bargaining systems'.[17]

Government economic policy throughout the period from 1979 to the mid-1990s was in direct contrast with that of the 1960s and 1970s, which, for most of these years, was based on Keynesian interventionist principles. Keynesianism incorporated: maintaining full employment in the labour market; using counter-cyclical fiscal and monetary policy instruments to facilitate macroeconomic management by influencing the demand side of the economy; and searching for a prices and incomes policy to keep annual wage settlements largely in line with national increases in productivity.

Macroeconomic policy during the 1980s and early 1990s, in contrast, focused on improving economic performance and business efficiency by improving the supply side of the economy, creating the market conditions necessary for economic prosperity and attempting to reverse Britain's relative economic decline. At intermediate or meso level, policy was aimed at revitalizing private enterprise, increasing the competitiveness of British businesses and strengthening the right to manage. Finally, at the micro level, governments wanted to strengthen consumer sovereignty in the market place, to promote personal responsibility in the family, at work and in

the community, and to free individuals from the 'dependency culture' of the welfare state.

The means by which successive Conservative governments attempted to achieve their strategic economic objectives consisted of increasing market competition, fostering an enterprise culture and creating conditions which they perceived to be conducive to business expansion. One policy instrument was the deregulation of capital and product markets. Another was reducing the size of the public sector, by privatizing public utilities, such as water, gas, electricity and telecommunications, and selling them off to private shareholders. 'Privatisation had the further advantage of raising additional revenue from the sale of state assets, so avoiding increases in general taxation to fund government expenditure.'[18] In other cases, public services, such as in central government, the health service and education, were hived off into public agencies, operating in quasi- or internal markets of 'providers' and 'purchasers', competing in some instances with the private sector. In yet other cases, public sector organizations, such as in central and local government, were required to 'market test' their services and to compete for their provision through compulsory competitive tendering with the private sector.

There were three main thrusts to governmental labour market and industrial relations policy during the 1980s and early 1990s. These were: deregulating the labour market and pay determination; restricting trade union power, especially the freedom of unions to take lawful industrial action against employers; and individualizing relations between employers and employees within the workplace.

Labour market deregulation in the private sector was facilitated by a number of devices, such as removing the protection of wages councils to low-paid, badly organized workers, rescinding the Fair Wages Resolutions and weakening the employment protection rights of individual employees, such as the legal right not to be unfairly dismissed. This was done, for example, by extending the period of continuous service required to qualify for this right. Most notably, continuous hostility was shown by government to multiemployer collective bargaining, for as Brown and Walsh comment:

> Since 1986 the Government has been increasingly outspoken in opposing multi-employer bargaining arrangements. They are criticized as being props for 'lazy' employers, establishing rigid national wage rates which restrict the

downward wage flexibility necessary to promote jobs in the high unemployment regions of the country.[19]

Similarly, in the public sector, public employers were put under increasing pressure to get rid of national pay bargaining machinery and to set up regional pay bargaining arrangements. This reversed a long tradition of centralized collective bargaining, embodied largely in the Whitley principles which were established immediately after the First World War. This regionalized pay determination strategy was advocated largely in terms of the marked geographical variations in employment and skills shortages existing in the 1980s and 1990s.

The restricting of trade union bargaining power, through the enactment of new legislation in Parliament, was in line with the 'free market' analysis of the Conservative governments in Britain after 1979. According to this analysis, unions are a prime cause of inflation, inefficiency and unemployment in the market economy. Further, because of their legal 'privileges' (known technically as statutory or legal 'immunities'), in not being able to be sued in tort by employers when they take damaging industrial action against them, unions are seen as wreaking unacceptable and unnecessary damage on firms, employees and the wider economy. For those supporting market individualism, therefore, the free market model suggests:

> that if union power could be broken by restrictive labour laws and tough management, and if at the same time the labour market could be generally deregulated, then economic benefits would follow, including more efficient working practices, higher productivity, and eventually the creation of more jobs.[20]

Moreover, union power, cohesion and solidarity were further reduced by successive Conservative governments who strengthened the legal rights of individual union members against their unions. This now includes the rights to be balloted in taking industrial action and not to be 'unfairly disciplined' by their unions, even where individual trade unionists fail to obey union instructions to take part in balloted industrial action.

Another contention of the market-oriented New Right in industrial relations is the device of the closed shop agreement. This is the arrangement whereby individual employees are required to be union members, as a condition of employment. The closed shop is singled out as being particularly objectionable and as the supreme example of coercive monopoly power associated with trade unionism. It is seen by free marketeers as being inimical to individual liberty, as destroying jobs and as reducing not only the employers' freedom to manage but also their profits. Like trade unions generally, the closed shop is perceived to be illegitimate in its intention, and unfair in its consequences, since its whole purpose is to restrict competition in the free labour market. According to those supporting the purist free market model, therefore, the employment relationship should be based on the individual contract, freely made between every employer and each individual worker, so as not to distort the workings of the free labour market or to infringe the personal liberties of individual employees, by coercing them into union membership. This process of individualizing employment relations was encouraged by successive governments in the 1980s and early 1990s, especially by importing private sector employment practices, such as personal contracts and performance pay, into the public sector.

Turning briefly to employer-led initiatives in restructuring and managing industrial relations since 1979, we observe not only the decline of multi-employer collective bargaining, and the corresponding growth of decentralized pay bargaining in the private sector, especially at employer or company level, but also the thrust by some employers for a 'union-free environment' through non-recognition and union derecognition policies. One factor leading personnel and industrial relations managers to devolve collective bargaining to corporate and site level is the development of business policies and corporate strategies which create devolved profit centres and local financial control systems. These result in the development of personnel strategies aimed at managing local internal labour markets more efficiently, raising labour productivity, increasing flexibility and reducing employment costs. Decentralized bargaining is seen as a viable industrial relations device to facilitate this. As Purcell and Ahlstrand conclude, on the basis of company case study evidence:

> motivations for changing bargaining levels derived from changes in a wider business structure/style and not for industrial relations reasons. . . . The stated aim has been to tie industrial relations and bargaining outcomes to the business performance of the operating units.[21]

Firms are also now increasingly likely to develop their own organizationally based personnel policies and employment systems. These derive from pressures in product and service markets for quality improvement and labour cost reduction. They are often linked with total quality management approaches, 'just in time' management systems and attempts by employers to establish employee commitment programmes, centred on individual employees, using staff appraisal, performance related pay and 'culture change' initiatives. Such organizations are less likely to see a role for trade unions in the managing of people function. Where they do, employers on greenfield sites might opt for single union recognition deals, whilst in other cases, non-recognition or even union derecognition are distinct policy choices on offer to management.

The evidence for union derecognition is not conclusive, though it does seem to be a growing trend. According to the 1990 WIRS, the number of cases of derecognition reported to it was small.

> Three per cent of all workplaces without any recognized unions in 1990 had previously had recognized unions at some time in the period 1984 to 1990. These amounted to just over 1 per cent of all workplaces in 1990. . . . [In the private sector] One per cent of managers . . . without recognized unions reported having recognized unions during the previous six years . . . Taking the whole of the private sector it amounted to less than 1 per cent. However, our limited data on the timing of derecognition, with a substantial concentration in 1989, was suggestive of a growing phenomenon.[22]

In a representative sample of 176 UK and overseas-owned companies in mid-1992, however, it was reported that almost one in five companies employing over 1 000 people had 'partially or wholly withdrawn trade union recognition in the past five years and a quarter of those did so at most of their sites'.[23] The most commonly cited factors leading to derecognition were falling union membership and privatization.

It would seem that the changing structure of employment and of workplaces, since the early 1980s, is a continuing threat to traditional patterns of union organization and therefore to collective bargaining arrangements with employers. These factors include: the decline of heavy manufacturing industry; the trend towards smaller employment units; the steady rise of the service sector; the contraction of the public sector; the rising proportion of overseas-owned companies; and the increase in part-time employment.

## 6.3   Bargaining Structure

Where collective bargaining has achieved a degree of permanence and stability, it is possible to identify a framework or structure in which negotiations between employers and trade unions take place. The term 'bargaining structure' is used to describe the 'stable or permanent features that distinguish the bargaining process in any particular system'.[24] Four interrelated features within any collective bargaining structure can be identified. 'These may be termed: Bargaining levels, Bargaining units, Bargaining forms and Bargaining scope'.[25]

The concept of 'bargaining levels', for example, describes the levels at which collective bargaining is conducted within an industry or an organization. In much of British industry, private and public, collective bargaining used to take place through multiemployer negotiations at national or industry level between employers' associations or other employer representatives, on the one hand, and federations of trade unions on the other. Such arrangements continue to exist but they are much less dominant now than in the past, with the growth of single employer bargaining. Collective bargaining also takes place at company or employer level and at enterprise or workplace level. In certain industries, agreements may be negotiated at several levels to determine different elements in the employment package. In some private sector industries, such as in chemicals, framework agreements on the pay and conditions of manual workers are determined at national level, even though not all employers are 'federated', and are then supplemented by company and workplace agreements on some matters. In the chemical industries, the Chemical Industries Association (CIA) has about 200 member firms, many of which operate nationally, accounting for about half of the industry's employment. CIA members that automatically apply the terms and conditions agreed nationally are known as 'conforming members', such as Albright and Wilson and RTZ. Those that do not, such as ICI, are commonly referred to as 'non-conforming members'. National agreements are closely adhered to regarding working hours, holiday entitlements, overtime premiums and holiday pay, whilst basic pay, shift pay and call out payments tend to be regarded as minima. According to the CIA, this system has many benefits. It is a major influence as a trend setter, by setting a floor of wages for the industry as a whole and by providing a solid framework for company agreements. But actual pay rates in member companies tend to be well above the national minima rates, with many companies enhancing the industry minima by incorporating regular bonuses or pay allowances into their basic rates. Bargaining levels, in short, may be high, intermediate or low, whilst in some industries there are a number of levels which may or may not be connected to one another.

Closely related to an industry's or an organization's bargaining levels are its 'bargaining units'. This term refers to the specific group or categories of employees covered by a particular agreement or set of agreements. Bargaining units are obviously connected with bargaining levels, but the latter concentrate on the managerial side of the negotiating table, whilst the concept of a bargaining unit is particularly concerned with the representative functions of trade unions. Individual unions or joint panels of unions, for example, act as bargaining agents for employees within given bargaining units. Bargaining units may be wide or narrow in coverage, and bargaining agents may be few or many in number. In chemicals and the textile trades, for example, there are relatively wide bargaining units with comparatively few bargaining agents nationally. In engineering, there can be either fairly wide bargaining units at national level covering all manual workers in a variety of trades or narrow units represented by a multiplicity of bargaining agents. Teachers in the 'old' university sector, on the other hand, have a fairly narrow bargaining unit and a single bargaining agent. Although there are nominally nine bargaining units in the National Health Service, most of these tend to be narrow in their coverage and they comprise a multiplicity of bargaining agents, especially among the professional and technical staff, with about 40 representative bodies. But there are also separate pay review bodies for doctors and dentists and for nurses, midwives and related grades which no longer have national collective bargaining arrangements on their terms of employment.

Bargaining units vary from bargaining level to bargaining level, especially in private industry. At company level, for example, negotiations may be conducted in a number of different bargaining units. There may be one set of agreements for craftworkers and skilled employees, another for process workers, and different agreements for supervisors and white collar workers where they are represented by trade unions. Furthermore, agreements on some items like the standard working week and holiday arrangements may apply to all employees within a company and the bargaining unit may be company-wide. However, where piecework payment schemes operate, there may be a multiplicity of small and separate bargaining units at enterprise level for the purpose of determining piecework prices.

The terms 'bargaining forms' and 'bargaining scope' are also closely connected. Bargaining forms focus on the ways in which an agreement or a set of agreements is recorded, that is whether it is written and formally signed, or unwritten and informal, whilst bargaining scope is used to indicate the range of subjects covered within a particular bargaining unit by its collective agreements. It would seem, generally, that the higher the bargaining level within an industry or organization, the more formalized its collective agreements are. Yet even where national or company agreements are written down and are fairly formal, they may leave some room for manoeuvre and interpretation through negotiation at lower bargaining levels or even by custom and practice in the workplace.

Similarly, as new subjects for negotiation are introduced and accepted within a bargaining unit, the range of subject matter in collective bargaining extends. Where bargaining scope ends, the right to manage or managerial prerogative begins. Although trade unions have traditionally pressed for extensions in the scope of collective bargaining, there are always certain subjects which management reserves the right to settle for itself, without having to obtain either union or employee agreement. Bargaining forms, in short, may be either written and formal or unwritten and informal, while bargaining scope may be either comprehensive or restricted in its range.

It is clear, therefore, that the structure of collective bargaining in Britain is diverse and heterogeneous, displaying contrasting degrees of formality and informality among, between and within particular bargaining groups, and over time. In these circumstances, the concepts of bargaining levels, bargaining units, bargaining forms and bargaining scope are useful analytic tools for comparing different collective bargaining structures. The bargaining structures within the engineering trades, for example, are quite different from those existing in other private sector industries, in the private services or in the public services. The engineering industry, for instance, covers a complex group of activities concerned with the manufacture, installation, maintenance and repair of metal goods. It includes work as wide ranging as metal founding and forging, scientific instrument making, motor vehicle assembling, constructional engineering, lamp and electronic manufacturing and so on. There are also a number of closely related industries like cutlery and edge tool manufacturing and lock, latch and key making which have their own negotiating machinery separate from that of the engineering industry.

The practice in engineering, at least till 1990, was for negotiations on major pay fluctuations and the main conditions of employment affecting manual workers to be conducted at national or multi-employer level between the Engineering Employers Federation (EEF), representing the employers, and the Confederation of Shipbuilding and Engineering Unions representing the many unions in the industry. Matters affecting the members of one union only, such as the electricians and plumbers, were also discussed at national level between the EEF and the union concerned. Similarly, issues affecting members of a particular group of unions could also be raised at national level by the unions involved. Such negotiations were conducted on an *ad hoc* basis at special conferences. The normal practice was for the trade unions making a claim to write to the EEF requesting a conference at which to present their case. This was then considered by the employers and a formal reply was given normally at a further conference. Negotiations continued either until agreement was reached or discussions broke down. In addition to these arrangements, the EEF conducted national negotiations on conditions of employment with unions representing certain white collar workers in the industry. However, the collapse in 1990 of national negotiations between the EEF and the CSEU marked the culmination of a process which began formally in 1968 but has been reflected in many other industries since, such as banking, cotton textiles and national newspapers.

In practice, however, national negotiations on pay and conditions in most of the private sector are increasingly marginal in their impact on the actual earnings of employees and on their conditions of employment at the place of work. This is because the major decisions on these matters are now generally taken at company or plant levels or at both. In these circumstances, it is local unions which take the initiative in making claims on behalf of their members to managerial representatives at both company and workplace, or either, level. Such negotiations are held on company premises, in company time and may or may not involve full-time trade union officers in the bargaining process. Furthermore, on some issues they normally take place continuously. Whilst there may be only one pay claim per

bargaining unit each year, other matters may be dealt with as they arise as the subject of separate agreements, of varying degrees of formality. The bargaining scope might include, for instance, holiday arrangements, payment by results schemes, shiftwork allowances, the amount of overtime, its allocation and so on.

Such local negotiations 'or "domestic claims" are the most personalized aspect of negotiations and for much of the time they deal not in economic claims but in disputes as to grievance procedures, dismissals, work practices, etc.'.[26] In the private sector, in short, both the collective bargaining structure and the elements within it are quite complex; bargaining is highly differentiated not only in its bargaining levels but also in its bargaining units among firms and within them. But there are also wide divergences in bargaining form and scope within the sector. These vary between considerable formality and comprehensive range, on the one hand, and unstructured informality and restricted range on the other.

By contrast, in the local authority sector in England and Wales, there are separate bargaining units for manual workers, white collar staff and other groups. These include the National Joint Council for Local Authorities (manual workers), the National Joint Council for Administrative, Professional, Technical and Clerical Staff and a variety of other joint committees and joint councils. A range of unions is normally represented on these bodies, which discuss a wide range of issues affecting both employers and employees. For manual and white collar staff, there are also a number of provincial councils which maintain links between bargaining levels and implement agreements and decisions made nationally. Control of terms and conditions in this sector, therefore, is more centrally determined than at establishment or workplace level. Nevertheless, it has been argued for some time that local government may have to consider how to retain the advantages of a national pay and conditions framework, 'whilst leaving appropriate discretion for councils to find their own solutions to particular local circumstances and problems'.[27] However, despite the fact that a small minority of local authorities in the South East broke away from national pay bargaining in the late 1980s, mainly on the basis of direct comparability with the local private sector, national pay bargaining arrangements remain firmly entrenched in the local authority sector.

*Table 6.1* Percentage of employees covered by collective agreements by major sectors 1980, 1984 and 1990.

| | All establishments | | | Private manufacturing | | | Private services | | | Public sector | | |
|---|---|---|---|---|---|---|---|---|---|---|---|---|
| | 1980 | 1984 | 1990 | 1980 | 1984 | 1990 | 1980 | 1984 | 1990 | 1980 | 1984 | 1990 |
| Manual workers | 55 | 62 | 48 | 65 | 55 | 44 | 33 | 38 | 31 | 76 | 91 | 78 |
| Non-manuals | 47 | 54 | 43 | 27 | 26 | 23 | 28 | 30 | 26 | 91 | 98 | 84 |
| All workers | 64 | 66 | 53 | 65 | 56 | 44 | 41 | 44 | 36 | 94 | 99 | 88 |

*Source*: WIRS 1992

## 6.4   Patterns of Collective Bargaining

Collective bargaining regulates both pay relations between employers and employees, through the intermediacy of trade unions, and managerial relations between managers and subordinates in the employment relationship. It is as a system of pay determination, however, that collective bargaining retains a major role in industrial relations. The incidence of collective bargaining in Britain varies according to a number of factors. These include: employment sector; the occupational status of workers; the size of employment unit; the ownership of the organization employing people; and various contextual factors, such as the economic and legal policies of the government in office. Another distinctive feature of the pattern of pay determination in Britain 'is the diversity and multiplicity of levels at which there is collective bargaining'.[28]

### The distribution of collective bargaining

Table 6.1 provides some indication of the general coverage of collective bargaining in Britain, by the major sectors of the economy, for 1980, 1984 and 1990. The data are taken from the Workplace Industrial Relations Surveys for these years. Table 6.1 shows, even though there have been changes in the distribution of bargaining during the past decade or so, that, first, collective bargaining is more likely to take place in the public sector than in the private sector, especially compared with the private services where collective bargaining and union recognition have never been very strongly established. Second, in the private sector, collective bargaining is more likely to be practised in manufacturing businesses than in services such as retailing, hotel keeping and finance and commerce. Third, collective bargaining is more likely to cover manual than non-manual employees, except in the public sector where bargaining for non-manual staff is generally well established.

There have, however, been some fairly substantial changes in the distribution of collective bargaining since 1980. First, collective bargaining among all workers, whilst increasing from just under two-thirds of all establishments in 1980 to two-thirds in 1984, then fell to just over a half of them in 1990. Second, the coverage of collective bargaining increased from just over half of all manual workers in 1980 to some three-fifths in 1984 but fell to under half of them in 1990. Third, for non-manual workers, collective bargaining covered just under a half of all establishments in 1980 and rose to over half in 1984, falling again to some two-fifths in 1990.

There have also been changes in the coverage of collective bargaining across the different sectors of the economy during the 1980s. First, in private manufacturing, the incidence of collective bargaining for manual workers fell dramatically from some two-thirds in 1980, to just over half in 1984 and to just over two-fifths in 1990. Second, although in the private services the coverage of collective bargaining rose from about a third of all manual workers in 1980 to almost two-fifths in 1984, by 1990 it had fallen back again to some third of this group. Third, there were, surprisingly, significant falls in the coverage of collective bargaining amongst non-manual workers in the public sector. The coverage for this group was over 90 per cent in 1980, rising to almost 100 per cent in 1984. In 1990, however, the figure had fallen to some four-fifths, largely on account of the removal from national collective bargaining arrangements of school teachers in 1987 and, in the NHS, nurses and midwives and the professions allied to medicine in 1983. Fourth, it is apparent from Table 6.1 that the coverage of collective bargaining for both manual and non-manual workers in the private services was never substantial at any time during the 1980s, varying between some 25 and 30 per cent of the workforce.

How can the distribution and coverage of collective bargaining arrangements in Britain be accounted for?

According to the workplace surveys, it is the ownership of establishments, establishment size and to a lesser extent enterprise size that are strongly associated with union recognition and collective bargaining. The surveys indicate that in the private sector the number of people employed in total by the enterprise of which the establishments were a part 'exercised strong independent influences upon the extent of trade union recognition'.[29] In the public sector, whilst size of establishment and size of enterprise are important influences on collective bargaining, it is enterprise ownership which tends to be the more significant factor.

## The private sector

In the private sector the pattern of collective bargaining is very complex. Several surveys of employing establishments provide useful evidence about the levels of bargaining which influence changes in rates of pay and other conditions of employment. They also attempt to identify the most important bargaining level having the greatest impact on pay rate changes. But there is no general agreement about what determines particular collective bargaining arrangements. 'The available literature on the subject has tended to view it as a decision taken by the parties on the basis of the various costs and benefits of alternative structures.'[30] The debate centres around whether it is employer or union organization which is the major factor. In Britain the 'literature starts from the assumption that management has the predominant influence'.[31]

For analytical purposes collective bargaining can be classified into 'multiemployer bargaining' and 'single employer bargaining', with single employer bargaining being further subdivided into 'centralized' and 'decentralized' bargaining. With decentralized bargaining, enterprises may have full delegated authority to settle pay claims and other conditions of employment; this is sometimes described as 'local autonomy bargaining'. In other cases, negotiations are conducted at establishment level, but within limits set by the corporate centre; this is sometimes known as 'co-ordinated local bargaining'. Private sector multiemployer bargaining is where a number of employers reach an industry-wide or national agreement on pay and conditions with the recognized unions in the industry as a whole, although there are a few rare examples where agreements continue to be negotiated at regional or district level, such as in cotton weaving. An increasing number of national pay agreements specify only minimum hourly rates or minimum weekly earnings rather than standard rates. Even where standard rates are laid down, provision is often made for company level or workplace productivity payments to be provided on top of standard earnings. The trend, however, is definitely away from multiemployer bargaining in the private sector to single employer bargaining, especially in large multiplant firms. This movement away from multiemployer bargaining was noted by the CBI in the late 1980s, after an analysis of its databank material on pay arrangements in the private sector, where it stated that 'The use of industry-wide agreements has declined, accelerating a trend under way before 1979'.[32] Examples of where multiemployer negotiating bodies have been dissolved since the mid-1980s include banking, cotton textiles, independent television, the bus and coach industry and Sunday newspaper distribution. In a series of relatively small industries like bacon curing, hosiery and knitwear, electrical cable making and roadstone quarrying, framework multiemployer agreements on pay and conditions continue to operate but the influence of local bargaining within them has been extended, either temporarily or permanently. There are a handful of private industries, however, where multiemployer bodies have been newly established. These include: the flax and hemp joint industrial council; the lace finishing joint negotiating committee; the retail food joint committee; and the national committee for registered clubs and associations.

Table 6.2 shows the basis for the most recent pay increase in private manufacturing for the years 1980, 1984 and 1990, based on the Workplace Industrial Relations Surveys. It indicates, first, the relative decline of collective bargaining in private manufacturing, for both manual and non-manual employees, between 1980 and 1990, although the decline among manual employees was far more dramatic than that among non-manual groups. Second, as indicated earlier, there was a relative decline in the importance of multiemployer bargaining among manual employees in this sector, with, by 1990, some two-fifths of this group having plant or establishment bargaining as the most important bargaining level. Third, and in direct contrast to this, the proportion of non-manual employees having multiemployer bargaining as the most important bargaining level increased from about one-fifth in 1980 to almost one-third in 1990, although only some quarter of this group were actually covered by collective bargaining arrangements at this time.

*Table 6.2* Basis for most recent pay increase in private manufacturing 1980, 1984 and 1990 (per cent).

| | Manual employees | | | Non-manual employees | | |
|---|---|---|---|---|---|---|
| | 1980 | 1984 | 1990 | 1980 | 1984 | 1990 |
| Result of collective bargaining | 65 | 55 | 45 | 27 | 26 | 24 |
| Most important level | | | | | | |
|   Multiemployer | 42 | 40 | 36 | 19 | 19 | 30 |
|   Single employer | 15 | 20 | 17 | 30 | 35 | 21 |
|   Establishment | 40 | 38 | 42 | 48 | 42 | 38 |
|   Other | 3 | 2 | 5 | 3 | 4 | 11 |
| Not the result of bargaining | 35 | 45 | 55 | 73 | 74 | 76 |

*Source*: WIRS 1990

The basis for the most recent pay increase for employees in the private services for 1980, 1984 and 1990 is shown in Table 6.3. This indicates, first, that collective bargaining is very weakly rooted in this sector. Second, where collective bargaining does take place, there has been a steady increase in the importance of single employer bargaining for manual employees since 1980, and even more so for non-manual employees, with some three-quarters of the latter affected by it in 1990. Third, there has been a slow increase in the importance of establishment level bargaining among manual employees in each of these years. However, whilst establishment bargaining had risen slightly in importance among non-manual employees in 1984, by 1990 it had once again regressed in importance and was even less important then than it had been in 1980.

It is clear from this brief analysis of collective bargaining levels that different employers and different sectors adopt their own strategic choices and policy options in managing collective bargaining and in dealing with trade unions in private manufacturing and the private services. There are, in short, a diverse and complex range of practices which are affected by economic, technological and representational influences in each case. There are obvious advantages and disadvantages for employers in determining particular bargaining levels. The advantages to employers of multiemployer bargaining include: the equitable treatment of all employees across the industry; making the best use of the employers' negotiating resources; preventing pay 'leap-frogging' by the unions; and leaving management at establishment level to focus on managing the business. There are, on the other hand, certain disadvantages to employers. These include: reducing the opportunity

for employers to negotiate domestic deals to cope with local labour market conditions; paying something for nothing to all employees, thus requiring changes in working practices and productivity to be negotiated locally; and some employers having to pay more than they can currently afford because of their business conditions. For the unions, multiemployer bargaining concentrates union negotiating power and negotiating skills, gets 'something' for all the union's members and legitimizes the union role throughout the industry. The main disadvantages to unions of multiemployer bargaining are reducing their ability to negotiate more advantageous deals for their members locally and not needing to maintain close day-to-day links with their members at company level.

For employers, centralized corporate bargaining has a number of advantages. These include: uniform terms and conditions within the company; more predictable labour costs; stable relationships between different negotiating groups; and fewer pay parity claims. Its major disadvantages are: accommodating the conflicting demands deriving from diverse product markets, labour markets and technologies; excessive formalization of collective agreements; extended lines of communication; and how to monitor workplace arrangements effectively. From the trade union viewpoint, centralized bargaining provides more effective and efficient use of union resources and negotiating skills and better co-ordination between bargaining groups. However, company bargaining, unlike workplace bargaining, can weaken the status and power of shop stewards and create tensions in decentralized unions, such as in the engineering workers union, where considerable autonomy is vested locally. Also smaller unions with full negotiating rights locally can find themselves

*Table 6.3* Basis of most recent pay increase in the private services 1980, 1984 and 1990 (per cent).

| | Manual employees | | | Non-manual employees | | |
|---|---|---|---|---|---|---|
| | 1980 | 1984 | 1990 | 1980 | 1984 | 1990 |
| Result of collective bargaining | 34 | 38 | 31 | 28 | 30 | 26 |
| Most important level | | | | | | |
|    Multiemployer | 56 | 53 | 35 | 43 | 37 | 20 |
|    Single employer | 29 | 32 | 52 | 36 | 50 | 73 |
|    Establishment | 9 | 11 | 13 | 7 | 10 | 4 |
|    Other | 6 | 4 | 0 | 14 | 3 | 3 |
| Not the result of bargaining | 66 | 62 | 69 | 72 | 70 | 73 |

*Source*: WIRS 1990

*Table 6.4* Major influences on collective bargaining levels.

| | Multiemployer bargaining | Single employer bargaining | |
|---|---|---|---|
| | | Centralized | Decentralized |
| Product market | Competitive | Homogeneous | Heterogeneous |
| Work organization | Labour intensive | Capital intensive | Capital intensive |
| Technology | Small batch | Homogeneous | Heterogeneous |
| Geographic location | Concentrated | Concentrated | Dispersed |
| Business structure | Many firms: small plant size | Multiplant: small plant size | Multiplant: large plant size |
| Union structure | Centralized: few unions | Centralized: various | Decentralized: multiunions |
| Payment system | Time payments | Job evaluated | Payment by results |

squeezed out of centralized negotiations where there is often strong competition for places in the union negotiating team because of multiunionism.

The advantages of decentralized bargaining for employers include the following: it enhances local managerial authority for industrial relations; it provides shorter lines of communication and aids speedier resolution of disputes; and it enables management to achieve a flexible approach to workplace change. On the other hand, decentralized bargaining often gives rise to claims for pay parity between different workplaces and negotiating groups, in addition to complicating the monitoring of labour cost control. For trade unions decentralized bargaining consolidates shop steward power and eases intraplant communications; but it can also weaken the authority of full-time trade union officers and intra-union or interplant solidarity.

Table 6.4 provides an indication of the major factors influencing multiemployer, centralized and decentralized bargaining. It must be repeated that the situation is highly complex and in many industries there are factors influencing employers and unions in more than one direction, as evidenced by the variety of mixed bargaining which takes place. In general, however, multiemployer bargaining is more likely in labour intensive industries which have large numbers of small firms that are geographically concentrated, with selling taking place in competitive product markets. Centralized employer bargaining is more likely in capital intensive industries which are either dominated by a single large firm or where there are relatively few firms each with a sizeable market share. Finally, other things being equal, decentralized bargaining is more likely than centralized bargaining where average plant size is high, where there is significant variation in plant size, 'where plants are geographically dispersed, where technology and the product market varies among plants and where the wage payment system relates pay directly to effort'.[33]

## The public sector

If the private sector has undergone substantial and rapid change during the 1980s and early 1990s, with the globalization of markets and industrial restructuring, then what has happened in the public sector since 1979 has been equally radical and far-reaching in its impact on employers, the unions and state employees. These changes and innovations include privatization, compulsory competitive tendering, structural reorganizations and the introduction of private sector management techniques into the public sector. In 1992, the total workforce of the public sector was 5.8 million, which is what it had been some 30 years earlier in 1961. By 1971, the public sector had increased to 6.6 million, rising to 7.3 million in 1976. Since then, it has slowly fallen to 7.2 million in 1981, 6.0 million in 1990 and 5.9 million in 1991. Despite the shrinkage of public sector employment since the early 1980s, therefore, total employment in public enterprises remains relatively high. Public employers are still large-scale, major employers of a variety of professional, technical, administrative and manual workers in Britain but, since 1979, the context of public sector employment has changed substantially and the central role of collective bargaining within it is somewhat less secure than it was previously.

Technically, public sector employment consists of those employed in central government, the civil service and the local authorities plus those in public corporations. The central government sector includes all bodies for whose activities a Minister of the Crown is accountable to Parliament. These include departments of state and bodies such as regional health authorities, national research councils, royal commissions and national museums and art galleries. The civil service comprises the home civil service and the diplomatic service, as well as those employed in the newly set up government agencies, such as the Employment Service, the Benefits Agency and the Driving Standards Agency. The local authority sector consists of all local authorities with power to raise funds by means of levies or local property taxes and includes the magistrates courts, the probation service and the police forces. Municipal bus companies and airports are now out of the local authority sector and are regarded as public corporations, whilst grant-maintained schools, further education colleges and the 'new universities' and colleges of higher education are counted as part of the private sector.

Public corporations are public trading bodies which have substantial degrees of financial independence from central government. They are publicly controlled to the extent that the Sovereign, Parliament or a Minister appoints, directly or indirectly, the whole or the majority of the boards of managements of public corporations. They are free, however, to manage their affairs without detailed control by Parliament. In particular, they have the power to borrow, within limits laid down by Parliament, and to maintain their own reserves. Some ten public corporations are designated as nationalized industries, including the Post Office, Nuclear Electric and London Regional Transport. Between 1982 and 1992, however, over 30 public corporations – including most of the former nationalized industries such as gas, telecommunications and electricity – were transferred to the private sector, amounting to a total of some 700 000 employees at the time of the privatizations. Finally, since 1 April 1991, NHS trust hospitals have been defined as public corporations.

Table 6.5 indicates those major parts of the public sector with collective bargaining arrangements for their staff. It excludes other public sector groups, such as higher civil servants, nurses, midwives and the professions allied to medicine, doctors and dentists, and the armed services, which do not have joint negotiating machinery but have their terms and conditions determined by pay review bodies appointed by government. Since 1987, under the Teachers' Pay and Conditions Act, some 400 000 schoolteachers in England and Wales have had their collective bargaining arrangements suspended and their pay determined by a pay review body. Collective bargaining remains, however, the major method for determining the pay and conditions of the vast majority of public employees in Britain.

In general, public sector collective bargaining has three main characteristics. First, in contrast to the private sector, 'the national-level, industry-wide bargaining structure . . . was essentially put in place either immediately after the First World War . . . or immediately after the Second World War',[34] though in the largely monopolistic public corporations, which are the sole buyers of labour, national agreements are not normally multiemployer agreements but single employer ones. There were attempts by some public sector employers, however, to regionalize and decentralize some bargaining groups in the 1980s and to move away from tightly controlled centralized negotiating arrangements, more on the private sector model, but with very limited degrees of success. Second, public sector industries or enterprises tend to have collective bargaining machinery

*Table 6.5* Major public sector collective bargaining groups 1993.

| Sector | Number of bargaining units | Number of employees* |
|---|---|---|
| *Central government* | | |
| Civil Service | 2 | 580 000 |
| National Health Service [†] | 9 | 350 000 |
| Universities | 5 | 110 000 |
| London Regional Transport | 20 | 45 000 |
| *Local government* | | |
| Manual staff | 10 | 1 000 000 |
| Administrative, technical and professional | 8 | 650 000 |
| Fire Services | 2 | 40 000 |
| Police | 5 | 200 000 |
| *Public corporations* | | |
| British Coal | 7 | 20 000 |
| British Rail | 7 | 120 000 |
| Post Office | 5 | 150 000 |
| British Broadcasting Corporation | 1 | 25 000 |
| Civil Aviation Authority | 1 | 7 000 |
| British Waterways Board | 2 | 2 000 |

* Approximate numbers only.
[†] Excludes groups such as doctors, dentists and nurses with pay review bodies.

for most groups of employees with clearly defined and sometimes large bargaining units. These are often divided into manual, craft, professional and technical, and other specialist groups typified, for example, by the British local authorities. The only major exceptions tend to be senior managers who are now generally on personal contracts of employment and performance-related pay. Third, Whitley bargaining machinery, based on the recommendations of the Committee on Relations between Employers and Employees in 1917–18, still provides the dominant model for conducting negotiations in much of the public sector.

Table 6.6 shows the basis for the most recent pay increase in the public sector for 1984 and 1990. The data are comparable with those provided in Tables 6.2 and 6.3 for private manufacturing and the private services respectively. Table 6.6 indicates, first, the very substantial drop in collective bargaining in the public sector in 1990, compared with 1984, especially that covering non-manual employees. Second, 'almost all of this fall was in multiemployer bargaining and was in the public services administered by local government'. Third, there was a

corresponding increase in the proportion of public sector establishments where pay was determined unilaterally by higher level management or by an external body, such as a pay review body. 'The large increase in this latter category in relation to non-manual employees, from 1 per cent to 11 per cent in 1990, reflects the changed arrangements for determining the pay of teachers, nurses and midwives', referred to above.[35]

The WIRS 1990 concludes that there are a number of notable differences in collective bargaining arrangements between the public and private sectors in the early 1990s. The first is 'the predominance of national pay-setting [in the public sector, which] was apparent whether we looked at the most important bargaining level as seen by our management respondents . . . or whether we took all the levels of negotiation' affecting a pay increase. Second, it is now common for non-manual employees in several parts of the public sector to have their pay 'partly determined by a national agreement and partly by a settlement confined to their own employer'. The WIRS, in short, detects a move towards more local pay-setting arrangements for some public service employees,

*Table 6.6* Basis for most recent pay increase in the public sector 1984 and 1990 (per cent).

| | Manual employees | | Non-manual employees | |
|---|---|---|---|---|
| | 1984 | 1990 | 1984 | 1990 |
| Result of collective bargaining | 91 | 78 | 98 | 84 |
| Most important level | | | | |
|     Multiemployer | 79 | 74 | 85 | 80 |
|     Single employer | 18 | 17 | 13 | 15 |
|     Enterprise | 1 | 1 | 1 | 0 |
|     Other | 2 | 8 | 1 | 5 |
| Not the result of bargaining | 9 | 22 | 2 | 16 |

*Source*: WIRS 1990

'although the contrast with the private sector remained strong'.[36]

National or industry-wide bargaining, therefore, still provides the most authoritative basis for determining pay agreements in the public sector, although there is growing scope for some local or establishment bargaining in certain parts of the sector. Varying proportions of the public sector, however, such as cleaning, catering and some professional services, are now contracted out to the private sector. This means that these workers are not covered by national agreements or, in some cases, by union recognition procedures, although the Acquired Rights Directive of the European Union casts some doubt on the legality of this.

The largest organization in central government is the National Health Service (NHS), where, for those employee groups covered by national Whitley collective agreements, there is only limited scope for local bargaining, mainly amongst craft and certain manual workers. In 1992, there were some 250 000 health service workers employed in over 150 self-governing NHS trusts (SGTs). These are now defined by national statistics as public corporations and, in theory at least, they have devolved discretion in determining locally which union(s) to recognize, if any, the term and conditions of their staff – who are 'trust' employees – and changes in payment systems. It is too early to conclude what patterns of industrial relations are likely to emerge eventually in SGTs, but it seems possible that some degree of regionalization or decentralization of collective bargaining could develop, incorporating different personnel management policies and industrial relations strategies in different parts of the country.

There have also been recent changes in pay determination in the civil service. By 1994, over 96 'Next Steps' agencies had been created, across the civil service, which have enabled a more fragmented approach to collective bargaining to be established for civil servants. This has led to questioning of the need for civil service wide terms and conditions of employment, agreed at central level. One result has been the negotiation of agency-specific pay structures and conditions of employment, incorporating pay flexibility, performance pay and new staff appraisal systems. Such developments 'reveal that the government's priority has been to keep staff costs down and to persuade individual civil servants that a more individualised approach to employee relations is to their advantage'.[37] A second consequence has been the fragmentation of union bargaining power in the civil service and the abandonment of the principle of 'pay comparability' – that is, comparisons with the pay of equivalent workers in the private sector. This has been replaced by the principle of 'what government can afford' or 'what it has to pay'. There is, in short, no longer a monolithic, centralized pay bargaining system in the civil service but a more fractionalized, diffuse one.

In the local authorities, there have been conflicting pressures on the collective bargaining system. Some authorities, and some unions, have wanted to continue with national pay bargaining, for both manual and non-manual groups, whilst others have wanted to abandon it and 'go local'. Most senior officers are on personal contracts and performance pay and some local authorities have opted out of national pay agreements for groups of specialist, non-manual staff. This happens, for example, where employers feel that national agreements constrain their own local authority from recruiting appropriate staff at 'industry' pay rates. Moreover, certain other professional groups, such as teachers in the 'new' universities (the 'old' polytechnics) and further education colleges in England and Wales, are no longer employed in the local authority sector but in 'corporations' in the private sector.

Among the remaining public corporations, pay bargaining is more likely to be at employer level than at establishment level. Where any local bargaining takes place it is normally over productivity, performance or local allowances for particular groups of workers, such as craftworkers. The tendency in public corporations in recent years, as in other parts of the public sector, has been to take senior managers out of collective bargaining arrangements and to relate their pay to performance, appraisal and job targets. It also seems that some remaining nationalized industries, such as British Rail and British Coal, are going to be privatized. Should this occur, it is probable that collective bargaining structures will be modified within them, post-privatization. What happens in practice will, no doubt, take account of market circumstances, managerial industrial relations objectives and the balance of bargaining power at the time.

It is Whitleyism, however, which provides the central feature of public sector collective bargaining. In outline, Whitleyism is firmly entrenched across the public sector except in organizations like the old universities and the British Broadcasting Corporation (BBC). The reasons why these sectors are not covered by Whitley negotiating arrangements are largely historical. Collective bargaining for traditional university teachers, for example, is of relatively recent origin and has no Whitley tradition. Similarly, collective bargaining in the coal and steel industries preceded nationalization. When these industries were taken into public ownership after the Second World War, they largely retained existing collective bargaining structures. Lastly, the BBC is a relatively small and specialist public enterprise with its own internal arrangements and traditions for industrial relations.

Basically, public sector Whitleyism provides a negotiating structure where there is 'a joint negotiating council at the national level for each major occupational grouping within each industry, while below these are councils at the regional, district, local or departmental levels'.[38] The negotiating machinery in local government, for example, is based on Whitley principles, with arrangements at national, provincial and local levels. At national level, there are two main national joint councils, and a number of

other central negotiating bodies or committees, for manual employees and white collar staff. These national bodies agree general terms and conditions for all employees in the appropriate categories. Whilst most local authorities tend to follow the terms of the national agreements, there is some scope for provincial and local negotiations. The various national negotiating bodies have employer representatives from the local authorities' associations, such as the Association of County Councils and Association of Metropolitan Authorities, as well as provincial council members.

At provincial council level, or intermediate between national and local authority level, there are separately constituted joint bodies in England and Wales, with representatives from local authorities and the trade unions. These consider matters referred to them by the main national councils, interpret and implement national agreements, and make recommendations to the national bodies. Provincial councils also negotiate agreement on local working practices, standby arrangements, training and on matters not dealt with by national agreements. At local authority level, in turn, there is a multiplicity of joint consultative committees. These deal with productivity issues, leave facilities, redundancy procedures, health and safety, and welfare, and are determined between local management and union representatives.

Another feature of public sector Whitleyism is that it operates on common negotiating principles, although details vary between sectors. Each joint council, for example, is a standing body which meets regularly and determines its own membership, without necessarily having equal representation from each side. Employer negotiators are normally known as the 'management side' and union negotiators as the 'staff side'. Each side has its 'leader', or chief representative, who is usually responsible for presenting their side's case at joint meetings. The detailed work of Whitley councils is usually carried out by appropriate subcommittees or joint working parties, at national, district or local levels. Largely because of this, the joint secretaries of these bodies play key roles in determining Whitley decisions. Plenary meetings often affirm what has already been agreed in committee.

Another major negotiating principle of Whitleyism is that decisions are normally taken by a majority of each side voting separately. This means in practice that no agreement can be made between the parties unless it is approved by a majority of both the employer and union representatives. This requires agreement within both sides, therefore, and neither side can outvote the other, thus compelling the acceptance of an agreement to which there is opposition. Though, on occasions, this makes joint agreement impossible, it has been a useful device for negotiators on both sides facing inflexible opposite numbers. In the past, at least, this convention has prevented determined employers from imposing unacceptable settlements upon union representatives against their will. More recently, however, government cash limit and cutback policies have effectively constrained the efficacy of public sector Whitleyism as an acceptable and fair method of pay determination. And the future of Whitleyism is in question as privatization continues, competitive tendering becomes more widespread and public sector organizations, such as the civil service and local government, are reorganized.

## Bargaining trends

Collective bargaining is a flexible process of conducting industrial relations. Indeed, it can be applied and adapted to a wide variety of contexts, where the parties want this. It varies in accordance with a number of factors. These include: the state of the economy; public and legal policy on industrial relations; the structure of industry; managerial objectives in industrial relations; the relationship of these to business strategy; technological imperatives; and the balance of bargaining power between employers and unions. For these and other reasons, collective bargaining is never static; it is constantly adapting in response to employer initiatives, union reactions and market pressures. Thus, compared with the 1960s and 1970s, the 1980s and 1990s have seen distinct changes in economic affairs, politics, social attitudes and the social structure. Bargaining structures, practices and outcomes, in turn, have been affected by these changes. One trend in collective bargaining, though by no means universal, has been for employers to resist union recognition claims, especially in greenfield sites. This is one reason why some employers have negotiated 'single union' and similar new-style agreements in their companies. Other employers have sought to individualize 'employee relations', by introducing employee commitment and involvement strategies into their organizations. In some cases, there have been examples of deunionization and derecognition, especially among management groups which formerly had bargaining arrangements. But as the Advisory Conciliation and Arbitra-

tion Service has commented on developments in 1992:

> Clear cases of de-recognition . . . remained infrequent: our staff became aware of about 80 cases over an 18-month period in which de-recognition was proposed by managements, covering fewer than 20 000 employees in total. In only about half of these did full de-recognition occur. A substantial proportion of these were in the South East and often involved technical, professional and other white collar staff.[39]

In the private sector, where multiunionism is common, some employers are increasingly determined to create 'single bargaining tables' where both manual and non-manual worker representatives sit and talk together. This means, in practice, in some companies, there are signs that new kinds of local forums may be emerging in which in-company representatives, not all of whom may be union members, are playing a greater and more authoritative role. However, while the 1990 WIRS shows that both multiple unions and multiple bargaining groups are becoming less common, 'there was no evidence of any *widespread* move towards "single table bargaining" where both manual and non-manual unions negotiated jointly'[40] (emphasis added). Overall, it would seem, employers and managements now have much greater confidence in handling collective bargaining issues than they appear to have had in the past. Indeed:

> managerial action, both directly and indirectly, is such a central influence on the unions that it is in some ways surprising that it is only in the 1980s that many organizations . . . realized that they [could] manage, rather than merely react to, the unions that they deal with.[41]

Employers and their representatives, then, are developing more strategic and planned approaches to collective bargaining units, levels, forms and scope. This is the case in both the private and the public sectors, where similar collective bargaining changes have taken place in a variety of organizations and enterprises.

Some managements, therefore, are taking deliberate initiatives to rationalize their bargaining units with the trade unions. Others are combining bargaining units into single table arrangements and others are derecognizing unions, where they can get away with it. The major trend in bargaining levels, as we have discussed earlier, is towards decentralization, either at corporate or at establishment level. All this is taking place in response to increasing pressures on employment costs and the need for cost-effective employment policies in organizations, whether private or public. What, then, are some of the trends in bargaining scope? Here we have some useful evidence from the WIRS 1990. Bargaining scope is not limited to pay. Other matters, such as hours of work and other conditions of employment, are negotiated between management and union representatives. As shown in Tables 6.7 and 6.8, other items, such as physical working conditions, redeployment, staffing levels, redundancy pay, recruitment and reorganization of working hours, are also negotiable.

The 1980 WIRS showed extensive bargaining on the first five items listed in Tables 6.7 and 6.8. But in the 1984 survey, there were very substantial falls in the extent of negotiation, in relation to both manual and non-manual workers. As the 1984 survey concluded:

> so far as manual workers were concerned, there appeared to be substantially less negotiation over non-pay issues in 1984 and the contrast was particularly marked at the work-place level. The decline in joint regulation appeared to be most marked in private services while nationalised industries seemed most immune from the trend. It was also very marked in manufacturing.[42]

According to the 1990 survey, however, there was little change in the amount of reported bargaining over non-pay issues between 1984 and 1990. For manual workers, there was a slight decrease, largely confined to manufacturing and the nationalized industries, but for non-manual workers no clear change was apparent. Further, whilst the extent to which such bargaining at workplace level declined between 1980 and 1984, this pattern was not repeated in the second half of the 1980s. There was no overall change in the extent of local bargaining affecting manual workers and there was a slight increase in relation to non-manual workers. As the WIRS 1990 concludes:

> Broadly speaking the results show a small convergence between the different sectors of the economy: those sectors with relatively extensive local negotiations about non-pay issues (manufacturing and the nationalized industries) showed, if anything, a decrease; sectors with less extensive local negotiations (the service sectors) showed mostly increases.[43]

Tables 6.7 and 6.8 also show some stability in the relative frequency on bargaining over the first five issues listed in 1984 and 1990, with the rank order remaining the same – for both manual and non-manual workers – whether the issue was negotiated at all or negotiated locally. Physical working conditions continued to be the most frequently negotiated issue and recruitment the least common one. The reorganization of working hours, asked in the 1990 survey, ranked highly in frequency and this was particularly the case for manual workers. 'In nearly 80 per cent of workplaces with recognized unions for manual workers managers reported that this issue was subject to joint negotiation.' There was also no change in the extent to which trade unions were involved in the introduction of new technology and major changes in work organization or working practices.

In 1984, 8 per cent of managers reported that changes involving new technology were negotiated with manual workers' representatives; in 1990 the equivalent figure was 6 per cent. In respect of changes in work organization or working practices the corresponding figures were 24 per cent in 1984 and 27 per cent in 1990.

Some new bargaining issues were reported in the 1990 survey by 11 per cent of the managers dealing with manual unions and by 8 per cent of those dealing with non-manual unions, with the greatest incidence being in the public sector. These issues ranged from fringe benefits and single status to payment systems, staffing levels and performance appraisal and training. Those matters most commonly mentioned were hours of work, fringe benefits and bonuses and payment systems. Overall, the impression given by the 1990 WIRS is that: 'in round terms over 90 per cent of workplaces with recognized unions bargained about the same range of issues as three years before'.[44]

These and related developments must not be overstated. But they do reflect the shift in bargaining power, and in negotiating initiatives, which has taken place in collective bargaining in recent years. Management, in short, is in the driving seat. Such developments also reflect the changes which have taken place in collective bargaining levels over the past decade or so. For example, there is little doubt that in many sectors, where national bargaining continues, national rates set only a floor and that wide variations exist between and within localities depending on local and plant agreements tailored to particular circumstances. Many managements

*Table 6.7* Managers' accounts of the extent of joint regulation with the largest manual bargaining unit over specified non-pay issues, by broad sector, 1984 and 1990 (per cent).

| | All establishments | | Private manufacturing | | Private services | | Nationalized industries | | Public services | |
|---|---|---|---|---|---|---|---|---|---|---|
| | 1984 | 1990 | 1984 | 1990 | 1984 | 1990 | 1984 | 1990 | 1984 | 1990 |
| Negotiated at some level: | | | | | | | | | | |
| Physical working conditions | 78 | 76 | 75 | 76 | 69 | 69 | 87 | 94 | 82 | 80 |
| Redeployment | 62 | 57 | 63 | 64 | 43 | 43 | 85 | 68 | 66 | 60 |
| Staffing levels | 55 | 50 | 47 | 34 | 40 | 32 | 77 | 80 | 62 | 69 |
| Size of redundancy pay | 46 | 42 | 51 | 45 | 44 | 46 | 37 | 21 | 48 | 41 |
| Recruitment | 38 | 32 | 31 | 24 | 21 | 18 | 41 | 12 | 49 | 50 |
| Reorganization of working hours | – | 78 | – | 88 | – | 72 | – | 98 | – | 74 |
| Negotiated at establishment level: | | | | | | | | | | |
| Physical working conditions | 39 | 42 | 64 | 58 | 33 | 42 | 63 | 72 | 24 | 28 |
| Redeployment | 33 | 32 | 55 | 50 | 27 | 26 | 69 | 35 | 19 | 26 |
| Staffing levels | 25 | 23 | 42 | 28 | 25 | 20 | 63 | 58 | 8 | 18 |
| Size of redundancy pay | 10 | 12 | 34 | 31 | 8 | 12 | 5 | – | 1 | 3 |
| Recruitment | 16 | 13 | 28 | 21 | 16 | 11 | 29 | 10 | 7 | 9 |
| Reorganization of working hours | – | 40 | – | 68 | – | 33 | – | 60 | – | 26 |

*Source:* WIRS, 1990

*Table 6.8* Managers' accounts of the extent of joint regulation with the largest non-manual bargaining unit over specified non-pay issues, by broad sector, 1984 and 1990 (per cent).

| | All establishments | | Private manufacturing | | Private services | | Nationalized industries | | Public services | |
|---|---|---|---|---|---|---|---|---|---|---|
| | 1984 | 1990 | 1984 | 1990 | 1984 | 1990 | 1984 | 1990 | 1984 | 1990 |
| Negotiated at some level: | | | | | | | | | | |
| Physical working conditions | 76 | 78 | 60 | 66 | 69 | 70 | 81 | 88 | 81 | 82 |
| Redeployment | 61 | 62 | 61 | 64 | 44 | 52 | 80 | 63 | 65 | 66 |
| Staffing levels | 55 | 56 | 42 | 41 | 32 | 36 | 77 | 90 | 62 | 65 |
| Size of redundancy pay | 49 | 51 | 51 | 59 | 53 | 72 | 38 | 36 | 48 | 41 |
| Recruitment | 39 | 40 | 26 | 22 | 25 | 22 | 38 | 37 | 48 | 51 |
| Reorganization of working hours | – | 46 | – | 84 | – | 32 | – | 88 | – | 45 |
| Negotiated at establishment level: | | | | | | | | | | |
| Physical working conditions | 30 | 34 | 48 | 43 | 18 | 32 | 50 | 46 | 27 | 33 |
| Redeployment | 26 | 30 | 51 | 43 | 18 | 22 | 52 | 26 | 20 | 33 |
| Staffing levels | 17 | 20 | 32 | 31 | 10 | 17 | 52 | 52 | 11 | 18 |
| Size of redundancy pay | 5 | 6 | 31 | 36 | 5 | 7 | 5 | 3 | 1 | 2 |
| Recruitment | 12 | 13 | 20 | 16 | 11 | 14 | 21 | 16 | 9 | 11 |
| Reorganization of working hours | – | 31 | – | 57 | – | 26 | – | 42 | – | 29 |

*Source:* WIRS, 1990

seek arrangements on pay and conditions which tie rewards to local labour and product market factors. Indeed, a number of companies and employers which until recently were parties to multiemployer or single employer centralized bargaining have moved to decentralized bargaining arrangements. Examples include road transport, electrical engineering and banking. Increasingly, it seems, companies are organized into discrete budget, profit and product centres. This requires unit managers taking responsibility for all operational activities. 'These developments provide a narrower focus for employment relationships, particularly in larger enterprises, and raise questions about how terms and conditions should be decided and co-ordinated'.[44]

Collective bargaining and industrial relations, then, are increasingly management and employer led. Indeed, Brewster and Connock claim that it is cost-effectiveness in industrial relations which is the touchstone against which management is being judged. This in turn requires coherent industrial relations strategies, with industrial relations and collective bargaining being closely related to the overall objectives of the organization. 'The notion of cost-effectiveness involves reduction in costs on the one hand and performance improvement on the other.' Thus the ultimate arbiter is the ability of firms to achieve sufficient returns on capital invested in the private sector, to allow for further investment in the future. Increased flexibility therefore becomes a key aspect of organizational management. This involves flexibility in task, working time and contractual arrangements. Pressures to improve cost-effectiveness are also leading to renewed emphasis on employee communications and 'may also require a focus on bargaining structures and trade union facilities'.

In these circumstances, collective bargaining and industrial relations policies and plans have to be adaptable and capable of adjustment. As Brewster and Connock write, for many organizations, 'the process of developing achievable objectives for labour relations in one, three or five years' time is becoming ever more vital – and increasingly widespread'. The emphasis is on the company's business objectives and how its industrial relations and collective bargaining strategies can contribute to business efficiency and success. Senior executives are looking at industrial relations 'in terms of costs, efficiency and flexibility; developing policies appropriate to these aims; and establishing monitoring and controls to make the policies operational'.[45]

## 6.5   Collective Agreements

Collective agreements are the output or result of the collective bargaining process. First, they provide constitutional frameworks by which the parties to collective bargaining can make, apply and monitor the industrial relations decisions affecting themselves and those on whose behalf they negotiate. Second, they define the market and managerial relations between employers and employees. If they are to be understood and adhered to by the parties, collective agreements need to be written and formalized. This is not to argue that formality of agreements in itself improves industrial relations. Indeed an overformal approach in collective bargaining inducing hairsplitting arguments over the meanings of words is not conducive to effective industrial relations between employers and trade unions or between managers and union stewards. Indeed, much collective bargaining is conducted informally, even when it is within the negotiating frameworks provided by regularized procedural arrangements. However, most collective agreements are more formalized than in the past and are put in writing where possible. This contrasts with those earlier 'agreements' in the 1960s and 1970s which were often based on 'shared understandings' and 'custom and practice' between negotiators at workplace level.

Written agreements largely overcome the problems arising in informal and poorly documented industrial relations situations when any of the main participants change for one reason or another. The continuity between the parties provided by written agreements is vital. Moreover, the stability which they introduce into collective bargaining can contribute to organizational and industrial relations change. But to repeat:

> Formal agreements are not a solution to all
> industrial relations problems. Their introduction
> can, however, herald a fresh start and can lead
> to industrial relations practices which, in the
> right conditions, should bring order into the
> working relationship from which could develop a
> genuine understanding.[46]

This is not to suggest that workers stop bargaining informally with management if they are powerful enough to do this. Indeed, informal practices are likely to be a permanent feature of industrial relations where there are powerful workgroups.

As outlined above, collective agreements are negotiated at various levels within different industries. They may even be struck at more than one level within an industry. These levels include: multi-employer, national or industry-wide agreements; regional or district agreements; single employer or company agreements; and plant and establishment agreements. Similarly, agreements may be negotiated between a single employer and a single union, as between the Post Office and the Union of Communication Workers for postal grades in the postal services; between one employer and a number of unions, as for manual grades in the Ford Motor Company; between a number of employers and a number of unions, as in the various local authority negotiating groups; between an employers' association and a single union, as in the electrical contracting industry; and between an employers' association and a number of unions, as in the chemical industry. Collective agreements are also negotiated between employer representatives and full-time union officers or between management representatives and union stewards.

Collective agreements are commonly classified as being either 'procedural' or 'substantive', although it is possible in practice to have both procedural and substantive elements within the same agreement. It has been suggested that:

> The procedural clauses of these agreements deal with such matters as the methods to be used and the stages to be followed in the settlement of disputes, or perhaps the facilities and standing to be accorded to representatives of parties to the agreement. Their substantive clauses, on the other hand, refer to rates of wages and working hours or to other job terms and conditions in the segment of employment covered by agreement. The first kind of rules regulate the behaviour of parties to the collective agreements – trade unions and employers or their associations, and those who act on their behalf; whereas the second kind regulate the behaviour of employees and employers as parties to individual contracts of employment.[47]

Procedural agreements, in other words, regulate relations between the parties to collective bargaining, define the bargaining units, and determine the status and facilities for trade union representatives in the bargaining process. Substantive agreements, on the other hand, regulate jobs, the pay for them, and the conditions under which they are performed. In practice, however, an agreement on the procedure for training union stewards, which also lays down the substantive payments they should receive whilst on union business, contains both procedural and substantive clauses. There is a tendency for procedural agreements to have a separate and a long-term existence. Substantive agreements tend to be altered more regularly to take account of changes in the employment relationship.

## Procedural agreements

There are a wide range of procedural agreements in practice. For example:

> There are jointly-agreed procedures for the negotiation of wage settlements, for the resolution of disputes, for settling individual pay and grading issues, for dealing with individual grievances, for handling disciplinary cases, for reaching decisions on dismissals, for recruitment, for training, for redundancy and indeed for any class of business which is brought within the area subject to negotiation.[48]

There is a tendency for the areas coming within the boundaries of collective bargaining to be constantly changed, wherever negotiating arrangements have been successfully concluded. The joint procedures governing negotiating behaviour and terms and conditions at work are influenced by a number of factors. These include: the industry; its technology; the size and geographical spread of establishments; the quality and style of workplace management; and the extent of trade union organization. They involve all the personal, local, historical and social forces helping to shape the patterns of collective bargaining within the individual industry and establishment.

It has been suggested that 'the cornerstone of collective bargaining in Britain is the procedure agreement'.[49] A procedural relationship between an employer and a trade union is established as soon as the union's right to represent the collective interests of its members is recognized. It is the practice of settling pay and conditions of employment through a negotiating procedure which frequently leads to the development of further joint procedures covering a wide range of areas of common concern to employers, trade unions and their members. In outline, the procedural act of recognition establishing negotiation rights is usually concerned: first, with defining the area in which the representative capacity of the trade unions is acknowledged; second, with indicating the subjects which are to be brought within the scope of joint regulation; and third, with specifying the steps by which agreement is to be sought and the procedure to be followed if there is a failure to agree between the parties. Obviously negotiating procedures do not conform to standard patterns and cannot be readily stereotyped. They vary by industry, the levels at which bargaining takes place, the characteristics and objectives of management and unions and so on. But the recognition agreement is the key one.

In private industry, for example, employers sometimes negotiate a comprehensive set of procedural agreements with trade union representatives at company or enterprise level. The items covered by such agreements include: defining the parties to the agreements; specifying the respective responsibilities of the parties; setting out the general principles of the agreements; and drawing up either a '*status quo*' or a 'right to manage' clause or both. The latter deal with how changes in working methods or employment conditions are to be handled. They are predominantly found in the engineering industries. A *status quo* clause, for example, usually states that when changes in working conditions are to be made by management, and when prior agreement has not been reached between management and the unions, the *status quo* shall prevail. Actions proposed by management, that is, shall not be implemented if objected to by the employees and their representatives, until either agreement has been reached by negotiation or the procedure to avoid disputes has been exhausted. The *status quo* also requires unions wishing to change working practices to make full use of the procedure for the avoidance of disputes before any departure from existing practices takes place. A right to manage clause, on the other hand, usually reserves the right of management to impose changes in employment or working conditions unilaterally, without negotiation or consultation of any kind. Right to manage clauses usually provide for consultation with the trade unions but not negotiation.

Other clauses in a set of comprehensive procedural agreements at company level might comprise: union membership arrangements; deduction of union contributions at source or the 'check off' system; and the appointment and function of trade union representatives, usually union stewards, within the procedures. There may also be redeployment and redundancy agreements and a disciplinary code. In the latter case, it is generally held that it is management's duty to maintain discipline within the workplace, whilst it is the union's duty to represent its members within the disciplinary framework. Management is also normally held responsible for taking the initiative

and ensuring that there are adequate disciplinary rules and procedures at the workplace, although trade unions are obviously interested in seeing that disciplinary arrangements are used consistently and fairly in the interests of their members.

The most important types of procedural agreement are the individual grievance procedure and the procedure to avoid disputes. 'Expressed in the broadest possible terms, procedures are both treaties of peace and devices for the avoidance of war.'[50] The grievance procedure, for example, is commonly regarded as the means by which individual employees can raise an issue of complaint to management about their pay or conditions of work. It lays down the steps for dealing with such matters. The aim of the grievance procedure is to resolve these issues – the amount of overtime payment received by an employee, the legitimacy or reasonableness of supervisory instructions, or the quantity of overtime allocated to an individual worker, say – as near as possible to the point of the original complaint. It is generally agreed that grievance procedures should be equitable in the ways in which employees are treated, simple to understand and rapid in their operation. Initially a grievance is normally discussed between an employee and his or her immediate superior. If the matter remains unresolved, the employee can then be accompanied at the next stage of the procedure by his or her workplace representative. If the issue is not settled at this level, it may then be taken to higher levels of management until either it is resolved, with or without trade union representation, or a 'failure to agree' is recorded.

In the engineering industry, for example, there are both domestic stages and external stages in the procedure for the avoidance of disputes with manual workers. The domestic stage has to be agreed in the establishment concerned and:

> This should cover such matters as the number of stages, the stage at which the shop stewards and, where recognised, the chief shop steward shall be involved, the level of management to be involved at each stage, the procedural level at which matters (whether individual, sectional or general) shall be raised by the party concerned, and the time limits within which different types of question shall be discussed.[51]

It is also agreed that where there is a 'Works Committee', it shall be the final stage in the domestic procedure. However, a works committee's decision on a particular issue does not prevent either party from referring the matter to an external conference for further discussion subsequently.

If an issue is not settled at the final domestic stage of procedure in the engineering industry, it can then be referred on behalf of either party to an external conference. This involves 'representatives of the employers' association and local officials of the trade union(s) concerned, as well as the management representative(s) and the shop steward(s) concerned'. Such conferences are supposed to be held within seven working days of receiving a written application from the party wishing to pursue the reference, although usually both parties agree a convenient date to suit their availability. It is also expressly agreed:

> In order to allow for the peaceful resolution of any matter raised by any party, there shall be no stoppages of work, either of a partial or general character, such as a strike, lock-out, go-slow, work-to-rule, overtime ban or any other restrictions, before the stages of procedure provided for . . . have been exhausted.[52]

Only after a 'failure to agree' has been recorded is either side free to take unilateral industrial action against the other. Matters concerning the interpretation or application of national agreements in engineering, on the other hand, are expected to be discussed at national level within seven working days on receipt of a written application, although this rarely happens now.

In practice individual grievances can give rise to collective disputes; thus, where trade unions are recognized, individual grievances and collective disputes are often dealt with through the same procedure. Alternatively, where there are separate grievance and disputes procedures, they are sometimes linked so that issues can pass from the grievance procedure into the disputes procedure. Disputes also occur through failure to agree on matters originating in the negotiating procedure. Hence in the event of differences arising between the parties, negotiating procedures commonly provide for these issues to be passed into the collective disputes procedure. The disputes procedure can therefore be a feature or an element in both a grievance and a negotiating procedure. Negotiating and grievance procedures with their associated disputes provisions, in other words, are sometimes kept separate; in other cases the disputes procedure is used to process all matters arising either from general negotiations or from the functioning of the grievance procedure.

If no distinctions are made between a negotiating procedure and a grievance procedure, it is usually in those situations where all the dealings with trade union representatives are regarded as a form of negotiation.

> Where there is a recognised distinction between negotiating and grievance procedures it may not be clear-cut in cases where the negotiating machinery is embodied as a stage in the grievance procedure or where an issue arising as a sectional grievance is adopted as the subject of a formal claim.[53]

The main objects of the machinery for resolving differences between management and trade unionists in Britain are to make, apply and interpret collective agreements, and to deal with grievances affecting either individuals or groups of employees. Typically most industrial relations procedures in Britain do not define the broad issues of rights and duties to be claimed under them in any exact way. Furthermore, it is not usual for a distinction to be made 'between the process of applying and interpreting existing agreements, as against the process of formulating new ones'.[54] The same procedures are used to process disputes of 'right' arising out of existing agreements and disputes of 'interest' arising out of matters not covered by existing agreements. Despite their constitutional diversity, British disputes procedures have three common features: they consist of a number of well-defined procedural stages; they lay down time limits for each stage of the procedure; and they are intended to preclude strikes or other forms of industrial action until all the stages of the procedure have been completed, including sometimes independent arbitration, and a failure to agree has been formally recorded.

## Substantive agreements

Substantive agreements vary widely according to the industry or organization in which they are determined. They may be broadly classified as: pay agreements; agreements on working conditions; and agreements on fringe benefits and other payments. Pay agreements for example cover: hourly rates of pay; salaries; pay structures; payment by results; productivity payments; incremental pay scales; minimum weekly earnings; overtime premiums; unsocial hours payments; shift-work pay; nightwork payments; maternity pay; holiday pay; call-out payments; length of service supplements; sick pay; and so on. Agreements on working conditions are mainly concerned with hours of work, length of the working week, holiday arrangements and annual leave, maternity leave, shift-work rotas, special work clothing, other allowances and so on. It is much more difficult, however, to specify the precise nature of fringe benefits and other payments. One reason for this is that what is initially regarded as a fringe benefit in an agreement, such as holiday pay or sickness pay, may once negotiated become a standard item in the employment package of the workers concerned. In this way, such benefits are open to continual improvement by further negotiation. More generally, however, fringe benefits include such items as retirement pensions, medical care, housing, social and recreation facilities, travelling and subsistence allowances, low-cost loans and so on.

## New-style agreements

During the 1980s, a number of 'new-style' collective agreements were negotiated between certain employers and some unions. These were variously described as 'single union' deals, 'no-strike' deals or agreements incorporating 'pendulum' arbitration arrangements. The major trade union involved in these new-style negotiations, the Electrical Electronic Telecommunications and Plumbing Union (EETPU), which is now part of the Amalgamated Engineering and Electrical Union, described them as 'high-technology' agreements. Roy Sanderson, national officer of the EETPU, is credited as the architect on the union side of most of the EETPU's new-style agreements. These new-style agreements generated some debate and dissent within the Trades Union Congress (TUC). Among the arguments made against such deals are that they:

exclude other unions who [sic] may have some membership in the unit covered by the agreement; or exclude unions which previously held recognition or bargaining rights; [and] lead unions to compete with each other for employers' approval which encourages dilution of trade union standards and procedures.[55]

Sanderson and others defend such agreements against allegations of 'sweetheart deals' by claiming that they enhance both the individual and collective rights of employees. New-style or high-technology agreements are justified, it is argued, because they are based on the view that:

the industrial relations system should be designed as a means of improving the quality of life of

employees, not as a means of waging a revolutionary struggle. [The] intention is to replace the adversarial approach and confrontation with co-ordination and co-operation with fair employers.[56]

Although there are examples of new-style agreements in the motor industry, such as between the engineering workers' union and Nissan, in newspaper production and elsewhere, the most notable examples involve Japanese high-technology companies and the engineers and electricians. They also typically involve green field sites. Ideally, the company begins operations with new site, plant, technology and industrial relations arrangements. Their distinguishing features may not be equally present in all greenfield sites, since employer motivations for starting afresh or anew vary widely.

But new-style agreements in greenfield site firms do have a common team approach to work organization, fewer managerial levels than most manufacturing firms, and an emphasis on two-way communication. Moreover, these firms utilize fewer manual grades than older manufacturing plants, data to support production targets, and a more open consultative management style. . . . Finally, the parties' advisory discussions generally encompass all aspects of organizational performance and employee welfare standards.[57]

The prototype new-style collective agreement was negotiated between Toshiba Consumer Products (UK) Ltd and the EETPU in April 1981. This agreement grew out of the closing of Rank Toshiba Ltd in 1980 and a loss of over 2 000 jobs at the Plymouth and Redruth plants, where the joint Anglo-Japanese venture came to an end in 1981. 'Toshiba Consumer Products (UK) Ltd arose out of the ashes to sign the first new-style agreement with the EETPU in April 1981.' Other employers and unions followed during the 1980s. The unions included the engineers, Transport and General Workers Union, the print-workers and the General Municipal and Boiler-makers. With their emphases on bargaining rights rather than interests, on co-operation and consensus rather than conflict, and on procedure rather than informality, the new-style agreements are probably more important than is suggested by the relatively small number of firms and employees they now cover. Whilst none of the individual elements of the new-style agreements is novel in itself, taken collectively 'they represent a radical departure from the traditional adversarial approach to [British] collective bargaining'. They also demonstrate that some fundamental changes are taking place in a number of British collective bargaining relationships, 'although it is difficult to predict how common these nontraditional agreements will become'.[58]

New-style agreements contain a number of common elements: single union recognition; single employment status; labour flexibility; consultative/ negotiating councils; no-strike or 'peace' clauses; and pendulum arbitration arrangements. Single union recognition provides that only one union is recognized for collective bargaining purposes. It does not preclude employees being members of other unions. Nor does it preclude employees being non-unionists. But only one union is accepted by management as the negotiating agent. Single status is aimed at reducing diversity in the terms and conditions of employment amongst factory, office and managerial employees. Where possible, conditions are harmonized, annual standard salaries are provided and status differentials are removed. This means that there is only one canteen, no reserved parking, the use of first names by all employees and identical uniforms for everyone, including managers.

Labour flexibility is achieved by a variety of means. These include: fewer job gradings compared with other firms; no job descriptions; pay geared to acquiring additional skills; and enhanced job security through the employer providing advanced training and retraining. It is expected that these arrangements will result in greater job satisfaction by staff and more commitment to corporate goals and objectives. Company joint consultative and negotiating councils provide the forums where pay is negotiated and employee representatives have the opportunity to influence how their companies are run. Normally, all employees are eligible for election to company councils, not just trade unionists or solely representatives of the single union with negotiating rights. In essence, company councils provide a channel for advice, consultation and information. In this way, both the union and the employee representatives become directly involved in discussions of the company's business plans, investment policies, operating efficiency and manpower or human resources planning. This is in addition to the customary topics of wages, hours and other conditions of employment.

No-strike or peace clauses in the new-style agreements are their most controversial element. The procedures in these agreements provide a mechanism which, it is claimed, 'offers the possibility of "strike free" agreements, and which reflect a harmonious or mutually convenient/complementary relationship between the parties rather than one of conflict'.[59] The object of these clauses is that the employer and the union commit themselves to resolve all disputes without recourse to industrial action. Such arrangements are not legally enforceable but an unauthorized strike by employees would constitute a breach of the parties' agreed procedure. In practice, of course, as ACAS concedes, no 'agreement in itself . . . can provide a guarantee that industrial action will never take place although it can emphasise the seriousness with which the parties undertake to seek to avoid disputes'.[60]

The device which is linked with the no-strike or peace provisions of the new-style agreements is pendulum or 'final offer' arbitration. Where conciliation fails, pendulum arbitration is used. This is illustrated in the Nissan agreement, which states:

> In the event of conciliation not producing a solution both parties may agree to arbitration. The arbitrator will be requested to determine positively in favour of one side or the other. The arbitrator will be asked to take account of those aspects which are already agreed. Both parties agree to accept the decision of the arbitrator.[61]

Final offer arbitration is designed to foreclose the possibility of striking by providing third-party, binding arbitration. After the parties have exhausted attempts to resolve a dispute by all other means, the arbitrator is expected to rule for one side or the other. He or she is precluded from making a decision which is a compromise between the two sides.

Grievance, discipline and dismissal disputes are resolved by the parties themselves, through the relevant procedures. It is impasses in negotiation which are referred to the arbitrator. Burrows suggests that the new-style agreements partially recognize the distinction between interest and rights issues. Thus the negotiating and disputes procedures in new-style agreements are based on the mutually accepted rights of the parties. 'The stated intention of the parties is to reconcile the few remaining differences of "interest" on substantive issues (notably pay) by in-company negotiations. Where a difference of "interest" persists, pendulum arbitration provides an outcome'.[62]

The claimed advantages of pendulum or final offer arbitration are that each side states its case and makes a reasonable offer. The arbitrator then tries to bring the two sides together by persuasion which, if it fails, enables a settlement for one side, or the other, to be made. It is argued that such a process causes little loss of face for either party, since the two sides are not far apart in the first place. One side is entirely satisfied, whilst the other does not feel that it has lost as much, or gained as much, as with conventional compromise arbitration.

It is also argued that new-style bargaining and new-style agreements provide advantages to all the parties involved. For the employer, there is only one union with which to deal, job flexibility and less likelihood of disputes. It can also expect more moderate pay claims. On the union side, there is negotiating security, full consultation and resort to pendulum arbitration. Employees, in turn, obtain single status, job security and involvement in decision making. However:

> specific objections by TUC affiliates to the practices of the EETPU [and single union deals] have concentrated on that union's willingness to sign single union agreements, particularly in circumstances which deprive other trade unions of their existing rights of recognition and negotiation.[63]

The novelty, extent and coverage of new style agreements must not be exaggerated, however, as shown by research by Industrial Relations Services (IRS) and Gall. According to IRS, for example, who looked at a number of case studies covering the 1980s, the industrial relations procedures incorporated in 'single union' organizations have developed in a range of formats, with no simple model becoming predominant. 'Moreover, no single element of the package is truly innovative or entirely "new" to arrangements already being practised by many companies in Britain'.[64] Gall, in turn, argues that only some 200 000 employees were covered by such agreements in 1993, out of a national workforce of some 24 million and some 9.5 million trade union members, with four companies – Tesco, ASDA, Midland Bank and the TSB – employing 165 000 of them. He concludes that 'numerically these "new style agreements" are still of negligible importance'.[65]

There is also convincing evidence that the rate of growth of new style agreements has declined since 1989, with the issue being transcended by others such as human resources management, employee involvement and employee communication. The reasons given for this are as follows. First, there has been a reduction in new inward investment because of world recession and therefore a reduction in greenfield sites and new style agreements. Second, simplified bargaining arrangements, such as single table bargaining, where multiunionism exists, are seen by some employers as alternatives to single unionism. Third, unions like the GMB and the transport workers have become increasingly dissatisfied with new style agreements, since they have found that they do not guarantee high membership levels and employee participation. This is because the employer selects the union to be recognized, thus undermining employee choice, and the negotiating structures which are created are often restrictive, thus rendering the union ineffective. Gall concludes that if the number of new-style agreements does not increase in the near future, 'they will still remain numerically a minor issue, although politically they may resume their former importance'.[66]

## 6.6   Industrial Action

The essence of the employer–employee relationship and the management–union relationship is that they are power-based. This means that unless there is a reasonable balance of power between the two sides, the stronger party might choose to use its power differential, or the threat of it, to impose its policies on the other weaker industrial relations participant. The purposes of industrial relations processes are to moderate the use of excessive power imbalances between the parties to the employment contract and to facilitate constitutional resolution of employer–employee and management–union conflict. The main implications of this power situation are, first, that each party seeks to impose on the other those conditions of employment – in their widest sense – which best suit its own interests. Second, where there is no agreement, consensus, or balance of power between the parties to the employment relationship as to what constitutes fair terms and conditions of employment between them, the stronger party seeks to impose its will unilaterally upon the weaker side. In order to achieve their respective goals, in other words, there is the likelihood of employers ultimately imposing sanctions on their subordinates; and of subordinate employees – either individually or collectively – ultimately imposing their own sanctions against their employers. Such sanctions may generally be described as 'industrial action'. Although industrial action is popularly associated with the use of the strike weapon against employers by trade unions, there is a wide range of industrial sanctions which management, unions and employees can use to further their immediate industrial relations objectives.

## Types of action

Historically, the balance of industrial power rested overwhelmingly in favour of the employer. Even the so-called change in the relative balance of industrial bargaining power to the advantage of organized workers in the 1960s and 1970s must not be exaggerated, although in the 1980s and 1990s, with high levels of unemployment and weakened trade unions, industrial relations was very much employer-led and management-driven. Some strategic groups of employees continue to have considerable short-term bargaining strength such as some computer operators, gas workers, railway signalworkers and similar groups, but this is not the general rule. Most employees do not have much collective strength and ultimately, even in the above named industries, long-term industrial power rests predominantly with the employers. Employers and management, in the final resort, can use a variety of industrial sanctions against their workers where they choose to do so. This is especially true where employees are weakly organized or are not organized at all.

Managerial sanctions against employees manifest themselves in the form of uncoordinated and individual actions or organized and collective actions. Uncoordinated and individual industrial action by management against subordinates, for instance, is typically found in non-union situations. It includes: close supervision; tight works discipline; discriminatory employment practices against certain employees; lay-offs; demotions; and the unofficial speeding up of work processes or job tasks. Organized and collective sanctions by management, on the other hand, include: the withdrawal of overtime; mass suspensions; the unilateral changing of work standards or piecework prices; the tactical precipitation of strikes; locking-out; the closing down of enterprises; and the removal of plant and machinery at the workplace.

The withdrawing of overtime or mass suspensions, for example, is sometimes used as a preliminary collective tactic by management to impress its intention on union negotiators that it proposes standing firm on a particular employment issue during negotiations. Similarly, the unilateral imposition of work standards by management over subordinates might be part of an overall strategy to precipitate a strike situation with the trade unions with which it

negotiates. This can happen, for instance, when order books are low but stock levels are high within a firm. In order to avoid having to pay lay-off money to its workers, or to prevent further stockpiling of its products, management is sometimes both instrumental and successful in precipitating strike action among its employees. This enables management, first, to run down its stocks and, second, to provide sufficient work for its employees, including overtime, when market conditions are more favourable. Precipitating strike action, of course, also makes it possible for management to appear the innocent party to an industrial dispute. In these circumstances, management can imply that it was union action in the first place which caused the industrial action to be taken.

Lock-outs by employers, whilst only one element in a total conflict situation, are in fact often difficult to distinguish from strikes. Yet the question of which party makes an initial declaration to act against the other is in practice immaterial. It seems likely, however, that nowadays employers only use the lock-out tactic very infrequently in order to achieve their industrial relations objectives. First, to do so might adversely affect their public images and inflame public opinion. Second, they can usually obtain the same ends by other means. Whilst employer lock-outs were more common in the past, especially in the private sector and usually when trade union power was weak, they are much rarer today.

The closing down of factories and offices, and certainly the threat by management to remove plant and machinery from their premises, is a much more likely managerial tactic in the circumstances of modern business organization. Some people would not even view such activities as coming within the ambit of organized industrial action. They would merely see them as legitimate managerial rights, either to liquidate uneconomic enterprises, thus necessitating redundancies, or to coerce uncooperative workers to comply with employer requirements at the workplace. Managerial actions of this sort can very occasionally lead to sit-ins and work-ins by employees.

Sit-ins and work-ins are mass occupations of employer premises by disaffected workers. They are used as alternative tactics to the more traditional forms of industrial action by trade unionists and workers. There are two types of occupation: a redundancy sit-in or work-in as a protest against the closure of a plant or company; and a collective bargaining sit-in to take the place of more traditional forms of industrial action such as working to rule, overtime bans, and all out strikes.

The two main characteristics of sit-ins and work-ins are the illegal occupation of an employer's premises against its wishes, and the exercising of countervailing control over the establishment by the occupiers. There seem to be three principal reasons why these tactics are sometimes favoured in preference to more traditional forms of organized industrial action by trade unionists. First, they offer some degree of control over the establishment being occupied, which is obviously important in redundancy situations where the removal of plant and machinery to other locations is being threatened. Second, since such actions take place on private property, this reduces the likelihood of conflict with the police. Third, by working-in or sitting-in, employees are better able to maintain their morale and group solidarity. Strikers, for example, often lose contact with their fellow workers, whilst some of them take up other jobs during protracted disputes. Normally employers tend to maintain a fairly low-key profile in dealing with trade union tactics of this sort. This is probably because of the long-term damage to industrial relationships which might be incurred in evoking the law, the cost to the company of the occupation, the effects on employees not involved in the action and the effect of the occupation on the organization's customers.

Other potential industrial actions which employees can impose on management are wide ranging. As in the case of managerial sanctions, a distinction has to be made between individual and unorganized actions on the part of workers and organized or group sanctions on the other.

Put simply, in unorganized conflict the worker typically responds to the oppressive situation in the only way open to him *as an individual*. . . . Such reaction rarely derives from any calculative strategy. . . . Organised conflict, on the other hand, is far more likely to form part of a conscious strategy to change the situation which is identified as the source of discontent.[66]

Unorganized industrial action, for instance, manifests itself in several ways. This includes: high labour turnover; bad time-keeping; excessive levels of absenteeism; withholding of effort; inefficient working; deliberate time-wasting and so on. Other symptoms of unorganized industrial action by individuals include continuous 'complaints, friction, infractions of rules, and similar evidences of low morale and

discontent'.[67] A study undertaken in four Lancashire coalmines found that among surface and underground workers 'low morale is associated with a high level of "unorganised" conflict and *vice versa*. On the other hand, we do not assume that high morale and "organised" conflict are necessarily opposed'.[68]

Organized and group industrial action against management is equally diverse and has similarly deep roots. The so-called Luddites or machine breakers, for example, were among the first groups of workers to collectively oppose the unilateral introduction of new technology into their factories by the early textile manufacturers in the nineteenth century. Nowadays, collective opposition by employees to managerial decisions is normally less violent. But it is no less serious for that, since management has to cope with its modern manifestations. At its blandest, organized industrial action by trade unionists can take the forms of working without enthusiasm, non-co-operation with management, going slow, or working to rule. A work to rule, for instance, usually involves an interruption of normal work processes by not carrying out what the employees regard as their non-contractual activities. It can entail the carrying out of managerial orders to the letter by the groups in dispute with management. It can result in workers strictly observing the safety or works rules which are normally disregarded by them, even though they are technically in breach of their contracts of employment. It is interesting to note that in working to rule, and where management's orders are obeyed, employees are not generally in breach of their contracts of employment. In deliberately going slow, however, employees are potentially open to action for such a breach, although employers rarely if ever seek legal remedies in such circumstances.

Another type of organized industrial action taken by workers collectively is the overtime ban. From the trade union viewpoint it is a weapon which needs to be used carefully. As a tactical weapon within a broader strategy it has great value. 'As a final weapon with no back-up, its usefulness is less certain, although it may work for less important issues'.[69] An overtime ban has the added disadvantages to trade unionists that it results in loss of pay, with corresponding financial gains for management. A ban on overtime, in other words, is only an 'intermediate' method of taking organized industrial action against employers. It is often used, for instance, to demonstrate to managements that the workforce is united and determined to take further collective action if their negotiating demands are not met. The

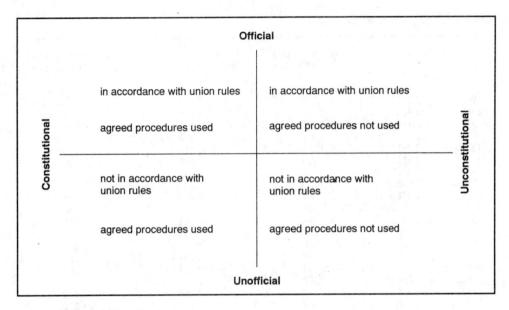

*Figure 6.1* Categories of strike action.

implication usually is that if the overtime ban fails to elicit the necessary responses from the employer, then tougher industrial sanctions will be imposed by the trade unions and their members.

The ultimate collective sanction used by trade unionists against management is the strike or industrial stoppage. Stoppages of work are normally connected with terms and conditions of employment: when initiated by employees they are described as strikes, when initiated by employers they are lock-outs. Strikes can be official or unofficial and constitutional or unconstitutional. Official strikes are where a union 'officially' supports its members in accordance with union rules during a dispute. A constitutional strike is one taking place after negotiations through the agreed procedure for avoiding disputes have been exhausted and a 'failure to agree' recorded. As shown in Figure 6.1 four main categories of strike action are possible.

## Stoppages

Information about the number of stoppages resulting from industrial disputes annually is collected by the Department of Employment's network of unemployment benefit offices. No distinction is made between strikes and lock-outs, with political strikes and small stoppages involving fewer than 10 workers or lasting less than a day excluded, except where the aggregate number of days lost exceeds 100. There is also a pos-

sible under-recording of disputes, particularly those near the margins of definition. As shown in Table 6.9, there were 369 recorded stoppages of work in the UK during 1991. This was about half the number in each of the previous three years, some three times less than in the early to mid-1980s and some eight times less than during the 1970s.

Because of the recording difficulties relating to numbers of stoppages, another measure – the number of workers involved in stoppages – is a better indicator of the impact of industrial disputes than is the number of stoppages themselves. The total number of workers involved in stoppages is obtained by aggregating the workers directly and indirectly involved in separate stoppages during that year. Any industrial action not affecting the usual working day, such as works to rule and overtime bans, are excluded, as are overtime working, weekend working which is not normal and public holidays. The number of workers involved in stoppages in progress in 1991 was 176 000. This was the lowest recorded level for 25 years, and especially low in comparison with the late 1960s and 1970s.

Another measure of stoppage activity is the number of working days lost in stoppages per year. These are estimates resulting from stoppages at establishments where the disputes occurred. As with other measures, a distinction is made between stoppages 'beginning in year' and those 'in progress in year', including those continuing from the previous

*Table 6.9* Stoppages in the UK 1967–91.

| Year | Stoppages | Workers involved in stoppages (000s) in progress in year | Working days lost in stoppages (000s) in progress in year | Working days lost per 1000 employees |
|------|-----------|-----------|-----------|-----------|
| 1967 | 2 133 | 734 | 2 787 | N/A |
| 1968 | 2 390 | 2 258 | 4 690 | N/A |
| 1969 | 3 146 | 1 665 | 6 846 | N/A |
| 1970 | 3 943 | 1 801 | 10 980 | N/A |
| 1971 | 2 263 | 1 178 | 13 551 | 612 |
| 1972 | 2 530 | 1 734 | 23 909 | 1 080 |
| 1973 | 2 902 | 1 528 | 7 197 | 317 |
| 1974 | 2 946 | 1 626 | 14 750 | 647 |
| 1975 | 2 332 | 809 | 6 012 | 265 |
| 1976 | 2 034 | 668 | 3 284 | 146 |
| 1977 | 2 737 | 1 166 | 10 142 | 448 |
| 1978 | 2 498 | 1 041 | 9 405 | 413 |
| 1979 | 2 125 | 4 608 | 29 474 | 1 273 |
| 1980 | 1 348 | 834 | 11 964 | 521 |
| 1981 | 1 344 | 1 513 | 4 266 | 195 |
| 1982 | 1 538 | 2 103 | 5 313 | 248 |
| 1983 | 1 364 | 574 | 3 754 | 178 |
| 1984 | 1 221 | 1 464 | 27 135 | 1 278 |
| 1985 | 903 | 791 | 6 402 | 299 |
| 1986 | 1 074 | 720 | 1 920 | 90 |
| 1987 | 1 016 | 887 | 3 546 | 164 |
| 1988 | 781 | 790 | 3 702 | 166 |
| 1989 | 701 | 727 | 4 128 | 182 |
| 1990 | 630 | 298 | 1 903 | 83 |
| 1991 | 369 | 176 | 761 | 34 |

*Source: Employment Gazette* (HMSO)

year. The figure of 761 000 working days lost in 1991 is less than a tenth of the 20-year average for 1971–90 of 9.6 million. However, the unusually high number of working days lost in certain years, such as 1972, 1979 and 1984, was to a large extent the result of large individual stoppages. In these cases, they were: a coalminers' dispute over a national wage increase, accounting for 45 per cent of the total for that year; another coalminers' pay dispute, accounting for 38 per cent of the total; and yet another miners' strike, in this case over pit closures, accounting for 82 per cent of the total. The relative impact of the largest stoppages, as proportions of total working days lost, for the years 1979–91, is indicated in Table 6.10.

There is no single satisfactory theory explaining stoppage trends in Britain. However, there was a distinct tendency for underlying levels of stoppage activity to rise in the immediate postwar period. But stoppages decreased substantially during the 1980s and 1990s, probably owing to high unemployment, weak trade unions and structural changes in the economy. A longitudinal study of strikes in Britain by researchers at the Department of Employment draws

three broad implications from its analysis. The first is that 'strikes appear to be over fundamental issues, in which economic pressures on participants are very important'. The two most prominent ones are pay and job security. This is confirmed in Table 6.11. This shows, for the period 1980–90, that stoppages over pay accounted for most working days lost in every year, except 1984 and 1985, when redundancy issues were the major cause; in 1991, redundancy issues came a close second to pay. The second implication is that strikes in the main 'are concentrated in a very small proportion of plants, typically the larger ones in certain industries and certain areas of the country'. The third implication is that industries and regions having high average plant size 'tend to experience relatively high rates of strike incidence and relatively high rates of strike frequency as well'.[70] The commonly held view that Britain is especially strike prone is not borne out by the empirical evidence, although the probability of strikes occurring is much higher in a few industries, and markedly high in some plants.

Industrial stoppages in the UK occupy an inter-

*Table 6.10* Largest stoppages as proportions of working days lost 1979–91.

| Year | Industry | Working days lost for these industries (millions) | Total working days lost nationally (millions) | Total working days lost nationally (%) |
|---|---|---|---|---|
| 1979 | Engineering | 16.0 | | 54 |
| | Health and public services | 3.2 | 29.5 | 11 |
| | Transport and communications | 1.0 | | 3 |
| 1980 | Steel | 8.8 | 12.0 | 74 |
| 1981 | Civil service | 0.9 | 4.3 | 20 |
| 1982 | Health service and railways | 2.3 | 5.3 | 43 |
| 1983 | Electricity, gas and water | 0.8 | 3.8 | 20 |
| 1984 | Coalmining | 22.3 | 27.1 | 82 |
| 1985 | Coalmining | 4.0 | 6.4 | 63 |
| 1986 | Public administration | 0.5 | 1.9 | 26 |
| 1987 | Telecommunications | 1.5 | 3.5 | 41 |
| 1988 | Postal services | 1.0 | 3.7 | 28 |
| 1989 | Local authorities | 2.0 | 4.1 | 49 |
| 1990 | Engineering | 0.3 | 1.9 | 16 |
| 1991 | Local authorities | 0.1 | 0.8 | 13 |

*Source*: *Employment Gazette* (HMSO)

*Table 6.11* Working days lost by cause, 1980–91 (percentage of total).

| | Pay | Duration/ pattern of hours | Redundancy issues | Trade union matters | Working conditions/ supervision | Staffing/ work allocation | Dismissal/ disciplinary measures | Total working days lost, all causes |
|---|---|---|---|---|---|---|---|---|
| 1980 | 89 | 1 | 3 | 2 | 1 | 2 | 2 | 11 965 |
| 1981 | 62 | 5 | 15 | 7 | 1 | 4 | 6 | 4 244 |
| 1982 | 66 | 5 | 16 | 2 | 1 | 6 | 3 | 5 276 |
| 1983 | 58 | 3 | 17 | 2 | 4 | 8 | 8 | 3 981 |
| 1984 | 8 | 0 | 87 | 1 | 0 | 2 | 1 | 31 051 |
| 1985 | 25 | 3 | 67 | 1 | 1 | 2 | 2 | 6 402 |
| 1986 | 59 | 3 | 15 | 3 | 3 | 13 | 4 | 1 920 |
| 1987 | 82 | 2 | 5 | 1 | 2 | 5 | 4 | 3 546 |
| 1988 | 51 | 0 | 7 | 4 | 1 | 33 | 3 | 3 702 |
| 1989 | 80 | 8 | 4 | 2 | 1 | 4 | 1 | 4 128 |
| 1990 | 58 | 25 | 2 | 2 | 3 | 8 | 3 | 1 903 |
| 1991 | 41 | 2 | 33 | 1 | 9 | 8 | 7 | 761 |

*Source*: *Employment Gazette* (HMSO)

mediate ranking position compared with other countries in the Organisation for Economic Co-operation and Development. This is indicated in Table 6.12 which shows, for the periods indicated, that the countries having the highest incidence of working days lost per 1 000 employees were Italy, Greece, Spain, Canada, Ireland and Finland. Those countries recording relatively few days lost per 1 000 employees included the Netherlands, West Germany, Norway, Sweden, Denmark, France and Japan. It is also clear from Table 6.12 that working days lost per 1 000 employees declined significantly for all the countries listed apart from Greece and Spain, which are relatively new democracies in Europe. Care must be taken when making detailed comparisons between countries, however, largely because of differences in methods of recording stoppages and their accuracy, but Table 6.12 provides a useful indication of the relative numbers of working days lost through stoppages of work between the countries listed.

*Table 6.12* Industrial disputes: average number of working days lost per 1 000 employees for selected countries 1974–91.

| Country | [1974–78] | [1977–81] | [1982–86] | [1987–91] |
|---|---|---|---|---|
| UK | 380 | 580 | 420 | 130 |
| Australia | 690 | 590 | 280 | 220 |
| Canada | 990 | 780 | 490 | 360 |
| Denmark | 90 | 140 | 260 | 40 |
| Finland | 490 | 540 | 530 | 180 |
| France | 210 | 140 | 80 | 50 |
| Germany | 60 | 50 | 50 | 10 |
| Greece | 660 | 940 | 560 | 7 640 |
| Ireland | 700 | 810 | 450 | 190 |
| Italy | 1 410 | 1 140 | 700 | 300 |
| Japan | 130 | 30 | 10 | 0 |
| Netherlands | 10 | 30 | 20 | 10 |
| New Zealand | 340 | 360 | 550 | 230 |
| Norway | 70 | 30 | 170 | 30 |
| Portugal | 130 | 220 | 150 | 70 |
| Spain | 1 030 | 1 440 | 520 | 650 |
| Sweden | 30 | 250 | 60 | 100 |
| United States | N/A | 230 | 120 | 70 |

*Source*: *Employment Gazette* (HMSO)

## 6.7   Summary Points

- Collective bargaining is a complex process with a labour market function which challenges management prerogative. It is a means of extending industrial democracy to employees by enabling them to influence those decisions affecting their daily working lives. For management, it shares control with unions, thus enabling employers to obtain legitimate joint agreement over certain employment decisions.

- The conditions necessary for collective bargaining are: freedom of association; unions independent of employer and state control; employer recognition; bargaining in good faith; and mutual acceptance of joint agreements.

- Union recognition has often been an intractable and recurrent problem faced by trade unionists, with the preference of trade unions being voluntary recognition, not use of the law.

- The extent and scope of collective bargaining was a major policy issue in the 1960s and 1970s. Donovan's prescription was to recommend voluntary procedural agreements at company and enterprise level. This would provide: structured bargaining negotiating machinery, intermediate between national and workplace levels; defined bargaining units; rationalized bargaining agents; documented bargaining forms; and extended bargaining scope.

- 'Fair Deal at Work' became the legal basis for reforming collective bargaining through the Industrial Relations Act 1971. The CBI strongly advocated more structured collective bargaining arrangements in the private sector during the 1970s and the synchronization and compression of the annual pay round. The Basnett plan for co-ordinating public sector bargaining in the late 1970s included the devolution and extension of joint negotiating machinery.

- Since 1979, pragmatic reforms to collective bargaining have continued in the private sector in conditions of relatively high unemployment. Changes have included decentralized bargaining, single table bargaining and new style single union deals. Other employers have moved away from the joint regulation of industrial relations, especially for white collar employees, to personal contracts, performance pay and employee involvement strategies.

- In the public sector, collective bargaining since 1979 has been influenced by strict cash limits, hardening attitudes to trade unions by government and the removal of pay negotiating rights of key groups such as school teachers, nurses, midwives and senior managers in the public services.

- Collective bargaining structure describes the stable and permanent features of any set of bargaining arrangements. These are bargaining levels, bargaining units, bargaining forms and bargaining scope. Levels are at multiemployer, single employer or establishment level. Units are the groups of employees covered by particular collective agreements. They may be wide or narrow in coverage and may consist of one or more bargaining agents. Forms describe whether agreements are written and formal or unwritten and informal. Scope focuses on the range of subjects covered in particular negotiations and may be comprehensive or restricted.
- The incidence of collective bargaining varies between employment sectors and is associated with size of employing establishment. Public sector employers are generally more likely to negotiate with trade unions than are private employers and bargaining between employers and manual workers is more likely than it is with non-manual workers.
- In the private sector, the pattern of bargaining is complex, with multiemployer and single employer structures coexisting to varying degrees. Single employer bargaining, in turn, may be either centralized or decentralized in multiplant companies.
- A number of factors influence the levels at which collective bargaining takes place. These include product markets, work organization, technology, geographic location, union structure, payment systems and labour markets.
- In the public sector, in contrast, multiemployer bargaining still predominates for most groups of employees, although the traditional Whitley system is weakening. A debate is emerging about the extent to which public sector bargaining should be regionalized or localized.
- The outcomes of collective bargaining are collective agreements. They are binding 'in honour' between the parties, employers and unions. Substantive agreements are concerned with the terms and conditions of employment, whilst procedural agreements define the relations between the parties. Substantive agreements centre on the pay, conditions and fringe benefits associated with particular jobs. Procedural agreements include: negotiating, grievance, disputes, disciplinary, redundancy, dismissal, recruitment and promotion procedures. These procedures provide the ground rules for negotiations between employers and unions in their dealings together.

- Where collective bargaining breaks down, usually over fundamental differences between the parties, such as pay, job security and union recognition, industrial action may be initiated by either side, with the final sanction being an industrial stoppage. National and international records of stoppages are kept. They record annually: number of stoppages; number of workers involved in stoppages; number of working days lost; and, for comparative purposes, the number of working days lost per 1 000 employees.
- The view commonly held, at least until the mid-1980s, that Britain is strike prone is not supported by the evidence. Strike trends are variable but strikes are more likely to take place in a few industries, such as mining, docks, car assembly and shipbuilding, with large establishment size and strong worker solidarity.

## 6.8   References

1. International Labour Office, *Collective Bargaining*, ILO, Geneva, 1960, p. 3.
2. Royal Commission on Trade Unions and Employers' Associations, *Report*, HMSO, London, 1968, p. 50.
3. N. Millward, Workplace industrial relations: results of a survey of industrial relations practices, *Employment Gazette*, July 1983, p. 281.
4. N. Millward and M. Stevens, *British Workplace Industrial Relations 1980–1984*, Gower, Aldershot, 1986, pp. 62–5.
5. N. Millward, M. Stevens, D. Smart and W. Hawes, *Workplace Industrial Relations in Transition*, Dartmouth, Basingstoke, 1992, p. 70.
6. A. Flanders, Collective bargaining: a theoretical analysis, in A. Flanders, *Management and Unions*, Faber and Faber, London, 1975, p. 239.
7. A. Fox, Collective bargaining, Flanders and the Webbs, *British Journal of Industrial Relations*, July 1975, p. 117.
8. R. Hyman, *Industrial Relations*, Macmillan, London, 1975, p. 26.
9. N. Chamberlain and J. W. Kuhn, *Collective Bargaining*, McGraw-Hill, New York, 1965, p. 113.
10. S. H. Slichter, *Union Policies and Industrial Management*, Brookings Institution, Washington, DC, 1941, p. 1.
11. Chamberlain and Kuhn, *op. cit.*, p. 138.
12. Royal Commission, *op. cit.*, pp. 36 and 262.
13. Conservative Political Centre, *Fair Deal at Work*, CPC, London, 1968, pp. 10, 56 and 62.
14. Confederation of British Industry, *The Future of Pay Determination*, CBI, London, 1977, pp. 5 and 11.
15. *Ibid.*, p. 25.

16. D. Basnett, A way out of warfare over pay, *The Sunday Times*, 4 December 1977, pp. 16 and 22.
17. J. Purcell, The rediscovery of the management prerogative: the management of labour in the 1980s, *Oxford Review of Economic Policy*, 7(1), 1991, p. 41.
18. D. Farnham and S. Horton (eds), *Managing the New Public Services*, Macmillan, Basingstoke, p. 20.
19. W. Brown and J. Walsh, Pay determination in Britain in the 1980s, *Oxford Review of Economic Policy*, 7(1), 1991, p. 45.
20. R. Lewis, Reforming industrial relations, *Oxford Review of Economic Policy*, 7(1), 1991, p. 62.
21. B. Ahlstrand and J. Purcell, Employee relations strategy in the multidivisional company, *Personnel Review*, 17(3), 1988, p. 6.
22. Millward *et al.*, *op. cit.*, p. 74.
23. Union regulation is spreading, *Personnel Management Plus*, 4(7), July 1993, p. 3.
24. P. A. L. Parker, W. R. Hawes and A. L. Lumb, *Department of Employment Manpower Papers Number 5, The Reform of Collective Bargaining at Plant and Company Level*, HMSO, London, 1971, p. 3.
25. *Ibid.*
26. C. Jenkins and B. Sherman, *Collective Bargaining*, Routledge and Kegan Paul, London, 1977, p. 63.
27. D. Thomas, Integrity of joint bargaining sacrosanct – but flexibility needed, *Local Government Chronicle*, 22 November 1987, p. 21.
28. W. W. Daniel and N. Millward, *Workplace Industrial Relations in Britain*, Heinemann, London, 1983, p. 177.
29. *Ibid.*, p. 25.
30. D. R. Deaton and P. B. Beaumont, The determinants of bargaining structure: some large scale survey evidence, *British Journal of Industrial Relations*, 18, July 1980, p. 203.
31. Advisory Conciliation and Arbitration Service, *Collective Bargaining in Britain: Its Extent and Level*, HMSO, London, 1983, p. 24.
32. See S. Palmer (ed.), *Determining Pay*, IPM, London, 1990, p. 17.
33. ACAS, *op. cit.*, p. 39.
34. P. B. Beaumont, *Public Sector Industrial Relations*, Routledge, London, 1992, p. 103.
35. Millward *et al.*, *op. cit.*, p. 232.
36. *Ibid.*, p. 234.
37. S. Horton, The civil service, in Farnham and Horton (eds), *op. cit.*, p. 143.
38. D. Farnham, Sixty years of Whitleyism, *Personnel Management*, July 1978, p. 32.
39. Advisory Conciliation and Arbitration Service, *Annual Report 1992*, ACAS, London, 1993, p. 18.
40. Millward *et al.*, *op. cit.*, p. 362.
41. C. Brewster and S. Connock, *Industrial Relations: Cost-effective Strategies*, Hutchinson, London, 1985, p. 140.
42. Millward and Stevens, *op. cit.*, p. 251.
43. Millward *et al.*, *op. cit.*, p. 253.
44. *Ibid.*, p. 254.
45. Brewster and Connock, *op. cit.*, pp. 165–9.
46. J. C. Ramsey and J. M. Hill, *Collective Agreements*, Institute of Personnel Management, London, 1974, p. 55.
47. A. Flanders, Industrial relations: what is wrong with the system? in Flanders, *op. cit.*, p. 86f.
48. N. Singleton, *Industrial Relations Procedures*, HMSO, London, 1975, p. 7.
49. Jenkins and Sherman, *op. cit.*, p. 24.
50. A. I. Marsh, *Royal Commission on Trade Unions and Employers' Associations Research Papers 2 (Part 1) Disputes Procedures in British Industry*, HMSO, London, 1966, p. 4.
51. *Agreement between the Federation and the Trade Unions Dated 1 March 1976, Operative from 5 April 1976: Procedure for the Avoidance of Disputes – Manual Workers*, Engineering Employers Federation/Confederation of Shipbuilding and Engineering Unions, London, 1976, para. 9.
52. *Ibid.*, paras 5 and 15.
53. Singleton, *op. cit.*, p. 17.
54. Marsh, *op. cit.*, p. viii.
55. Trades Union Congress, *Meeting the Challenge*, TUC, London, 1989, p. 9.
56. G. Burrows, *No-strike Agreements and Pendulum Arbitration*, IPM, London, 1986, p. 55.
57. L. Rico, The new industrial relations: British electricians' new-style agreements, *Industrial and Labor Relations Review*, 41(1), October 1987, p. 68.
58. *Ibid.*, pp. 68 and 78.
59. Burrows, *op. cit.*, p. 7.
60. Advisory Conciliation and Arbitration Service, *Annual Report 1986*, ACAS, London, 1987, p. 20f.
61. *Nissan–AEU Agreement* (nd), clause 4(e).
62. Burrows, *op. cit.*, p. 7.
63. *Ibid.*, p. 59.
64. Industrial Relations Services, Single union deals in perspective, *IRS Employment Trends*, November 1992, p. 6.
65. G. Gall, What happened to single union deals? *Industrial Relations Journal*, 24(1), 1993, p. 7.
66. *Ibid.*, p. 74.
67. A. Kornhauser, R. Dubin and A. M. Ross (eds), *Industrial Conflict*, McGraw-Hill, New York, 1954, p. 14.
68. W. H. Scott, E. Mumford, I. C. McGivering and J. M. Kirkby, *Coal and Conflict*, Liverpool University Press, 1963, p. 40.
69. E. Johnston, *Industrial Action*, Arrow Books, London, 1975, p. 25.
70. C. T. B. Smith, R. Clifton, P. Makeham, S. W. Creigh and R. V. Burn, *Strikes in Britain*, HMSO, London, p. 89f.

# PART THREE

## The State and Industrial Relations

# 7

# The Politics of Industrial Relations

Industrial relations in Britain cannot be divorced from party politics. On the one hand, there is the long-established connection between some major trade unions and the Labour Party, with the unions providing the greater part of Labour Party finance, sponsoring candidates in general elections and being deeply involved in Party policy making and political activity. On the other hand, there is the Conservative Party which by ideological inclination, social contacts and financial support is closely related to the business community, especially big business. At another political level, we have union and employer pressure groups, notably the Trades Union Congress (TUC) and the Confederation of British Industry (CBI), which seek to influence whichever major political party is in power to follow policies and party programmes which will best serve their members' interests. It is these institutions and traditions which provide an ideological and political framework within which British industrial relations takes place.

## 7.1 Trade Unions and the Labour Party

Trade unions were created in Britain and developed long before the Labour Party was formed. Unions for skilled workers, for example, and later unskilled workers, developed and grew steadily throughout the nineteenth century and the TUC was established in 1868, more than a generation before the Labour Party. In 1871 the trade unions had gained some protection at law under the Trade Union Act and to some extent the long struggle to prove that they were law abiding, respectable, constitutional organizations had been won. The trade union leaders of the time maintained 'a strong presumption in favour of the *status quo*', distrusted innovation and had a liking 'for distinct social classes', with 'each man being secured and contented in his station of life'.[1] They did not want their hard-won acceptance by Victorian

society to be lost by political adventuring. Up till this time the TUC had been content to use its Parliamentary Committee to protect union interests. It maintained links with the Liberal Party and supported a handful of trade union Members of Parliament (MPs) to protect and further the interests of the trade unions through specific legislation. Before 1880, however, labour or working-class representation in Parliament was sparse: 'what representation there was was by courtesy of the Liberal Party'.[2]

By the turn of the century, a number of fundamental social changes had occurred which would inescapably involve the unions in political activity from which they would never be able to withdraw. First, there was the gradual extension of the political franchise to almost all adult males. Second, there had been a dissemination of socialist ideas and programmes for political change by groups of social reformers. Third, trade unionists had come to recognize that the law-making powers of Parliament could be used to protect their collective interests and to obtain those other political and social objectives which collective bargaining alone could never achieve. This latter had been emphasized by the threat to union security arising from a series of legal decisions against the unions in the 1890s. Finally, there was the growth of the so-called 'new unionism' amongst sections of the relatively unskilled labourers in the docks, gas companies and transport sector from the late 1880s.

It was these developments which led to a demand by the TUC for better representation of labour and working people in Parliament. The outcome was the creation of the Labour Representation Committee (LRC) after a conference called by the TUC in 1900. With the election to the House of Commons of 28 members of the LRC in the 1906 general election, the name of the party was changed and the modern Labour Party was born. The Labour Party and the trade unions have been represented there ever since, albeit with fluctuating fortunes. The logic of these historical and social forces probably made the creation of a broad-based political party representative of working people's interests inevitable. However, once such a party had been formed by the trade unions, and if they were to accept the constitutional constraints of parliamentary democracy, it followed that the trade unions were creating an organization which they could never completely control. They could only seek to guide, influence and lobby within it. Besides, the unions' chief preoccupation both then and now has always been safeguarding their own existence and their members' incomes, jobs and working conditions. They have also largely financed the Labour Party, but:

> the heart of British unionism is still in these jealously revered organizations that stand guard over the collective economic interests of each group – the jobs and the working conditions that go with the jobs.[3]

Many socialists in 1900 would have preferred to have established an independent socialist party free of trade union domination, since they regarded the unions as inherently reactionary and conservative institutions in their social and economic outlooks. Nevertheless, a new political party representing working-class interests could not realistically have been launched without trade union support, finance and organizational strength. As a result there has frequently been an uneasy and tense relationship between the trade unions and the Labour Party, especially with sections of the Parliamentary Labour Party (PLP). The roots of this tension lie essentially in the contradictory desires of the unions. They wish to operate as autonomous and separate economic agents, whilst at the same time wanting to shape a legislative programme for the Labour Party which, at times, has effectively constrained their freedom of economic action on behalf of their members. The necessarily narrower economic objectives of the unions in protecting their members' jobs and employment interests have inevitably conflicted at times with the efforts of the Labour Party to give itself national appeal to win majorities in the House of Commons.

> For the unions the historic connection with the Party provides a political lobby to protect their industrial role: for the Party the connection provides the finance to maintain its political organization.[4]

The 'labour movement' in Britain consists of two elements: an industrial wing, the trade unions affiliated to the TUC; and a political wing, the Labour Party, consisting of a coalition of labour interests including party affiliated trade unionists, individual members, the socialist societies such as the Fabians, and the PLP. The theory of the 'Labour Alliance' is that its two wings, the trade union movement and the Party, are interdependent and integral parts of the larger working-class movement seeking economic, political and social justice for all working people and their families, both as workers and citizens. The trade union role is to protect the jobs and to advance the terms and conditions of employment of trade unionists through collective action, as well as funding the Party. The Labour Party's role as set out in Clause 4 of its constitution is:

> To secure for the workers by hand or by brain the full fruits of their industry and the most equitable distribution thereof that may be possible upon the basis of the common ownership of the means of production, distribution, and exchange, and the best obtainable system of popular administration and control of each industry or service.[5]

The genesis and development of the Labour Party as the 'child of the trade union movement' does not only signify a rejection of the view that trade unionism and politics do not mix. It also explicitly accepts that party affiliated unions have interests overriding purely industrial and occupational ones and that the Party is an organization in which union and non-union elements have to live together. The implications of this for the wider labour movement and British party politics were less evident in the first half of the twentieth century when the unions were weak economically and numerically, and when the Labour Party had not achieved governmental office. But with the growth in economic power of the unions after 1945 and the increased political significance of the Labour Party, whether actually in government or as the major opposition party in Parliament, the situation changed significantly. To quote the TUC:

> Trade unions and political parties do . . . perform quite distinct functions and their preoccupations can be quite different. The growth of the Labour Party to the point where it became the Government of the country has entailed a significant divergence of function. The existence of common roots yet distinct functions is therefore the most important relationship between the trade unions and the Labour Party.[6]

The formal relationship between the affiliated unions and the Labour Party has generally reflected moderate and constitutional thinking among trade unionists, democratic and reformist convictions amongst Labour politicians, and a presumption that the goals of instrumental trade unionism and parliamentary socialist democracy are compatible. Many however have disputed these views. Fundamentalist socialists have often argued that Parliament is a social and political quagmire where middle-class Labour MPs, time-honoured procedures, constitutionalism and civil service influence effectively inhibit the implementation of genuine socialist policies. Marxists argue, for example, that the election of Labour or Conservative governments makes no difference in the class struggle in capitalist countries like Britain. It is also suggested that parliamentary alliances, and the need for the Labour Party to present itself as representing the national interest rather than sectional industrial and political groupings, invariably create disillusionment with parliamentary activities amongst its supporters, thus leading militant trade unionists towards direct action instead. However it is analysed, the British labour movement is a complex social organism incorporating myriad internal tensions and conflicts. 'The Labour Alliance is formally a reality, but its unity is a myth'.[7]

## Political funds

The key to understanding the trade union–Labour Party connection is the device of political funds. The Trade Union and Labour Relations (Consolidation) Act 1992 enables trade unions or unincorporated employers' associations to include the furtherance of political objects in their rules and to adopt political fund rules providing for expenditure on such objects. The proposal to do so must be endorsed by a simple majority of members in a ballot held under rules approved by the Certification Officer. The 1992 Act requires unions with political funds, and those wishing to continue spending money on political objects, to hold political fund review ballots of their entire memberships at least once every 10 years.

The 1992 Act lays down a number of requirements for union rule books incorporating political funds and objects. First, union expenditure in furthering union political objects has to be made out of separate political funds, not general funds. Second, any union members giving notice of their objections to political funding in accordance with the Act must be exempt from any obligation of contributing to that fund. In other words they must be free to 'contract out' of paying political contributions or the 'political levy' as

it is generally known. Third, exempt members must not be excluded from any benefits of their union, or placed under any disability or disadvantage compared with other members, except in relation to controlling or managing the political fund. Fourth, admission to the union shall not be conditional on paying the political levy.

Union members wishing to claim exemption from contributing to union political funds must give notice of their objection in the form laid down by the 1992 Act. Unless contributions to the political fund are collected by a separate levy, exempt members must be relieved from paying the political element of normal contributions. Union rules must provide for such relief to be given as far as possible to all exempt members when paying their union subscriptions. They must also enable members to know what portion if any of their contributions goes to union political funds. Any union members alleging breaches of political fund rules may complain to the Certification Officer under Section 82(2) to (4) of the 1992 Act. Having heard the complainant, and given the union an opportunity to be heard, and if it is considered that a breach of rules has occurred, the Certification Officer may make an order remedying it. Appeals against the Certification Officer's rulings may be made to the Employment Appeal Tribunal on a point of law.

As can be seen from Table 7.1, at the end of 1991 there were 52 unions with political funds. They had over seven million members contributing to union general funds, of whom some 6 million, or 84 per cent, paid political levies. This represented about 73 per cent of trade unionists in unions affiliated to the TUC which, in 1991, had '74 affiliated unions with a total membership of 8 192 664'.[8] The percentage of members per union contributing to union political funds varies widely. In 33 of these unions, over 90 per cent of their members paid political levies; in 11 unions between 60 and 89 per cent did so; and in the remaining eight unions less than 59 per cent did so. Twenty-three of these unions each had over £100 000 in their political funds at the end of 1991, the four largest funds being those of the General Municipal Boilermakers and Allied Trades Union, the Transport and General Workers Union, the National and Local Government Officers Association and the National Union of Public Employees with £2.3 million, £4.8 million, £3.9 million and £1.4 million respectively.

Union political fund expenditure is used for three main purposes: '(1) to affiliate to the Labour Party;

*Table 7.1* Union political funds 1991.

| | Number of members contributing to the political fund [d] | Number of members exempt from contributing to the political fund [d] | Percentage of members contributing to the political fund (approx.) [d] |
|---|---|---|---|
| Amalgamated Engineering Union | 397 071 | 225 551 | 64 |
| Associated Society of Locomotive Engineers and Firemen | 18 055 | 811 | 96 |
| Association of Her Majesty's Inspectors of Taxes | 2 406 | 113 | 96 |
| Bakers Food and Allied Workers Union | 33 419 | 909 | 97 |
| Broadcasting Entertainment Cinematograph and Theatre Union | 5 879 | 9 [c] | 100 |
| Ceramic and Allied Trades Union | 25 214 | 69 | 98 |
| Civil and Public Services Association | 1 | – | – |
| Communication Managers Association | 16 782 | 510 | 97 |
| Confederation of Health Service Employees [c] | 186 267 | 15 726 | 92 |
| Educational Institute of Scotland | 44 610 | 1 605 | 97 |
| Electrical Electronic Telecommunication and Plumbing Union | 267 921 | 42 396 | 86 |
| Fire Brigades Union | 36 693 | 11 530 | 76 |
| Furniture Timber and Allied Trades Union | 30 346 | 4 439 | 87 |
| General Union of Associations of Loom Overlookers | 334 | 341 | 49 |
| GMB | 735 033 | 63 915 | 92 |
| Inland Revenue Staff Federation | 52 995 | 2 298 | 96 |
| Institute of Professional Managers and Specialists | 78 995 | 2 402 | 97 |
| Iron and Steel Trades Confederation | 30 758 | 7 930 | 80 |
| Manufacturing Science and Finance Union | 274 307 | 329 693 | 45 |
| Musicians Union | 33 442 | 1 903 | 95 |
| National and Local Government Officers Association [c] | 630 109 | 46 806 | 93 |
| National Association of Colliery Overmen Deputies and Shotfirers | 5 696 | 54 | 99 |
| National Association of Colliery Overmen Deputies and Shotfirers Durham Area | 478 | – | 100 |
| National Association of Schoolmasters and Union of Women Teachers | 100 285 | 58 795 | 63 |
| National Association of Teachers in Further and Higher Education | 63 711 | 2 796 | 96 |
| National Communications Union (Engineering and Clerical Groups) – Engineering Group | 86 151 | 22 801 | 79 |

*Table 7.1 (continued)*

| | Number of members contributing to the political fund[d] | Number of members exempt from contributing to the political fund[d] | Percentage of members contributing to the political fund (approx.)[d] |
|---|---|---|---|
| National Communications Union (Engineering and Clerical Groups) – Clerical Group | 31 754 | 3 131 | 91 |
| National Graphical Association (1982)[a] | 57 790 | 43 102 | 57 |
| National League of the Blind and Disabled | 1 601 | 73 | 96 |
| National Union of Civil and Public Servants | 111 644 | 1 117 | 99 |
| National Union of Domestic Appliances and General Operatives | 650 | 12 | 98 |
| National Union of Insurance Workers | 15 631 | 3 025 | 84 |
| National Union of Knitwear Footwear and Apparel Trades | 52 500 | 849 | 98 |
| National Union of Lock and Metal Workers | 4 646 | 46 | 99 |
| National Union of Mineworkers | 40 703 | 65 316 | 38 |
| National Union of Public Employees[c] | 535 406 | 15 759 | 97 |
| National Union of Rail Maritime and Transport Workers | 112 104 | 2 034 | 98 |
| National Union of Scalemakers | 2 | 1 039 | – |
| National Union of Tailors and Garment Workers[b] | 56 395 | 10 235 | 85 |
| Power Loom Carpet Weavers and Textile Workers Union | 2 149 | 18 | 99 |
| Rossendale Union of Boot Shoe and Slipper Operatives | 2 252 | 21 | 99 |
| Scottish Carpet Workers Union | 760 | – | 100 |
| Society of Graphical and Allied Trades 1982 (SOGAT)[a] | 82 731 | 74 610 | 53 |
| Society of Telecom Executives | 13 712 | 11 315 | 55 |
| Society of Union Employees (NUPE) | 164 | – | 100 |
| Transport and General Workers Union | 997 182 | 21 786 | 98 |
| Transport Salaried Staffs Association | 34 150 | 5 880 | 85 |
| Union of Communication Workers | 179 634 | 11 988 | 94 |
| Union of Construction Allied Trades and Technicians | 171 947 | 23 013 | 88 |
| Union of Democratic Mineworkers | 14 690 | 82 | 99 |
| Union of Shop Distributive and Allied Workers | 311 905 | 29 444 | 91 |
| Union of Textile Workers | 1 887 | 64 | 97 |
| Total for the 52 unions with political funds for 1991 | 5 990 947 | 1 167 361 | 84 |

[a] These unions amalgamated 30 September 1991 to form the Graphical Paper and Media Union.
[b] This union transferred its engagements to GMB on 1 March 1991.
[c] These unions amalgamated 1 July 1993 to form UNISON.
[d] It should be noted that columns 1 and 2 do not necessarily add up to a union's total membership. The numbers of members exempt relates only to those members who have completed a political fund exemption notice.
*Source:* Certification Officer, *Annual Report for 1992* (HMSO, 1993)

(2) to finance parliamentary candidates; and (3) to finance local political activities'.[9] In practice it is only the Labour Party to which trade unions can affiliate, since all other parties are based on individual membership alone. In 1992, the claimed membership of the Labour Party was just over five million members. This consisted of 4.8 million affiliated trade union members from 29 trade unions, some 260 000 individual members in constituency Labour parties (CLPs) and about 53 000 members of socialist societies and co-operative organizations. Union affiliated membership of the Labour Party, therefore, outweighs individual membership by almost 20:1, though a small number 'of those who are members through their union's affiliation are individual members as well'.[10] The real significance of union affiliation fees paid by affiliated unions to the Labour Party is that they go to the central funds of the Party. They provide the basis of Labour Party financial stability and a leading role which trade union delegates play at Labour Party conferences. The unions are also represented by delegates on the Party's National Executive Committee.

The second major purpose of union political funds is to promote and maintain parliamentary representation. This expenditure takes two forms:

> There is the making of regular, and, at general election times of what are often large contributions to the Labour Party's election funds, and there is the promotion and maintenance of the union's own direct parliamentary representation.[11]

In the 1979 general election, for example, 269 Labour MPs were elected. Of these 133 were sponsored by affiliated unions. After the 1983 general election 209 Labour MPs were returned of whom 112 were union sponsored. At the 1987 general election, there were 164 union-sponsored candidates. Of these 129 were elected MPs, out of a total of 229 Labour MPs in 1987. In 1992, only 15 trade unions sponsored successful Labour candidates, compared with 22 unions in 1987. This reduction was owing to a number of union mergers between 1987 and 1992. The unions sponsoring most candidates in 1992 were the TGWU with 38 candidates, the GMB with 17 and the NUM with 14. One hundred and forty-three union-sponsored MPs were elected in the 1992 General Election, which represented 53 per cent of all Labour MPs, compared with 56 per cent in 1987. Twenty-two of the union-sponsored MPs were women – over a third of the total number of women in the House of Commons. In addition to contributing to election expenses, the affiliated unions sometimes supplement the salaries of elected parliamentary representatives. Different methods are used for this. These include: direct annual payments; reimbursement of travelling and other expenses incurred in discharging their parliamentary duties; assistance with constituency expenses and clerical and research assistance. Which methods are adopted depend on union preferences, the local constituency and the specific needs of individual MPs. Naturally the unions prefer sponsoring those candidates likely to be parliamentary winners. Apart from the EETPU, of whose ten sponsored candidates only three were elected, most sponsored candidates were elected in 1992.

The third main purpose of union political funds is to finance local political activity. This includes contributions by union branches to CLPs or local trades councils. Union political funds are also used to support candidates in local authority elections. Sometimes fixed sums are allocated from central funds which are then drawn on by union branches for approved expenditure. In other cases there are established local political funds which union branches use. Occasionally, there are separate local funds to which, by union rules, a fixed proportion of all political funds received must be allocated. Whatever the arrangements, the precise rules defining the scope of local political expenditure 'are likely to be fairly rigid'.[12]

## Structure and organization

Figure 7.1 provides an outline of the main structural features of the British labour movement. The trade union wing consisted of 29 Labour Party affiliates in 1992, with almost five million trade unionists paying the political levy. In 1991 the TUC had 74 affiliated unions, comprising a total TUC membership of over nine million members, which meant that Labour Party affiliation among the major trade unions represented about 60 per cent of TUC membership at that time. Labour Party affiliation enables these unions to send delegates to the Labour Party Conference to influence Party policy; to have representation on the Party's National Executive Committee (NEC); and to sponsor Labour MPs.

The Labour Party consists of the PLP and the extra-parliamentary party, namely the trade unions, the CLPs and the socialist societies, whose diverse elements only come together at the Party's annual conference. In theory, the annual conference is the

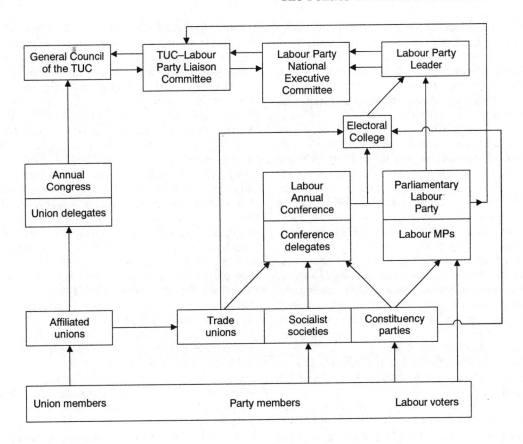

*Figure 7.1* Unions and the Labour Party.

Party's sovereign body. In practice the main power centres are the PLP, the unions and the CLPs, and often bitter conflicts emerge between them in Party debates and on policy issues. It is at Conference that formal Party policy is determined and the NEC is elected. Currently, the NEC consists of 29 members and 'shall, subject to the control and directions of the Party Conference, be the administrative Authority of the Party'.[13] In addition to Party officials and the Party Leader, seats on the NEC are allocated by election to three main groups: the trade unions, with 12 members; the CLPs, with seven; and women members of whom there are five.

By convention a block voting system was used at the annual Conference, with the unions accounting for nearly 5 million votes and the CLPs some 260 000 in 1992. This meant that the unions had a powerful voice at Conference. They could also dominate 18 of the 29 seats on the NEC if they so wished through their collective voting strength. More significantly,

after the changes in Party rules in 1981 when an Electoral College was created with the responsibility for electing the Labour leader, the trade unions had a great influence on the choice of leader. The Electoral College votes were divided according to a predetermined formula: 40 per cent to the trade unions and 30 per cent each to the PLP and CLPs.

The dominant institutional position of the trade unions within the Labour Party has always been controversial. The four consecutive defeats of the party in the general elections from 1979 to 1992 were attributed, in part, to its association with the trade unions. At the party's annual conference in 1993 the then leader of the party, John Smith, staked his authority on winning agreement to significant constitutional reform. This involved five rule changes.

First, the union 'block vote' in conference debates is weakened, by forcing unions to split their votes between individual delegates, although unions will be able to mandate their representatives in advance. The unions' 70 per cent of the conference vote will reduce to 50 per cent if party membership increases from 260 000 to 300 000.

Second, the party leader and deputy leader will be elected by an electoral college, with the trade unions, MPs and MEPs, and constituency members having one-third of the votes each.

Third, Labour Parliamentary candidates will be selected on a one member one vote (OMOV) basis. Individual members, voting by single transferable vote in their constituencies, will replace the former joint selection by individuals and affiliated trade union branches. Union members, who pay the political levy, will be able to vote if they pay £3 to join the party. Trade union branches will retain the right to nominate candidates and to subsidize MPs.

Fourth, in future, in 50 per cent of Labour-held seats that fall vacant, all-female candidate shortlists will be drawn up. A resolution seeking greater black representation on candidate shortlists was defeated, however. This rule change may well be difficult to implement in practice, as it appears to contravene equal opportunities legislation.

Fifth, less controversially, conference agreed a cut in party membership subscriptions from £18 to £15 annually.

These constitutional changes were carried by very narrow margins. The OMOV, or Rule Change E, was won by only 3.2 per cent, 47.5 per cent to 44.3 per cent. The two largest unions, the TGWU and the GMB, voted against and the MSF delegation, which commanded 4.5 per cent of the vote, abstained. Their abstention, supported by only 17 to 15 among their delegates, was because they wanted to see the changes favouring more women MPs.

The institutional links between the trade unions and the Labour Party have clearly been diluted by these reforms. John Smith and other 'modernizers' within the party and the trade unions argued that change was necessary to improve the chances of the Labour Party winning the next election. John Smith said in his conference speech:

> Let me make it absolutely and totally clear. It is not a choice between one member one vote and a role for the trade unions. It's the chance for more trade unionists than ever before to take part in all the decisions and campaigns of the Labour Party. . . . This party was founded by the trade unions. The links between us have always been strong and I believe they are as important today as they ever have been.[14]

Labour Party 'traditionalists' were more sceptical of the future relationship between the two wings of the labour movement, seeing the Labour Party moving away from both its trade union roots and its socialist credentials, although still dependent on union financial support.

Trade unions are the main financiers of the Labour Party. According to one authority, 'the trade unions have long provided nearly 80 per cent of the income of the Party'.[15] Not all of the income goes to the central bodies. Some goes to the area organizations and local parties but the national party relies heavily upon union money. One reason why the Labour Party is poorer than the Conservatives is that the CLPs are less efficient money-gathering machines than their Conservative counterparts. Party finance is nevertheless insecurely based, and for many years 'the party's normal activities have been running at a deficit'. This has resulted in 'a continued and heavy borrowing from the bank'.[16] The situation is worsening, since the unions have their financial problems too, with falling memberships, rising costs and squeezes on their financial resources since the late 1970s. Managing the union–Party alliance is delicate enough. Managing its difficult financial position effectively is equally challenging for the Labour Party and its leaders in conditions of change and political uncertainty.

Another institutional device sustaining the union–Labour Party connection, until 1991, was the TUC–Labour Party Liaison Committee linking the General Council, the NEC and the PLP. It was created in the mid-1970s to build closer formal links between the TUC unions and the Labour Party, when relations between them had deteriorated. In 1983, the Committee issued a policy statement declaring its underlying aims:

> Our primary objective is to offer work – and the rights, status and dignity that go with it – to all our people. Our approach is based on a partnership between a Labour Government and the trade union Movement, harnessing into common cause the skills of managers and all those who can help in the drive for full employment and better social provision. Only by creating this new partnership in society can we bring together all resources, talents and expertise to find practical solutions to the problems we face.[17]

After 1991, the Committee ceased to meet on a formal regular basis. It now meets unofficially and irregularly, reflecting the more fractured relationship between the TUC and the Labour Party in the early 1990s.

To sum up, British trade unions have gained greatly from their close partnership with the Labour Party:

> Since 1906 this has constantly provided Members of Parliament to defend trade union interests and keep the issues of special interest to trade unionists before the House. When Labour has been in office it has legislated to remedy unwelcome rulings of the courts, repeal obnoxious enactments, or extend the scope of trade union action.[18]

Conversely, the Labour Party has benefited from the trade union connection, by being provided with a very high proportion of its current income for expenditure on its political purposes. The relationship, however, was never without its tensions and never were they more evident than in the 1990s.

## 7.2 Employers and the Conservative Party

Just as there is a strong identity of interest between trade union leaderships and the Labour Party, there is an equally strong political connection between those running private sector businesses and the Conservative Party. Whilst, however, the political connections between trade unionism and the Labour Party have been overt, those between private businesses and the Conservatives are more subtle, covert and fragmented. There appear to be three main areas where the interests and activities of employers and the Conservative Party interrelate, overlap and are mutually supportive. These are: their preferred ideologies and economic policies; the social networks existing between big business, the City and Conservative politicians; and the donations provided by some leading employers to the Conservative Party.

The modern Conservative Party has been, and remains, the political party protective of the privately owned enterprise sector and of the market economy as the prime means for allocating and distributing resources in society. As the *Conservative Manifesto* put it in 1983:

> We want to see an economy in which firms, large and small, have every incentive to expand by winning extra business and creating more jobs. This Conservative Government has been both giving these incentives and clearing away

obstacles to expansion. . . . Only a government which really works to promote free enterprise can provide the right conditions for that dream to come true.

The manifesto also expressed the necessity of reforming the nationalized industries by continuing 'to expose state-owned firms to real competition', by transferring 'more state-owned business to independent ownership' and by seeking means 'of increasing competition in, and attracting private capital into, the gas and electricity industries.' The Conservatives are supportive, too, of small businesses and claim that the recent 'climate for new and smaller businesses in the UK has been transformed and is now as favourable as anywhere in the world'.[19]

These themes recurred throughout the late 1980s and early 1990s. Shortly after becoming Prime Minister in November 1990, for example, John Major stated his continued commitment 'to promote enterprise by companies large and small, and to help create more jobs' and 'to take privatisation further, and bring private business skills to the aid of the public sector'.[20] At the same time, the Conservative Party set out on its industrial strategy with four aims for business. These were reducing the burdens on business, by fulfilling 'its promise to reduce . . . tax rates [on business]', 'opening market opportunities for British industry and commerce', providing business with 'the benefits of free competition' and building partnerships with business. In this respect, it claimed, 'it is vital that the Government works closely *with* business, rather than agree with Labour's policy of *forcing* companies to train, using their Jobs Tax as a whip'.[21]

Crouch argues that in opposition and in the early months of government:

> Conservatives tend to hanker after the abolition of organized structures of government planning and a return to free-market policies. The solution to industrial relations problems is seen as automatically taken care of by the level of unemployment, perhaps backed by legislation that will make strike action more difficult. Industrial relations are then depoliticized; trade unions settle down to a non-political role of industrial bargaining; and the government can revert to a role of occasional consultation in difficult disputes, not having to bother with incomes policy or troublesome tripartite deals that smack of corporatism and concede too much power to the unions.[22]

Table 7.2 Social background of Conservative and Labour MPs 1979, 1987 and 1992.

| | Conservative | | | Labour | | |
| | % 1979 | % 1987 | % 1992 | % 1979 | % 1987 | % 1992 |
|---|---|---|---|---|---|---|
| Professions | 45 | 42 | 39 | 43 | 40 | 42 |
| Business | 34 | 37 | 38 | 5 | 10 | 8 |
| Public school | 73 | 68 | 62 | 17 | 14 | 14 |
| University | 68 | 70 | 73 | 57 | 56 | 61 |
| Working class | – | 1 | 1 | 35 | 29 | 22 |

Source: A. Ball, *British Political Parties* (Macmillan, 1981), D. Butler and D. Kavanagh, *The British General Election of 1987* (Macmillan, 1987) and D. Butler and D. Kavanagh, *The British General Election of 1992* (Macmillan, 1992)

This contrasts with the alternative strategy favoured by more moderate Conservatives, 'towards which Conservative governments tend to gravitate'. This involves 'some use of free-market policies, but supplemented by corporatist measures for incorporating the unions' into governmental policy making.[23] In practice, of course, these two approaches have been radically reversed since 1979, as successive Conservative governments have taken explicitly right-wing ideological and policy stances on fundamental economic and industrial relations issues, and traditional reformist Conservatives have been virtually excluded from influencing party policy and government action. Whichever wing of the Conservative Party predominates, however, 'the vast majority of business executives in Britain support the Conservative Party; the party has also benefited from donations from companies'.[24]

Turning to the social networks between employers and the Conservative Party, we observe that the evidence is more circumstantial and tenuous, and less rooted in empirical detail. It has to be recognized in the first place that like the trade unions and the Labour Party, neither employers nor the Conservatives are homogeneous groupings. Employers may be large or small, manufacturing or non-manufacturing, whilst the Conservative Party is itself a heterogeneous collection of big business, City, small business, shopkeeper and landed interests. The social composition of Conservative MPs reflects this. According to Ball, Conservative MPs remain 'totally unrepresentative in social background of the electors who vote Conservative'.[25] Table 7.2 illustrates the predominantly public school, university, professional and business background of Conservative MPs in recent Parliaments, certainly in comparison with Labour MPs.

The Conservative Party, however, is not exclusively the party of big business, or even of small business. Electorally, the Conservatives can only win general elections by attracting lower-middle-class and working-class votes, as well as those of higher business executives, professional workers and City or financial interests. Further, farmers and landowners have traditionally been a very powerful and influential group in the Conservative Party and remain so today. The leader of the Conservative Euro-MPs at Strasbourg in the 1980s was a former President of the National Farmers Union (NFU), probably one of the most effective employers' associations and employers' lobbies in Britain. Also, until 1984, when it rescinded its political fund rules, the NFU maintained its own political funds.

Additionally, the British business sector is itself divided, not only between big business and small business but between 'manufacturing industry and finance capital'.[26] It is the CBI which purports to speak for the corporate manufacturing and service sectors, and key public enterprises, but it does not represent Britain's financial institutions and 'it is finance rather than manufacturing which seems the more influential in Britain'.[27] Further it is finance capital or City interests which now appear to have the closer links with the parliamentary Conservative Party. Conservative MPs 'are members of firms in the City; the numerous lawyers who are Conservative MPs also have closer links with the City than with the manufacturing industry'.[28] At the end of 1985, for example, it was disclosed that:

At least 37 peers and MPs, mostly Conservative, have business ties with companies involved in the four consortia fighting for the multi-billion pound Channel Link contract . . . [Moreover] more than a third of the peers who spoke in the Lords debate on the channel link had a direct business interest in one of the consortia.[29]

Both the Euro Route and Channel Tunnel Groups contained two Conservative MPs, including two former cabinet ministers, whilst another Conservative backbencher was parliamentary adviser to Sea Containers, part of the Expressway consortium. It was also reported that a Conservative MP had had to apologize to the Speaker of the House of Commons for failing to reveal, in the Commons register of MPs' interests, 'that he was employed by Grayling, a public relations company working for Flexilink',[30] which was an anti-Channel link group of shipping interests.

With the decline in the relative strength of the landed interest in the Conservative Party, as well as those in the party who were former officers in the armed or colonial services, there has been a significant rise in influence and power of those representing City interests, especially in the parliamentary party in the House of Commons. This has been accompanied by a shift away from the old-fashioned paternalistic Conservatism of past administrations towards the neo-*laissez-faire* ideologies and policies associated with the 'New Right' in the Conservatives which has been ascendent since the mid-1970s. The heavy toll that economic recession had on manufacturing industry and small businesses in the early 1980s seemed to have aroused surprisingly little sympathy among the parliamentary Party. The rise of City interests in the Party partly explains this. Although more concern for industry was expressed during the recession of the early 1990s, MPs were fired more by the effects on the City. Further, the rise of the professional London-based Conservative MP 'has reduced even further the influence of local business executives, often the bedrock of local constituency parties'.[31]

Despite changes in its composition in Parliament, and amongst its supporters in the electorate, the Conservative Party continues to be the main beneficiary from company political donations. In 1984 almost £3 million was provided by companies as political donations, with about £2.25 million going directly to the Conservatives. During the election year of 1987, 428 companies gave £5 536 268 to the party. This was a significant increase over the 235 companies which gave £2 094 619 in 1986. It is usual for the number of donations to increase in election years and to drop off in between but a Labour Research analysis in 1993 revealed that 'company donations to

*Table 7.3* Eleven largest corporate donors to Conservative Party funds 1992–93.

| Company | Donations (£) |
| --- | --- |
| United Biscuits | 130 000 |
| Taylor Woodrow | 124 500 |
| Hanson | 115 000 |
| Glaxo | 102 000 |
| P & O | 100 000 |
| Rothmans International | 100 000 |
| Forte | 80 500 |
| Allied Lyons | 80 000 |
| Caledonia Investments | 79 000 |
| Barings | 70 000 |
| Scottish & Newcastle Breweries | 70 000 |
| Total | 1 051 000 |

All these donations went to the Conservative Party, except £15 000 of Hanson's donation and £12 000 of Glaxo's which went to the Centre for Policy Studies. *Source*: Labour Research Department, *Labour Research*, July 1993

the Tories plummeted in the period up to the last [1992] general election compared with the equivalent period before the 1987 one.'[32]

There were 240 recorded company donations to the Conservative Party in 1992, totalling £3 733 522. This was far below the 1987 figure and one of the reasons was the collapse or failure of previous donor companies during the recession of the early 1990s. Eleven companies which had given almost £1 000 000 in the 1987 campaign did not contribute in 1992. However, some 71 new companies made donations, including Rothmans, Rolls-Royce and the recently privatized Thames Water. Most corporate donations were small and under £5 000. Table 7.3 shows the 11 largest corporate donors, headed by United Biscuits and Taylor Woodrow. These 11 companies gave over £1 000 000 in total, which was about one-quarter of all the official donations to the party in that year.

Most corporate political donations go direct to the Conservative Party, as Table 7.4 shows. Only 23 of the 263 donations recorded did not go directly into party funds and of these 18 went to pro-Conservative bodies. The political or economic agencies supporting the Conservatives include the Centre for Policy Studies (CPS), Aims of Industry and, up to 1993, the British United Industrialists (BUI) and the Economic League (EL). BUI was an organization which existed in part to raise money for the Conservative Party and to launder donations between companies and the party. In 1987–88, BUI received about £200 000

*Table 7.4* Political donations 1992–93.

| Recipient | Number of donations | Total cash received £ |
|---|---|---|
| Conservative Party | 240 | 3 733 552 |
| British United Industrialists | 5 | 74 500 |
| Centre for Policy Studies | 11 | 65 500 |
| Aims of Industry | 1 | 17 050 |
| Liberal Democrats | 2 | 12 000 |
| Economic League | 1 | 3 700 |
| Unspecified | 3 | 1 300 |
| Total | 263 | 3 907 602 |

*Source*: Labour Research, July 1993

from 17 companies and in 1992–93 there were five donations totalling £74 500. About 80 per cent went to the Conservative Party before BUI folded. The CPS, a Conservative think-tank, received £81 500 in 1987–88 and £65 500 in 1992–93. EL and Aims of Industry, both pressure groups dedicated to advancing the causes of private enterprise, received donations of £53 000 and £22 000 respectively in 1987–88 and £17 000 and £3 000 in 1992–93. The EL went into liquidation in April 1993.

What has been a significant trend in recent years has been the growing 'grey area' of money going to the Conservative Party which is not attributable to corporate donations. The Conservative Party's accounts for the financial year ending March 1992 show donations of just over £19 million. Nearly £15 million or 80 per cent of party donations, therefore, remained unaccounted for at that time. Some of this money, it came to light, had been given by foreign businessmen and companies which are not required to disclose their contributions under either British or international law. A great deal of adverse publicity surrounded the disclosure of money received from the Turkish Cypriot businessman Asil Nadir. Notwithstanding these corporate political donations, the Conservative Party was over £19 million in deficit in 1993.

Although the bulk of corporate political donations go to the Conservatives, the Liberal and former Social Democratic parties have also benefited. One of the largest political donations of £188 000 went to the Liberal Party in 1983. This was made by the British School of Motoring (BSM) and was 'equivalent to half the Liberals' central expenditure in 1983 (excluding a separate general election account)'.[33] In 1984 'both Alliance parties continued to be recipients of other company donations'.[34] Thirteen companies

were involved, with the largest sum of £49 000 passing from BSM to the Liberals. All the other sums were relatively small, with another of £5 100 going to the Liberals and £9 500 to the Social Democratic Party (SDP). In 1987–88, the SDP–Liberal Alliance received, prior to its break-up, '25 donations totalling £114 248 from 23 companies in the year to March 1988'.[35] In 1992–93 the Liberal Democrats received only two donations of £12 000 and the Labour Party only one. This probably underestimates the real contributions of smaller businesses.[36]

In view of the fact that trade unions with political funds are required to hold political fund review ballots at least once every 10 years, it is interesting to observe that an LRD survey in 1985 found only six companies asking for shareholders' consent at the AGM to make donations. A report by the Constitutional Reform Centre proposed a voluntary code of practice for companies making political donations. It proposed, first, that companies making political donations should obtain shareholder consent at their annual general meetings (AGM). Second, that company boards wishing to make donations should provide shareholders with a statement of why such actions are in the interests of the company and its shareholders, and that they should seek approval of that statement at their AGMs at least once during the life of a Parliament. Third, companies making political donations should do so openly, without using institutional conduits like the BUI. By law companies must now declare donations of £200 or more and their recipients.

## 7.3 The Trades Union Congress
### Background

The TUC is one of the longest established political interest groups in Britain, having been founded in Manchester in 1868. Previous but unsuccessful attempts had been made in 1833 and 1845 to establish a central organization to represent the collective interests of working men and of the trade unions. The London Trades Council or the 'Junta', which was established in 1860, had emerged as the representative of the exclusive amalgamated societies of the 'labour aristocracy' but it lacked wider representation, particularly within the new northern industrial cities. The call for a trade union 'Congress' in 1868 reflected the intense concern of existing unions towards the Royal Commission which had been appointed in the previous year to 'inquire into and Report on the

Organisation and Rules of Trade Unions'. Representatives of the unions gathered in Manchester and were anxious to present a responsible, constitutional and moderate image of trade unionism to the Royal Commission. They wanted legislation to ensure that trade unions were no longer regarded as criminal conspiracies, and that their funds would be protected from embezzlement by dishonest officials. The first Congress, although poorly attended, agreed upon the necessity of a central trade union body which would meet annually.

The initial and unstable existence of the TUC was transformed by the publication of the Trade Union Bill in 1871. This Bill fell so far short of trade union expectations, still leaving many of their activities potentially criminal, that a new collective determination to protect their interests steadily hardened. At the well-attended Congress of 1871, a Parliamentary Committee of the TUC was established. This was the forerunner of the TUC's modern General Council and was of great influence in the formation of the Labour Party in 1900. From 1871 until the First World War 'the Secretary had only one clerk to assist him in carrying out the work of the Congress; between them they constituted the complete TUC establishment!' The TUC was thus materially ill-equipped to fulfil the duties which the early unions and their leaders expected of it. In 1919 Ernest Bevin, the main architect in the formation of the Transport and General Workers Union, complained that the trade union movement was 'a great shapeless mass, all the time struggling to co-ordinate its efforts, but finding itself without a head to direct'.[37]

Eventually, in 1920, Bevin persuaded Congress to abolish the Parliamentary Committee and to establish a General Council of 30 members representing 17 industrial or trade groups. The first General Council, elected in 1921, possessed much greater power and authority over the policies of the trade union movement than did the former Parliamentary Committee. Increased affiliation fees, for example, were to be used to provide additional staff and better research facilities. It was the General Strike of 1926 and its aftermath, however, which had the most profound effect upon the TUC and its developing General Council.

The collapse of the 1926 General Strike was of course a landmark in the history of the TUC. Immediately it resulted in a severe fall in union membership and morale, but far more than that it meant an urgent need for a reappraisal of the role of Congress and indeed of the movement as a whole.[38]

This 'reappraisal' meant, in the long term, that the TUC turned away from outright political confrontations with governments and employers. Instead, it concentrated its attentions on extending collective bargaining and on improving the machinery of industrial relations for its member unions. Political reform on a broad front was left to the political wing of the Labour movement: that is, the Labour Party. But Congress continued to be concerned with securing government policies and amendments to the law benefiting working people and their families. By the Second World War the TUC was playing an active part in promoting the war effort, with Ernest Bevin occupying a vital role in the War Cabinet as Minister of Labour, but there had been very few significant changes in the fundamental structure and organization of the TUC since 1921. The considerable growth of the TUC's power and influence between 1945 and the late 1970s resulted not from changes in its internal organization and structure, but from a growth in trade union membership and from changes in the impact of trade unionism upon the national economy during that period.

Congress also gained from fundamental shifts in industrial and political power in Britain in the 1970s and from the intervention by successive governments in the private sector of industry.

The standing of Congress therefore depends on the extent and direction of government intervention in the economy and on the ability of the General Council both to influence the government's actions and to bring the unions along with them.[39]

Certainly until 1979, after the election of the first Thatcher administration, few postwar governments failed to consult the TUC before taking major policy decisions on economic or social affairs, or before introducing legislation affecting the interests of the trade union movement. Since 1979, however, Conservative ministers and senior civil servants have effectively excluded the TUC from influencing government policy and have rarely sought the opinion of the TUC before taking major policy initiatives. In effectively depoliticizing British industrial relations and moving towards a more market model of individualized 'employee relations', successive Conservative governments during the 1980s and 1990s have succeeded in neutralizing the role of the TUC and marginalizing its political influence.

Nevertheless, the purposes of the TUC remain what they have been since it was first incorporated into the policy-making process during the Second World War. These are, first, to act as a voice for affiliated unions and for all working people in Britain; second, to advance the interests of affiliated unions and their members by the most appropriate means; and, third, to try to influence government policy in ways beneficial to affiliated unions and their members. The TUC also seeks a voice in international labour affairs. It was, for example, a founder member of the International Confederation of Free Trade Unions in 1949 and is the British workers' delegate to the International Labour Organisation. The TUC also belongs to the European Trade Union Confederation, which deals with issues of interest to working people both inside and outside the European Union, and the Trade Union Advisory Committee of the Organisation for Economic Co-operation and Development.

The main means used by the TUC to further its aims and objectives include: lobbying MPs, government departments and ministers; maintaining close links with the Labour Party and senior Labour MPs; nominating trade union representatives to national, regional and local bodies; and publishing and disseminating research papers, discussion documents and policy statements. It also uses the media and appropriate public relations techniques to publicize its activities.

## Structure and activities

Britain is one of the few countries to have a single trade union confederation representing all major trade unions. In many other industrial nations in the western world, 'trade unions and their national centres are divided on the basis of party politics or on religious grounds'. In others the division is between a national centre for manual workers' unions and one for non-manual unions. 'The trade union Movement in Britain is fortunate in having only one national centre',[40] the TUC. The basic unit is the affiliated union; collectively they provide the TUC with its representative authority and its organizational finance, each union paying an annual affiliation fee based on its total membership. Table 7.5 shows that in 1991 the TUC had 74 affiliated organizations comprising a membership of over eight million trade unionists. Between 1979 and 1991, the number of affiliated organizations fell from 112 to 74 and total membership by one-third. A major reason

*Table 7.5* TUC affiliated organizations and membership 1979–91.

| Year | Number of affiliated organizations | TUC membership |
| --- | --- | --- |
| 1979 | 112 | 12 128 078 |
| 1980 | 109 | 12 172 508 |
| 1981 | 108 | 11 601 413 |
| 1982 | 105 | 11 005 984 |
| 1983 | 95 | 10 510 157 |
| 1984 | 89 | 10 082 144 |
| 1985 | 91 | 9 855 204 |
| 1986 | 89 | 9 580 502 |
| 1987 | 87 | 9 243 297 |
| 1988 | 83 | 9 127 278 |
| 1991 | 74 | 8 192 664 |

*Source*: TUC, *Annual Reports* (TUC 1979–89)

for the fall in the number of TUC affiliates was the incidence of amalgamations and mergers taking place between some unions during these years. These arose largely out of economic necessity especially for those unions which, for various reasons, experienced membership decline and financial pressures on their organizational resources. This influenced, for example, the merger between the National and Local Government Officers Association, the National Union of Public Employees and the Confederation of Health Service Employees to form a new union, UNISON, with over a million members, in July 1993. The fall in total union membership amongst TUC affiliates since 1980 is a reflection of the increased levels of unemployment: unions have lost members as jobs have disappeared through redundancy, natural wastage and early retirements, especially in manufacturing industry.

The supreme policy-making body of the TUC is its annual Congress which meets at Blackpool on the first Monday in September, remains in session for five days and is presided over by the Chair of the General Council. Affiliated unions are entitled to send delegates to Congress on the basis of one for every 5 000 members 'or part thereof'. They total some 1 000 and are nominated by individual unions at branch or area level. They are normally mandated to support at Congress those policies democratically determined at their own union conferences. Congress has three main functions: it considers the work done and reported on by the General Council during the previous year; it discusses and takes decisions on motions forwarded to it for the agenda by affiliated unions; and it appoints the General Council for the coming year.

The report of the General Council covers key areas: relations between unions; trade union organization and industrial relations; equal rights; social insurance and industrial welfare; environment; education and training; trade union education; international affairs; economic policy; industry committees; the European Union; press and information; and finance and resources. Policy debates at Congress result from motions submitted for the agenda by affiliated unions. Where several unions submit similar or associated motions, they are combined together or 'composited'. Amendments to motions are also submitted by individual unions. Before Congress opens, the General Council meets to determine its position on agenda items. If it agrees with a motion it says so. If it disagrees, a member of the General Council is selected to move its rejection or for it to be 'remitted back' to the General Council for its consideration. This usually means the motion will be lost in all but name. Where the feelings of Congress are clear on a motion, the Chair of Congress asks for a vote by show of hands. But if there is sufficient demand for a 'card vote' from delegates, the Chair normally concedes it. This means that each trade union leader holds up a card representing its total affiliated membership. The total 'votes' cast are then counted. This is known as the 'block vote' which enables each union to influence voting decisions in proportion to its total membership.

One of the most important functions of Congress is to elect the General Council for the forthcoming year. The General Council has a number of duties. The main ones are:

(a) The General Council shall transact the business in the periods between each annual Congress, shall keep a watch on all industrial movements, and shall, where possible, co-ordinate industrial action.
(b) They shall watch all legislation affecting labour, and shall initiate such legislation as Congress may direct.
(c) They shall endeavour to adjust disputes and differences between affiliated organisations.
(d) They shall promote common action by the trade union Movement on general questions, such as wages and hours of labour, and any matter of general concern that may arise ... and shall have power to assist any union which is attacked on any vital question of trade union principle.[41]

Until 1981–82, the General Council was organized into 18 'trade groups' with an additional group for women. At their 1981 Congress, however, delegates resolved that a new system of determining the composition of the General Council was necessary, since the trade group principle was becoming less relevant to the changing composition of affiliated membership. After 1982 the General Council consisted of three sections but by 1992 this had increased to four sections. Section A consists of representation for all affiliates with over 200 000 members each. Unions with between 200 000 and 399 999 members have two seats each; those between 400 000 and 649 999 three seats each; those between 650 000 and 899 999 four seats each; those between 900 000 and 1 199 999 five seats each; and those between 1 200 000 and 1 499 999 six seats each. Section B consists of members from those organizations with a membership of 100 000 up to 199 999, with each union having one General Council seat each. Section C consists of representatives of all unions with fewer than 100 000 members. The total number of representatives is related to the total numerical membership of those smaller unions on a sliding scale. Thus there are 11 seats for unions with a total membership of between 1 600 000 and 1 759 999, regressing to six seats for unions with a total membership between 800 000 and 959 999. Section D consists of four women members, all of whom are members of affiliated organizations with fewer than 200 000 members each.

Between Congresses, the General Council is not merely the custodian of Congress decisions, it also has to respond to events. In this way, it has an inescapable leadership function which has to be exercised cautiously, given the General Council's representative capacity and its responsibility for the trade union movement as a whole. Occasionally the General Council uses the device of convening special conferences of union national executives where vital policy decisions of national importance to the trade unions have to be made between Congresses. Examples include the TUC's opposition to the Industrial Relations Bill in 1971 and the Employment Bill in 1982, and in 1986 when the TUC convened a special conference to reconsider the movement's policy towards government funding for trade union ballots.

The General Council meets monthly and is served by eleven standing committees one or more of which are attended by General Council members and the General Secretary. These committees are: Finance and General Purposes; International; Education and Training; Social Insurance and Industrial Welfare; Employment Policy and Organization; Economic; Equal Rights; Trade Union Education; European Strategy; Environment Action Group; and the Women's Committee. Each committee is serviced by one or more of the TUC's departments and their professional staff, which in recent years has placed a heavy burden of work on departmental personnel. This has been compounded by having to adjust to continual changes in the economy, the law and government policies. Delegates at Congress regularly urge the TUC to provide more and better services to affiliated unions, to conduct additional research and to provide more information to them, whilst at the same time normally opposing moves to increase affiliation fees proportionally.

The work of the TUC is also assisted by eight industry committees covering: construction; energy; financial services; health services; local government; textiles; clothing and footwear; and transport. These committees bring together all TUC unions with members in these industries and co-ordinate collective bargaining and industrial relations policies among them. Some of these industry committees have replaced federations of trade unions which previously acted independently of the TUC. The TUC also has five joint committees covering a wide range of activities with external bodies. These are: pensioners; public services; race relations; regional councils; and a youth forum.

Despite the fact that the TUC covers the whole of England and Wales – Scotland has its own TUC – it does not possess a strong regional structure. Traditionally, it is local trade councils representing the interests of trade union branches from affiliated unions at local level which provide TUC representation outside London. Trade union branches can affiliate to their local trades council, sending delegates to them according to the size of their branch membership. The trades council is then registered by the TUC. Trades councils in England and Wales act as local agents for the TUC. Funds are provided from affiliation fees paid by local union branches. Trades councils operate model rules, approved by Congress, devised to prevent them from subscribing to the funds of breakaway unions or to the Communist Party and other proscribed organizations.

Many trades councils in the large industrial cities were established long before the TUC itself, and they continue to provide a valuable forum for grass roots union debate on local and regional affairs.

The TUC also organizes a conference of trades councils each year and issues an annual report dealing with their activities. Nevertheless, despite TUC supervision some trades councils are taken over by proscribed bodies. In other instances, they follow courses of action which offend declared TUC policies. As a result, they are sometimes suspended. The TUC admits that trades councils are often ignored or poorly supported by trade union branches and that some branches are 'unwilling to become associated with trades councils because of their belief that some trades councils are unrepresentative of the mainstream of the trade union movement and tend towards extremist views'.[42]

Because of the unwillingness of affiliated unions to pay increased affiliation fees, the TUC's regional councils depend upon voluntary officers to run them, obviously limiting their effectiveness. The TUC has voiced its concern at the lack of adequate full-time officer support for the regional structure. Hence the TUC is almost unique among national bodies in not having a strong regional organization.

Although the TUC's direct impact on the government has diminished substantially since 1979, it is still represented on a number of bodies created by government. Senior members of the TUC serve, *inter alia*, on the Health and Safety Executive, the Equal Opportunities Commission, the Council of the Advisory Conciliation and Arbitration Service, and the boards of certain public corporations. Service on these nationally important bodies places a considerable burden on the members of the General Council and on the TUC staff who brief and service them. Further, members of the General Council are either general secretaries or national officers of individual unions, with all the heavy work burdens which this involves.

In order to fulfil its wide responsibilities on behalf of the trade union movement, the TUC continuously seeks a more responsive and representative General Council, and means of providing better representation for women members. It also accepts the need periodically to review its committee system, its provision of educational services and its internal organization. Its legal, research and information services are regularly updated too. This is in keeping with the TUC's established involvement in the various public agencies created by successive governments. Whilst it seems generally agreed that the TUC reacts only slowly to institutional change, it has nevertheless adapted itself to the varying circumstances facing member unions. Critics believe its central weakness to be its lack of executive authority over affiliated organizations. Its supporters emphasize its considerable moral authority over affiliates. The TUC's political influence on government policy, however, tends to be greater and more effective under Labour governments; under Conservative ones the TUC's impact is generally weaker and tends to fluctuate or diminish.

## 7.4 The Confederation of British Industry

The first successful attempt to establish a central organization of employer interests was during the First World War, when the Federation of British Industries was formed in 1916. Its main purpose was to advance the commercial interests of member firms. The formation of earlier organizations had not achieved any permanent or co-ordinated central association of employers in Britain up till that time. But the monopoly interest of the Federation of British Industries was short lived, since immediately afterwards the National Union of Manufacturers – later known as the National Association of British Manufacturers – was formed. Its major focus was the special interests of small manufacturers. In the meantime:

> Some of the employers' organisations, particularly the key Engineering Employers' Federation, were suspicious of the quasi-syndicalist ideas of some of the FBI's leaders and eventually formed a separate organisation to deal with labour matters, latterly called the British Employers' Confederation.[43]

Thus by the end of the First World War, three separate central organizations of employers were claiming to represent the collective interests of private sector businesses in Britain – the Federation of British Industries (FBI), the National Association of British Manufacturers (NABM) and the British Employers' Confederation (BEC).

Since the NABM always had a larger proportion of small firms amongst its members compared with the other two employer organizations, its policies and activities often conflicted with those of the other two bodies. Moreover, the separate existence of the Confederation with its main interests focused on industrial relations, and the Federation with its principal concerns centred in commercial affairs, continually provoked difficulties between the two organizations for many years. Furthermore, the

interventionist policies of the wartime coalition government between 1940 and 1945, and the postwar Labour government immediately afterwards, created new areas in which co-ordinated consultation between government and all major private sector employers was increasingly necessary. Despite attempts to amalgamate these two central organizations of employers during the 1940s, no agreement on terms could be reached between them. In these circumstances, 'the BEC lived a predominantly defensive life, the FBI a largely promotional one'.[44]

The main impetus leading up to the merger between the Confederation, the Federation and the small business manufacturers to form the CBI in 1965 was the renewed interest which took place in economic planning in Britain after 1960. Accordingly, the need for creating more effective and co-ordinated arrangements for the representation of industrial opinion than hitherto became more pressing.

> Thus, in July 1963, the Presidents of the FBI, the BEC and the NABM appointed Sir Henry Benson and Sir Stephen Brown to prepare a report on the way in which the three organisations could be merged into one National Industrial Organisation.[45]

As things turned out, the FBI was generally in favour of the Benson–Brown proposals, since the new body was to operate under the Federation's revised charter. Elements within the BEC, however, initially opposed the proposals for a merger among the three bodies. The Engineering Employers Federation, for example, was especially hostile. Amongst other things, its leaders disliked the suggested constitution:

> because it would allow direct membership and representation on the labour committee to individual firms. If companies paid subscriptions to the new body, the Federation argued, they might not also wish to pay to their employers' organisation, particularly if they could exercise influence through the labour committee.[46]

Although in the end the Engineering Federation withdrew its objections because it did not wish to be made the scapegoat for a breakdown in negotiations among the parties, it had made its point.

The NABM, on the other hand, proved a much more difficult body to fit into the new organization than its two other constituents. Many of its members felt that the particular interests of smaller businesses would not be defended by the CBI, since it would be predominantly made up of larger employers. They were also opposed to the proposal to admit the nationalized industries into membership. The question of admitting nationalized industries into the CBI was contested on two fronts. First, there were those private sector firms opposed in principle to nationalization. Second, there were those individuals who saw nationalization as a fundamental socialist measure. They were equally opposed to public sector organizations joining a predominantly private sector body. In the event, a breakaway organization, the Society of Independent Manufacturers, was formed which later became the Smaller Businesses Association.

The CBI came into being by amalgamation among the three constituent organizations on 30 July 1965. Its initial membership comprised '12 600 firms, the main nationalised industries, 104 employers' organisations and 150 trade associations'.[47] The set of events which tipped the balance in favour of the merger was the approach made by the newly elected Labour government to British industrial representatives at the end of 1964. The freshly appointed Secretary of State and Minister of Economic Affairs, George Brown, soon made it clear that he wanted to discuss industrial matters and to pursue his productivity policy with only one body of employers, not three. Moreover, the increasing influence of the TUC in economic and political affairs clearly demonstrated to the diehards of private industry that the collective interests of their members and of employers in Britain generally could only be maintained and developed on a unified basis through a common central organization.

Under the terms of its Royal Charter, the principal objects of the CBI are:

(a)  to provide for British industry the means of formulating, making known and influencing general policy in regard to industrial, economic, fiscal, commercial, labour, social, legal and technical questions, and to act as a national point of reference for those seeking industry's views;

(b)  to develop the contribution of British industry to the national economy;

(c)  to encourage the efficiency and competitive power of British industry, and to provide advice, information and services to British industry to that end.[48]

The Confederation's functions on behalf of its member organizations, therefore, are much wider than those in the field of industrial relations alone.

Unlike its counterparts in Italy and Sweden for example, the Confederation is not a collective bargaining agency and its main task on behalf of member organizations in industrial relations and other fields is to formulate general employer policy for implementation by its constituent bodies. Its preferred policies are communicated to government, the general public and the TUC. The CBI, therefore, is not only concerned with giving its members an opportunity to voice their opinions, 'it must also ensure that those opinions are aggregated into a policy which is well-informed as well as representative of industrial opinion'.[49]

## Membership and organization

The CBI claims to be the 'recognized voice of British business'. It exists primarily:

> to voice the views of its members in ensuring that governments of whatever political complexion – and society as a whole – understand both the needs of British business and the contribution it makes to the well-being of the nation.[50]

It seeks to create a climate of opinion in which business can operate efficiently and profitably. It campaigns to lessen the burdens on business, tackle handicaps in competition and help to improve the performance of companies. The four basic aims of the CBI are:

- To uphold the market systems and the profit motive that sustain them.
- To bring home to the public at large that no other system offers comparable opportunities for growth with such freedom of choice and action for the individual.
- To oppose further encroachments on the private sector whenever this is inconsistent with the proper functions of the market system.
- To press for greater freedom from Government interference for the existing nationalised sector and permit its proper commercial development.[51]

The CBI is consulted by government, the civil service and the media on major national issues. An important part of its task is to represent business interests at regional and local levels too.

Like most other employer bodies, the CBI is made up of corporate members, with membership drawn from many sectors of British business. It claims to represent the interests of more than a quarter of a million firms and organizations that embrace all sectors of industry and commerce in the UK. These include manufacturers, accountants, bankers, surveyors, building societies, transport and distribution companies, hotels, vehicle manufacturers, textile companies, exporters, publishers, solicitors, wholesalers and retailers and advertisers. Many members are multinational businesses or parent companies with numerous subsidiaries but over half are companies with 200 employees or fewer. Prior to the privatization of the nationalized industries after 1983, many of those bodies and the public corporations were also members. Some 200 employer organizations, trade associations and commercial associations representing individual manufacturing industries, local trade associations and Chambers of Commerce are also members of the CBI.

Although the CBI claims to speak for the whole business sector, many small firms continue to see it as an organization dominated by larger firms. They are reluctant to join it, even though there is a Smaller Firms Council designed to promote and protect their interests. During the recessions of the early 1980s, late 1980s and early 1990s, many manufacturing firms felt that the CBI was ineffective in promoting their interests as the manufacturing sector contracted by nearly 20 per cent. In an attempt to cater more specifically for manufacturing firms, the CBI set up a National Manufacturing Council in 1993. This was to act as the voice of the UK's manufacturers and to seek to ensure that the UK entered the twenty-first century with a manufacturing base matching the best in the world. Apart from the nationalized industries and public utilities, other parts of the public sector, including central and local government, have not joined. Despite its claim to represent industry, therefore, the CBI is largely representative of sections of private manufacturing industry and commerce. Wide gaps in its potential membership remain.

Figure 7.2 provides an outline of the CBI's organizational structure. The CBI's governing body is its Council, normally chaired for two years by a President who is elected by the membership. Council consists of elected office holders, such as a deputy president, two vice-presidents and the last six past presidents, and the chairpersons of its Standing Committees. Other representatives on the CBI's Council come from employer, trade and commercial organizations, the public sector, its Regional Councils, the Smaller Firms Council and individuals drawn from member organizations of all sizes and activities. All these people are senior professional

managers or owner-managers from the private and public sectors. As the ruling body of the CBI, Council takes all policy decisions but in doing so is advised by its Standing Committees. Additionally, the annual National Conference enables delegates to debate policy issues and make their contribution to policy determination. CBI policy has two aspects:

> In the long term, the aim is to make a constructive contribution to attitudes and forward thinking on issues affecting business. In the short term, the CBI has to be equipped to react quickly and positively to any proposals by Government or others, which have a bearing on industry and commerce.[52]

Because of its size, Council is too large a body to decide policy details. These are determined by the Standing Committees. The CBI's Standing Committees cover every aspect of business life and are responsible for most of its detailed work on policy making. They put forward ideas, draft policy proposals and present them to Council, drawing on the views of Regional Councils, the Smaller Firms Council and individual members. Each Standing Committee covers a specific area of policy, with the President's Committee having wider terms of reference. It consists of leading CBI figures, including the chairpersons of key Standing Committees and the Smaller Firms Council. 'Its role is to advise the President on major policy issues and to keep the CBI's public position and overall strategy under constant review.'[53]

The CBI's Standing Committees are important bodies. Some are purely representative and are concerned with obtaining consensus on general policy. Others are specialist committees focusing on particular aspects of policy, whilst others are co-ordinating committees which attempt to keep different policies in line with one another. Each council, committee or group of committees is serviced by one of ten internal directorates. These are: Administration; Company Affairs; Education and Training; International Affairs; Economics; Employment Affairs; Environmental Affairs; Public Affairs; Manufacturing Industries; and Membership. The Director-General, assisted by two Deputy Directors-General, is the CBI's chief executive. The Director-General heads the permanent staff of around 300, communicates regularly with the media and the public, and leads negotiations with government and the civil service on specific issues.

The CBI is also divided into regions and regards

**PRESIDENT**

In addition to chairing the monthly CBI Council, the President leads major CBI delegations to see Government Ministers. He normally holds his appointments for a two-year period. Sir Michael Angus, Chairman of Whitbread plc, succeeded Sir Brian Corby as President in May 1992. Previous holders of the office include Sir Trevor Holdsworth, Sir David Nickson, KBE, DL, Sir James Cleminson, MC, DL, Lord Pennock, Sir John Hedley Greenborough, the Rt Hon. the Viscount Watkinson, CH, Sir Ralph Bateman, KBE, Sir Michael Clapham, KBE.

**DIRECTOR-GENERAL**

The CBI's chief executive, the Director-General, heads the CBI's permanent staff of around 300 who carry out the bulk of the day-to-day work of running the CBI, preparing policy and negotiating with Ministers and civil servants. He is appointed by the President with the approval of CBI Council. In June 1992 Mr Howard Davies succeeded Sir John Banham, Director-General since March 1987; his predecessors were Sir Terence Beckett (1980/87), Sir John Methven (1976/80), Sir Campbell Adamson (1969/76) and Mr John Davies (1965/69)

**SENIOR STAFF**

Director-General: Howard Davies.
Deputy Director-General and Secretary: Maurice Hunt
Deputy Director-General: Richard Price

**COMPANY AFFAIRS**

Company law
Competition policy
Government contracts
Corporate responsibilities
Commercial law
Consumer affairs
Industrial policy
Utilities
Water supply
Production and productivity

**ECONOMICS**

Economic and financial policy
Liaison with the City
Taxation policy
Accounting standards
Economic situation and forecasting, including Industrial Trends Surveys
Statistics policy

**EDUCATION AND TRAINING**

Links between business and schools, universities, polytechnics and colleges
Education and training policy

**INTERNATIONAL AFFAIRS**

Overseas trade policy
EC policy
International relations
Trading conditions in individual countries
Overseas investment
Export promotion policy and export credits
Development aid

**EMPLOYMENT AFFAIRS**

Industrial relations
Conditions of employment
Pay determination, pay databank
Social Security, National Insurance and sick pay arrangements
Pensions
Employee participation and communication
Employment information services
Employment law
European and international industrial relations
Disabled employees

**ENVIRONMENTAL AFFAIRS**

Environment
Health and safety

**ADMINISTRATION**

Secretariat servicing CBI Council, Finance and General Purposes Committee and the Presidents Committee
Finance, personnel, data processing and central management services
Conferences and special events
Publications and marketing
Publicity activities
CBI News
Project excellence
Library Services

**PUBLIC AFFAIRS**

Relations with press

**MANUFACTURING INDUSTRIES**

Manufacturing sector issues
Marketing
Research and technology
Technical barriers to trade
Standards policy

**MEMBERSHIP**

CBI In the Regions
Regional Councils and Members' Groups
Consultation with membership
All aspects of CBI's activities dealing with smaller firms
Impact of legislation, taxation, industrial stategy and regional, economic and financial policy on smaller firms
Membership recruitment and retention

Source: CBI (1993)

*Figure 7.2* Organizational structure of the CBI.

its regional organization as an important means of keeping headquarters staff, councils and committees in touch with local opinion. Each region has its own Regional Council which acts as a sounding board for membership opinion, whilst facilitating personal contact amongst local members.

> The Regional Councils regularly discuss national issues and the results of these discussions are reported to the CBI Council by their representatives so that regional problems can be taken into account in policy formation.[54]

Regional Councils also provide machinery for consultation with local government and central government officials in their own regions.

## Activities

The two major groups of activities in which the CBI is involved are membership services and membership representation. Membership services are wide ranging. The CBI is, for example, an important source of information for daily business needs. It has specialist staff in company law, industrial relations, employment legislation, taxation, education and training, and overseas trade. Members draw on staff expertise thereby keeping themselves up to date on a variety of matters affecting their businesses. The relevant information is communicated by publications, telephone, the Directorates, or the nearest CBI regional office. The Pay Data Bank, for instance, enables member firms to have an accurate and authoritative picture of current pay awards. The Employee Communication Unit draws on wide experience in briefing companies on the best way of ensuring information flows to their workforces, whilst Regional Councils regularly update local trading situations affecting their members.

In representing members' interests, the CBI has extensive contacts in Westminster and Whitehall, locally and internationally. The CBI is represented, for example, on the Advisory Conciliation and Arbitration Service (ACAS), the Health and Safety Commission, the Commission for Racial Equality (CRE) and the Equal Opportunities Commission (EOC). The CBI also lobbies ministers, government departments and MPs. The earlier government policy making can be influenced the better it is for the CBI and its members. To do this:

> The CBI has to be aware of the thinking of Ministers, the research aims of the political parties, back-bench MPs and civil servants on a continuous basis to ensure its views are put forward at the best possible opportunity.[55]

The process continues as government proposals or consultative documents are published and as bills pass through Parliament. Constructive working relationships are also maintained with the TUC both directly on *ad hoc* issues and through joint membership of public bodies like ACAS. Like the TUC, however, the CBI found it much more difficult to influence government policies in the 1980s and 1990s. This resulted from governments moving away from a corporatist policy making framework to a more market-centred one, effectively excluding CBI and TUC initiatives in the process.

Local issues and local government are equally important target areas for the CBI. Its regional offices and regional councillors, for example, are in constant contact with local authorities, MPs, MEPs and government departments. The CBI also maintains close links with international bodies. These include the European Commission, the European Parliament, the UK Delegation and various European Union institutions through its Brussels office. As the major central organization of employers in Britain, the CBI is a member of the Union of Industrial and Employers' Confederations of Europe. In more general terms, the CBI seeks to put forward CBI policies to the wider public, both at home and abroad. It therefore maintains close contacts with newspaper, radio and television journalists, with the aim of establishing a better general understanding 'of the wealth-creating role of business and of the opportunities within industry and commerce for satisfying work'.[56]

In its short history, there is little doubt that the CBI has had a major impact on economic and industrial affairs as the major central organization of employers in Britain, even though its views have been less well received by governments since 1979. Its members include many of the large manufacturing companies in the country and some important service ones. Moreover, like the TUC, the CBI has a degree of access to political lobbying, and to appointments on bodies like industrial tribunals and the Council of ACAS, which few other political interest groups can equal. However, it also has its weaknesses. For example, it has not yet extended its membership coverage across the whole of British industry as widely as some of its advocates have suggested. It is strongest among large firms; it is weakest among smaller firms. It has successfully recruited in manufacturing industry; it has been less successful in parts of the service sector. It is also argued that, in comparison with some of its European counterparts, the CBI is under-financed in relation to the wide range of tasks which it attempts to undertake. Finally, the CBI is not a tight and cohesive body but, like the TUC, a coalition interest group with all the advantages and disadvantages which this type of organization brings. According to one authority:

> there is always potential tension in the CBI between those members who would prefer to see the organisation follow a 'strategy of responsibility', cooperating with government in the implementation of its policies in the hope of securing concessions, and those who would like the CBI to engage in more frequent and more outspoken criticisms of government policy even if this impairs the organisation's ability to negotiate concessions from government.[57]

## 7.5    The Electorate and Changing Political Alignments

The party political preferences which voters express in parliamentary elections every four or five years determine the outcome of general elections. The outcome of general elections, in turn, enables the leading party in the House of Commons to take office and to implement its economic, social and industrial relations policies. These policies and governmental programmes have major implications for everyone whether as citizens, workers or trade unionists. As we indicate in this chapter, political divisions in Britain are based largely on social class interests, especially occupational ones. Throughout the immediate post-war period in the 1950s and 1960s, the backbone of Labour Party political support was the manual working class, substantial parts of which were strongly unionized. The backbone of Conservative support was the professional and business middle classes which tended not to be unionized and were generally hostile to trade unionism, although without the support of one-third of the working class the Conservatives would never have been elected to office. Since the 1970s, the occupational structure, the distribution of union membership and political allegiances within the electorate have changed. What was predominantly a blue-collar labour force which was strongly unionized is steadily becoming a white-collar and less well-organized one. And what was

*Table 7.6* Class composition of the electorate 1964 and 1983.

| Class | 1964 % | 1983 % |
|---|---|---|
| Salariat | 18 | 27 |
| Routine non-manual | 18 | 24 |
| Self employed | 7 | 8 |
| Supervisors and technicians | 10 | 7 |
| Manual working class | 47 | 34 |

*Source*: A. Heath *et al.*, *How Britain Votes* (Pergamon 1985)

predominantly a two-party political system seems to be shifting towards a more multiparty one. These economic and political changes have important implications not only electorally but also for the politics of industrial relations.

Table 7.6 provides a five-fold occupational classification of the electorate and shows how its class structure changed substantially between 1964 and 1983. The manual working class was the largest occupational group in both years. But whereas in 1964 it constituted nearly half of the electorate, and was almost three times the size of the salariat of managers, administrators and professional workers, by 1983 the working class and salariat 'were almost of the same size'. Further, whilst the salariat and routine non-manual workers made up 36 per cent of the electorate in 1964, they constituted 51 per cent in 1983. Britain is still divided by social class and occupational differences but 'the shape of the class structure has changed, with important electoral implications particularly for Labour.'[58] In other words, between 1964 and 1983 Britain was transformed from a largely blue collar workforce to a predominantly white collar one, with corresponding changes in trade union membership and in the political allegiances of the electorate.

Table 7.7 shows the relationship between class and voting in the 1964 and 1983 general elections. In 1983 the Conservative vote was lower among the salariat and routine non-manual workers than in 1964 but higher among supervisors and technicians and the manual working class, whilst the self-employed were consistently 'the most Conservative class, and indeed by far the most united class in its politics'. The Labour vote was lower across all classes, particularly among supervisors and technicians and the manual working class. The Alliance vote was higher across the classes, notably among the manual working class

*Table 7.7* Class and vote 1964 and 1983.

| Party | Salariat | | Routine non-manual | | Self employed | | Supervisors/ Technicians | | Manual working class | |
|---|---|---|---|---|---|---|---|---|---|---|
| | 1964 | 1983 | 1964 | 1983 | 1964 | 1983 | 1964 | 1983 | 1964 | 1983 |
| | | | | | % | | | | | |
| Conservative | 61 | 54 | 54 | 46 | 74 | 71 | 40 | 48 | 23 | 30 |
| Labour | 20 | 14 | 31 | 25 | 12 | 12 | 44 | 26 | 70 | 49 |
| Liberal/Alliance | 18 | 31 | 14 | 27 | 13 | 17 | 15 | 25 | 7 | 20 |
| Others | 1 | 1 | 1 | 2 | 1 | 0 | 1 | 1 | 0 | 1 |

*Source*: A. Heath *et al.*, *How Britain Votes* (Pergamon 1985)

where it rose from 7 per cent in 1964 to 20 per cent in 1983. 'Over the 1964 to 1983 period as a whole the dominant impression is one of "trendless" fluctuation rather than steady dealignment'. Yet if 1964 was the high point of relative class voting, 1983 was remarkable for 'the challenge it posed to the long-standing and overwhelming dominance of the Conservative and Labour parties within British electoral politics'.[59]

Table 7.8 outlines how Britain voted in the general election of 1987. It indicates that whilst the correlation between social class and voting behaviour had weakened 'divisions between the manual and working classes remain important'. According to Mass Opinion Research Investigations (MORI) 54 per cent of the middle class voted Conservative, compared with 18 per cent voting Labour. Similarly, 48 per cent of unskilled manual workers voted Labour, compared with 30 per cent voting Conservative. The most significant feature of the Conservative Party's support in this election was its strength amongst the working class. Here 'it gained 36% of the vote (compared to Labour's 48%), its largest post-war share'. As in 1979 and 1983, Conservative support

was built on the 'new working class'. These are manual workers, living in the south, who are house owners, employed in the private sector and not union members. Other features of Table 7.8 are the Alliance parties' consistent share of the vote across all social classes, all age groups, all trade unionists and between the sexes.

Table 7.9 shows the pattern of voting in the general election of 1992. Here one can discern both a slight revival of class voting and a qualified endorsement of two-party politics. The Labour Party increased its vote among skilled workers (class C1) from 36 per cent in 1987 to 40 per cent in 1992 and among unskilled workers (DE) from 48 per cent to 49 per cent in 1992, whilst the Conservative Party won back some support among the salariat (AB and C1). The Labour Party sharply improved its vote among the professional and managerial classes (AB), which was up by 9 per cent from 1987, with both main parties taking votes from the Liberal Democrats, whose support fell among all classes.

In the elections between 1945 and 1970 the two major parties took nearly 90 per cent of the vote between them. From 1970 to 1987 that share fell to

*Table 7.8* How Britain voted in 1987.

| | Class | | | | Sex | | Age | | | | |
|---|---|---|---|---|---|---|---|---|---|---|---|
| | ABC1 | C2 | DE | Union members | Men | Women | 18–24 | 25–34 | 35–54 | 55+ | All |
| All | 43 | 27 | 30 | 23 | 48 | 52 | 14 | 19 | 33 | 34 | 100 |
| Conservative | 54 | 40 | 30 | 30 | 43 | 43 | 37 | 39 | 45 | 46 | 43 |
| Labour | 18 | 36 | 48 | 42 | 32 | 32 | 40 | 33 | 29 | 31 | 32 |
| Alliance | 26 | 22 | 22 | 26 | 23 | 23 | 21 | 25 | 24 | 21 | 23 |
| Other | 2 | 2 | 2 | 2 | 2 | 2 | 2 | 2 | 2 | 2 | 2 |

*Source*: *British Public Opinion: General Election 1987* (MORI, 1987)

*Table 7.9* How Britain voted in 1992.

| | AB | C1 | C2 | DE | Union member | Council tenant | Men | Women | 18–24 | 25–34 | 35–54 | 55+ | Total |
|---|---|---|---|---|---|---|---|---|---|---|---|---|---|
| All | 19 | 24 | 27 | 30 | 23 | 23 | 49 | 51 | 14 | 19 | 13 | 34 | 100 |
| Conservative | 56 | 52 | 39 | 31 | 31 | 24 | 41 | 44 | 35 | 40 | 43 | 46 | 43 |
| Labour | 19 | 25 | 40 | 49 | 46 | 55 | 37 | 34 | 39 | 38 | 34 | 34 | 35 |
| Lib Democrat | 22 | 19 | 17 | 16 | 19 | 15 | 18 | 18 | 19 | 18 | 19 | 17 | 18 |
| Con–Lab swing | 3 | 1½ | 2½ | 0 | 2 | 1½ | 3½ | ½ | ½ | 1½ | 3½ | 1½ | 1½ |

*Source*: Butler, D. and Kavanagh, D., *The British General Election 1992*, p. 277, Macmillan: Basingstoke

75 per cent but increased to 78 per cent in 1992. Since 1970 neither the Conservative Party nor the Labour Party have managed to win office with more than 43 per cent of the total votes cast. Throughout the period the Liberals – or the Liberals and their allies or more recently the Liberal Democrats – have gained between 18 and 25 per cent of the vote and have offered an alternative to the two major parties. Tactical voting has become a feature of British elections and 'proved to be more widespread and more important [in 1992] than in previous elections. Tactical voting on its own probably halved Mr Major's majority'.[60]

In spite of the slight revival of class voting in 1992, a degree of class de-alignment has occurred amongst the British electorate over the past 20 years and, in particular, the Labour Party has been less attractive to its traditional voters. There are a number of explanations for this trend. One is that the social composition of the classes has changed and this is reflected in changed voting behaviour. Deindustrialization and the growth of white collar professions, especially in the public sector, have led to growth in the middle classes. The 'new middle classes', however, are a fragmented and heterogeneous group. They consist of people with working class origins and partisan loyalties and those who are committed to liberal values and favour public service and professional standards over commercialism and wealth creation. This subgroup is attracted more to those parties which support social reform and the welfare state rather than the market. But within the new middle classes, there are also those who identify with free enterprise, the market and the existing social structure. These individuals are more likely to find their natural political home with the Conservatives.

Second, Labour's traditional support base, the manual working class, has been shrinking in size for some years now. Between 1979 and 1992, the working class declined from 41 per cent to 34 per cent of the electorate, whilst the professional and managerial salariat grew from 26 per cent to 29 per cent. Although the working class is still the largest social and occupational grouping in Britain, it has declined owing to technological changes and the relative long-term contraction of the manufacturing sector of the economy. This has resulted in an increase in the size of the service sector, a contraction of the old staple industries – like coal, iron and steel and shipbuilding – and an expansion of the routine non-manual workforce relative to manual employment. These trends have weakened Labour's traditional voting strongholds.

The manual working class, however, has never voted solidly Labour, with one-third traditionally supporting the Conservatives. Explanations of this working class Conservatism have emphasized 'either the notion of working class deference or that of inherited party loyalties'.[61] It is evident that inherited party loyalties now play a less significant part in people's political socialization than in the past and that other factors explain their political support. Although social class may still be important, non-class cleavages are significant too. Housing and whether people are home owners or council house tenants appear to affect the way that people vote. Only 24 per cent of council house tenants voted Conservative in 1992, compared with 55 per cent for Labour. The major growth in home ownership recently has clearly meant a loss of votes for Labour. There also appears to be a link between type of employment and voting behaviour. It has been suggested, for example, that:

those who depend on the state for employment or for substantial consumption provision tend to subscribe to a 'statist' ideology which has become associated with the Labour Party, while private sector workers and those who buy their key consumption requirements in the private market tend towards an 'anti-statist' ideology which has become associated with the Conservatives.[62]

A third trend has been the changing structure of trade union membership, which is also a significant factor in voting behaviour. Until 1979 a majority of trade unionists voted Labour. In 1983, only 39 per cent of trade unionists voted Labour, whilst in 1987, 42 per cent did so, with nearly 60 per cent voting either Conservative or Alliance. In 1992, MORI estimated that 46 per cent of trade unionists supported Labour but that was out of a greatly reduced trade union membership, since the number of trade unionists had fallen from over 13 million in 1979 to below 10 million in 1993.

Concealed within those overall figures are the changes in white and blue collar union membership. In 1965 white collar unions represented only 15 per cent of TUC membership. In 1988 they represented about half and by 1993 they were the majority. There are different political allegiances between white collar and blue collar trade unionists, with the former being more likely to support the Conservative and Liberal Democratic Parties and the latter the Labour Party.

All these social and economic trends have weakened working class solidarity and working class loyalty to the Labour Party. The new working class of home owners, non-unionists or white collar unionists, and those living in the South, are much less likely to vote Labour and more likely to vote for either Conservative or Liberal Democratic candidates, since as voters they have no strong partisan identification.

The developments outlined in this section have obvious implications for the political system, industrial relations and the politics of industrial relations: whether Labour can win back its traditional voters and gain new ones; how the wider labour movement adapts to changes within the social structure; the emerging pattern of trade unionism and its members' political allegiances; the financial relationship between the Conservatives and big business; and whether the third force in British politics, the Liberal Democrats, can succeed in changing politics and the politics of industrial relations. All these are key political and industrial relations issues but their possible outcomes remain uncertain in the 1990s, after the fourth consecutive election victory of the Conservative Party in 1992.

## 7.6  Summary Points

- The formal political relationship between some of the major unions in Britain and the Labour Party is a long established one. It was the trade unions which were instrumental in forming the LRC in 1900 and a few years later it became the Labour Party.

- It is the device of union political funds which enables unions to establish political fund rules and to raise a political levy from their members to spend on political objects. Members wishing to contract out of the political levy must be allowed to do so and admission to a union must not be conditional on paying the political levy. Union political expenditure is used for three main purposes: to enable unions to affiliate to the Labour Party; to sponsor Labour MPs; and to finance political activities and campaigns.

- Labour Party affiliated unions currently provide some 4.8 million Labour Party members and the bulk of Labour Party finances. Affiliated unions send delegates to the party's annual conference, influence debates and vote there, have elected members on the party's NEC and comprise one-third of the electoral college which elects the party leadership. Since the 1993 Labour Party conference, Labour Party parliamentary candidates are selected locally on a 'one member one vote' basis. In the 1992 election, 143 union-sponsored candidates were elected to the House of Commons.

- Relationships between employers and the Conservative Party tend to be less formal and more personalized. Many Conservative MPs sit on company boards, whilst City interests, rather than manufacturing interests, appear to have closer links with the Conservative Party today. Other links are provided by common social backgrounds, membership of the same business and social clubs, family connections and informal personal networks. The Conservative Party is also the major beneficiary of corporate political donations which account for a large part of Conservative central funds, though some monies are channelled to the Conservatives by conduit bodies such as the CPS and Aims of Industry.

- The TUC is the only central trade union confederation in Britain representing the major unions. In the early 1990s, it had over 70 affiliated unions, with a total membership of more than 8 million trade unionists. TUC policy is made at its annual Congress, which meets for a week in September. Congress also selects the TUC's General Council, which implements TUC policy and keeps a watching brief on trade union and labour affairs. For the larger unions membership on the General Council is automatic; for smaller unions and women members it is by election. The TUC's strategic role has been weakened in recent years.

- The CBI, in contrast, was only formed in 1965. Since then the CBI has established itself as the central organization representing employer interests in Britain. It has broadened its membership base and represents business interests to government, local authorities and the EU. Its membership is drawn from private sector, industrial, service and commercial enterprises, public employers, employers' associations and chambers of commerce.

- The complex internal organization of the CBI includes its Council, various standing committees and regional councils. The membership services provided by the CBI are wide ranging, nationally and locally. These are backed up by skilled professional advice from lawyers, accountants and tax specialists.

- Since the 1970s, significant changes appear to have taken place within the social, occupational and trade union structures. Though the manual working class remains the largest single class, the salariat, routine non-manual workers, supervisors and technicians now constitute over 60 per cent of the electorate. Similarly, the trade union movement is becoming less a blue collar than a white collar one. These developments are being reflected in the changing political allegiances of the electorate. In recent elections, traditional ties between the Labour Party and some union members seem to be weakening, as do those of some of the professional middle classes to the Conservative Party.

## 7.7   References

1. S. and B. Webb, *Industrial Democracy*, Longmans, London, 1902, pp. 596–9.
2. A. Ball, *British Political Parties*, Macmillan, London, 1987, p. 44.
3. Selig Perlman, quoted in I. Richter, *Political Purpose in Trade Unions*, Allen and Unwin, London, 1973, p. 22.
4. D. Farnham, The Labour alliance: reality or myth?, *Parliamentary Affairs*, 29(1), Winter 1976, p. 46.
5. Labour Party, *Constitution and Standing Orders of the Labour Party*, London, 1982, Clause IV (4).
6. Trades Union Congress, *Trade Unionism*, TUC, London, 1966, p. 56.
7. Farnham, *op. cit.*, p. 46.
8. Trades Union Congress, *Report of 123rd Annual Trades Union Congress 1991*, TUC, London, 1992, p. 1.
9. B. C. Roberts, *Trade Union Government and Administration in Great Britain*, Bell, London, 1956, p. 373.
10. *Ibid.*
11. *Ibid.*, p. 376.
12. *Ibid.*, p. 380.
13. Labour Party (1982), *op. cit.*, Clause IX (i).
14. Quoted in *The Independent*, 30 September 1993, p. 6.
15. Ball, *op. cit.*, p. 206.
16. Eric Varley speaking at the Labour Party Conference 1982. See *Report of the Annual Conference of the Labour Party*, Labour Party, London, 1983, p. 34.
17. TUC–Labour Party Liaison Committee, *Policy Statement: Partners in Rebuilding Britain*, TUC–Labour Party, London, 1983, para. 2.
18. H. Phelps Brown, *The Origins of Trade Union Power*, Clarendon, Oxford, 1983, p. 56.
19. The Conservative Party, *The Conservative Manifesto 1983*, CPC, London, 1983.
20. Conservative Party, *Transforming Britain*, CPC, London, 1992, p. 65.
21. Conservative Party, *The Government's Industrial Strategy*, CPC, London, 1992, pp. 5–8.
22. C. Crouch, *The Politics of Industrial Relations*, Fontana, London, 1979, p. 133.
23. *Ibid.*, p. 134.
24. G. K. Wilson, *Business and Politics*, Macmillan, Basingstoke, 1985, p. 60.
25. Ball, *op. cit.*, p. 192.
26. Wilson, *op. cit.*, p. 60.
27. *Ibid.*, p. 66.
28. *Ibid.*, p. 61.
29. R. Taylor, Tories with a stake in the Channel, *The Observer*, 15 December 1985.
30. *Ibid.*
31. Wilson, *op. cit.*, p. 61.
32. Labour Research Department, Who paid for the Tory victory?, *Labour Research*, July 1993, p. 7.
33. Labour Research Department, Company cash for the Liberals, *Labour Research*, May 1985, p. 117.
34. *Labour Research*, August 1985, p. 202.
35. *Labour Research*, December 1988, p. 8.
36. *Labour Research*, July 1993, p. 13.
37. J. Lovell and B. C. Roberts, A Short History of the TUC, Macmillan, London, 1968, pp. 57 and 59.
38. *Ibid.*, p. 92.
39. H. A. Clegg, *The System of Industrial Relations in Great Britain*, Blackwell, Oxford, 1970, p. 405.
40. TUC (1966), *op. cit.*, p. 1.
41. TUC, *Rules and Standing Orders*, Rule 8, quoted in *Report of the Annual TUC*, TUC, London, 1992.

42. TUC, *Consultative Arrangements within the TUC*, TUC, London (nd), p. 20.
43. W. Grant and D. Marsh, *The Confederation of British Industry*, Hodder and Stoughton, London, 1977, p. 20.
44. S. Blank, *Government and Industry in Britain*, Saxon House, Farnborough, 1973, p. 49.
45. Grant and Marsh, *op. cit.*, p. 25.
46. E. Wigham, *The Power to Manage*, Macmillan, London, 1973, p. 216.
47. Confederation of British Industry, *Evidence to the Royal Commission on Trade Unions and Employers' Associations*, CBI, London, 1965, p. 7.
48. *Ibid.*
49. Grant and Marsh, *op. cit.*, p. 87.
50. Confederation of British Industry, *Britain's Business Voice*, CBI, London, 1985, p. 3.
51. Confederation of British Industry, *Britain's Business Voice*, CBI, London, 1993.
52. CBI (1985) *op. cit.*, p. 7.
53. *Ibid.*, p. 10.
54. Grant and Marsh, *op. cit.*, p. 92.
55. CBI (1985), *op. cit.*, p. 6.
56. *Ibid.*, p. 7.
57. Grant and Marsh, *op. cit.*, p. 211.
58. A. Heath, R. Jowell and J. Curtice, *How Britain Votes*, Pergamon, Oxford, 1985, pp. 35 and 39.
59. *Ibid.*, pp. 20, 35 and 3.
60. D. Butler and D. Kavanagh, *The British General Election of 1992*, Macmillan, Basingstoke, 1993, p. 280.
61. J. Dearlove and P. Saunders, *Introduction to British Politics*, Polity Press, Cambridge, 1984, p. 200.
62. *Ibid.*, p. 203.

# 8

# Public Policy and
# Industrial Relations

Public policy is the term used to describe the mixture of legislation, current government political priorities and the broad policy directives pursued by the civil service and public agencies at any given time. Public policy changes as government political priorities change and when governments change. Some public policies endure over a long period of time, despite changes of government. This is because there exists a general public and political consensus about them. Other public policies have a very short life. This chapter concentrates on public policy on industrial relations in the early 1990s and, to a lesser degree, on how public policy has developed during previous decades.

The existence of a clear public policy on industrial relations is important for all those concerned with developing and maintaining good relations between employers and trade unions and between managers and employees. It is also essential that the general public should clearly understand the nature of a government's attitude towards the conduct of industrial relations and its impact upon the country's economic prosperity and social welfare. The state of public opinion on such matters as trade union power, the right to strike and picket, and the responsibility of government to ensure fair play between employers and employees, changes over time. This leads eventually to political change and to new public policies. Public policy is, therefore, largely the result of changing political opinion and emerging political policies over comparatively long periods of time.

## 8.1 The Traditional Role of Government in Industrial Relations

### The role of the State

The State intervenes in industrial relations in Britain by four main methods: through the law and the courts; through its economic policies; through its industrial relations institutions or agencies; and in the way the State regulates relations with its own employees. Public policy has, since Britain became a member of the European Community, been increasingly shaped and determined by EC (and later EU) law and policies. The principal purpose of labour law, for example, is 'to regulate, to support and to restrain the power of management and the power of organised labour',[1] though the traditional view of the role of the State and the law in British industrial relations emphasizes the abstentionist or voluntarist tradition. This contends that public or legal interference in the practical conduct of industrial relations rarely benefits the parties concerned. This view, however, is misleading if applied outside the areas of collective bargaining and the freedom to organize which – compared with many other countries – continue to be relatively free from legal regulation. However, since 1980, the freedom to strike and trade union immunities have been effectively narrowed and constrained by legal intervention from the State, but not to the point where they would violate the Convention of the International Labour Organisation or the European Social Charter. The law, government and its agencies have also been interventionist in other aspects of industrial relations for many years. These include: ensuring safe working conditions in particular industries; regulating employment among young people and female workers; establishing minimum wage levels in certain trades; and creating machinery for State intervention in industrial disputes. More recently, laws have been enacted guaranteeing a series of statutory employment rights for individuals against discrimination in their employment on the grounds of race or of sex, against unfair dismissal by their employers, establishing the right to redundancy payments and for other purposes.

In considering the role of the State in regulating employment and industrial relations, commentators often forget that the State intervened in the fixing of wages in the reign of Elizabeth I. The development and application of the common law by the judges subsequently resulted in combinations of trade unionists, infringing the so-called 'restraint of trade' doctrine, being limited by the law. And it was not until the early stages of the industrial revolution that the doctrine of *laissez-faire* strongly discouraged government interference in economic or industrial affairs. This was on the grounds that if individuals were left to pursue their own self-interest, this would benefit both them and society generally. State interference in business affairs and in industry, including relations between 'master' and 'servant', it was held, could only lead to the malfunctioning of the market system and to a reduction in the production of goods and real wealth in society. The concept of *laissez-faire* was the predominant social ideology associated with early capitalism and was reflected in the laws of Parliament and the judgments of the courts. Its adoption as a creed for successful business practice during the early stages of the industrial revolution gave powerful approval to the belief in individualism and disapproval of collective action including trade unionism. This dualism remains an important moral and political issue even today.

The unregulated growth of the factory system, however, led to horrifying working conditions, intolerable exploitation at work, and disturbing manifestations of human degradation in the home and in the early factories. The State, with its moral obligation to ensure the health and prosperity of its citizens, could not for long stand completely aside whilst the working and living conditions of the newly created industrial working classes deteriorated. As a result, a series of parliamentary statutes were passed advancing at least minimum standards of factory safety, industrial welfare and personal morality at work. The consequences of the rigid application of *laissez-faire* principles were clearly incompatible with social and political stability, on the one hand, and with the moral duties of government on the other.

Attitudes to government and State intervention in economic affairs and industrial relations, however, depend largely upon differing philosophies of the State. Those favouring minimum State intervention think that government should create only a few of its own institutions and should employ as few people as possible. The chief functions of the State, it is argued, should be confined to ensuring national security from external threat and law and order internally. This view of the State, along with the belief in *laissez-faire* economics, has endured as a powerful social philosophy for a very long time. Less government, by this view, is equated with good government, with the State being regarded as largely neutral in the application of its power. This 'benevolent-neutral'

view of State power suggests that government only needs to intervene in industrial relations to protect the employment interests of individuals when no other means are available, or to uphold the wider interests of society as a whole when these appear to be threatened by particular industrial pressure groups.

Many people reject such a benevolent view of the State. They argue that the State is the political arm of the ruling classes. They believe that State power reflects the political hegemony of the ruling elite, as well as predominantly serving its interests. This view of the State, the 'coercion' view, holds that State intervention in industrial relations, whether by government, law, the courts or the agencies of law enforcement and social order, is mainly designed to ensure that the interests of private capital and the ruling classes are advanced to the detriment of working people and their representative organizations. Yet regardless of which view of the State is correct or acceptable to individuals and citizens, the aim that the roles of government and the State should be small and minimal has not been achieved. Indeed the size and the role of the State have grown ever larger and penetrate almost every aspect of present-day social and economic life. By the late 1980s, for example, about one quarter of the labour force was employed by the public sector, whilst the State controlled and utilized vast capital resources. But the State also has the duty to uphold the interests of its citizens generally. With such a growth in the economic roles of government and of the public sector, the pressures for State intervention in industrial relations have been both cumulative and inevitable.

Until recently, State intervention in industrial relations and the legal regulation of trade union activities in Britain owed much more to judicial interpretations of the common law than they did to Acts of Parliament. In the early nineteenth century, for example, judges concluded that trade unions were criminal conspiracies. When the struggles against criminal liability had been won by the trade unions, and legislation had been passed relieving them from this threat, the judges and the courts subsequently interpreted trade union activities as being liable at civil law. This in turn was remedied by the Trade Disputes Act 1906 which, apart from 1971–74, remained the legal *status quo* until the 1980s.

It became possible to speak of 'non-intervention' in collective labour relationships because the Acts of 1871, 1875 and 1906 aimed to push back the boundaries of illegalities in the common law that would hamstring the unions.[2]

Those favouring the benevolent-neutral theory of the State see the decisions of the judges as being impartial interpretations of the law. Those regarding the State as an instrument of class hegemony and political coercion see the judges' decisions on labour matters as expressions of the use of the law by the ruling classes as limiting the power of organized labour.

Whatever the truth of these views, it is hard to believe that in making their decisions, judges are not deeply influenced by their own social backgrounds, upbringing, education and perhaps even their political preferences.

Judges do their honest best but the great majority 'define the public interest inevitably from the view point of their own class', one that puts priority on maintenance of order, protection of private property and 'containment of the trade union movement'.[3]

Until the passing of the Industrial Relations Act 1971 and the considerable volume of other labour law enacted in the 1970s, it is reasonable to conclude that most parliamentary statutes in the area of collective labour law did little more than restore to the trade unions, and to their members, some of the legal rights which had previously been taken away from them by judicial decisions. Indeed trade unionists have often expressed the fear that the rights given to them by new statutes have been reduced or made invalid by the subsequent interpretations of the common law by the courts and by the judges. What Parliament has given to the unions, they argue, the courts have frequently taken away. Since 1979, however, a further series of statutes have been passed by Parliament, weakening trade union bargaining power, organization and activities. At the same time, other agencies of the State, such as the police and the courts, have become periodically embroiled in bitter trade disputes and industrial conflict, thus paradoxically politicizing such events.

The case for continuing the traditional policy of non-intervention in industrial relations by the State and its agencies is no longer practicable or tenable. Indeed in the face of the massive volume of recent individual, collective and protective labour law – under the Wilson, Callaghan, Thatcher and Major administrations in the 1970s, 1980s and 1990s – it is difficult to maintain the myth that the role of the State is any longer rudimentary in British industrial

relations. Perhaps the root of the myth that the State in Britain plays a passive and residual role in industrial relations stems from the fact that there is little legislation in Britain controlling collective bargaining. But this is certainly no longer true in relation to trade union organization and membership, the freedom to strike, the operation of closed shops or the taking of industrial action. However, whenever attempts are made to introduce laws or to impose State regulation over such activities, the trade union movement normally presents vehement and united opposition against such proposals. Having gained most of their legal rights and collective freedoms after long and difficult struggles against the common law, criminal and civil liability, bitterly hostile employers, and adverse decisions of judges, many British trade unionists intuitively resist any form of legal or State limitation on their freedom to bargain collectively, on their freedom to take part in industrial action and on their freedom to organize. The role of the State in industrial relations, therefore, remains a problematic one. Where the State's role is perceived to be bipartisan and balanced, it is legitimized and non-controversial. Where it is partisan and explicitly biased, on behalf of employers, unions or the ruling elite, it becomes overtly political and disputable.

## Model employer

The government, as custodian of State authority and power, is also in overall terms the largest employer in Britain, being responsible directly or indirectly for about five million employees or some 20 per cent of the workforce. The areas of employment controlled by government include the civil service, local government, police, fire services, national defence, education, the National Health Service, what remains of the nationalized industries and a range of recreational and cultural services including the BBC, national libraries and museums. Since at least the First World War, all governments have accepted the responsibility to act as a 'good' or 'model' employer and to provide their employees with adequate terms and conditions of employment. They have also been willing to recognize trade unions and to negotiate and consult with their representatives. Government or public employees were amongst the first to be provided with pension schemes, sick pay and workplace procedural agreements covering discipline, grievance handling and grading appeals. Shortly after the First World War, the government accepted the recommendations of the Whitley Committee that, in the interests of good employer–employee relations and industrial peace, joint industrial councils (JICs) should be established as representative of both employers and trade unions. The government made it public policy that managers in the State sector should make it clear that trade union representation, and therefore membership of trade unions by individual employees, was desirable in order that negotiations at JIC level should enjoy broad support.

The result, by the time of the Second World War, was that trade union membership and the joint determination of terms and conditions of employment for most public sector workers was far more advanced than in much, but not all, of the private sector. After 1945, this trend was further encouraged by the development of the welfare state and the nationalized industries, where trade union membership and collective bargaining became strongly entrenched. By the time of the Donovan Commission's inquiry in the mid 1960s, industrial relations in the public sector were generally regarded as satisfactory and the bulk of the Donovan report's recommendations were devoted to measures aimed at improving industrial relations in the private sector.

> The analysis and recommendations of the Donovan Commission (1965–68) viewed the problem of British industrial relations as being very much problems of the private sector. . . . The result was that the public sector hardly figured at all in discussions of the desired direction(s) of reform in British industrial relations in the 1960s.[4]

In terms of public policy, then, a succession of governments from the end of the First World War to the late 1970s continued, in various degrees, to foster the essential characteristics of public sector industrial relations. It was these which were held in such high esteem at the time of the Donovan inquiry. Many at that time believed that if only those parts of the private sector which seemed so endlessly involved in disputes and bitter industrial relations wrangles, such as in manufacturing and heavy engineering, would emulate the arrangements and attitudes in the public sector, all might be well.

By the late 1970s, the position of the government as a model employer was generally acknowledged. The government's chief characteristics as a model employer were: the automatic recognition of the right of trade unions to represent the government's employees; the acceptance of collective bargaining –

largely at national level – for the determination of pay and conditions of employment; and the widespread use of joint consultation procedures. Government employees were among the earliest of employees to receive pensions, reasonable holidays, career training and security of employment. Governments also accepted and implemented the recommendations of the International Labour Organisation. Considerable efforts were also made, in the period 1945 to 1979, to ensure that the pay of public sector employees was broadly comparable with that of the private sector. The general election of 1979, however, marked a clear change in the attitude of government to this role of model employer.

## Industrial peacekeeper

Substantial sections of the general public, and perhaps more importantly the electorate, have seen the settlement of damaging and socially disruptive industrial disputes as a direct responsibility of government and the prime minister of the day. A sense of unease and even of alarm grows in the public mind when the combatants in an intensely bitter and prolonged strike are left alone by the government to fight it out to the finish. In the late 1970s and during the 'Winter of Discontent' of 1978–79, for example, public opinion moved heavily against the Labour government, led by the then Prime Minister, James Callaghan, because it appeared either powerless to control the unions or unwilling to do so. Many were concerned that:

> Trade unions may exploit their power in order to extort monopolistic gains for particular groups; obstruct changes that the whole economy greatly needs; discriminate against particular persons, or worsen the prospects of employment for whole categories; inflict heavy losses on firms and persons not party to the original dispute; and disrupt public services, or even hold up the whole economy.[5]

The failure of James Callaghan to deal quickly and firmly with the strikes in the public sector in 1978–79 played a large part in the defeat of the Labour Party in the general election of 1979 and the success of the Conservative Party which promised the electorate it would 'deal with the unions' and 'return the unions to their members'.

There has been a long tradition in Britain of government and prime ministers taking direct steps to seek a satisfactory outcome to bitter strikes. Before the First World War, Lloyd George, as probably the most powerful Cabinet Minister in the Asquith Liberal government, took well-publicized steps to try to end several national strikes. This was seen by many to be a natural and desirable role for the government to fulfil and it established a pattern which survived until 1979. Stanley Baldwin used his position as premier to try to bring about a peaceful end to the miners' dispute which led to the General Strike of 1926. Harold Macmillan in the 1950s invited the leaders of trade unions involved in what were perceived to be prolonged and damaging strikes to Downing Street, where long meetings, sustained by 'beer and sandwiches', took place in an attempt to achieve conciliated settlements between the unions and employers.

Governments seeking to secure the settlement of disputes have sometimes in the past successfully used courts of inquiry or appointed leading non-political public figures, such as judges or academics, to conduct investigations and make recommendations. The bitter trade union recognition dispute at the Grunwick Film Processing Laboratories in 1976, for example, led to the appointment of Lord Scarman, a senior judge, to conduct an inquiry. Hugh Clegg, a professor of industrial relations, was also appointed in the late 1970s to investigate the comparability claims for pay increases of those working in the public services such as refuse collection, sewerage and the National Health Service. In previous decades other highly respected public figures had been appointed to conduct inquiries into the circumstances which had given rise to large-scale strikes in the docks, railways and coalmines. This traditional approach by government to their perceived responsibility for settling large-scale industrial disputes came to an abrupt end after 1979.

## 8.2 The Changing Role of Government in Industrial Relations

For over 30 years following the Second World War, there was a remarkable degree of political consensus on the economic role of government in regulating the economy, its relations with the trade unions and the handling of industrial relations. The essential elements of that consensus were: the maintenance of full employment and the welfare state; continuing State ownership of the industries nationalized between 1945 and 1951; high levels of public expenditure; the continuation of the legal-abstentionist or voluntarist tradition of industrial relations; and the

involvement of the Trades Union Congress (TUC) in government decisions affecting the welfare state and the management of the national economy. This political, economic and social consensus has been aptly described as the 'Post-War Settlement'.

> Its aims could be summed up as government intervention in the economy to promote full employment, a Welfare State of equal rights to health care, education, a job or subsistence. Its means were to be the fuller involvement of labour in its achievement both industrially and politically.[6]

During the 1970s the basis on which the postwar settlement rested was increasingly criticized and, after the 1978–79 Winter of Discontent, it relapsed. This left the way open for the first Thatcher administration, in 1979, to establish a new relationship between government and the trade unions.

The basic elements of this new relationship between government and the unions were: an abandonment of the commitment to full employment; the exclusion of the TUC from the governmental policy making process; new trade union laws reducing immunity for industrial action and picketing and restricting the closed shop; a wide range of measures aimed at depoliticizing industrial relations; and policies designed to weaken collective organization and industrial action, which was the cornerstone of traditional industrial relations. This was to be replaced by a system emphasizing the individual relationship between employers and employees and between unions and their members.

> The trade unions with their traditional role in wage determination, and collectivist pursuit of their goals, were seen as seriously impeding individualism and the working of free labour markets. The outcome was a legislative package (underpinned by complementary policies, especially towards the public sector) which sought to subordinate labour law and the trade unions to the government's economic goals. This marked a sharp rejection of the 'abstentionist' tradition.[7]

After 1979, successive Conservative governments reversed traditional public policies on industrial relations in two main areas: the role of government as a model employer and the role of government as an industrial peacekeeper. The first Thatcher administration, for example, made it transparently clear that it wanted to severely diminish both the size and the influence of the public sector. It believed in private ownership, free enterprise and unfettered market competition, in which consumers ruled, not State ownership dominated by producer interests. The civil service was reduced in numbers; pay comparability with the private sector was largely abandoned; and efforts were made to decentralize the civil service pay bargaining structure in favour of local bargaining and performance-related pay for individual civil servants. This was followed by policies which split off many parts of the civil service into autonomous 'agencies', and by 'market testing', which required the civil service to identify services and departments suitable for privatization. The hostility of the three Thatcher administrations of the 1980s to trade unionism, and to pay determination by national collective bargaining, became an established part of public policy. The Water Act 1983, for example, which abolished the National Water Council, ended national collective bargaining in the water industry in favour of regional bargaining. Similar trends took place in the steel industry, in the Post Office and at British Shipbuilders, where yard-level agreements supplanted national agreements. The Transport Act 1985 was followed by the abolition of national bargaining in favour of company-level agreements for bus operatives with similar decentralization taking place within British Rail.

At GCHQ, Cheltenham, in 1984 the government ended the right of employees to be union members on grounds of national security. In 1987, the government during a long dispute with the schoolteachers ended their system of national collective bargaining and imposed pay settlements by passing the Teachers' Pay and Conditions Act 1987. In the hope that the private sector would follow its example, the government, as employer, was instrumental in ending the closed-shop arrangements at British Rail, British Gas, British Telecom, the Post Office and in the water supply industry.

On taking office in 1979, the first Thatcher administration made it clear that the privatization of large areas of the public sector would follow. This policy was vigorously pursued throughout the 1980s, with over 15 major public sector organizations being privatized. These included: British Gas; British Telecom; Associated British Ports; British Aerospace; Britoil; and National Freight. In the early 1990s the government expressed its intention to privatize British Rail and British Coal. In what remained of the public sector, the government used new legislation to enforce the contracting-out of

certain services such as catering, cleaning and security through competitive tendering.

The trend established during the 1980s by the government as an employer was one of antipathy towards trade unionism and national collective bargaining, with little general sympathy for joint management–employee decision making. This antipathy was not only towards trade unions and collective bargaining, but also towards joint agreements on how work was organized and executed. This was seen to be an exclusive management function. Not unnaturally, the public sector unions reacted with some hostility and the situation at the time of Donovan in the 1960s was reversed in the 1980s, with the public sector being the major area of disputes and manager–employee conflict. By the mid-1980s industrial conflict in the public sector appeared endemic.

> Since the present government came to power in 1979, there have been instances of national strike action in the public sector in virtually every year. The predictable result has been that the public sector has tended to account for the majority of working days lost through strike action in those years.[8]

By the early 1990s, it was difficult to detect what the model employer role of the government was, other than being hostile to trade unionism and national collective bargaining. If a 'new model' is being fashioned, however, it would appear to have the following features: it places managers in positions of indisputable authority, with employees playing only a consultative and supporting role in organizations; it supports pay determination based on individual performance and personal appraisal; and it expects acceptance of new technologies and new working practices by employees without opposition or complaint. The new model requires public sector industrial relations to copy those developed in the private sector during the 1980s, not *vice versa*.

> The present Conservative government, which entered its third term of office following the June 1987 election, [enjoyed] a reputation second to none of being 'anti public sector'. And . . . it [was] clearly trying to make the public sector more like the private sector in many of its industrial relations arrangements and practices.[9]

Since 1979, the four Conservative administrations have decisively rejected any positive role in industrial peacekeeping and have poured scorn on the idea of settlements being arrived at over 'beer and sandwiches' in 10 Downing Street. Disputes, the government believed, no matter how bitter, must be left to the two sides to resolve and to the operation of market forces to achieve a sense of reality. While public opinion appears to have condemned James Callaghan for not taking direct interventionary action in the public service strikes of 1978–79, it paradoxically appeared to support Margaret Thatcher for not personally or directly bringing the year-long miners' strike of 1984–85 to an end.

Since 1979, too, the four Conservative administrations have not used the time-honoured method of seeking a compromise solution to large-scale industrial disputes. The public might have expected such a peacekeeping approach to have been offered to employers and unions in the steel strike of 1980, the health workers' dispute in 1982, water workers in 1983, the miners in 1984–85, the teachers in 1986, and the printers' dispute with News International at Wapping in the same year. Instead, the government allowed those disputes to continue until one side or the other won – which in every case was the employer. It would appear then, from the evidence available, that since 1979 Conservative governments not only abandoned the traditional peacekeeping role of government during major disputes, but also adopted economic policies which led directly to strikes, particularly in the public sector. They sought and achieved considerable reductions in steel and coal production that led to bitter strikes which the unions lost. They imposed by law new contracts of employment and pay increases on teachers who took the strongest industrial action in their history. They passed six Acts of Parliament restricting the legal rights of trade unions to take industrial action, to picket, to operate closed shops and to run their own internal affairs as they wished. They pursued economic policies, at a time of worldwide recession, which resulted in the highest levels of unemployment and redundancies since the 1930s. Yet they achieved and retained, after the Falklands campaign, high levels of public support and won the general elections of 1983, 1987 and 1992 with substantial parliamentary majorities, but only some 40 per cent of the votes cast.

It would appear that a substantial proportion of the general public, whilst perhaps uneasy at the confrontational style of the Thatcher governments between 1979 and 1990 when dealing with the trade unions and with large-scale strikes, nevertheless did not express outright disapproval. This was because they apparently accepted that a fundamental restructuring of the economy, cuts in public expenditure growth, reductions in public sector employment, and the enactment of laws restricting trade union rights could not be achieved without strikes and high unemployment. It is difficult to believe that a government committed to such painful policies, which inevitably resulted in angry union action, could have enjoyed so much public support at three general elections unless, rightly or wrongly, the public accepted that there were no real alternatives. There also existed, however, a very substantial body of opinion which believed that the Thatcher governments pursued misguided economic policies and that the resulting conflicts and inequalities – as well as the failure of the prime minister to accept the role of peacemaker in society – had caused deep and bitter social divisions within Britain.

## Individualizing employee relations

Seen historically, both the political and legal systems in Britain have been defenders of individual freedom and rights but hard critics of collectivities seeking advantages for groups of people sharing common interests. Individualism and individual rights are commonly associated with free market capitalist enterprise. This stresses the need for free individuals to follow their own talents, abilities and energies within a broad but unobstructive framework of law. Individualism is, therefore, associated with the right of the political spectrum. The collectivist tradition, on the other hand, emphasizes the value of co-operation, shared beliefs and values, and the need to use the State to achieve collective improvements. It claims that individualism leads to selfishness and a society sharply divided between rich and poor. Collectivism, therefore, is associated with the left of the political spectrum. In practice, however, all governments in Britain in the twentieth century have preserved and enhanced both individualist and collectivist values and traditions. But governments of the left have emphasized collectivism, whilst those of the right have stressed individualism. During the 35 years after 1945, during which the postwar settlement dominated the political system, the emphasis generally favoured collectivist values and action. After the general election of 1979, and during the 1980s, the emphasis shifted sharply towards the individualist tradition and this involved a process of individualizing employee relations.

It can be argued that the essence of British politics since 1979 has centred on the issue of what is the most suitable balance between the values and objectives of individualism and collectivism. It is still far from clear that a consensus between the two has been achieved.

The three Thatcher administrations of the 1980s sought to impose upon Britain a set of individualistic values stressing the need for a new economic realism. This entailed creating an 'enterprise culture' where individuals would seek business success and be allowed to keep the rewards they gained. The free market, where the customer reigns supreme, was to be the testing ground of individual success in business. It was believed to be essential, therefore, that product and labour markets should not be impeded by so-called monopoly trade union power. Individual employees were expected to understand how vital it was for their firms to meet the demands of the market, and that their personal future and salary position were dependent upon market success. It was seen to be the task of management to motivate individual employees to play a part in securing the company's success in the market place. This ideology of economic individualism, and employee commitment to the enterprise, regards the collectivist values and methods of trade unionism as inimical to the enterprise culture. Governments during the 1980s, and to a lesser degree after 1990, therefore sought to encourage the adoption by employees of a cultural identity with market and commercial success, rather than with trade union values. They encouraged individual employees to develop property acquisition attitudes by emphasizing home ownership, by facilitating council house sales and by widening share ownership and profit sharing. Salary increases were only to be seen as being earned if productivity and profits had been improved. During the years of large-scale redundancy and high unemployment in the early 1980s, the apparent switch from trade union values to those of an enterprise culture, and a belief in the efficacy of market forces, were undoubtedly assisted by the fear of unemployment and the belief by many workers that unions were powerless to protect them.

The breakdown of collectivist working-class culture in Britain was also hastened during the 1980s by important social changes. The traditional manual working classes employed in the old 'smokestack' industries, working in large factories, steelworks, docks, railway centres and coal mining went into sharp numerical decline. So did several of Britain's great Victorian industrial cities and their working-class districts. With these profound socio-economic changes came a decline in the very basis upon which trade unionism, socialism and the collectivist culture of the working classes were founded. Yet the seeds of the decline of the collectivist values, which had underpinned the postwar settlement, had possibly been sown earlier, even before the individualist values of the enterprise culture were openly advocated by governments in the 1980s.

During the first two or three years of the 1980s, employers, managers and trade unions were very uncertain of what was taking place other than that it involved recession, redundancies, factory closures and high unemployment. After an uncertain and brief flirtation with something which was referred to as 'macho' management, some leading organizations seized the opportunity to marginalize or by-pass trade unionism at work. They did so by seeking to increase employee identity with the organization and by introducing a range of management practices such as staff appraisal, customer satisfaction awareness, performance-related pay, quality management, single-status employment conditions and flexible working practices. Most of these practices were introduced either with union willingness or their reluctant, if not actually hostile, acceptance. The impact of these practices, when seen against the end of the postwar settlement and the enterprise culture campaign by the government, was to further weaken the collectivist hold of the trade unions and strengthen employee individualism and their identity as part of the organization. How deep and permanent these changes are remains to be seen. Should a government with a different ideology be elected and full employment return, the collectivist traditions of the postwar settlement could, perhaps, once again re-emerge.

The trade union legislation introduced by the 1984, 1988 and 1993 Acts also reinforced the individualist tendencies brought about at the workplace by management practices and the values of the enterprise culture. By making it a legal requirement that union leaders and union executive bodies must be elected by secret postal ballot, and that industrial action can only be taken after a successful secret postal ballot, the government ensured that the relationship between unions and their members was made more individualistic. It was no longer possible for elections of union leaders to be held at branch meetings or for strikes to be agreed by a show of hands at mass meetings. This further undermined the traditional collectivist practices of trade unions.

A few unions, on the other hand, have now openly embraced the enterprise culture, and the new economic realism, and have abandoned some of the traditional collectivist patterns of behaviour of the old trade unionism. Unions such as the Electrical Electronic Telecommunications and Plumbing Union (EETPU), which was expelled from the TUC, made new-style agreements with companies starting up on green-field sites. These agreements not only involve single union recognition and strike-free arrangements, but also actively urge their members to identify with the commercial aims, market policies and management styles of the employer. This new brand of trade unionism claims to recognize and value the enterprise culture and has adapted its own values, organization and bargaining objectives to it. But how significant this trend is and how many unions will follow the EETPU example, albeit silently and discreetly, remains to be seen. It would appear, however, that the trade union and industrial relations policies of the four Conservative governments since 1979 have shifted the emphasis on public policy, as well as workplace practices, substantially away from collectivist values towards individualist values and the enterprise culture. According to one commentary:

> managers are not simply concerned to change working practices and other workplace arrangements by exploiting a favourable balance of power, but are also concerned to change employee attitudes. In pursuit of this goal it could be argued they have implemented a series of institutional changes: the revitalisation, or creation of joint consultative committees, the introduction of quality circles and the reform of reward systems to incorporate profit or performance related pay and share ownership. [And] . . . For this variant of new industrial relations the most salient attitudes are towards labour-management cooperation in pursuit of productivity, towards management itself, and towards unions.[10]

## Depoliticizing industrial relations

Since 1979 it has been public policy to reduce, wherever and whenever possible, the element of politics in both the activities of trade unions and the conduct of industrial relations. It was believed by government not only that the handling of relationships between employers and employees had become too political in itself but also that the role of the

trade unions in society was unnecessarily infused with politics. A long-term policy of reducing the political aspects of trade union behaviour, collective bargaining and workplace industrial relations was, government believed, essential in order to make the relations between employer and employee one of mutual understanding of the realities of economics and competitive markets. In brief, the historical concern of trade unions with the political issues of industrial power, socialism and capitalism, the distribution of profits and wages and industrial democracy were, if possible, to be replaced with a concern for commercial viability, appreciation of market situations, an understanding of the legitimacy of profits, and mutual respect and cooperation between managers and workers.

It was hoped by government that the ideological culture of industrial relations could be changed so that employees, and their unions if possible, would identify more closely with the objectives and methods of capitalism operating within a dynamic enterprise culture of innovation and competitive markets. For this to become possible, worker commitment to trade unionism and belief in socialism had to be marginalized, if not eliminated. This process of depoliticizing industrial relations during the 1980s followed seven clearly definable paths. First, the TUC and the trade unions were refused any meaningful role in the process of national government or in the major decisions affecting the national economy. Second, workers were to be convinced, if possible, of the material and social benefits which private enterprise capitalism could bring them. Third, the government would not attempt in any way to regulate incomes or prices as governments had attempted to do in the 1960s and 1970s. Fourth, the trade union political levy and political fund, which linked the unions to the Labour Party and provided it with the bulk of its finance, would have to be determined by secret ballot. Fifth, the law on trade union immunity when taking industrial action was changed so that political strikes became extremely hazardous for the union concerned. Sixth, the public sector was to be reduced in size, with large public corporations being privatized and competitive tendering, contracting out and agency decentralization being introduced into the public services. Finally, trade union leaders and union national executive bodies would be required by law to be periodically elected by secret postal ballot of all their members. These measures, it was believed, if given sufficient time to become widely accepted and understood, would not only reduce the political content of industrial relations, but also radically transform the attitudes and behaviour of the British labour force.

During the 35-year period between the end of the Second World War and the general election of 1979, the TUC had played an increasingly powerful role in the economic and welfare state decisions made by central governments. The TUC was consulted on all major issues affecting the economy, and successive chancellors, regardless of political party, listened carefully to the views of the TUC before making vital economic decisions. Similarly, the views of the TUC on the size and distribution of public expenditure were carefully noted by governments. Powerful union general secretaries were seen entering and leaving Downing Street during economic crises and the media eagerly sought their views on events. Such was the power of the TUC to influence the thinking and behaviour of governments during the 1960s and 1970s that political observers referred to the governmental process of Britain as one of 'tripartism' involving government, the TUC and the Confederation of British Industry (CBI). Others saw the system as a corporate State, with government taking place through consultation with major corporate bodies such as the TUC and the CBI, and with Parliament and elected representatives at all levels playing a secondary role. This process became so highly developed that it continued regardless of the political party in power, though Labour governments had a closer working relationship with the TUC than Conservative ones. The political role of the TUC by the late 1970s was very powerful indeed.

After the general election of 1979, this pattern of government changed abruptly, with the TUC frozen out of the governmental process. Successive Conservative chancellors did not even consult the TUC before making vital economic and budget decisions. Union leaders were no longer invited to Downing Street and only rarely did they meet formally with members of the government. As the influence of the TUC on government waned, so did the interest of the media in the TUC. It is hard not to conclude that the political power and influence of the TUC on government is now a mere shadow of what it was.

The Prime Minister spoke scornfully of the irrelevance to the nation's economic problems of 'beer and sandwiches at No. 10' (as she called talks with trade union leaders). Tripartism was abandoned. Union leaders and the TUC were simply not consulted about relevant government policy, or their views and advice were ignored.[11]

The second path taken towards the depoliticization of industrial relations lay in Prime Minister Thatcher's ideological campaign throughout the 1980s to convince the nation that economic prosperity and national revival were only possible if everybody accepted the need to create an enterprise culture. The essential elements of this enterprise culture were seen to be: co-operation, trust and a mutuality of interest between managers and workers in achieving efficiency and high productivity; the need to produce high-quality goods and services ensuring consumer satisfaction; the recognition of the importance of being competitive; and the acceptance of market forces as the final arbiter of business success or failure. Welfare state provision, for all but the very needy, was attacked as creating a culture of dependency. If an enterprise culture could be established, it was argued, economic prosperity would be assured for all sections of society. The political campaign to establish the values of this enterprise culture was seen as a battle for the heart and mind of the nation. If the struggle was to be won, then the allegiance of workers to their trade unions and socialist beliefs had to be weakened. At a practical level the sale of council houses, and a wider spread of home ownership, were seen as vital starting points. The government in the 1980s also sought to extend share ownership downwards in society and urged the development of profit-related pay schemes and manager–worker buyouts. The more workers felt they had a property stake in the enterprise economy the less likely, it was believed, they would respond to trade union and socialist values.

The third policy for reducing the political significance of industrial relations after 1979 lay in the government's complete rejection of any form of prices and incomes policy. During the previous 20 years, a wide variety of prices and incomes policies had been used to try and achieve full employment, economic growth and low inflation. While this is not the place to assess the success or otherwise of past incomes policies, they gave the TUC a position of political power, as governments of all persuasions had to win the support of the unions if their policies were to succeed. Instead of incomes policies, the Conservative governments of the 1980s relied initially upon measures aimed at the strict control of the money supply to control inflation, regardless of its impact upon industry and employment. But by denying a central role to the unions in running an incomes policy, governments removed much of the political power and status that the TUC had established over the past two decades. The public were quick to note that the political power of the TUC and the unions had declined sharply during the 1980s.

A more direct and open attack on the political influence of the trade unions came with the passing of the Trade Union Act 1984. This required all unions with political funds, and those wishing to establish a political fund, to hold secret ballots of all their members at least once every 10 years. Only if a majority votes for a political fund can the union establish or retain such a fund. This requirement was seen by many as a somewhat crude attempt to move quickly after the 1983 general election to weaken the political link between the trade unions and the Labour Party, since the election had revealed a sharp fall in the number of trade unionists supporting the Labour Party. It was clearly hoped by the government that many unions would not be able to convince a majority of their members to vote for the retention of political funds and to maintain their Labour Party link. The result of the ballots on political funds, after 1984, must have been a great disappointment for the government. Indeed:

> The results of political fund ballots exceeded the unions' wildest dreams. During the 12 months from April 1985 to March 1986, 37 balloted, and with, by the standards of union elections, a reasonably high turn-out of 51 per cent, only two unions failed to achieve an affirmative level of support of less than 70 per cent of those voting. Indeed in 21 out of the 37 unions, the vote in favour of maintaining a political fund exceeded 80 per cent.[12]

The legal requirement that political fund ballots be held at least once every ten years means that the opinion of trade union members will have to be tested again in the mid-1990s – probably just before a general election.

Political strikes are seen as those strikes undertaken by a trade union and its members to express opposition to a policy being constitutionally pursued by an elected government. Such strikes are contentious, because they often do not directly involve the pay and conditions of those taking strike action, but are called to oppose the policies of a constitutionally elected government. Examples of political strikes can perhaps be found in strikes opposing privatization or cuts in certain areas of public expenditure, such as the

National Health Service. The Trade Union and Labour Relations Consolidation Act 1992 (TULRCA 1992) strictly confines trade union immunity for industrial action to trade disputes between 'workers and their own employer'. Moreover, the law now requires a strike to be 'wholly or mainly' related to clearly defined industrial relations issues involving workers and their employer. These restrictions mean that strikes involving people or organizations, other than the strikers' own employer, or about matters other than industrial relations, do not normally possess immunity from civil action, thus enabling employers and, since 1993, ordinary consumers and members of the general public to obtain court injunctions against the unions. Political strikes clearly fall into the category of industrial action not covered by legal immunity.

The obvious effect of these legal changes was to make most trade unions extremely cautious about calling disputes which could result in a court order being served against them. If such orders were ignored, this could result in unions paying heavy fines in contempt of court. If these legal changes result in a decline in politically motivated strikes, such as opposition to privatization proposals, despite their undeniable infrequency, a further step will have been taken in the process of depoliticizing industrial relations.

Privatization of substantial areas of public sector employment, and the legal requirement for public sector organizations to contract-out certain services, such as cleaning and catering, has transferred large numbers of employees from public to private sector employment. This change has meant that the government is no longer their employer, even in an indirect sense, and cannot therefore be called upon to increase public expenditure to finance pay increases or to make good trading losses. The privatized gas, electricity supply, telecommunications and docks industries, for example, must now have regard to market conditions and formal financial considerations when deciding on pay increases. Similarly, those local government employees, for example, whose work went out to competitive tendering and who lost the contract, but who became employed by the private sector company winning the contract, are no longer public sector employees. In both cases the government can no longer be the legitimate target of complaint to finance pay increases by increasing public expenditure. These changes have depoliticized industrial relations further.

Finally, the requirements of the Trade Union Act

1984 and the TURER Act 1993 for the election by secret postal ballot of union leaders and national executive body members will, the government hopes, greatly reduce the number of so-called unrepresentative left-wing candidates being elected. The previous systems used by many unions which involved elections at branch meetings or at annual conferences led, it was believed, to positions of power and influence being usurped by unrepresentative candidates for high office. By requiring all senior trade union positions to be filled by secret postal ballot of all those members entitled to vote, the 1984 Act, it is believed, will result in more moderate leaderships being elected. Such leaders, it is hoped, will be less concerned with socialist politics and left-wing ideology, and more concerned with achieving practical improvements for their members. Whether or not this legislation will achieve the changes intended is still difficult to ascertain.

In summary, it would appear that the seven major policy steps taken by the four Conservative administrations since 1979 to depoliticize industrial relations and trade unionism might well have been collectively successful. This is despite the fact that many of the measures were seen as highly political in themselves and undeniably anti-union in their emphases at the time.

## 8.3 Wages Councils and Pay Review Bodies

Unlike some countries, Britain has never introduced a statutory minimum wage covering all employees. This is not only because of the problem of defining low pay and of administering, inspecting and enforcing national minimum wage provisions, but also because of the apparent lack of trade union enthusiasm for such legislation, until relatively recently. In the general election of 1992 the Labour Party was committed to the introduction of minimum wage legislation. Yet the State has long recognized the human and social consequences of allowing intolerably low levels of pay to go unchecked in particular industries. Public opinion in the closing decades of the nineteenth century, for example, revealed deep concern at the conditions of many workers in the so-called 'sweated trades'. The Committee of the House of Lords which examined these industries in 1889–90 revealed:

a rate of wages inadequate to the necessities of the workers or disproportionate to the work

done; excessive hours of labour; the insanitary state of the houses in which the work is carried on. These evils can hardly be exaggerated. The earnings of the lowest classes of workers are barely sufficient to sustain existence.[13]

These sweated trades existed in most large cities and were concentrated in bootmaking, tailoring, furniture making, chain and nail making, and lace and net production. It was in these trades that the present system of wages councils and wage regulation orders originated. State regulation of low wages on an industry by industry basis is a good example of public policy maintained over more than 80 years despite very many changes of government. The policy was, however, terminated in 1993.

The first Trade Boards Act was passed in 1909. Its main purpose was to raise wages in a limited number of industries. It was largely an experimental measure which applied to four trades and covered only a minority of workers employed in the sweated trades. These initial trade boards had the strictly limited function of fixing minimum legally binding time rates of wages, although a wages inspectorate was set up to enforce compliance with the legal determinations of the boards. In 1917, the Whitley Committee recommended an extension of trade boards to other trades and industries where employer and trade union organization was weak. This was achieved by the Trade Boards Act 1919 which gave powers to the Minister of Labour to establish further boards 'if he was of the opinion that no adequate machinery existed for the regulation of wages in the trade in question'.[14] It was the hope of the Whitley Committee that the trade boards would encourage the development of trade unions and employers' organizations in these industries. This could then lead to the regulation of wages and of conditions of employment in these trades by collective bargaining machinery.

This hope, many times repeated since 1917, has not in the main been fulfilled. By 1938, there were some 50 trade boards – with employer, union and independent members – covering about one and a half million workers. In addition to these trade boards, minimum wage regulation was also achieved in agriculture by the creation of the Agricultural Wages Board of England and Wales in 1924. This was extended to Scotland in 1937, whilst the whole scheme was further strengthened by the Agricultural Wages Acts of 1948 and 1949. These gave powers to the Agricultural Wages Boards to order wage increases without reference to the Minister of Labour, unlike the existing trade boards, which had to obtain that approval.

Subsequent legislation in 1946 and 1959 renamed the trade boards wages councils. Their coverage was extended, with piecework rates, overtime rates, holidays and holiday pay, as well as minimum hourly rates of pay now coming within their scope. The Industrial Relations Act 1971 established the principle that wages councils should move towards their own collective bargaining arrangements where this was possible. To this end, the Commission on Industrial Relations was given the responsibility of examining questions relating to the modification or abolition of wages councils. In total, the Commission looked at wages council industries employing some two million people with a view to encouraging trade unions and collective bargaining within them, although it was not greatly successful in doing this.

The Wages Councils Act 1979, until it was amended by the Wages Act 1986, contained several measures making wages councils more effective and more independent of the State. First, representative organizations, such as trade unions nominated by the Secretary of State for Employment, could appoint their own members to wages councils. Each wages council comprised equal representation of trade unions and employers plus three independent members whose votes could determine decisions. The chairperson of each council was drawn from the three independent members. Second, the powers of wages councils were extended to fix most other terms and conditions of employment other than wages, working hours and holidays. Third, wages councils were permitted to make their own wage regulation orders as well as determining their operative date. Finally, the Advisory Conciliation and Arbitration Service (ACAS) was given the duty of inquiring into wages council matters on reference from the Secretary of State for Employment. It could recommend, for example, the establishment of statutory joint industrial councils (SJICs) without independent members. The aim of these bodies was to replace wages councils as an intermediate step between statutory pay determination and full collective bargaining between employer and trade unions. None in fact were established between 1979 and 1986.

The Wages Act 1986 limited the powers of the wages councils to fixing a single hourly and overtime rate of pay for employees aged 21 and over. Holiday rates and pay differentials above the minimum rate were left to be settled by contract of employment. The 1986 Act permitted the Secretary of State for Employment to abolish or vary the responsibilities of wages councils by order, after consultation with interested parties. The 1986 Act did not contain any provision permitting the setting up of new wages councils. In 1988, the Government published a White Paper proposing the complete abolition of wages councils on the following grounds: that they create inflexibility within the labour market which prevents new jobs, albeit low paid, from being created; that modern welfare benefit systems make them unnecessary; that they are 'shot-through' with anomalies and are anachronistic; and that they would be unable to cope with the demands which would be made when a single European market came into being in 1992.

The 1993 Trade Union Reform and Employment Rights Act abolished the Wages Council system from 30 August 1993. After that date the determination of wages and other conditions of employment is a matter for employees and prospective employees to settle with the employer. However, contracts of employment largely determined by Wages Council Orders issued before 30 August 1993 will continue in existence unless renegotiated to the satisfaction of both parties. New employees, however, may be offered pay and conditions below those of existing employees.

The abolition of the Wages Council system marks a major break in public policy on low wages and the exploitation of largely unskilled labour, which has been in existence for most of the twentieth century. Whether or not the benefits in terms of greater labour market flexibility and the creation of many more low-paid jobs will outweigh the loss of the legal protection previously offered to many of the most vulnerable people in the labour market remains to be seen.

A relatively small yet significant number of employees in the public sector have their pay regulated through pay review bodies, which are appointed by the prime minister. They make their recommendations on pay increases to the prime minister for final decisions on their implementation. The importance of pay review bodies lies in the political convenience which they provide for governments. Whilst on the one hand government tries to keep pay increases for the vast majority of public sector workers to no more than the rate of inflation, pay review bodies permit higher awards to go to those holding very senior positions in the public services. They also enable higher awards to be made to those, such as nurses, whom the government wishes to be seen rewarding for refusing to take industrial action.

The doctors' and dentists' review body was first formed in 1962 to advise the prime minister on the remuneration of doctors and dentists in the National Health Service (NHS). It was re-established in 1971. It is independent and takes evidence from the Health Department, the NHS and the professional bodies representing doctors and dentists. Whilst governments do not have to accept the recommendations of the review body, they invariably do so. The top salary review body functions in broadly the same manner as the review body covering doctors and dentists. It reports to the prime minister annually recommending salary increases for: the top grades of the civil service, some 600 people in number; the 200 most senior officers in the armed forces; and about 1 000 members of the judiciary. Considerable public interest is taken in the awards made to these 'top people' because of the relatively high salaries they receive, and because the increases invariably exceed the average increase in earnings of all employees as measured by the Department of Employment. The increases recommended by the top salary review body are normally justified on the grounds of comparability with the salaries paid to senior people in the private sector.

In 1983, the prime minister, with the full agreement of the professional bodies concerned, established the Review Body for Nurses Midwives Health Visitors and Professions Related to Medicine. Its task is to recommend pay increases for over half a million people employed by the National Health Service. The review body, however, does not consider terms and conditions of employment other than pay. These remain a Whitley Council responsibility. The pay review body for nurses and others served the politically convenient purpose in the mid-1980s of removing some half-million essential NHS staff, who enjoyed high public esteem, sympathy and support, from the stringent measures imposed by government on public sector pay increases. The fact that the Royal College of Nursing (the nurses' trade union), the Royal College of Midwives and the other professional bodies covered by the review body refused to take strike action in support of pay demands was undoubtedly a major factor in the government's decision to establish it. The essential role played by the prime minister in accepting the case for relatively high pay increases for nurses was, in part, intended to show that the government would value and reward those public sector employees who renounced strike

action. The reform of the NHS after 1990, which created largely autonomous NHS Hospital Trusts, made the future of the Review Body for Nurses Midwives Health Visitors and Professions Related to Medicine problematic. The reforms were, *inter alia*, intended to decentralize the Whitley pay bargaining system and make individual trusts responsible for pay increases.

Acceptance by the trade unions and the professional bodies concerned of the right of the review bodies to make independent recommendations on pay increases, and the undisputed right of the prime minister to accept or refuse a recommendation, clearly abrogates their collective bargaining freedoms. However, few commentators or observers believe they would have achieved the same results through conventional negotiations or by taking militant industrial action against their employers.

## 8.4 Conciliation, Arbitration and Inquiry

Despite the fundamental reluctance of most governments to intervene directly in the regulation of collective bargaining between employers and trade unions, the historical realities of endemic industrial conflict have compelled the State to provide a permanent system of third-party intervention in industrial disputes in Britain. This has included conciliation services, arbitration bodies, and facilities for courts of inquiry in particular disputes. Third-party intervention by State agencies, especially when apparently intractable industrial conflicts seem to threaten economic and sometimes social stability, has proved to be an effective way of resolving such issues. It is often the only way in which disputants feel that they can ultimately reach an honourable compromise.

### Origins and development

It is a major principle of third-party intervention that the parties to an industrial dispute are first encouraged to apply their own formal machinery for the settlement of industrial conflict. This usually means exhausting the voluntarily agreed disputes procedure for resolving differences between the parties which both sides are expected to use before engaging in either strikes or lock-outs. Such voluntary procedures normally follow a closely defined series of stages which culminate at the national or industry level, where national collective bargaining exists, although increasingly disputes procedures apply to the individual workplace or company. By these arrangements, it is the intention of the parties that industrial action will only take place after all stages of the agreed disputes procedure have been formally observed and constitutionally applied. It is only when this final stage has been reached, and when the chances of a negotiated settlement are slender, that third-party intervention is usually felt to be appropriate. Such intervention is generally successful because it is believed that the conciliators or arbitrators are as unbiased and impartial as human personality permits and that the political and external influences in settling the dispute are minimized. It is the intention of third-party intervention to obtain a settlement acceptable to both sides in the conflict, by bringing them together to resolve their differences, or by suggesting the basis for a settlement or, with the participants' consent, by making an arbitration award.

The origins of conciliation and arbitration in Britain are to be found in the hosiery industry in the middle of the nineteenth century. In 1860 A. J. Mundella, a wealthy Nottingham hosiery manufacturer, called a meeting of local employers to avoid a threatened lock-out by hosiery manufacturers in retaliation for a series of strikes by their workers. He persuaded both sides to establish a permanent Board of Conciliation and Arbitration as a means of settling future disputes between them. This Board was so successful that it was subsequently used as a model by other industries. To the modern observer, it might appear an obvious development. But at that time, it was a considerable step forward in industrial relations 'for employers' and workers' leaders to sit round a table discussing their differences on equal terms'.[15]

These first national conciliation boards not only set the pattern for the settlement of trade disputes through joint regulation in their own trades, but also provided the basis for the future development of national and local collective bargaining machinery in their industries. Mundella, who later became a Liberal MP, strongly advised the political leaders of the day that the State could not willingly stand aside from damaging industrial disputes, if the parties themselves could not resolve their differences. As a result of changes in public opinion, growing numbers of employers, trade unions and workers began to favour the creation of some form of independent conciliation and arbitration machinery which only the State could effectively provide.

It was in 1893 that the Labour Department of the Board of Trade was first established. This followed over a decade of industrial unrest in which cabinet ministers, the clergy, and even W. E. Gladstone as Prime Minister had been forced to intervene as industrial peacemakers. In the same year that Parliament passed its first Fair Wages Resolution, the Royal Commission on Labour under the chairmanship of the Duke of Devonshire was established. Its main recommendation was that a system of State-sponsored conciliation should be provided in those disputes which the parties could not resolve themselves. Accordingly, the Conciliation Act 1896 provided that the Board of Trade might inquire into the causes and circumstances of trade disputes and would make provision for third-party conciliation and arbitration if the parties agreed. It was not welcomed by the majority of employers, however, who saw the Act as an unwarranted interference with their established rights over their property and employees. Lord Penrhyn, for example, owner of large slate quarries in North Wales, whose treatment of his striking workers and their families had disturbed late Victorian public opinion, refused a Board of Trade offer of conciliation under the new Act. Like other employers of the time he was firmly of the view that 'my acceptance of it would establish a precedent for outside interference in the management of my private affairs'.[16] Nevertheless, the provisions of the 1896 Conciliation Act gradually became accepted as valuable mechanisms for resolving intractable industrial disputes.

In 1917, the needs and conditions of war led to the creation of the Ministry of Labour which soon collected a wide range of duties and responsibilities in industrial and labour matters. In 1918, the fourth Whitley report on conciliation and arbitration, while recommending both the extension of conciliation and the introduction of a new 'Standing Arbitration Council', stressed that it should be voluntary in nature. It rejected the imposition of an elaborate system of conciliation and arbitration upon industry, 'in place of the present well-recognised voluntary conciliation and arbitration machinery which exists in so many of the important trades of the country'.[17] In consequence, the Industrial Courts Act 1919 provided a system of voluntary arbitration giving the Minister of Labour powers to refer a trade dispute to arbitration provided that, first, the parties were willing to do this and, second, the relevant disputes procedure had been exhausted. Such arbitration could be provided either by the new Industrial Court or by one or more persons appointed by the Minister.

In the latter case, they would act as a board of arbitration chosen by the parties under an independent chairman nominated by the Minister. Under Sections 4 and 5 of the 1919 Act, the Minister could also set up courts of inquiry into particular disputes. Thus the Conciliation Act 1896 and the Industrial Courts Act 1919 formed the basis of voluntary third-party intervention by the State in trade disputes until the enactment of the Industrial Relations Act in 1971, although between 1940 and 1959 the Minister of Labour could refer a dispute to the Industrial Court for compulsory arbitration under Orders 1305 and 1376.

This system worked tolerably well for many years. Both sides of industry trusted and respected the impartial integrity of the Ministry's panel of arbitrators, on the one hand, and the skilled services of the Ministry of Labour's conciliation officers on the other. This enviable reputation largely depended upon the absence of overt political interference by government in the State's conciliation and arbitration services. After 1964, however, this independence became more questionable. With the introduction of formal incomes policies, the advice of conciliators and the decisions of arbitrators frequently conflicted with the pay norms and incomes policy guidelines then in operation. Moreover, the system of State intervention in industrial relations became more legally regulated under the provisions of the Industrial Relations Act of 1971, particularly through the agencies of the National Industrial Relations Court and the reformed Commission on Industrial Relations (CIR).

Although the 1971 Act was repealed by the Trade Union and Labour Relations Act in 1974, and a new system of conciliation and arbitration was established under the Employment Protection Act in 1975, the long-established voluntary system of State conciliation and arbitration almost ceased to exist between 1970 and 1975. At the very least, it no longer enjoyed its previous high standing and reputation of being free from direct political influences. In the meantime, in the late 1960s, the Ministry of Labour was renamed the Department of Employment and Productivity. Subsequently, it became the Department of Employment and substantial parts of it were hived off to form the independent Manpower Services Commission with responsibilities for national manpower planning and job training. At the same time, the Employment Services Agency became responsible for the labour exchange services of the Department of Employment. These were renamed as job centres and they also took over the other employment services of

the former Ministry of Labour. In 1974, responsibility for industrial health and safety was transferred to the Health and Safety Commission. Lastly, the process of dismemberment of the old Ministry of Labour was largely completed by the establishment of ACAS in 1974. This last measure finally removed from Ministerial control the State's conciliation and arbitration functions which successive governments had exercised for over 80 years.

## The Advisory Conciliation and Arbitration Service

The origins of ACAS derived during the protracted struggles over the passing of the Industrial Relations Act in 1971. In this and the subsequent period, when the trade unions did all in their power to render that Act unworkable, a body of opinion emerged, representative of both trade unions and employers, which called for the establishment of a conciliation and arbitration service independent of government control and of civil service influence. The result was ACAS, which took up its formal duties in September 1974. Its activities were placed on a recognized legal basis by Sections 1–6 and Schedule 1, Part 1, of the Employment Protection Act 1975. Its chairperson is appointed by the Secretary of State for Employment and it has a council of nine members. One third of these are nominated by the TUC, one third by the CBI and the remaining third are independents, mainly academics with special knowledge of industrial relations.

Basically ACAS was created as the embodiment of the voluntary approach to industrial relations. It was charged:

> with the general duty of promoting the improvement of industrial relations and, in particular, of encouraging the extension of collective bargaining and the development and, where necessary, reform of collective bargaining machinery.[18]

The TURER Act 1993 removed this duty from ACAS and replaced it with the more general and less contentious duty to promote and improve industrial relations. This is a significant change in public policy.

ACAS provides a wide range of services, but basically they fall into six categories. First, there are its conciliation duties. ACAS can intervene in industrial disputes, for example, at the request of one or more of the parties to a dispute, with a view to bringing about a settlement through collective conciliation between employers and trade unions. Pay and other terms and conditions of employment are usually the most frequent causes of such disputes. But disputes over trade union recognition are also subject to collective conciliation on a voluntary basis. In its collective conciliation work ACAS follows the long-established practice of encouraging the parties to a dispute to use their agreed procedures where they exist. As an independent body, ACAS has continuously maintained that it will not act as an interpreter of incomes policy or government recommended maximum percentage pay increases in the public sector as they affect particular disputes. The collective conciliation service provided by ACAS appears to be valued by employers and unions. Research published in the mid-1980s found:

> Much of the work done by ACAS conciliators is carried out quietly and unobtrusively in the regions. For the most part those employers and trade unions who use conciliation do so to try to settle minor issues rather than major disputes. Moreover, it is only a tiny minority of negotiations that ACAS conciliators are asked by the parties to help. Nevertheless, our survey evidence suggests that when ACAS does intervene both sides have a high regard for the service which it provided and would use it again if a similar issue arose. Thus the general picture which emerges is one of limited demand being met satisfactorily.[19]

There is every reason to believe that most employers and trade unions still held ACAS in high esteem a decade later.

ACAS also offers conciliation in cases arising between individual employees and employers. Since the mid-1970s, there has been a considerable extension of statutory employment rights for individuals with their employers. Individual employees who contend that their statutory rights have been infringed can make complaints to industrial tribunals. It is the duty of ACAS conciliation officers to attempt to settle such complaints prior to these being referred to a tribunal. Complaints about unfair dismissal embodied in the Employment Protection (Consolidation) Act 1978 provide the great majority of the cases handled by ACAS conciliation officers. Individual conciliation is also offered in questions of employees' rights embodied in the Equal Pay Act 1970, as amended by new regulations in 1983, the Sex Discrimination Act 1975, the Race Relations Act 1976, the Employment Act 1980, the Wages Act 1986, the Employment Act 1988 and TURER Act 1993. Some of the individual complaints made under these Acts are eventually heard by industrial tribunals, some are settled by ACAS officers, others are settled privately and the rest are withdrawn. The TURER Act 1993 permits, for the first time, a conciliated settlement acceptable to tribunals to be agreed providing the applicant has received advice from a legally qualified person. Previously, such 'out of court' settlements could only be arranged by ACAS officers.

The second function of ACAS is to provide facilities for arbitration, mediation and investigation into trade disputes. Arbitration is offered at the request of one or more of the parties, but only with the consent of all the parties to the dispute. It is usually done through single arbitrators appointed by ACAS, but it can also take place through boards of arbitration. ACAS can also refer issues for arbitration on a voluntary basis to the Central Arbitration Committee (CAC). Other responsibilities of ACAS relate to industry-wide arbitration. For example, it has responsibility for the Post Office Arbitration Tribunal; for the Railway Staff National Tribunal; and for the Police Arbitration Tribunal. Additionally, ACAS also offers mediation, which is a method of settling disputes 'whereby an independent person makes recommendations as to a possible solution leaving parties to negotiate a settlement'.[20] Mediation is sometimes used where the parties are reluctant to bind themselves in advance to accepting an arbitration award. Having noted an external mediator's recommendations, they then undertake further negotiations between themselves.

The third function of ACAS is advisory work with employers, and to a lesser extent with trade unions and employers' associations. This takes the form of either short advisory visits on specific questions, or longer-term in-depth advisory projects and surveys. The subject matter on which advice is sought is wide ranging. It includes: information relating to general industrial relations matters; grievance, disputes and disciplinary procedures; industrial relations legislation; and contracts of employment. Other advice which ACAS provides is on: pay and payment systems; job analysis; job evaluation and work study; and personnel policies. Although most advisory work is carried out in establishments employing fewer than 300 workers, some very large employers such as the National Health Service and local authorities have also used the facilities of ACAS as an aid to improved industrial relations at local level. Research conducted into the advisory role of ACAS found that a clear majority of those employers and trade unions who sought ACAS advice on a wide range of issues were satisfied with the service.

To the client group the impartial provision of sound advice appears to be what matters most and to the interested parties group it is the combination of impartiality and independence that primarily attracts clients to ACAS for advice.[21]

Closely related to its advisory work is ACAS's fourth duty, under Section 199 of the TULRCA 1992, to issue codes of practice containing practical guidance for promoting improvement in industrial relations between employers and employees. By the late 1980s, ACAS had issued three codes. These dealt with disciplinary practice and procedures in employment, disclosure of information for collective bargaining purposes, and time off work for trade union duties and activities. Following approval by the ACAS Council, such codes are submitted to the Secretary of State for Employment and are laid before Parliament. They are then taken into account in hearings at industrial tribunals. In 1987 after very careful research and consultation, ACAS decided that its code of practice on disciplinary procedures in employment, published and approved by Parliament in 1977, needed updating and expanding in the light of 10 years' experience of operating the 1977 code. In 1987, therefore, it issued a supplementary handbook on discipline at work which it hoped would be used by employers, trade unions and employees to establish sound disciplinary practices and procedures. ACAS stresses, however, that the 1987 handbook does not replace or supplant the 1977 code, which industrial tribunals are required to take into account when hearing cases of alleged unfair dismissal. The usefulness of the 1987 handbook can perhaps be judged from the fact that within a year of its publication requests had been made by employers and others for 170 000 copies.

The fifth major activity of ACAS is to undertake inquiry work aimed at improving industrial relations. Other than inquiries into industrial disputes and questions of trade union recognition, inquiry teams are concerned with in-depth inquiries into important changes and developments taking place in the fields of personnel management, labour utilization and industrial relations. During the 1980s, ACAS conducted inquiries into the flexible use of labour, appraisal systems, labour turnover and absence, employee involvement, handling redundancy situa-

tions, the use of quality circles and the growing problem of alcohol abuse by employees. Much of this in-depth research is distilled by ACAS into practical advisory booklets. Employers use them to assist them to improve their industrial relations and personnel management practices.

In-depth inquiries by ACAS, however, are not to be confused with facilities for *ad hoc* courts or committees of inquiry or investigations into particular industrial disputes provided by the Industrial Courts Act 1919. Committees of inquiry tend to be used for more general purposes than committees of investigation, whilst committees of investigation are less formal than courts of inquiry. Moreover, unlike courts of inquiry, committees of investigation have no obligation to lay their reports before Parliament. In each case, these bodies usually comprise a chairperson, an employer and a union representative. The appointment of courts of inquiry, for instance, chaired by a judge, is a time-honoured method of looking into disputes of a particularly serious and prolonged nature. 'The object of such an inquiry is to establish the facts of the dispute and, by publishing its findings, to focus opinion on the shortcomings of either or both sides.'[22] Courts of inquiry are appointed by the Secretary of State for Employment and have played a major part in resolving some of this country's most difficult industrial disputes over the last 60 years.

Since 1979, however, Secretaries of State in the four Conservative administrations have not appointed a single court of inquiry into a major industrial dispute, preferring instead either to leave the disputants to come to an agreed settlement or for a clear winner to emerge. This process, or policy, was followed during the 1980s when prolonged and bitter strikes took place in the steel and coalmining industries, in the civil service, between schoolteachers and the local authority employers, in the national daily newspaper industry, in the shipping industry, and in the National Health Service. In none of these disputes did the government feel it to be either necessary or desirable to appoint a committee of inquiry, despite the often violent nature of the disputes. The most likely reason why the governments of the 1980s did not appoint courts of inquiry is that they hoped employers would make use of the Employment Acts 1980 and 1982 and the Trade Union Act 1984. These had narrowed trade union immunity when unions took industrial action and made it relatively easy for employers to obtain court injunctions against the unions concerned. The trade union legislation of the 1980s could, therefore, have marked the end of government-appointed courts of inquiry into major industrial disputes.

An early and famous example of the usefulness of courts of inquiry was the 1924 court of inquiry into dockers' wages and conditions. It was here that Ernest Bevin's advocacy of the dockers' case earned him the accolade of 'the dockers' KC'. Other examples include: the Devlin reports on the docks and port transport industry in the 1950s and 1960s; the Pearson reports on the electricity supply and the shipping industries in the 1960s; the Wilberforce report on miners' pay in 1972; and the Scarman report on the Grunwick dispute in 1977. Such reports prove invaluable;

> where (i) the bulk of workers in the industry is concerned and a national strike is threatened; (ii) where there is a likelihood of strike action which would have a disruptive effect on a wide section of the public; (iii) (occasionally) where an isolated dispute looks like having severe secondary effects; (iv) where persistent disputes reveal the existence of an underlying problem, producing a trouble spot. . . . (v) where no further arbitration or negotiation machinery is left.[23]

During the 1980s, ACAS evolved its services to meet the needs of a rapidly changing industrial relations climate. While the bulk of its work continued to be with individual and collective conciliation, and in providing mediation and arbitration on a voluntary basis, it steadily developed an impressive range of advisory, consultative and training services. These were aimed at helping employers, employees and trade unions to use modern management practices. ACAS has become less involved with issues of trade union recognition and collective bargaining, and more concerned with assisting organizations to improve their personnel management practices. These include: effective recruitment and selection of employees; establishing and operating equal opportunities policies; creating schemes for the involvement of employees using quality circles and small group activities; improving communications and joint consultation; and developing the skills managers need to successfully introduce changes in work organization, flexible working practices and performance-related payment systems. The TURER Act 1993 requires ACAS to charge, where appropriate, for its services, which were previously largely free.

In short, ACAS has reflected the general trend in industrial relations away from collective approaches and towards more individualized relationships between employers and employees. Also in keeping with the trend of the 1980s, ACAS has devoted more of it resources to assisting small private sector organizations with the development of good employee relations practices. In its 1987 annual report, ACAS acknowledged that important changes were taking place in employee relations:

> We noted . . . that, in line with moves to increased flexibility, an increasing number of personnel managers were giving greater weight to what are sometimes called 'employee directed' policies which have as their main objective the establishment of a closer relationship between the employer and the employee. Such a relationship is seen as providing a greater commitment to the enterprise and its success, a personal identification with the quality of the product or service it provides and through these a greater understanding of the need to accept changes in working practices and organisation.[24]

In its 1992 annual report ACAS observed that:

> Economic pressures and changes in business structures continued to raise questions for employers in 1992 about the role and functions of trade unions. We have noted the way in which organisational changes . . . have been leading managements not only to question the appropriateness of the structures and procedures through which they relate to trade unions, but in some cases the need to recognise all, or indeed any, of the unions which have represented their employees.[25]

## 8.5 Other State Agencies

### The Certification Officer

The Certification Officer, whose powers derive from the Trade Union and Labour Relations (Consolidation) Act 1992 and the TURER Act 1993, has the duty of discharging the responsibility for maintaining a list of all trade unions and employers' associations and for seeing that these organizations keep adequate accounting records. They must also have their accounts properly audited and submit annual returns to the Officer, returns which are open for public inspection. The Certification Officer also has the duty of ensuring that certificated unions meet with the legal definition of 'independence'. If a trade union is under the domination or control of an employer, it will not receive a certificate of independence. The main advantage to a trade union in being listed as an independent certificated union is the ability to secure tax relief on parts of its income and expenditure.

Under the TULRC Act 1992 and TURER Act 1993, the Certification Officer is responsible for seeing that the statutory procedures for transfers of engagements, amalgamations and changes of name are complied with, and for dealing with complaints by members about the conduct of fully postal, merger ballots supervised by an independently named scrutineer. Under a transfer of engagement, only the members of the transferrer organization vote. But in the case of an amalgamation, a favourable vote by members of each amalgamating organization is required. After voting has taken place, a period of six weeks must elapse before the new organization is registered. During this time, any member of any one of the organizations involved can complain to the Certification Officer that the law governing the balloting arrangements was breached.

The Employment Act 1980 empowered the Certification Officer to reimburse certain expenditure incurred by independent trade unions in conducting secret postal ballots of members for legally specified purposes. The scheme did not cover non-postal or workplace ballots. During 1987, for example, 42 unions applied for refunds in respect of 526 ballots. The Certification Officer rejected 19 of these applications on the grounds that they failed to meet the regulations covering the scheme. The total sum paid in 1987 to unions to cover ballot expenses was £1 158 000. In the early 1980s, the TUC threatened to expel trade unions which applied for money to cover secret ballots. By the late 1980s most unions were in fact applying for balloting refunds. In 1993 the government announced that the public funding of fully postal ballots would end. The expenditure, which is not inconsiderable, will now be borne by individual trade unions.

It is the duty of the Certification Officer to deal with complaints by members that a trade union has failed to comply with its legal obligations, which impose duties on a trade union to hold secret postal ballots for the election of members to its principal executive body and to maintain an accurate register of its members. If a member does not receive a ballot paper, or the ballot paper is posted to a wrong address, a member can complain to the Certification Officer, or to the courts, that the union is not maintaining an accurate and up-to-date record of members for voting purposes. The law does recognize, however, that many factors which are beyond the control of the trade union might make it difficult to maintain accurate records. It is the duty of the Certification Officer to investigate such complaints and, if justified, to make a declaration that the union has failed to keep accurate membership records.

The Certification Officer is also charged with the legal duty of ensuring observance of the statutory procedures governing the setting up and operation of political funds. There is also the duty of approving the conduct of political fund review ballots in accordance with the law, as well as for dealing with complaints by members about breaches of political fund rules. The Certification Officer must ensure that a union's political fund rules make clear the legal definition of 'political objects' and that expenditure is of necessity confined to those objects. There is also the necessity of ensuring that the political fund is separated from the union's general funds. A proposal for the continuation or establishment of a political fund must be approved by a simple majority of those voting by fully postal secret ballot. Any trade union member who wishes to complain about an alleged breach of the political fund rules may do so to the Certification Officer or to the courts. If, after investigation, the Certification Officer considers that a breach has occurred, an order for remedying it may be issued. In 1987, for example, the Certification Officer received seven complaints that unions had acted in breach of their political fund rules. Four of these were upheld. These few complaints should be seen against the background of over 50 trade unions holding and using legally constituted political funds of a total value in 1990 of over £14 million, with a contributing membership of about six million trade unionists.

## The Central Arbitration Committee

Unlike the workload and legal responsibilities of the Certification Officer, which expanded considerably during the 1980s, those of the Central Arbitration Committee (CAC) declined markedly. By the early 1990s, it was providing voluntary arbitration in a handful of cases and hearing a small number of complaints by trade unions that employers were not disclosing information to them for collective bargaining purposes. This obvious and perhaps inevitable decline in the legal scope and workload of the CAC suggests that its continuation in its present form is open to question.

The present legal responsibilities of the CAC are laid down in the TULRC Act 1992. These are the provisions of an arbitration service for those voluntarily wishing to use it and to hear allegations that employers have not disclosed information necessary for collective bargaining purposes to independent trade unions. During the 1980s, the CAC ceased to be responsible for five major legal duties. In 1980, Parliament repealed the provisions in the Employment Protection Act 1975 giving the CAC the task of determining claims by trade unions that an employer should recognize them for collective bargaining purposes. It also repealed, under Schedule 11 of the Act, the right of unions to make claims that an employer was not giving workers the terms and conditions of employment prevailing in that industry or occupation. In 1983, Parliament rescinded the Fair Wages Resolutions and the CAC lost its responsibility for deciding issues related to it. The Wages Act 1986 relieves the CAC of its legal duties in relation to wages councils. And in 1987, it ceased to be responsible for the examination of collective agreements to ensure that they did not contain discriminatory clauses which contravened the sex discrimination legislation. In 1993 CAC was required in certain circumstances to charge for its services.

The major responsibility, other than arbitration, now remaining with the CAC is to hear complaints by independent trade unions that an employer refuses to disclose information which they believe should be disclosed to them for collective bargaining purposes, as required by the 1992 Act. In hearing disclosure cases, the CAC has to decide if the information really is necessary for effective collective bargaining. It also has to decide: if the information sought is relevant to that purpose; if the union would be materially impeded in its bargaining if it did not receive it; and if an employer's claim that the disclosure of certain information would injure its commercial interests is well founded. If it decides the employer should disclose certain information and the employer refuses to do so voluntarily, it can issue a disclosure award in favour of the union. In practice, most complaints by trade unions are settled by conciliation by ACAS and are not referred to the CAC. Of the small number of disclosure cases which receive a formal hearing before the CAC, only a handful result in disclosure awards being made. It would appear that the trade unions in general either have little difficulty in getting employers to disclose the bargaining information

they require or that they do not require detailed information in order to bargain effectively.

The CAC also has the duty under the TULRC Act 1992 to provide voluntary arbitration where the two parties wish to either avoid a dispute or to end one. As ACAS can also provide an arbitration service on request, the CAC is normally only used to arbitrate in issues of national importance. As the tendency since 1979 has been for the two sides in national disputes to settle the issue one way or the other, regardless of how bitter the dispute became and because that process also appeared to be the one preferred by government, very few disputes of national importance are referred for arbitration to the CAC.

## Commissioner for the Rights of Trade Union Members

The new office of Commissioner for the Rights of Trade Union Members was created by the Employment Act 1988 (now the TULRC Act 1992). The role of the Commissioner was seen as vital by the government in ensuring that the rights given by legislation to individual union members, principally under the Trade Union Act 1984, could be enforced through the courts. It is the duty of the Commissioner to assist individual union members to take complaints that their unions have not fulfilled their legal obligations before the courts. The role of the Commissioner is modelled on the part played by the Commission for Racial Equality in race discrimination cases, and the Equal Opportunities Commission in sex discrimination cases. Such comparisons are seen as odious and misleading by the trade unions. It was the belief of the government, in guiding the 1988 Act through Parliament, that union members had to be both determined and courageous in seeking legal redress, if they believed their union had not complied with the legal requirements of the Trade Union Act 1984. Just as those who are discriminated against on grounds of sex or race should receive help in seeking a legal remedy, the government believed that individual trade union members should be entitled to the same assistance. The comparability between race and sex discrimination and the unfair treatment of individual trade union members remains open to question.

The 1992 Act empowers the Commissioner to provide assistance to individual union members by paying for legal advice, by arranging for the complainant to receive legal advice, by arranging and paying for the complainant to be legally represented before a court, and by defraying the complainant's personal expenses in pursuing a case. No means-testing of the individual union member is applied in granting financial assistance. In general, the Commissioner is empowered to exercise discretion when deciding whether or not to support a complaint. The Commissioner shall have regard to: whether the case raises a question of principle; whether the legal and factual complexities of the case would make it unreasonable for the complainant to proceed unaided; and whether the case involves what the Act describes as a matter of 'substantial public interest'. Clearly, the powers of the Commissioner are extensive.

The matters where the 1992 Act empowers the Commissioner to give legal and other assistance to individual union members include:

- failure by the individual's union to hold a ballot before industrial action;
- failure to hold a political fund ballot in keeping with the rules laid down by the Certification Officer;
- failure by the union to hold properly conducted ballots for the election of the members to its principal executive body;
- the right to inspect a union's accounts;
- the unlawful use of a union's property by its trustees;
- use of union funds for the indemnification of unlawful conduct;
- the use of a union's political funds for purposes other than those established by the law;
- failure to maintain an accurate register of union members;
- applications to the courts to recover union funds which have been used to indemnify unlawful conduct.

The Commissioner is also empowered to give assistance and legal advice to trade union members seeking to bring proceedings against a trade union where it is alleged that union rules relating to the following matters have been breached:

- the expulsion, removal, appointment or election of a person from any office or position;
- disciplinary proceedings taken against a member;
- the authorization or endorsement of industrial action;
- the balloting of union members;
- the use of union funds and property;

- levies imposed to support or sustain industrial action;
- proceedings at any level in a union which are in breach of its rules (e.g. branch, committee or conference activities).

When deciding whether or not to give assistance to a union member alleging a breach of union rules, the Commissioner must be satisfied that either the breach of rules complained of would also affect other union members, or that similar breaches have also been committed, or could be committed, against other union members. The Commissioner does not possess a 'roving brief' to investigate unions at will to see if their rules are being broken, but can only act in response to a complaint by individual union members. The essential task of the Commissioner on receiving a complaint regarding alleged breaches of union rules is to decide if an issue of principle is involved, whether the union member requires assistance or should proceed unaided, and whether or not a case involves a matter of 'substantial public interest'. Where the Commissioner decides to assist a union member to bring a complaint, the union, or other body, against whom the action is being taken must be informed of the Commissioner's role.

## Commissioner for Protection against Unlawful Industrial Action

The Commissioner for Protection against Unlawful Industrial Action has been created by the Trade Union Reform and Employment Rights Act 1993. This public office marks a new direction for public policy. The Commissioner is required, after due consideration, to assist any person, including members of the general public, to exercise a Citizen's Right under the 1993 Act to seek damages from a trade union where it is alleged that unlawful industrial action has involved them in a loss; that is, where industrial action not taken in accordance with legal requirements has resulted in a person failing to receive goods or services or where goods or services have been delayed.

If members of the public believe they have suffered damages as the result of unlawful industrial action they can seek the assistance of the Commissioner in bringing legal proceedings. The 1993 Act, therefore, creates a Citizen's Right to damages arising out of unlawful industrial action. The Commissioner, before granting legal or financial assistance or both to the person concerned, must be satisfied that it would be unreasonable to expect the person to proceed unaided or that a matter of substantial public interest is involved. If the Commissioner decides to provide the person concerned with assistance the trade union against which the action will be brought must be informed of this decision.

## 8.6   Summary Points

- Public policy on industrial relations comprises the legislation and the clearly declared political, social and economic policies which the government in power espouses, as implemented by the courts, the civil service and other state agencies.
- Public policy, generally speaking, reflects the social and ethical values of the government in power and public opinion.
- Public policy on industrial relations between the end of the Second World War in 1945 and the election of the first Thatcher Conservative government in 1979 enjoyed a considerable degree of consensus, continuity and stability. It became part of what has been called the postwar settlement.
- For industrial relations the postwar settlement, which dominated public policy for almost 35 years, was founded on: a belief in a minimum of State and legal interference in industrial relations or the voluntarist tradition; the commitment of government to full employment policies; public support for collective bargaining; the example set by government as a 'model employer'; and the close involvement of the TUC and the CBI in government management of the economy and wages policies. This postwar settlement and consensus came to an end in 1979.
- Since 1979 public policy on industrial relations has been characterized by very different values and policies: the abandonment of government commitment to full employment; increased legal control of the trade unions and their activities; the privatization of the State corporations and much of the public sector of the economy; a clear anti-trade union ideology; the almost total exclusion of the TUC and CBI from government economic policy making; and the abandonment by the State of its role as model employer. By the early 1990s public policy on industrial relations had been fundamentally transformed.
- One of the greatest changes in public policy concerned the role of the State as industrial peace-keeper and the use of the office of Prime Minister and the Cabinet to prevent, deter or end bitter

strikes which endangered the public interest. Since 1979 the participants to industrial disputes have been left alone to settle their differences. Attempts at settlements at 10 Downing Street over 'beer and sandwiches' were abandoned. Increasingly employers used the 'labour injunction' and the trade union laws passed since 1979 to prevent or end strikes.

- During the 1980s and the early 1990s public policies encouraging the individualization and depoliticization of industrial relations were pursued. The values and institutions of collectivism were rejected in favour of the individual interests of employers and employees, which sought to forge an ever greater personal relationship between the two. Employees were encouraged to loosen their allegiance to the collectivist values of traditional trade unionism, in favour of a personal commitment and involvement in the commercial objectives and values of the organization employing them.
- The personal links between individual employees and their employers were further strengthened by the use of share ownership schemes, profit-related pay, pension and health care insurance arrangements, performance related pay, performance appraisal reviews, and a range of management schemes to increase the personal involvement and commitment of employees to their work and their employer.
- Public policy since 1979 has also sought, through legal changes, 'to give unions back to their members' through the compulsory use of the secret postal ballot, by the implementation of measures designed to weaken or end the use of trade union funds for political purposes, and by attempts to replace the collectivist values of trade union solidarity with the economic ideology of an 'enterprise culture' and individual responsibility and initiative. State social security provision was castigated as a 'dependency culture'.
- All attempts by government to control pay increases by the use of incomes policies were abandoned after 1979, in favour of economic policies of deflation and the strengthening of market forces and the supply side of the economy.
- Wages councils, first established in 1909 to regulate the pay and conditions of the lowest paid people in Britain and supported by every government for three-quarters of a century as public policy, were abolished in 1993 as anachronistic and distortive of the labour market.

- The Advisory Conciliation and Arbitration Service, representing continuous public policy since the nineteenth century, but expanded in the 1970s to fulfil wider industrial relations objectives, had its responsibilities narrowed in 1993.
- The legal duties and responsibilities of the Certification Officer, who took over from the previous Registrar of Trade Unions, embody continuous public policy since 1871. In the 1980s and early 1990s these duties and responsibilities were considerably expanded by legislation. The Officer now plays an increasingly important role in the regulation of the internal affairs of trade unions.
- The duties and responsibilities of the Central Arbitration Committee have declined drastically as government policy has been to regulate industrial disputes by legal means rather than by voluntary recourse to third-party intervention.
- The office of Commissioner for the Rights of Trade Union Members was created in 1988 to assist union members to take before the courts complaints that their union has not fulfilled its legal obligations in relation to them as individuals. In particular, the Commissioner has been empowered to assist union members to further complaints relating to the use of secret postal ballots.
- In 1993 the office of the Commissioner for Protection against Unlawful Industrial Action was founded to assist an individual deprived of goods or services by unlawful industrial action to seek legal redress. The 1993 Act creates a Citizen's Right for this purpose.

## 8.7  References

1. O. Kahn-Freund, *Labour and the Law*, Stevens, London, 1977, p. 4.
2. Lord Wedderburn, *The Worker and the Law*, 3rd edn, Penguin, Harmondsworth, 1986, p. 18.
3. J. A. G. Griffiths, *The Politics of the Judiciary*, 3rd edn, 1985, pp. 185 and 234, quoted in Lord Wedderburn, *op. cit.*, p. 21.
4. B. Towers (ed.), *A Handbook of Industrial Relations Practice*, Kogan Page, London, 1987, p. 39.
5. H. Phelps Brown, *The Origins of Trade Union Power*, Oxford University Press, Oxford, 1986, p. 304.
6. J. MacInnes, *Thatcherism at Work*, Open University Press, Milton Keynes, 1987, p. 18.
7. Towers, *op. cit.*, p. 10.
8. *Ibid.*, p. 55.
9. *Ibid.*, p. 57.
10. J. Kelly and R. Richardson, Annual Review Article 1988, *British Journal of Industrial Relations*, March 1989, p. 145.
11. MacInnes, *op. cit.*, p. 140.
12. Towers, *op. cit.*, p. 290.
13. *Fifth Report from the Select Committee of the House of Lords on the Sweating System* (1980) quoted in E. H. Phelps Brown, *The Growth of British Industrial Relations*, Macmillan, London, 1965, p. 197.
14. Ministry of Labour, *Written Evidence to the Royal Commission on Trade Unions and Employers' Associations*, HMSO, London, 1965, p. 114.
15. E. Wigham, *Strikes and the Government 1893-1974*, Macmillan, London, 1976, p. 1.
16. *Ibid.*, p. 13.
17. Ministry of Reconstruction, *Report on Conciliation and Arbitration*, HMSO, London, 1918, p. 3.
18. Advisory Conciliation and Arbitration Service, *Annual Report 1981*, HMSO, London, 1982, p. 6.
19. M. Jones and L. Dickens, Resolving industrial disputes: the role of ACAS conciliation, *Industrial Relations Journal*, 1983, p. 17.
20. Advisory Conciliation and Arbitration Service, *op. cit.*, p. 19.
21. E. Armstrong, Evaluating the Advisory Work of ACAS, *Employment Gazette*, April 1985, p. 143.
22. R. W. Rideout, *Principles of Labour Law*, Sweet and Maxwell, London, 1976, p. 54.
23. *Ibid.*
24. Advisory Conciliation and Arbitration Service, *Annual Report, 1987*, ACAS, London, 1988, p. 15.
25. Advisory Conciliation and Arbitration Service, *Annual Report, 1992*, ACAS, London, 1993, p. 18.

# 9

# Individual Employment Law

In this chapter and the following one on collective labour law, we provide an outline description of the main statutes which, at the time of writing, govern the legal aspects of industrial relations in Britain. It is not the intention in these two chapters to attempt a philosophical explanation of the role of the law in regulating labour relations in an advanced market economy like Britain. Neither is it our intention to provide detailed legal analyses of the law of industrial relations. Those seeking to extend their knowledge can find many more learned expositions of labour law written by members of the legal profession and by academic specialists in the field. What the following two chapters seek to achieve is a concise and introductory guide for students and practitioners of industrial relations to the considerable number of complicated statutes which have been enacted in recent years. In this chapter, we focus on that legislation regulating the individual employment relationship between employers and employees. In Chapter 10, we turn to the collective aspects of labour law, such as the law on industrial disputes, trade unionism and collective bargaining.

## 9.1  The Contract of Employment

### The common law background

Considering how essential the principle of contract and the legal rights and penalties which this term implies are in an industrial society, it is somewhat surprising that the first specific Act of Parliament covering the contractual relationships between employers and employees was the Contracts of Employment Act 1963. Hitherto, a body of common law had emerged over a long period of time which, to a limited extent, regulated the duties of employees and the responsibilities of employers in their employment relationships. It is not unreasonable to conclude that historically the relative social and economic power of the 'master' or employer far exceeded that of his 'servants' or employees in their contractual rela-

tionships. Although the common law did not alter that fundamental balance of power, it clarified the duties and responsibilities of both parties to the employment contract. The most effective method, however, of redressing the imbalance in power between employer and employee has been trade unionism, not common law or parliamentary statute. 'As a power countervailing management the trade unions are much more effective than the law has ever been or ever can be.'[1] Since 1979, however, trade union power, though still substantial, has waned and that of the law has waxed.

The main components, or constituent parts, of the contract of employment between employer and employee are outlined in Figure 9.1. As far as the common law is concerned, employees have a duty to be ready and willing to work, to offer personal service to their employer and to take reasonable care in the exercise of that service. Employees are also required not to disrupt wilfully their employer's undertaking, to obey reasonable orders given by the employer or its agents, and to work for the employer in the employer's time. They are also expected to respect the employer's trade secrets, to safeguard the employer against any loss incurred during their service and not to disclose certain information relating to the employer's business. It is becoming increasingly commonplace for employers to write into the contracts of employees a clause forbidding them to disclose confidential information concerning clients or processes to competitors. Many place restrictions or restrictive covenants on certain employees to prevent them from taking jobs with a close competitor or from setting themselves up as competitors. The common law duties of the employee may or may not be contractually specified, but where they are they often derive from custom and practice. The employer in return agrees to pay the agreed wages for the willingness to work and to provide reasonable opportunity to earn the agreed wages, although it appears to be legally uncertain whether an employer is actually obliged to provide work. Employers have a duty to take every

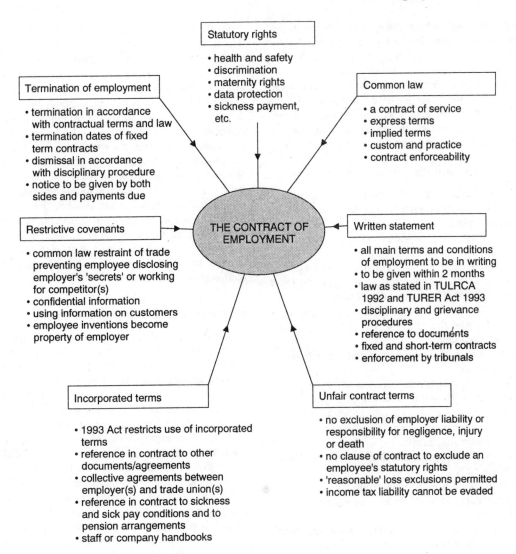

*Figure 9.1* Constituent elements of the contract of employment.

reasonable care to ensure their employees' safety, to treat their employees with proper courtesy and to indemnify them for injury sustained during employment. The importance of these common law requirements, however, has steadily diminished as the former absolute powers of the employer have declined. They have also diminished as the employer's statutory obligations have been more clearly defined and as the statute law has made the employers' responsibilities to their employees more specific.

The Employment Protection (Consolidation) Act 1978 (sections 1–6), as amended by the Trade Union Reform and Employment Rights (TURER) Act 1993,

requires that all those employees who work eight or more hours per week are given a written statement of the terms of their employment within two months of their engagement. The 1993 Act now requires that a contract of employment, as embodied in the statement of its main terms, be given to the employee in full. While some aspects of the contract, such as terms relating to sickness and pension rights, can be covered by reference to other documents, all other parts of the contract must be given in writing directly to the employee. This change will mean that the contract of employment will become both more detailed and comprehensive, and more legalistic.

Employees who work for fewer than eight hours per week are not normally covered by the legislation. Whilst the legislation covers apprentices, it does not cover people who are under contract to supply a service such as freelance agents or self-employed persons; neither does it cover seafarers. If the employer does not give a written statement within the two-month period, the employee may make a complaint to an industrial tribunal and seek a remedy.

The written particulars required by law include:

- names of the parties to the contract;
- date of commencement of employment;
- place or places of work and address of employer;
- date when any previous relevant continuous employment began;
- if employment is not permanent, the length of period it will continue for, or if it is for a fixed term, the date employment will terminate;
- any collective agreements which directly affect the contract and the names of the parties by whom they were made;
- scale or rate of remuneration and the method of calculation;
- intervals at which remuneration will be paid;
- hours of work and normal working hours;
- holidays, public holidays and holiday pay;
- matters concerning sickness and sick pay;
- pension arrangements;
- length of notice on both sides on termination of employment;
- job title or a brief job description;
- disciplinary and grievance arrangements and procedures;
- where an employee is required to work outside the UK for more than one month, details of length of period, rate of pay, currency to be paid in, and the terms relating to return to the UK.

Whilst employees need only give a minimum of one week's notice to terminate their contract, unless it specifies a longer period, employers are required to give employees with four or more weeks' service at least one week's notice, and those with two years' service at least two weeks' notice. Employees are then entitled to a minimum of an additional week's notice for each year of continuous employment up to 12 years. Where an employer fails to give the legally required minimum notice, or payment in lieu of notice, employees can bring a case of 'wrongful' dismissal against their employer, as distinct from 'unfair' dismissal, to an industrial tribunal.

Two further points need to be made. First, for details relating to pensions, sickness entitlement, discipline and grievance procedures, employers can refer employees to any relevant documents incorporating the required information, providing they give them a copy. It is now increasingly the practice of employers to cover all aspects of employment in a comprehensive company handbook which is issued to all employees. Second, the written statement itself is not the contract of employment. It has no direct legal force at all, though its terms can be used as evidence before an industrial tribunal in unfair dismissal cases. It is merely information about what the employer believes to be some of the main terms of the contracts of employment of individual employees. The provisions of the 1993 Act, however, require the employer to give more specific and detailed information on contracts of employment.

## Express terms and implied terms

In statute law, a 'contract of employment' means a contract of service whether it is express or implied, and (if it is expressed) whether it is oral or in writing, between an employer and an employee. The express terms of a contract of employment pose few problems. Indeed, the written particulars provided by the employer to each of its employees are the best evidence of the express terms of an employment contract. They normally include the terms and conditions of employment, such as the pay, hours of work, holiday entitlements, pension rights and so on. Although collective agreements between employers and trade unions are not directly legally enforceable unless the parties specifically state so in writing, the terms within collective agreements are normally incorporated into the individual contracts of employment of employees. This is done either by express incorporation or by implied incorporation.

> The collective agreement is, however, meant to affect the individual contracts; otherwise the elaborate structure of bargaining would have no legal effect at all. . . . The best way is for the employment contract to incorporate the collective terms *expressly*.[2]

The 1993 Act now requires the written statement of the main terms and conditions of employment given to the individual employee to state clearly whether or not collective agreements are involved and the persons by whom they were made. The contract of employment should, therefore, expressly define who is and who is not covered by collective agreements. It is doubtful, however, that the 1993 Act, in requiring a full and detailed written statement of the main terms of the contract, will exclude the common law aspects of the contract of employment which have been established by legal judgments over several centuries.

The implied terms of contract of employment are more complex. Broadly, terms may be implied from the relations between the parties, from custom and practice, and by the law. The courts and tribunals, for example, are prepared to imply a term into the contract 'in circumstances where the parties did not expressly insert a term to meet a particular contingency'.[3] Custom and practice, on the other hand, may only be implied as a term in a contract of employment provided that it is 'reasonable, certain and notorious'. It must, in short, be recognized as such by the courts or by industrial tribunals, be capable of reasonably precise definition or description and be well known to the parties.

## Incorporated terms

Although works rules and disciplinary codes are also incorporated into individual contracts of employment, the latter are now regulated to a considerable extent by statute. Statutory implied terms include, for example: the equality clauses under the Equal Pay Act 1970; guaranteed payments in respect of lost working days; and the terms and conditions imposed by the Central Arbitration Committee (CAC) where an employer has refused to disclose information needed for collective bargaining purposes. These statutory terms governing the contract of employment are rarely if ever expressly incorporated into individual contracts of employment. Employers have a duty to observe them as the law of the land, whilst employees can obtain enforcement of their statutory legal rights by due process of the law. Many of these statutory implied terms in the contract of employment, such as health and safety and unfair dismissal legislation, now effectively supersede the common law requirements.

Under current employment legislation, employers are obliged to give all employees working eight hours or more itemized pay statements. This provides employees with: a clear statement of how their gross pay is made up; its methods of calculation; the details of the variable or fixed deductions involved; their net pay; and the method and intervals of payment. Where some deductions are fixed these need not be itemized every time a payment is made, provided that employees are given a standing statement of these deductions. This sets out the amount, the intervals between each deduction and why they are made. Such detailed pay statements are obviously of considerable use in cases taken before industrial tribunals.

## Variation of contract

Contracts of employment change or are varied all the time. Whenever there is a pay increase, a reduction in working hours, a reallocation of work duties, a change in work location or an agreed move to shiftwork, for example, the conditions of the contract are changed. Where these changes are agreed by trade unions as part of the collective bargaining process, even though both the express and implied terms of the contract of employment are changed, there is no need to issue amended written statements. But there is a statutory obligation to change the written statement when it becomes inaccurate. The 1993 Act requires the employer to give individual employees written notification of any changes to be made in the written statement of the contract of employment within one month. Where the employment situation is fluid with changing places and hours of work, and where flexible working methods make precise job descriptions difficult to determine, the contract can make specific provisions to cover the requirements of changing work situations. Where the contract specifically permits the employer to require employees to accept spatial and functional mobility and flexible working hours, for instance, it should be clearly stated and applied in a reasonable manner.

If employees are dismissed for refusing to accept change which their contracts clearly require, such as movement to new work sites or a reallocation of duties, it is unlikely that they will be able to contest successfully a case for redundancy payment or unfair dismissal. Where substantial variations in the contract must first be agreed between the parties, this intention should be made quite clear – preferably in writing and notice of one month given to the employee that the changes will take place. With collective bargaining this presents few problems, but without it individual employees must give their consent for any major changes of this sort. If a change takes place, and the employees adhere to the new arrangements without protest, it is deemed that they have accepted the change voluntarily. But as one tribunal has pointed out 'voluntary acceptance of new terms must be distinguished from taking Hobson's choice'.[4]

## Constructive dismissal

The law relating to changes in the contract of employment and legal judgments in individual cases suggest that the situation is extremely complex. However, where an employer substantially varies the terms and conditions of employment of its employees, and where their contracts clearly do not permit this to be done, or where it happens in spite of the protests of the employees concerned, that employer is breaking or repudiating the contracts. In such cases, if employees are dismissed for refusing to accept the arbitrary changes made by an employer to their contracts, or where they leave their employment in protest, they might well be able to successfully contest a case of constructive dismissal at an industrial tribunal. However, the courts have decided that where a substantial variation of contract is unavoidable, because of extreme and pressing adverse financial circumstance, for example, employees can be obliged to accept it. In the event of dismissal, the employer would be required to prove to a tribunal that the financial circumstances constituted a dire threat to the organization.

## Fixed or short-term contracts

So far we have dealt with contracts of employment of indefinite duration, since most employees and employers expect the contract to continue until one of them decides to terminate it. Many employees, however, commence employment for a fixed period which they understand to be the principal condition of employment. When this is the case, the period of employment needs to be clearly stated along with the fixed date of termination. Every effort should be made to ensure that the employees understand that the job is for a fixed period only. Where a fixed term contract lasts for more than one year, the right of the employee to seek a legal remedy for unfair dismissal can be waived providing it is in writing. Where the contract is for more than two years the right to redundancy payments can be waived. These restrictions on a legal right must, however, be clearly stated in the contract. Further, in certain cases where a number of consecutive fixed term contracts have been given to an employee, the courts might decide that the employee's employment was continuous and that he or she should be

treated at law as a permanent employee with full legal rights.

The 1993 Act for the first time extends employment protection rights, including contract of employment rights, to members of the armed forces. These rights include: written statements of employment particulars; itemized pay statements; time off for antenatal care; maternity rights; and unfair dismissal rights.

## 9.2    Unfair Dismissal

## Origins and scope

At common law, employers have traditionally possessed wide powers to engage and to dismiss their employees at will. Until the Industrial Relations Act 1971, which gave most employees the legal right to claim compensation for 'unfair dismissal' for the first time, the power of employers to dismiss their employees was only restricted by trade union organization and by collective agreements incorporating established dismissal procedures within them. In theory, any employees who were not given due notice, or payment in lieu of notice, when dismissed by their employer could sue that employer for 'wrongful dismissal', that is, alleged breach of the contract of employment, under their common law rights through the civil courts. But in practice this rarely happened because of the heavy legal costs involved and the generally accepted right of the employer to hire and fire with relative impunity. Where trade unions were strongly organized, however, they could usually threaten strike action if any of their members were unreasonably dismissed. But where trade unionism was weak or non-existent, employers possessed virtually unlimited powers of dismissal. The insecurity of employment thus created, whilst perhaps tolerated in the nineteenth century, proved completely unacceptable in the second half of the twentieth century.

It was the Industrial Relations Act 1971 which introduced for the first time the right of legal redress for what it defined in law as unfair dismissal. It also permitted individuals who claimed that they had been dismissed unfairly to bring their cases before an industrial tribunal rather than the ordinary courts. The comparative informality of industrial tribunals, it was believed, with their emphases upon common sense and the realities of industrial relations, rather than upon the formality and legal pedantry associated with the civil courts, together with their speed and relative cheapness from the employee's

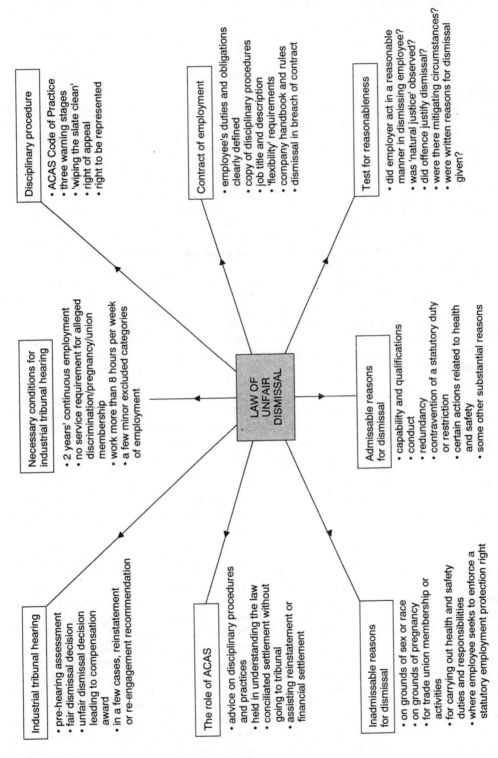

**Disciplinary procedure**

- ACAS Code of Practice
- three warning stages
- 'wiping the slate clean'
- right of appeal
- right to be represented

**Contract of employment**

- employee's duties and obligations clearly defined
- copy of disciplinary procedures
- job title and description
- 'flexibility' requirements
- company handbook and rules
- dismissal in breach of contract

**Test for reasonableness**

- did employer act in a reasonable manner in dismissing employee?
- was 'natural justice' observed?
- did offence justify dismissal?
- were there mitigating circumstances?
- were written reasons for dismissal given?

**Necessary conditions for industrial tribunal hearing**

- 2 years' continuous employment
- no service requirement for alleged discrimination/pregnancy/union membership
- work more than 8 hours per week
- a few minor excluded categories of employment

**LAW OF UNFAIR DISMISSAL**

**Admissable reasons for dismissal**

- capability and qualifications
- conduct
- redundancy
- contravention of a statutory duty or restriction
- certain actions related to health and safety
- some other substantial reasons

**Industrial tribunal hearing**

- pre-hearing assessment
- fair dismissal decision
- unfair dismissal decision leading to compensation award
- in a few cases, reinstatement or re-engagement recommendation

**The role of ACAS**

- advice on disciplinary procedures and practices
- held in understanding the law
- conciliated settlement without going to tribunal
- assisting reinstatement or financial settlement

**Inadmissable reasons for dismissal**

- on grounds of sex or race
- on grounds of pregnancy
- for trade union membership or activities
- for carrying out health and safety duties and responsibilities
- where employee seeks to enforce a statutory employment protection right

*Figure 9.2* Main aspects of the law of unfair dismissal.

point of view, was deemed to be a more suitable vehicle for hearing cases involving unfair dismissal.

Figure 9.2 illustrates the main aspects of the law of unfair dismissal. It is probable that at least half a million dismissals for all reasons take place each year but only about 40 000 cases are registered annually with industrial tribunals and of these some two-thirds either settled by conciliation or withdrawn. Of the cases proceeding to a tribunal hearing, about two-thirds are rejected as being registered beyond the legal time limits or 'out of scope' or – as in most cases – the dismissals are found to be fair and the cases are dismissed. Only one-third of the 10 000 or so cases which are heard annually by tribunals are upheld as unfair dismissals and only about half of one per cent result in the reinstatement or re-engagement of the dismissed employee. The remedy awarded by the tribunals in the majority of cases declared to be unfair dismissals is monetary compensation, with the median award being £1 800 in 1990–91.

A detailed analysis of unfair dismissal cases in 1985–86 by the Department of Employment found that a majority of unfair dismissal cases arose in private, non-manufacturing workplaces, particularly in the distribution sector. The median workplace in which unfair dismissal cases arose employed 40 people and did not recognize trade unions. A majority of unfair dismissal claims were made by manual workers, especially the semi-skilled. The median unfair dismissal applicant had four years' service, with the median wage of those bringing unfair dismissal cases being below the median wage for full-time employees as a whole. Union members were less likely to be successful at a tribunal hearing than their non-union counterparts.

## Those covered

With the repeal of the Industrial Relations Act 1971 and the 'consolidation' of the individual rights under the Employment Protection Act 1975, the main body of statute law concerning unfair dismissal is provided by the Employment Protection (Consolidation) Act 1978, as amended by the Employment Acts of the 1980s and the TURER Act 1993. With the exception of a few classes of employees, all those with more than two years' continuous employment with an employer have a statutory right not to be unfairly dismissed. The qualifying period of continuous employment was raised from six months to 12 months in 1980 and to two years in 1985. Under current UK

legislation, this right exists either if employees work 16 or more hours per week for their employer, or if they have worked eight or more hours per week for the same employer for at least five years continuously. Due to House of Lords judgements in 1994, however, and the requirements of EU equality laws, it is likely that part-time employees will be able to take a case of unfair dismissal to an industrial tribunal. This means that current legislation in the UK is incompatible with European law. Employees on fixed-term contracts of one year or more, whilst excluded in respect of the expiry of their contract, may bring a case for unfair dismissal unless they have accepted a contract which clearly waives their right to claim legal remedy for unfair dismissal. Employees covered by a negotiated dismissal procedure which qualifies for an exclusion order from the Secretary of State are also excluded from the unfair dismissal provisions of the 1978 Act where 'the remedies provided by the agreement . . . are on the whole as beneficial as . . . those provided in respect of unfair dismissal'[5] by section 65 of the Act.

Between 1980 and 1985 employees working in small firms, which throughout their period of employment had employed 20 or fewer employees, could not make a claim of unfair dismissal if they had not completed two years' continuous employment at the time of their dismissal. Workers in firms of more than 20 employees at this time only needed 12 months' service to qualify. The requirement of continuous employment for all employees, regardless of the size of the firm employing them, was raised to two years in 1985. In hearing cases of unfair dismissal in small firms, tribunals are now required to take into account the employer's size and administrative resources when considering whether the dismissal was carried out fairly.

## Code of disciplinary practice

In cases of unfair dismissal reaching a tribunal, great importance is attached to the reasonableness of the employer's actions and whether or not a satisfactory disciplinary procedure was followed. In 1977, Parliament approved its first code of practice on disciplinary practice and procedures in employment, prepared by the Advisory Conciliation and Arbitration Service (ACAS). In 1987, ACAS issued an advisory handbook on discipline at work. It complements the 1977 code and contains detailed practical guidance to employers and employees on how to handle disciplinary and dismissal situations. This

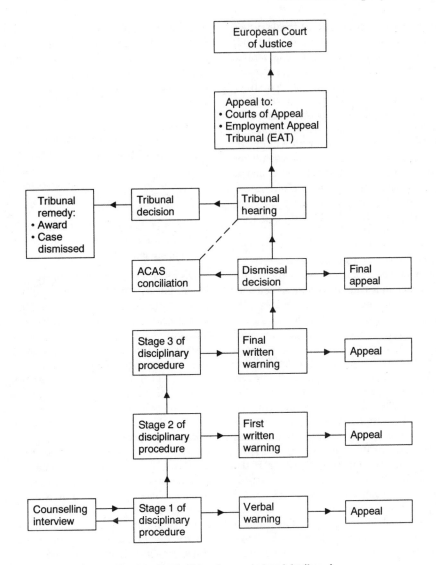

*Figure 9.3* Disciplinary procedure and unfair dismissal hearings at industrial tribunals.

handbook updates the code of practice and does not replace or supplant it. It is based on valuable experience gained over a 10-year period. Both the code and the handbook give 'practical guidance on how to draw up disciplinary rules and procedures and how to operate them effectively'.[6] They are intended as guides for employers, employees, trade unions and industrial tribunals in establishing and assessing the operation of disciplinary procedures within organizations. The 1977 code must be considered by tribunals in determining their decisions, and outlines behaviour which can be interpreted as constituting an offence, enabling tribunals to decide whether an employer has

acted reasonably in dismissing an employee. Figure 9.3 illustrates in diagrammatic form the procedure a disciplinary hearing should follow.

The code stresses, among other things, that disciplinary procedures should be in writing; they should specify to whom they apply; they should provide speedy action; they should indicate the disciplinary actions which may be taken; they should give individuals a chance to state their cases; and they should ensure that a sensible system of warnings and a reasonable period of time are provided for employees to improve their behaviour. The code recommends very careful use of the powers of dismissal, emphasizes the need for an appeals system and suggests how it should be conducted. The code also stresses the importance of verbal and written warnings, of disciplinary transfers where possible and of keeping adequate records on disciplinary matters. There is also the need to provide the opportunity to 'wipe the slate clean', for disciplined employees, after a suitable period of good behaviour. Above all, the code emphasizes, there is a need for all employees, including management, to be fully aware of the disciplinary procedure and the possible consequences of infringing it. Where employers have clearly failed to observe the general standards advised in the code, an industrial tribunal may well conclude that their actions have been unreasonable.

The obligation of employers to act in a reasonable manner in disciplining and dismissing employees not only means that employers should follow the ACAS code. It also means that employers should consider whether the situation and the employee's offence merit dimissal, and whether there are mitigating circumstances for which 'natural justice' demands should be taken into account when making decisions of this kind. Did the employee understand the rules and warnings received, for example? Did the employee have a chance to explain the conduct in question, and was the actual manner of dismissal satisfactory? The law also requires that an employer should give employees, if requested, written reasons for their dismissal or for the failure to renew a fixed term contract of employment, within 14 days of the request being made. Where an employer refuses to do this, or where the reasons for not doing so are believed to be inadequate or untrue, employees may complain to an industrial tribunal. If the tribunal finds an employee's claim to be justified, it can make an award against the employer of two weeks' pay. Where a dismissal letter is given, it can be used as evidence at a hearing before an industrial tribunal.

## Reasons for dismissal

Section 57 of the Employment Protection (Consolidation) Act 1978 lays down the main grounds on which dismissals can be judged as either 'fair' or 'unfair'. What constitutes fair or unfair dismissal is largely a matter of legal and not moral definition. Before the Employment Act 1980, the onus of proof that the employer had acted both reasonably and fairly in dismissing an employee lay with the employer. It is now the responsibility of the tribunal to decide whether the employer acted reasonably

given all the circumstances. This change significantly reduced the burden of proof on the employer when appearing before a tribunal. Apart from 'some other substantial reason', it is only 'fair' to dismiss an employee for one of the following 'admissible' reasons:

(a)   related to the capability or qualifications of the employee for performing work of the kind which he was employed to do, or
(b)   related to the conduct of the employee, or
(c)   that the employee was redundant, or
(d)   that the employee could not continue to work in the position which he held without contravention (either on his part or that of his employer) of a duty or restriction imposed by or under an enactment.[7]

Dismissal on grounds of incapability means that if employers follow adequate disciplinary procedures and act reasonably, they can fairly dismiss employees, even after two years' continuous employment, on the grounds of an employee's incapability, inadequacy, incompetence or lack of skill in the job. It is essential that employees are allowed a reasonable time in which to improve their performance and, if practicable, are offered suitable alternative employment by their employer. If a case is brought before a tribunal, it can require the employer to produce substantive proof of the employee's lack of capability. Dismissal on grounds of incapability due to sickness, for instance, demands considerable evidence that the employer acted in a reasonable manner. The employer must show that the agreed sick leave arrangements have been exhausted and that every chance has been given to employees to recover sufficiently to undertake their contractual duties. Where absence is continuous over a long period, employees must be warned of the possible consequences. Where necessary, doctors' reports need to be obtained before the process of dismissal is initiated. Where the evidence suggests that an employee is unlikely to be healthy enough to do the existing job again, he or she should if practicable be offered suitable alternative employment and a new contract.

One of the most common reasons for dismissal is on grounds of improper conduct by employees at work. Where misconduct is alleged, the employer must take care to ensure that an adequate disciplinary procedure has been used, and that all the necessary warnings have been made by the supervisory staff and by management to the employee. If the case goes before a tribunal, the employer can be required to produce convincing evidence that misconduct actually took place. An employer also has to show that it acted reasonably in disciplining and in eventually dismissing the employee and that the employee was given every chance to redeem the conduct. In cases of gross misconduct, however, employees can still be summarily dismissed if they are first given a chance to explain their behaviour. This can sometimes result in evidence being produced justifying a breach of expected disciplinary standards. This usually happens where employees act very much out of character and where they are clearly suffering from personal stress. For an employer to justify dismissal on the ground of gross misconduct, therefore, it is essential that employees understand exactly what constitutes such behaviour. It is now regarded as good practice to suspend employees immediately when they commit acts of gross misconduct and send them home whilst an enquiry takes place to decide within a few days whether or not to dismiss.

Dismissed employees may also bring cases of unfair dismissal before a tribunal concurrently with claims for redundancy compensation under Part VI of the Employment Protection (Consolidation) Act 1978. In certain circumstances, cases of unfair dismissal may be brought against an employer on the grounds of redundancy. But this is only possible where the employer fails to rebut the presumption both that the dismissal was for redundancy and that it was unfair. Where an employee is unfairly selected for redundancy on the grounds of personal discrimination by the employer, or where the redundancy selection process is in breach of an agreed redundancy procedure, the employee can also bring a claim of unfair dismissal against the employer. In this case, the aim is to refute the employer's contention that dismissal is entirely on the grounds of redundancy. Where an employer dismisses an employee on clear grounds of redundancy, however, the dismissal is fair under the law.

If dismissal takes place on the grounds that to continue to employ the person would result in a breach of statutory requirements, a dismissal is generally regarded as being fair. For example, if employees are specifically engaged to drive motor vehicles and they lose their licences through drunken driving, they can be fairly dismissed. Even in these cases, the employer is expected to consider whether the person can be offered alternative work before the decision to dismiss is finally made. Similarly, an employer is permitted to dismiss a person for 'some other substantial reason'.[7] Although this appears to allow employers

to escape the main rigours of the legislation on unfair dismissal, in practice this has not been the case. Indeed, tribunals require considerable evidence to be presented by an employer before they uphold cases for fair dismissal on the ground of 'some other substantial reason'. However, where relevant evidence is produced, fair dismissal can be established on the grounds of economic necessity or commercial security, or because the dismissal took place in order to prevent excessive disharmony at the workplace.

The law requires that in certain cases dismissal is automatically unfair. For example, an employer must never dismiss an employee for an 'inadmissible reason', such as for trade union membership, or nonmembership, or on the grounds of sex, pregnancy or race. The 1993 Act has created four new grounds where a dismissal related to a health or safety issue will qualify as automatically unfair. Neither can employees be dismissed or selected for redundancy on the grounds of trade union activity. The 1993 Act also protects employees from dismissal if the reason was that an employee had brought proceedings against the employer to enforce certain statutory employment protection rights under the Wages Act and the TULRC Act 1992. Where employees believe that they have been dismissed for an inadmissible reason, they can apply to a tribunal for a quick hearing or 'interim relief'. This requires the tribunal to recommend the person's immediate re-employment or suspension on full pay until the case has been properly heard. Such a recommendation may be made provided the case looks *prima facie* reasonable, and that the individual's union supports the claim and gets it to a tribunal within seven days of the dismissal. Moreover, under existing sex and race discrimination legislation, it is also automatically unfair, in most circumstances, to dismiss any employee on the grounds of sex, race, colour and ethnic or national origins. The law relating to the unfair dismissal of women on the grounds of pregnancy has been considerably strengthened by the Trade Union and Employment Rights Act 1993, which implements the main terms of the EU Directive on the Protection of Pregnant Women at Work. It is now automatically unfair to dismiss a woman, regardless of her length of continuous employment, if the reason or principal reason for dismissal is pregnancy or any reason related to pregnancy or childbirth. UK law and ECT judgements now protect a pregnant women from dismissal in almost every possible circumstance.

It is unfair to dismiss employees for non-membership of a union where a closed shop exists. Until the Employment Act 1982, it was also unfair to dismiss employees for taking part in industrial action if they were unfairly selected for dismissal. Now, however, it is not unfair to dismiss employees for taking part in a strike or other industrial action where an employer, first, has dismissed all those taking part and, second, has not offered re-engagement to any of them within three months of their dismissal. Moreover, the TULRC Act 1992 now prevents an employee dismissed for taking part in 'unofficial' industrial action from complaining to an industrial tribunal that he or she has been unfairly dismissed 'if at the time of dismissal he was taking part in an unofficial strike or other form of industrial action'.[9]

## Constructive dismissal

Finally, dismissal is unfair if an employer behaves in a way calculated to lead either to the eventual dismissal of any employee, usually on the grounds of misconduct, or to the resignation of employees because they find it impossible to remain with the employer. Such enforced dismissals or resignations are said to be 'constructed' by the employer and they are legally described as constructive dismissals. In cases of constructive dismissal, however, there is a heavy burden on the employee(s) to present sufficient and substantial evidence that constructive dismissal did in fact take place. The principal test for constructive dismissal at a tribunal hearing is whether or not the employer acted in breach of contract of employment. This is the so-called 'contractual test'.

## Criminal offences

In the case of employees dismissed for committing a criminal offence outside their place and hours of employment, dismissal is only considered fair if the nature of the offence strikes at the root of the contract of employment. For example, a conviction for stealing would probably justify the dismissal of an employee whose honesty and trustworthiness were regarded as essential elements by the employer. The same type of conviction might not in different circumstances justify dismissal if the tribunal did not accept that it was fair given the circumstances of the person's employment. Generally, however, a custodial sentence which prevents employees from attending their place of work is regarded as 'frustration' of the contract of employment and may thereby end it.

## Complaint to tribunal

If a claim for unfair dismissal proceeds to an industrial tribunal, and it becomes apparent that the employee was actually dismissed, the tribunal usually follows four broad procedural steps. First, in cases of dismissal for admissible reasons, it determines if the application is in order by establishing, in the first instance, whether the applicant was a full-time employee with more than two years' continuous employment and whether the application for a hearing was made within three months of the dismissal. Second, the tribunal requires the employer as the respondent to state the principal reason given for the dismissal at issue. Third, the tribunal considers whether the reason for dismissal was fair or unfair at law and whether the employer acted reasonably and in accordance with the rules of natural justice. Lastly, the tribunal determines the remedy which can be awarded if a claim of unfair dismissal is upheld against an employer.

If a tribunal finds in favour of the applicant, it can order the reinstatement of the employee into the original job – thus ensuring continuity of service – or re-engagement into another job of a similar nature with the same employer. In doing this, the tribunal considers three factors: first, the wishes of the employee; second, whether the employee contributed to the dismissal; and third, how 'practicable' it is for the employer to take the employee back. (In practice, tribunals only rarely consider reinstatement or re-engagement of the unfairly dismissed employee.) The 1993 Act now allows an industrial tribunal to award compensation where an employer has failed to comply with a reinstatement or re-engagement order. In addition to the remedy of getting the job back, a tribunal can also award compensation to the dismissed employee, or compensation alone. There are three types of compensation: a basic award; a compensatory award; and an additional award. The basic award is for the fact of the dismissal and is dependent upon the age of the employee and years of continuous employment. A compensatory award is based on the loss of pay and other benefits by the employee. However, if the tribunal decides that the employee partially contributed to the dismissal, it reduces its assessment accordingly. Finally, an additional award is payable where an employer fails to comply with an order to reinstate or to re-engage a dismissed employee. Normally, this amounts to between 13 and 26 weeks' pay. However, if dismissal was on the grounds of sex or race discrimination the additional award of between 26 and 52 weeks' pay can be added to the other compensation already determined. For unfair dismissals arising out of trade union membership, non-membership or trade union activities a special award can be made.

## 9.3 Redundancy Rights

The Redundancy Payments Act 1965 introduced for the first time the principle of a 'property right' in a job. It enabled compensation to be claimed by employees made redundant through no fault of their own.

> Just as a property owner has a right in his property and when he is deprived he is entitled to compensation, so a long-term employee is considered to have a right analogous to a right of property in his job, he has a right to security and his rights gain in value with the years.[10]

This Act was intended not only to bestow a property right in employment, but also to encourage a level of occupational mobility compatible with the needs of an advanced industrial economy. It also sought to discourage overmanning in the older trades and to permit the maximum flow of labour resources to the newer high-technology industries. The transfer of Undertakings (Protection of Employment) Regulations 1981 were introduced to implement the EC Acquired Rights Directive (77/187). The Directive, now largely covered by the 1993 Act, provides for continuing employment rights when an undertaking is transferred to a new employer.

### Meaning of redundancy

Redundancy is defined in the EPC Act 1978 as being where an employee, and only an employee, has been dismissed because the employer has ceased or intends to cease business in the place at which the employee was contracted to work. Dismissal on the grounds of redundancy also occurs where an employer has to reduce its labour force because the requirements of the business to carry out work of a particular kind have ceased or diminished. This takes place where the business or part of it is closed and where the business or work is transferred elsewhere. Redundancy can also take place where a fixed-term contract is ended without being renewed, unless the contract was for more than two years and included a waiver clause. Similarly, employees can claim redundancy compensation if they are laid off or put on short-time work-

ing for four consecutive weeks, or for six weeks in a three-month period. This is provided the reason for short-time working is not industrial action. In these circumstances, employees have to serve written notice to the employer of their intention to claim dismissal on the grounds of redundancy within four weeks of the lay-off period. The 1993 Act has amended the definition of redundancy, at least for the purposes of consultation, which means that where dismissal is for a reason not related to the individual concerned it can be regarded as redundancy. The implications of this change can only be assessed when cases are brought before tribunals and the courts of appeal. The 1993 Act also requires employers to consult with trade union representatives with a view to reaching agreement on the transfer of contracts of employment.

The best practical test of redundancy is 'Has the job disappeared?' If the dismissed employee is replaced by someone else doing the same job, redundancy cannot usually be claimed, although a case of unfair dismissal against the employer on grounds other than redundancy might result. Where a proprietor dies, or a business is sold or transferred to other owners without loss of employment, the employees maintain their continuity of employment. Where redundancy takes place within the meaning of the 1978 Act, as amended by the 1993 Act, the principles upon which the amount of compensation is based depend upon the age, length of service and average earnings of the employees. This amounts to: half a week's pay for each year of employment between the ages of 18 and 21; one week's pay for each year between the ages of 22 and 40; and one and a half weeks' pay for each year between 41 and State retirement age. A maximum weekly wage is fixed by the Secretary of State and reviewed annually (£205 in 1992). But employers wishing to pay in excess of the statutory scheme are free to do so. Redundancy payments are not normally subject to income tax. The rebate scheme for employers was terminated in 1986.

### Qualifying status

With the major exceptions of Crown servants, share fishermen, domestic servants, employees working abroad and close relatives of an employer, all employees over the age of 18 – normally working for more than 16 hours per week and with at least two years' continuous employment with the employer – are entitled to redundancy payments if dismissed by their employer on the grounds of redundancy. As in the case of unfair dismissal claims, recent decisions by the House of Lords and the European Court of Justice, strongly suggest that all employees, irrespective of hours worked, could qualify for redundancy rights. Employees can also bring their case to an industrial tribunal if they believe that they are entitled to redundancy payments which have not been paid to them. Redundancy payments are not made to those over normal retirement age. Moreover, at the age of 64, redundancy entitlements diminish by one-twelfth with the passing of each month, until at the age of official retirement all redundancy entitlements are lost. It is clear that where employees are declared redundant and express the wish to go to another job before their periods of notice expire, they may do so without loss of their redundancy entitlements. This can be done as long as they put their requests in writing to the employer and the employer agrees to their requests. If an employee leaves the job early without prior agreement of the employer, on the other hand, redundancy entitlements may be forfeited.

## Suitable alternative employment

When redundancy situations arise, an employer is expected to take every reasonable step to find the employee or employees suitable alternative employment. If the employees do not accept this alternative work, they may lose their redundancy entitlements. Obviously whether or not the offer of alternative work is suitable and reasonable depends upon the conditions applying in each case. But generally the offer of alternative work has to be of at least similar status and payment to the previous employment. Where the alternative work is accepted, new contracts of employment have to be agreed.

Under the Employment Protection (Consolidation) Act 1978, an employee can agree to undertake a trial period of not more than four weeks in the new post offered by the employer. At the end of the trial period, both the employee and the employer have to agree that the post is suitable, and then a new contract of employment can be drawn up. Where necessary, the trial period, which might involve formal training, can be extended. Where a four-week trial period in a new post is offered and accepted, it is best done in writing. It needs to specify the date of the end of the trial period and the terms and conditions of employment applying after the end of the specified period. If an employee unreasonably refuses an offer of a trial period in a suitable alternative post, any entitlement to redundancy payments may be lost. Contested cases go before industrial tribunals.

## Handling redundancy situations

The Employment Protection (Consolidation) Act 1978 lays down the methods and procedures which employers are obliged to observe for handling redundancies when dealing with independent recognized trade unions. These procedures apply to all employees being made redundant regardless of the length of service or the number of hours they work each week. The employer must also consult the trade unions, even where the people being made redundant are volunteers and not trade union members. These procedures, however, do not apply to employers which do not recognize independent trade unions for collective bargaining. Where, however, the employer does not recognize and negotiate with trade unions, it is nevertheless required to consult with those employees it is intending to make redundant. Where an employer recognizing independent unions finds the redundancy of some or all of its employees to be unavoidable, it must consult with the trade unions and with the Department of Employment 'at the earliest opportunity'. Where more than 10 but fewer than 100 employees are to be made redundant within a period of 30 days or less, the employer is required to commence consultations with the unions at least 30 days before the first intended dismissal. Where more than 100 employees are to be made redundant within a period of 90 days or less, then consultations with the independent unions must take place at least 90 days before the first dismissal occurs.

> The employer must disclose, in writing, to the trade union representatives the reasons for the redundancy, the number it is proposed to dismiss and the number of employees of that description at the establishment in question, the proposed method of selection and the proposed method and period for carrying out the dismissals. It should be noted that he does not have to disclose the precise identity of those it is proposed to dismiss. The employer must consider the representations of the union.[11]

If an employer fails to observe these consultative requirements before the redundancies take place, only the recognized trade unions can make a claim to a tribunal. If the tribunal upholds the complaint, it can issue a protective award. This protects the employment of those involved for up to a maximum period of 30 days in cases involving more than 10 but fewer than 100 employees, or 90 days where more than 100 employees are to be made redundant. In those instances involving fewer than 10 employees, a protective award may be issued for up to 28 days. If the employer fails to comply with an award, the employees are entitled to receive pay from the employer for each week of the 28-day, 30-day or 90-day period during which consultations should have taken place. Except in cases involving fewer than 10 employees, employers are also required to give the same periods of notice of pending redundancies to the Secretary of State for Employment, who can call for further information on the matter. If an employer fails to meet these obligations, it can be fined on summary conviction. Moreover, where an employer either selects employees unfairly for redundancy, or fails to follow the customary procedures or agreed redundancy agreement, the individuals can bring cases of unfair dismissal against their employer. In these circumstances, a claim for unfair dismissal can run concurrently with a claim for redundancy entitlements.

The 1993 Act implements the EC Collective Redundancy Directive of 1975, which was extensively revised in 1992, and the new amendments to EU law concerning companies operating in more than one member state. These changes require employers to give more information concerning the need for redundancies. Employers are also obliged by these EU requirements to consult with unions about ways of avoiding redundancies and the number of people to be dismissed. Importantly, employers will now have to consult 'with a view to reaching agreement with the trade union representatives'.

In 1994, the ECJ ruled that UK legislation was in breach of European law. The ruling concerned a 1977 EC Directive, guaranteeing workers the right to consultation during mergers, takeovers, privatization and the sub-contracting of public sector work. In a related judgement, the ECJ declared that the UK had contravened EU law on consultation with workers over redundancies.

## Complaints to tribunals

When employees are given notice of dismissal due to redundancy they are, under the 1978 Act, entitled to reasonable time off with pay to look for another job during working hours or to seek suitable training for future employment. Only those employees with two or more years' continuous employment and who work for more than 16 hours per week are entitled to this provision. Complaints concerning the failure of employers to grant reasonable time off are heard by tribunals.

If an employer either fails to pay the required redundancy compensation or rejects the claim that redundancy has taken place, employees can make a claim to an industrial tribunal. The complaint has normally to be made within six months of the effective date of the redundancy. Employers used to bear only a proportion of the total redundancy payment awarded. They could apply to the Department of Employment for a rebate from the Redundancy Payments Fund to offset the cost of redundancy payments. The rebate stood at two-thirds in 1965, was later reduced to half, then to 41 per cent in 1977, before falling to 35 per cent in 1985. The Fund was abolished by the government in 1986.

Between the enactment of the Redundancy Payments Act in 1965 and the creation of the National Industrial Relations Court in 1971, the lack of an effective system of appeal from the decisions of industrial tribunals led to many inconsistent decisions in redundancy cases. Since 1975, the Employment Appeal Tribunal (EAT) has had appellate jurisdiction on matters of law referred to it by industrial tribunals. It has helped to clarify the law of redundancy by guiding the decisions of the tribunals through reference to its appeal cases. When either party to a tribunal decision on redundancy wishes to give notice of an appeal to the EAT, it may do so on a point of law only. As with industrial tribunals, there is a right of representation there by any person, but the EAT does not normally award costs except where the proceedings are considered to be either vexatious or unnecessary. Figure 9.4 attempts, in diagrammatic form, to demonstrate the complex interplay between the law of redundancy, the consultative process and the management of redundancy situations.

## 9.4 Equal Opportunity

### Equal pay and sex discrimination

The Equal Pay Act 1970, the Equal Pay (Amendment) Regulations 1983, the Sex Discrimination Acts 1975 and 1986, the Employment Act 1989, the Trade Union and Employment Act 1993, along with the EU's rules on equal pay and equality of opportunity, as in article 119 of the Treaty of Rome, constitute the major legislation protecting employees, mainly women, from being discriminated against on the grounds of their sex or marital status in relation to their terms and conditions of employment. The Sex Discrimination Act 1975, for instance, seeks to prevent discrimination both in employment and in the

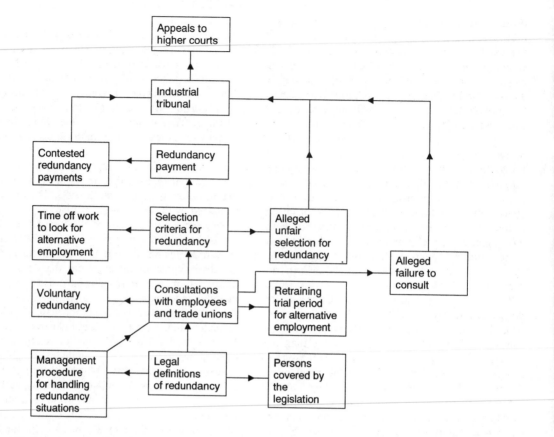

*Figure 9.4* Managing redundancy within a legal framework.

provision of goods, facilities, services and education on the grounds of sex alone. It is a principal purpose of this legislation to prevent the more obvious types of sex discrimination in employment and fundamentally to change social attitudes concerning the role of women in society and in the world of work. Indeed, the sex discrimination legislation has been described by one distinguished observer as 'a major attempt to change the social mores of a nation'.[12]

## Legal requirements

The Equal Pay Act 1970, which came into force with the Sex Discrimination Act on 31 December 1975, is intended to prevent discrimination in the terms and conditions of employment between men and women. Where men and women are employed on 'the same or broadly similar work', both sexes are entitled to the same contractual terms regarding pay, hours of work, holidays, terms of notice, sick pay schemes, and most other conditions of employment. The Act covers

all men and women employed in Britain regardless of their hours of work or length of service. It establishes the right of individual employees, regardless of their sex, to equal terms and conditions of employment if they are doing work of the same or broadly similar nature. They also have this right when jobs have been given an equal value under a discrimination-free analytical job evaluation exercise. The Act does not, however, lay any obligation on employers to carry out job evaluation exercises. Furthermore, the law only applies if the terms and conditions of employment of both sexes are determined by a job evaluation rating. Since 1984 claims for equal pay can be heard by tribunals on the grounds that the job evaluation method used was discriminatory on grounds of sex and should be disregarded.

Due to a number of adverse judgments by the European Court, which involved claims made by British female employees, the 1970 and 1975 Acts have been amended. The Equal Pay (Amendment) Regulations 1983 widen the scope for claims of equal pay based on 'work of equal value'. The Sex Discrimination Act 1986 brings UK legislation into line with the Treaty of Rome by requiring employers to set a common retirement age for both men and women. It also ends restrictions which women might face in obtaining work-related training, as well as removing some of the restrictions on the hours that women can work. This is extended by the Employment Act 1989, which ends other restrictions on the hours which females work, the jobs which they can do and the industries in which they are employed.

## Enforcement process

Initially, a person seeking equal pay and conditions of employment has to take their case to the employer. If the employer denies the claim, the matter may be referred to an industrial tribunal or a county court. There is no minimum period of employment to qualify in claiming this statutory right. To obtain a remedy, however, the employee must have been in the job for at least six months before applying to the tribunal. No claim can be referred to a tribunal more than six months after the job has ended. The Equal Opportunities Commission (EOC) has authority to assist applicants and to provide guidance and advice to the parties in dispute. Where an industrial tribunal finds in favour of the woman or man, it can award pay or damages for up to two years before the date at which proceedings were initiated.

The Equal Pay Act has been modified by Section 8 of the Sex Discrimination Act 1975. This provides that every contract of employment shall be deemed to contain an 'equality clause' which will automatically modify any term of a contract of employment 'less favourable to a member of one sex than to a member of another'.[13] This equality clause has the effect of modifying any less favourable contractual provisions where a woman is employed in like work with a man in the same employment. Where a woman believes that the equality clause, which the law assumes is expressly incorporated into the woman's contract of employment, has been contravened, she may make a claim to an industrial tribunal.

## Impact of European law

Following a successful claim in 1982 before the European Court of Justice that the Equal Pay Act 1970 did not fully comply with the European directive on equal pay, the British government introduced the Equal Pay (Amendment) Regulations 1983, which came into force in January 1984. These regulations widen the scope of the 1970 Act by permitting industrial tribunals to hear cases based on claims of equal pay for work of 'equal value' between the sexes at the same place of employment or closely connected place of employment. This permits, for example, a qualified female cook to make a claim that her work is of equal value to that of a skilled male craft worker at the same establishment, regardless of the fact that their jobs are very different and not covered by the same job evaluation scheme. Previous to the 1983 Regulations, tribunals could only hear claims involving 'like work' or those employed on 'the same or broadly similar work'. A female making a claim under the amended 1970 Act can obtain the assistance of the EOC to prepare and present her claim.

The employer can resist an 'equal value' claim at a tribunal on the grounds that a 'genuine material factor', presented by the employer, justifies different rates of pay for men and women. Possibly acceptable 'material factors' can involve business and commercial necessities or labour market shortages justifying differences in pay between the sexes. Considerable evidence is required by a tribunal before it accepts that a 'genuine material factor' justifies differences in pay between men and women.

Rules governing the procedures to be followed by industrial tribunals when hearing cases involving the 1983 Regulations have been issued so that a tribunal can, if it feels the case justifies it, appoint an independent expert in job evaluation to measure and compare analytically the job of the female claimant with the job of the male employee or comparator with whom she is claiming equality of pay. Before the tribunal finally decides whether or not to accept the independent expert's report and conclusions the report, but not the expert, can be challenged and probed by both the claimant and the employer. The final decision is for the tribunal to make. If it finds in favour of the claimant it can make an award of equal pay which can be backdated for two years. Appeals against tribunal decisions, on points of law only, are made to the Employment Appeal Tribunal and to the higher courts, with the right to further appeal in certain cases to the European Court of Justice under EU law.

## Discrimination in employment

The Sex Discrimination Acts 1975 and 1986 largely completed the legal processes aimed at removing sex discrimination in employment begun by the 1970 Equal Pay Act. These Acts extend the prohibition on sex discrimination across the whole field of employment relationships. The Acts cover: employees of all ages; all employers regardless of the number employed; trade unions and employers' organizations; bodies awarding qualifications; the writers and publishers of job advertisements and job descriptions; contractors of outside labour; employment agencies; and Crown employees. Those not covered include private households and the clergy. The 1975 Act distinguishes between direct and indirect sex discrimination. Direct discrimination occurs when an employer treats a man or woman less favourably than it treats or would treat a person of the opposite sex in the same circumstances. Indirect discrimination takes place when an employer applies a job condition equally to both sexes, but in circumstances where the proportion of one sex in the labour force which can comply with it is substantially less than the proportion of the other sex. This can happen, for instance, where an employer requires that employees should normally be of a minimum height or capable of lifting and handling certain objects or weights. Indirect discrimination also occurs when an employer treats either men or women unfavourably on the grounds of their marital or domestic circumstances.

Men and women must also be treated equally under the 1975 Act in respect of job recruitment, the advertisement of vacancies, the selection of candidates, application forms and job interviews. Once employed, men and women are to be treated equally in terms of their promotion opportunities, job transfers, job training, pension rights, age of retirement and fringe benefits. It is unlawful, for example, for an employer to refuse any of these rights on the grounds of a person's sex, or marital status. The law does not apply, however, where the police and prison services stipulate minimum height or other requirements, or where national security is involved.

The 1975 Act, however, does permit discrimination in favour of married couples where both are required, for example, as wardens of children's homes. The concept of positive discrimination is also established within this Act as a means of permitting certain public bodies, such as colleges of further education, to provide training facilities specifically designed for one sex if the trainees have been out of the labour market for domestic reasons. In the same way, where the work done at a place of employment has traditionally been the exclusive prerogative of one sex, positive discrimination can be exercised as a means of allowing access to the job by the other sex. Single-sex training is legally permissible, for example, where few of that sex were performing the work during the

previous year. This could benefit women who want to become engineering fitters, for instance, or men who want to undertake secretarial training.

## Justifiable discrimination

Section 7 of the Sex Discrimination Act 1975 also establishes that where sex is a 'genuine occupational qualification for the job' discrimination is lawfully permitted. The 1975 Act very carefully defines such situations. They fall into six main categories. The first is where the essential nature of the job calls for a man or woman for physiological reasons such as for authenticity in entertainment. Second, it is justified for reasons of privacy or decency as in public toilets for example. Third, discrimination is acceptable where only single-sex accommodation exists and where sleeping or sanitary facilities are not provided for the other sex and it would be unreasonable to expect the employer to provide them. Fourth, discrimination is permitted in jobs in single-sex hospitals, hostels or prisons, or for people needing special care. Fifth, where jobs in welfare, education or other personal services can more effectively be provided by either a man or a woman, sex discrimination can legitimately take place without breaking the law. Finally, discrimination can occur when advertising jobs abroad, where the laws and customs of the land prevent a man or woman doing a particular job as in some Middle East countries. These exceptions do not apply, however, where the employer is already employing enough people of the same sex and they could be reasonably expected to do the job without undue inconvenience.

When either a man or a woman believes that discrimination has occurred on the grounds of sex, they can take their case to an industrial tribunal or make use of the conciliation services provided by ACAS. The EOC, which was set up under the Sex Discrimination Act 1975, also carries out investigations, conducts research, issues guides and codes of practice, provides education, reviews the legislation, and makes policy recommendations. It is also required to produce an annual report. In addition it can bring complaints to a tribunal, issue non-discrimination notices, and ultimately obtain injunctions. The EOC also attempts conciliation and helps individuals with their cases. Furthermore, it provides advice to employers. An industrial tribunal upholding a case of sex discrimination against an employer can award compensation to the worker, and it can recommend that the employer takes the necessary

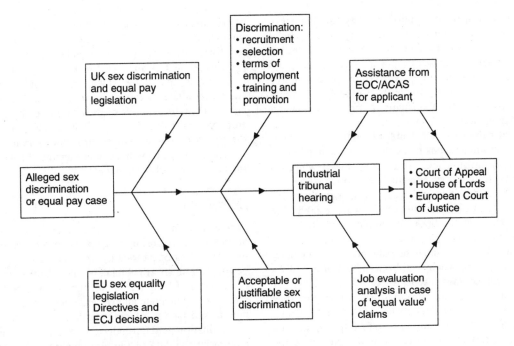

*Figure 9.5* Equal opportunities in employment, equal pay and the legal processes.

steps to reduce or to obviate the discrimination at issue. Contrary to the procedures used in cases of unfair dismissal, it is the applicants in sex discrimination cases who are required to produce evidence that discrimination has in fact taken place. It is the employer's responsibility to refute the charge.

## Race relations

Britain has acquired a substantial non-white population since the end of the Second World War and the problems of racial discrimination in the hiring of employees, working conditions, job opportunities, training and promotion have become increasingly acute. Until the Race Relations Act 1968, discriminatory practices against racial minorities could only be discouraged through moral and political condemnation. That Act has now been considerably strengthened by the Race Relations Act 1976 and the establishment of the Commission for Racial Equality (CRE). Whilst it is probable that the law can play a positive and influential role in the prevention and correction of racial discrimination in employment, racial discrimination laws – like those concerned with sex discrimination – are primarily intended to modify public attitudes and personal behaviour in this field. The 1976 Act makes it unlawful for any employer in

Britain, including the self-employed, to discriminate against a person of a particular racial group on the grounds of colour, race, nationality, citizenship or ethnic origins. The Act does not, however, make it unlawful to discriminate on grounds of religious or political belief, age or sexual orientation. The Act covers all employees irrespective of their age, sex, or length of service, although domestic servants in private households, partnerships of five or less, and persons and seafarers recruited for employment abroad are specifically excluded from it.

## Forms of discrimination

The 1976 Race Relations Act, like the Sex Discrimination Act of 1975, carefully distinguishes between direct and indirect discrimination. Direct discrimination occurs when an employer treats a person on racial grounds less favourably than others in the same circumstances. This can occur, for example, by refusing to train or to promote an employee solely because of that person's colour or race. Indirect discrimination, on the other hand, occurs when an employer applies a condition of employment which adversely affects a particular person or racial group considerably more than it does persons of other racial origins. This could happen, for example, by formally testing an applicant's English language in such a way so as to discriminate indirectly against a racial minority when recruitment takes place. Such testing could result in a smaller proportion of the group passing the test than other persons or groups in the general population. Obviously, indirect discrimination is much more difficult to prove than direct discrimination.

Under the 1976 Act, employers must not discriminate on the grounds of race, colour or nationality when advertising jobs, recruiting, interviewing, selecting, training, transferring, promoting, disciplining or dismissing employees. It is unlawful, for example, to discriminate racially when establishing the terms and conditions of employment. It is also unlawful for an employer to give instructions for subordinates to discriminate racially, or to aid somebody to discriminate racially within an employing establishment. Employment agencies, for instance, must not discriminate on racial grounds in the terms that they offer in jobs or the services they provide their clients. Neither are they permitted to refuse to provide any of their services on racial grounds. Nor does the 1976 Act permit an employer to discriminate when recruiting on the grounds that it already has a high proportion of non-white employees and that it wishes to preserve a 'balanced' workforce.

## Acceptable discrimination

Racial discrimination in employment is permitted, however, in a few very closely defined and restricted circumstances. It is allowable, for example, where a person of a particular racial group is needed for authenticity, such as in acting, modelling, or working as a waiter or waitress in an ethnic restaurant. Racial discrimination is also permissible where a certain type of community worker is required to promote the welfare of a particular racial group. It might be necessary, for instance, to appoint a West Indian to run a youth club catering largely for young people of Caribbean origin. Where an employer already has a sufficient number of employees of the specified racial group required to do the job, it must use one of them and not recruit a new employee of that race, if this can be done without undue inconvenience.

Positive or reverse racial discrimination is also permitted by employers or training bodies in certain circumstances. It is permissible, for instance, if they are providing training for a particular racial group or a nationality for the express purpose of enabling that group to take up employment in occupations or areas of employment in which it is under-represented. But it is clearly unlawful under the 1976 Act for anybody to discriminate against individuals, or to bring pressure to bear on them, for seeking to assert their statutory rights under race legislation. Where employees allege that an employer has discriminated against them on grounds of their race or colour, the employer must not victimize those persons. Indeed, the employer may be required to show an industrial tribunal that it did not discriminate against them once the allegation had been made.

## Enforcement

Where individuals believe that they have been discriminated against by an employer on the grounds of race, colour or nationality, they may bring a case before an industrial tribunal. As in the other types of hearings determined by tribunals, ACAS first attempts to conciliate and to settle the matter to the mutual satisfaction of both parties. Complaints of discrimination need normally to be made within three months of the date of the discriminatory act. At a tribunal, the applicant may be represented by anyone of their choosing, including a representative of the CRE if the organization agrees. In cases involving direct or indirect discrimination and victimization, the applicant has in the first instance to provide sufficient evidence of the claimed discriminatory act or its circumstances. It is then for the respondent to refute this evidence. It has to be shown in the case of indirect discrimination, for example, either that the employer's action is justifiable within the meaning of the 1976 Act, or that one of the Act's exceptions apply. If the tribunal finds in favour of the applicant, it has to consider what remedies to award. The tribunal can award either an order declaring the rights of the parties, or an order requiring the respondent to pay compensation to the applicant. Alternatively, a recommendation can be made that the respondent takes a particular course of action. Any appeal on a point of law against a decision of a tribunal has to be considered by the Employment Appeal Tribunal.

In 1983 the CRE issued a code of practice aimed at eliminating racial discrimination and promoting equality of opportunity in employment. The CRE issued the code under powers given by Section 47 of the 1976 Act. Whilst the code itself is not legally enforceable, its contents can be used as evidence at tribunals which take its recommendations into account when hearing claims of racial discrimination in employment. The code gives practical advice to employers, employees, trade unions and employment agencies, not only on how to avoid discriminatory racial practices, but also on the development of positive policies for the enforcement of equality of opportunity. The code declares it to be the responsibility of employers and trade unions to develop equal opportunity policies which are widely understood and accepted by the whole of the workforce within employing establishments.

## Disabled persons

The Disabled Persons (Employment) Act 1944, as amended by the 1958 Act, establishes a register of disabled people which used to be kept by the Manpower Services Commission (MSC) but is now kept by the Employment Service of the Employment Department. Disablement Resettlement Officers of the Employment Service issue certificates of registration to disabled persons which they can show to employers when seeking work. Disabled persons possessing these certificates are commonly referred to as 'green card' holders. The 1944 Act requires employers with 20 or more workers to employ a quota of disabled people which is set at 3 per cent of their total workforce. It is not, however, an offence under the Act to be below the 3 per cent quota, but when employers are in that position they should not engage anyone other than a registered disabled person without first obtaining a permit to do so from the local job centre. In practice, however, the requirements of the 1944 Act are either ignored or disregarded on an extremely wide scale and very few employers are ever prosecuted or fined. Even the government, in its capacity as employer, does not conform with the Act.

The 1944 Act also reserved certain designated occupations for disabled persons such as car park attendants and electric lift attendants. The employer must also keep careful records of all the disabled persons employed for inspection by the relevant officials of the Employment Service. Committees for the Employment of Disabled People were established at local level by the 1944 Act to advise the Secretary of State on matters relating to the employment of disabled persons. They also encouraged local employers to be more conscious of their responsibilities towards the disabled and to fulfil the 3 per cent quota. The Companies (Directors' Report) (Employment of Disabled Persons) Regulations 1980 require the annual directors' report of firms employing more than 250 people to contain a statement of their policy on the employment, training, career development and promotion of disabled employees. These Regulations, whilst applying to private companies, also impose similar obligations on public sector employers.

Largely because of the ineffectiveness of existing legislation and regulations aimed at protecting and furthering the interests of disabled employees and unemployed disabled persons, in 1984 at the government's request the MSC, later the Training Services Commission, produced a code of practice on the employment of disabled people. The code, which was supported by the government, the Confederation of British Industry and the Trades Union Congress, urges employers in both the public and private sectors to accept their social responsibilities for disabled employees and sets out a list of good practices and policies for employing them. Whilst observance of the code is voluntary, it is hoped that employers, trade unions and others will use it as a guide or model when reshaping their policies towards the disabled. This is normally done within the framework of an equal opportunities policy.

## 9.5    Other Individual Rights

### Union membership and non-membership rights

The Trade Union and Labour Relations (Consolidation) Act 1992 provides a statutory right for all employees to belong or not to belong to an independent trade union of their choice and to take part in its activities. It also provides remedies against employers for dismissal on the grounds of trade union membership or non-membership and for any actions short of dismissal which they might take to prevent (or to force) employees becoming or not becoming members of independent unions. Similar remedies are available if employers attempt to discriminate against employees for being members of unions or for taking part in appropriate trade union activities. If employees who are trade unionists are dismissed, and they believe that the dismissal arose out of their trade union membership or their activities as trade union members, they can request 'interim relief' from an industrial tribunal. This must take place within seven days of the incident, and the applicants may be awarded reinstatement or suspension on full pay until a full hearing of the complaint is held. It is, therefore, automatically unfair to dismiss employees on the grounds of either trade union membership or non-membership or for taking part in appropriate trade union activities.

Section 137 of the 1992 Act provides those people refused employment on the grounds of trade union membership or non-membership with the opportunity to seek a remedy before an industrial tribunal. It is not, however, unlawful for an employer to refuse employment on the grounds of an applicant's past record as a trade union activist. It is, however, often difficult to distinguish between trade union membership and activities, so a refusal of employment on the grounds of union activities could still result in a case being heard on the grounds of union membership.

The 1992 Act seeks to prevent employers from discriminating against employees who, as lay officials of their union, seek time off work for their trade union duties and activities and for training purposes. This means that in practice employers are obliged to allow time off work for union stewards and other lay officials of independent recognized unions: to negotiate with employer representatives; to hold approved union meetings at the workplace; and to meet full-time union officers in working time. Both employers and trade unionists are expected to observe the recommendations of the ACAS code on time off, though the Employment Act of 1989 narrows the employer's obligations.

The 1993 Act regulates the use of the 'check-off', whereby an employer deducts the employee's union subscription from his or her pay. It is now necessary for the employer to secure the permission in writing of the employee before making deductions. The employee can withdraw consent at any time providing it is done in writing. Moreover, the employer must secure renewal of permission to continue to deduct union subscriptions at least once every three years. Deductions made without the consent of the employee can be recovered by application for a tribunal hearing.

Any employees or job applicants who consider that their trade union membership or non-membership rights have been infringed by an employer may seek a remedy through an industrial tribunal, within three months of the employer's discriminatory act. Such action can be taken by employees regardless of their length of service with an employer. When a tribunal hears cases of discrimination on grounds of trade union membership, non-membership and activities, the onus of proof is on the employer to show that it has not infringed the employee's or job applicant's rights. If a tribunal finds a complaint to be well founded, it makes a declaration to that effect. It can

also award compensation, including substantial sums for injury to feelings, to the employee to be paid by the employer. If the tribunal considers it appropriate, it can 'join' an employment agency to the case, or a trade union, where it is believed that either, or both, such bodies are closely connected with the alleged dismissal or action short of dismissal or refusal of employment. Figure 9.6 summarizes the overall position.

## Maternity rights

The Employment Protection (Consolidation) Act 1978, the Social Security Acts 1986 and 1992 and the Trade Union Reform and Employment Rights Act 1993 provide female employees with the statutory rights: not to be dismissed for reasons related to pregnancy; to receive maternity payments and maternity leave; and to return to their jobs after the birth of a child if they so wish. The legislation also enables a pregnant employee regardless of length of service not to be unreasonably refused time off work for antenatal care and to be paid for this time off. This protection for pregnant women at work has been considerably extended and clarified by the Trade Union Reform and Employment Rights Act 1993, which largely implemented the EU directive on the Protection of Pregnant Women at Work. In giving to *all* pregnant women at work legal rights, the 1993 Act builds on and does not greatly alter or remove the rights of pregnant women with more than two years' continuous service, which are already embodied in the EP(C) Act 1978 as amended. The 1993 Act ensures that:

- *all* pregnant women employees are entitled to 14 weeks' maternity leave regardless of length of service (those with 2 years' or more service continue to have the right of up to 40 weeks' leave);
- the 14 week maternity leave period normally starts from the date the woman is absent from work owing to pregnancy, unless leave commences prior to the eleventh week before the expected date of confinement;
- maternity leave can be extended beyond 14 weeks if a legal restriction, such as a health at work regulation, prevents the woman returning to work;
- in order to secure the right to maternity leave, a pregnant woman must give the employer 21 days' written notice before commencing maternity leave, unless it is not reasonably practicable to do so;

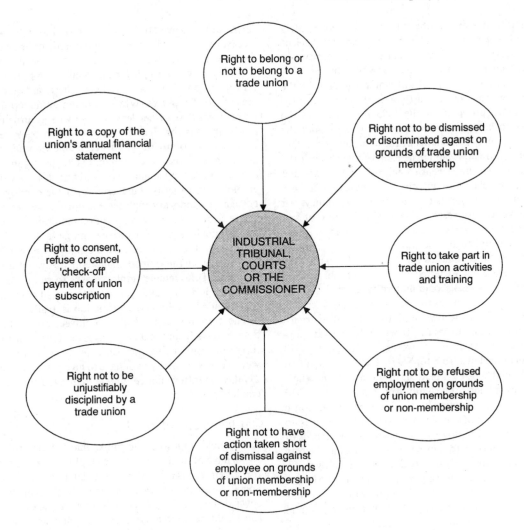

*Figure 9.6* Trade union membership and non-membership rights.

- the pregnant woman must supply her employer with a certificate from a doctor or midwife stating the expected week of childbirth if so requested;
- in the event of a woman on maternity leave being made redundant, the employer, if possible, must offer her suitable alternative employment;
- the employer is obliged to meet the contractual employment rights of women, including those regarding pay, during the 14 weeks' maternity leave;
- the 1993 Act requires the employee on maternity leave to give the employer seven days notice of her intention to return to work before the end of her maternity leave;

- women who have a general right to maternity leave under the EPC Act 1978, or contractual right, as well as the right to claim the rights provided by the 1993 Act, may choose the rights they deem to be the most favourable;
- the dismissal or selection for redundancy of a woman, regardless of her length of service, because of pregnancy or on maternity-related grounds is automatically unfair.

Any pregnant woman wishing to claim her rights under the EPC Act 1978, as amended, earning not less than the lower earnings limit for national insurance purposes and with 26 weeks' continuous service with her employer, ending with the week immediately preceding the fourth week before the expected week of confinement, is entitled to statutory maternity pay (SMP) and to maternity leave. However, the law does not create a statutory right of maternity leave for the pregnant employee, other than the 14-week leave for all women provided by the 1993 Act. It leaves the issues to be agreed between the employer and the employee under the terms of the contract of employment. To qualify she must normally work until the beginning of the eleventh week before the expected birth, and she must inform her employer that her anticipated absence is because of her pregnancy. An employer cannot restrict these rights because of any views its managerial agents might hold about pregnancy, morality or marital status. If a pregnant employee, who qualifies for SMP, works to the 11th week before her expected confinement, she is then entitled to 18 weeks' paid maternity leave.

Where a woman has two years' continuous service, and earns above the lower limit for national insurance purposes, she qualifies for six weeks' higher-rate payment on nine-tenths of average earnings, plus 12 weeks at the lower rate for SMP. Those not qualified for the higher rate are paid the lower rate for the whole 18-week period. The employer recoups the SMP payments by deducting the total sum paid each month from the national insurance payments it makes to government. Employers must keep careful records of SMP payments for inspection by social security officers. Appeals against decisions by employers on the rights of female employees to receive SMP are made to social security tribunals. Employers may request employees to apply for maternity pay and maternity leave in writing. They are also entitled to ask for medical certificates providing evidence of pregnancy and the expected date of confinement.

## Returning to work

If a woman wishes to return to work after her confinement, she must inform her employer of her intention to do so in writing at least 21 days before leaving work, or as soon as it is reasonably practicable to do so. To claim this right, she must normally work to the 11th week before the expected confinement. If the woman has two or more years of continuous service, she is normally expected to return to work within 29 weeks of giving birth, but a four-week extension period is permitted if adequate medical evidence is produced. This means in effect that a woman can be away from work on the grounds of pregnancy, con-

finement and leave after birth for a total of up to 44 weeks, during which time the employer is obliged to keep her job open for her, if she wishes to return to it. Conversely, the employer can delay an employee's return by another four weeks if there are good reasons for doing this. When a woman on maternity leave, regardless of her length of service, returns to work, she has the right either to be given back her previous job or to be given acceptable alternative employment. The latter is required to be a job of similar status and conditions, without any loss of employment benefits. Furthermore, if the employer engages a temporary replacement during the period that a female employee is absent on maternity leave, that person must be informed in writing that he or she will have to leave, if a suitable alternative job cannot be found when the woman on maternity leave returns to work. If the female employee asks to return to a part-time job, the employer should permit her to do so, provided a suitable part-time job is available.

The employer can ask the employee, not earlier than 21 days from the date it was given for the birth, to confirm in writing that she intends to return to work. The woman does not have to give the employer 21 days' written notice unless requested by the employer to do so.

## Enforcement of rights

Any female employee who thinks that her maternity rights have been infringed by an employer may apply for a remedy through an industrial tribunal or a Social Security Appeals Tribunal. Such remedies cover disputes arising over maternity pay, maternity leave and reinstatement rights, if they are made within three months of the event. If attempts by ACAS at voluntary conciliation fail, tribunals are then empowered to award compensation to aggrieved female employees and to reinstate them where this is practicable. If a woman is made redundant during pregnancy leave, she is also entitled to redundancy payments and to any other legal rights which she has accumulated under the law. Where an employer can satisfy a tribunal that it is not practicable to offer the employee her original job back, and that she has unreasonably refused suitable alternative work, her claim for unfair dismissal fails.

## Guarantee payments

Guarantee wage payments are now available to all employees who are on short-time working or are laid off by their employers. These provisions are covered by the Employment Protection (Consolidation) Act 1978 as amended by the Employment Acts 1980 and 1982. An employee is entitled, in certain circumstances, to guarantee payments by an employer:

> Where an employee throughout a day during any part of which he would normally be required to work in accordance with his contract of employment is not provided with work by his employer by reason of – (a) a diminution in the requirements of the employer's business for work of the kind which the employee is employed to do, or (b) any other occurrence affecting the normal working of the employer's business in relation to work of the kind which the employee is employed to do.[14]

All employees with more than four weeks' continuous employment with their employer are entitled to guarantee wage payments. The main excluded categories of employee are those employed for a fixed term of three months or less to perform a specific task, and those whose contracts of employment do not stipulate regular hours of work.

Those employees who are either on short-time working or are laid off are not entitled to guarantee payments if they unreasonably refuse an offer of suitable alternative work. Nor are they entitled when the short-time working or lay-off results from a trade dispute involving other employees of the same or an associated employer. Moreover, payment is only made in respect of each complete working day lost, and guarantee payments are not provided in respect of a day in which some work is provided – even if that work is provided outside normal working hours. Furthermore, there is a maximum entitlement of guarantee payments for five working days per quarter, and these are not cumulative. The calculation of the day's pay depends upon the payment laid down in the individual's contract of employment. It is subject to an upper limit which the Secretary of State for Employment reviews annually. Where employees are covered by a collective agreement which lays down guarantee payments at least as favourable as those of the Act, the parties may jointly apply to the Secretary of State for an exemption from the requirements of the Act. As with the other individual provisions under the 1978 Act, employees not receiving guarantee payments to which they believe they are entitled may bring a case, within three months, to an industrial tribunal. If the complaint is upheld, the tribunal can order the employer to make the appropriate payments.

## Medical suspension payments

Employees covered by special occupational health and safety regulations are entitled to receive regular payments from their employer whilst suspended from normal work for medical reasons arising directly from the nature of their work. The Employment Protection (Consolidation) Act 1978 requires employers to make weekly payments to any of their employees who are suspended on medical grounds because of the nature of the work which they do. Schedule 1 of the 1978 Act, as amended by the Secretary of State when new occupational hazards are confirmed, lists those compulsory health regulations with which employers are obliged to comply. The Control of Lead at Work Regulations 1980, for example, require employers involved in the manufacture of lead products to suspend employees on medical advice where their health is jeopardized. Suspension is also necessary where illness has already been caused by exposure to lead manufacturing processes. In this and similar cases, employers are obliged to suspend the employees concerned and to provide them with payment for a statutory maximum period of 26 weeks from the day of their suspension.

> It is most important to realise that this right to a certain period of payment of wages does not apply to ordinary absence because of incapacity as a result of sickness. Indeed, it does not apply to any period of absence, even upon a compulsory suspension where the employee is actually incapable of work by reason of sickness or injury.[15]

The right to receive payment during medical suspension applies to all employees with more than four weeks' service. It operates in those industries and occupations covered by the health order in Schedule 1 of the 1978 Employment Protection (Consolidation) Act, and by those codes of practice issued under Schedule 16 of the Health and Safety at Work etc. Act 1974. Where an employer dismisses a suspended employee, an award of unfair dismissal can almost certainly be made by an industrial tribunal. If dismissal takes place during medical suspension, a claim of unfair dismissal can be brought by an employee with four weeks' service instead of the customary two-year qualifying period. Where an employer offers a suspended employee who is capable of doing other work suitable alternative employment, the employee is obliged to accept it. This is provided that a doctor confirms that the employee is medically fit to perform that work. If the employee unreasonably refuses such an offer of suitable alternative employment, he or she may lose entitlement to medical suspension payments. In the case of dismissal for refusing suitable alternative work during medical suspension, a tribunal may decide that fair dismissal has occurred when taking all the factors into account.

Complaints by employees of non-compliance by employers with the medical suspension requirements of the 1978 Act must normally be made within three months of the day of suspension. Where a case is upheld, the tribunal can order the employer to make the necessary payments to the employee. Those employers appointing temporary replacements to do the work of suspended employees must tell the temporary employees that their employment will be terminated on the return to work of the suspended workers. The number of employees currently covered by the health orders, codes of practice and medical suspension clauses involves only a small minority of the total labour force. But as more health hazards are identified, the lists of occupations covered by medical suspension orders by the Health and Safety Commission grow.

## Employer insolvency

If an employer becomes bankrupt or goes into receivership, the Employment Protection (Consolidation) Act 1978, as amended by Schedule 6 of the Insolvency Act 1986, and Schedule 2 of the Employment Act 1990, provides for the payment of those sums owed to the employees by the insolvent firm. The debts which employees can recover include arrears of payments up to a maximum fixed by the Secretary of State for Employment for a period not exceeding eight weeks. These payments include wages, salaries, commissions, guarantee and medical suspension benefits provided under the Employment Protection (Consolidation) Act 1978, remuneration for time off work for trade union duties, and remuneration under a redundancy protective award. Other insolvency entitlements are holiday pay, payment in lieu of notice and any payments outstanding from a basic award for unfair dismissal made by an industrial tribunal. All employees, including part-timers, are entitled to insolvency payments irrespective of their length of continuous service. These rights, however, do not extend to the wife or husband of an employer. Thus, with respect to the monies owed to employees where 'an employer becomes bankrupt or insolvent, the general rule is that wages

or salary due to an employee in respect of the four months before the bankruptcy or insolvency are a preferential debt'.[16]

The Employment Protection (Consolidation) Act of 1978 also provides that where employees are covered by an occupational pension scheme, and where due to insolvency the employer has not paid its contributions, these can be paid by order of the Secretary of State for Employment up to certain maxima. Those employees wishing to make a claim for debts arising out of their employers' insolvency have to apply to the receiver or liquidator. If payment is not forthcoming after the claim has been made, former employees can refer the matter to the Secretary of State for Employment.

> If the Secretary of State fails to make . . . payments a complaint may be made to an industrial tribunal. . . . If the tribunal thinks that the payment ought to be made, it shall make a declaration to that effect and state the amounts which the Secretary of State ought to pay.[17]

## Legal right to time off work

The legal right to reasonable time off work with pay for trade union representatives was first established by the Employment Protection Act 1975. The intention was to assist workplace representatives to carry out their industrial relations duties and to provide them with appropriate training. ACAS issued a code of practice to guide employers, trade unions, shop stewards and industrial tribunals on how to interpret the legislation, and to guide all the parties in seeking to reach common ground when requesting time off work and granting it.

The Code stresses that the objective in granting time off work for trade union representatives is to improve relationships between employers and trade unions, and that the Code may be used in evidence at industrial tribunal proceedings.

The 1975 Act and subsequent legislation also provided employees, other than trade union representatives, with: the right to time off work to perform public duties, such as elected councillors; the right to time off work to look for a job while under notice of redundancy; and the right to time off work for a pregnant employee for ante-natal care. Figure 9.7 illustrates the scope of the legislation.

The right to time off work for industrial relations purposes, training and public duties is now embodied in the TULR Act 1992. In 1991, ACAS issued a new

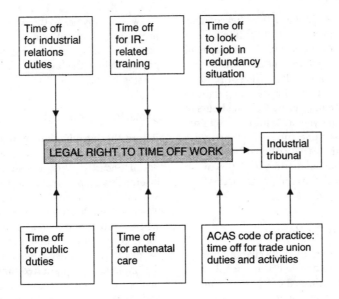

*Figure 9.7* Legal right to time off work.

Code of Practice on *Time Off for Trade Union Duties and Activities*, which more narrowly defined what was covered by the legislation than did the previous Code. The 1991 Code recommends that reasonable time off work should be granted to trade union workplace representatives for functions related to:

- terms and conditions of employment, including physical conditions of work;
- the engagement, non-engagement or termination of employment;
- allocation of work/duties of employment as between workers or groups of workers;
- matters of discipline;
- trade union membership or non-membership;
- facilities for workplace representatives so that they can fulfil their duties;
- negotiations, consultation and other procedures.

The Code also stresses that reasonable time off work should be granted to trade union representatives to prepare for negotiations with the employer, or its representatives, and for reporting back on the progress of negotiations to members. Legitimate activities can also include attending appropriate union meetings, meetings with trade union full-time officials and policy-making bodies of a trade union.

The Code emphasizes the need for workplace union representatives and the employer to discuss and agree on the most reasonable frequency and quantity

of time off work, so as not to disrupt or damage the organization in question. Union representatives should provide management with as much notice as possible of their need for time off work, in order that the employer can organize work cover and other arrangements to avoid disruption to production or service to the public. Where possible, the Code advises trade unions and employers to negotiate a formal agreement on time off work which provides clear guidelines, enables planning to take place, helps to avoid misunderstandings and clarifies the issues related to pay while carrying out union duties.

Where employees are members or officials of an independent trade union recognized by the employer and are refused time off work or pay in appropriate circumstances, they can seek a remedy from an industrial tribunal. If such a complaint is not resolved by conciliation through ACAS, the industrial tribunal takes the code of practice into account when hearing the case and making its decision.

The 1978 and 1992 Acts also provide those persons undertaking certain public duties and those under notice of redundancy to be given time off work which is 'reasonable in all the circumstances'. The public duties relate to those employees who are justices of the peace, members of local government authorities, members of statutory tribunals, members of regional or district health authorities and members of educational governing bodies. Employers are obliged to give the holders of such public offices 'reasonable' time off work. There is no legal obligation to pay them as many of these offices qualify for payment allowances from the organizations on which they serve. Where employees are under notice of redundancy, the 1978 Act gives them the statutory right to reasonable time off with pay during working hours to look for alternative employment. Whilst the Act does not stipulate what 'reasonable' time off during notice of redundancy is, an industrial tribunal is only permitted to award a maximum of two-fifths of an employee's weekly pay if a complaint is successfully made to a tribunal.

## Rehabilitation of offenders

One of the main objectives of the Rehabilitation of Offenders Act 1974 is to enable certain people who have been convicted of criminal offences to conceal their records when applying for jobs. The aim is to rehabilitate offenders into society by assisting them to obtain jobs, whilst at the same time protecting the general public. Before past offenders can claim the protection of the 1974 Act their convictions must be 'spent' – meaning that a legally determined period free of any further convictions must have followed their original conviction. In other words they must have 'gone straight' for periods closely defined by the Act. If persons with spent convictions apply for jobs, the 1974 Act entitles them not to answer any question about previous convictions or to deny that they have ever been convicted. Moreover, if an employer becomes aware that persons in its employment have a spent conviction and dismisses them for failure to disclose a criminal record at the appointment interview, such a dismissal could well be found unfair by an industrial tribunal. Not all jobs and occupations, however, are covered by the Act.

Convictions of life imprisonment or for periods in excess of 30 months can never be spent and are not therefore covered by the 1974 Act. Periods of imprisonment of more than six months, but less than or up to 30 months, are not spent until a conviction-free period of 10 years has passed. A period of imprisonment not exceeding six months requires a conviction-free period of seven years and a fine or other sentence five years. There are also many occupations and employments excluded from the 1974 Act, where rejection for employment or dismissal for failing to disclose a conviction are deemed to be reasonable by employers. The exceptions are specifically listed by Order and include

Crown employment, the Post Office, the medical profession, the legal profession, the police, the probation services, teachers, social work, work with people below the age of 18 and employment in nursing homes.

## Statutory sick pay

Before the introduction of the Statutory Sick Pay (SSP) scheme in 1983, as amended by subsequent Social Security Acts, employees claimed national insurance sick pay from the Department of Health and Social Security (DHSS) on an individual basis which did not directly involve the employer. The SSP scheme transferred a great deal of the responsibility for and the cost of administering and making sick payments for absence from work from the State to the employer, and permitted substantial financial and manpower savings for the State in terms of money and numbers of civil servants. The SSP scheme also substantially reduced the burden on general practitioners by permitting employees to write their own sick notes – known as 'self certification' – which gives the employer their reasons for being absent from work.

SSP is available to all employees under the Statutory Sick Pay Act 1993, except those on very low earnings, casual workers, those over pensionable age, women receiving maternity benefits and those taking industrial action. Sick pay is not provided for the first three days of sickness, which are known as 'waiting days'. Benefit only starts after the fourth qualifying day. It is only after the fourth day of sickness that a 'period of incapacity to work' and the right to payment are established. Payment can only be made for normal working days or 'qualifying days'. The qualifying days have to be clearly designated working days and part of the individual's contract of employment. For the vast majority, but by no means all of the labour force, the qualifying days are Monday to Friday inclusive. Where there are two or more linked periods of incapacity within a 56-day period – including Saturdays and Sundays – exceeding three days, entitlement to sick pay starts on the fourth day.

When employees are sick they must inform the employer without delay and in accordance with the employer's rules. If they do not do so the employer is entitled to withhold SSP. They must produce, as soon as is practicable, written reasons for their illness or self certification. Only after a period of incapacity for work of seven days do employees have to obtain and produce evidence of sickness from a doctor or any other approved practitioner such as an osteopath or acupuncturist. In the case of illness lasting less than seven days, it is the employer's responsibility to decide whether or not to accept the self certification reasons given by the employee. If the employer rejects or disbelieves the reasons provided by the employee and does not therefore provide sick pay, the employee has the right to appeal against the employer's decision to a DSS insurance official. In the case of sickness lasting for more than seven days, the employer can require the employee to produce further doctor's sick notes at reasonable intervals. The employer then continues to provide sick pay up to a maximum of 28 weeks. After 28 weeks the employee is transferred to the DSS State sickness scheme which then provides the sick payments.

The rate of sick pay depends upon the employee's average gross weekly earnings but an upper and lower limit, which is reviewed annually, is set by the Secretary of State. The daily rate of SSP is calculated by dividing the weekly rate by the number of qualifying days in the relevant week. The SSP scheme lays a firm obligation on employers to keep adequate records for at least three years of all sickness and sick payments for inspection by the DSS. The employer is responsible for making all sick payments to employees up to a maximum of 28 weeks, in any one tax year. Until the 1993 Act, the employer was entitled to recoup 80 per cent of the costs of sick payments (100 per cent for small employers) by making deductions from the national insurance payments made by both employer and the employees to the Inland Revenue. Employers are now obliged to meet the full costs of SSP, excepting those who qualify for 'small' employer's relief.

## Employee data protection

The Data Protection Act 1984 enables employees to obtain access to personal data held by their employer on computers. The 1984 Act applies only to computer data, however, and not to data stored in written form. The Act entitles an employee, or data subject, to be informed by the employer, or data user, of any personal data held on computer. The data subject must make a reasoned and reasonable request for the data which must be given in an intelligible and understandable form. The data subject must make the request in writing and where appropriate pay a statutory fee.

The data user can only refuse to supply the data

subject with a copy of any personal data where the request is not made in writing, the recognized fee is not paid, there is no clear evidence of the applicant's identity, it involves disclosing information about other people without their permission, or the data subject makes too many requests for information. Where these conditions are met, the information must be supplied within 40 days. The data user does not, however, have to explain why the data is being held on computer, or what use it is intended to make of it. All it has to do is to supply a copy of the data information to the data subject.

All computer data users are required by the 1984 Act to register with the Data Protection Registrar and provide the Registrar with the following information: the name and address of the data user; a description of any person(s) it is intended to disclose the personal data to; a description of the data it is intended to hold and for what purposes; a description of the sources it is intended to obtain the personal data information from; and the names of any countries outside the UK to which it is intended to transfer the data. Data users are required to observe a number of basic protection principles: personal data will only be used for specified and lawful purposes; the data will only be obtained fairly and lawfully; adequate and not excessive data will only be held; and the data user will protect personal data against unauthorized access, alteration, accidental loss or destruction. Those data users failing to observe these principles can be refused registration, deregistered, and served with enforcement notices or transfer prohibition notices by the Data Protection Registrar. Appeal against decisions by the Registrar can be made to the Data Protection Tribunal and High Court.

Certain types of personal data are exempt from registration or disclosure to data subjects. They include data on how employee pay or pensions are calculated or how and for what reasons deductions from pay are made. Data users can, however, be required to give personal data on employees for use in medical research into occupational health and injury. Users of personal data are also excluded under the Act from disclosing data which involves national security or the prevention or detection of crime. Where a data user, such as an employer, refuses a data subject, such as an employee, access to personal data, the employee can seek a court order to obtain the information. And where a data subject suffers damage or distress due to the use of personal data which is misleading or inaccurate, or where the data had been disclosed or destroyed without proper authorization, the individual may apply to the courts for compensation.

## Payment of wages and deductions from pay

Section 1 of the Employment Protection (Consolidation) Act 1978 requires employers to give employees a written statement of the main terms and conditions of their employment which informs them how much they will be paid, how their pay is calculated and when they will be paid. If employees are required to work overtime, the overtime hourly rate must be stated. Similarly, conditions related to pay bonuses and shift-working must be clearly stated. Employers are also obliged under the 1978 Act to give to employees at regular intervals, an itemized pay statement, clearly indicating gross pay and how it is constructed, and net pay, including a separate list of all deductions made.

Since the repeal of the Truck Acts in 1986, which obliged employers to pay employees in coin and notes if they wanted this, the choice of how wages are to be paid is now left to the contract of employment. If the employees wish to be paid in cash, the employer must agree to that condition contractually. If payment is to be made by credit transfer, which is now the method by which the vast majority of employees are paid, then that too must be part of the contract of employment. Payment in kind, such as subsidized housing, free food, low-interest loans and company cars, for example, can be contractually agreed, subject to Inland Revenue disclosure.

The Wages Act 1986 lays down the legal requirements on employers in making deductions from the pay of employees. Deductions from pay which the employer is obliged to make by statute include income tax payments, national insurance contributions and court orders made under the Attachment of Earnings Act 1971. All other deductions which the employer makes to the employee's wages must be mutually agreed between them, and form part of the written contract of employment. All deductions from pay must, therefore, be determined either by statute or by the contract of employment. There are, however, some important exceptions where deductions can be made without being covered by the contract of employment. If an employee is overpaid because of a genuine error of intention or calculation, for example, the sum paid in error can be deducted from pay, providing the employer does so in a reasonable manner. The same applies to expenses paid in error.

Deductions from pay which are then passed on to a third party – such as union 'check off' payments, savings or social club subscriptions – are permitted, provided they are agreed in writing by the employee. Deductions from pay can also be made in the event of an industrial dispute.

The Wages Act 1986 carefully distinguishes between deductions which can be made from the wages of employees in the retail trades, for cash shortages or stock deficiencies, and deductions from all other employees. Employers in the retail trades must not deduct more than one-tenth of gross pay on any one pay day. Where the sum to be deducted – because of, say, a cash shortage in the till or for missing stock for which the employee is responsible – exceeds one-tenth of the employee's gross pay, then the remaining sum has to be deducted on subsequent pay days until the total sum has been recouped. If employees leave their employment before the total sum has been deducted, however, then the employer can deduct the remainder in full from the final wage payment. If there is still an outstanding sum, the employer has to resort to the civil courts. Deductions from pay for cash shortages or stock deficiencies must be made within a period of 12 months following the occurrence. If a cash shortage or stock deficiency is discovered more than 12 months after the event, the employer is not entitled to make pay deductions, unless the employee agrees voluntarily in writing. The employer is not debarred, however, from taking appropriate disciplinary action.

Deductions from the pay of workers not employed in the retail trades are not governed by the one-tenth maximum or the 12-month period. Deductions for these employees must follow what has been agreed in their contracts of employment, or what is agreed in writing between the employer and individual employees. Where employees believe that the employer has made illegal deductions from their pay under the Wages Act 1986, they can seek a remedy at an industrial tribunal. Such a claim, however, must be made within three months of the deduction having been made. An employee in the retail trades can also complain that deductions in excess of one-tenth of gross wages have been made, or that deductions began more than 12 months after the cash shortage or stock deficiency occurred. If the tribunal finds the complaint to be well founded, it can order the employer to repay the illegal deductions to the employee.

## Access to medical records

The Access to Medical Records Act 1988 establishes the right of prospective employees, existing employees, former employees and agency workers to have access to the medical reports and records compiled by medical practitioners for submission to employers for employment purposes. The fundamental purpose of the Act is to ensure that inaccuracies and damaging statements on medical records do not follow individuals throughout their working lives, thereby detracting from their job and career prospects. Since January 1989, individuals have a right of access to their medical records which a medical practitioner has provided to an employer for employment purposes. Such medical reports or records can be requested by an employer from the individual's general practitioner, a specialist consultant or the company doctor, after the employer has obtained the agreement of the individual.

Before seeking a medical report, the Act requires the employer to notify the individual in writing that it is seeking a medical report and that it can only do so with the individual's written consent. The employer must also inform the individual that there is a right to withhold consent and a right to see the report before it is submitted to the employer. The employee can also request written changes to the report. The employer must also inform the medical practitioner whether or not individual consent has been given and whether the individual wishes to see the report before it is sent to the employer. The employer must tell the medical practitioner that the report must not be submitted until the individual has had access and consented to it. If the individual, after reading the medical report, wishes the medical practitioner to make changes or amendments to it, this may be requested. Individuals may also prepare their own comments on the report, which must be attached to it, if it is submitted to the employer. Where individuals do not follow through their original request to see the report, the medical practitioner must wait 21 days before submitting it to the employer.

The medical practitioner is empowered by the Act to exclude from the scrutiny of the individual those parts of the report or medical records which might cause serious harm to the physical or mental health of the individual. Moreover, if the medical practitioner believes that the whole report should be withheld from the individual, in that person's interests, the doctor is empowered to refuse the individual access to

it. In cases where the medical practitioner refuses to change the report at the request of the individual, or where the individual is refused access on medical grounds, the report will not be submitted to the employer. When this happens, it usually unavoidably causes the employer to draw its own unsubstantiated conclusions concerning the health of the individual. The issue is likely to be particularly difficult where alcohol-related illness or drug abuse are suspected, or where it is thought that an employee has a disease likely to be greatly feared by other employees. Where individuals believe either that an employer or that a medical practitioner has not complied with the Act, they can apply to the county court for a hearing. If the court agrees that the Act has not been followed it may make a compliance order.

## 9.6 Industrial Tribunals

Tribunals of various types provide a predominantly flexible means whereby individuals, preferably without the assistance of a lawyer, can obtain redress from administrative decisions or the interpretation of the individual rights which legislation provides for them. The first tribunals in Britain were established in 1911. They were set up to adjudicate on complaints for compensation arising out of the National Insurance Act of that year. Shortly afterwards, during the First World War, an extensive system of tribunals was established to hear cases arising out of the Munitions of War Acts, whilst at the end of the war, a system of War Pension Tribunals was also set up to determine war pension rights. After 1945 further tribunals were created. The measures which they were able to consider included: individual complaints arising out of nationalization legislation; rents; social security matters; national insurance benefits; and income tax imposition.

Such was the proliferation of these administrative tribunals that the Government appointed a Royal Commission to investigate them in 1955. In 1957 its report recommended the continued use of tribunals as effective, inexpensive, rapid and relatively informal means of settling disputes arising out of legislation affecting the ordinary citizen. The Commission was less satisfied, however, with the operation and proceedings of some tribunals. It suggested that certain operational criteria and safeguards should be followed by all tribunals. Two independent Councils of Tribunals were created to give guidance and to oversee the working of existing tribunals. But their role was to be supervisory, not appellate.

## Industrial tribunals

Somewhat surprisingly, 'industrial tribunals' were not created until 1964. They were established in the first instance to hear complaints arising out of the training levies paid by employers under the Industrial Training Act 1964. From the following year, the Redundancy Payments Act 1965 con-siderably expanded the work load of industrial tribunals, when they began to determine redundancy payments for employees made redundant by their employers. The Industrial Relations Act 1971 extended their jurisdiction still further by giving them the task of determining cases of unfair dismissal brought before them by dismissed employees against their former employers. Although the Industrial Relations Act was repealed in 1974, the range of statutory rights for employees at work has been considerably widened since the 1970s. Individual employees can now bring claims to industrial tribunals on a variety of issues arising out of current labour law.

Table 9.1 shows the number of cases in each of the main categories of jurisdiction which tribunals dealt with in 1990–91. A majority of complaints, 55 per cent, involved unfair dismissal. Table 9.1 also shows that a comparatively small proportion of complaints reach a full hearing before a tribunal, and that in 1990–91 only 2 530 cases of unfair dismissal, for example, were successful out of 19 554 originally registered cases, the vast majority of cases being settled by ACAS, withdrawn by the people concerned or dismissed by a tribunal for legal reasons. The most common legal reasons were 'out of scope' (i.e. jurisdiction) or 'out of time'.

Unfair dismissal cases, while remaining the main work of tribunals, have been dropping as a propor-tion of all cases in recent years: from 75 per cent in 1986–87 to 55 per cent in 1990–91. During the same period, the number and proportion of cases concern-ing complaints arising from redundancy and the pay-ment of wages has increased.

Table 9.2 shows the compensation awarded by tribunals in successful cases of unfair dismissal in 1990–91. The table, however, gives no indication of the amounts received by those people who accepted a money settlement, largely through the conciliation work of ACAS, from their former employer instead of proceeding to a tribunal hearing, such settlements being private to the parties concerned.

The statutes under which industrial tribunals have jurisdiction to hear cases include:

- Equal Pay Act 1970 (as amended by the Equal Pay (Amendment) Regulations 1983) (also affected by EU law and ECJ decisions);
- Health and Safety at Work etc. Act 1974 and the Safety Representatives and Safety Committee Regulations 1977;
- Sex Discrimination Act 1975 (as amended by the Sex Discrimination Act 1986 and the Employment Act 1989) (also affected by EU law and ECJ decisions);
- Race Relations Act 1976;
- Employment Protection (Consolidation) Act 1978 (this Act contains the majority of all the points of law which come within the jurisdiction of industrial tribunals);
- Transfer of Undertakings (Protection of Employ-ment) Regulations 1981 (for implementation of EC Directive 77/187 on acquired rights of employees);
- Employment Act 1982;
- Insolvency Act 1986;
- Wages Act 1986;
- Employment Act 1989;
- Employment Act 1990;
- Social Security Act 1992;
- Trade Union and Labour Relations (Consolida-tion) Act 1992;
- Trade Union Reform and Employment Rights Act 1993 (this Act creates several additional points of law which become the jurisdiction of industrial tribunals, namely: further complaints regarding trade union membership or non-membership rights; complaints concerning 'check-off' deductions; greater protection for pregnant women in employment; the right of all employees to written statements of terms of employment; the right not to be unfairly dismissed on grounds relating to health and safety; the extended right of trade unions and their representatives to be consulted over proposed redundancies; and the determination of claims by employees of breach of contracts of employment).

Industrial tribunals are also required by law to take into account several Codes of Practice issued by ACAS, the EOC and the CRE and approved by Parliament:

- ACAS Code of Practice 1: Disciplinary Practice and Procedures in Employment;
- ACAS Code of Practice 3: Time Off for Trade Union Duties and Activities;
- EOC Code of Practice for the Elimination of

Table 9.1 Outcome of industrial tribunal cases, 1990–91.

| | Total Number of registered cases disposed of | ACAS conciliated statements | Withdrawal | Successful at tribunal hearing | Dismissed at tribunal hearing | Disposed of otherwise |
|---|---|---|---|---|---|---|
| Other provisions of the Employment Protection (Consolidation) Act 1978 | 1 732 | 495 | 578 | 318 | 288 | 53 |
| Redundancy provisions of the Employment Protection Act 1975 | 240 | 46 | 110 | 61 | 22 | 1 |
| Equal pay | 508 | 64 | 246 | 10 | 25 | 163 |
| Insolvency pay | 94 | 0 | 44 | 17 | 29 | 4 |
| Redundancy pay | 5 022 | 0 | 3 044 | 1 273 | 610 | 95 |
| Race discrimination | 926 | 185 | 371 | 47 | 269 | 54 |
| Sex discrimination | 1 078 | 335 | 424 | 78 | 220 | 21 |
| Unfair dismissal | 19 554 | 7 329 | 5 807 | 2 530 | 3 536 | 3 352 |
| Wages Act | 6 238 | 1 730 | 2 344 | 1 107 | 832 | 225 |
| Others | 434 | 13 | 238 | 62 | 96 | 25 |
| All | 35 826 | 10 197 | 13 206 | 5 503 | 5 927 | 993 |

*Source: Employment Gazette* (HMSO, 1991)

*Table 9.2* Compensation awarded by tribunals – unfair dismissal cases*, 1990–91.

|  | Numbers | Per cent |
|---|---|---|
| Less than £100 | 13 | 1.01 |
| £100–£149 | 9 | 0.70 |
| £150–£199 | 11 | 0.86 |
| £200–£299 | 20 | 1.56 |
| £300–£399 | 47 | 3.67 |
| £400–£499 | 37 | 2.89 |
| £500–£749 | 103 | 8.04 |
| £750–£999 | 87 | 6.79 |
| £1 000–£1 499 | 136 | 10.62 |
| £1 500–£1 999 | 105 | 8.20 |
| £2 000–£2 499· | 77 | 6.01 |
| £2 500–£2 999 | 71 | 5.54 |
| £3 000–£3 999 | 105 | 8.20 |
| £4 000–£4 999 | 66 | 5.15 |
| £5 000–£5 999 | 51 | 3.99 |
| £6 000–£6 999 | 38 | 2.97 |
| £7 000–£7 999 | 19 | 1.48 |
| £8 000–£8 999 | 23 | 1.79 |
| £9 000 and over | 23 | 1.79 |
| Unspecified | 240 | 18.74 |
| All | 1 281 | 100.00 |
| Median award | £1 773 | |

* These figures do not cover unfair dismissal on grounds of trade union membership or activities, or non-membership of a trade union; pregnancy, or refusal of the right to return to work after pregnancy; or in a strike or lock-out situation.
*Source: Employment Gazette* (HMSO, 1991)

Discrimination on the Grounds of Sex Marriage and the Promotion of Equality of Opportunity in Employment;
CRE Code of Practice for the Elimination of Racial Discrimination and the Promotion of Equality of Opportunity in Employment.

Some idea of the growth in the work and activities of industrial tribunals can be gauged from the fact that whilst in 1965 these tribunals registered about 1 300 cases, this had risen to more than 30 000 cases annually by the early 1990s. From employing some 40 staff in two offices in their early days, industrial tribunals were employing over 500 staff in about 24 centres in all parts of the country at an annual cost of about £10 million in the late 1980s. In practice, only a minority of applications made to tribunals result in actual hearings and decisions. For example, in 1990, of all tribunal applications only one-third were actually heard by tribunals and disposed of. The other two-thirds were settled by agreement between the parties or withdrawn. In most cases conciliated settlements were achieved by officers of ACAS. Of those unfair dismissal cases heard by tribunals in 1990–91 the applicant was successful in fewer than half, with fewer than 1 per cent of cases resulting in reinstatement or re-engagement for the applicant.

## Tribunal procedures

We now turn to the methods and styles of operation favoured by industrial tribunals and the main regulations governing their procedures. In the first place, they have deliberately sought to establish a reputation for fair and impartial hearings. They do this with as much informality and speed as is consistent with their being courts which apply oaths and administer the laws of the land. Hearings are held in conventional accommodation but ordinary though sober clothing is worn by the chairpersons of tribunals and their staff. The parties bringing and contesting a case are described as the 'applicant' and the 'respondent' respectively. Applicants are normally employees, or former employees; respondents are usually employers. Each is encouraged to present his or her own case without the often unnecessary and expensive assistance of solicitors or barristers. In order to assist the lay advocate the atmosphere is as relaxed and as informal as possible. In recent years, however, tribunals have been increasingly criticized for becoming more legalistic with a steadily rising use of solicitors – particularly by employers. In general, applicants are represented by lawyers in about one-third of all cases and respondents in about one-half.

The procedures within industrial tribunals are orderly and everyone has the right and the opportunity to put his or her point of view. Each tribunal has a chairperson who is legally qualified with at least seven years' legal experience. The chairperson is normally advised by two lay advisers, or assessors, each of whom has had considerable experience in industrial relations and employment matters. One adviser is drawn from a panel nominated by employers and employers' organizations and the other from a panel nominated by trade unions and employee organizations. It is the chairperson's job to interpret and to apply the law after listening to both sides of the case and to the expert opinions of the two advisers.

The 1993 Act now permits a range of cases to be heard either by the chairperson sitting with one other lay member, or by the chairperson sitting alone, instead of by all three members, provided the parties to the hearing consent. Similarly, certain appeals to the EAT can be heard by a judge sitting with one other appointed member or by a judge sitting alone. These changes are intended to expedite hearings and reduce waiting times and costs.

Although the tribunal chairperson has considerable discretionary powers over the ways in which an actual tribunal operates, tribunals are obliged to observe the Industrial Tribunals (Rules of Procedure) Regulations 1985. These regulations embody several main rules. Broadly, the general regulations governing industrial tribunals require first of all that applicants make an originating application. This is normally done by completing a standard form – called an IT1 – which is available at most offices and job centres administered by the Employment Agency. This form, which gives basic information identifying the parties and stating the ground on which a remedy is sought, is forwarded to a Central Office of Industrial Tribunals, one of which is in London, the other in Glasgow. At this stage, a decision is taken whether or not the case comes within the jurisdiction of an industrial tribunal. Care is also taken to ensure that both the applicant and the respondent are correctly identified. In order to reduce the time spent at a hearing in establishing the basic facts, current regulations require applicants and respondents to set out their preliminary cases in much greater detail than in the past. Since 1980, the tribunal may in some cases consider, by means of a pre-hearing assessment, the contents of an originating application. Its purpose is to discuss whether the case has substance or not. If the tribunal at a pre-hearing assessment believes the case to be ill-founded or to have little chance of succeeding, it can advise either party not to proceed to a full hearing. It cannot, however, prevent either party from proceeding if they ignore its advice. The tribunal can warn them that if they persist they may be liable for costs. Pre-hearing assessments (PHAs) in the early 1990s were only held in about 2 per cent of all cases. The 1989 Employment Act empowered the Secretary of State to make regulations permitting tribunals to hold pre-hearing reviews (PHRs), to consider apparently ill-founded cases. Where it was felt the case should not proceed after holding a PHR, the tribunal could require a deposit, from either party, of £150. This procedure has not yet been imposed by the Secretary of State.

The 1993 Act gives tribunals and EAT discretionary powers to prevent hearings concerning allegations related to sexual misconduct, harassment or sexual orientation being reported in the media, which prevents the persons concerned being identified until the restriction is lifted or the case concluded. The intention is to prevent fear of media publicity from deterring individuals from bringing such cases.

The Central Office forwards originating applications to the appropriate Regional Office of Industrial Tribunals. The respondent in each case is then informed by the Regional Office of the contents of the originating application with which it is concerned and is given 14 days to decide whether or not to contest the application. This is termed 'a respondent's notice of appearance', and a respondent not entering an appearance is not normally entitled to take any further part in the proceedings unless called upon as a witness by another person. If conciliation between the parties fails, the tribunal has the power to require written particulars relating to the case to be made available. In addition, the parties may request – in writing to the chairperson – that certain documents relating to the case may be disclosed to the tribunal. This is done by an order for discovery of documents. Finally, the time and place of the hearing are decided and these are communicated to the parties by way of a notice of hearing.

## The hearing

The conduct of a hearing at an industrial tribunal is largely determined by the tribunal chairperson and the case normally takes place in public. The chairperson can accept written admissions from or on behalf of either of the parties for consideration by the tribunal if they are unable to appear. Tribunals also have the power to ask for further particulars when they consider this to be necessary. A tribunal can order, at the request of one of the parties, that copies of documents be made for its own use. It is also accepted that both parties have the right to be represented at a tribunal. This is usually done through a manager, a trade union officer, an employers' association representative, a knowledgeable third party, a lawyer or a friend. The chairperson permits each party to make their opening statements, to give evidence, to call witnesses, to examine them and to address the tribunal. If one of the parties fails to appear or to be represented, the tribunal may dispose of the application in its absence. Tribunals also have the power to dismiss a case when an applicant fails to attend a hearing. Once all the evidence has been presented, the chairperson decides, in consultation with the assessors, when to conclude the hearing so that they can make their

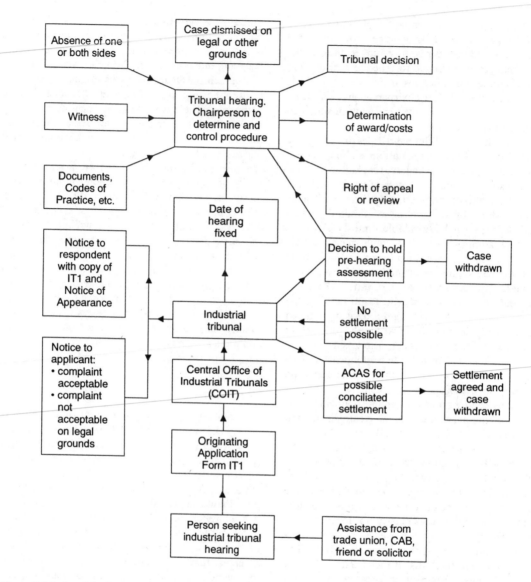

*Figure 9.8* Industrial tribunal processes and procedures.

decision in favour of either the applicant or the respondent.

The decision may be unanimous or a majority one. It is the chairperson who decides on the legal issues and the assessors who contribute their views as to the industrial relations factors involved. The decision is then formally recorded, including the reasons leading to it, and it is conveyed to the parties. This is usually done on the day of the case. In more complex cases, a decision may be reserved and notified in writing later. Such decisions, although not binding on other tribunals, are made available for public inspection. A tribunal may review its decisions, where it has committed an error, 'misdirected itself', or where a party did not receive notice of the proceedings, or where a decision was made in the absence of a party or person entitled to be heard. It may also do so when new evidence has become available, or where the interests of justice require such a review. Such instances are rare however. Similarly, a tribunal can review a decision of another tribunal where, because of the death or illness of one of its members for example, it is not practicable to review its own decision.

Industrial tribunals possess powers to determine remedies for employees who are either unfairly dismissed or otherwise discriminated against by employers in violation of labour law. These include the power to order reinstatement, re-engagement or compensation if the applicant's case is upheld. Although an award in respect of legal costs is not ordinarily made, the general impression is that individuals are not normally deterred from bringing a case before a tribunal for this reason, since witness allowances are made and travelling costs reimbursed. Tribunal cases do not qualify for legal aid but limited legal advice is available for those on low incomes. As noted in Table 9.1, the majority of claims brought before industrial tribunals concern: unfair dismissals; redundancy payments; equal pay; maternity leave and maternity payments; and sex discrimination. A few cases involve the determination of contracts of employment; itemized pay statements; time off work for trade union and public duties; protective redundancy awards; discrimination at work in respect of trade union activities; suspension from work on medical grounds; the rights of employees when their employer becomes insolvent; and racial discrimination in employment. As already implied, when an application is made to an industrial tribunal under one or more of these headings, it is the duty of ACAS, which is kept informed of originating applications and of appearance notices, to approach the parties in the first instance. This is done with a view to obtaining an 'out of court' settlement so that the case need not proceed to a tribunal.

## Role of ACAS

The efficacy of ACAS conciliation methods is probably indicated by the fact that about two-thirds of originating applications do not reach a tribunal hearing. It is the task of ACAS conciliation officers to make quick and informal contact with the parties after an appearance notice has been instigated. The aim is to obtain, in an unfair dismissal claim, for instance, the reinstatement or re-engagement of the employee, or a financial settlement which will permit the application for a tribunal hearing to be withdrawn. Conciliation officers must be careful not to make value judgements or to adjudicate on the issue. Their purpose is to seek a resolution of a situation which is mutually acceptable to both parties. ACAS

can also take part in discussions between the parties leading to a financial settlement. If this is done, the applicant has to drop the claim against the respondent. Where conciliation occurs but is unsuccessful, and the case proceeds to a tribunal, anything said or written during the attempted conciliation is not normally permitted to be used as evidence. Only where a party agrees to this material being used can it be heard as evidence. The conciliation process, in short, is confidential. Without the skilled services of ACAS conciliation officers, industrial tribunals would become grossly overloaded. Consequently, the backlog of cases would mean intolerable delays before hearings could take place.

The 1993 Act permits a legal settlement between applicant and respondent to be made without the involvement of ACAS, provided the applicant has received advice from a qualified lawyer and the final agreement is in writing. It is intended that these changes will provide a quick and simple means of reaching binding settlements without the case going before a tribunal.

## Appeals process

One of the most obvious shortcomings of industrial tribunals, from their inception in 1964 until the creation of the National Industrial Relations Court (NIRC) in 1972, was the absence of a court of appeal which could clarify the new labour laws and establish a useful but not inflexible body of case law. From 1972 until 1974, appellate jurisdiction from the decisions of industrial tribunals was available through the NIRC, which ceased to exist after the repeal of the Industrial Relations Act 1971 by the Trade Union and Labour Relations Act in 1974. The Employment Appeal Tribunal (EAT) was initially established under the Employment Protection Act 1975. Its present statutory basis is largely to be found in the Employment Protection (Consolidation) Act 1978 and its jurisdiction and procedures are covered by the Employment Appeal Tribunal Rules 1980 and 1985. First, it hears appeals on any questions of law stemming from the proceedings of an industrial tribunal, with the overwhelming bulk of EAT's work concerning appeals dealing with unfair dismissal and redundancy, equal pay, contracts of employment, sex and race discrimination and any other individual rights under labour law. In 1990, 524 appeals against tribunal decisions were made to the EAT. Of these, 400 were dismissed, withdrawn or remitted to the tribunal for a rehearing. Not all matters decided by industrial tribunals can be taken to the EAT. It does not have jurisdiction, for example, in appeals against improvement or prohibition notices brought under Section 24 of the Health and Safety at Work etc. Act 1974. In all other matters, further appeals from the EAT are possible to the Court of Appeal (or Courts of Session in Scotland) in the first instance and, ultimately, to the House of Lords and the European Court of Justice.

The second function of the EAT is to hear appeals against the decisions of the Certification Officer on questions of law, or of fact, in relation to the granting of certificates of independence to trade unions under the Trade Union and Labour Relations (Consolidation) Act 1992. The EAT also bases appellate jurisdiction on matters of law concerning the political levy, trade union political fund and trade union amalgamations under the TULRC Act. Appeals can be made to the EAT on certain trade union ballots.

The EAT is presided over by a High Court judge. Although it is described as the Employment Appeal Tribunal, it is possible for the EAT to sit in more than one location at any one time. Normally it is centred in London and in Glasgow but it also goes on circuit. The EAT, like the industrial tribunals, comprises a lawyer – in this case a High Court judge – and two non-lawyers appointed for their specialist knowledge of industrial relations. The non-lawyers who are members of the EAT are appointed by the Lord Chancellor from nominations made by the Secretary of State for Employment. In effect, this means that they are nominees of either the CBI or the TUC. The rules of the EAT, moreover, permit non-lawyers to argue cases there. In summary, then, the EAT is a court in the fullest sense of the word.

The 1993 Act gives the EAT new powers to deal with vexatious litigants. It is intended that these powers will only be used when clear evidence exists that the litigant's behaviour self-evidently justifies it. The litigant, however, has the right of appeal. The 1993 Act also permits EAT to hear cases by a judge sitting alone if the case is one of appeal from a tribunal which was also heard by the chairperson sitting alone.

The EAT has developed a strong definition of its role as only hearing appeals from tribunals on points of law and not on the substantive facts of the case.

> Appeal on a point of law is thus tightly circumscribed and the point has been made repeatedly that the EAT must exercise considerable self-restraint in cases where it disagrees profoundly with the decisions of the

tribunal on the facts but where there is no definable error of law; in such a case it must not interfere. Likewise, there have been repeated warnings . . . that points of fact are not to be dressed up in the garb of points of law in order to bring an appeal.[18]

## 9.7   European Union Labour Law

Employment law in the UK has been influenced, changed and amended by European Union (EU), and formerly EEC and EC law, and its related processes, since the accession of the UK to the Treaty of Rome in 1972, and the passing by Parliament of the European Communities Act 1972. A referendum on the UK's membership of the then EEC, held in 1974, was approved by a substantial majority of the electorate.

In 1986 the Single European Act was passed by Parliament, making the UK an integral part of a single EU-wide market without barriers by 1992. Most, if not all, of the legislation was concerned with the economic rather than the social development of the EU. However, Articles 117, 118 and 119 of the Treaty of Rome had clear implications for certain aspects of employment and labour law. And Article 100 enabled the Council of Ministers to issue 'social' Directives to member states in order to 'harmonize' employment relations across the Community. After 1972 the UK was obliged to acknowledge at law the following 'social' Directives:

- Equal Pay Directive 1975;
- Collective Redundancies Directive 1975;
- Equal Treatment Directive 1976;
- Acquired [employee] Rights Directive 1977;
- Social Security Directives 1979 and 1986;
- Insolvency [of employer] Directive 1980;
- Written Statement of Contracts of Employment Directive 1991;
- Protection of Pregnant Women at Work Directive 1992.

The Trade Union Reform and Employment Rights Act 1993 implements, to a greater or lesser degree, the requirements of the above social Directives.

### Enforcement of EU labour law

Despite clear opposition by the UK government to nearly all of these Directives a few employees were, with great difficulty and legal complexity, able to take test cases through the UK's courts and to the European Court of Justice (ECJ) for judgment. This process, which mainly concerned the enforcement of the rights of women employees, slowly established the supremacy of the EU labour law and Directives over much of the UK employment law.

> The effect of this enactment [the 1972 Act] was to commit UK law to a body of Community law as it evolves. Instead of two separate systems, we had now entered a new legal order. . . .
> However, the commitment to Community law went beyond the legislative level. It also applied to the case law developed by the Court of Justice interpreting the legislation.[19]

## Development of the 'social dimensions' of the EU

After the passing of the Single European Act in 1986, a strong body of opinion developed in most EU member states that greater emphasis should be placed on the 'social dimension' of the Community. The intention was that labour in general should share some of the benefits anticipated to flow from the single market. This led eventually to agreement at Strasbourg in 1989 for a 'Social Charter' or the *European Charter of Fundamental Social Rights of Workers*, to give it its formal title. And, in order to implement the Charter, a Social Charter Action Programme was launched. (Britain refused to 'adhere' to either the Social Charter or the Action Programme.) The Action Programme concentrated on the following areas:

- health and safety of workers;
- working hours;
- protection of young workers;
- disabled employees;
- consultation and participation;
- 'atypical' contracts of employment.

The whole processes of development and closer political integration took a fundamental leap forward in 1992 with the signing by heads of states at Maastricht of a treaty on European union. The Maastricht Treaty was approved by the UK Parliament in 1993. The treaty included an *Agreement on Social Policy*, which became commonly known as the 'Social Chapter'. Britain secured agreement from the other 11 member states for it not to be a party to the Social Chapter. The other 11 member states made it clear that the Agreement on Social Policy, contained in the Maastricht Treaty, was to continue along the path laid down by the 1989 Social Charter. The main areas of the social policy added or re-emphasized by the Maastricht Treaty were:

- improvements in the working environment to protect workers' health and safety;
- working conditions;
- information for and consultation of workers;
- equality between men and women with regard to labour market opportunities and treatment at work;
- social security and social protection of workers;
- protection of workers when their employment is terminated;
- conditions of employment for third-country nationals legally residing in Union territory.

Importantly, however, the Agreement excludes from action on social policy considerations concerning pay, the right of association, the right to strike or the right to impose lock-outs.

The list of 'areas' or 'fields' of social policy agreed at Maastricht are to be adopted by means of Directives or by requiring member states to achieve laid down minimum standards.

## Implementation of the Maastricht Agreement on Social Policy

It is likely that the most far-reaching aspect of the Maastricht Treaty's Agreement on Social Policy will be the acceptance that the implementation of Directives on the areas agreed upon at EU level will largely be left to management and labour to implement by agreement at the level of the member state. It would appear to be the intention of the EU that the future development of labour law should be the result of a collective bargaining process. This process for the future implementation of EU labour law has been arrestingly described as 'bargaining in the shadow of the law'.

> (2) . . . before submitting proposals in the social policy field, the Commission shall consult management and labour on the possible direction of Community actions. (3) If, after such consultation, the Commission considers Community action advisable, it shall consult management and labour on the content of the envisaged proposal. Management and labour shall forward to the Commission an opinion or, where appropriate, a recommendation.[20]

It is not difficult to see why, after more than a decade of anti-trade union legislation, the deliberate exclusion of trade unions from all the processes of government, deep opposition to collective bargaining and policies designed to reinforce the free operation of the labour market, a Conservative government should have so strongly resisted both the 1989 Social Charter and the 1992 Social Chapter of the Maastricht Treaty. Regardless, however, of whether or not at some time in the future the UK does accede to the Social Policy of the Maastricht Treaty, there will be three vital outcomes for the future of EU labour law:

1. The implementation of Community labour law through collective bargaining within Member States is explicitly recognised.
2. A role for the social partners at EC [sic] level is introduced. The procedure is that of 'bargaining in the shadow of the law' . . .
3. If the social partners at EC level reach agreements, it appears that Member States are obliged to implement these agreements within their national legal orders; it is not clear how this is to be accomplished.

The future of European labour law lies with the instruments agreed by the Member States at Maastricht: directives and EU level collective agreements, to be implemented within Member States, and enforced, *inter alia*, using the techniques developed to enforce Community law.[21]

## 9.8   Summary Points

- Since the 1970s a very wide range of individual employment rights has been introduced by both Labour and Conservative governments. The existence of these employment rights has greatly changed the contractual relationship between employer and employee. Almost all these employment rights can be enforced by local industrial tribunals.
- The contract of employment has become more formal and legalistic, while the importance of the common law relationship between employer and employee has declined. The right of the employer to control and command the employee, while still substantial, has abated; while the role of the law and that of the formal and written aspects of the contract of employment have increased.
- The law relating to unfair dismissal has become the most important of the many employment rights created since the early 1970s. A majority of all cases heard by industrial tribunals concern unfair dismissal. The existence of the legislation on unfair dismissal, and the obligation laid on

employers to provide and use adequate and sensible disciplinary procedures, has made most employers careful and cautious when disciplining and dismissing employees. It is probable that the implementation and use of sound disciplinary procedures have brought more security and greater equity to the employment relationship than the legal right to bring a complaint of unfair dismissal conferred on employees.

- A considerable body of legislative rights now exists which seeks to ensure that discrimination on grounds of sex and race does not take place at work. The most used and apparently important aspects of this equal opportunity legislation concern discrimination against women in recruitment, selection, promotion and terms of employment. The right to equal pay with men has also been vigorously progressed. Equal opportunities rights, including maternity rights, have been greatly reinforced by EU law, Directives and judgments of the European Court of Justice.
- During the 1980s Conservative governments used legislation to establish the right of the employee to be or not to be a member of a trade union. There is little, if any, conclusive evidence to show that this legal right caused a decline in trade union membership. The impact on the closed shop, which prior to the 1980s had been a powerful and deep-rooted aspect of British industrial relations, was considerable. The closed shop has now virtually ceased to exist. Whether or not the 1993 Act will be the final word on the legal regulation of trade union membership remains to be seen.
- UK legislation concerning the rights of pregnant women employees now largely complies with EU law and Directives and with the judgments of the ECJ. All women, regardless of their hours and length of employment, are now entitled to maternity leave and other rights.
- Industrial tribunals now possess jurisdiction on a very wide range of legal rights which are central to the relationship between employer and employee. There is a widespread, though imprecise, understanding by both employers and employees of the role tribunals play and the legal powers they possess. A constant complaint levelled against tribunals is that despite their efforts to provide hearings which are as informal and relaxed as is compatible with their being courts, they have become increasingly legalistic and formal.
- The role played by ACAS in helping both parties, before a tribunal hearing, to understand the law,

and to reach a conciliated settlement rather than proceed to a hearing, is invaluable. The impact of the changes in the 1993 Act, which could reduce the role of ACAS in securing 'out of tribunal' settlements, remains to be seen.

- The impact of EU law, Directives and ECJ judgments on UK employment law and the legal rights of employees has been weighty, pervasive and cumulative. Despite the fact that the UK government has rejected the EU Social Charter and the Maastricht Treaty's Agreement on Social Policy, it is unlikely that UK employment law will be able to remain unaffected by the changes which these EU-wide developments will create.

## 9.9  References

1. O. Kahn-Freund, *Labour and the Law*, Stevens, London, 1977, p. 10.
2. Lord Wedderburn, *The Workers and the Law*, 3rd edn, Penguin, Harmondsworth, 1986, p. 330.
3. N. M. Selwyn, *Selwyn's Law of Employment*, 7th edn, Butterworths, London, 1991, p. 64.
4. Incomes Data Services, *Employment Contracts*, IDS, London, 1976, p. 65.
5. Employment Protection (Consolidation) Act 1978, c. 44, s. 65(2)(d).
6. Advisory Conciliation and Arbitration Service, *Code of Practice, Disciplinary Practice and Procedures in Employment*, HMSO, London, 1977, p. 1.
7. Employment Protection (Consolidation) Act 1978, c. 44, s. 57(2).
8. *Ibid.*, s. 57(1).
9. Trade Union and Labour Relations (Consolidation) Act 1992, Section 237.
10. *Wynes* v *Southrepps Hall Broiler Farm Ltd.* (1968), quoted in R. W. Rideout, *Principles of Labour Law*, Sweet and Maxwell, London, 1976, p. 176.
11. R. W. Rideout and J. Dyson, *Rideout's Principle of Labour Law*, 4th edn, Sweet and Maxwell, London, 1984, p. 296.
12. Kahn-Freund, *op. cit.*, p. 156.
13. Rideout and Dyson, *op. cit.*, p. 304.
14. Employment Protection (Consolidation) Act, c. 44, s. 12(1).
15. Rideout, *op. cit.*, p. 107.
16. I. T. Smith and J. C. Wood, *Industrial Law*, 4th edn, Butterworths, London, 1989, p. 114.
17. N. M. Selwyn, *Law of Employment*, Butterworths, London, 1991, p. 117.
18. I. T. Smith and J. C. Wood, *op cit.*, p. 239.
19. Steven D. Anderman, *Labour Law, Management Decisions and Workers' Rights*, Butterworths, London, 1992, p. 15.
20. Treaty on European Union (Maastricht) 1992, *Agreement on Social Policy*, Article 3, paragraphs 2 and 3.
21. Brian Bercusson, Maastricht: a fundamental change in European labour law, *Industrial Relations Journal*, Autumn 1992, p. 188.

# 10

# Trade Union Law and the Law on Industrial Action

Before 1979 the use of the law to regulate the collective relationships between trade unions and employers, in terms of collective bargaining, industrial disputes, picketing and closed shops, was relatively limited. During the latter part of the nineteenth century and up until the 1960s, the State preferred to leave the regulation of industrial relations to collective bargaining, with the law playing a largely abstentionist role. The nineteenth-century belief in the economic doctrine of individual *laissez-faire* was extended to cover industrial relations as collective *laissez-faire*. When judges declared that trade unions and strike action were in breach of the common law doctrine of restraint of trade, Parliament passed Acts which gave trade unions legal immunity against such actions.

As the trade unions were relatively weak (and even more so the workers they represented) compared with the power possessed by the employers in the period before the Second World War, the State was seen to be redressing the balance of industrial power by giving trade unions the legal freedom to organize, to bargain with the employers collectively and to take industrial action without the fear of legal consequences. This tradition of State neutrality, or legal abstentionism, in the conduct of industrial relations gave rise to the view that the role of the State was merely one of ensuring some balance of power between employers and the trade unions. Writing about this period, Kahn-Freund commented:

> The law seeks to restrain the command power of management. How far it succeeds in doing so depends on the extent to which the workers are organised. The law also seeks to restrain the power of the unions. How far it can do so depends on the attitude of the employers.[1]

This view of the State as regulator of the balance of power between employers and trade unions suggests some degree of neutrality and of objectivity in its role. But laws are made by governments and governments are formed from political parties. Views as to

what constitutes a proper balance of power between labour and capital, or employers and trade unions, depend to a great extent upon the political views and ideologies of the political party forming the government at any given time. A great deal therefore depends upon public opinion regarding the conduct of industrial relations and above all on the moral justification for strike action and picketing.

During the second half of the nineteenth century and the first half of the twentieth century, it can be reasonably argued, middle-class opinion favoured the improvement of the standard of living and working conditions of working people, provided this could be done without greatly disturbing the economic and social structure. If this could be achieved through the development of moderate trade unionism and collective bargaining, then the common law, it was argued, should not be allowed to prevent it. Moreover, the State as an employer should set an example by recognizing the rights of trade unions to negotiate the terms and conditions of State employees. This voluntarist view of industrial relations, and of the abstentionist role of the law in the collective relationship between employers and trade unions, was reinforced by public opinion and some degree of political consensus until about the 1960s, when the issue of trade union power became a matter of serious political debate. It was increasingly argued by some commentators during the 1960s and 1970s that trade union power was excessive and that the actions of trade unions, and particularly of shop stewards, were greatly reducing the efficiency, capacity and competitiveness of the British economy. In short, the British economy and the standard of living of the people were being damaged by the unfettered use of ever-growing union power. Those who believed that the trade unions were responsible for Britain's poor postwar economic performance argued that the time had come to reduce trade union power by new laws restricting industrial action and the closed shop, and democratizing the ways in which trade unions were run. The balance of power would be readjusted in favour of employers, managers and the individual trade union members.

In their election manifesto of 1979 the Conservative Party argued that:

> Between 1974 and 1976 Labour enacted a militants' charter of trade union legislation. It tilted the balance of power in bargaining throughout industry away from responsible management and towards trade unions, and sometimes toward unofficial groups acting in defiance of their official union leadership.[2]

While there was undoubtedly a substantial sector of the British public which did not agree with that statement, the Conservative Party nevertheless won the 1979 general election and set about reforming trade union law to strengthen the power of employers and managers. It is clear, however, that the statutes passed since 1979 – the Employment Acts 1980, 1982, 1988, 1989, 1990 and the Trade Union Acts 1984 and 1993 – have substantially restricted the power of trade unions to take industrial action, to picket disputes and to enforce closed shops. In making these legal changes, the four Conservative governments since 1979 have clearly departed from the legislation of the late nineteenth and early twentieth centuries, which had restricted the power of the employer in favour of the emergent trade unions. British industrial relations by the early 1990s are increasingly regulated by law. This is in terms not only of the individual relationship between employers and individual employees but also of collective relationships between employers and trade unions.

> Although one can set the legal changes descriptively within sophisticated academic debates around issues of voluntarism or interventionism in British industrial relations the central strategic objective behind government legislative policies since 1979 has been a simple one: *to shift the balance of power from trade unions to employers.*[3]

## 10.1    Trade Unions and the Law

### Union membership

Internationally, it has long been acknowledged that freedom of association in relation to the right to belong or not to belong to a trade union is a fundamental human freedom. This belief is embodied in the International Labour Organisation (ILO) Convention of 1948, and in the European Convention of Human Rights and Fundamental Freedoms, both of which are formally recognized by the United Kingdom. While both these declarations, in upholding the freedom of association, imply both a right to belong to a trade union and a right not to belong, the right to belong is given far greater emphasis. The European Community Charter of the Fundamental Rights of Workers (1989), however, unambiguously states the belief in the right of non-membership.

It is one thing, however, to give and to recognize a human freedom in a negative sense by approving a statement of principle. It is quite another matter to ensure that an abstract freedom becomes a reality by providing positive legal guarantees or rights which prevent employers from obstructing their employees from becoming trade union members. Conversely, many countries protect the right of individual employees not to be trade union members. Both principles are now incorporated in British labour law in the Trade Union and Labour Relations (Consolidation) Act 1992 (TULRC Act 1992).

In Britain, the struggle to obtain the legal right to organize and join trade unions was long and bitter. The repeal of the Combination Acts in 1824, for instance, whilst making trade unions no longer criminal associations, did not remove the threat that certain of their activities could be construed as criminal conspiracies. Such criminal activities included demanding wage increases and calling and supporting strikes. The uneasy and uncertain state of the law continued until the Conspiracy and Protection of Property Act 1875. Although this statute removed the threat of criminal liability from the act of trade union organization and from certain actions of their members, such as striking, it continued to leave the unions open to possible claims for civil damages from employers. Civil liability for certain torts by trade unionists 'in contemplation or furtherance of a trade dispute' was not finally removed until the Trade Disputes Act 1906.

Although the 1875 and 1906 Acts became cornerstones of the legal rights of trade unions until the short-lived Industrial Relations Act 1971, they only conferred a set of freedoms or legal immunities from common law prosecution on trade unionists. There was little that workers could do if their employers sought to dismiss or to victimize them for being members of unions. Neither were they protected if their employers required them to sign a document as a condition of employment, stating that they would not become trade union members. It was little use appealing to the law for enforcement of a human freedom, since the courts only normally enforce specific positive rights contained in Parliamentary statutes and common law. Trade unions, therefore, did not look to the law for the protection of what is now internationally recognized as a basic human right. They preferred, instead, strong organization and militant industrial action to achieve their ends. As a result, the traditional trade union attitude towards the law and the courts has been one of hostility and intense suspicion, and this continues to be the case today.

Because of dissatisfaction with the so-called freedom to join trade unions, some people see the law as an alternative method to ensure positive guarantees of trade union membership and the right of their members to participate in union activities. Legislation introducing the right of employees not to be prevented or deterred from joining a trade union and, where appropriate, from taking part in trade union activities was first established by the Employment Protection (Consolidation) Act 1978. These rights have now been modified by the TULRC Act 1992 and the Trade Union Reform and Employment Rights Act 1993 (TURER Act 1993), where the right to belong or not to belong to a trade union is dealt with at law. Similarly, the right of trade unionists to time off work to take part in appropriate trade union activities and to receive relevant training are protected by law. The Acts which have now been consolidated into the Trade Union and Labour Relations (Consolidation) Act 1992, in part or in whole, are:

Conspiracy and Protection of Property Act 1875
Trade Union Act 1913
Industrial Courts Act 1919
Trade Union (Amalgamation etc.) Act 1964
Industrial Relations Act 1971
Trade Union and Labour Relations Act 1974
Employment Protection Act 1975
Trade Union and Labour Relations
    (Amendment) Act 1976
Employment Protection (Consolidation) Act 1978
Employment Act 1980
Employment Act 1982
Employment Act 1984
Employment Act 1988
Employment Act 1989
Employment Act 1990

Trade unionists can exercise these legal rights by applying to an industrial tribunal for a remedy if their employer dismisses them, or takes action short of dismissal, on the grounds of their membership or non-membership of a trade union or of their legitimate activities connected with a union. The TULRC Act 1992 makes it unlawful for an employer to refuse employment on the grounds of membership or non-membership of a trade union or to dismiss or take action short of dismissal on membership grounds. The legislation also covers employment agencies. It is unlawful for a trade union to unreasonably refuse trade union membership or to expel from membership without good cause. Furthermore, the 1993 Act introduces a new right whereby a union shall not exclude or expel a person save on narrowly defined grounds. The 1993 Act also restricts the right of a union member to claim that action short of dismissal has been taken by the employer which affects his or her financial position because of trade union membership. An example could be where the employer will only pay an increase to employees agreeing to have their pay regulated on a personal basis and not by collective bargaining. Where a tribunal is satisfied that the employer's purpose was to change its bargaining relationship with its workforce such action should not be taken as intended to deter union membership.

The issue of whether or not the right to trade union membership should be matched or balanced by the reverse right not to belong has been fiercely contested. The right to belong and not to belong was first embodied in the 1971 Act but it was not retained in the Trade Union and Labour Relations Act 1974, the Employment Protection Act 1975 or the Employment Protection (Consolidation) Act 1978. The Trade Union and Labour Relations (Amendment) Act 1976, however, clearly established that employees could be fairly dismissed in closed-shop situations, and that they would be unlikely to receive a remedy if they brought a case of unfair dismissal before an industrial tribunal. The position has now been reversed by the TULRC Act 1992.

Equating the right to join a trade union with the right not to join has been the subject of much legal, moral and political controversy. Those supporting the two rights as necessarily equal and opposite ones argue, in terms of individual liberties, that the right to join a union must be logically and morally matched by the right not to join. One without the other is perverse. On the other hand, those who support the legal right of employees to join the union of their choice object to the legal right not to join on the grounds that such legislation is really aimed at weakening trade unions and their collective bargaining role. They also see it as further evidence that the law and judges attach undue emphasis to individual employee rights at the cost of the collective rights of employees as represented by trade unions. 'In a collective bargaining system based on the single channel of trade union representation, the legal right to dissociate may be regarded as the equivalent of a right to disorganise the union.'[4]

The TULRC Act 1992 appears not only to have settled the controversy in legal terms, but also to have effectively ended the political and moral debate as well. It would also appear that because the EU Social Charter, which is strongly supported by the TUC, gives equal moral standing to both the right to union membership and the right to non-membership, that this controversy is unlikely to be reopened.

## Rights of union members

The TULRC Act 1992 and the TURER Act 1993 establish a number of legal rights for individual union members, including the right to apply to the courts for an order restraining a union from inducing a member to take industrial action in the absence of a properly conducted secret ballot. There is a right of complaint to an industrial tribunal for compensation, where a union has allegedly unjustifiably disciplined a member for refusing to take part in industrial action, for protesting that a union official is in breach of union rules or for seeking the assistance of the Commissioner for the Rights of Trade Union Members (the 'Commissioner'). Under the 1992 and 1993 Acts, a member can make a complaint to the Commissioner or the courts that a union is not complying with the legal requirements concerning the election of union general secretaries, presidents and the members of the union's principal executive committee. The Acts also give the right to members who are candidates in an election to a union's principal executive committee to prepare an independent election address and have it sent out with the voting papers at no cost to themselves. Any members who believe that a union has failed properly to conduct a secret postal ballot may make a complaint to the Commissioner or to the courts for a decision. Finally, the 1992 and 1993 Acts give members the right of access to their union's accounting records and the right to stop the employer deducting union subscriptions from pay on request. Members also have the right to take legal action against the union's trustees, where they use union funds or property for unlawful purposes.

The changes in the 1993 Act concerning the deduc-

tion of union subscriptions, the 'check-off', from pay could prove particularly important for trade union membership. The employer, under the 1993 Act, may only lawfully deduct subscriptions from pay provided the employee has agreed in writing within the previous three years.

In order to assist union members, if not actually to encourage them, to secure their legal rights through application to the courts, the office of the Commissioner for the Rights of Trade Union Members is created by the TULRC Act. The Commissioner is empowered by the Act to assist members bringing a legally justified complaint, by making available free legal advice and assistance and, in the event of the action failing, meeting any costs or expenses awarded against the member. The 1993 Act contains additional rights for trade union members in relation to their union, by which they can seek the assistance of the Commissioner in bringing, or seeking to bring, a legal action. Figure 10.1 illustrates the most important rights which trade union members can legally pursue in relation to alleged breeches.

## Union legal status

A great deal of legal interest has centred on the statutory definition of a trade union, although in day-to-day industrial relations it does not appear to be of any great practical significance. It merely reflects the lawyers' understandable search for conciseness and legal definition, which usually play little tangible part in real-life industrial relations. The Trade Union Act 1913, largely following the Trade Union Act of 1871, defined a trade union in law as comprising:

> any combination, temporary or permanent, under the constitution of which the principal objects are: the regulation of the relations between workmen and workmen, masters and workmen, or masters and masters, or the imposing of restrictive conditions on the conduct of any trade union or business.[5]

The Trade Union and Labour Relations (Consolidation) Act 1992 now defines a trade union as any organization which:

> consists wholly or mainly of workers of one or more descriptions and is an organisation whose principal purposes include the regulation of relations between workers of that description or those descriptions and employers or employers' associations.[6]

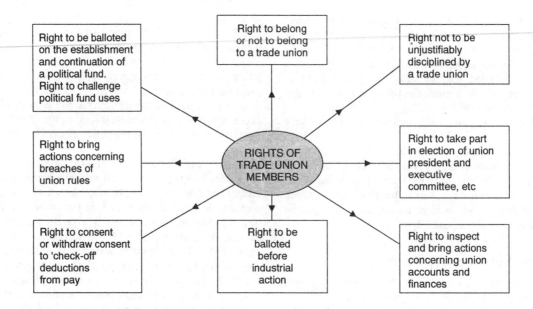

*Figure 10.1* Rights of union members.

Since the legal definition of a trade union has changed little during more than a century of profound political and industrial change, it can be safely assumed that the real importance of its statutory definition lies in the abstract corporate personality which it confers upon them. In other words, it is a

> technical device of the law to ensure that a body of individuals can, as an entity, enter into contracts, own property, be liable in contract and tort, sue and be sued in court, be prosecuted for an offence, and be subject to the enforcement of judgements. Whether these practical results are achieved through the techniques of corporate personality or through some other technique is a matter devoid of general interest.[7]

The 1906 and 1974 Acts made it clear, beyond all reasonable doubt, that unions could not be sued as corporate bodies. The 1992 Act, however, largely removed this immunity for liability in tort, making it possible for unions to be sued in their own name. And the 1993 Act creates a 'Citizen's Right' whereby any member of the public many bring an action for personal damages allegedly caused by unlawful industrial action, where the action causes loss of goods or services or the prevention of receiving goods or services. The 1993 Act also creates a Commissioner for Protection against Unlawful Industrial Action to

assist litigants. It would appear that the process started in 1979 has reached full circle.

Of much greater practical importance than any formal legal definition of trade unions and their status are the requirements they must fulfil to become certificated unions under statute law and their legal obligations to produce annual returns and financial accounts. Trade union registration was first introduced by the Trade Union Act 1871. Under that Act registration was wholly voluntary, and although registration provided very few legal advantages, most unions registered. All the Registrar of Friendly Societies required was a copy of the union rule book and its annual financial returns. The Industrial Relations Act 1971 radically changed the system of registration by making it a necessary condition for unions wishing to use the legal procedures provided by the 1971 Act. Those unions which did not register under this Act lost their entitlement to tax relief on their investment income. The Trade Union and Labour Relations Act 1974 abolished the method of registration established by the 1971 Act. It required the Certification Officer to grant certificates of independence only to those trade unions which can demonstrate that they are independent of the control and influence of the employers with which they deal. 'The certificate is conclusive evidence of the independence of the union.'[8]

## Trade union finances

The Trade Union and Labour Relations (Consolidation) Act 1992 requires every trade union within the definition of the Act to send the Certification Officer details of its annual returns and internal affairs. These include: its revenue accounts; balance sheets; current rules; superannuation accounts; and the auditors' report. Trade unions are also required to keep proper accounts and to establish a satisfactory system of control over income, expenditure, receipts and remittances. These detailed financial requirements have probably helped to improve the methods of internal accounting and financial control used by many trade unions. The accounts of all certificated trade unions can now be seen by any member of the public on request.

Furthermore, the 1993 Act requires a union to include in its annual financial returns to the Certification Officer details of the salaries and benefits provided to the president, general secretary and each member of the executive, a statement of the number of names on the union's membership register and the number of names without a known address. All union members are to receive reasonable details of the union's annual financial statement. The 1993 Act also stipulates the legal processes whereby any possible legal irregularities in a union's financial affairs can be investigated. The Certification Officer is empowered to appoint inspectors to investigate alleged or suspected cases of financial impropriety, with any findings to be used as evidence if legal proceedings later take place.

The financial affairs of trade unions are now subjected to detailed regulation by the 1993 Act, which *inter alia* empowers the Commissioner to examine any documents relating to a union's finances, scrutinize its accounts and provide information requested. Failure to comply with the Commissioner's orders may lead to criminal conviction.

## Membership applications and expulsions

The common law has long provided the trade union member, albeit somewhat unsatisfactorily, with the right to seek legal redress against a trade union should he or she be expelled without justification or in contravention of the rule book. Such a route, however, is protracted, legally complex and expensive. Alternatively, the TUC seeks to ensure that union members are only expelled in fair and reasonable circumstances, by requiring affiliated unions to meet certain standards for their rule books in general, and for their disciplinary and expulsion rules in particular. Where an individual member feels that the rule book has been ignored, flouted or misinterpreted in arriving at an expulsion or disciplinary decision, he or she can appeal to the TUC Independent Review Body. However, neither the common law nor the TUC provides a channel of redress for those people who apply to become members of a trade union and are refused.

The TULRC Act 1992 and the 1993 Act confer legal rights regarding application for trade union membership, the disciplining of union members and the expulsion of union members. The 1993 Act now requires a union to admit all who apply for trade union membership except for those who do not meet certain narrowly defined criteria such as profession, trade, occupation, qualifications or occupational description. Other cases are where the union cannot represent them because it only operates in a particular part of the country or where it only represents the employees of a particular employer. A union may also refuse membership or expel a member on clear evidence of unacceptable conduct. The 1993 Act, however, makes it clear that unacceptable conduct does not include current or former membership of another trade union, current or former employment with a particular employer, membership of a political party or failure to have taken part in a strike. The legal changes are widely regarded by the trade unions as potentially damaging to them and that they will make the 'poaching' of members between unions impossible to control.

Trade union members who allege they have been unfairly expelled or disciplined by a trade union can seek the assistance of the Commissioner for the Rights of Trade Union Members in bringing a case before an industrial tribunal. Likewise, any person refused membership of a union can seek the help of the Commissioner in order to obtain legal redress. In making a decision regarding refusal of trade union membership or expulsion from membership, a tribunal will require the union to show that it has acted according to its rule book and that its conduct was reasonable. The person refused membership or expelled is not required to demonstrate his or her right to membership or why he or she should not have been expelled. If the tribunal finds in favour of the complainant, compensation can be awarded, providing the case was brought within six months of the date of expulsion or refusal of membership.

## Union mergers and amalgamations

The number of British trade unions has declined from over 1 000 at the turn of the century to fewer than 300 by the early 1990s. Whilst the decline in the number of trade unions can be partially explained by the extinction of many small trade unions, the main reasons for the reduction in numbers can be accounted for by amalgamation and mergers. The Trade Union Amendment Act 1876, for example, required the assent of at least two-thirds of the members of each union before amalgamation could take place. The Trade Union (Amalgamation) Act 1917 reduced this by requiring:

> that at least 50 per cent of those entitled to vote should do so and that the votes of those in favour should exceed by at least 20 per cent the votes of those against. Initially this easing of the requirement had a marked effect and a considerable number of smaller unions were absorbed.[9]

This Act probably assisted the creation of the Transport and General Workers Union and other important mergers in the early 1920s.

The Trade Union (Amalgamations etc.) Act 1964 (now part of TULRC Act 1992), reduced the voting requirement of the 1917 Act still further to a simple majority of those voting in each union. This Act enabled many more mergers to take place. Most unions had before 1964 experienced considerable difficulties in getting 50 per cent of their members to vote on amalgamation proposals. Currently, the Certification Officer is responsible for the accuracy and acceptability of amalgamation proposals and for hearing objections and complaints concerning the conduct of merger ballots. Unions which do not accept his decisions may appeal, on a point of law, to the Employment Appeal Tribunal. When an amalgamation is satisfactorily completed the Certification Officer registers it.

The 1993 Act greatly increases the legal regulation of union merger ballots by requiring the ballot to be fully postal and to be subject to control by an independent scrutineer who will carefully regulate the ballot. The Act also permits the Certification Officer to refuse approval of a union merger ballot if it is accompanied by any statement making a voting recommendation or expressing an opinion about the proposed merger.

## 10.2   Industrial Action and Legal Immunities

It is now generally accepted that the freedom of all but a very small minority of employees to withdraw their labour, either as individuals or as members of organized groups, is not only a fundamental human freedom but also an essential condition for the existence of effective collective bargaining. As Lord Wright said in the famous *Crofter* case in 1942:

> Where the right of labour is concerned . . . the rights of the employer are conditioned by the rights of the men to give or withhold their services. The right of workmen to strike is an essential element in the principle of collective bargaining.[10]

If this legal freedom is accepted, it has to be conferred by Parliament, for if the workers could not in the last resort collectively refuse to work, they could not bargain collectively.

> The power of management to shut down the plant (which is inherent in the right of property) would not be matched by a corresponding power on the side of labour.[11]

Only totalitarian societies forbid the use of strikes or make striking a direct criminal offence. Most parliamentary democracies accept that the imposition of criminal sanctions, as distinct from civil sanctions, on strikers would violate the European Social Charter. This, however, does not prevent the use of either 'cooling off' periods or 'no-strike' clauses in collective agreements. Neither does it prevent those countries which are signatories to the Social Charter from imposing law which requires protracted ballots before a strike can take place which is largely immune from actions for civil damages. It is also clear that because the freedom to strike is conferred by the law as a basic democratic freedom, it does not follow that all strikes are morally defensible. Indeed, public opinion might be outraged at the use of the strike weapon in certain circumstances where, for example, life or property is deliberately endangered. It is the task of politicians, trade unions, employers' associations and public opinion to establish a social climate and a legal framework of industrial relations which, whilst retaining the freedom to strike, reduces such courses of action to a minimum.

## Historical background

Prior to 1979 the law was not generally thought to be an effective means of reducing strikes, so legislation designed to promote good industrial relations practices was enacted to facilitate the activities of the Advisory Conciliation and Arbitration Service (ACAS) and its codes of practice. Furthermore, whilst the freedom to strike is extended to all employees, other than the police, certain civil servants and the crews of ships on the high seas, strikes are often strongly discouraged by the government and public opinion where they obviously damage either the social life of the community or the vital economic performance of the nation. For some 50 years before 1979, the view of strikes held by Kahn-Freund commanded widespread political support.

> Industrial stoppages cause losses to the economy, and hardship to men and women. Everyone, except those on the lunatic fringe, wants to reduce their number and magnitude ... The important thing to do is to find out why strikes occur, and remove their causes. It is more fruitful to promote collective bargaining ... than to sharpen the tools of repression.[12]

Such attitudes have only developed in comparatively recent times, since historically this view took some time to become acceptable. Throughout the early nineteenth century, by their interpretation of the common law, the courts declared strikes to be criminal until the enactment of the Trade Union Act 1871. This gave unions legal immunity from the common law doctrine of restraint of trade, whilst the Conspiracy and Protection of Property Act 1875 protected trade unions from charges of criminal conspiracy when taking strike action. The courts then exposed trade unions to claims for civil damages when their members engaged in strike activity, until the Trade Disputes Act 1906. The 1875 Act made it quite clear that strikes were not collectively actionable on criminal grounds if such actions were not criminal if done by a single individual. The 1906 Act, which reversed the Taff Vale judgment of the House of Lords in 1901, protected trade unions from certain civil actions by expressly forbidding the hearing of such cases arising out of trade disputes as defined by that Act. The Industrial Relations Act 1971 largely removed the civil immunities for trade unions and for trade unionists provided by the 1875 and 1906 Acts. It substituted, instead, the statutory and specific wrongs of 'unfair industrial practices'.

When this Act was eventually repealed by the Trade Union and Labour Relations Act 1974, the law effectively reverted to the pre-1971 position by restoring the specific trade union immunities from civil damages given by the 1906 Act. By defining the scope of a trade dispute very widely to include almost any form of industrial action, the 1974 Act effectively restored trade union immunity from civil actions. The legal definition of trade disputes contained in Section 29 of the 1974 Act included: all disputes arising out of terms and conditions of employment; engagements, non-engagements, suspension or termination of employment; allocation of work duties between workers or groups of employees; matters of discipline; membership or non-membership of trade unions; facilities for trade union officials; trade union recognition; and disputes arising out of the machinery for negotiation or consultation and other agreed procedures. The Employment Act 1988 subsequently removed immunity from trade disputes aimed at establishing or maintaining closed shops. Such industrial action is now unlawful.

This very broad and general definition of trade disputes only prevented trade union industrial action from being the subject of legal claims for civil damages as long as such actions were protected by Section 13 of the 1974 Act. (The TULRC Act 1992 and the TURER Act 1993 now contain the law relating to industrial action.) The 1974 Act stated that acts in 'contemplation or furtherance of the trade dispute shall not be actionable in tort'. This legal phrase, which is commonly known as the 'golden formula', renders trade union industrial action 'immune' from civil proceedings which could take place if the common law was applied. This immunity was closely defined in Section 14 of the 1974 Act. Changes to Section 14, therefore, modified the protection from civil actions largely enjoyed by trade unions since 1906. The key in the 1974 Act to changing and restricting the civil immunities provided in the 'golden formula' lay in the repeal or amendment of Section 14.

Section 15 of the Employment Act 1982 repealed Section 14 of the 1974 Act. Section 15 of the 1982 Act makes it clear that 'acts in contemplation or furtherance of a trade dispute' are liable to civil damages if they are not covered by the new definitions of trade disputes contained in Section 18 of the 1982 Act. Only trade disputes narrowly defined as being 'between workers and their employer' now possess the clear protection of the golden formula. Disputes between 'workers and workers' have lost their immunity and, instead of matters being merely 'connected with' the list of defined trade disputes in Section 29 of the 1974 Act, they must now be 'wholly or mainly' related to them. The protection given by the 1974 Act to disputes occurring outside Britain has been more narrowly defined too.

While the law relating to industrial action is undoubtedly complex and detailed, the general effect of the changes introduced since 1979 is, nevertheless, relatively clear.

> After 1970, the law became deeply involved in industrial relations in ways which broke dramatically with the tradition of voluntarism . . . in certain well-publicised disputes it played a direct role, and it may have encouraged unions to be more circumspect in their behaviour, notably in the use of strikes. . . . One key limitation was that the law merely placed weapons in the hands of the employers who had to choose whether to use them . . . many chose not to do so.[13]

## Civil damages

Where proceedings are brought against a trade union for civil damages under the 1992 Act, if the union is to be protected, the law requires that the decision to take industrial action, following a ballot, is authorized or endorsed by a 'responsible person' from the union involved. According to the Act, such persons include a union's 'general secretary', 'president', 'officials' or 'principal executive committee'. This introduces the legal concept of 'vicarious responsibility' into civil actions arising out of trade disputes. In practice, this means that if a 'responsible person' – as defined by the 1992 Act – repudiates the trade industrial action not approved by ballot, the claim for damages might fail. Repudiation of the trade dispute by a responsible person representing the trade union, such as its general secretary or president, must take place as soon as is reasonably practicable. It also requires that the person or persons involved in the dispute are notified in writing of this repudiation as soon as possible. In general terms, this is seen as making trade unions 'responsible' for the actions of their members. Since the passing of the 1993 Act all ballots of union members relating to industrial action must be fully postal. The 1993 Act also requires the union conducting the industrial action ballot to keep the employer involved fully informed of all matters related to the ballot.

Limitations are placed on the damages the courts can award against a trade union by the 1992 Act. These limits are based on the number of members in the union. For unions of fewer than 5 000 members, the limit is £10 000; for unions of between 5 000 and 25 000 the limit is £50 000; for unions between 25 000 and 100 000 the limit is £125 000; and for unions with more than 100 000 members the limit is £250 000. These limits can be varied by order of the Secretary of State for Employment. They have, however, remained unchanged since 1982. Where damages are awarded, they can only be recovered from certain assets of the union. They cannot be recovered by the courts from 'protected property', such as union provident funds which are used to pay sickness benefit and superannuation to members. Neither can the courts recover damages from union political funds.

The essence of these changes to trade union legal immunity for civil damages arising out of trade disputes appears to be to retain protection for obvious and genuine disputes between workers and their direct employer which have been clearly approved by a membership postal ballot, and to narrow protection for all other types of dispute; for example, so-called 'secondary' or 'sympathy' strikes. The protection afforded by the 1974 Act to those workers involved in a trade dispute with a Minister of the Crown, because of the political policy he or she is pursuing, was removed by the 1982 Act. Such strikes could be construed as 'political' in their purpose and nature. Nevertheless, the problem of defining other than the most blatant examples of political strikes would appear to be extremely difficult. The 1988 Act closed the legal loophole whereby trade unions representing civil servants and Crown employees, who did not have contracts of employment normally defined by the law, could not be considered as having urged their members to break their 'contracts' by taking industrial action. The law now deems civil servants and Crown employees to possess contracts, in the event of court action for liability for inducing breach of their contracts.

## Labour injunctions

The passing of the 1980 and 1982 Acts and the narrowing of trade union immunities 'in contemplation or furtherance' of trade disputes presents British employers with a new situation. Using the law to limit or defeat industrial action is a clear break with the past, where employers had, in general, accepted that the law was not very constructive in solving industrial relations issues. Employers have had little taste for bringing civil law cases before the courts in order to seek damages from unions engaged in unlawful industrial action no longer protected from actions for civil damages since the 1980s. They have, however, found the court injunction a more acceptable and speedy device for stopping a dispute – or making it very expensive for the unions to proceed – without resort to protracted legal wrangles for damages before the civil courts. Employers have also discovered that the courts grant injunctions speedily in the majority of cases and that when they are granted the union's wrath is usually directed against the courts and the judges and not necessarily against the employer. Evidence of this can be found in the use of the court injunction, following the passing of the 1980 and 1982 Acts, in disputes involving British Telecom, provincial and national newspapers, the motor vehicle industry and the coalmining industry. Since 1980, employers have successfully sought to obtain labour injunctions aimed at restraining strike actions which, it is alleged, could be shown to be unprotected by legal immunity if the cases were heard by a court.

Injunctions are court orders instructing people or organizations to cease a particular activity or to refrain from following a course of action whilst a civil court hearing of the disputed matters is being processed. Injunctions, therefore, give temporary relief pending a full court hearing. Judges in chambers grant injunctions on the arguments presented by the parties and on the balance of convenience. They grant them when they believe that an arguable case has been made that the party making the application is likely to suffer considerable damage, if the activity being objected to is allowed to continue until a full court hearing takes place. This might, indeed, be weeks if not months away. It is always stressed that the granting of an injunction does not prejudice the outcome of the case. Injunctions, if granted, are served on the other party by solicitors and not by the police who are not usually involved in civil law cases. Where the injunction is not obeyed, the person or organization granted the injunction can return to the court and start contempt of court proceedings against the offending party. If the court agrees, an order of contempt is then issued and, unless the other party obeys the injunction, fines or imprisonment can follow. Appeals can be made against injunctions granted by the High Courts to the Court of Appeal and the House of Lords. Since the passing of the 1980 and 1982 Acts, such appeals have been processed

with a speed not usually associated with English courts.

Following contempt of court proceedings, if the injunction is still not obeyed by the trade unions to which it is directed, and the industrial action the court has instructed to stop continues, heavy fines can be imposed. If the unions still refuse to pay the fines, the courts can order seizure of their funds and assets by sequestration order. Financial assets of the unions can then be taken from banks and their property sequestrated.

The use of what can now be called the labour injunction has, since the passing of the 1980 and 1982 Acts, become a powerful new tool in the hands of employers seeking to end industrial action which does not enjoy immunity under the new legislation. It is the use of the injunction itself, and not the civil action for damages which might or might not follow, which is decisive. In those cases in recent years where the injunction has been used against unlawful strike action, the successful use of the injunction has rarely been followed by a court action for civil damages. The injunction, having served its purpose, is not followed by a court action which would merely exacerbate the breakdown in industrial relations between the parties. Figure 10.2 demonstrates schematically the legal procedure a union must follow if industrial action is to be lawful.

## 10.3   Picketing

### The background

The law relating to the physical conduct of strikes and the rights of strikers to assemble, to communicate information and to persuade others to help or to join them, is commonly referred to as the law of picketing. In most strikes, it is a common practice for the unions to appoint official pickets to stand outside the workplace where the dispute is taking place. This is done to make it clear to employees, management, the public, and other workers delivering or collecting goods and materials there, that a strike is in progress. In furthering their trade dispute, the strikers seek to impose the maximum economic sanctions upon the employer. The law permits them to do this with certain provisions: that physical force is not used; that people and vehicles are not stopped against their will; and that their conduct does not threaten a breach of the peace in the eyes of the police. Picketing is also confined to those employees directly involved in the dispute and to their place of work, or to a clearly

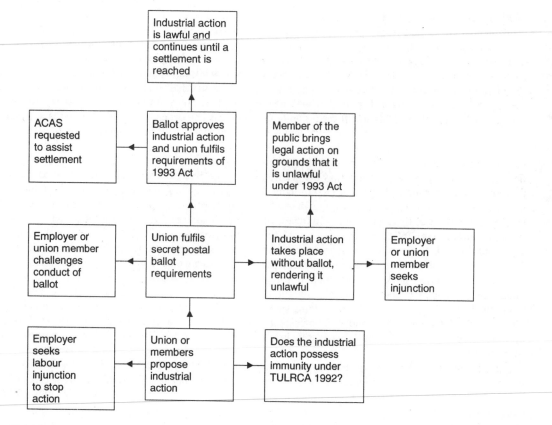

*Figure 10.2* The law and industrial action.

connected establishment. Since the Employment Act 1980 (TULRC Act 1992), secondary picketing is not protected by the law. Within these constraints, pickets remain free to advertise their case and to persuade others of the justice of it. They can do this as long as they do not obstruct and assault others, create a nuisance, trespass, or conspire to commit a breach of the peace. The arbiters of their conduct in each instance are the police.

Picketing was, by implication, first made legal by the Conspiracy and Protection of Property Act 1875. This permitted pickets to attend a house or a place of work 'in order merely to obtain or communicate information', provided that such activities 'shall not be deemed a watching and besetting'.[14] The intention of this Section of the 1875 Act was to deter and to discover criminal conspiracies rather than to control picketing which did not appear to present any serious law and order problems at that time. The Trade Disputes Act of 1906 extended the protection for picketing by explicitly making it:

lawful for one or more persons, acting on their own behalf or on behalf of a trade union . . . in contemplation or furtherance of a trade dispute, to attend at or near a house or place where a person resides or works or carries on business or happens to be, if they do so attend merely for the purpose of peacefully obtaining or communicating information, or of peacefully persuading any person to work or abstain from working.[15]

## Present law

Following the enactment of the Employment Act 1980, Parliament issued a code of practice on picketing. This aims to provide practical guidance on picketing in trade disputes for those contemplating, organizing or taking part in a picket and for employers and members of the general public who may be affected by it.

The law on picketing remained largely unchanged

from the end of the last century until the Employment Act 1980, despite the revolution which had occurred in road transportation. It was largely because the law was designed to enable pickets peacefully to persuade workers walking to work and those delivering goods by horse-drawn vehicles – *not* drivers of cars, buses and heavy lorries – that the law of picketing was claimed by some to be inadequate. It is difficult to persuade and to communicate with people travelling inside modern motor vehicles. Furthermore, the nature of picketing had undergone fundamental changes in the intervening period. It had changed, for example, from the picketing of the employer's premises by those directly involved in a dispute, to the use of large numbers of mobile or 'flying' pickets, picketing consumers of the product made by the strikers. The national coalmining strikes of the early 1970s and 1980s saw not the picketing of coalmines, which was plainly unnecessary, but of power stations and coal and coke depots to prevent the generation of electricity and the delivery of fuel to consumers. At the same time, the use of mass picketing by thousands of people, a majority of whom might not even be directly involved in the dispute but were merely sympathizers, led to considerable problems for the police who sought guidance from the picketing laws, which were clearly not intended for such situations. A classical example of this was during the long, violent and emotive union recognition dispute at the Grunwick Processing Laboratories in 1977. Yet the mass confrontation between the police and strikers during the national coal strike of 1984–85 was not resolved by the laws regulating picketing in the 1980 Act and the code of practice on picketing. This was achieved by the massive deployment of police equipped and trained to control mass picketing and by the injunctions and sequestration orders, granted by the courts, to stop unlawful picketing.

The Employment Act 1980, by amending Section 15 of the 1974 Act, brought major changes to the law regulating the conduct of peaceful picketing. The right to picket is clearly retained but lawful picketing is almost exclusively confined to those workers in dispute picketing at or near their own place of employment. So-called 'secondary picketing', mass picketing and flying pickets are not provided with legal protection. Trade union officials can picket any place of work where their members are in dispute and engage in peaceful picketing. Special provisions are made in the 1980 Act to enable those persons whose employment does not provide them with a fixed place of work, for example lorry drivers and commercial travellers, to picket any premises of their employer from which they work or from where their work is administered.

When pickets behave in a manner judged by the police as likely to cause offence or a disturbance, they can be arrested. Such behaviour includes threatening violence, causing an affray, damaging property, disturbing the peace, using abusive language, obstructing the police in the execution of their duties, criminal trespass or carrying an offensive weapon. Pickets may not obstruct the highway, though they can signal drivers to stop so that they can talk and explain their case. A great deal depends upon the judgment, skill and experience of the police officers involved and on the co-operation they receive from union office holders among the workers in dispute. Any person who wishes to cross a picket line must be allowed to do so.

## Legal enforcement

Where picketing takes place and is not protected by the 1974 and 1980 Acts, and is deemed by an employer to be interfering with its contracts, it may start a civil action for damages against those pickets whom it believes to be responsible. This is done by seeking an injunction – or in Scotland an interdict – from the courts. If granted, the injunction is served on those persons believed to be responsible for the organization of the picketing. On receipt of the injunction, the pickets must cease picketing or possibly place themselves in contempt of court. If the pickets do not obey the injunction, it is the employer's responsibility to commence contempt of court proceedings before continuing with an action for civil damages. In practice, the injunction alone serves the purpose of preventing picketing. It is not the function of the police to be involved with civil actions or to serve a court injunction against pickets. Enforcement of a court order is a matter for the courts and their officers. Whilst the police do not normally assist the employer in identifying pickets or by serving the order themselves, they do assist the officers of the court if they think there might be a breach of the peace.

## Code of practice

The Code of Practice on Picketing, issued by Parliament in 1980 to provide practical guidance on the law and on how to ensure peaceful picketing, does not itself impose any legal obligations on pickets. But its provisions are admissible in evidence in proceedings before any court. The code contains guidance on the practical organization of picketing, on the right of any persons to cross a picket line and on allowing the passage of essential supplies and services. It also emphasizes the dangers that can result when a large number of pickets are involved. The code recommends that in general the number of pickets should not exceed six, though there are no references to the number of pickets in any Act of Parliament. During the coalmining dispute of 1984–85, however, the High Court ruled that no more than six people could picket at any one colliery gate.

It has long been a practice of workers in dispute to extend their actions to the suppliers and customers of the employer and to persuade workers in related factories to break their contracts of employment. Such secondary action and secondary picketing was protected by Section 13 of the 1974 Act under 'acts in contemplation or furtherance of a trade dispute'. Section 17 of the Employment Act 1980 removed the immunity of Section 13 for secondary action and secondary picketing. The immunity was retained, however, where the workers of an employer in dispute with that employer seek to persuade other workers in its associated yet geographically distant factories to take sympathetic industrial action, including the 'blacking' of goods and services. From a legal viewpoint, it was very important that such action was specifically targeted, so that the connections between the primary and secondary actions were obvious and clear. Where the secondary action or picketing is not directly connected, the employer could seek civil damages through the courts. The 1990 Employment Act ended legal immunity for secondary industrial picketing, regardless of its relationship to the primary action. Pickets can now only picket their own place of work. If they work for an employer with many different establishments, picketing must be carried out only by those people who work in those establishments.

Where an employer is successful in obtaining a court injunction stopping unlawful picketing and the pickets and their unions ignore it, the employer can commence contempt proceedings. If the pickets and their union still ignore the injunction the court can order the seizure of their assets and property. Examples of the use of injunctions to stop mass secondary picketing are to be found in the disputes between Messenger Newspapers Ltd and the National Graphical Association at Warrington in 1983, between British Coal and the National Union of Mineworkers in 1984–85 and between the print unions and News International at Wapping in 1986. In all three disputes, the unions refused to obey court injunctions obtained by the employers requiring them to stop mass picketing and were declared to be in contempt of court. Eventually, union funds were sequestrated. The speedy effect and considerable power of the labour injunction is now well understood by both employers and trade unions.

## 10.4   The Closed Shop

In many countries, such as France, Germany, Italy and Switzerland, the closed shop is either effectively unlawful or severely restricted: the freedom not to organize is on a par with the freedom to organize. 'If everyone, so it is argued, has the fundamental right to join a union, he has the equally fundamental right not to do so'.[16] While this right is contained in the European Convention of Human Rights, and is the subject of specific legislation in many countries, the closed shop, or union shop, in Britain was neither directly banned nor unduly restricted at law until the Employment Acts 1980, 1982, 1988 and 1990. Under these Acts, the rights of individual employees not to be unfairly dismissed for refusing to join a trade union or to remain a member in a closed-shop situation is protected. Likewise, the rights of a person applying for a job and refused on the grounds of non-union membership are protected.

The law now protects the person who applies for employment but is refused on the grounds that he or she is not a member of a required union, or one of the number of specified unions, or refuses to join a union. The law also protects the employee who refuses to join a union, or one of a number of specified unions or leaves a union, while in employment, by providing redress for unfair dismissal. The practical effect of the present legal position is to render both the pre-entry and the post-entry closed shops 'technically' unlawful.

In post entry union shop arrangements the new legal rules will mean that employers will be careful of what they say in interviews but will not necessarily welcome non-union employees. On the other hand, they are unlikely to be willing to dismiss non-union employees given the legal penalties. . . . In some instances this may lead to a tacit acceptance of non-unionists continuing to work alongside unionists.[17]

## Development of the closed shop

Traditionally, closed shops developed over many years in a number of industries, including printing, dockwork, coalmining, shipping, electricity supply, manufacturing, the theatre, construction and road haulage. Closed shops were concentrated in the public sector and in large establishments employing mainly manual workers. It has been estimated that by the early 1980s nearly one-quarter of the working population were in some form of closed shop. A few closed shop agreements between employers and unions – which were then legally described as union membership agreements (UMAs) – were informal understandings that non-union labour would not be employed. It was also understood that employees who left their union, or lost their membership in some other way, would be dismissed if they did not rejoin the union or if they were not accepted back into membership. In pre-entry closed shops, estimated in the early 1980s to cover over a million employees, it was the normal practice of employers only to engage existing union members, usually with the approval of the union(s) concerned. Where post-entry closed shops operated, newly engaged employees were given a set period in which to become members of the specified union(s). In most employment situations where a closed shop existed, the closed shop was the subject of a formal written agreement between the employer and the union(s) concerned. This was done so that the union(s) could make it quite clear to other unions that only their members were to be employed on certain types of work.

## The case for and against the closed shop

For more than 20 years, between the publication of the Donovan Report in 1966, which tacitly supported the closed shop, and the passing of the Employment Acts 1988 and 1990, which finally made the closed shop unlawful, a political, legal and moral battle took place. Those who supported the closed shop argued that it was justified as a means, developed over more than a century by workers, of collectively counterbalancing the economic power of employers. The closed shop enabled workers and their unions to secure good wages, reasonable working conditions and security of employment. Those workers who refused to join the union were dismissed as 'freeloaders', willing to accept the benefits of the closed shop but seeking to avoid paying the union subscrip-

tion. Any attempt by employers, governments or the law to break or weaken the closed shop would be bitterly contested.

Those who opposed the closed shop argued that it was a violation of human freedom and the right of free association. Those who refused to join the specified union were refused employment or faced dismissal if already in employment. Thousands of people, it was claimed, were forced against their will and moral judgement to become union members in order to secure employment and remain in employment. Moreover, argued its opponents, the closed shop led to economic stagnation as it prevented or restricted market competition, led to highly restrictive labour practices, distorted the labour market and prevented technological development.

The closed shop was eventually made unlawful by a step-by-step approach with the passing of the Employment Acts 1980, 1982, 1988 and 1990, and by a code of practice on closed shop arrangements issued by Parliament. Since the late 1980s the controversy over the closed shop has died away, with little indication that either the TUC or the Labour Party now wishes to change the present legal position. It is not unlikely that the fact that the present legal position on the closed shop in the UK is broadly in line with the requirements on union membership and non-membership in the EU Social Charter has played a part in their thinking.

## Enforcement

Where applicants are declared by a tribunal to have been unfairly dismissed for refusing to become or remain a trade union member, they can be awarded substantial compensation in excess of awards for other forms of unfair dismissal. Where an employer argues before a tribunal that the act of dismissal or refused employment was the result of trade union pressure and took the form of industrial action, or the threat of industrial action, it can use its legal right of 'joinder' and make a request to the tribunal for the trade union to become a party to the proceedings. Where the tribunal finds the employer's claim to be well founded, it can order the joined party to contribute to the compensation. Even where the pressure upon employees to become union members against their belief or will stops short of dismissal, they can still bring cases before a tribunal.

Employees have the right not to be unreasonably expelled or excluded from a trade union whilst in employment. Where employees feel they have been unreasonably expelled or excluded, they can take a complaint to an industrial tribunal. The tribunal will make a decision based on the individual circumstances and merits of each case. The tribunal takes into account the rules of the union, but does not necessarily base its findings on whether or not the rules were observed. Where a tribunal makes a declaration that an employee was unreasonably expelled or excluded from union membership, that individual is entitled to claim compensation from the union. Such an application for compensation cannot be made before the union has had time to reconsider the case and to admit or re-admit the person involved. This process does not prevent individual members taking a case to the ordinary courts under the common law, if actions taken against them by their trade union are contrary to the union's own rules or in violation of natural justice. The TULRC Act 1992 provides union members with the right of complaint to a tribunal that they have been unjustifiably disciplined by a union, with the Act defining what unjustifiable disciplining is.

## Commercial contracts

The TULRC Act 1992 contains a prohibition on union membership requirements in commercial contracts. The objective of these sections is to make unlawful and void any clauses in commercial contracts for goods or services requiring another employer to guarantee that it will only use trade union labour. This form of pressure, whilst still not a common practice, grew in the 1960s and 1970s. It was usually associated with the printing industry and with strong closed shop situations. The union aim was to prevent an employer placing orders and contracts with firms not employing trade union labour and not operating closed shops. Firms or suppliers must not exclude, or fail to consider, tenders for commercial contracts on the grounds that the firm concerned does not employ union members. Conversely, contracts must not contain requirements that only non-union labour is to be used, though conditions of this nature are almost unknown. Trade disputes or any other form of industrial action, or threat of action, to enforce union labour-only clauses in contracts are not protected by legal immunity and are therefore potentially actionable in tort.

## 10.5   Collective Bargaining and the Law

### Recognition and collective agreements

To some extent the history of collective bargaining in Britain is the history of the struggle for trade union recognition. The classical method used by manual workers during the nineteenth century for this purpose was to increase their level of trade union membership and their strength of organization to the point where they were confident that formal recognition from their employers could not be refused. If their employers agreed, there was no problem. But if the employers decided not to concede recognition, nor to abandon their unilateral determination of pay and conditions of employment, the unions had to decide whether to take strike action or to present a further request for recognition at some later date. This process of attrition was virtually unregulated by law and continued in slightly modified form until the Industrial Relations Act 1971. This Act provided for the first time a limited legal procedure which could be used by those trade unions, registered under the Act, that wished to obtain formal recognition agreements from their employers.

Recognition disputes remained one of the most bitter and protracted forms of industrial conflict between trade unions and employers well into the twentieth century but their incidence declined as trade union membership grew and as the institution of collective bargaining became more firmly established. Government also played a positive role in extending collective bargaining. It did this by recognizing the right of its own employees to belong to trade unions and by negotiating with them. By promoting the development of collective bargaining machinery after the First World War, the Whitley reports (1917–18) also played a crucial part in persuading many employers to recognize trade unions and to negotiate with them.

The Employment Protection Act 1975 provided, under Sections 11–16, a legal procedure by which independent certificated unions could try to obtain formal recognition agreements from employers without resort to overt industrial conflict. This did not mean, or course, that unions did not continue to use the strike weapon as a means of obtaining recognition if they preferred that method to one of due legal process, or that employers were legally obliged to negotiate recognition agreements. This legal procedure, which involved the Advisory Conciliation and Arbitration Service and the Central Arbitration

Committee, was repealed by the Employment Act 1980.

Statute law is not now involved with trade union recognition which is left to be determined voluntarily by the good sense, or otherwise, of trade unions and employers. Providing a ballot of all members involved has been conducted according to the requirements of the TULRC Act 1992, a recognition dispute involving industrial action would not normally be actionable at law. This does not mean that the courts do not have to decide whether or not a union is recognized by an employer. In many cases the courts are obliged to settle the question of union recognition in order to decide a union's right to claim such basic legal entitlements as the right to be consulted on impending redundancies, to be consulted about the transfer of an employer's undertaking, to receive bargaining information and to appoint safety representatives. The courts have had to decide the criteria which constitute union recognition by the employer in order to decide whether or not a union is legally entitled to its statutory rights.

## Collective agreements and the law

Formal contractual association lies at the heart of all business transactions within market-based economies like that of Britain. The law encourages the drawing up of formal business contracts between freely consenting parties. This is done on the assumption that both sides expect the other to meet their contractual obligations with mutual goodwill and acceptance. If either side fails to fulfil its obligations then redress and compensation can be sought by the other party through the civil courts. That is, both sides to the contract or agreement *intend* it to be legally binding. On this basis, innumerable contracts are agreed daily between producers and wholesalers, for example, between shipbuilders and shipping companies, between local authorities and road construction companies, between housebuilders and house purchasers and so on.

Collective agreements, however, are not legally enforceable between employers and unions because they are not commercial contracts between consenting parties but are highly complex social and economic agreements regulating the working lives of millions of people in the organizations in which they are employed. Such agreements do not easily meet the general criteria of the law of commercial contract. It is clearly not the intention of unions or employers in negotiating collective agreements to regard them as legally enforceable contracts, unless they take the highly unusual step of declaring in writing that the collective agreement they have negotiated is legally enforceable. The voluntary and non-contractual nature of collective agreements was upheld by the civil courts in 1969 in the *Ford Motor Co.* v *Amalgamated Union of Engineering and Foundry Workers* decision. Here it was 'held that an agreement between the Ford Motor Co. and a number of unions could not be enforced as a contract'.[18] The decision was based on the factual finding that there was no contractual intent. Furthermore, the nature and uncertain wording of collective agreements and particularly their aspirational character, it was felt, would 'present grave problems of enforcement'.[19]

Collective agreements, therefore, are better understood, not as legally enforceable commercial contracts but as 'an industrial peace treaty and at the same time a source of rules for terms and conditions of employment, for the distribution of work and for the stability of jobs'.[20] This view of collective agreements was endorsed by the experience of the Industrial Relations Act between 1971 and 1974, when all collective agreements were presumed to be legally enforceable unless clearly indicated otherwise by the parties. The TUC response was to insist that affiliated unions put clear disclaimers in all written agreements which they signed. At the same time, employers showed little interest in persuading the trade unions to make collective agreements legally enforceable. One reason was that employers were aware of the impracticability of suing unions or employees for compensation for breach of contract, to say nothing of the damaging effects which such litigation would have on personnel management and industrial relations. Thus Sections 179 and 180 of the Trade Union and Labour Relations (Consolidation) Act 1992 now state unambiguously that any collective agreement:

> shall be conclusively presumed not to have been intended by the parties to be a legally enforceable contract unless the agreement–
> (a) is in writing, and
> (b) contains a provision which (however expressed) states that the parties intend that the agreement shall be a legally enforceable contract.[21]

## Collective bargaining and the state

The law has played an important and positive role in encouraging and fostering the growth of voluntary collective bargaining and the development of jointly agreed negotiating machinery in Britain. The historical evidence strongly suggests, for example, that the Trade Union Act 1871, the Conspiracy and Protection of Property Act 1875 and the Trade Disputes Act 1906 powerfully fostered the growth of voluntary collective bargaining machinery in Britain. The Royal Commission on Labour in 1894, which led to the Conciliation Act 1896, along with the influential Whitley reports which appeared at the end of the First World War, played considerable parts in encouraging the growth of voluntary collective bargaining as an effective means of determining mutually acceptable terms and conditions of employment between employers and employees. Moreover, the Nationalization Acts enacted after 1945, and the growth of public sector employment, have clearly encouraged the growth of voluntary collective bargaining as a principal method of regulating employer–employee relationships. It is reasonable to conclude that the State, over a very long period of time, has supported the development of voluntary, responsible collective bargaining as the best way of ensuring stable and peaceful industrial relations between employers and employees and their representatives.

It has generally been the intention of the legislators, at least before 1979, not to make collective agreements legally enforceable, but to encourage the responsible development of voluntary collective bargaining in Britain. The Whitley reports, for instance, were implemented in this voluntary spirit by the Ministry of Labour immediately after the First World War. They did much to encourage the development of national collective bargaining machinery through the establishment of joint industrial councils representative of both employers and trade unions during the interwar period. More recently, ACAS has been given the statutory duty of promoting good industrial relations through encouraging the extension of collective bargaining and joint negotiating machinery in industry.

Since 1979, however, government opinion has turned against voluntary collective bargaining on the grounds that it is inflationary, that it is abused by powerful trade unions and workgroups, and that it is inflexible in the face of changing product and labour market conditions. In so much as government now supports collective bargaining, it believes it should be clearly decentralized and far more responsive to changing economic circumstances, and that pay increases should be closely related to the personal work performance record of individuals. This belief

has been given concrete expression in the 1993 Act, which removes from ACAS one of its main functions of promoting the extension, development and reform of collective bargaining, in favour of the more general duty to promote the improvement of industrial relations.

## Disclosure of information for collective bargaining purposes

The trade unions have long argued that employers should disclose certain information to them so that they can negotiate more realistically together. They have wanted this information to check both the veracity of management's financial statements and any claims that their employers cannot afford to meet their pay demands. The unions' requests for information have usually been a claim that management should 'open the books' for inspection. Some employers wishing to foster responsible collective bargaining have voluntarily given union representatives such commercial, financial and production information when this has been requested. Where employers have refused to disclose this information, some unions have proved very resourceful in obtaining the evidence they require. They have obtained this from annual company reports, newspapers such as the *Financial Times* and the stockbroker financial information services. They have also used the trade union research services provided by the Trades Union Congress, Ruskin College at Oxford and the Labour Research Department.

The legal right of independent recognized trade unions to request employers they conduct negotiations with to disclose information for collective bargaining purposes was first established by the Employment Protection Act 1975. The legislation on the disclosure of information is now contained in Sections 181 to 185 of the TULRC Act 1992. There is also a legal procedure enabling independent trade unions to complain if an employer refuses such information. As a general guide to these sections of the Act, ACAS issued a code of practice on disclosure of information to trade unions for collective bargaining purposes in 1977, subsequently approved by Parliament. This, it is hoped, provides a guide for trade unions, employers and the Central Arbitration Committee (CAC) when considering the information that can legitimately be requested for collective bargaining purposes.

The 1992 Act applies to every employer, including the public services and government departments, and lays a general duty on employers to disclose on the request of representatives of independent trade unions:

> all information relating to his undertaking as is in his possession ... without which the trade union representatives would be to a material extent impeded in carrying on ... collective bargaining with him, and ... information which it would be in accordance with good industrial relations practice that he should disclose to them for the purposes of collective bargaining.[22]

The trade unions must be independent and recognized by the employer for the purpose of collective bargaining. If the employer rejects the union's claim that it recognizes them, the issue can be determined by conciliation. The information disclosed by the employer has to be in writing or confirmed in writing. Although the Act is not specific on what information should be disclosed, it clearly states that the ACAS code is to be the general guide for both parties and for the CAC in determining whether or not the employer has complied with the requirements of the Act.

The legislation places certain restrictions on the general duty of employers to disclose information. Information is restricted, for example, where it: endangers national security; contravenes another law (such as the Official Secrets legislation); breaches confidential sources; relates specifically to individuals without their agreement; or causes substantial injury to the undertaking. The employer needs only to give the information in a form which it believes to be most suitable. It can refuse information 'where the compilation or assembly would involve an amount of work or expenditure out of reasonable proportion to the value of the information in the conduct of collective bargaining'.[23] Where an employer appears to refuse unreasonably to disclose the requested information, an independent trade union may present a complaint to the CAC in writing that 'an employer has failed to disclose ... information which he is required to disclose'.[24] The complaint is usually first referred to ACAS for conciliation but, if this fails, the CAC hears the complaint and decides whether it is well founded, stating the reasons for its findings. If the CAC finds the complaint well founded, it specifies the information which the employer should disclose and a date by which the employer has to provide the information. If the employer still refuses to disclose the required information, the union can, under Section 20 of the Act, submit a further complaint. This leads to a CAC award making the

disclosure of the specified information part of the terms and conditions of each individual employee's contract of employment, which can be enforced through the courts.

The ACAS code is not concerned with the legal process whereby the law can be enforced. Its aim is to provide practical guidance on the most reasonable ways in which information can be requested and conceded for the purposes of collective bargaining. The code states that the Act imposes no specific items of disclosure on employers, but leaves it to the code to recommend what actual information should be disclosed in the interests of good industrial relations. Failure to observe the code does not itself render anyone liable to proceedings, 'but the Act requires any relevant provisions to be taken into account in proceedings before the Central Arbitration Committee'.[25] The code is clearly a 'relevant provision'.

The code of practice recommends employers to disclose information on pay, conditions of service, manpower levels, company performance and productivity, and on the employer's general financial situation. It suggests, too, that managements formulate a policy on disclosure and make formal joint agreements on disclosure arrangements with the trade unions with whom they negotiate. It advises trade unions to undertake training to ensure that negotiators know what information to ask for and that they are equipped to use the information effectively.

> Misunderstandings can be avoided, costs reduced, and time saved, if requests state as precisely as possible all the information required, and the reasons why the information is considered relevant. Requests should conform to an agreed procedure. A reasonable period of time should be allowed for employers to consider a request and to reply.[26]

## Transfer of undertakings

The Transfer of Undertakings (Protection of Employment) Regulations 1981 and 1987 issued by Parliament, which were intended to put into effect the EC Acquired Rights Directive 77/187, gave most but not all employees new legal rights when their employers sell or transfer their businesses or undertakings. These Regulations were extended and clarified in 1993 by the Trade Union Reform and Employment Rights Act. It is believed that the relevant sections of this Act now fully implement the EU directive. Almost all employees, including those in the public sector, should now enjoy continuity of employment along with their existing contracts of employments and union recognition rights when their employers transfer the business. Employers are also required to inform and consult recognized unions about proposed transfers or mergers and their likely effects on employees. Any dismissals arising out of a transfer or merger are considered unfair unless the employer can show that they were necessary for economic, technical or organizational reasons. This requires the employer to disclose all relevant information relating to redundancies arising out of the transfer. If employers do not comply with the law, recognized unions but not individual employees may complain to an industrial tribunal. Where a complaint is upheld, the tribunal may award up to four weeks' pay to each employee. However, the law currently is complex and in a state of transition, as the EU Directive is being amended and the ECJ develops further case law.

## 10.6   Union Ballots

As we have already indicated, individual trade unionists can appeal to the courts for redress if their union treats them in ways which do not accord with the union's rule book. Trade unions must also submit details of their internal organization, methods of operation and accounts to the Certification Officer if they wish to become a certified independent union under the 1992 Act. Until the Employment Act 1980, the question of internal trade union democracy was considered to be their own private business. The 1980 Act, however, enabled the Secretary of State for Employment to approve public money for independent trade unions to conduct certain secret ballots. Trade unions were not obliged to make use of this provision and the Secretary of State had discretion in financing such ballots. The objectives of these provisions were to enable vital decisions taken within trade unions to be determined by secret postal ballots of their memberships and, in theory, to 'improve' internal union democracy. In 1993 the government gave notice that the scheme to reimburse unions for costs incurred in holding secret ballots was to end. This will impose on the unions a not inconsiderable cost.

Matters on which unions are legally obliged, under the TULRC Act 1992, to hold secret postal ballots of members include: the election of certain principal union officers; amending the rules of a union; seeking approval for trade union amalgamations; and establishing and retaining a political fund. The TULRC

Act 1992 and the 1993 Act lay down in considerable detail how union membership elections must be conducted. The most stringent requirement concerning all union membership ballots, however, stipulates that they must be fully postal with ballot papers being sent by post to each member and the member being able to vote in secret and post his or her ballot paper. The stationery, printing, administrative and postal costs are not inconsiderable.

The process begun by the 1980 Act to ensure that vital internal trade union decisions are democratically determined by secret postal ballots of the whole membership was enlarged by the Trade Union Act 1984 (now the TULRC Act 1992). The 1992 Act has three major provisions: secret ballots for the election of trade union leaders and principal executive bodies; secret ballots before taking industrial action; and secret ballots for political funds and objects.

### Election of officers

The 1992 Act requires trade unions to elect, by secret ballot of the whole membership, union general secretaries and presidents, members of principal executive committees and those persons attending principal executive committees regularly. Elections must take place at least once every five years. This requirement applies 'notwithstanding anything in the union's rules'. The 1992 Act lays down the minimum requirements for the conduct of elections to a union's principal executive body. Outgoing members of an executive may remain in office for a handover period not exceeding six months. All union members entitled to vote must be given equal voting rights. The union must keep accurate records of all its members' names and addresses and keep them up to date. Unions must have complete and accurate registers of members.

Voting must be by secret postal ballot and members must be given every opportunity to vote. Voting must take place without interference from, or constraint imposed by, the union or any of its members, officials or employees, and the votes must be fairly and accurately counted. Executive members must not be elected indirectly by conference delegates or regional committees or by any 'block vote' system. All members of the union are entitled to vote but certain exceptions laid down in the union's rules can be made, including: those in arrears with union dues; new members with less than three months' standing; and apprentices, trainees and students. Where appropriate, a union can divide its membership by geographical area, trade groups, occupation or clearly separate sections, and elections can take place for executive members by all the union members within these defined divisions.

The 1992 Act requires all union members, except for a small number of members usually excluded by union rules, to be eligible to stand for election to the union's principal executive. Unions may set reasonable lower and upper age limits on candidates or require a minimum period of membership. But they must not stipulate that candidates are required to belong to a particular political party. Any union member who qualifies under the 1992 Act to vote or stand in union elections and is prevented from doing so can make a complaint to the Certification Officer or to the courts. The member can also complain that the union does not keep an adequate register of members. Union members who believe their union has not complied with the Act must make a complaint within one year of the election result being announced. The member makes the complaint to the Certification Officer and need not be involved in any legal expenses. Union members are required to give specific evidence of election malpractice. They can also request help and legal assistance in preparing and presenting their cases from the Commissioner for the Rights of Trade Union Members.

If the Certification Officer determines that the union has broken the Act's requirements, a declaration can be made to that effect. Where such a declaration is made, the member can take the complaint to the courts, unless the union accepts that it has broken the Act's requirements and has put the matter right. However, if the union does not accept the Certification Officer's findings, the member can proceed with a complaint to the courts. Where the courts accept the Certification Officer's declaration, they can order the union to hold a fresh election, take steps to remedy the infringement, such as recounting the votes or updating its membership register, or in cases of minor infringements order the union not to commit the offence again. Where a union refuses to recognize the court's order, or refuses to accept its right to make such an order, the court can declare the union to be in contempt and may impose a fine, followed possibly by further fines and orders leading eventually to the sequestration of the union's assets.

## Industrial action ballots

The TULRC Act 1992 and the 1993 Act require trade unions to hold secret ballots before authorizing or endorsing official industrial action by their members. Failure to hold ballots before taking industrial action can result in the loss of legal immunity by the union in the event of any action for civil damages. Where union members intend taking industrial action involving a breach of their contracts of employment, they must first hold a secret postal ballot of those members directly involved in taking the action. The ballot must be held not more than four weeks before the start of the industrial action and a majority of those voting must be prepared to take the action. Where these two conditions are met, the action should be immune from civil actions for damages. Where the union wishes its members to take action short of striking, as well as strike action, a separate question for each must be contained on the ballot paper and immunity for both forms of action depends upon separate majority votes in favour of each. The 1992 Act also gives the legal right to all union members entitled to vote in a ballot proposing industrial action to appeal to the courts for an order restraining their union from inducing them to take industrial action in the absence of a properly conducted ballot. These members can seek the assistance of the Commissioner for the Rights of Trade Union Members in taking their cases to court or in seeking an injunction against the union.

The 1993 Act makes several important changes to the law relating to industrial action ballots:

- all ballots to sanction industrial action to be fully postal, with each worker entitled to receive a ballot paper at his or her home address, which he or she must return by post for the vote to be valid;
- the union to give the affected employer(s) seven days' notice of the proposed ballot and a sample copy of the ballot paper;
- the union to specify to the employer(s) the opening date of the ballot, and describe those people the union believes are entitled to vote in the ballot so that the employer can identify them;
- the union to give the employer details of the result of the ballot;
- the ballot to be subjected to independent scrutiny with the named scrutineer making a detailed written report on the conduct of the ballot within four weeks;
- the union to give the employer seven days' written notice of the start of industrial action and notify the employer of the employees who will be taking part;
- the union to indicate to the employer(s) whether

or not the action will be 'continuous' or 'discontinuous', and if the action is to be continuous, the days on which it will take place;

- any individual person, that is a member of the general public, who, as a result of unlawful industrial action, is prevented from receiving goods or services, or receives goods or services of a reduced quality, will be able to apply to the High Court for an order requiring the union in question to cease industrial action;
- the 1993 Act provides for the appointment of a Commissioner for Protection against Unlawful Industrial Action, who will be able to assist members of the public to bring actions against unions involved in unlawful industrial actions.

Where union members take industrial action not authorized or endorsed by the union following a secret ballot which complies with the detailed requirements of the 1992 and 1993 Acts, the union will be held responsible unless the action is clearly repudiated by the union's principal executive, the general secretary or the president. The repudiation must be put in writing as soon as possible. The persons or person legally permitted to make the repudiation must not, following the repudiation, behave in a manner which is inconsistent with the repudiation.

Where a union fails to fulfil the requirement to hold secret postal ballots before taking official industrial action, it loses its immunity in legal proceedings for civil damages. Actions may be brought by employers who can prove that their employees have broken their contracts of employment without first having gone through a successful ballot, or where commercial contracts have been interfered with, that they have suffered financial loss. Customers and suppliers who can show that their contracts have been interfered with can also bring civil actions. Employers and others affected by the industrial action can seek an injunction to have the industrial action called off, which, if not complied with, can lead to contempt of court fines and the sequestration of union funds and assets. The scale of damages which the courts can award was fixed at an upper limit of £250 000 for the largest unions in 1984, and has remained unchanged since then. If an employer seeks and obtains an injunction, it does not mean it must proceed with a case for civil damages. Nor is it necessary to seek an injunction before proceeding with a civil action. An employer can seek civil damages against a union which did not hold the

necessary ballot, after the industrial action has been resolved, though past experience suggests that this is extremely unlikely.

The law stipulates those union members entitled to vote in a ballot on industrial action and how the ballot should be conducted. Only those members called upon to take such action are entitled to vote. Employees not eligible to take part in the ballot cannot be lawfully asked to take industrial action at a later date without a further ballot. The ballot paper must state specifically that members are being asked to take part either in strike action in breach of their contracts of employment or in industrial action falling short of a strike. The questions must be framed to require a straight 'yes' or 'no' answer. Voting must be in secret and fully postal. The votes must be fairly and accurately counted and the results made public to those entitled to vote. The results must declare the number of votes cast, the number of 'yes' votes, the number of 'no' votes and the number of spoiled or unacceptable ballot papers.

The 1993 Act establishes the right of any member of the public to exercise a new Citizen's Right to commence civil law proceedings if they can prove they have suffered damages arising out of an industrial dispute which has not complied with the requirements of the law. The 1993 Act creates the office of Commissioner for Protection against Unlawful Industrial Action with the duty to assist a person exercising his or her Citizen's Right in order to take redress.

In 1990, the Secretary of State for Employment issued a detailed code of practice on trade union ballots on industrial action, which had been approved by Parliament. Its guidelines have to be carefully considered by the courts in deciding cases where it is alleged that secret industrial action ballots have not been properly conducted. The code contains over 50 sections of detailed guidance on how industrial action ballots are to be conducted by trade unions. The code makes the preparation and conduct of industrial action ballots a drawn-out and complex matter. It also makes it relatively easy for union members, employers or any third party affected by a proposed dispute to seek an injunction on the grounds that the code has been breached.

## Political fund ballots

The TULRC Act 1992 permits unions to set up separate political funds and to use the money in those funds for political objects, providing they first hold a membership ballot. Monies kept in a union's general fund cannot be used for political purposes. Members who wish to contribute to the political fund pay a small addition to their basic union subscription known as the political levy. If they do not wish to pay the political levy, they have to 'contract out' in writing. The 1992 Act enables those unions with a political levy to provide the Labour Party with most of its finance as well as providing for expenditure on parliamentary and local government elections involving union-sponsored candidates. The 1992 Act lays down the requirements which unions have to comply with in order to establish and use a political fund. The union has first to hold a ballot of its members before a political fund can be established. It is then required to adopt a number of political fund rules approved by the Certification Officer.

The 1992 Act requires all unions with political funds established under the Act to hold review ballots at intervals of not more than 10 years after the initial ballot. The review ballots must be conducted in accordance with rules laid down by the Certification Officer. If a union fails to hold the required review ballot, any member of the union may bring a common law action before the courts, which may then order the union to comply. Failure to obey the courts could lead to contempt of court proceedings. Where a review ballot rejects continuing the political fund, the union must: take immediate steps to stop collecting the political levy; refund levy payments made after the ballot, if so requested by members; stop all expenditure on political objects within six months; and transfer the existing monies in the political fund to other funds held by the union. Where a union fails to do these thing after a 'no' vote by a majority of the union members in a review ballot, any member of the union may seek an order requiring the union to comply with the Act's requirements.

The 1992 Act also clarifies and updates the definition of 'political objects' contained in the Act. Only expenditure falling within the Act's definition is lawful. Expenditure is lawful under the Act if it is incurred: for contributions to a political party; for expenses, services and property provided for a political party; for costs involved in the selection and election of candidates for political office; for the support and maintenance of those holding political office; for political meetings or conferences and the expenses of delegates; and for producing, publishing and distributing literature, films and advertisements intended to persuade people to vote or not to vote for a candidate or a political party.

The claimed objective of the Trade Union Act 1992 is to 'return trade unions to their members'. The main instrument intended to achieve this is the secret postal ballot. Opposition to the Act is largely a rejection of the arguments that existing trade union rules, balloting systems and internal democratic procedures are faulty in any major way. In opposing the original 1984 Act, the TUC initially rejected the use of public funds to pay for trade union elections, and unions applying for financial assistance were faced with possible expulsion from the TUC. This policy was subsequently modified, however, to permit unions to claim public money to offset secret ballot costs. In 1993, the government announced that state financial contributions would end. It is as yet unclear whether or not the legislation is working as intended and whether it has resulted in more moderate trade union leadership and less militant attitudes to industrial action, as well as reduced involvement with party politics.

## 10.7  Health and Safety at Work

### Historical background

The early factory system which grew out of the industrial revolution during the opening decades of the nineteenth century created wretched working conditions, especially for the many young children and women employed in textile factories and the coalmines. The prevailing economic and political philosophy of *laissez-faire* initially discouraged Parliament from passing protective legislation, but the social outcry and shock to the Christian conscience of such working conditions eventually led the State to intervene. Thus laws controlling the length of working hours for children were enacted and women were not allowed to be employed in mines, 'dragging trucks of coal to which they were harnessed by a chain and girdle going on all-fours, in conditions of dirt, heat and indecency which are scarcely printable'.[27]

The early factory legislation of 1802 and 1833 was not characterized by a concern for the safety of life and limb. It focused, rather, on the excessively long hours worked by women and children in particular industries, and on the morality and religious education of the industrial revolution's new working classes. One of the main problems of this legislation was the enforcement of the standards established by Parliament in the new factories of the North. This led in 1833 to a limited form of State factory inspection which was steadily strengthened by successive Acts of

Parliament. Safety legislation throughout the nineteenth century and well into the present century did not develop along coherent and consistent policy lines. It was enacted in a piecemeal manner to deal with public concern and worker agitation over specific matters such as working hours and dangerous conditions of work in factories, mines, railways, shipping, glass manufacture, baking and road transport. This piecemeal approach to safety legislation continued after the Second World War, though greater effort was subsequently made to codify existing legislation along industrial lines and to strengthen the powers of the various inspectorates.

By 1970, there were nearly 30 Acts of Parliament dealing specifically or partially with industrial safety, some 500 legal regulations, and seven separate inspectorates. The principal legislation, still largely in force, was: the Agriculture (Poisonous Substances) Act 1952; the Mines and Quarries Act 1954; the Agriculture (Safety, Health and Welfare Provision) Act 1956; the Factories Act 1961; and the Offices Shops and Railway Premises Act 1963. The responsibility for enforcing safety standards laid down by the various statutes was divided between seven largely autonomous inspectorates: the Factory Inspectorate; the Mines and Quarries Inspectorate; the Agricultural Safety Inspectorate; the Explosives Inspectorate; the Nuclear Installations Inspectorate; the Radio Chemical Inspectorate; and the Alkali and Clean Air Inspectorate. Additionally, local authority health and safety inspectors were also responsible for the enforcement of a range of health and safety legislation, including the Office Shops and Railway Premises Act 1963.

During the late 1960s, increasing concern was expressed by the public, the trade unions, and employers about Britain's poor record in industrial health and safety matters. There was also concern about the plethora of disconnected, confusing, overlapping and often antiquated legislation, and the outdated and inadequate systems of inspection and legal enforcement of minimum safety standards. In 1970, the Committee on Safety and Health at Work was appointed under the chairmanship of Alfred Robens. Its terms of reference were: to review the provisions made for securing health and safety at work; to consider what changes were needed in existing legislation; to examine the nature and extent of voluntary action by management and employees in securing safe working conditions; and to state what steps could be taken to protect the safety of the general public as well as of employees.

The report of the Committee on Safety and Health at Work marked a completely new approach to industrial safety. It stressed the apparently surprising viewpoint that health and safety at work could not be adequately secured by existing legislation or inspectorates. It would be best pursued, it argued, by creating a climate in which government, management and employees were jointly responsible for the voluntary attainment and supervision of adequate safety standards.

> We have stressed that the promotion of safety and health at work is first and foremost a matter of efficient management. But it is not a management prerogative. In this context more than most, real progress is impossible without the full co-operation and commitment of all employees. How can this be encouraged? We believe that . . . workpeople . . . must be able to participate fully in the making and monitoring of arrangements for safety and health at their place of work.[28]

The report also criticized the volume of overlapping and confusing legislation which dealt piecemeal with the specific safety problems of different industries. It criticized too: the weaknesses of the different small and autonomous inspectorates; the inadequacy of fines and the legal enforcement of safety standards; and the lack of a powerful centralized agency with responsibilities for research, education and the establishment of specific standards of health and safety at work for all employees.

## The 1974 Health and Safety Act

The Health and Safety at Work etc. Act 1974 closely follows the recommendations of the Robens report. Part I of the Act establishes in broad terms the general duties of employers, the self-employed, and employees in achieving acceptable safety standards at work. It states:

(1)  It shall be the duty of every employer to ensure, so far as is reasonably practicable, the health, safety and welfare at work of all his employees.

(2)  Without prejudice to the generality of an employer's duty under the preceding subsection, the matters to which that duty extends include in particular –

(a)  the provision and maintenance of plant and systems of work that are so far as is reasonably practicable, safe and without risks to health;

(b)　arrangements for ensuring, so far as is reasonably practicable, safety and absence of risks to health in connection with the use, handling, storage and transport of articles and substances;

(c)　the provision of such information, instruction, training and supervision as is necessary to ensure, as far as is reasonably practicable, the health and safety at work of his employees;

(d)　so far as is reasonably practicable as regards any place of work under the employer's control the maintenance of it in a condition that is safe and without risks to health and maintenance of means of access to and egress from it that are safe and without such risks;

(e)　the provision and maintenance of a working environment for his employees that is, so far as is reasonably practicable, safe, without risk to health, and adequate as regards facilities and arrangements for their welfare at work.[29]

The 1974 Act lays the responsibility on employers for issuing a written policy statement on health and safety within their organizations and for devising means of implementing it. This policy statement has to be brought to the attention of all the workforce. Where safety representatives are appointed by recognized independent trade unions, employers are obliged to consult them on all safety matters. By making these general duties for health and safety applicable to 'every employer', including the self-employed and the controllers of premises, the 1974 Act ensures that no employers are excluded from the general legal obligation of ensuring satisfactory health and safety standards at work. These general duties on employers are also extended to protect members of the public, thereby giving the Act extremely wide application.

Part I of the 1974 Act similarly lays a general duty upon all employees to take 'reasonable care' whilst at work not only for their own health and safety, but also for those of other employees. Employees are required, for example, to co-operate with all those persons in supervisory capacities charged with carrying out the general duties laid upon the employer by the Act. The Act continues the common law practice of holding employees responsible for the observance

of necessary safety measures, the avoidance of reckless behaviour, and the interference with or misuse of 'anything provided in the interests of health, safety or welfare in pursuance of any of the relevant statutory provisions'.[30]

Section 6 of the 1974 Act imposes for the first time a general duty on designers, manufacturers, importers and suppliers of certain products to ensure that the articles which they offer for sale are designed, constructed and tested to be safe when properly used. They also have to ensure that information is available about the article, the testing of it, and how it should be correctly used. Finally, they are required to carry out any necessary research to discover, eliminate or minimize any risks to health and safety related to the product which they are designing, manufacturing, importing or supplying.

Sections 10 to 14 of the 1974 Act create a new and centralized Health and Safety Commission (HSC) to direct the general policy of health and safety at work and to implement the many long-term implications of the Act. It comprises a full-time independent chairperson and nine part-time commissioners made up of three union-nominated members, three employer-nominated members, two from the local authorities and an independent member. The Commission has taken over the responsibilities for most occupational health and safety matters formerly divided among several government departments. It is also responsible for forming a powerful and unified inspectorate, undertaking research and providing training, education and general information to those requiring it. Control of general policy is in the hands of the mainly part-time HSC. The day-to-day responsibility for health and safety matters, the implementation of the HSC's policies and the general administration and enforcement of safety standards at work rests with the Health and Safety Executive (HSE), which is staffed by civil servants. It is a basic duty of the HSC and the HSE to propose ways of consolidating existing and overlapping legislation. They are also expected to issue safety regulations and codes of practice to be observed by employers, employees and the courts. Ultimate control over the HSC and HSE is vested in the Secretary of State for Employment who may 'give to the Commission at any time such directions as he thinks fit with respect to its functions . . . or expedient to give in the interests of the safety of the State'.[31] An example of the power which this right to issue new regulations confers on the HSC is the Control of Substances Hazardous to Health (COSHH) Regulations which came into force in 1989. These regulations have very wide application and apply especially to the control of substances which could have a long-term effect on the health of employees and others who might come into contact with them.

## Enforcement

Sections 18 to 26 of the 1974 Act provide for the appointment of inspectors by the HSE, with powers to enforce the administration of all safety legislation and the required standards of health and safety at work. It is an offence for any employer or for any other person to obstruct or to prevent the entry of inspectors to premises which they are legally entitled to inspect. The main instruments of enforcement open to the inspectorate are 'improvement' and 'prohibition' notices which can be served on employers by individual inspectors. If inspectors consider that a law has been broken in respect of health and safety at work, they can issue an improvement notice to the responsible person requiring that the contravention be remedied within a certain time. If the necessary action is not taken within the specified time, a prohibition notice may then be issued stopping the particular work operation. Inspectors also possess the power to issue prohibition notices if there is an immediate risk or danger to workers or to the general public.

Employers may appeal against these notices to an industrial tribunal. But until the tribunal makes a decision the prohibition notice applies. Where an inspector thinks there is no immediate risk, a 'deferred prohibition' notice may be served upon an employer giving it time to take the necessary remedial steps without stopping production. Non-compliance with improvement or prohibition notices can lead to fixed maximum fines imposed by magistrates' courts, or unlimited fines by higher courts in the case of trial by indictment and even imprisonment in exceptional cases. The HSC, the HSE and the inspectorates also possess powers under Sections 27 and 28 of the 1974 Act obliging persons and organizations to disclose necessary information relating to health and safety matters to them. These powers may only be used with the consent of the Secretary of State for Employment.

Part II of the 1974 Act establishes the Employment Medical Advisory Service (EMAS) and defines its responsibilities and functions. EMAS is an organization of doctors and nurses whose task is to give advice about occupational health, and to help to prevent ill

health caused by bad working conditions. Employers, employees, self-employed persons or accredited trade union representatives can all request the assistance of EMAS with any occupational health problems. It advises individuals on the type of work which best suits them or on the work that they should avoid on health grounds. EMAS also gives advice to the inspectorates and to the HSE on long-term policy recommendations on occupational health. Where certain industrial health regulations are in force, or where people are employed on known hazardous work, EMAS gives medical advice and conducts medical examinations of employees. EMAS is also concerned with the measurements of physical and environmental work hazards such as noise, vibration, dust and mental stress and in setting standards and acceptable levels of exposure to such health hazards. Finally, EMAS carries out long-term research into various aspects of occupational health about which little or nothing might be known.

Part III of the Act makes detailed changes to the building safety regulations to improve health and safety specifically in the building and construction industries, which have bad safety records. Lastly, Part IV of the Act deals with other miscellaneous and general matters including, for example, those relating to radiological protection and fire precautions at work.

## Promotion of health and safety at the workplace

The safety regulations and codes of practice, issued under the 1974 Act, require the obligatory appointment of employee safety representatives and statutory safety committees at the workplace. The Robens report clearly stated that predominant reliance on a system of external health and safety inspection had not proved to be particularly successful. This should be strengthened, it recommended, in order to underpin an internal system of regulation, control and inspection by management and employees jointly. This fundamental change in emphasis to the monitoring of health and safety standards at work cannot be stressed too strongly, since the Health and Safety at Work etc. Act 1974 is largely founded on this principle.

> We recommend, therefore, that there should be a statutory duty on every employer to consult with his employees or their representatives at the workplace on measures for promoting safety and

health at work, and to provide arrangements for the participation of employees in the development of such measures ... Guidance should, however, be given in a code of practice outlining model arrangements, including advice on joint safety committees and the appointment of employees' safety representatives.[32]

This general duty of management to consult with employees and to recognize the appointment of trade union safety representatives and the formation of safety committees is embodied in Section 2 of the 1974 Act. It is also to be found in the regulations on safety representatives and safety committees and the code of practice on safety representatives approved by the HSC and by the Secretary of State for Employment in 1977. In order to facilitate the emergence of competent safety representatives, the HSC has issued a code of practice on time off for training safety representatives. The regulations and codes became operative in October 1978. Independent recognized trade unions are given the legal right to appoint safety representatives from among their members at their workplace, without obstruction or interference from the employer. At the written request of any two union-appointed safety representatives, an employer is obliged to form a safety committee. Section 116 and Schedule 15 of the Employment Protection Act 1975 abolish the right of employees, other than those who are members of independent recognized unions, to elect safety representatives within the meaning of the regulations and codes. This does not however prevent the appointment of safety representatives, and the establishment of safety committees, at workplaces where unions do not exist. This is providing the workers and the employers agree voluntarily to their creation. But the legal power to compel an employer to have a safety committee is confined to trade union safety representatives.

The code of practice on safety representatives recommends that safety representatives take an overall and general view of their duties, rather than the narrow one of only representing their own union members. The code goes on to advise that the number of representatives appointed within an organization should bear some relationship to several factors. These include: its total number of employees; its variety of occupations; the size of the workplace and its locations; the operation of shiftwork; the types of work activity; and the degree of inherent danger within them. Other factors to be considered when appointing safety representatives are: the rate of

change taking place in working conditions; its technology and manpower levels; and the problems of workplaces with high risks such as in steel and in chemicals, and those with low risks but with specific danger areas within them. Where possible, safety representatives are expected to have at least two years' experience of the workplace or similar workplaces with the same safety problems.

The advised functions of safety representatives include keeping themselves informed of the general legal requirements on health and safety at work and the specific legal hazards facing the employees whom they represent. They are expected to know the best precautionary measures available to protect employees. They should conduct regular inspections of the workplace and investigate the circumstances relating to accidents and known high-risk work situations. Safety representatives must also be fully aware of their employer's safety policy and should help keep it up to date as well as encouraging co-operation with its objectives by all employees. They are advised to bring all known safety hazards to the attention of the employer and to assist in taking measures designed to reduce such hazards. Where possible, safety representatives are encouraged to keep standard written records and to make them available for inspection by all those concerned with health and safety matters at the workplace.

When Safety Inspectors visit a workplace, management and safety representatives have to be given copies of their reports and of any advice provided. Current safety regulations make it clear that criminal charges cannot be brought against safety representatives when accidents happen or when failures to meet the requirements of any safety legislation occur. According to the HSC:

> the Commission have directed that the Health and Safety Executive shall not institute criminal proceedings against any safety representative for any act or omission by him in respect of the performance of functions assigned to him by the Regulations or indicated by the Code of Practice.[33]

The regulations strongly recommend the establishment of voluntary joint management and safety representative committees. If an employer refuses to establish a safety committee, a complaint can be made to an industrial tribunal by the safety representatives of independent recognized trade unions. The tribunal can then issue an award compelling the employer to establish a safety committee within a three-month period, after consultation with the safety representatives and union officials. Notices must be published for the attention of all employees, announcing the formation of the safety committee, its membership, the area which it covers and the safety policy that it has to implement. The HSC advises that specific safety committees shall be established and that health and safety matters should not be made a subsidiary or additional responsibility of, say, a works negotiating committee. It also advises the establishment of separate safety committees for clearly distinguishable geographical establishments. In very large workplaces it may be necessary to have more than one safety committee.

## Duties of safety committees

The functions of safety committees are largely determined by management and safety representatives. It is suggested that their functions should include the following: a careful statistical study of accidents; health trends; notifiable diseases; known hazards and 'near misses'; and the formulation of precautionary policies to reduce the incidence of accidents. Further functions include: safety audits; joint safety inspections at regular intervals; the consideration of Inspectors' reports on the workplace; the reports arising out of special inspections and investigations by safety representatives; the joint production of works safety rules and safe working systems; the organization of safety training and of visits by health and safety experts; and annual inspections of the complete workplace by the whole safety committee. Lastly, the HSC advises that the composition of safety committees:

> should be settled in consultation between management and the trade union representatives concerned through the use of the normal machinery. The aim should be to keep the total size as reasonably compact as possible and compatible with the adequate representation of the interests of management and all the employees, including safety representatives. The number of management representatives should not exceed the number of employees' representatives.[34]

Under the powers given by the 1974 Act, the HSE has issued a stream of major regulations, codes of practice, guidance notes and consultative documents. Regulations which greatly extend the duties and responsibilities of employers cover such things as:

the classification, packaging, labelling and use of dangerous substances; the transportation by road of dangerous substances; dangerous and noxious emissions into the atmosphere; first-aid requirements at the workplace; the protection of young people on government training schemes; poisonous agricultural substances; the notification of accidents and dangerous occurrences; and many other matters vital to the safety of working people.

The emphasis of the HSC's concerns during the 1980s has shifted towards a growing awareness of the need to safeguard the long-term health of workers. This is where their type of work, or contact with potentially dangerous substances, could cause serious health problems later. The greatest force for change is now coming from the EU and there is a stream of Directives for improving health and safety at work.

## 10.8   Emergency Powers, Public Employees and Political Strikes

## Public safety

Governments have long recognized that extensive and prolonged strikes or strikes which endanger life, essential services, public health, national security and property cannot be permitted to go unchecked. Yet this presents considerable political and legal difficulties in a country where the liberty to strike, after due observance of the legal requirements, has been firmly established. Virtually all industrial countries possess some legislative provisions to protect essential services, 'or to deal with the problem of the termination of supplies or the withdrawal of the means of supply by reason of industrial action.'[35] But in Britain the tradition of voluntarism in industrial relations, especially in the freedom to strike and the process of collective bargaining, has ensured until recently that government possesses relatively fewer controls in these respects than in most other western industrial countries. Section 5 of the Conspiracy and Protection of Property Act 1875 (now contained in TULRC Act 1992), however, still allows for criminal prosecutions where any workers breaking their contracts of employment are likely to cause serious bodily harm or injury to valuable property. This criminal provision is little used yet it remains on statute.

## Emergency powers

The Emergency Powers Acts of 1920 and 1964 enabled governments faced with severe disruptive industrial action to declare a state of emergency. This is where it appears that:

> there have occurred, or are about to occur, events of such a nature as to be calculated, by interfering with the supply and distribution of food, water, fuel or light, or with the means of locomotion, to deprive the community, or any substantial portion of the community, of the essentials of life.[36]

Such a declaration of an emergency can only be made by Parliament and lasts for one month, although the period can be extended if Parliament decides. In practice, such emergencies have not lasted very long. During an emergency period, orders in council can be issued to secure the preservation of peace and the maintenance of essential supplies and services. Such orders, giving wide powers to governments, must be laid before Parliament and last for seven days at a time. Such orders, however, cannot forbid strikes or peaceful picketing or require a person to return to work. Moreover, existing criminal law may not be changed and orders seeking to impose fines and imprisonment upon striking employees without trial are not permitted by the Act.

The aim of the 1920 Act is to facilitate direct government action during emergencies, without introducing new and arbitrary criminal sanctions against any section of the community. It does not restrict the right of Parliament to control the use of emergency powers and the length of time for which they remain in force. The Emergency Powers Act 1964 further extends the powers of the 1920 Act by permitting a government to use the armed forces on 'urgent work of national importance' without any consultation with Parliament. This Act is primarily intended to deal with natural catastrophes. But it could be used in damaging trade disputes, as, for example, where the withdrawal of their labour by fire-fighters requires the government to use the armed forces to fight fires and to save lives and property. In fact, emergency powers and orders issued under the emergency powers legislation have been used only twelve times since 1920 – during the General Strike of 1926, in four dock strikes and in strikes involving electricity workers, railway workers, seafarers and mineworkers.

The most determined, though subsequently abort-ive, attempt by government since the Second World War to place severe restrictions on industrial action 'in the public interest' were contained in the Industrial Relations Act 1971. This gave powers to the Secretary of State for Employment to apply to the National Industrial Relations Court (NIRC) (now EAT) for an order directing those responsible not to organize strike action for a period of up to 60 days. These provisions for a 'cooling off' period were aimed at preventing strikes which could, among other things, be 'gravely injurious to the national economy' or 'create serious risk of public disorder'. This Act also permitted the Secretary of State to apply to the NIRC, in similar circumstances, for a compulsory ballot of union members, under the supervision of the Commission on Industrial Relations, asking them if they wished to support a strike called by their union's executive or its leaders. Both these devices were clearly an extension of the powers of the State to prevent damaging strikes. These powers, along with the 1971 Act, were repealed by the Trade Union and Labour Relations Act 1974.

## Public employees

Only a minority of people would deny the freedom to strike granted to the vast majority of workers to groups of employees doing essential public service jobs, such as firefighters or ambulance drivers. Few, equally, would deny to government the right to use the armed forces to provide a skeleton service in those areas of employment where life, limb and property are placed in jeopardy by striking workers. It is a question of public opinion and political judgement when to invoke emergency powers whose use could easily exacerbate an already difficult strike situation, on the one hand, but whose absence would equally result in the breakdown of essential public services and public order on the other.

There have also been limitations placed in the past on the freedom to strike of some public sector employees. The Conspiracy and Protection of Property Act 1875, for example, provided criminal sanctions against workers in the water and gas industries who:

> wilfully and maliciously broke a contract of service with that authority knowing or having reasonable cause to believe that the probable consequence of his so doing, either alone or in combination, would be to deprive the inhabitants of the area covered by the authority of the whole

or the greater part of their supply of that commodity.[37]

The electricity supply industry was added to this list in 1919. The Merchant Shipping Acts of 1894 and 1970 similarly provided criminal sanctions against striking seafarers on board ship, implicitly linking such strikes with the concept of mutiny on the high seas. Seafarers can strike, however, providing that 48 hours' notice is given after their ship has reached port in the United Kingdom and they comply with the law requiring a secret ballot approving the taking of industrial action under the TULRC Act 1992.

The police, but not prison officers, also are forbidden to strike by the Police Act 1919, which was enacted following a police strike in that year. This Act made it unlawful for members of the police forces to join a trade union, but the Police Act 1964 permits them to join the Police Federations, which represent police officers over pay and conditions of service. Whilst not technically trade unions the Police Federations act very much like them. Members of the British armed forces can join a trade union but they cannot take any form of industrial action. Similarly, the Post Office Act 1953 makes it an offence for post office workers to interfere with the delivery of mail for political or sympathetic strike purposes. In this case, it is only the Attorney-General who can initiate a prosecution against postal workers. The Industrial Relations Act 1971 repealed those provisions in the Conspiracy and Protection of Property Act 1875 threatening workers in essential public services with criminal proceedings for taking strike action. It is now only the police, therefore, who are explicitly forbidden by law to strike or to take part in other industrial action against their employers.

The Energy Act 1976 gives government considerable powers enabling it to ensure that electricity supply is maintained. This Act was passed after the miners' strikes of 1972 and 1974. It was not used during the year-long miners' strike of 1984–85, since the power stations were not directly involved and police action prevented pickets closing them. The only group of employees, other than the police, who are prevented from either joining a union or taking part in industrial action are those in the secret services and, since 1984, civil servants employed at the Government Communications Headquarters at Cheltenham (GCHQ). The government took this step on the grounds that union membership and the freedom to strike were incompatible with national security. This caused fierce opposition and con-

troversy but the decision was upheld by the courts, including the House of Lords.

## 'Political' industrial action

It is common for governments to try to draw a distinction between 'political', 'economic' and 'ordinary' strikes. Strikes in pursuit of purely economic objectives, such as higher pay or better working conditions, for example, are usually regarded as being normal and even acceptable. However, strikes aimed at social objectives such as those to advance nationalization, to oppose privatization or to combat public spending cuts are regarded by some as being political, unfair and unconstitutional methods of achieving the ends. Yet it is extremely difficult if not impossible in practice to distinguish between economic and political strikes. An attempt to redistribute income from profits to pay, for example, can be seen as a political activity in much the same way that redistributive changes in income tax are political. Many trade unionists declare that it is impossible to separate economic from political aims in industrial relations.

Furthermore, governments intervene in so many aspects of economic activity today that any attempt to draw a meaningful distinction between politics and economics almost certainly ends in failure. At the same time, some trade unions have long held social objectives such as increased old age pensions, full employment policies, the nationalization of key industries and high levels of public spending on welfare provisions, although these have generally been pursued through the manifesto commitments of the Labour Party rather than by direct industrial action. The question could also be asked whether a strike by employees in pursuit of a pay claim in excess of a maximum stipulated by a government as an essential element of its pay policy is an economic strike or a political one. It would appear, then, that the concept of the political strike owes more to ideological distinctions rather than to any clear analytical separation between what are political ends and means and what are economic ones.

It has often been held, for instance, that general strikes are political because they aim to bring down a constitutionally elected government or are designed to make it abandon a legislative course of action. The General Strike of 1926 was held by the then government to be political, unconstitutional and unlawful, whilst the TUC insisted that it was a sympathy strike aimed at helping the mineworkers resist a wage cut caused by the withdrawal of coal subsidies by the government. After its victory in the General Strike, the Conservative government passed the Trade Disputes and Trade Unions Act 1927 making general and sympathetic strikes unlawful; the Act was repealed in 1946. Other examples serve to illustrate the confusion which exists over what constitutes a political strike. A strike by dock workers in 1970, for example, sought to advance the nationalization of the docks at a time when a Bill for a partial nationalization was before Parliament. In 1966, at the height of the seafarers' official strike for higher pay in breach of the government's current incomes policy, the prime minister declared in Parliament that it was a strike against the State by a tightly knit group of politically motivated men. Sporadic strikes occurred during and after the passing of the Industrial Relations Act 1971 by unions and by groups of workers opposed to it. Also after the election of the first Thatcher government in 1979, some trade unions organized strikes, rallies, marches and national days of protest against the Employment Acts of 1980 and 1982, cuts in public expenditure and plans to privatize some of the nationalized industries.

The coal dispute of 1984–85 was portrayed by the government as a direct challenge to the authority of the State and as a thinly disguised attempt to overthrow a constitutionally elected government. Those taking part in the strike and those supporting it were described by the Prime Minister as 'the enemy within'. The leadership of the National Union of Mineworkers asserted that the strike was only intended to prevent the closing of mines and the loss of coalmining jobs. The outcome of this strike, a return to work without a settlement, was determined without recourse to the Emergency Powers Acts. It was probably the most bitter, violent and prolonged dispute since the strikes of 1910–14. The miners' defeat was made possible by the success of the police in containing the picketing and the movement of miners across the country. The miners were also weakened by lack of direct support from the TUC, closely related unions and the Labour Party. The laws on secondary picketing, contained in the Employment Act 1980, also helped to make the use of emergency powers unnecessary. This experience probably made the Conservative government realize the limited effectiveness of the emergency powers legislation, compared with other devices of State power and social control.

In all these cases, it would appear that the strikers could not or would not distinguish between the political objectives of these strikes and their own economic self-interest. Whilst political strikes, general strikes and sympathetic strikes in Britain are not criminal, the TULRC Act 1992 appears to render political strikes liable to actions for civil damages by redefining a trade dispute in Section 244. This limits lawful trade disputes to those between workers and their employer. Further, a union only possesses legal immunity in a trade dispute which 'relates wholly or mainly to' those matters defined in Sections 178 and 244 of the 1992 Act, rather than being only 'connected with' them. The general effect of these two changes is to make it possible for employers to bring cases for civil damages in trade disputes, where it is claimed that the dispute is not between the employer and its workers, or where the strike is not closely connected with those matters listed in Section 178 of the 1992 Act. To date, very few employers have chosen to do so. Obviously, many of the examples of so-called political strikes given above would be potentially open to civil action should employers wish to take it. Equally, these two changes in the legal meaning of a trade dispute make sympathy strikes potentially actionable for civil damages. More importantly, perhaps, these legal changes make it possible for employers to obtain injunctions stopping strike action which they argue is political in its nature and intent. As a practical method of stopping strikes, since 1982 employers have found injunctions more attractive than bitter and protracted court actions. If injunctions serve their purpose of stopping a strike, little is achieved by proceeding with civil actions for damages against the unions.

## 10.9  Summary Points

- Collective labour law regulating the relationship between trade unions and the State, trade unions and their members, trade unions and employers, and industrial action has gone through three historical stages since the early nineteenth century: first, legal control through the application of the common law; second, legal abstentionism, 'voluntarism' or collective *laissez-faire*; third, close regulation by statute, or 'juridification'.

- In order for trade unions to exist, for collective bargaining to develop and for workers to take industrial action, the law has had to acknowledge their legitimacy and fundamental rights; and, while requiring the observance of detailed legal requirements in their practice, provide the means for the legal enforcement or protection of these rights.

- Much of the legislation concerning trade unions passed since 1979 has been aimed at providing union members with the means to determine and control the policies and activities of their union. The principal legal device fashioned for the achievement of this purpose has been the secret fully postal ballot.

- After decades of political and moral struggle and debate, mainly about the closed or union shop, the law now equates the right of a person to be a member of a trade union with the right not to be a member. The present legal position on trade union membership is likely to stand, because it complies with most international and European conventions on human rights.

- The right of trade unions to call industrial action, and the right of union members to take industrial action, are now very closely regulated by a web of legal requirements, which, if not carefully observed, can expose trade unions to the granting of labour injunctions and damages by the courts to employers and others. At the heart of the legal processes which a union must closely observe in order to take lawful industrial action lies the secret postal ballot of members.

- For industrial action, including picketing, to be lawful it must take place between an employer and its employees and 'relate wholly or mainly' to certain aspects of the relationship between employer and employee. So-called secondary and sympathy industrial action is unlawful. The key to the enforcement of this legal position by employers has, since 1979, proved to be the labour injunction.

- Changes in the law since 1979 have greatly enhanced the rights and powers of individual union members who seek redress for alleged unfair treatment by their union, expulsion or refusal of membership. In order to prosecute their case, they can seek the assistance of the Commissioner for the Rights of Trade Union Members.

- The law relating to picketing during an industrial dispute is now narrowly confined to those workers who are in dispute with their employer at their place of work, or closely related place of work. The number of pickets can be confined to as few as six if the police and the courts so decide. Experience during the 1980s suggests, however, that it is planning and action by the police which prevents or stops 'mass' picketing, and the use of 'flying' pickets, rather than the law and the courts.

- Somewhat surprisingly given the deeply interventionist nature of the labour law passed since 1979, collective agreements between trade unions and employers remain unenforceable at law, unless an agreement states in writing that it is the intention of both the parties that it should be legally enforceable. However, all governments since 1979 have made clear through public policy their dislike of collective bargaining and have sought to dismantle it in the public sector. Government has also removed from ACAS the duty to promote collective bargaining. What government intends to replace collective bargaining with, as a means of determining the pay and conditions of very large numbers of employees, is still unclear.

- The Health and Safety at Work Act 1974 has proved to be one of the most effective, durable and creative pieces of legislation in the field of employment since the Second World War. Above all, it has largely shifted the responsibility for the enforcement of health and safety law, regulations, codes and standards from the State and its enforcement agencies to employers and employees. In recent years the major concern of the State, employers, trade unions and employees has shifted from accidents and injuries to the long-term effect on the health of workers of exposure to dangerous substances and working practices. Major initiatives now emanate from the EU, rather than Parliament.

- Experience during the 1980s in controlling protracted and bitter industrial disputes, which threatened public order and/or essential services, suggests that the use of court injunctions, the control of secondary strikes, and rapid and strong police action were more effective than resort to emergency powers legislation.

- Almost all the legislation now regulating collective labour law and the trade unions, including that dating from the late nineteenth and early twentieth centuries, is to be found in the Trade Union and Labour Relations (Consolidation) Act 1992.

## 10.10  References

1. O. Kahn-Freund, *Labour and the Law*, Stevens, London, 1977, p. 9.
2. *Conservative Party Manifesto*, Conservative Central Office, London, 1979.
3. K. J. Mackie, Changes in the law since 1979: an overview, in B. Towers (ed.), *A Handbook of Industrial Relations Practice*, Kogan Page, London, 1987, p. 254.

4. R. Lewis, Collective labour law, in G. S. Bain (ed.), *Industrial Relations in Britain*, Blackwell, Oxford, 1983, p. 383.

5. K. W. Wedderburn, *The Worker and the Law*, Penguin, Harmondsworth, 1971, p. 410.

6. Trade Union and Labour Relations (Consolidation) Act 1992, s. 1.

7. Kahn-Freund, *op. cit.*, p. 220.

8. R. W. Rideout, *Principles of Labour Law*, Sweet and Maxwell, London, 1976, p. 257.

9. *Ibid.*, p. 263.

10. *Crofter Hand Woven Harris Tweed Company Limited* v. *Veitch* (1942), quoted in Wedderburn, *op. cit.*, p. 340.

11. Kahn-Freund, *op. cit.*, p. 225.

12. *Ibid.*

13. Anthony Ferner and Richard Hyman, *Industrial Relations in the New Europe*, Blackwell, Oxford, 1992, p. 17.

14. Trade Union and Labour Relations (Consolidation) Act 1992, s. 241.

15. Trade Disputes Act 1906 6 Edw. VII c. 47, s. 2.

16. Kahn-Freund, *op. cit.*, p. 193.

17. Steven D. Anderman, *Labour Law, Management Decisions and Workers' Rights*, Butterworths, London, 1992, p. 253.

18. Kahn-Freund, *op. cit.*, p. 127.

19. Rideout, *op. cit.*, p. 59.

20. Kahn-Freund, *op. cit.*, p. 122.

21. Trade Union and Labour Relations (Consolidation) Act 1992, ss. 179 and 180.

22. *Ibid.*, s. 181.

23. *Ibid.*, s. 182.

24. *Ibid.*, s. 183.

25. Advisory Conciliation and Arbitration Service, *Code of Practice 2. Disclosure of Information for Collective Bargaining Purposes*, HMSO, London, 1977, p. 1.

26. *Ibid.*, p. 4.

27. S. Webb, Introduction to Hutchins and Harrison, *A History of Factory Legislation*, 1903, p. vii, quoted in K. W. Wedderburn, *op. cit.*, p. 241.

28. Report of the Committee, *Safety and Health at Work* (Robens Report), HMSO, London, 1972, p. 18.

29. Health and Safety at Work etc. Act, 1974, c. 37, s. 2.

30. Rideout, *op. cit.*, p. 386.

31. Health and Safety at Work etc. Act 1974, c. 37, s. 12.

32. Robens Report, *op. cit.*, p. 22.

33. Health and Safety Commission, *Safety Representatives and Safety Committees*, HMSO, London, 1977, p. 15.

34. *Ibid.*, p. 39.

35. Rideout, *op. cit.*, p. 334.

36. Emergency Powers Act 1920, quoted in *ibid.* p. 335.

37. Conspiracy and Protection of Property Act 1875 38 and 39 Vict, c. 86.

# PART FOUR

## Industrial Relations in Practice

# 11

# Management and Employment Practices

'The right to manage', also known as 'managerial prerogative', 'managerial rights' or 'managerial functions', is at the centre of industrial relations decision making. The right to manage has always been jealously guarded by those managing organizations whether as owner managers or as professional managers of corporate employers. Similarly, trade unions, their representatives and union members have continuously coveted, challenged and sought to share through collective bargaining those managerial prerogatives most affecting employee interests at corporate and workplace level. Having indicated in Chapters 9 and 10 how externally generated labour law affects the unilateral right to manage by managers within organizations, we turn in this chapter to examine the nature of managerial prerogative and those areas of enterprise decision making where it remains strong today. Indeed, the evidence shows that since the early 1980s the right to manage in Britain has been firmly reasserted by managers, in both the private and the public sectors. This is indicated by the development of firm-specific labour market and organization-based employment systems. These contrast with the traditional reliance by employers 'on the external labour market for labour supply, and on industry-wide wage-fixing institutions for the determination of basic terms and conditions of employment'. Through deregulation of the labour market, management has increasingly been able to achieve its aims in labour management 'through a rediscovery of the management prerogative'.[1]

## 11.1 The Right to Manage

The right to manage relates to those areas of corporate and workplace decision making which managements consider to be exclusively theirs and hence are not subject either to collective bargaining with trade union representatives or to legal regulation. Such rights were traditionally taken to include the hiring and firing of employees, promotion, discipline, manning, production control, overtime alloca-tion and other job-related issues. Marsh argues that the notion of managerial prerogative 'carries with it the implication that there are actions or areas for action so essential to management that these must remain unilaterally the property of management if management itself is to continue to exist'.[2] However, since recognized trade unions seek to constrain unilateral managerial control within work organiza-tions, the question arises whether there is any logical limit to the extent to which trade unions can penetrate into the traditional functions of management. Where unions are recognized for collective bargaining purposes, therefore, the right to manage is never absolute. Even where there are no trade unions, works councils and informal customs and practices can effectively constrain the right to manage in many areas of job decision making. Nevertheless, with weakened trade unionism since the early 1980s and with changes in the law favouring employers, there is little doubt that managerial prerogative has been reinforced in recent years, with managerial confi-dence in industrial relations decision making growing accordingly.

Any definitive description of managerial pre-rogative is problematic, since the term has a number of different meanings. In practice, there is no clear distinction from one industry to another of what exactly constitutes a solely managerial function. The industry where the struggle to retain the so-called right to manage has been most bitterly fought in Britain is engineering. After the national lock-out in the industry in 1897–98 and under the terms of settle-ment dated 28 January 1898, the federated employers insisted they would 'admit no interference with the management of their business'. They also reserved the right to introduce into any federated workshops, at the option of the employer, any condition of labour operational at the beginning of the dispute. The agreement did not apply, however, to the determina-tion of hours of work or rates of pay. Similarly, in the Managerial Functions Agreement of 1922, the parties agreed that 'The Employers have the right to manage their establishments and the Trade Unions have the right to exercise their functions'.[3]

The reasons why engineering employers have continuously asserted their right to manage are not difficult to identify, although they derive largely from nineteenth century circumstances. The first justification for the right to manage was the claim that private owners of industrial capital, or their appointed agents, had the right to do as they wished with what they owned or were responsible for. More importantly, the insistence by the engineering employers on their managerial functions was also a product of nineteenth century craft trade unionism. The early craft unions in the engineering trades did not wish to negotiate with employers on terms and conditions but wanted to impose their own common rules of the trade upon employers unilaterally. They wanted in other words: to determine union pay rates for the job; to prevent 'de-skilling'; to lay down their own manning levels; to control overtime; and to regulate the supply of apprentices into their trades. They were also opposed to management introducing piecework payment systems. The engineering employers, in short, considered that they were being opposed by craft organizations which would accept no compromises with them. If trade union craft controls were to be rigidly insisted upon, the employers held, then there was no alternative other than to maintain their own exclusive right to manage within their enterprises. It remains a strong tradition in engineering and related industries today. A further justification of the right to manage is the 'economic efficiency argument'. This holds that professional managers alone, whether in private or public enterprises, have the necessary expertise and knowledge to make the 'right' decisions within their organizations. According to Storey, since managers are merely taking 'technical' decisions in their enterprises in the best interests of all parties, 'it would be wrong to prejudice their judgement with considerations of a partisan, political nature'.[4]

Seen in these contexts, the doctrine of managerial prerogative is not an easy orthodoxy to view sympathetically in modern democratic societies. Yet the struggle to maintain managerial prerogative continues in most work organizations. 'In a very real sense the conflict over managerial prerogative and functions is part of the struggle . . . for status and recognition'[5] by the employers' managerial elite: an elite based not on property rights, but on its claimed knowledge and skills of management techniques and business administration. The struggle is also

part of the conflict between management's need to innovate within enterprises and the employee's need for job security and job control. Ever since the early trade union challenges to management's virtually unrestricted powers in industry over a hundred years ago, managers have used the managerial prerogative argument in their own defence against further trade union and worker encroachments into managerial functions and of their responsibility for enterprise efficiency and success. Any restriction on this prerogative, they argue, is bound to result in lower economic performance and loss of managerial control. Contemporary employer opposition to the European Union's Charter of Fundamental Social Rights of Workers has to be seen in this context.

Notwithstanding these points, the union role is by definition primarily one of attempting to limit the powers of managements to make decisions unilaterally within both private and public enterprises in matters affecting their members' employment and job interests. By its very nature trade unionism is a device aimed at containing managerial prerogatives. Yet despite the restrictions put on management's right to manage by trade unions, economic performance within work organizations does not seem to have been unduly hampered by their presence. It could be argued, in fact, that management's capacity to adapt itself to the conditions imposed by the presence of trade unions is generally underestimated by many managers, even today. Indeed, it has been suggested 'that further restrictions on managerial prerogative by the workers would be more likely to improve than to endanger organizational performance'.[6] It is also clear that although many managers continue to assume that there are some prerogatives which trade unions must never be allowed to encroach upon, they are increasingly hazy about their boundaries. Taken to its logical extreme:

> Within a system of management by agreement there would no longer exist any area of management decision-taking where management itself could claim an absolute and unilateral right to resist union influence in any form.[7]

Managerial prerogative today, then, may most usefully be defined as 'the residue of discretionary powers of decision left to management when the regulative impacts of law and collective agreements have been subtracted'.[8] Although some unions disclaim any desire to participate in management, just as management contests the right of trade unions to obviate its own functions, the extent to which collective bargaining, in containing managerial prerogatives, becomes participation in management is a matter of degree. Further, where collective bargaining affects any aspects of organizational decision making, a form of worker participation in management exists, but only if trade unions are recognized for collective bargaining purposes by employers.

In short, although trade union penetration of managerial prerogatives is likely to be greatest in those areas most closely associated with personnel management – such as in pay determination, conditions of employment, job security and methods of working – only practical and balance of power considerations place actual limits on trade union interest in the technical aspects of present day managerial functions. What were the boundaries of managerial rights in the past are natural areas of collective bargaining today. Furthermore, what seem to be the boundaries of managerial rights today might well be natural areas of collective bargaining and participation in the future. Whilst employees do not appear to demand participation in all managerial decisions, it is 'neither practicable nor desirable to draw up a list of decisions which should be for ever exclusively management's business'.[9] It has to be recognized, however, that with high unemployment and weakened trade unionism for over a decade now, the right to manage has been strengthened and the balance of decision-making power has swung strongly in management's favour at corporate and workplace levels.

## 11.2 Discipline, Dismissal and Company Handbooks

It is not generally realized the extent to which the growth of early market capitalism imposed severe constraints on the daily working lives of ordinary people. These included strict rules on time-keeping, regular attendance at work, maintaining standards on the job, obeying unquestioningly the orders of their 'masters', and generally conforming to the rules of the workplace. Adjustment to these new circumstances of work did not come easily and one of the early prerogatives imposed by the 'masters' on their 'servants' was a harsh and rigid industrial discipline. Well into this century, conditions of employment were strictly regulated in most workplaces and employees were tightly controlled by managerial authority alone. In the railway workshops at Crewe around 1900, for example:

No smoking was allowed. Suspension was the usual penalty . . . on one occasion a man was dismissed on the spot for knocking out an unlit pipe against a door-post. Employees were not allowed to wash their hands, under pain of instant dismissal. Two visits to the lavatory in one day could mean suspension.[10]

Clearly, the main purposes of disciplinary rules of this sort were to deter and to deal out retribution to recalcitrant workers within a system of rigid managerial control. Today disciplinary rules serve different purposes and are normally incorporated, together with works rules and other sources of corporate information, in company handbooks.

### Company rules

The old style of industrial discipline derived from the belief that it was solely management's prerogative to make decisions, especially on disciplinary matters, and that there should be no restrictions on this right, particularly from subordinates. Such a view of workplace discipline was invariably combined with either an authoritarian or a paternalistic style of management. It normally coincided with a set of disciplinary rules harshly administered, inconsistently applied and arbitrarily enforced. As employing establishments grew in size, and as employers were forced to delegate their disciplinary authority to lower levels of management, it was first line supervisors who emerged with almost absolute powers of hiring and firing subordinate workers. The main written sources of these disciplinary regulations were the so-called 'works rules', now normally called 'company rules'. These were usually a comprehensive code of written rules drawn up unilaterally by the employers to regulate the behaviour of subordinates in their establishments. They were regarded by the courts as express terms of the contracts of employment between individuals and their employers, infringements of which could result in fines, suspension from duty, or instant dismissal.

A detailed examination of works rule books in the engineering industry concludes that they are full of wide-ranging claims of the rights of management and strongly worded clauses referring to the obligations of employees. They cover five main items at the workplace: engagement; the employee's duties and the authority of management; pay and welfare services; explicit rules of workplace behaviour; and suspension or termination of employment. It is suggested that they serve 'contractual', 'precautionary', 'regulative', 'informative' and 'expressive' purposes. Through the latter, for instance, managements seek legitimacy for their works rules and for administering them. 'In the light of these considerations works rule books seem to operate as one of the most explicit instruments of enterprise government at the workplace'.[11] Some organizations are now bringing their works rules into the area of joint regulation, by attaching them to written local agreements negotiated with trade unions.

Works rules or company rules, then, continue to exist in most establishments today but are no longer the sole source of disciplinary authority. In law 'works rules seem to have a kind of intermediate place between the collectively regulated parts of the employment contract and the parts which are purely individual'. Nowadays, company rules are intended to do a great deal more than merely to make known to employees an employer's disciplinary requirements. They are found in a variety of forms. In some cases, they are simply occasional notices fixed to works notice-boards informing employees of general instructions from management. In other cases, the separate instructions are collected together in a booklet described as the 'Works Rules Book', 'Conditions of Employment', or the 'Employee Handbook'. With successive revisions the text expands to become 'an amalgam of disciplinary rules, warnings, advice, claims to managerial "rights", pension fund regulations, information about the firm's welfare benefits, and so on'.[12]

## Disciplinary and dismissal procedures

For a number of reasons, disciplinary practices have changed considerably in recent years. Capital invested in the training of employees, for example, has increased the value of human resources at work, 'making the indiscriminate use of disciplinary action, especially dismissal, even more wasteful'.[13] Furthermore, most full-time employees have a statutory right not to be unfairly dismissed by their employers after two years of continuous employment. Also, management's powers to take unilateral decisions on disciplinary matters have been curtailed by the challenge of trade union organization, where unions are recognized. At the very least, where unions are recognized, they normally have the right to represent their members when disciplinary action is taken against them. In these circumstances, the unilateral managerial right to discipline employees is no longer

absolute. On the one hand, punitive managerial sanctions against employees suspected of disciplinary infringements have given way to corrective action being taken against them. This is, first, to win their co-operation and, second, to promote self-discipline on their part. On the other hand, most managements now take a less authoritarian approach to disciplinary matters in any case. They do this by not only trying to develop fair and consistent disciplinary policies, but also accepting the legitimacy of union involvement in administering them, for categories of employees with negotiating procedures.

Broadly, there are eight main categories of workplace offence which can lead to disciplinary action against employees: negligence; unreliability; insubordination; interfering with the rights of other employees; damaging corporate property; endangering safety; immoral conduct; and theft. Although company rules, the employee handbook and, to a lesser extent, collective agreements constitute the formal sources of management's disciplinary authority, custom and practice or unwritten understandings in the workplace also have an important influence on management's reactions to alleged infringements of works discipline. The two main approaches which management uses to achieve improved standards of discipline within the workplace are preventative and corrective. Preventative measures include effective recruitment, selection and promotion procedures and fitting the person to the job within an organization. Training and communication systems are also important means of preventing disciplinary problems arising amongst employees. New recruits particularly need to be made aware of the standards of workplace discipline required by their employers.

The corrective approach to discipline at work is now more common. Its purpose is to give individuals the chance to change and modify their behaviour through a series of warnings and progressively more severe penalties after repeated instances of misconduct. The potential penalties available to management vary in their severity and in their impact. They include verbal and written warnings, fines, suspensions, job transfers and ultimately dismissal. Verbal warnings, for instance, can be either informal or formal and are normally used as a minor penalty. Somewhat more serious is the written warning, set down on a special form to ensure that the recipient knows the consequences of repeating the same or worse offences. Among unionized workforces, it is common for written warnings to be given to employees in the presence of their workplace representative. Other sanctions used by management are fines and deductions on employees such as non-payment for time missed when an employee is late. In other cases, suspension is used for more serious offences. Similarly, demotion is occasionally applied in response to proved carelessness in a job, whilst job transfers are used to avoid indiscipline rather than as a penalty against it.

Dismissal is the ultimate sanction available to management in disciplinary cases against employees. Since many employees have a statutory right not to be unfairly dismissed by their employers, together with the right to challenge such dismissals before an industrial tribunal, the development of effective disciplinary rules and procedures within enterprises is vital to management and employees alike. In its code of practice on disciplinary procedures in employment, for example, the Advisory Conciliation and Arbitration Service (ACAS) advises that disciplinary procedures should not be viewed primarily as a means of imposing sanctions upon employees but should be designed to improve their personal conduct. Such procedures should also:

(a) Be in writing
(b) Specify to whom they apply
(c) Provide for matters to be dealt with quickly
(d) Indicate the disciplinary action which may be taken
(e) Specify the levels of management which have the authority to take the various forms of disciplinary action, ensuring that immediate supervisors do not normally have the power to dismiss without reference to senior management
(f) Provide for individuals to be informed of the complaints against them and to be given an opportunity to state their case before decisions are reached
(g) Give individuals the right to be accompanied by a trade union representative, or by a fellow employee of their choice
(h) Ensure that, except for gross misconduct, no employees are dismissed for a first breach of discipline
(i) Ensure that disciplinary action is not taken until the case has been carefully investigated
(j) Ensure that individuals are given an explanation for any penalty imposed
(k) Provide a right of appeal and specify the procedure to be followed.[14]

ACAS strongly recommends that formal, written and recognized disciplinary procedures are established within enterprises. Management usually initiates the drawing up of such procedures. But, where trade unions are recognized for bargaining purposes, it is essential that they accept the fairness of the disciplinary rules applying to their members. Where management has an agreed disciplinary procedure with the trade unions, it needs to decide whether or not non-unionists have the same rights under it as do employees belonging to the recognized unions. Evidence provided by the workplace industrial relations surveys suggests that 'in 1990, as in 1984, it was clear that disciplinary procedures had been agreed in 90 per cent of establishments where trade unions were recognized'.[15]

Disciplinary procedures, it is suggested, comprise two distinct but interrelated parts. On the one hand, there is the enforcement of discipline by a system of progressively more severe sanctions administered by successive levels of management; this can be called the *administrative* procedure. 'On the other hand, there is a corresponding series of stages which allows employees recourse to appeal against the disciplinary sanctions imposed; in other words, the *appeals* procedure'.[16] The key features of such procedures are, first, that the responsibility for taking disciplinary action rests with management. It is management which investigates the case, sets the penalty to be enforced and informs the employee of this intention. Second, employees have the right not only to be represented by their trade unions at disciplinary hearings but also to appeal against any penalty imposed by management if they consider this to be unfair.

In most disciplinary matters, it is normal practice for the supervisor or first line manager to give a series of verbal warnings to the offending employee. If the employee's behaviour fails to improve, the next stage of a typical procedure is for the supervisor, in consultation with the employee's workplace representative, to issue a formal written warning to the employee. After repeated minor offences, or a more serious offence, the employee receives a final written warning from the departmental manager after consultation with the workplace representative. Further offences can lead to the suspension of the employee by the departmental manager, following consultation with the senior workplace representative and the personnel department. In practice, because of the wide variety of behaviour constituting misconduct, and because of the need for consistency in dealing with these matters, the personnel department often becomes involved at an early stage in the procedure to avoid disputes and to ensure that the proper procedures are being followed. Finally, where additional infringements of disciplinary rules by the offending employee or gross misconduct occur, the ultimate sanction is dismissal. It is normally the responsibility of senior management to take this decision after it has consulted with the senior workplace representative and the personnel department.

At all stages of the disciplinary procedure, the employee normally has recourse to a parallel appeals procedure. This can either be a separate procedure, or more usually, the grievance procedure through which issues are raised by trade union members and their representatives. At each disciplinary level, an appeal against disciplinary sanctions by management can be taken up by the employee's trade union representative, where this is asked for. Such appeals are heard by higher management, culminating with an appeal to top management.

A typical chain of appeal from supervisory level upwards is through the disciplined employee's workplace representative to the departmental manager in the first instance. If this is unsuccessful, it is followed by an appeal to senior line management through the senior workplace representative. The last internal appeal is usually made to top line management, again through the senior workplace representative. In some cases, final access can also be obtained to independent third-party arbitration or to the national disputes procedure – although this is not often used. In a few unusual instances, some organizations have joint appeals procedures. These have equal representation of both managerial and trade union nominees. Normally, such committees are obliged to reach a unanimous decision. There are an even smaller number of organizations which have even more participative approaches to discipline. They use joint procedures for managing discipline. In these cases, both the administration of discipline and the hearing of appeals are jointly determined. These necessitate workplace representatives sitting with managerial representatives on formal joint disciplinary committees. The purpose of these joint committees is to investigate all reported disciplinary cases and, if necessary, to take disciplinary action against offending employees.

Most managers would view the joint approach to discipline as implying either a weakening of their own prerogative to discipline subordinate employees, or reflecting failure on the part of management to manage. Many workplace representatives are equally suspicious of joint disciplinary procedures,

because they fear that they could become too closely associated and incorporated with management in the workplace. In practice, a joint approach to discipline in both its administrative and its appeals aspects is only normally effective where relations between employers and unions are openly conducted, and where there is mutual trust between them and a tradition of good industrial relations.

To sum up, it is clear that the traditional right of management to discipline employees unilaterally is now constrained not only by statute law but also by the development of appeals procedures within properly designed disciplinary codes. Employers are expected to develop appropriate disciplinary and dismissal procedures and to use them in a reasonable and fair manner when dealing with employees. This last point was reinforced by the Polkey case in 1987, which is widely regarded to be of central significance for complaints of unfair dismissal. It has also influenced the way that employers and employees weigh up their chances before deciding whether to proceed to a tribunal or not. For some time it has been open to tribunals to find a dismissal fair, even where disciplinary procedures had not been followed by an employer. This was justified on the grounds that following a fair procedure would have made 'no difference' to the individual, because the individual would have been dismissed anyway. In the *Polkey* v *Dayton Services* decision, the House of Lords overturned the 'no difference' principle. Attention instead is focused on what the employer knew at the time of dismissal and whether the employer's procedure was reasonable. The effect of this is that a failure to follow a fair disciplinary procedure is likely to lead to a finding of unfair dismissal against the employer.

## Company handbooks

Company handbooks, sometimes known as 'employee handbooks' or 'organizational manuals', are used by employers for a variety of purposes. These include: as a source of reference; in fulfilling an employer's statutory requirements; as a means of communication; and as an aid to induction training. All employees need information about the organization which employs them, its rules and regulations, its safety and security requirements and its fringe benefits. Although prepared by management:

> No employee handbook should be a unilateral declaration by management. If employees are to take a serious interest in it, they should be

involved in deciding the content and their opinions sought on different methods of presentation.[17]

Since a company handbook is a means of providing intracorporate communication, such communications are improved when the parties communicating meet to discuss the aims, meanings and implications of the messages to be communicated. A company handbook is a useful source of reference on the organization. It provides background information on the company, on employment matters, on policies and procedures and on amenities. The sort of background information on the organization and on its products or services which is supplied includes: the employer's name and address; company history; products, services, markets and workforce; organization chart; and directors and senior management.

Since all employees working for eight or more hours a week are entitled to written particulars of their main terms and conditions of employment from their employer within two months of starting work, many companies and organizations find it useful to set these out in a company handbook. These include: payment method, intervals and deductions; periods of notice; lay-off arrangements; holiday entitlements; and so on. Other employment matters covered in company handbooks are: pensions; sickness and accident benefits; time off work provisions; maternity leave and payments; and various company rules. These include rules on: attendance and absence; accidents; security; safety; hygiene; and dress. Most company handbooks also specify employee benefits such as special loan arrangements, special leave arrangements, staff purchases and bonus payments.

Procedures and policies incorporated in company handbooks cover such areas as: health and safety; union membership, representation, recognition and collective bargaining; equal opportunity in relation to gender, race and age; workplace communications; discipline and grievances; training; retirement; and so on. Amenities and services are concerned with canteen, transport, social and sports club, parking and creche facilities. As a method of communication, company handbooks provide employees with information they need to know about the employer and indicate what kind of organization they work for. Handbooks emphasize the company's special needs, such as the importance of hygiene in food preparation or of customer service. They also make positive contributions to effective industrial relations and

ensure that misunderstandings about the employer, and its policies, are avoided. As an aid to induction training, company handbooks provide essential corporate information, assisting employees to settle into their jobs as smoothly and easily as possible.

Various formats of handbooks are used. Sometimes they are loose-leaf, enabling them to be amended quickly and cost-effectively. They can also be pocket-sized; this means that they are convenient, portable and the personal possession of each employee. Whatever the format, handbooks need to be regularly updated with supplements, additions and amendments. Systematic preparation of a company handbook is a useful contribution to effective employment policies and practices. Committing policies to writing helps identify the central issues and ensures that these are widely known by all employees in the organization.

## 11.3 Traditional Payment Systems

In the early days of market capitalism, the ways in which workers were paid for their labour services and their pay relationships were usually determined by the master alone. Both the wage payment system and the pay structure within the firm were unilaterally regulated by the owner managers and were claimed as a managerial prerogative. This is still the case in parts of private industry, especially within medium-sized and smaller companies which are not unionized. In general, however, payment systems and pay structures are mutually agreed where trade unions are recognized. Pay rates and pay relationships are then jointly determined by managerial and union representatives, within the appropriate collective bargaining machinery. But it remains the responsibility of management to administer the payment system and the pay structure in each case. Pay is a reward for employees, on the one hand, and a cost to employers on the other.

> For managers the pay system applied to employees may be seen as an important instrument of management policy; while employees may be more likely to see it in terms of maximising rewards and its impact on standards of living and job security.[18]

In selecting a particular payment system for a group of workers, management has traditionally adopted two main criteria. It has sought that method of payment which gives it the greatest degree of cost control and of supervisory power over subordinate employees, as well as providing the best incentive for efficient job performance by the employees themselves. In essence, management has had three choices. It can use a time rate system of flat-rate wages or salaries; it can pay employees by results; or it can combine both methods. A time rate payment system, for example, provides a standard level of pay for a given amount of time spent on the job, whether by the hour, day, month or year. There has normally been no direct link between payment received and the effort put into the job by employees on time rate payments systems. Payment by results (PBR) schemes, on the other hand, are 'based either on payment per piece produced or on a form of time allowed/time taken basis' which 'have in the past seemed a certain way of ensuring or improving output'[19] from the workforce.

## Wages and salaries

The traditional straight time rate payment system is the salary. The differences between a wage and a salary are both economic and social. Wage earners, for instance, are normally manual workers who are paid a basic hourly or weekly rate of pay, with supplements to their basic rate such as overtime, shiftwork, or bonus payments often negotiated between management and trade unions. The hourly paid are usually paid in cash directly for the work which they do, and the way in which it is done, rather than for what is done.

By contrast, salary earners – or 'the staff' as they are sometimes described – are normally white-collar employees. They receive a fixed flat-rate payment weekly, monthly or sometimes quarterly by cheque or credit transfer directly into their bank. Although some scales are negotiated for salaried employees, others are not. Even where they are, the point at which salaried employees are placed within these scales when starting employment often depends entirely upon management discretion. Salaried employees may be clerical, professional, technical, or managerial staff who usually have expectations of advancement based on age, seniority, qualifications, experience, or performance, to higher levels of monetary reward. The wage earner's expectations are much more limited.

The distinctions between traditional wage and salary payments emerged mainly for historical reasons. With the growth of market capitalism in the nineteenth century, wage payment systems provided flexibility for employers in response to fluctuating

work loads within their enterprises. In this way, they could relate wage payments to output, to productivity, or to the amounts of overtime worked by subordinates. By varying staffing levels in relation to the quantity of orders for their products, employers could control their labour costs and keep them as low as possible. Compared with manual workers, however, the number of white-collar workers within these organizations was fairly small. In return for their loyalty and commitment to the business or to the individual proprietor, these employees were given more favourable hours of work and better working conditions than were manual workers. These included security of employment, regular salaries, and better promotion chances. But they were also expected to work additional hours when necessary, with little or no extra payment for it.

Traditional salary payments are characterized:

by pay progressions, whether published or unpublished, related to increasing experience, quality of performance and career expectations, whether through the use of incremental scales, pay ranges, merit additions or promotions.[20]

A traditional salary system has two main features: first, it comprises a pay structure of differential payments and a related job structure; and second, it provides a set of rules and procedures defining the relationships between the pay and the job structures, the qualities necessary for movement within and between these structures, and the processes by which decisions are made when there is competition for limited promotion opportunities amongst individual employees. The essence of a traditional salary system is not only to relate the pay and job structures satisfactorily, but also to ensure that they are administered fairly and equitably.

The main characteristic underlying the administration of traditional salary payment schemes, which largely distinguishes them from traditional methods of wage payment, is their use of incremental scales. Salaries which have incremental scales provide a range of annual additions to employee pay. Although these incremental scales are sometimes collectively determined through collective bargaining, as in the public sector, they are normally administered under direct employer and managerial control.

Incremental pay arrangements can be expressed in terms either of scales within definite incremental steps or ranges, and the latter can be 'closed' (i.e. have minima and maxima) or 'open-ended' (i.e. have either minima or maxima, but not both). For the purposes of analysis we have found it useful to classify systems with salary scales as 'fixed' systems and systems based on ranges, whether closed or open-ended, as 'variable'.[21]

Fixed schemes generally allow for some degree of flexibility in their operation, variable schemes place more constraints on managerial options. Furthermore, fixed systems are more supported in the public sector, whereas private sector employers generally prefer variable systems – especially for senior staff. The fixed–variable dichotomy represents the opposite ends of a spectrum, since there are three subdivisions within each of the fixed and variable categories. Fixed salary scales may have automatic progression for employees like those engaged in routine clerical work; limited flexibility such as for some professional staff; or automatic progression to a fixed point with controlled discretion beyond it, such as for managerial staff. Similarly, variable progression may be through a range of increments according to guidelines; through a range of increments but with no definite guidelines such as for junior managers and technical staff; or through variable progressions without incremental ranges such as for senior managers in the private sector. Research suggests that traditional white-collar salary systems vary along the following lines:

- senior management staff – with open ended salary bands, progression through which is discretionary to the employer;
- junior management – with fixed range salary bands, again with discretionary progression, perhaps tied more closely to some form of performance appraisal system;
- clerical and technical staff – with fixed range salary bands, sometimes involving fixed increments to the mid-point of a band, and flexible elements beyond, sometimes based on performance appraisal;
- incremental scales for all staff, through which the individual moves by regular and specified steps. In such cases it is the range in the scale which determines the rate for the particular job.[22]

Three things stand out about traditional salary payments. First, what management expects from its salaried employees is frequently less easy to measure and to monitor than what is required from its wage earners, mainly because of the nature of the work

which they do. Second, the choice of traditional salary systems within an enterprise is related to a number of characteristics of the organization. These include: the nature of its work; its technology; its corporate objectives; its style of management; the role of the pay system in rewarding ability and effort; and the environment in which it operates. Third, the administration of traditional salary systems provides management with a considerable degree of discretion and control in the ways in which they are operated. Thus although some traditional salary structures are negotiable, the processes by which decisions are made in placing individuals within a salary range, and in promoting individuals between incremental scales once they are appointed, invariably remain a managerial prerogative. In other words, both the efficient administration and the equitable application of most traditional salaries and their job structures rely heavily on effective managerial control and fairness on management's part.

## Payment by results (PBR)

Traditional wage payment systems for manual employees normally comprise a number of elements. The first is the basic hourly rate which might be determined on an industry-wide basis through national collective bargaining or in other cases by employer or workplace agreements. A time rate payment system by itself, however, provides only a limited incentive to improve productivity, efficiency or output. Thus whilst time rates are widely applied in managerial and non-manual work, in complex process industries and the service sector, a payment by results element may be superimposed upon a time rate. Hence, in addition to the basic time rate for the job, a manual worker's weekly earnings might include PBR, overtime payments, shiftwork allowances, other special premia like seniority increments and – where PBR does not operate – some kind of payment 'in lieu' of a direct bonus. Obviously, managerial control over traditional wage payments is much less than over salaried worker's employment packages, since collective bargaining has made considerable inroads into unilateral managerial regulation of wage payment systems.

The clearest difference between traditional wage payment systems and traditional salary payments is the scope given within the former for some form of payment by results. Although some salaried employees, such as sales personnel, are paid by results, PBR 'may be broadly interpreted to mean any system of wages or salaries under which payment is related to factors in a worker's performance other than time spent at his employer's disposal'.[23] Management's underlying assumption, in using PBR schemes, is that where employees vary the output of their jobs according to effort, this can be related to payment received. In this way, it is hoped, the prospect of higher earnings results in greater effort on the part of employees. Payment by results is also attractive to employers wishing to vary their wages bills as demand for their products changes. There are various PBR schemes. Moreover, in most PBR schemes the total wage packet is made up of a number of elements. These may include a fixed basic element, a variable output bonus and a fall-back provision. The bonus element can be calculated on a daily, weekly or monthly basis. In other cases it is paid over an even longer period of time or of output. Under some PBR schemes, the weekly bonus is paid on the average output of the previous month or quarter. This aims to reduce the effects of fluctuations in work output from one week to another on employee earnings.

Basically, there are three types of PBR: individual PBR, group PBR and measured day work (MDW). Individual PBR comprises two main systems: piecework and incentive bonuses. The oldest of these is straight piecework. This is where an employer pays a standard price for each piece or unit of output produced by individual employees. Under this method, pay and output are directly proportional. Nowadays, most piecework systems also incorporate a time rate element. Fall-back rates guarantee a minimum level of weekly earnings irrespective of output, and 'waiting time' is paid when piece workers are held up by interruptions of work beyond their immediate control. Individual piecework earnings may also be supplemented by fixed hourly, daily or weekly payments to preclude excessive fluctuations in earning levels.

Where employee effort is measured in terms of the time taken to do a job, rather than in the quantity of output produced, and a standard time is allowed to complete it, incentive bonus changes are brought into effect. Although there are a variety of such systems, an incentive bonus scheme is essentially used where an employee is paid a basic time rate with a standard time set for completing the job. A bonus is then paid in relation to the time saved in actually doing the job or to the extra product produced in the time allowed for doing it.

Under these systems, the fixing of a price for the work to be done and the determination of work-loads for particular tasks are formally separated. A wage is negotiated in terms of units of time and the times allowed for different tasks are then fixed separately.[24]

The main differences among these traditional PBR systems lie in the varying relationship between pay and output which they utilize. They comprise: proportional straight line, progressive, geared, stabilized, regressive, or variable schemes. Their aims include encouraging learners, discouraging excessively high performance or safeguarding management against errors in standard setting. All these schemes are normally based on work study standards. The British Standards Institution employs a scale of performance: 75 performance corresponds with a normal level of effort which an employee on a time rate would achieve. The standard level which employees on PBR would be expected to achieve corresponds with a 100 performance. Under a proportional straight line incentive scheme, for example, guaranteed minimum earnings are normally paid at 75 performance, whilst a 100 performance results in a $33\frac{1}{3}$ per cent increase in earnings, with earnings at other performance levels pro rata. Examples of other types of schemes are provided in Figure 11.1.

The Taylor Differential Piece Rate system is progressive in that it yields a higher rate of pay for above standard performance. In practice, however, the majority of individual PBR schemes in Britain, whether piece based or time based, tend to be regressive such as the Bedaux scheme, with the effective price per unit of output declining as worker output rises. Under these schemes, gross earnings rise at a lower rate than total output. This means that unit labour costs diminish with increased levels of output. Thus employers are protected against rising unit costs resulting from falls in output, whilst employee earnings are less liable to fluctuation than under proportional or progressive schemes.

Individual PBR is most suitable in jobs which have a high manual content, a repetitive nature, short cycle operations, and where there are no marked fluctuations in the product market. Individual PBR works most successfully: where the proportion of average earnings comprising a variable output bonus does not exceed 25 per cent; where performance standards are properly work measured; and where learning and improvement factors are also taken into account when establishing work standards. It is preferable with PBR systems to determine internal differentials

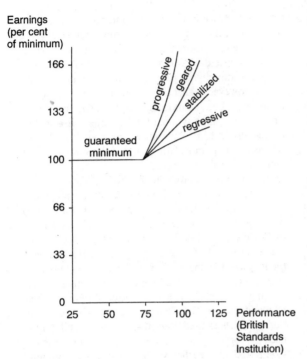

Earnings
(per cent
of minimum)

166

133

100 — guaranteed minimum

66

33

0

25  50  75  100  125  Performance (British Standards Institution)

progressive
geared
stabilized
regressive

*Figure 11.1* Progressive, geared, stabilized and regressive incentive bonus schemes.

by systematic job evaluation and to regularly revise the suitability and administration of the bonus system being used. The work being done needs to be measurable and directly attributable to the individual, whilst the pace of work should be controlled by those doing it rather than by the job technology. Management also needs to ensure that subordinates receive a steady flow of work, not subject to frequent changes in methods of production or in its use of materials and equipment.

Group PBR operates where the production process makes it difficult to attribute job performance or work output to individual workers. It is also used to encourage workgroups to work co-operatively. In these cases, normal PBR schemes may be applied to groups with bonus payments allocated among group members equally or in a predetermined ratio. Workgroup members need to be reasonably competent but the motivational effort of group PBR can diminish as workgroup size increases.

Another incentive payment is the 'lieu' bonus. These are additional payments, in place of bonuses, paid to timeworkers who cannot be employed on PBR directly. They are a form of pay compensation

to employees like maintenance workers not able to supplement their weekly earnings by normal PBR. Lieu bonuses are often calculated according to the average bonus of direct workers and are paid in the belief that if total production increases, indirect workers have contributed to the productivity of the direct workers. In practice, the most common reason for paying lieu bonuses is to prevent any major changes occurring in pay relationships and earnings between skilled time-workers, on the one hand, and less skilled piecework or bonus workers on the other. Consequently, lieu bonuses are rarely related to effective work measurement.

Measured day work is the generic term given to those wage payment systems occupying a midway position between individual and group PBR, especially with 'banded' ranges of payment, on the one hand, and day rate schemes based on high time rate payments, on the other. Under MDW pay is fixed on the understanding that employees 'maintain a specified level of performance, but the pay does not fluctuate in the short term with . . . actual performance'.[25] To work effectively MDW relies heavily on some form of work measurement and job assessment to define the required level of performance by employees and to monitor the levels of job performance. In outline, MDW comprises: either a time rate payment for specified job performance; or a time rate payment and a bonus payment for a specified performance; or a series of options by which employees maintain one of a series of performance levels to which differing rates of pay apply. The essence of MDW is that a specific effort bargain is struck between employer and employees. By it, employers agree to pay an agreed level of wages in return for a specified level of job performance by their employees.

Various reasons are suggested for adopting MDW. These include: the prevention of sectional wage bargaining; the elimination of leap-frogging pay claims; the preclusion of wide fluctuations in employee earnings; and the maintenance of rational pay structures. Changes to MDW from PBR are most commonly conducted when PBR has decayed to such a degree that industrial relations have become seriously affected by it. This is reflected in the increased rejection of job times, in job mobility by employees and by steady loss of managerial control over workplace earnings. Employees may also be concerned at the instability of their earnings and the inequities in practice between their pay rewards and job effort. MDW is then seen as a means by which management can secure standard effort and 'of employees securing stable earnings. It can thus meet the immediate objective of both sides'.[26] It is a mixture of industrial relations criteria, management and employee needs, and technological factors which usually contribute to the introduction of MDW payment systems.

An alternative to standard MDW is the premium pay plan (PPP). This is a stepped or graduated form of MDW requiring detailed work measurement and administrative machinery. It is designed to overcome the major shortcomings of individual or group PBR, whilst allowing individual employees some choice of job performance and of movement between pay bands for themselves. It does not rely solely on financial incentives to ensure high performance but demands high standards of managerial supervision. Under PPP, employees improve their pay in two ways. Either they achieve a higher level of performance over a specified period in their existing jobs, or they move to another job with a higher pay-rate and increased work-performance classifications. The closely specified procedures and highly structured nature of PPP, however, necessitate continuously strict checks by management on employee effort. Its characteristics suggest that operating PPP demands high managerial standards and that management does not abdicate its monitoring responsibilities as so often happens with other forms of PBR.

## 11.4    Trends in Payment Systems

In its 1988 study of developments in payment systems, ACAS found a wide range of arrangements being used and drew four main conclusions. First, it found that payment systems which emphasized stability of earnings, such as straight time rates, were still in widespread use. Second, employers in its sample 'were showing increasing interest in all forms of incentive payment', with traditional PBR systems continuing on some scale but with increasing interest being shown in 'merit pay' schemes, linking pay to individual performance. 'A third, more general, conclusion is that many managers were reviewing existing arrangements to suit their changing market and organizational structures and goals'.[27] A fourth and final conclusion was that a wide variety of approaches were being operated together in many establishments.

A number of changes have taken place in payment systems since then. In their search for more cost-effective industrial relations, in response to product market and labour market factors, more sophisti-cated private sector employers, and even some public sector ones, have moved away from traditional payment systems to more flexible systems. These flexible payment systems link remuneration to performance, output, productivity, profits or labour market conditions. However, whilst these systems are seen as being instrumental in containing employment costs and improving company profitability, they also relate to the difficulties experienced by some employers of recruiting, motivating and retaining suitable employees in the workplace.

In research conducted by the Policy Studies Institute (PSI) for the Department of Employment in 1990, in a 'modern' industrial area (Reading) and in a 'traditional' one (Leicester), six main categories of flexible and incentive payment systems were identified. The study found that the use of flexible payment systems in these organizations was widespread, with over 80 per cent of the organizations sampled relating all or part of their employees' remuneration to performance. Over half of them used individual bonuses, others used collective bonuses, whilst most used a combination of flexible payment systems. Compared with earlier studies of payment systems, the PSI concluded that by the early 1990s the evidence suggests:

there might have been a movement away from collective incentive systems and systems which relate remuneration to the performance of a group, towards individual incentive systems and systems which relate remuneration to the performance of the individual employee and management's appraisal of his/her worth or contribution. Whether this will be a sustained phenomenon, or whether it is merely a response to conjectural circumstances in the labour market is uncertain.[28]

It was also apparent from the PSI survey that in about a half of the organizations studied the pay of at least some of the employees was determined by collective bargaining. In two-thirds of these organizations, the pay for some of their employees was determined nationally, in a half of them at organizational level and in some fifth of them at both national and organizational levels. Not surprisingly, organizations recognizing trade unions were more likely to apply collective flexible payment systems, whilst organizations where pay was determined uni-laterally by management were more likely to apply individualized systems. There were also differences in the application of payment systems between the modern area, Reading, and the traditional one, Leicester. Thus the survey found that:

- with its more heavily service-oriented economy and tighter labour market, together with a lower level of unionization, Reading showed a greater use of individualized forms of wage setting than did Leicester;
- management determined the pay of some employees on the basis of individual performance in 73 per cent of Reading organizations but only 51 per cent of Leicester organizations;
- fewer than 25 per cent of Reading organizations were party to national agreements on pay compared with 43 per cent of organizations from Leicester.[29]

The evidence suggested, therefore, that 'an individualisation of payments had indeed occurred'. One in five organizations was making greater use of bonuses based on individual performance and two in five were linking pay more closely to the assessment of individual performance. In many instances, this individualization of pay applied primarily to basic pay, 'rather than to additional bonuses', but only a few organizations claimed that the use of flexible payment systems that were targeted on the totality of their workforce, or on predetermined groups within them, 'had grown'.[30]

## Current management perceptions of pay and payment systems

There is evidence to show that some organizations are experiencing changing perceptions about the relationship between pay rewards and pay equity. Indeed, since the mid-1980s, some employers have been 'trying to reassert control over the economics of remuneration and are linking it to external factors such as performance requirements and business ambitions'. Such employers are becoming less concerned with established payment systems and pay structures and more concerned with attracting and retaining the right individuals in the workplace, in reaction to the skills shortages facing them. As one consultant has put it:

Pay packages are increasingly being individually tailored to meet the requirements of key employees, particularly at the top. Pay is being geared to individual potential and performance, through merit-pay systems and variable cash

bonuses, and to incorporate performance through group incentive schemes.[31]

Both private and public sector organizations are facing unprecedented and accelerating rates of change – market, technological and social. The private sector is confronted with shorter product cycles and competitive markets, whilst the public sector is faced with pressures from limits on public spending and substantial culture change. The pressures are on many employers to recruit from an increasingly limited supply of high quality people. The result is a shift in pay philosophy by such employers. For them, pay is no longer perceived as a bureaucratized administrative process but as a means of facilitating organizational change and adaptation to internal and external pressures acting on companies. A number of factors are taken into account by employers in determining payment systems, rates and structures. These include: job size; personal characteristics such as age, experience, qualifications, skills, contribution, performance and potential; market factors; unit and total labour costs; remuneration philosophy; collective bargaining arrangements; union bargaining power; and so on.

In the 1960s and 1970s, it was job size that was probably the main determinant of relative pay, with general pay levels being fixed by collective bargaining, reference to market surveys and successive incomes policies. Now, individual factors relating to job skills and company circumstances reflecting competitive market positions are paramount. The forces at work are:

changing labour markets and career structures; more devolved pay practices leading to diverse and fragmented pay markets; more flexible and personalised reward arrangements for individuals; a widening of differentials; the move towards payment for performance; more ownership stakes in profits and shares; a blurring of the distinction between revenue . . . and capital stakes in business participation; and much more vigorous performance management.[32]

In parts of the private sector, pay policy is being based increasingly on three basic principles. First, pay policy and practices should reflect and support the business objectives and strategies of the firm. Second, pay matters should be regarded as part of a wider human resources strategy, focused on meeting the changing people needs of the enterprise. Third, pay policy and practices need to be consistent with the dominant culture of the organization. Employers in the public sector, in turn, have not been uninfluenced by what is happening in the private sector, with pay for performance, especially for management grades, being introduced in the health service, local government and civil service.

Some large employers are breaking down their centralized pay structures and devolving pay determination to their operational units. This means that employees doing the same jobs with similar experience, but in different parts of the organization, are being paid differently. This is because the business units to which they belong have differing levels of added value and profitability. They therefore structure their pay policies and payment systems accordingly. Part of this so-called revolution is that it is 'overthrowing the assumption that people should be paid the same even though their contribution and circumstances are different'.[33]

During the 1960s and 1970s, various influences on pay determination resulted in a weak link being established between pay and performance. These influences included incomes policies, collective bargaining and equity in pay relativities. Since the early to mid-1980s, employers have found that they can only reward performance after results have been achieved. Output 'started to replace input as an important compensable factor'. At the top, it is being gauged in earnings per share, whilst for senior and middle management, it is geared to achieving personal and corporate targets. Among non-managerial employees, there has been a steady stripping away of input-based bonuses in many cases. These have 'been replaced by output-based schemes, with manual, craft and supervisory rewards related to financial results'.[34]

### Flexible starting pay

Employers, in determining the starting pay of new employees, sometimes take into account either local labour market conditions or the qualifications or experience of individual new starters. Varying the levels of starting pay for these purposes results in pay differences amongst individuals but does not mean that remuneration contains a discernible incentive element.

### Local and regional allowances

Local and regional allowances are used by employers to supplement pay in areas where labour market conditions are tight or where the cost of living is relatively high. These payments normally consist of a fixed sum, discernible from basic pay, which is paid to employees working in a particular location. Such allowances are most often used by public sector employers and companies in the market services, such as building societies, banks and insurance companies.

### Performance related pay

Performance related pay (PRP), or merit pay, means that management's assessment of an individual's job performance, usually through a performance appraisal system, enables the pay of individual employees to be varied according to management perceptions of an individual's worth and contribution to the organization. This can take the forms of lump sum payments, percentages of basic pay or predetermined cash increments. PBR enables managers to apply discretion in deciding the criteria which determine an individual's pay and is typically related to the pay of managerial, professional and non-manual workers. In more formalized performance appraisal schemes, operated by larger organizations, the criteria are likely to be explicitly defined. In smaller organizations, pay is more likely to be determined by management's subjective assessment of each employee alone.

With PRP, remuneration decisions become more complex and possibly controversial. Further, effective implementation of PRP, since it is based on employee performance and market forces, depends for its effectiveness partly on the ability of the personnel function to communicate the rationale of such approaches to the workforce. Adopting PRP has implications, in the private sector, for a company's relations with its shareholders too. They are likely to demand information about the size of bonus elements in pay awards and the basis on which they are calculated. Moreover, whilst PRP is comparatively easy to justify, install and monitor when a company's profits are buoyant, the real test comes when profitability is low and businesses turn in poor financial results.

## Individual bonuses

These are traditional PBR systems, such as piece-work, output and target-based bonuses and sales commission, which are aimed at individual workers. Such bonuses are based on the performance of individual workers and are discernible from basic pay. Individual bonuses are paid as a fixed sum on attaining a given level of output or of sales (threshold bonuses), or as payments which vary according to the precise level of output or of sales (variable or flexible bonuses). With threshold bonuses, employees expect to obtain them for what they deem to be a 'reasonable' amount of work and effort, whilst flexible bonuses are more sensitive to individual performance.

## Collective bonuses

Collective bonuses are of two types: group or departmentally based bonuses and those based on the output or value added of an organization. As with individual bonuses, collective bonuses are of the threshold or flexible types. One type of company-wide bonus, for example, is based on added value (AV). AV is the sales revenue of a company, less its expenditure on wages, salaries, administrative costs and profits. AV is a useful indicator of corporate efficiency, so any increase in its value demonstrates an improvement in overall company performance. The Rucker share of production plan uses the ratio of wages to AV on which to base bonus payments. Any improvement in this ratio results in the distribution of a bonus payment to all employees. The expectation is that the desire of employees to increase the bonus pool available induces them to accept changes in working methods, thus raising overall efficiency.

## Collective incentives based on profits

The implementation of profit sharing and employee share plans within companies has been encouraged by successive governments, and by legislation, from the mid-1980s. As a result of this, they have expanded since then. Profit related pay provides employees with an opportunity to share in the commercial success of the businesses for which they work, by linking part of their pay to company profits. In some cases, the amount paid is by management discretion, in others by a fixed percentage of profits and in others by some other method. Employee share ownership schemes provide opportunities for employees to become shareholders in the companies for which they work, often with tax concessions, through such schemes as 'save-as-you-earn' and executive share option arrangements.

Difficulties with collective incentive schemes of these types arise where profits are low and the amount to be shared out is of little or no consequence. Most share schemes are limited to companies whose shares are quoted on the Stock Exchange. There are impediments to private companies wishing to create employee shareholdings, where there is no open market for shares. Further, employees can lose their savings under these provisions where their companies either go out of business or are taken into receivership.

## Simultaneous usage of bonus schemes

It is clear from research, and anecdotally, that some employers combine different bonus schemes within their organizations. The 1990 PSI survey found, for example, that 'two-thirds of organisations were found to use one or more [systems]',[35] with well over a third using three or four. Two-thirds of the organizations using a single type of bonus scheme related basic pay to management assessment of individuals, whilst a large majority of organizations, using two or more types, included PRP as part of the package.

## Pay structures

Payment systems are also related to internal pay structures.

> At any place of work a network of differentials exists between the various occupations or skills and between those who share those same occupations and skills. A wage structure consists of the pay relationships of all the groups or individuals in a firm.[36]

These are connected in turn to a network of external pay relativities varying by occupation, industry and region. There is normally a continual struggle amongst all workgroups within an enterprise to maintain their internal differentials and to get them 'right'. In other cases, the structure of differentials within and among bargaining groups is reasonably rational and orderly. In many cases it is not so, as pay differentials change in accordance with market and bargaining factors.

Changes in internal differentials are caused by many factors. These include labour market shortages, product market fluctuations, trade union bargaining power, employer independence and the impact of government policies on existing differentials. Formerly, it was management alone which determined an organization's internal pay differentials in the light of market forces. Whilst in non-union firms this remains a managerial prerogative, internal pay structures are more likely to be determined jointly with unions, frequently in a number of bargaining units. This makes the whole issue of establishing equitable internal differentials a highly inflammatory and extremely contentious one. At least 13 different sequences have been identified as playing some part in producing a given pattern of pay levels within an organization at any one time.

> They are considerations of labour-market rates, career aspirations, beliefs about fair payment, wage-bargaining processes, overtime pay, wage drift, productivity bargains, age increments, merit payments, length-of-service increments, working conditions allowances, attempts to avoid grade distortion and attempts to restore differentials.[37]

Even where job evaluation is used, getting internal differentials 'right' can be a difficult and conflict ridden process.

## 11.5   Employment Practices

The development of an organization's employment practices emerges out of its personnel management, human resources or industrial relations policies. And these, in turn, derive from the corporate philosophy of the enterprise towards its employees. It is increasingly recognized by employers that all organizations depend upon the effective use of their available resources to achieve their corporate goals, whether they are financial, material or human. It is also accepted by most large-scale employers that effective employment policies contribute to the achievement of these goals but are only likely to succeed where they are acceptable to the workforce and are seen as compatible with their interests.

Clearly formulated employment policies are seen to be important because they help ensure that organizational decisions affecting employees are well thought out, understood and consistently and fairly applied within enterprises. These policies are also expected to contribute to the development of productive working relationships between employers and employees and, where they are recognized, their

unions. Explicit employment policies normally take account of a number of internal and external influences. These include legislation, policies in other areas of corporate activity, collective agreements and prevailing good practices. They express an employer's intentions and objectives about the whole range of employment matters affecting the employer and its workforce. Good employment practices are expected to follow from appropriate employment policies, thus contributing to organizational efficiency and employee well-being. A selection of these practices are outlined and described below. They are neither exclusive nor exhaustive but they illustrate the sorts of employment and human resource areas of concern to line and personnel managers currently.

### Recruitment and selection

Many employers, especially the larger, more sophisticated ones, spend considerable time and money ensuring that, as far as possible, they recruit the right persons for the jobs and tasks needing to be done in their organizations. In many enterprises, both private and public, responsibility for choosing new employees rests with line managers, assisted by personnel managers. One result of effective recruitment and selection is reduced labour turnover and good employee morale. Recruiting ineffectively is costly, since poor recruits may perform badly or leave their employment, thus requiring further recruiting and employee replacement to be undertaken. A planned recruitment system is normally effective, efficient and fair. It is deemed to be effective where it produces enough suitable candidates and enables the selectors to distinguish between suitable and unsuitable applicants. It is efficient where it uses the most cost-effective advertising and recruiting sources and methods. A fair recruitment system maintains the employer's good name with both existing employees and potential recruits. It does this by dealing fairly, honestly and courteously with all job applicants and job enquiries.

Recruiting suitable applicants for an appointment requires drawing up a job description, providing a person specification and attracting applications. A job description outlines the main tasks and responsibilities of a job. It covers job purpose, job tasks and job scope, and in doing this identifies what the job entails. It also enables managers to decide what kind of person is needed for the post. By analysing the tasks in terms of knowledge and skills needed to do them, the managers can write a person specification.

This describes the ideal person to fill the job and provides a profile of the personal skills, knowledge and characteristics to be sought in the recruitment and selection process. Also the use of a person specification, as a basis for the job interviews, reminds interviewers to be realistic and as objective as possible in their assessment of candidates.

Searching for suitable candidates is done internally or externally. Internal recruitment, for example, provides opportunities for the development and promotion of existing employees. It ensures that trained and valuable employees are retained rather than lost by the employer. Recruiting externally requires the identification of a suitable recruitment medium and the design of an appropriate advertisement. Using application forms has a number of advantages. These include helping in the initial sifting of candidates, providing the basis for the job interview and acting as a guide to the candidates' suitability.

In selecting the best candidate from the employer's shortlist, the selectors' major problem is to establish how closely the applicants match the ideal set out in the person specification. Where the job is straightforward, a short interview and perhaps a simple practical test is all that is needed. For more senior appointments, in-depth interviewing, group exercises, assessment centres or psychological tests are used, with employment records, biodata, certificates of qualifications and other accomplishments being taken into account. Personnel specialists are generally responsible for the early stages of selection, with line managers becoming more involved in the final stages and in the interviewing procedures.

Despite its clear and apparent limitations as a selection device, the interview is still the most common method of employee selection. If fair and effective selection decisions are to be made by the interview method, systematic interviewing is necessary. Preliminary and final interviews are the norm. After the selection decision has been determined, candidates are informed of the selectors' choice and an offer of a contract of employment is made. These conditions are generally set out in a letter of appointment which becomes part of the individual's contract on starting the job.

There is some evidence, again among more sophisticated employers, of a growing trend by management to use more systematic selection procedures and to link these with staff appraisal. Townley claims that 'careful selection screening and regular formal monitoring of performance' are no longer confined to managerial levels but 'are becoming the experience of those at lower levels in the organizational hierarchy, especially blue-collar employees'. This is in response to the changing economic contexts of companies and to an increasing emphasis on the attitudinal and behavioural characteristics of employees. 'Selection and appraisal, in other words, are identified as contributing to an *overall approach to the handling of labour relations*'.[38]

## Induction

Inducting new employees or 'new starters' into an organization consists of any systematic process by which individuals commencing their employment are familiarized with their job, work surroundings, the people with whom they will be working and the firm and industry in which they are employed. Since starting a new job is an anxious time for most people, it is generally accepted that it is good practice for the employer to help new employees settle down in their work as soon as possible. It benefits the individual, the employer and the organization as a whole. Unless they are given time to settle down and get involved with their jobs quickly, new employees are unlikely to respond effectively to the demands and responsibilities of their work tasks and activities. Moreover, discontented employees are likely to be ineffective workers and a potential cause of poor industrial relations. Effective induction programmes help employees settle into their new jobs, help them to establish good working relationships with their colleagues and enable them to see where they fit into the organization. Induction begins, in part, when employees are recruited and selected and continues during the first weeks of their employment. The aim of systematic induction is to cover as much ground as possible in the shortest effective time. Once employees become established in their jobs, it is more difficult to arrange time off for induction.

Whilst induction is generally a fairly informal activity, it is best carried out in a systematic way. It covers such topics as: organizational layout; departmental structure and practices; conditions of employment; education, training and promotion arrangements; safety and first aid; employment rules and procedures; employee involvement and communications; welfare and employee benefits; and organizational structure and developments. The overall plan for induction is often drawn up in consultation with first line managers, the personnel department, safety officer and union and employee representatives. Induction normally involves the new recruits in meeting and listening to people talking about aspects of the organization, watching activities and asking questions. Information is provided by a variety of methods, including corporate documents, the company handbook, visual aids and group discussion. An especially valuable contribution can be made by a work colleague or 'mentor' who acts as a friend and sponsor of the new employee during the first weeks of employment.

Employees needing special attention during induction include school-leavers, women returning to work, disabled employees, management trainees and members of minority groups. School-leavers, for example, lack work experience and may be particularly vulnerable to workplace accidents. Women returners can find it difficult adapting to work organizations after several years absence from them. The induction of disabled workers needs careful attention since they may have problems of access and may need special facilities, whilst minority groups may adopt social conventions of which the employer may be unaware. Overall, then, effective induction has positive benefits for all the parties involved. Although it needs to be systematic, it need not be overformalized; done effectively it contributes to effective working, workforce stability and good industrial relations.

## Harmonization

The differences in payment systems continuing to exist between white collar salaried staff and hourly paid manual workers derive from largely outdated historical, social and economic factors. Moreover, they are reflected not only in the methods of employee payment but also in the total remuneration package and in the conditions of employment between the two groups generally. According to ACAS:

> The most significant differences in current terms and conditions are to be found in the coverage and basis of pension and sick pay schemes, the liability of manual workers to lay-off and short time working, basic working hours, and holiday entitlements. In general, most manual workers are still treated considerably less favourably than non-manual workers in all these areas, and full harmonisation would be costly.[39]

Differences are also found in the contribution of overtime and PBR to total pay, fringe benefits, workplace facilities and clocking in.

Harmonization of conditions of employment within organizations and the introduction of staff status for all employees, however, are of increasing interest to management, unions and employees. Although the cost of harmonization is often the main obstacle in introducing staff status for manual workers, the principle has become of growing importance to the parties to industrial relations during recent years. Experience shows that introducing harmonization can improve not only industrial relations but also corporate efficiency, provided it has the acceptance of the employees affected – both manual and non-manual, including managers – and involves if not single status at least a significant degree of harmonization.

Where harmonization is introduced it is generally a management initiative. Full and open consultation is normally essential wherever it is contemplated, which is a time-consuming process. In doing this, management relinquishes yet another of its prerogatives: rewarding specific employee groups differently. Yet attempts to harmonize conditions of employment produce their own industrial relations problems. In drawing up agreements of this sort the parties have to consider:

> Whether to retain an incentive payment scheme and a guaranteed week, the disparity of hours between blue and white collar employees and the effect on absences and timekeeping. Finally, there is the disparity between what management hope to achieve and what can reasonably be expected in terms of increasing employee involvement.[40]

Moving towards integrating manual and non-manual payment systems and conditions of employment produces its own difficulties, such as staff opposition to losing their relatively advantaged employment status. Effective harmonization ultimately requires fundamental changes in employee attitudes and in managerial attitudes to the two groups, with sometimes radical changes in working methods.

Harmonization is normally one element in the negotiation of 'new-style' collective agreements, where single-union recognition is provided on greenfield sites, and is used to facilitate employee motivation. In recruiting employees in such firms, employers seek enthusiasm, idealism, commitment, expertise and attention to detail. They also want employees to function well under open-style management. In these circumstances, the selection process is used to produce a labour force 'that can function well where individual responsibility, self-monitoring through "make-and-check" procedures, ability to work in small teams, and self-motivated behavior are expected'.[41]

## Workplace communications

Effective workplace communication is a two-way process requiring a two-way flow of information between management and its workforce. Workplace communication usually refers to the provision and passing of information and instructions enabling an employing organization to function efficiently, with employees being properly informed of developments, managerial plans and current events. Managers have a responsibility to communicate with all their employees and with the unions and their members. Good channels and procedures, it is argued, promote more effective management practices, more committed employees and greater trust within the organization between employer and employees. Employees need to be informed about their duties, obligations and rights. They also have to communicate with managers and be able to ask questions about their work and about developments within the enterprise, and to get answers to their questions. Employees are communicators too. They have to pass on job-related information to others as part of their work. They may also wish to contribute to the job environment in which they are located and to the personnel and other policies affecting their welfare and interests in employment.

Good practice suggests it is primarily management's responsibility to create the conditions and establish the necessary policies and procedures for promoting effective communications with employees. This process requires a lead from top management. Where a senior manager is made responsible for ensuring that the policy is put into practice and is maintained and reviewed regularly, it is more likely to succeed. The principal links in workplace communications are line managers. They are responsible for passing information in both upward and downward directions. Managers also have to exchange information with other managers, which necessitates horizontal as well as vertical communication structures. In larger organizations the personnel function, in addition to line management, has an interest in providing information to employees and getting feedback from them. Personnel managers are particularly well placed to identify needs, advise on policy and monitor arrangements.

The sort of information which employers com-municate to their employees includes information about conditions of employment, about employees' jobs and about the organization. Information about an employee's conditions of service is normally provided in the statutorily required 'written particular'. Job-related and operational information covers a range of items. These include: operating and technical instructions; health and safety; general information about the workplace; background information about the company; information about work objectives and performance standards; and information about key personnel on site. The operating and technical instructions given to employees cover such matters as: the work to be carried out; standards to be met; the use of machinery and equipment; and the health and safety regulations and precautions to be observed.

Employees also require information about the workplace generally. This includes supervisory and managerial arrangements, administrative procedures, social and welfare facilities, and, where they exist, trade union agreements. Other information related to union matters covers time off work for trade union duties and activities, access to management, the recruitment of new union members, and collection of union subscriptions. These matters are normally incorporated in written agreements negotiated between the employer and the recognized trade unions.

Most employees have a strong interest in what is happening in the company or organization in which they work. Where best practice is observed, the sort of information given to employees about the organization covers: corporate objectives and policies; past and the present performance and progress; and future plans and prospects. The main details feature financial performance, changes in staffing and human resources, the state of the order book, technological developments and investment plans. Interest is sometimes shown in income and expenditure figures, profit-and-loss accounts, added value, share price movements and so on. In non-commercial enterprises, employees are interested in financial data of a different sort, for instance for comparison with similar organizations with which they are familiar. Job security is another matter of major concern to all employees, so advance information and discussion of the enterprise's prospects help alleviate anxiety and assist in adaptation to change.

To be effective, workplace communications should be clear, concise, presented objectively, systematic, relevant and open to question. Various methods are used to communicate, either by face-to-face approaches or in writing. Face-to-face communications have the advantages of directness and quickness; these include meetings, conferences, seminars and audio-visual aids. Written communication is most effective where: the need for information is permanent; the topic requires detailed explanation; the accuracy and precision of wording are essential; and the audience is large and widespread. The main methods of written communication are: company handbooks; reports; house journals; in-house newsletters; bulletins; notices; and letters to individual employees.

## Appraisal and employee reviews

Increasing interest has been shown by employers in staff appraisal and employee reviews in recent years. Appraisals regularly assess employee performance, and potential and development needs, while performance reviews provide managers and employees with opportunities to discuss how employees are progressing. They examine what improvements in employee performance can be made, as well as helping to build on their strengths and enabling them to perform more effectively in the future. Reviews of the potential and the development needs of employees predict the level and type of work which employees will be capable of doing in the future. These reviews make proposals on how employees can be best developed for their future careers, with the maximum contribution accruing to the organization. Reward reviews determine the rewards that employees will get for their past work. These are normally separate from appraisal but are often assisted by information from the performance appraisal.

The claimed benefit of appraisal is that it helps improve employee job performance. It does this by identifying employees' strengths and weaknesses and by determining how their strengths can be best used by their employer and how their weaknesses can be overcome. Appraisal can also provide information for human resource planning purposes, assist in succession planning and assess the suitability of employees for promotion. It can improve communications by giving employees the opportunity to talk about their ideas and expectations. This, it is argued, can improve the quality of working life by increasing mutual understanding between managers and employees. Whilst appraisal is traditionally associated with white collar jobs, it is increasingly

used in manual jobs and can improve the motivation of blue-collar workers as well. Moreover, with growing interest being shown by managers in flexible working practices, new technology, quality improvement and the harmonization of conditions of employment, many enterprises are extending appraisal to all their employees. In most organizations, employees are appraised by their immediate manager. This is on the grounds that those who delegate work and monitor performance are best placed to assess performance and potential. But it is sometimes undertaken by higher-level managers in the organization. The frequency of formal appraisal depends on the nature of the enterprise but where it takes place, it is often done at least annually and sometimes more frequently.

For appraisal to work effectively, a number of conditions are necessary before a system is installed. First, senior managers must be committed to it. Second, senior managements are recommended to consult with their managers, employees and union representatives before introducing a scheme. Third, schemes should be as straightforward as possible. Fourth, a timetable should be fixed for implementing the scheme. Fifth, all managers who carry out appraisals should receive training to help them assess performance effectively and put that skill into practice. Sixth, a senior manager should be appointed to ensure that managers carry out the appraisals. To provide written records of appraisal, a number of techniques are used. These include 'ratings', 'comparisons with objectives', 'critical incidents', 'narrative reports' and 'behaviourally anchored rating scales'. To preserve the credibility of appraisal, there is often an appeals procedure built into the system. Further, since the main aim of appraisal is to help employees improve their performance, appraisals should not be used to discipline poor performers. On the other hand, nor should they be used as a device for employees to negotiate better gradings or performance payments through the appeals procedure.

Assessing potential is based upon either past performance, or self-assessment, or reports from assessment centres. Reports from an employee's immediate manager, and observations from more senior managers, are an important, although incomplete, way of assessing employee potential. Self-assessment should where practicable be followed up by plans to realize potential through training courses, assignments and planned experience. In recent years, there has been an increase in the use of assessment centres to assess the potential of staff. These are staffed by trained assessors who use a variety of group and psychometric tests to examine the potential of employees.

Reward reviews provide for salary increments, money bonuses and similar incentives which are awarded on the basis of employee performance. Merit pay, for example, is an additional payment, over and above basic pay, linked to a systematic assessment of employee performance. The reward review is normally a separate process from the appraisal interview, which is likely to be more constructive and not involve pay. There are four main variants of reward review. The first involves fixed incremental scales with limited flexibility. In the second, performance pay is linked to an incremental scale, based on a satisfactory performance rating. A third is where pay increases are based on performance ratings awarded by a series of fixed percentage points. The fourth comprises a lump sum payment which is not consolidated into the employee's salary. In most of these cases, a common practice is to supplement 'across the board' pay increases with reward payments.

There are, however, some organizations operating staff appraisal and employee review systems without clearly thought out objectives. Others operate appraisal systems incorporating a variety of objectives, some of which may be incompatible and conflicting. Staff and performance appraisal, for example, can be undertaken with the following objectives in mind:

- to let employees know where they stand;
- to recognise good work;
- to warn employees they must improve;
- to communicate to some employees the direction in which they should improve;
- to develop employees in their present jobs;
- to develop employees for higher jobs;
- to help develop a participative environment to set performance targets;
- to examine problem areas;
- to form the basis for individual merit payments;
- to identify individuals with potential for promotion.[42]

Research suggests that a number of conditions are necessary for effective staff appraisal to take place: the organizational culture should be one based on high trust, support, openness and involvement; the appraisal system should be based on a code of ethics; appraisal should be appreciated as a key link in a proactive human resources management strategy; the relevance of appraisal to the development of the organization and to individual needs to be recognized; and appraisal should be recognized as an important vehicle for employee involvement. Above all, the objectives of a staff appraisal system should be clearly thought out, properly set out and understood by all.

## Quality improvement

A recent development in employment practices is managerial commitment to improving the quality of products and services in their organizations, through involving employees in quality improvement programmes. This commitment to 'total quality' within enterprises is in response to increasing competition and to rapid economic and technological change. It is argued that those organizations which succeed, whatever their business, are those making the best use of their people, or human resource assets. Quality improvement programmes are introduced and maintained by a variety of methods, including quality circles, quality improvement groups and quality development teams. Whatever name is chosen, improving quality through group involvement processes reflects corporate culture, with an emphasis on quality management at all organizational levels. Effective employee involvement in quality improvement often challenges traditional management views about delegation. This is because quality improvement groups identify their own problems and select and implement their own solutions. Participation in these programmes is about changing attitudes at all levels, not just amongst subordinate non-managerial employees.

Quality groups comprise six to ten employees, normally involved in related work. They meet regularly, under the direction of a trained leader, to select problems, propose solutions and – when appropriate – implement their own solutions. Each group agrees ways of improving quality, productivity, service to customers and other departments, and other aspects of their daily working arrangements. Group involvement methods use the knowledge of those who are closest to the work and are best placed to suggest improvements. The introduction of new working methods is more effectively achieved, it is argued, where the staff performing the work have been involved and consulted. Employee involvement in quality improvement is likely to result in: cost savings by developing more effective working methods; improved competitiveness; reduced labour turnover; and improved vertical and horizontal communication. Other claimed benefits of group participation and involvement include: increases in revenue potential; improved ways of doing the job; and better morale from increased motivation. What many managers of effective quality improvement programmes value most is the change in employee attitudes and more positive approaches to change.

There are a number of prerequisites for increasing the commitment of managers and staff at all levels in quality improvement programmes. These include: communication about the roles and benefits of the programme; the appointment of a facilitator or group co-ordinator; the commitment of the board and senior management; the involvement of middle management and supervisory management; and the support of trade union and staff representatives. Other factors include the provision of adequate training, the monitoring and communication of results, and continuing managerial support to provide guidance and to reward efforts. An effective approach to increasing employee participation in quality improvement is to commence with a pilot study. Where this is successful, the subsequent publicity normally increases participation in the programme.

A further aspect of management's concern with quality improvement in recent years is 'total quality management' (TQM). There is no generally agreed definition of the term but the Institute of Management Services defines it as:

a strategy for improving business performance through the commitment and involvement of all employees to fully satisfying agreed customer requirements, at the optimum overall cost, through the continuous improvement of the products and services, business processes and people involved.[43]

Such quality improvements take place within the whole organization, beginning in the vertical structure, such as in departments, sections and work teams. But since many quality issues cut across these vertical units, organizational arrangements for co-ordinating quality improvements horizontally are also required. Hence cross-functional co-operation is an essential feature of TQM. One principle of horizontal activity is that of the 'internal customer'. This means that organizational units have to discuss the quality of their performance with other units who receive their output (their 'customers') in order to improve the service they provide.

According to ACAS, implementing a TQM strategy often requires a change in organizational culture. This includes:

* the internalization of quality and continuous improvement as a goal of all activities;
* more open communications, so that those further down are listened to by those further up;
* the greater involvement of a wider range of people in the decision making process.

TQM is, however, not a set of management techniques. It is rather a fundamental change in the way an organization is run. It is not a process which can ever be completed, since it involves a commitment by everyone in the organization to permanent improvement. Top management commitment is essential in implementing TQM. Senior managers must not only state their belief in TQM but also demonstrate their own commitment to it by their behaviour. They should be seen as champions and facilitators of the total quality cause. 'Above all they must communicate with employees and display dedication to [total quality] and culture change'.[44] Unlike quality circles, TQM is management driven, from the top, and is a strategic issue for corporate management, not just an issue for lower levels of the management hierarchy. Managers therefore have to initiate an educative approach to gain employee commitment to and enthusiasm for TQM which relies heavily on teamwork and co-operation within the organization to make it work.

## Equal opportunities

The provision of equality of opportunities in employment, and the elimination of discrimination in employment practices on the grounds of sex, marital status or ethnic origin – and sometimes age, disability and sexual orientation – has become an issue of prime importance for employers over the last two decades. Employer concern with equal opportunities policies and practices is not solely due to employers' self-interest in protecting themselves from the legal consequences of infringing the legislative requirements in terms of sex and race discrimination. Increasing pressure has been brought to bear on employer attitudes and practices from outside forces, such as interest groups, trade unions and professional management associations. Moreover, employers also derive positive benefits from creating, applying and monitoring equal opportunities in employment. These include: making full use of the talents of all members of the workforce; improving job motivation and employee performance; widening the talent base in organizations, by developing people's potential; improving employer–employee communications; and improving the external image of the organization.

A number of steps are necessary for implementing an equal opportunities programme. These are: allocating responsibility for it; consulting; policy making and publicity; training; examining procedures and criteria; monitoring; and taking positive action. Most employers embarking on an equal opportunities employment policy allocate overall responsibility to a senior member of the management team, such as the personnel director. Nevertheless, it is essential that equal opportunities are seen to have the active support of senior management as a whole, if they are to be carried out by all staff in the organization. Hence whilst recognizing their own prime responsibility for ensuring equal opportunities in the workplace, most employers acknowledge that the effectiveness of such policies and programmes are dependent on the support and co-operation of all the employees and parties involved. This implies that consultations need to be held with managerial and supervisory staff, elected worker and union representatives and other interested groups at an early stage.

Many employers draw up policy statements setting out clearly and publicly the organization's commitment to ensuring equal opportunities. These can then be distributed to employees, displayed on noticeboards, included in employee handbooks and collective agreements, and publicized more widely. Some employers refer to their policy in their job advertisements, on application forms and in relevant promotional literature. These make clear both to potential job applicants and to the general public the employer's commitment to equal opportunities. Areas covered include: guarding against preconceptions; recruiting and selecting; training; promoting; terms and conditions; monitoring; and handling grievances and victimization.

The importance of training as a key element in an equal opportunities programme is increasingly recognized by employers. Training is provided as a means of ensuring that employees understand fully their responsibilities under the law, as well as under the organization's policy. It is especially important for those involved in making key decisions in such areas as recruitment, selection, appraisals and promotion. The sort of topics covered in equal opportunities training include: the nature of discrimination and how it occurs; the relevant legislation; special interest groups; and reviewing the equal opportunities programme and its practical implications. Employers sometimes find that implementing an equal opportunities programme raises implications for other types of training and identifies previously neglected training needs.

When developing programmes to implement an equal opportunities employment policy and relevant practices, employers have to examine existing personnel procedures and activities. In doing this, employers often recognize that some of their existing procedures and criteria are operating unfairly, however unintentionally, against a particular employee group. Indeed, they may constitute unlawful discrimination. As a result of this examination or review, where unfair and potentially unlawful employment practices are exposed, they have to be changed and removed to ensure that equal opportunity is provided. Most employers find in this respect that it is useful to examine their existing procedures and criteria by analysing their record-keeping data and updating it, where necessary.

Many employers adopting comprehensive equal opportunities employment policies and practices use, as a means of reviewing the progress of their policy, some system of statistical monitoring. These monitoring systems are generally based on the collection and analysis of appropriate employee and job application data. The use of such data enables employers to gain a picture of what is actually happening in their employment structure and thus base their programmes implementing equal opportunities on precise factual information. By analysing the composition of their labour force, employers are able to identify areas of significant under- or over-representation of particular employee groups. Where appropriate, employers can then make the necessary changes to their employment practices in accordance with their equal opportunities policy and programme. Analysis of the relative success rates of candidates from different employee groups in selection decisions can also be used to identify potential discrimination in this area, and enable steps to eliminate it.

Increasingly, employers committed to implementing an equal opportunities employment policy are recognizing that they might need to take positive action to eliminate employment and job discrimination practices. They can do this, for example, under the provisions of the Race Relations Act 1976. Its provisions permit employers, for instance, to take positive measures to redress any under-representation of particular ethnic groups within the workforce or within specific fields of employment. Job advertisements designed to reach members of such groups, for instance, can be used to encourage job applications from them. Other measures to help ethnic groups include: recruiting school-leavers to meet any special training needs; encouraging members of such groups to apply for promotion and training for promotion; and providing skills for training them.

The Institute of Personnel and Development (IPD), as the leading professional body of personnel managers in Britain, has issued an equal opportunities code. It argues that as the professional body concerned with the most effective use of human resources at work, the IPD has a role and responsibility to promote fair practices in the managing of people at work. The IPD believes that personnel managers have a special and leading role to play in combating discrimination in employment. Its code covers sex and racial discrimination in employment, as well as discrimination on the grounds of age and against people with disabilities. The Institute recommends, for example, that personnel departments obtain the commitment of senior management to the employment of people with disabilities and that they train line managers not to assume that all people with disabilities are unemployable. It also recommends that organizations carry out a review of the employment levels of all people with disabilities and not just the registered disabled. In the area of age discrimination, the IPD believes that, for most jobs, automatically excluding entire age groups is not only wasteful for organizations but also damaging to individuals. As a general rule, the IPD recommends that age should not be used as a primary indicator in recruitment, selection, promotion and training decisions. Organizations should also consider incorporating in their equal opportunities statements their commitment not to discriminate arbitrarily on the grounds of age, whilst encouraging self-development for old and young employees.

## The flexible firm

There is research evidence showing that large numbers of employers introduced enhanced labour flexibility into their organizations during the 1980s. Indeed, a survey conducted by ACAS in the late 1980s concludes that 'certain kinds of flexible working practices are becoming more widespread in Britain'. It also suggests that 'some forms of flexibility which were previously thought to be confined largely to the service sector are now being widely adopted in manufacturing industry'.[45] A significant number of large organizations, in particular, appear to be developing a growing range of flexible working practices. A number of factors are forcing employers to examine the ways in which they operate and their needs for enhanced labour flexibility. First, the economic recession of the early 1980s was much more severe in Britain than in most other developed countries. In consequence, there were considerable reductions in employment levels. Second, the increasing pace of technological change is opening up new market opportunities for British firms, with the corresponding need to innovate in production and operational methods. Third, manufacturing industry in particular is having to respond to intensifying international competition in retaining both its domestic and overseas markets. Markets have become more volatile and uncertain, thus requiring firms to develop manning levels and working practices enabling them to adjust quickly to unpredictable fluctuations.

There are a number of corporate reasons why firms and employers, not only in the manufacturing sector, are wanting increased labour flexibility. These include: to increase productivity; to reduce labour costs; to meet fluctuating demands for their products or services; to react to increased competition; and to cope with technological change. Other reasons include to improve work relations, to raise staff morale and to attract and recruit satisfactory workers. Nevertheless, since manufacturing industry was badly affected by the recessions of the early and late 1980s, it is not surprising that it is here that flexibility has been introduced primarily to reduce labour costs, to meet fluctuations in demand and to increase competitiveness.

There are various forms of labour flexibility in the 'flexible firm': a useful way of categorizing them is by: numerical flexibility; functional flexibility; flexibility in hours of work; and flexibility in labour costs and rewards. Flexibility in numbers allows employers to increase or reduce the size of their workforces in accordance with seasonal and other fluctuations in the demand for their goods or services. The measures which they use to achieve numerical flexibility include using: part-timers; job sharers; temporary workers; subcontractors; fixed-term contracts; and homeworkers. Most use seems to be made of temporary workers, part-timers and subcontractors. Far less use is made of homeworkers and fixed-term contracts.

Functional flexibility is achieved by getting greater flexibility among craft and skilled workers. This leads to relaxed demarcations between different crafts or between craftworkers and non-craftworkers such as production staff. There may also be a blurring of distinctions between white collar and blue collar employees.

Most employees still work in regular blocks of seven or eight hours. The supply of work is rarely so regular, however, since most employers are affected by seasonal pressures and varying customer demand. Optimal utilization of capital equipment is likely to encourage employers to seek to maximize their returns on investment in new technologies. This is leading to a growth in shiftworking and to new and more flexible shift patterns. According to ACAS, shiftworking is the most common form of flexibility in hours of work, with relatively few organizations introducing other types of flexibility. In the ACAS survey, 'only three per cent [of respondents] had introduced annual hours working, one tenth had established job sharing and 14 per cent had set up flexible working hours'.[46]

As shown earlier, many employers in recent years have sought greater flexibility in relating labour costs to enterprise outputs through a closer relationship between pay and performance. The objective is that pay and reward systems should contribute more directly to corporate goals. This involves a continued shift to enterprise bargaining and widening differentials between skilled and unskilled workers. It also results in the displacement of the 'pay rate for the job' by payment systems rewarding flexibility in tasks and in acquiring and practising skills which are at least partly based on performance assessment. There has also been increasing interest in merit pay schemes, covering not only white collar employees but blue collar ones too. These changes appear to be leading to more integrated pay structures in some organizations, covering all white collar or all blue collar staff. Some companies are already moving towards plant-wide integrated job evaluation schemes, embracing all employees. The 'equal pay for work of equal value' regulations 'are also giving a boost to the use of analytical job evaluation techniques and perhaps towards harmonisation of terms and conditions of employment'.[43]

Further research by the Employment Department in the late 1980s aimed to find out the reasons why employers employ non-standard labour (NSL) – such as part-timers, temporary employees, agency temporary workers and the self-employed – the costs of doing so and whether increased labour flexibility is the result of a 'new' management strategy of labour utilization. The main reasons given by employers for recruiting NSL were traditional ones. These were: to cater for tasks requiring limited time inputs; to match demand for products or services; and to take advantage of the preference for part-time work among some groups of workers. Employers were, however, more likely to give new rationales for increasing their use of NSL. These included greater productivity, more flexibility, reduced labour costs and lower unionization. The study showed, however, that only a small minority of employers used NSL as a result of strategic considerations based on the concept of the 'core–periphery' model. This research suggests, therefore, that 'the prospects for changes in the extent and nature of non-standard employment are likely to depend for the most part on fairly traditional influences rather than decisions of personnel strategists'.[48]

The direct costs of employing NSL were not significant in distinguishing between full-time and other forms of labour. The hourly rates of pay for full-timers, part-timers and temporary workers doing similar jobs were the same for nearly 90 per cent of employees. Coverage of the most important non-pay benefits, such as sick pay and pensions, was, however, significantly lower for part-timers compared with full-timers and for temporary workers relative to part-timers. On the other hand, more than half of the employers in the survey thought labour turnover and absenteeism rates were the same for full-timers as for part-timers, though about a quarter of them thought that part-timers had lower rates of turnover and absenteeism.

A series of case studies undertaken by the Employment Department's research team revealed a number of features associated with the use of NSL. These included, first, that the employers' choice among different types of NSL was affected by three factors. These were: the predictability of demand for the product or service; the time intervals between peaks of demand; and the degree of skill or job knowledge required. Second, employers rarely had a clear human resources strategy to guide decisions on the different types of labour they employed. For many their policy followed from an overiding business strategy. Third, it was also apparent that a number of employers who had taken advantage of some form of labour flexibility had gone back to more conventional forms of labour usage, after having problems with labour quality and performance. It was also clear that NSL was not homogeneous. Two distinct groups of NSL could be identified.

> The first comprised skilled or technically qualified personnel, mainly male, working freelance or through an agency, usually because they wished to. The second, larger group, was mainly women, seen as having low or easily replaceable skills, working for low rates of pay, and divided in the extent to which they accepted such employment as a matter of preference.

The main research finding of the case studies was that there was 'little evidence to support the argument that increased labour flexibility is the result of a new management strategy for manpower utilisation'. What was prevalent in the mid-1980s 'was a compulsive drive from the side of business strategy in the private sector, and from the budgetary constraints in the public sector'. There is, in fact, 'little sign of strategic thinking about labour utilisation in British industry – employers typically improvise'.[49]

## 11.6   Non-union Firms

The non-union firm has provided an increasing focus of interest in industrial relations, since the early 1980s. But, compared with studies of unionized environments, research in the area of the non-union firm is relatively inconclusive, small scale and focused on particular geographical regions of Britain. Some interest, for example, has been shown in high technology establishments which, it is claimed, are generally identified with lower than average levels of union recognition and union density. A survey of Scottish electronics plants in the late 1980s, however, disputes this and concludes that six out of ten employees in this sector worked in unionized workplaces, with four out of ten employees being union members. A survey of 115 hi-tech firms in the south-east of England, on the other hand, found that:

> 80 per cent of establishments did not recognise unions; 56 per cent of employees in the sample were employed in non-union establishments; over two-thirds of establishments not recognizing trade unions (accounting for 39 per cent in the sample) also had no union members; where unions were recognized membership density was typically over 50 per cent for manual workers but less than 25 per cent for non-manual; and finally, there was little evidence during the 1980s of widespread union recruitment activity or,

conversely, of derecognition of unions by employers.

The authors conclude that a 'human resource management' approach to labour management within such firms was only one of the ways in which employees were managed. Employers exhibited, rather, a range of approaches, manifested in different management styles, 'which appear to be related to, but not determined by, both labour and product market factors as well as factors such as the size and age of establishments'.[50]

For more general evidence relating to the extent of non-unionism and the characteristics of non-union firms, it is necessary to turn to the Workplace Industrial Relations Surveys (WIRS). The most rudimentary question to consider is whether establishments have any union members. The findings of the 1980 and 1984 WIRS show that there was virtually no change in the proportion of establishments having trade union members for these years, with 73 per cent in both 1980 and 1984. By 1990, however, the proportion had fallen to 64 per cent overall, with a drop from 68 to 58 per cent for manual workers and from 58 to 51 per cent for non-manuals. 'The clear picture is of a sizeable decline in the number of workplaces with trade union members between the early 1980s and the end of the decade',[51] with all of this decline in the private sector.

Another striking change in union membership trends between the 1984 and 1990 surveys was the increasing proportion of establishments with no union members at all. This proportion increased from 27 to 36 per cent of all employees, from 32 to 42 per cent of manual employees and from 42 to 49 per cent of non-manual employees. Moreover, there is a ratchet effect on union membership which makes a change from low to zero union density more probable than a change in the reverse direction.

The main determinants of union membership include: size of establishment and size of enterprise, with large ones more likely to have union members than small ones; age of establishment, with old ones more likely to have union members than young ones; and workplaces with high proportions of manual and full-time employees more likely to have union members than those having non-manual and part-time ones. Other factors, such as absence of product market competitors, are also associated with higher rather than lower levels of union membership. Above all, the contrast in union membership levels amongst establishments in the private sector where management recognized trade unions and those where they did not between 1984 and 1990 is particularly striking. 'In 1984 the density figures were 67 per cent and 5 per cent respectively. In 1990 they were virtually unchanged at 66 per cent and 4 per cent respectively.'[52]

Non-union firms are found in a variety of private sector enterprises: small firms; medium size firms; and a few large companies, especially in service sectors such as hotels and catering, banking and insurance, and finance. In private services in 1990, for example, only 31 per cent of establishments in the WIRS recognized unions for manual workers and 26 per cent for non-manual workers. Further, partially non-union firms are not uncommon. This means, in practice, that many larger firms, whilst recognizing trade unions for their manual staff, are less willing to do so for their professional, technical and managerial employees. They operate selective union recognition policies, comprising full recognition for production, maintenance and clerical workers combined with a non-recognition policy for all other staff. The 1990 WIRS shows, for example, that whilst 44 per cent of establishments recognized unions for manual workers in private manufacturing only 23 per cent did so for non-manual workers.

An examination of the 1990 WIRS indicates that, in private manufacturing, there was a fall in the proportion of workplaces with recognized trade unions, from 56 to 44 per cent, which continued a trend already in train during the early 1980s. In the private services, the fall in union recognition was smaller than that in manufacturing: 'from 44 to 36 per cent between 1984 and 1990 and from 41 to 36 per cent over the ten years covered by [the] surveys'. As in manufacturing, the decline in the extent of recognition in private services was mainly confined to smaller establishments, with under 200 employees each. It was more pronounced in: independent establishments than those belonging to larger enterprises; foreign owned than indigenous workplaces; and 'those establishments employing substantial numbers of ethnic minority workers, a trend that was already apparent in the private sector between 1980 and 1984'.[53]

In both small and medium-sized companies, therefore, union recognition for some or all of their employees is less likely to be conceded than in larger firms in the manufacturing sector. Whether such non-recognition policies are explicit or not is difficult to determine. More probably, it is an implicit assumption by those owning, directing and managing such enterprises that unions are unnecessary in representing employee interests, for some or all of their employees, and are obstructive to the right to manage. In the smaller firm, close links are often claimed between management and non-managerial employees who sometimes share common unitary perspectives of the enterprise. In other cases, both these groups and supervisory staff do not always readily identify with trade unionism and employees can be difficult to organize into union membership. They believe that their employment interests are best advanced by individual effort and compliance with managerial expectations, rather than by collective representation and challenging management's right to manage through trade union organization. Where this is combined with a paternalistic or even *laissez-faire* style of management, employee demand for union representation is weakened and management's claim to the unilateral right to manage without interference from trade unions is strengthened.

Large non-union firms such as Marks and Spencer PLC and International Business Machines (UK) Ltd (IBM UK) are the exception rather than the rule, even though their influence is growing in importance. Large non-union firms are more likely to be American or privately owned, to be involved in non-manufacturing or service activities, to employ predominantly skilled or partially skilled white-collar workers, to be commercially successful in expanding product markets and to have covertly non-union personnel policies. Senior managers within such organizations would argue that their firms are not 'anti-union' but are 'non-union' because they claim that their employees see no real need for union organization or collective representation in employment matters. With enlightened and sophisticated paternalist personnel policies and 'people centred' managerial styles, such managers claim, unionization and collective bargaining are irrelevant to organizational success and employee welfare.

The reality is more complex, however, since tight screening in the recruitment and selection of employees, cohesive management control systems, in-company propaganda and training programmes, and attractive employee benefits undoubtedly contribute to employee commitment and loyalty within large non-union employers of this type. This managerial style has been described as 'sophisticated paternalism' and is characterized by a deliberate attempt to avoid collective bargaining and often a refusal to recognize trade unions. A main aim of such companies is to pre-empt industrial relations conflict between management and their employees, not through jointly agreed constitutional procedures, but through the skilful application of proactive neo-unitary personnel management techniques and policies; being successful companies, they can normally afford the financial costs of doing this.

Len Peach, when Director of Personnel and Corporate Affairs of IBM UK, claimed, for example, that IBM's personnel relations policy has six key elements conducive to its successful implementation. First, there is the 'practice of Full Employment'. This means that, on the one side, the company offers alternative employment to employees whose jobs are eliminated by economic or technological change. In turn employees must be willing to undertake training, move location and change jobs should the employer deem these to be necessary in the interests of the company. This policy was challenged, however, by the large-scale redundancies which took place in IBM UK in the early 1990s, when thousands of IBM employers were offered attractive packages to retire early or leave the company voluntarily, because of substantial losses owing to product market factors. Second, the company is committed to 'Single Status' with all employees under the same conditions of service and with the same employee benefits irrespective of skill. This reflects the willingness of IBM management, it is said, to judge people 'according to their contribution and not to a pre-defined pecking order – which is the essence of a company alert to and willing to change'. Third, the pay system is identical for most employees. It is based on a job evaluation scheme, with a monetary value placed on each job according to the company's policy of paying its employees 'favourably compared with other leading companies – in other words to occupy a high position in the market place'.

The fourth essential feature of IBM's personnel policy is the company's commitment to 'performance assessment and career counselling and planning'. Its main objective is to provide regularly 'a balanced statement of each employee's performance against objectives' assessed by their manager and validated by his or her superior. To this end all IBM managers 'average one week's management training in people skills . . . for every year of their careers'. Fifth, downward communication takes place through such mechanisms as the company newspaper, annual statements, location newspapers, bulletin boards and video tapes of messages from top management. Upward communication is provided through periodic attitude or opinion surveys of employees, with a biennial survey testing the company's communication processes themselves.

Finally, IBM has two main devices for processing employee grievances and appeals within the company. One is the 'Open Door' system enabling aggrieved employees who are dissatisfied with a managerial decision to appeal against it either through the management hierarchy or by a direct appeal 'to any level of management, by-passing intervening levels'. Twenty-five per cent of these, Peach suggests, are upheld in favour of the employee. The other device is the 'Speak Up' programme allowing individuals – or sometimes groups – to submit anonymous written complaints or requests for more information on a policy question to management and to obtain a formal reply from the person in the company best qualified to answer it. The company apparently receives more than 1 000 'speak ups' per year. These provide, Peach argues, early warnings of problems 'which, unheeded, might cause much distress to both individuals and the company'.[50]

## 11.7   Summary Points

- Management prerogative is the right to take unilateral decisions within organizations, subject only to limitations placed on it by the law and collective agreements.
- Normally, however, and with few exceptions, management can only manage effectively and successfully with the agreement and consent of subordinate employees.
- Where unions are recognized, there are few prerogatives, rights or functions at the workplace in the payment, deployment and disciplining of labour which remain exclusively management's. The right to manage in many enterprises, therefore, continues to rest on the right to initiate organizational and industrial relations change rather than to impose it unilaterally.
- The character of works rules has also been modified in recent years. Previously they were a major source of management's disciplinary authority within enterprises. Nowadays, company rules and handbooks serve much wider purposes than the regulation of disciplinary issues alone. These include advice about the organization's pension funds, its welfare provisions and other related matters. Disciplinary practices have also been affected by codes of practice, labour law and trade union membership. Trade union representatives regard discipline as not subject to managerial discretion alone. The

emphasis is generally on preventing disciplinary offences and on their correction, rather than on retribution and punishment.

- Dismissal remains the ultimate managerial sanction, with disciplinary procedures being more formalized than in the past. Today a series of administrative procedures has to be undergone within the disciplinary code before an employee can be dismissed. This enables those disciplined to appeal against disciplinary actions taken against them by line management, usually through their union representative.

- Where trade unions are recognized, there is less managerial control over traditional payment systems, since management has to negotiate pay structures with union representatives. A major distinguishing feature of salary payment systems is their incremental pay structures. Wage payment systems are less amenable to unilateral management regulation, because they comprise a number of variable elements such as basic rates, shiftwork allowances and overtime payments.

- Traditional PBR systems include individual PBR, group PBR and measured day work (MDW). Individual PBR comprises piecework and incentive payments, including a time rate and guaranteed earnings. The variable or bonus element can be regressive, proportional or progressive. MDW is a wage payment system which is intermediate between time rate systems and pure incentive schemes. It guarantees payment for a specific output or level of job performance, with a premium pay plan (PPP) offering individuals a choice of job performance and pay bands.

- Owing to economic, market and other factors, some employers have adopted more flexible payment systems since the mid-1980s. These include flexible starting pay, local and regional allowances, PBR, individual bonuses, collective bonuses and incentives based on profits or share ownership, although some employers combine more than one bonus scheme in a payment package.

- Current employment practices emerge out of management's human resources and personnel policies. Effective recruitment and selection procedures are essential, since mistakes are costly and not easy to rectify, with planned recruitment systems normally being both efficient and fair. Proper induction procedures are necessary to enable new employees to fit into their work roles, become integrated into the workplace and understand where they fit into the organization structure.

- Moves towards harmonization proceed where there are fundamental changes in managerial and employee attitudes, combined with marked changes in working arrangements.

- Effective employment practices are facilitated by proper workplace communication procedures. These encourage two-way exchanges of ideas and information between management and the workforce and their representatives.

- In designing and implementing employment policies, more managements are using appraisal and performance review systems. These include performance review, reviews of potential and development needs and reward reviews. Various techniques are used to assess employee performance and how this contributes to corporate success.

- Other current employment practices are concerned with extending equal opportunities in organizations and improving quality, including attempts by some managements to move towards total quality management (TQM) systems. These have implications for employee relations practices.

- There is evidence that many employers are now using non-standard labour (NSL) and employment flexibility to attract and retain workforces appropriate to their needs. These include part-timers, temporary employees, agency temporary workers and the self-employed. This is in response to labour and product market pressures. The direct costs of employing NSL appear to be not greatly dissimilar from those of standard labour, with labour turnover and absentee rates in line with those of full-time employees.

- NSL is not homogeneous. Skilled freelance workers tend to be males who want flexible employment, whilst less skilled, low-paid NSL tend to be female who have less choice in the labour market. There is little evidence that employers are adopting a strategic approach to labour utilization and labour management in the 1990s. They tend to improvise in managing human resources in response to their immediate business strategies.

- In non-union firms, management's right to manage remains relatively unchallenged, though constraints are placed on it by externally generated labour law. Different managerial philosophies seem to distinguish the small to medium-size non-union firm from its larger counterpart. In the former, managerial attitudes are more defensive of the right to manage, with no predetermined scheme for union avoidance. In larger firms, a more sophisticated approach to employee relations is more observable. This takes the form of more assertive, proactive personnel policies and practices, specifically aimed at obviating union representation and union organization in these enterprises.

## 11.8 References

1. J. Purcell, The rediscovery of the management prerogative: the management of labour relations in the 1980s, *Oxford Review of Economic Policy*, 7(1), 1991, p. 33.
2. A. Marsh, *Concise Encyclopedia of Industrial Relations*, Gower, London, 1979, p. 186.
3. Quoted in A. Marsh, *Industrial Relations in Engineering*, Pergamon, Oxford, 1965, pp. 250 and 272.
4. J. Storey, *The Challenge to Management Control*, Business Books, London, 1980, p. 45.
5. G. F. Bloom and H. R. Northrup, *Economics of Labor Relations*, Irwin, Homewood, Illinois, 1965, p. 173.
6. Organisation for Economic Co-operation and Development, *Workers' Participation*, OECD, Paris, 1976, p. 42.
7. W. E. J. McCarthy and N. D. Ellis, *Management by Agreement*, Hutchinson, London, 1973, p. 96.
8. Storey, *op. cit.*, p. 41.
9. OECD, *op. cit.*, p. 42.
10. K. Hudson, *Working to Rule*, Adams and Dart, Bath, 1970, p. 59.
11. E. O. Evans, Work rule books in the engineering industry, *Industrial Relations Journal*, Summer 1971, p. 63.
12. *Ibid.*, pp. 56–7.
13. R. T. Ashdown and K. H. Baker, *Department of Employment Manpower Papers Number 6. In Working Order: A Study of Industrial Discipline*, HMSO, London, 1973, p. 5.
14. Advisory Conciliation and Arbitration Service, *Disciplinary Practice at Work*, ACAS, London, 1987, p. 5.
15. N. Millward, M. Stevens, D. Smart and W. Hawes, *Workplace Industrial Relations in Transition*, Dartmouth, Aldershot, 1992, p. 194.
16. Ashdown and Baker, *op. cit.*, p. 26.
17. W. Marks, *Preparing an Employee Handbook*, IPM, London, 1978, p. 6.
18. D. Grayson, Payment systems for the future, *Employment Gazette*, March 1984, p. 121.
19. B. Conboy, *Pay at Work*, Arrow, London, 1976, p. 6.
20. National Board for Prices and Incomes, *Report No. 132. Salary Structures*, HMSO, London, 1969, p. 5.
21. Office of Manpower Economics, *Incremental Payment Systems*, HMSO, London, 1973, p. 4.
22. Grayson, *op. cit.*, p. 122.
23. National Board for Prices and Incomes (NBPI), *Report No. 65. Payment by Results*, HMSO, London, 1969, p. 3.
24. *Ibid.*, p. 4.
25. Office of Manpower Economics, *Measured Daywork*, HMSO, London, 1973, p. 8.
26. *Ibid.*, p. 23.
27. Advisory Conciliation and Arbitration Service, *Developments in Payment Systems*, ACAS, London, 1988, p. 24.
28. B. Casey, J. Lakey and M. White, *Payment Systems: A Look at Current Practice*, Employment Department, London, 1992, p. 34.
29. B. Casey, J. Lakey, H. Cooper and J. Elliott, Payment systems, *Employment Gazette*, August 1991, p. 454.
30. *Ibid.*, p. 457.
31. B. Curnow, The creative approach to pay, *Personnel Management*, October 1986, p. 70.
32. *Ibid.*
33. *Ibid.*, p. 71.
34. *Ibid.*, p. 72.
35. Casey *et al.*, *op. cit.*, p. 22.
36. Conboy, *op. cit.*, p. 57.
37. T. Lupton and A. M. Bowey, *Wages and Salaries*, Penguin, Harmondsworth, 1974, p. 19.
38. B. Townley, Selection and appraisal: reconstituting social relations, in J. Storey (ed.), *New Perspectives on Human Resource Management*, Routledge, London, 1989, p. 92.
39. Advisory Conciliation and Arbitration Service, *Developments in Harmonization*, ACAS, London, 1982, p. 9.
40. Institute of Personnel Management, *Staff Status for All*, IPM, London, 1977, p. 61.
41. L. Rico, The new industrial relations: British electricians and new style agreements, *Industrial and Labor Relations Review*, 41(1), October 1987, p. 71.
42. G. James, *Performance Appraisal*, ACAS, London, 1988, p. 3.
43. Institute of Management Services, *Total Quality Management*, IMS, London, 1992, p. 5.
44. Advisory Conciliation and Arbitration Service, *Total Quality Management*, ACAS, London, pp. 4 and 6.
45. Advisory Conciliation and Arbitration Service, *Labour Flexibility in Britain*, ACAS, London, 1987, p. 35.
46. *Ibid.*, p. 22.
47. *Ibid.*, p. 5.
48. A. McGregor and A. Sproull, Employers and the flexible workforce, *Employment Gazette*, May 1992, p. 233.
49. L. Hunter and J. MacInnes, Employers and labour flexibility, *Employment Gazette*, June 1992, pp. 308, 314 and 315.
50. I. McLaughlin and S. Gourlay, Enterprise without

unions: the management of employee relations in non-union firms, *Journal of Management Studies*, 25(5), 1992, pp. 675 and 686.

51. N. Millward, M. Stevens, D. Smart and W. Hawes, *Workplace Industrial Relations in Transition*, Dartmouth, Aldershot, 1992, p. 60.

52. *Ibid.*, p. 65.

53. *Ibid.*, pp. 72 and 73.

54. L. Peach, Employee relations in IBM, *Employee Relations*, 5(3), 1983, p. 3.

55. *Ibid.*, pp. 18 and 19.

# 12

# The Personnel Function

The essence of the modern personnel function is to enable management to organize the efforts of the people working in enterprises 'to attain the highest levels of efficiency, adaptability and productivity'.[1] In most small organizations the personnel function is exclusively the responsibility of line or functional managers, although there might be someone at senior level 'charged with overall responsibility for personnel matters and who will see that policy and guidelines are agreed and laid down'.[2] In larger organizations, 'managing people' is mainly a line management responsibility but there is normally a specialist personnel management function too. This is staffed by personnel professionals providing policy advice, guidance and support to line managers in their daily dealings with subordinate employees.

Wherever there is an awareness of the importance of people as 'human resources' in their organizations, rather than just as 'economic inputs' or 'wage labour', managers have to concern themselves with the human aspects of management. This gives rise to the need for the expertise and skills of professional personnel managers and has 'led to the establishment of personnel management as a significant and distinct field of management studies'.[3] Personnel management and human resources management are that part of the function of management arising out of the fact that enterprises employ people, even though the personnel function exists quite independently of whether specialists are employed or not. The focus of this chapter is the professional personnel role within enterprises, its part in policy making and implementation and its relationship with line management.

## 12.1 The Nature of the Personnel Function

The emergence and growth of personnel management within private and public enterprises has been largely shaped by the politico-economic contexts within which personnel policies and practices have developed in Britain. In general, with the economy in recession, the specialist personnel role is weakened, 'hard' and control centred. With the economy growing, and with skill shortages in the labour market emerging, personnel management is strengthened, 'soft' and welfare centred. Personnel activity is also affected by government policy, employment law and trade union power. The more interventionist government policy and the stronger trade union power then the greater is the need for professional personnel management.

A major expansion of the professional personnel management function took place in many medium and larger organizations during the 1960s and 1970s. This was in response to increasing trade union organization and power, the growth in employment legislation and relatively tight labour markets, where labour demand tended to exceed labour supply. It has been estimated that in 1963, for example, there were about 10 000–15 000 personnel managers in Britain. By the late 1970s, this had risen to a claimed 50 000 personnel specialists.[4] During the early 1980s, the number of personnel specialists stabilized. This was mainly because of the economic recession at that time, and the large shake-out of labour from manufacturing industry, when the recruiting, training and developing of human resources within enterprises shifted to 'assessing, excluding and retiring them'.[5] A recent estimate of the numbers of personnel specialists working in Britain puts the figure at some 150 000 in 1992, with 'employee relations' accounting for some third of the total.

According to the 1990 Workplace Industrial Relations Survey, personnel management activity, whether performed by personnel specialists or others, tends to be associated with foreign-owned companies, those recognizing trade unions and those with substantial concentrations of white collar employees. But the key factor associated with personnel management operations is the total number of employees: the larger the number of employees, the more likely the organization is to have personnel specialists. The job titles of personnel managers in the 1990 survey varied but interestingly only a small proportion of them had 'human resources' in their titles, with their activities 'covering no more than 130 thousand employees' in the representative sample. Earlier surveys, in 1980 and 1984, had shown substantial increases in the extent to which designated personnel managers had formal qualifications, at 49 and 58 per cent respectively. By 1990, the proportion had fallen slightly to 54 per cent of the sample, although the qualifications of 'non-designated' managers, spending a quarter or more of their time on the personnel function, had increased over the same period.

## Perceptions of the personnel function

Perceptions of the personnel management function within enterprises vary widely. Some commentators have been highly critical of specialist personnel management, arguing that in the 1970s, for instance, personnel management began with great promise 'but at the beginning of the 1980s the promise remained unfulfilled'. This critic, Manning, argues that whilst the importance of the efficient and effective managing of human resources within enterprises has not receded, personnel management as a discipline has not made the significant impact in organizations which it should have done. Compared with marketing and production, for example, personnel management has the weakest conceptual base, it is claimed, and the poorest technology in relation to some other managerial functions. 'What is needed is the sort of analytic and creative thinking that has been demonstrated so successfully in disciplines like marketing and finance'. Manning tries to explain the apparent apathy of some line managers towards personnel. To the average manager, he writes, 'personnel all too often seems distant from the immediate problems of achieving his budget and from the wider business needs of the company'.[7]

In the organizations studied by Legge two major points were noted. First, there was a general absence of systematically formulated personnel policies within them. Second, line management tended to neglect the personnel aspects of their decision making roles. She claims that senior management, whilst accepting the need to develop appropriate personnel policies, was often unable to think through and develop consistent personnel strategies. She also found that line managers:

> while recognizing that much of their work was a form of personnel management tended to

operate in the area in an *ad hoc* manner, without any clearly thought out and articulated framework to which to relate their activities. As a result, in company decision-making, the personnel management considerations involved in production, marketing and finance decisions were not so much overruled . . . as went by default.[8]

The sometime chairman of ICI, John Harvey-Jones, also criticized the role of personnel professionals. He was not greatly impressed by the ways that some personnel departments were run by those in charge of them. Although personnel managers are the custodians of most of the theory of management, he writes, all too often in his view their activity 'appears to be directed towards offering advice to others, rather than practising within their own house'. He is also doubtful whether prolonged exposure within the specialist personnel function provides an appropriate background for generating 'an all-round businessman with the particular qualities which are required for the highest positions in industry'. Whilst believing that line managers should work in personnel for a period, he does not consider that personnel management should be primarily a specialist activity but 'should be the responsibility of every line manager'.[9]

Other senior executives and corporate leaders are on record as being more supportive of the specialist personnel function and perceiving it in more progressive and proactive terms. The former chairman of British Rail, Peter Parker, for example, views the professional personnel role in humanistic terms as the 'agent of change' within the enterprise. He looks to the personnel function to help managers and unions understand the 'different cultures of enterprise and of the community'. The personnel manager's 'new role', he claims, is 'the co-ordinator of two cultures', emphasizing the mutuality of the industrial and social purposes of work. Parker argues that the major responsibility of the personnel function is to sustain the effectiveness of an organization's human resources, whilst extending every individual's sense of scope of work. If an enterprise is to achieve its objectives Parker claims, 'I see personnel increasingly involved in the effort to clarify the social policy of an enterprise'. In Parker's analysis, 'industry cannot separate its own working relationships and values from those of the community in which it operates and serves'.[10]

Parker believes that personnel managers should be moved around managerial functions and that line managers should get a feel for personnel work by experiencing it for themselves. Further, the personnel function needs to be fully integrated into organizational structures 'by being absolutely clear about it as supportive of line management'. Parker expects three things from personnel managers: professionalism; to be 'outward looking'; and to operate on two time scales:

> Personnel must develop long-term policies and strategies and it must also be in there pitching when day-to-day problems arise, when tough negotiations are being faced, when line managers need their skill and experience to the full. In a sense, there is the creative philosophical role, the preventive role and the day-to-day role.[11]

Whilst he does not see the personnel department primarily as a 'fire fighting' agency, Parker concedes that even with the best long-term strategies, personnel 'fires' sometimes have to be put out.

A leading senior executive in the private sector, Alex Jarrett, sometime chairman of Reed International, put forward equally strong views about the importance of the personnel function. For him personnel managers and personnel directors are the people 'with special knowledge and skills about what is the most important asset of our business – the people we employ'. He identifies three issues vitally affecting industrial relations and the success of a company. These are collective bargaining and pay determination, employee involvement, and the career development and remuneration of management. In any company or group of companies, he argues, these are crucial matters on which the business must establish clear policies and strategies. In Jarrett's view the personnel department and its professional staff have, with their specialist knowledge and skills, a major contribution to make to organizational effectiveness. It is individual line managers, however, who carry the prime responsibility for industrial relations in their own departments and the outcome of pay negotiations. Personnel professionals also have a role in developing and implementing appropriate employee involvement policies. In Jarrett's experience, 'both industrial relations and [employee] involvement are matters of good management in which personnel has a vital part to play'.[12]

These few contrasting classical analyses of personnel management provide some insights into the different perceptions about the personnel function amongst general management practitioners. They also show that there is no consensus as to what con-

stitutes personnel's central thrust and direction, apart from its concern with the human aspects of management. This should not be surprising, given the diverse origins and different ideological roots of the personnel role in British management. For example, a major ambivalence within personnel management lies between the so-called 'welfare role' of personnel and the 'management control role', with 'the one paternalistically oriented towards the welfare of employees and the other rationally derived from corporate needs to control'.[13] The welfare role, for example, was the earliest type of personnel activity to emerge in Britain and was associated with the altruistic concern for the corporate and social welfare of their employees by a handful of paternalistic employers such as Rowntrees, Cadburys and W. D. and H. O. Wills at the beginning of the century. These firms were the first to appoint 'factory welfare workers' whose duties included raising standards of factory welfare, ensuring factory legislation was implemented, providing personal counselling to employees and looking after employee amenities such as canteens, rest rooms and recreation grounds.

Seebohm Rowntree saw factory welfare workers as representatives both of their firms and of employees. In representing the employer they were expected to devise improvements in conditions of work and keep the 'personal element' prominent in relations with employees. As representatives of employees, Seebohm wrote:

> it is the duty of the social helpers to be constantly in touch with them [employees], to gain their confidence, to voice any grievances they may have either individually or collectively, to give effect to any reasonable desire they may show for recreative clubs, educational classes, etc and to give advice in matters concerning them personally.[14]

In these twin roles welfare workers were seen as intermediaries between employer and employees but were not to be subordinate to either, even if they were to be seen to serve both. Today the welfare role is largely a residual one and is a relatively minor part of the personnel function. The main exceptions are those non-union employers, often with predominantly female workforces, who adopt paternalistic styles of management. Welfare work has, however, left a marked impact on the image of British personnel management giving some people the mistaken view that personnel managers are 'social workers' in industry.

The management control role, in contrast, is rooted in managerial concern for economic efficiency at work. In its control role, personnel management aims to get the best out of the human resource within organizations, minimizing its unit cost, maximizing its productive output and, where possible, integrating individual employee needs with those of the employing organization and its managerial decision makers. This perception of the personnel function clearly identifies personnel work, whether performed by line managers or personnel specialists, firmly within a managerial and employer frame of reference. Whilst implying a more executive role for personnel managers, the management control role also raises questions about the respective allocation of personnel activities between line and personnel managers. It means in practice 'that personnel managers may become involved in an extremely wide range of activities sometimes executive, sometimes advisory, but always a part of the managerial team'.[15]

Further perceptions of the personnel function include the 'third-party role' and the 'professional role'. Just as the personnel manager claims some kind of independent status from that of the employer in carrying out a welfare role by acting as an intermediary between the parties, and as a corporate conscience for management, especially in understanding the concerns of employees and their needs, so too does the third-party role of personnel management. With the expansion of employment legislation in recent years, for example, the personnel function becomes an important source for interpreting the law and spelling out its implications for employers and employees. By using this legislation to justify certain personnel policies and practices, personnel managers are adopting a third-party intermediary role, based on their expert knowledge and understanding of the law, with 'an implicit assumption that the law enshrines the values of society as a whole in contradistinction to the immediate self-interest of any particular employer'.[16]

The professional role of personnel management is the one largely advocated by the Institute of Personnel and Development (IPD), which is the professional association aiming at improving personnel practice in Britain. The professional role sees personnel managers as managerial resources having specialist knowledge and skills but also possessing values and concerns which exist independently of a specified organization. By this view, the specialist personnel manager is expected to have a series of transferable occupational skills, and a set of professional values, enabling both economic efficiency for the employer and social justice for employees to be achieved simultaneously within the employing organization. It differs from the third-party role by being explicitly identified with employer interests and operating only informally as the corporate conscience. 'The range of activities may be considerable, but they could become predominantly advisory rather than executive'.[17]

Another perception of the personnel function is provided by Tyson. He argues that close examination of the social constructs used by personnel managers in dealing with personnel problems reflects organizational cultures rather than occupational norms and beliefs. In his research he identifies similarities in beliefs and values between personnel staff in the same organizations and considerable differences between personnel staff in different organizational settings. The real specialism of personnel management, he claims, 'could be described as the capacity to survive, to be adaptable, and to facilitate senior managerial actions'. In his view the role of the personnel specialist leads to an accommodation between organizational and personal values, partly because it is a processing and facilitating role and partly because personnel specialists represent organizational interests and define its identity and character. He concludes that 'personnel managers could be described as specialists in ambiguity'. Such a role, however, 'clearly limits the possibility of developing a capacity to contribute to managerial strategic thinking'.[18]

One of the most influential perceptions and analyses of the personnel function is provided by Torrington and Hall. They trace the development of the personnel function 'by suggesting a general self-image, which obtained at different periods'. These are: 'the social reformer', who supported workers in their dealings with the early factory employers; 'the acolyte of benevolence', who dispensed paternalist employer benefits to employees; 'the humane bureaucrat', who was concerned with employee selection, training and placement; 'the consensus negotiator', who used bargaining expertise to deal with strong trade unions on behalf of management; 'the organization man', who was preoccupied with the effectiveness of the organization as a whole; 'the manpower analyst', who quantified 'manpower' supply and demand; and, most recently, the 'human resources manager', who is resource centred and aims to satisfy management needs for human resources, rather than being workforce centred and acting as an intermediary between employer and employees. For Torrington and Hall, however, modern personnel management is a synthesis and needs to integrate the mutual needs of employer and employees within the workplace. They therefore suggest that:

> Personnel management is a series of activities which: first enable working people and their employing organizations to agree about the objectives and nature of their working relationship and, secondly, ensures that the agreement is fulfilled.[20]

The Personnel Management Standards Lead Body (PSLB), whose purpose is 'to provide world-class standards and qualifications for personnel which make a valuable contribution and are cost effective', provides one of the most up-to-date and possibly controversial perceptions of the personnel management function. It sees personnel predominantly as 'an enabling activity'. For the PSLB, the key purpose of personnel is 'to enable management to enhance the individual and collective contributions of people to the short and long term success of the enterprise'. As an activity concerned with 'creating an environment which enables management to recruit, train and motivate the people they need for today's and tomorrow's jobs', personnel is central to organizational success. The PSLB also sees personnel, when carried out by a specialist unit, as needing to add 'real value' to the business decision making process and to contribute to the profitability of 'the business'. The PSLB goes on to argue that personnel is responsible for promoting organizational values in relation to people at work, by identifying their importance to the success of the enterprise. These 'core values' include:

- dealing with people fairly;
- maximizing the development and training of the workforce to meet the current and future needs of the enterprise;
- providing equal opportunity for all as a continuing feature of management practice and personnel processes;
- handling disciplinary matters within the principles of natural justice;
- creating and maintaining a safe and healthy working environment.

## Power and authority in personnel

The power and authority in any managerial function are normally related to how its activities and tasks are seen as contributing to enterprise efficiency and organizational effectiveness. Some management functions such as production, finance and marketing find it relatively easy to claim a clear relationship between their activities and enterprise success compared with the personnel department. The difficulty arises for personnel management in part because personnel managers are more concerned 'with means rather than ends and inputs rather than outputs, and in situations where it is difficult in determining the relationship between the two'.[21] As functional specialists, personnel managers are involved with obtaining, maintaining and discharging an organizational resource – people – through which corporate objectives are achieved. They are not concerned with the objectives themselves. Further, the personnel function deals with people as complex, sometimes unpredictable individuals who are not amenable to manipulation like inanimate objects such as finance, technology and other material resources.

Another problem inherent in the personnel role is its concern with providing and maintaining human inputs which are utilized in other parts of the enterprise where they are employed. The organizational outputs which employees generate, in association with capital and other resources, are often seen as achievements of other parts of the enterprise, not of the personnel department. If improved or more efficient employee effort is a product of effective personnel practices, such as successful recruitment, sound training or well-designed remuneration packages, the personnel department seldom receives the credit. Indeed, the specific contribution which professional personnel management makes to enterprise success is, it is argued, normally difficult 'to measure and isolate from effects of market and other organizational factors'.[22]

Another difficulty which the personnel role encounters in gaining organizational power and status is the widespread nature of the function. This presents difficulties in defining the boundaries between personnel management and other managerial activities. There is also the problem of arriving at realistic definitions of what the personnel department's unique contribution within an organization is. Because every managerial activity has personnel elements, it is argued, it is difficult for the personnel department to claim that its specific contributions facilitate organizational success. Even where personnel outputs are quantifiable and measurable, such as low absenteeism, few employee grievances or strike-free industrial relations, they are not necessarily attributable to the professionalism of personnel specialists and are rarely credited to the personnel department.

Where there appear to be few personnel problems within an enterprise, line managers can even claim that they deserve the credit for effective personnel management, not the personnel department; but they can blame the personnel department if things go badly. In either case, the diffusion of the personnel function into line management activities 'sometimes leads line managers to question whether the personnel function needs a specialist presence within an organization at all'.[23] Indeed, effective 'people management' by line managers can undermine the status of the specialist personnel role because personnel work does not then appear to be a specific activity requiring professional knowledge, skills and expertise. Further, although the personnel department is often responsible for designing and setting up particular personnel systems, such as payment systems, job evaluation and staff appraisal schemes, it does not normally implement them. This is the responsibility of line and functional managers whose success or failure in these tasks is removed from the direct control of personnel staff.

Recruitment, for example, is a main area where personnel departments are judged by other managers.

> This usually seems to them to be unfair because they cannot manufacture people, and they frequently feel that their failure to recruit is due more to management's refusal to accept their advice on personnel policy than their own incompetence at recruiting ... Few aspects of the personnel function show up fundamental weaknesses more clearly than does the problem of recruitment.[24]

Because of these factors, personnel departments can have a low status in the eyes of line management and a 'vicious circle of information denial, lack of support and credibility is set up'.[25] This undermines the authority of the personnel function which, in its quest for organizational power and managerial recognition, has to devise appropriate strategies aimed at influencing corporate decision making, contingent to organizational circumstances, rather than assuming its role is automatically legitimized by all managers and managerial groups.

## Personnel professionalism

Whether personnel management is a profession 'will continue to be debated within the more general discussion of whether any managerial occupation could qualify given the usual template applied'.[26] In the classical sense, that of a high-status occupational group with full professional autonomy providing personal services to individual fee paying clients, personnel management is clearly not a profession. If, however, professionalism exists where an occupational group 'makes a claim for power and authority in specified areas of occupational performance, then personnel management can be regarded as a professionalized activity'.[27]

This model of professionalism has two main elements. The first is common occupational interests among practitioners, even though the professional group itself is heterogeneous. The second is that its practitioners claim and demonstrate high standards of competence and expertise in carrying out their specialist activities and tasks. The first point is made in Watson's study of personnel managers. He claims that there is a common consciousness among personnel specialists, especially in their concern with gaining status with senior management. In his view there is a coherence within the occupation which is far greater than he expected when carrying out his research.

> To find personnel officers and managers in banks, engineering companies, co-operative societies, council offices and so on, speaking in such similar ways on aspects of their jobs was a considerable surprise to me.[28]

Being professional in their jobs, on the other hand, requires personnel managers to be competent and expert in their organizational roles and to provide tangible evidence that they are contributing positively to the effective managing of human resources. It does not necessarily mean being members of a recognized professional body with its underlying assumptions of specialist education and training and high occupational status and prestige. It requires, rather, the demonstration of specialist skills and expertise in managing the increasingly complex employment relationship between employers and employees in an organizational setting. In this sense experience indicates a strong identification by personnel managers with organizational needs and corporate objectives, rather than with those of employees or the wider society. 'What the notion of professionalism symbolises for the contemporary personnel specialist is . . . competence in the meeting of general managerial goals'.[29] Personnel professionals, in this sense, are seen largely as contributing effectively to the successful management of the enterprise, not as being an elite group of externally accountable practitioners.

## 12.2   Personnel and Human Resources Management (HRM)

There is considerable debate about the changing nature of personnel management since the mid-1980s. One writer has described personnel managers in 1993 as being 'in a crisis of confidence', arising largely from Britain being in slump and with unemployment standing at some three million. He identified the main personnel issues and priorities which this sort of environment generated as follows.

- **Workforce restructuring:** major redundancy, early retirement and redeployment programmes as enterprises withdraw to core businesses and shed the unprofitable.
- **Increased decentralization of decision making and accountability:** including pay bargaining and employee relations, especially noteworthy now in the public sector through the Next Steps agencies, contracting out, local pay systems in local government and so on.
- **Productivity programmes of all sorts:** teamworking and flexibility, performance management, incentive schemes, quality schemes, working time changes.[30]

The main thrust of personnel work was conditioned by a recessionary economy at that time and this combined with other factors to encourage employers to seek downward pressure on overall employment costs, to maintain organizational survival and viability.

One response to the challenges facing the personnel function during the 1980s and the 1990s has been the emergence of 'human resources management' (HRM). Guest describes HRM as the 'new orthodoxy' of personnel management/industrial relations, whilst questioning the future survival of the professional model of personnel management. 'For at least two decades, the dominant orthodoxy was the pluralist Donovan model. . . . In the 1980s this was challenged by the emergence of human resource management.'[31] Torrington and Hall, on the other hand, argue that it is wrong to suggest that the 'new' HRM has taken over from the 'old' personnel management. They see both approaches as present in the same organization, though they concede that 'there is a tendency for human resources management to increase at the expense of personnel management'.[32] The reasons for this include: the devolution of personnel duties to line managers; widespread unemployment and the use of non-standard labour; the appeal of HRM as a means of making the personnel function more influential in organizations; the range of 'mini-expertise', external to the employer, needed in personnel management; reduced union power; the weakening effects of employment legislation; and the need for personnel to justify itself in cost terms.

### Current conceptions of the personnel function

In a study of the changing nature of personnel management in the 1980s, Torrington and Mackay note that there is an underlying trend for the term 'personnel management' to be replaced by 'human resources management' amongst personnel specialists. They see personnel management as being directed mainly at the organization's employees and not being totally identified with managerial interests. Indeed 'there is always some degree of being "in between" the management and the employees, mediating the needs of each to the other'.[33] A similar point is made by Watson, who argues that personnel managers frequently have to appear to be facing two ways at the same time. To maintain credibility with employees, they have to show concern for employee welfare. 'But to justify their existence with management they must show to their managers a concern for the *efficiency* of labour utilisation', as well as 'ensuring that staff interests are always subvervient to those of organisational *effectiveness*, and for *controlling* the workforce'.[34]

HRM, in contrast, is directed mainly towards managerial needs for people resources in organizations, with greater emphasis being placed on 'planning, monitoring and control, rather than on problem solving and mediation'. Whilst traditional personnel management is underpinned by the ideas that employees need looking after, and are only effective when their needs are being met, HRM reflects a different set of beliefs. These are 'that getting the deployment of correct numbers and skills at the right price is more important than a patronizing involvement with people's personal affairs'. Although some of Torrington and Mackay's respondents were impressed by a human resources emphasis in personnel, others only 'reluctantly acknowledged its increasing importance'. Its greatest benefit appears to be the wider recognition given to the specialist personnel function by senior line management where an HRM approach is adopted.[35]

Tyson identifies four 'traditions' of personnel and three 'models'. Taken together they provide a useful framework for examining the modern personnel function. According to Tyson, the 'welfare tradition' originated in the industrial betterment movement of the late nineteenth century, whilst the 'employment management' tradition emerged out of the bureaucratization of work stimulated by two world wars. The more recent 'industrial relations' and 'professional' traditions respectively arose out of the tight labour market conditions of the postwar years and the professional association activities of the Institute of Personnel Management (IPM). The latter encouraged the view that 'personnel specialists possess a separate occupational identity, and should be accorded a professional status based on a knowledge of the social sciences, of personnel techniques and on employment law'.[36]

Tyson's three models of personnel are the 'clerk of works', the 'contracts manager' and the 'architect' models, also referred to as the 'administrative support', 'systems reactive' and 'business manager' models. Where the specialist personnel function operates on clerk of works lines, for instance, it is an administrative support activity with no business planning involvement. Personnel authority is vested in line managers, as the principal activities are recruitment, record-keeping and welfare. The contracts manager approach to personnel is a 'system model' which is part of a comprehensive policy framework acting on behalf of line managers. Personnel managers are especially valued for their capacity in making quick decisions and informal agreements with the unions to maintain organizational harmony. The architect model of personnel aims to create and build the organization as a whole. It is a creative view of personnel and contributes to corporate success 'through explicit policies which seek to give effect to the corporate plan, with an integrated system of controls between personnel and line managers'. A key feature of the architect model is that 'personnel executives take the management of change, and the use of social science techniques to be the cornerstone of their approach'.[37]

For Tyson and Fell, an HRM philosophy emerges wherever people are perceived not as a cost for doing business but as the 'only resource capable of turning inanimate factors of production into wealth. People provide the source of creative energy in any direction the organization dictates and fosters.' For them, HRM has a base in the behavioural sciences, is concerned with the induction and development of individuals and enhances organizational performance. HRM changes personnel from the role of a 'control-oriented supplier of labour to an overall human resource planning, development and utilization agency'. It integrates and co-ordinates people planning with strategy formulation and takes a pro-active view of human resources activities in an organizational setting. Moreover, within the architect model, HRM is 'directed at achieving the symbiosis which is seen to exist between the organization and its goals and an effective use of the human resources the organization needs to achieve those goals'.[38]

Fowler identifies two main themes in HRM thinking. These are, first, 'that every aspect of employee management must be wholly integrated with business management', thus reinforcing corporate culture. The second is 'a dominant emphasis on the common interests of employers and employed in the success of the business'. This, it is believed, will release 'a massive potential of initiative and commitment within the workforce'. Yet Fowler is sceptical about the concept of HRM. He argues that what is new about HRM is not what it is but who is saying it. 'In a nutshell, HRM represents the discovery of personnel management by chief executives.' He suggests that the success of some of the companies held up as models of HRM practices and corporate excellence owes as much 'to the covert skills of their corporate lawyers and international marketeers as to the undoubted high morale of their factory and office staff'.[39]

Fowler is also cautious about two other aspects of HRM. One is whether an HRM culture is appropriate for all organizations, given that different business environments have their own organizational and cultural characteristics. His second reservation is the North American origin of much HRM literature and practices. 'At the heart of the concept is the complete identification of employees with the aims and values of the business – employee involvement, but on the company's terms.' He questions whether it is really possible to claim mutuality at work between managers and managed, when ultimately it is the employer which can decide whether to close the company down or to sell it to outsiders. In his view, the HRM literature largely ignores power in employee relations and the role of trade unions in protecting employee interests at work. Whilst accepting the need for compatibility between personnel practices and corporate culture, effective leadership and recognizing individual potential at work, Fowler believes that some HRM enthusiasts may be over-simplifying the issues. 'Are they genuinely concerned with creating a new, equal partnership between employer and employed, or are they really offering a covert form of employee manipulation, dressed up as mutuality?'[40]

Michael Armstrong argues that Fowler's reservations are only valid 'if HRM is regarded as something completely different from personnel management, which of course it is not'. He believes that they share many of the same roots. What is needed is 'a revised concept of HRM which links its worthwhile elements with the best personnel management practices'. He does not therefore see HRM as threatening personnel management. In tracing the behavioural roots of HRM, Armstrong posits that 'it is possible to develop an HRM concept which is not as crude as it has sometimes been portrayed'. For him, HRM is based on four fundamental principles. First, human resources are an organization's most important assets. Second, personnel policies should make a major contribution to achieving corporate goals and objectives. Third, corporate culture exerts a major influence on achieving 'excellence' and must therefore be managed. Fourth, whilst integration of corporate resources is an important aim of HRM, it has to be recognized *that all organisations are pluralist societies in which people have differing interests and concerns which they may well feel need to be defended collectively*.[41]

## Critiques of personnel management

A number of critiques of personnel management were made in the 1980s. Manning argues, for example, that in many companies in the early 1980s personnel departments faced growing disenchantment and a steady decline in influence. He believed that personnel departments had failed to make the significant inroads into corporate affairs expected of them. To rectify the widespread apathy of line managers towards the personnel department, and to allay the fears that personnel seems to be too remote from line management's problems, Manning recommends four ways of developing the role. The first is to challenge the principles underlying current thinking in the function. The second is to establish personnel in the strategic management of companies. The third is to

create a body of coherent and credible technology to support that strategic role. 'And the final item is the effective use of computers to record and measure organizational performance.'[42]

Thurley asks whether personnel management in the 1980s was sick and whether it required 'urgent treatment'. He suggests that any claimed sickness rested on three allegations. First, it is asserted that personnel specialists are caught in a mismatch between abstract models of HRM and real-life activities which go unrecognized by other managers. Second, it is argued that though personnel specialists cope by using their professionalism instrumentally, they really conform with organizational norms. Third, personnel finds it difficult to develop overall strategies to break out of this situation 'due to constraints under which organizations have to work'. Thurley's conclusion is that personnel is 'not particularly sick but is certainly suffering from stunted growth'. The reasons are, first, that personnel management has failed to generate an overall set of political and economic objectives acceptable to major decision makers. Second, there has been a failure to provide 'the R and D necessary to make social science operationally useful'. Third, personnel managers have neglected to organize the personnel function effectively to 'facilitate innovation and higher performance' in enterprises.[43]

Looking back to the 1970s from a practitioner's perspective, Cowan concludes that the 1970s were wasted years for the personnel management profession. 'In fact we can look back on a decade that is the modern wasteland of personnel management.' Cowan identifies what did not happen: industrial democracy came and went; the social impact of Europe never materialized; new forms of work organization and work structuring proved illusory; harmonization of terms and conditions was very limited; and equal opportunities did not make as much progress as expected. Above all virtually no progress was made 'in finding a solution to Britain's industrial relations problems'. Cowan believes that what went wrong was a tendency to overestimate the rate of change in social affairs. 'So, although the strategies for the '70s may well have been based on a social analysis of probable future developments, it was assumed that they would take place much more quickly than they did.'[44]

Writing several years later, Cowan adds that examining the growth of personnel management in the 1970s reveals a major paradox. During this period, the personnel function gained considerable power and influence. This stemmed from increased union strength and new labour laws which highlighted the importance of industrial relations. Yet in hindsight, 'this greater power and influence did little, if anything, to improve the effectiveness of line management and, because of this, business overall'. With this experience in mind, Cowan argues that personnel management needs to increase its power and authority, and hence its contribution to business effectiveness, 'through the achievement of total management efficiency which means without blunting the thrust of line management'. It might then be possible 'to describe the years ahead as the "non-negotiating" nineties to reflect the environment that is likely to be experienced in that decade'.[45]

Further criticism of personnel comes from a novel direction. Peter Armstrong's basic concern is that the personnel function is not responding sufficiently to the challenges posed to it by the business dominance of the management accountancy profession. According to Armstrong's analysis, the contracts manager personnel role is being replaced by a polarized profession 'consisting of a mass of "clerk of works" ... and a few elite "architects" of strategic human resources policy who continue to operate at the corporate headquarters level'. His diagnosis is that the current problems 'faced by the personnel profession have as much to do with the increasing dominance of management accounting systems in British companies as with the recession'.[46] Armstrong concludes that the architect or business manager model of personnel management 'is relevant only to those companies which have expanded around a recognisable "core" of operational activities'. In those more typical highly diversified companies, there are no grounds whatsoever for supposing that the personnel function is going to escape 'the general process of devolution and subordination to financial control which has been the fate of other managerial specialisms'. For Armstrong, the strategy of survival for the personnel profession in most large British companies lies in a 'modest and practical version of "deviant innovation"'. As Legge and Exley indicate, this requires personnel managers to act proactively and skilfully, not as 'conformist innovators' by making their activities conform to the dominant values associated with organizational success. It involves them, rather, in attempting 'to change this means and ends relationship by gaining acceptance for a *different set of criteria* for the evaluation of organizational success and their contribution to it'.[47] This approach recognizes the fact of accounting

controls within companies but 'seeks to exploit their problematic aspects as means for promoting intervention by the personnel profession'.[48]

## The HRM response

During the 1980s and 1990s, for a variety of organizational, technological and market reasons, some firms developed an HRM response to personnel management problems. The trend was by no means universal, and should not be exaggerated, but it has been commented on by both students and practitioners of personnel management. Guest, for example, in a seminal article on the topic identifies six underlying pressures behind the rising interest in HRM in Britain. They are: the search for competitive advantage; models of excellence in corporate enterprise; the 'failure' of personnel management to promote the potential benefits of effective management; the decline in trade union pressure; changes in the workforce and the nature of work; and the availability of 'new models' of management involving a subtle blend 'of some of the "best" elements of scientific management and human relations'.[49]

Guest suggests that there are three ways in which the term HRM is being used. These are: a retitling of personnel management; a reconceptualizing and reorganizing of personnel roles, especially in the conceptual framework of the Harvard Business School; and a distinctively different and new approach for managing people. In analysing the nature of HRM as a philosophy of managing people, Guest sees it as only one approach among several, with others being equally 'legitimate and likely in certain contexts to be more successful'. Further, given the evidence that only some workers will seek out and respond to work environments providing 'challenge, autonomy, learning opportunities and self-control', Guest argues that HRM, being based on these assumptions, is only viable in those organizations employing workers with such orientations. In fact, drawing on survey evidence from the London School of Economics, on what respondents viewed as ideal models 'of good personnel management practice', Guest concludes that the HRM model 'was by no means the dominant one and it is interesting to note that the largest number of companies fell within the professional model'.[50]

One of the most interesting aspects of Guest's essay is his theoretical analysis of HRM. He sees HRM as having four policy goals. These are: integration; employee commitment; flexibility; and quality.

Integration has four components: management strategy; 'vertical integration between strategic concerns, management concerns and operational concerns'; the attitudes and behaviour of line managers; and the view that all employees should be fully integrated into the business for which they work. Underlying these four elements of integration is a general proposition. This is that if personnel management is integrated into strategic planning, 'if human resource policies adhere, if line managers have internalized the importance of human resources' – and this is reflected in their behaviour – 'and if employees identify with the company, then the company's strategic plans are likely to be more successfully implemented'. As a result change is facilitated and resistance to it weakened.

The goal of employee commitment is to develop feelings of involvement with the organization in individual employees. This is seen to make them more satisfied, productive and adaptable workers. The theoretical proposition is that 'organizational commitment, combined with job-related behavioural commitment will result in high employee satisfaction, high performance, longer tenure and a willingness to accept change'. The theoretical proposition behind the goal of flexibility is that flexible organizational structures 'together with flexible job content and flexible employees will result in a capacity to respond swiftly and effectively to change, thus ensuring the high utilization of human and other resources within the organization'. The goal of quality has a number of elements, including quality of staff, performance, management practice and public image, especially the employer's human resources policies. To ensure high quality, considerable attention is normally given in HRM to recruitment and selection, training, appraisal, goal setting and job design. In these ways, human resources are fully utilized 'by providing high quality challenging jobs for high quality staff'. The theoretical proposition is that the pursuit of policies designed 'to ensure the recruitment and retention of high quality staff to undertake demanding jobs, supported by competent management will result in high performance levels'. Having identified these goals, Guest warns that many British companies may not want to practice HRM. The opportunity for change 'seems most likely to arise when a new chief executive is appointed, when a major crisis arises which creates opportunities for change or at a greenfield site'.[51]

Beaumont argues that the literature on HRM is very much dominated by organizational practice and academic work originating in the USA. He identifies the components of a fairly sophisticated, cohesive and integrated HRM package as being:

- relatively well developed internal labour market arrangements (in matters of promotion, training and individual career development);
- flexible work organization systems;
- contingent compensation practices and/or skills or knowledge-based pay structures;
- relatively high levels of individual employee and workgroup participation in task-related decisions;
- extensive internal communications arrangements.

The key messages in the US literature are the 'strategic' focus of HRM and the need for HRM practices to be consistent with overall business strategy. There is also the need for the components of an HRM strategy to reinforce one another and to be congruent with corporate culture. 'Team work', 'flexibility', 'employee involvement' and 'employee commitment' are the 'leading watchwords of this approach'.[52]

A series of case studies conducted at the University of Warwick's Centre for Corporate Strategy and Change indicate that companies undertaking developments in HRM do so under strong competitive pressures. According to these findings, HRM in such firms has not developed in a vacuum. In practice, 'a complex set of business environment changes have led to a series of generic strategic responses', with seven 'interdependent' responses driving developments in HRM. These are: competitive restructuring; decentralizing of decision making; internationalization of markets; acquisitions and mergers; quality improvement; technological change; and new concepts of service and distribution management. Thus complexity of externally inspired change creates 'needs for new operating structures and systems, new skills, knowledge and capability from staff at many organisational levels and in a variety of functions'. The origins of HRM issues, in other words, are 'manifestly connectable to the business and technical changes in the outer context of the firm'.[53]

The Warwick research team also identifies the main internal characteristics of firms where HRM changes are likely to take place. These include: changes in their top leadership; the implementation of major redundancy programmes; the creation of 'performance-oriented cultural change'; improvements in product quality and customer relations; attempts to create an overall 'culture for change'; the complementary development of strategic management and people management skills; and the 'decentralisation of responsibility for HRM activities' to line management. Such internal and external changes appear to have been managed by responses across the whole range of personnel activity. These include: skill supply; human resources development; selection and retention; rewards management; and employee relations.

It is sometimes claimed that HRM thrives more in non-union environments than in unionized ones, if only because HRM is seen as being unitarist and individualist in focus. Geoffrey Armstrong argues that commitment through employee relations is the key to corporate success. In his view, there are many dramatic examples of companies that have made themselves successful through major shifts in their strategic direction. This has been done by changing radically their approach to their employees, equipping and training them for change, and organizing and motivating them to contribute effectively to the competitiveness required. To get the competitive edge, he argues, it is the quality of people which makes the crucial difference. 'Increasingly competition is between workforces, not just between products.'[54]

Armstrong identifies several organizational features of successful businesses in the 1980s. These include flatter management structures, smaller corporate headquarters, multiskilled managers, effective strategic planning and dynamic board leadership. It is the latter above all which creates success. Such enterprises also share, in Armstrong's view, common features in the ways they manage people. They create, for example, a sense of common purpose and shared values, emphasize the primacy of customers, invest heavily in training and, most importantly, 'treat their employees as respected contributors to organisational success, not just as necessary costs of production'. Additionally, they stress employment security based on employee flexibility, harmonization of conditions, 'encouragement of share ownership, "open-door" communications policies, opportunities for progression' and 'rewards for improving performance'.

This is not to say that there is no role for trade unions and collective bargaining, which there is. 'But it has to be based on a joint acceptance of the communal imperative that an organisation that fails to satisfy the needs of customers is dead in the water.' He has no time for adversarial industrial relations, where the right to bargain takes precedence over the needs of customers and the competitive needs of the business. In the 1960s and 1970s, Armstrong

believes, too many managers had lost sight of their firms' business goals within which, and in support of which, British industrial relations was supposed to operate. There is no looking back, Armstrong argues, and management will fail commercially, in the increasingly turbulent and changing conditions of business, unless it gets better 'at convincing our people that we know what we're doing, where we're going and how we're going to get there'.[55]

A number of case studies, examining changes in the ways in which people are managed, was undertaken by Storey. They covered organizations in both the private and public sectors, focusing on mainstream employers in the 'heartland territories of the British employment scene', not 'special cases' like IBM, Marks and Spencer and Nissan. Storey argues that some of the more significant changes bearing on the employment relationship appear to be driven from 'organisational changes which, on the surface, are not always self-evidently industrial relations or personnel management initiatives'. These studies seem to highlight a 'degree of commonality in the kind of organisational change processes' taking place in Britain in the late 1980s and indicate 'the way that the approach to "people management" is shifting in emphasis'.[56]

According to Storey, the concept of HRM is a controversial one. He claims that the term has four meanings. First, it is sometimes used as a synonym for 'personnel management'. Second, it may signal that personnel management techniques are being used in an integrated and more coordinated way. Third, it is sometimes used to signal a more business oriented and business integrated approach to the managing of people, with the emphasis being placed on the concepts of 'resources' and 'management' rather than on 'human'. 'In consequence, it suggests the potential of gaining added value through the sophisticated use of this factor rather than simply viewing it as a problematic arena in which the best that might be hoped for is quiescence.' The fourth meaning of the term HRM is 'the desideratum that not only ought ... integration [of personnel management techniques and of personnel and business policy] be in evidence' but also 'there needs to be some extra qualifying factor such as an underlying logic in pursuit of employee "commitment" or some similar characteristic feature'. For Storey, however, two faces of HRM are particularly noteworthy. These are the 'soft version', where HRM relates to the 'human relations movement', and the 'hard version', which emphasizes the calculative, business-like treatment of labour. But both versions share the presumption that 'decisions about the human resource are deserving of strategic attention because both start from the premise that the way in which this resource is managed will be critical to the success of the business plan'.[57]

Storey concludes, on the basis of his case study material, that there was clear evidence of extensive, innovatory HRM activities being directed at the managing of employees in these organizations, across the private and public sectors. These changes were management initiated and management led and 'the touchstones were a retreat from proceduralism, an emphasis on adaptability, direct communication with employees, "managerial leadership", and the moulding of a more tractable employee stock'. Moreover, the overall trend was towards more 'individualized [employment] arrangements' between employers and employed. It also appears that 'labour relations "firefighting" had been pushed to the very margins of [employer] concern'. It is the roles of line and general managers, rather than personnel managers, that have been central to these people management changes: 'both as drivers/devisers of new patterns and as implementers/deliverers of the preferred approaches'. Any sources of variation between the cases appeared to derive from differences in sectors of production, organizational structures and ownership, although in some instances 'human resource management type initiatives had been "bolted on" to the embedded system'. Further, any interest in the personnel department's 'claim to mediate or interpret shopfloor and union perspectives and values had waned'. Nevertheless, although Storey acknowledges the considerable changes recorded in 'HRM' recently, he also notes the limits to these changes. 'As described [here], there has been no "transformation" in these British cases.'[58]

Recent shifts of emphasis within the personnel function, then, should not be exaggerated. Some organizations have experienced far greater change than others. Even where managements have introduced job flexibility, performance-related pay and direct communications with the workforce, all does not change overnight because of such initiatives. Indeed, Torrington and his colleagues point out, in examining the time distributed by personnel specialists amongst different areas of personnel work, 'the pre-eminence of employee relations is clear: greatest discretion, most time, most important and growing in importance'. The trend they perceive in personnel management 'is a gradual increase in emphasis on manpower control at the same time as a high commitment to employee relations, but the two are not necessarily found in the same place at the same time'.[59] Where change has occurred in the personnel function, it seems, it is incrementalist and evolutionist in nature, not a major paradigm shift.

What is being observed, as research extends our knowledge and understanding of the personnel function, is the overwhelmingly contingent nature of personnel philosophies and practices. Personnel management styles and activities, in other words, strongly reflect the cultural and contextual circumstances in which they originate. HRM, which is itself heterogeneous and diverse in its emphases, is best described as a business-oriented approach to managing people, within which the personnel function adapts. And it arises from specific organizational circumstances. These include pressures for change, often deriving from product market competition, technological imperatives and corporate needs for success. HRM developments also require top managerial initiatives aimed at integrating corporate resources, including the company's 'human resources', to enable them to work together with a sense of common purpose and collective identity. But HRM is not appropriate to all organizations. The danger is to view HRM as a *universal* set of strategic prescriptions for all personnel management situations, at all times. What seems to be emerging, then, is a 'new model' of the personnel function in some organizations, the HRM model and its variants. According to Gowler and Legge, this 'derives from a model of employees as actors capable of exercising choice and initiative . . . and whose commitment has therefore to be won, as overt control of performance is likely to prove counterproductive'.[60]

## The limitations of HRM as a personnel management process

Despite the wide range of analyses of HRM in recent years, there is considerable scepticism amongst most British academic commentators about the universality of HRM as a personnel management phenomenon. Derek Torrington argues that 'there is no more trite remark than that the most valuable resources of a business are its human resources'. For him, 'HRM is no revolution but a further dimension to a multifaceted role'. He believes that HRM will improve the authority of personnel management in two ways: 'by finally making training important and by helping managers grant more dignity to working people by concentrating more on getting the contract right and less on supervision and motivation'. For him, personnel management remains a distinctive management specialism whose practitioners derive their expertise 'from an understanding of one or more of the ways in which people, individually and collectively, engage with the need to be employed and the needs of organizations to employ them'.[61]

According to Storey and Sisson, British managers continue to approach the management of employment in characteristically *ad hoc* ways. They argue that the degree of the shift to 'strategic human resource management' remains strictly limited and that, on balance, there are considerable limits to the 'full-blown version of HRM in Britain'. Although there is no single explanation for British management's general failure to adopt a strategic approach to HRM, they identify four considerations accounting for the limited penetration of HRM into British management policy and practice. The first is the relative underprovision of management education and training in Britain, with the result that few British managers have the opportunity to be exposed to formal planning processes. 'In the British context, planning, for too many managers, simply means budgeting.' The second factor is that British business strategies have tended to focus on traditional domestic markets, with too many companies relying on business structures and strategies which were 'state of the art' in the 1960s rather than in the late 1980s. Third, compared with countries like Germany and Japan, management in Britain has been, and is, dominated by the finance function with its focus on people as costs and commodities, rather than as investments and assets. Fourth, unlike in Germany and Japan, where corporate ownership is largely in the hands of the banks, it is investment trusts and pension funds which hold the bulk of voting rights in British companies. This means that 'evaluation periods for individual post-holders tend to be short-run even though, overall, funds in aggregate are viewed on their long term performance'.[62]

There is also the rhetoric of HRM. As Keenoy writes: 'at the heart of the HRM rhetoric is the idea that it represents a novel form or approach to the management of people' and that it 'emphasises employee commitment and involvement and a relatively caring concern for employees while simultaneously integrating HR policy and practice with strategic objectives'. Yet there is little evidence that employers actually practise 'a form of employment regulation which remotely resembles the

rhetorical model'. For Keenoy, the rhetoric of HRM could well be intended to reconstruct the motivation to work and to re-legitimize managerial authority in contemporary Britain. He suggests that: 'the *primary* purpose of the rhetoric of HRM might be to provide a legitimatory managerial ideology to facilitate an intensification of work and an increase in the commodification of labour',[63] as part of the solution to Britain's economic difficulties.

The reality of HRM to Keenoy is that the emergence of HRM coincided with a significantly changed economic and political context. With the search for competitive edge in the private sector, and the rolling back of the state and the seeking for control of public spending in the public sector, since the early 1980s, Keenoy suggests that it is 'these economic and political forces [which] have had far more influence on HR practices than the rhetoric of HRM'. In short, 'the dominant values which appear to have informed the reality of HR practice have been those of cost-effectiveness in response to an increasingly competitive environment'.[64]

Yet there are also contradictions and ambiguities in HRM practices and the HRM model of personnel management. On the one hand, employees are to have personal contracts, performance-related pay, performance appraisal and personal responsibility for budgets. Yet, on the other, they are expected to become team players through team briefings, quality circles and cascading communication initiatives. There are also:

> the behavioural implications of the contradiction between the notion of HRM as a method of maximising the economic return of the labour-resource by integrating decisions about its utilisation and management into business strategy and the notion of HRM as a method of releasing the untapped reserves of labour-resourcefulness by facilitating employee responsibility, commitment and involvement.

More fundamentally, the HRM literature fails to address and marginalizes two key issues regarding the employment relationship. One is what structures employer–employee relationships and the other is the impact of organizational structures and managerial ideologies on behaviour at work. The first derives from the differential in power and the potential for conflict in the employment relationship, between those selling and buying labour in the market place. The second is the assumption that unitary, or neo-unitary, theory is central to the rhetoric of HRM.

*Table 12.1* Classification of the personnel function.

| Selected characteristics | Dominant models of the personnel function | | |
| --- | --- | --- | --- |
| | Paternalist welfare model | Professional personnel model | HRM model |
| Orientation | Welfare, moral and humanist | Occupational, service and manpower control | Managerial, market and human resource utilization |
| Ideology | Paternalist | Collectivist | Individualist |
| Role of personnel | Person management | System management | Resource management |
| Relationship with line management | Administrative | Advisory/executive | Strategic |
| Generic activity | Human relations | Industrial relations | Employee relations |
| Status of workforce | Workers | Employees | Professionals |
| Contract with workers | Social | Legal | Psychological |
| Role of unions | Marginal | Adversarial | Collaborationist/absent |
| Change | Slow | Moderate | Continuous |
| Market position | Protected | Stable | Competitive |
| Attitude to workforce | Cost containment of labour | Cost-effectiveness of workforce | Investment in human resources |

*Source*: D. Farnham, *Personnel Management in Context* (1990)

'Both require reference to power-relations and the institutionalisation of socio-economic conflict',[65] factors which HRM analyses generally ignore.

Finally, it is interesting to note that when the WIRS looked at the particular job titles used by designated specialists in its 1990 questionnaire, it found that nearly all reported that 'personnel', as opposed to 'human resources', appeared in their job titles. 'Only one in a hundred, rather fewer than in 1984, said that their title concentrated on "industrial", "staff" or "employee" relations. And an even smaller minority, of less than 1 per cent, said that they were called "human resource" managers.'[66] Interestingly, this last group was not confined to larger, multi-establishment organizations but was found in small numbers in a cross-section of sectors, enterprises and establishments.

## Classifying the personnel function

It is clear from the literature and from recent personnel management practices that a variety of 'models', 'traditions', 'perspectives' and 'theories' of the personnel function have been proposed. Of these the term 'model' is probably the most useful concept on which to build, since it provides images of the structure, form and content of modern personnel management. Using the word in this sense, one can identify in effect three dominant models of the modern personnel function. These are the 'paternalist welfare' model, 'professional personnel' model and 'HRM' model. Although variants of each of these could be developed, these three 'ideal' types, and their selected characteristics, provide a useful framework for analysing and classifying contemporary personnel management. This is illustrated in Table 12.1. In practice, of course, few 'pure' models of the personnel function exist. Although in some organizations either the paternalist, or the professional, or the HRM model predominates, in others the personnel function contains elements of two or more of the models and is mixed. Of these three dominant models, the paternalist and the professional are rooted in the culture and practices of traditional personnel management in Britain. This started with the appointment of factory welfare officers at the beginning of the century.

The HRM model, which is neo-unitary, growing in importance, but by no means universally practised, is seen by some to be the 'emergent "consensus" functionalist image of personnel management in the 1990s'. As such it aims to justify personnel's current power base, because its power bases of the 1970s 'have been undermined by declining traditional union power, changed legislative direction' and a reserve army of the unemployed. By becoming 'centrally involved in the management of the organisation's symbolic order "in search of excellence"', this new model of the personnel function lays claim to an expandable area of activity. Moreover, it is 'one associated with images of leadership rather than the threatened downgraded position associated with recession'.[67] The modern personnel function, then, is infinitely adaptable to specific organizational, cultural and market circumstances. What the evidence indicates, therefore, is that a new model of personnel management, 'human resources management', is gaining ground in a group of successful, well-managed businesses. These are often dominated by market volatility and change. In many other cases, however, the professional personnel management model continues to operate, providing a more traditional base for personnel work. This means, in practice, that 'both the "new" and "old" models of personnel management appear to coexist – normally in different organizations'.[68]

## 12.3   Personnel Strategy and Policy

### Interventionist strategies

Karen Legge suggests that in their search for functional authority within organizations personnel managers need to adapt their behaviour to the situational contexts and constraints facing them. If the personnel department wishes to gain power and influence in corporate decision making, she argues, personnel managers have to derive authority from any of three paths. She calls these 'conformist innovation', 'deviant innovation' and that of the personnel 'problem solver'.

Conformist innovation is defined as the attempts by the personnel manager 'to demonstrate a closer relationship between his activities (means) and organizational success criteria (ends)'. In adopting this approach personnel managers accept the dominant values and bureaucratic structures of their employing organizations and try to show the importance of personnel management activities in advancing corporate goals. In doing this, personnel practitioners highlight their role in facilitating, if only indirectly, organizational success. They do this by tackling obstacles to enterprise efficiency and effectiveness. This includes reducing labour

turnover, for example, improving staff training or extending management development. Personnel's contribution to enterprise success 'becomes less important than its role in anticipating, preventing or rectifying a range of organizational malfunctions'.[69]

As conformist innovators, personnel managers emphasize their 'auditing' and 'stabilization' relationships with management, not their advisory ones. Auditing relationships evaluate whether particular managerial actions conform with corporate policies and procedures. Stabilization relationships result in approving managerial decisions, on the basis of specialist expertise, taking corporate objectives into account. These aim to cope bureaucratically with problems of control and co-ordination by scrutinizing managerial decisions before, during and after they are taken. Both auditing and stabilization relationships require personnel managers to minimize the costs of potentially inconsistent and inappropriate personnel decisions by line managers.

In adopting the conformist innovation strategy, personnel specialists develop an appreciation 'that their contribution will appear more tangible if presented in financial terms'. Conformist innovators therefore attempt to justify personnel work in cost–benefit terms – including costing labour turnover, evaluating training programmes, estimating the financial benefits of new payment systems and so on. They also encourage human asset accounting and the use of the computer in the personnel function. As conformist innovators, personnel managers accept line management's definition of how organizational activities should be determined and what their priorities should be. They do not seek to change them but to facilitate their efficiency and effectiveness.

Whilst conformist innovators accept their ends and adjust their means in the personnel role:

> the deviant innovator, rather than making his activities conform to the dominant values about what constitutes success, attempts to change this means/end relationship by gaining acceptance for a different set of criteria for the evaluation of organizational success and his contribution to it.[70]

In the role of deviant innovator, in other words, the personnel specialist seeks acceptance of personnel policies and procedures on altruistic grounds as well as utilitarian ones. Personnel managers can argue, for example, that work should satisfy individual ends as well as instrumental organizational ones. In doing this, they introduce external reference groups into

organizational decision making so as to evaluate
the effectiveness and acceptability of particular personnel activities. The personnel manager can even act
as the 'interpreter and advocate' of societal norms to
the enterprise, showing that its dominant norms and
values are not necessarily the same as those held in
society as a whole.

Personnel specialists using the deviant innovation
strategy base their activities, their professional relationships and their authority more on a third-party
consultancy role than on an exclusively managerial
one. They define the personnel needs of line managers and then decide how these needs should be met
rather than allowing line management to do so. They
do this by applying their professional expertise and
values to personnel issues in accordance with what
they see to be appropriate standards within their
enterprises. They expect their managerial clients,
in turn, to accept personnel's definition of what
activities are to be provided rather than asserting
their own right to do so. In practice few personnel
managers are able to change dominant organizational
values so fundamentally, since these are usually
derived from commercial needs. Nor are they normally able to exert control over line management.
Some control takes place, however, when personnel
managers advise line management on appropriate
courses of action arising from the requirements of
employment law.

Normally, 'neither of these attempts to gain "professional" authority is fully viable'. Many personnel
activities are difficult to quantify and evaluate in
economic terms, so it is difficult for conformist
innovators to demonstrate personnel's contribution
to enterprise success. Similarly, attempts by deviant
innovators to initiate alternative corporate values are
likely to provoke resistance amongst line managers
accepting the existing ones. In practice, 'personnel
specialists tend to oscillate between these two paths to
"professional" authority'. In deflationary conditions
conformist innovation strategies are likely to be more
acceptable, whilst in periods of boom 'the climate for
experimentation of all kinds is likely to be more
favourable than at other times'.[71]

Legge concludes that whilst conformist innovation
and deviant innovation may be perceived as distinct
and separate interventionist strategies, they may also
be regarded as different styles of performing the
role of the personnel manager as 'problem solver'.
It is in their role as problem solvers, she claims,
whether directed towards conformist innovation or
deviant innovation solutions, that personnel man-

agers are most likely to influence personnel policy
effectively. She concludes that 'diagnostic problem
solving' requires a contingent approach to personnel
management, with the design and implementation
of personnel policy matching or contingent upon
organizational circumstances. A contingent approach
to personnel problem solving, she argues, 'brings with
it the combined advantages of flexibility . . . with
a sensitivity to the political dimensions of organizational life'.[72]

## Strategic HRM

Traditionally, the influence of industrial relations
on corporate business practice in Britain has been
minimal. One reason for this disparity is that top-
level managements have not normally seen industrial
relations issues as matters of corporate concern.
Miller argues, however, that industrial relations
should be an important strategic corporate issue, and
he provides a definition of industrial relations,
derived from the business policy literature. He also
attempts to clarify a definition of strategic HRM.

For Miller, 'non-strategic' industrial relations
management implies a personnel function which is:
separate from the business; reactive; short term; of
no interest to boards of directors; and 'constrained by
a legalistic and institutional definition such that it is
concerned principally with unionized employees and
is concerned principally with lower-level employees'.
Strategic HRM, in contrast, whose origins lie in the
USA, he argues, must be linked to the organization's
product market, if it is to contribute to the firm's
competitive advantage and organizational success.
For as the American study of Kochan and Capelli
claims:

> Changes in the competitive environment can
> occur gradually as products change in response
> to changing consumer demand . . . or as low-cost
> competition grows. The environment can also
> change abruptly because of competitive shocks
> such as deregulation . . . or the introduction of
> new products . . . and technologies. Regardless
> of the cause, a sharp increase in competitive
> pressures forces firms to make a series of
> decisions whose effects reverberate through the
> organization and its industrial relations system.[73]

It follows, therefore, that strategic HRM is concerned with those decisions and actions, affecting the
management of employees at all levels in the business,
which 'are related to the implementation of strategies

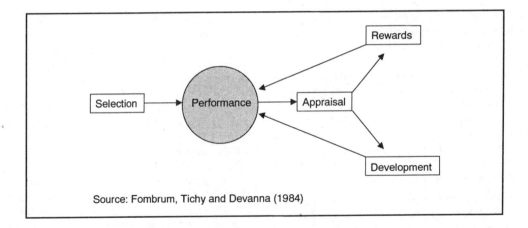

Source: Fombrum, Tichy and Devanna (1984)

*Figure 12.1* The human resource management cycle.

directed towards creating and sustaining competitive advantage'.[74]

In tracing the emergence of HRM in Britain in the mid-1980s, Hendry and Pettigrew point out that, unlike in the USA, HRM presented itself as a more or less fully formed set of values and prescriptions. It emerged in Britain largely in response to economic recession, loss of competitiveness and the political climate associated with market-led Thatcherism. But there was also an often repeated criticism of the personnel function: that it lacked a strategic approach to employment issues in such matters as new technology, forms of flexible working, industrial relations management and personnel management generally. In what was claimed to be one of the first published reviews of HRM to appear in Britain, the 'strategic' theme in HRM, identified by Hendry and Pettigrew, was seen to comprise four elements. These were:

1.  The use of planning.
2.  A coherent approach to the design and management of personnel systems based on an employment policy and manpower strategy, and often underpinned by a 'philosophy'.
3.  Matching HRM activities and policies to some explicit business strategy.
4.  Seeing people of the organization as a 'strategic' resource for achieving 'competitive advantage'.

Following American analyses of strategic management and of strategic HRM, Hendry and Pettigrew accept the view that 'the critical management task is to align the formal structure and the HRM systems so that they drive the strategic objectives of the organisation'. As shown in Figure 12.1, the firm's key human resource systems and processes, 'the human resource management cycle', focus on organizational performance. The HRM systems to be developed and integrated, for organizational effectiveness, are the areas of employee selection, appraisal, training and development, and rewards. These 'should be aligned in specific ways to channel behaviour and create an appropriate organizational culture (or "dominant value")'. Hendry and Pettigrew conclude that there are two ways in which strategic HRM can be approached:

(a) through an 'a priori' definition of what constitutes it as a special variant of personnel management, in which case one is likely to be evaluating selected manifestations against the touchstone of a particular discipline or ideology; or (b) treating it as a range of things affecting the employment and contribution of people, against the criteria of coherence and appropriateness (a less rigid term than 'fit'), and monitoring changes therein.

Strategic HRM, in short, is concerned with the question of how personnel management is able to contribute to business effectiveness and business strategy change. Further, what makes strategic HRM distinctive is the need for managements to address the changes deriving from turbulent product market conditions, with the emphasis shifting 'away from formality, and the imperatives of juridification . . . and arbitration . . . as the focus of employment management'.[75] This requires different skills and competences, as compared with the traditional ones, among personnel professionals.

The view that human resource management is becoming more strategic and integrated, especially in the management of change, is reinforced by Storey's recent research into developments in the managing of human resources across a wide spread of British organizations. He concludes, from his series of 15 'core case' companies and 25 'panel' companies, that the process of managing change within then 'was becoming more strategic' and that:

> The human resource elements – new policies on selection, appraisal, reward, communications, deployment, utilization and development – were increasingly seen as integrated. And this integrated approach was more likely to have an exposure at senior levels – including the board.[76]

## Policy

An espoused personnel, human resources or industrial relations policy is an attempt by management to define its proposed courses of action in dealings with employees and trade unions. Policy in this sense provides a set of guidelines within which management plays a positive proactive role in personnel management rather than an *ad hoc* reactive one. Positive personnel policies normally provide links with other policy areas such as production, finance and marketing, as well as forming an integral part of the overall strategy by which senior management seeks to achieve its corporate goals and objectives. An espoused personnel policy, in short, provides a strategic framework by which management takes the initiative and seeks to act consistently in all personnel and industrial relations matters. It is claimed that the main purpose of a defined policy is that it:

> promotes consistency in management and enables all employees and their representatives to know where they stand in relation to the company's intentions and objectives. It further encourages the orderly and equitable conduct of industrial relations by enabling management to plan ahead, to anticipate events, and to secure and retain an initiative in changing situations.[77]

It has been argued that the decision to produce an explicit personnel policy 'leads logically to the sort of written policy which some companies have produced and trained their managers to use'. There are a number of advantages, it is claimed, in producing written policy statements. First, the processes involved in producing such documents focus managerial attention and energies on their purposes and objectives. They clarify intentions and remove uncertainties where reliance would otherwise be placed on custom and practice, improvization or where policy is a matter of surmise. Second, written documents provide clear reference points in communicating policy guidelines to managers, employees and employee representatives. Third, by creating the starting point of policy, written statements provide a basis for policy changes and reviews as circumstances require or permit. By being written it is 'easier to change than policies which are embedded in custom and practice, tradition and precedent'.[78]

The first requirement for formulating a corporate personnel policy is that the organization's governing body and senior management team give commitment and attention to the task. It is, after all, they who exert a major influence on it and on its integration with other policy areas. It is also sensible to involve line managers and employees in the policy process, since without the agreement and acceptance of those who implement policy, and are affected by it, it is unlikely that the policy guidelines will be authoritative. This necessitates effective procedures ensuring that senior management, operational management and employees are kept fully informed about what is happening and that they are able to influence policy determination from the outset.

It is further argued that personnel policy formulation also requires the guidance and co-ordination which the industrial relations specialist should supply. The specialist contribution is based on its functional responsibility for personnel management and industrial relations, the time it can devote to the tasks, and the skills, knowledge and expertise of professional personnel specialists. Those employed within the personnel function need to undertake an overall study of corporate needs and consult and involve the people who are required to carry out policy at various levels. They are in a position to produce proposals, ensure their discussion and secure agreement to them. This course argues for the appointment at board level, or equivalent, of personnel directors or personnel 'strategists' able to influence and formulate policy at the highest organizational levels.

The processes by which formal personnel policies are created and developed are complex. Top management has a key part to play but its approach is affected by the philosophy and style of management it adopts, as well as by the importance it attaches to particular policy issues. The extent of its activity is also affected by corporate size, organizational structure and other internal factors. It is increasingly recognized that whilst line management, employees and their representatives have distinctive roles to play in determining and applying policy, boards must 'assume final responsibility for authorising policy in industrial relations or in other areas'.[79]

A useful checklist for determining personnel policies issues is provided by the Department of Employment's code of practice on industrial relations. It states that 'the principal aim of management is to conduct the business of the undertaking successfully', but a major objective should be 'to develop effective industrial relations policies which command the confidence of employees'. The code interprets 'industrial relations' in its widest sense, not just confining it to collective bargaining and negotiating machinery. It says that there are two main themes underlying the code:

i   the vital role of collective bargaining carried out in a reasonable and constructive manner between employers and strong representative trade unions; [and]

ii  the importance of good human relations between employers and employees in every establishment, based on trust and confidence.[80]

It therefore stresses the need for policies in both collective employment matters and those directly affecting individual employees in performing their normal job tasks.

The major policy areas which the code emphasizes are employment policy, communication and consultation, collective bargaining, and grievances and disputes, with disciplinary matters now covered by a separate code of practice and a handbook issued by the Advisory Conciliation and Arbitration Service. In examining employment policies, for example, the code stresses the importance of establishing good working relationships between management and employees in order to make 'the most effective use of its manpower resources and give each employee opportunity to develop his [or her] potential'. It recommends that management initiates and accepts primary responsibility for these policies. 'But they should be developed in consultation or negotiation, as appropriate, with employee representatives.' Such policies should not be influenced by 'age, sex or other personal factors except where they are relevant to the job'.[81]

The employment issues where management is recommended to pay particular attention in policy determination are: the planning and use of human resources recruitment and selection; training; payment systems; the status and security of employees; and working conditions. In operating its human resource policies, for instance, management is advised to avoid unnecessary fluctuations in employment levels and to record information helping it to identify the causes of absenteeism and labour turnover. In recruitment and selection, it is expected that management will consider filling vacancies by transfer or promotion from within the enterprise, base selection on suitability for the job and ensure that those who are given the responsibility to make selection decisions are competent to do so. Management is recommended to ensure that new employees are given induction training, with other job training being provided to supplement education, training and work experience.

Turning to payment systems, it is argued that these should be kept as simple as possible, based on some form of work measurement and jointly negotiated with trade unions where these are recognized. They should be kept under review ensuring that they suit current circumstances and take account of any substantial changes in the organization of work or job requirements. It is also considered advisable to provide stable employment and job security for employees, consistent with operational efficiency, and that fluctuations in the level of employee earnings should be avoided where possible. Further, differences in conditions of employment and employee status, and in the facilities available to them, 'should be based on the requirements of the job', not on personal grounds or for non-economic reasons. Similarly, a redundancy policy for dealing with reductions in the workforce is recommended and 'should be worked out in advance so far as practicable and should form part of the undertaking's employment policies'.[82]

Communication and consultation are considered to be essential in all establishments to promote efficiency, mutual understanding and job involvement, especially in periods of change. The most important method of communication, it is argued, is by word of mouth, supplemented by written information and meetings for special purposes. Management particularly needs to ensure that information is provided to employees about their jobs, trade union arrangements, opportunities for promotion, welfare facilities and health and safety. It is suggested that management initiates the setting up and maintenance of

consultative arrangements best suited to the circumstances of the establishment, in co-operation with
trade unions and their representatives. These arrangements, however, 'should not be used to by-pass or
discourage trade unions'.

Advice on collective bargaining begins with bargaining units. It is recommended that a bargaining
unit should cover as wide a group of employees as is
practicable, since too many small units make it difficult for related groups of employees to be treated
consistently. Whilst the interests of employee groups
need not be identical, there 'should be a substantial
degree of common interest' amongst them, taking
account of minority interests. A number of factors
should be taken into account in defining bargaining
units: the nature of the work; common interests;
employee wishes; location of the work; the matters
to be bargained about; and whether separate bargaining units are needed for 'particular categories of
employees, such as supervisors or employees who
represent management in negotiation'.

When considering trade union recognition, management is recommended to examine the support
for the claim among employees and the effect of
granting recognition on any existing bargaining
arrangements. After recognition, it is argued, relations between management and unions should be
based on jointly agreed industrial relations procedures providing clear rules and a basis for resolving
differences between them. Regular contacts between
management and unions are recommended, not just
when trouble arises. Agreements 'should be in
writing and there should be agreed arrangements
for checking that procedural provisions have not
become out of date'. There is also advantage in
agreeing at industry level those pay–work issues
covering the industry as a whole. These include: terms
and conditions suitable for general application;
guidelines for negotiating at lower levels; and a procedure for settling disputes, 'either for the industry as
a whole or as a model for individual undertakings to
adopt by agreement'.

It is also recommended that management and
trade unions should agree the number of workplace
representatives required in an establishment and the
workgroups for which each representative is responsible. To encourage union members to vote in
steward elections, 'management should offer the
trade unions facilities to conduct elections . . . and to
publicise the date and details'. Whilst the extent and
nature of shop steward facilities can be agreed between management and unions, other facilities can be

provided by management. These include: lists of new
employees; accommodation; telephones; and offices.
Management and unions can also review the training
most appropriate for steward needs 'and take all
reasonable steps to ensure that stewards receive the
training they require'.

Since employees have a right to seek redress for
grievances relating to their employment, management is expected to establish with employee representatives arrangements for raising grievances and
having them settled fairly and promptly. Such
procedures should be in writing, have a number of
stages or levels and a right of appeal. Where unions
are recognized, management is recommended to
establish a procedure for settling collective disputes
with them. This should be in writing and:

i    state the level at which an issue should first be
     raised;
ii   lay down time limits for each stage of the proce-
     dure, with provision for extension by agreement;
iii  preclude a strike, lock-out, or other form of
     industrial action until all stages of the proce-
     dure have been completed and a failure-to-agree
     formally recorded.[83]

## 12.4   Personnel Work

The work of the specialist personnel function can be
examined in terms of its activities and tasks, its
varying roles and its functional organization. The
activities and tasks of personnel management, for
example, incorporate the specific duties and job skills
of personnel practitioners in fulfilling their corporate
and operational responsibilities. Their roles cover the
executive, advisory or administrative actions which
they undertake as experts in personnel management.
The functional organization of the personnel department emerges from the ways in which personnel
activities, tasks and roles are structured within enterprises in order to achieve personnel objectives and the
implementation of personnel policy.

### Activities and tasks

There are several ways of classifying the work of
personnel specialists. Moxon was the first to attempt
a comprehensive classification. He did this in a
pamphlet published by the IPM at the end of the
Second World War in which he defined personnel
management as the 'function of management concerned with what is commonly called the human

*Table 12.2* Most common tasks of personnel staff.

| Personnel activity | Most common tasks |
| --- | --- |
| Direction and Policy Determination | Developing policy proposals; managing subordinate personnel staff; developing external relations |
| Personnel Planning and Research | Participating in corporate planning |
| Industrial Relations | Attending negotiating meetings; applying agreements on terms and conditions; acting as workplace industrial relations specialists; providing advice to managers on the law; participating in disciplinary, grievance and disputes procedures |
| Pay and Benefits Determination | Proposing employment packages; determining and implementing employment packages |
| Payment Administration | Initiating pay transactions; dealing with individual pay complaints |
| Organizational Design and Development | Producing job descriptions |
| Manpower Planning and Control | Maintaining records of manpower numbers; controlling levels of manpower |
| Personnel Information and Records | Determining personnel records requirements |
| Training and Development | Identifying individual training needs; instructing/lecturing |
| Recruitment and Selection | Determining selection methods; defining recruitment requirements; job advertising; processing job applications; interviewing candidates; taking part in selection decisions; organizing selection programmes; making offers of employment; taking up references |
| Employee Communications | Planning employee communications; operating communications procedures |
| Health, Safety and Welfare | Employee counselling and welfare; liaising on company health services; advising on pensions |

*Source*: D. Guest and R. Horwood, *The Role and Effectiveness of Personnel Managers* (LSE, 1980)

factor'. He went on to identify six major personnel activities: 'Employment, Wages, Joint Consultation, Health and Safety, Employee Services and Welfare, [and] Education and Training'. He subdivided these activities into 48 separate individual tasks.[84] Since then the scope of personnel work has expanded considerably. Nowadays, a typical range of personnel activities encompasses: corporate planning including the integration of the personnel function with other managerial functions to achieve enterprise objectives; organization structure; manpower planning; manpower development; remuneration; industrial relations; and employee services.

A more detailed analysis of current personnel activities and a breakdown into their separate tasks is provided by the London School of Economics (LSE) classification reported by Guest and Horwood. In their study of the personnel role in a manufacturing company with 40 work units and 31 000 employees and a regional health authority (RHA) employing 61 500 health service staff, they identified 12 major personnel activities incorporating 85 separate personnel tasks. The 12 activities were: direction and policy determination; planning and research; industrial relations and collective bargaining; pay and benefits determination; payment administration; organization design and development; manpower planning and/or control; personnel information and records; employee development and training; recruitment and selection; employee communications; and health, safety and welfare. In this study the researchers also identified 31 out of the 85 personnel tasks within the main activity areas that were most commonly undertaken by over 50 per cent of the personnel respondents. These are summarized in Table 12.2 as a guide to what personnel staff normally do.

According to this research, there was a considerable degree of common ground in the tasks undertaken by the personnel staff in both organizations, especially in recruitment and selection. There were, however, also marked contrasts reflecting the greater degree of centralized administrative work in the RHA compared with the manufacturing organization, where personnel staff were 'more concerned with day to day grass roots issues including aspects of industrial relations, communications and welfare.' It was also shown that a much higher proportion of the personnel staff in the manufacturing plants engaged 'in a wide range of tasks related to Pay and Benefits Determination, Training and Development, Industrial Relations and, to a lesser extent, Manpower Planning and Control' than did their counterparts in the RHA. It appears that the personnel function in the RHA retained 'much of the tradition of an administrative staffing activity', with personnel staff in the manufacturing organization being more likely to be 'engaged in a full range of advisory, executive and administrative activities'.[85]

Guest and Horwood make an interesting distinction between the activities performed by personnel managers in the two organizations and their personnel subordinates. They define 'generalist' personnel managers as those in charge of personnel activity reporting to line management, with personnel 'specialists' or 'subordinates' reporting to someone within the personnel function. Personnel generalists, for example, were found to be more 'heavily involved in industrial relations' and in direction and policy determination in both organizations than were subordinates. Generalist personnel managers were also identified as those concentrating on training and development in the manufacturing organization and on recruitment and selection in the RHA. Amongst specialist subordinate staff 'only Recruitment and Selection and Training and Development figure[d] prominently' in the manufacturing organization but, in the health authority, personnel subordinates were also involved 'in Pay Determination and Administration, Training and Development and Recruitment and Selection'.

Table 12.3 A classification of contemporary personnel work.

*Personnel management and oganization*
  Human resource planning
  Organization structure
  Organization culture
  Authority, leadership and management
  Organizational communication
  Interpersonal communication
  Procedures for administrative action and mutual control
  Computers in personnel work
  Consultancy and consultants

*Employee resourcing*
  Labour markets
  Forms of employment and the contract of employment
  Job analysis
  Recruitment strategy and employment documentation
  Selection methods
  Employment interviewing and decision making
  Health, safety and welfare
  Equalizing employment opportunity
  Termination of the employment contract

*Training and development*
  The training framework
  Work design and motivation
  Learning principles and training skills
  Management development
  Performance assessment and the appraisal interview

*Employee relations*
  Trade union recognition and employee participation
  Negotiating agreement
  Grievance and discipline
  Preparing for tribunals

*Pay*
  Payment administration
  Job evaluation
  Pensions and sick pay
  Incentives, performance pay and fringe benefits

*Source*: D. Torrington and L. Hall, *Personnel Management* (Prentice-Hall, 1991)

Another major difference between the activities of generalist personnel managers and specialist personnel subordinates was that the managers were 'involved in a wider variety of types of activity than their specialist subordinates'. Of the 85 personnel tasks on the researchers' checklist, 41 were 'undertaken by over 50% of the generalists in the manufacturing company compared with only 19 undertaken by over 50% of the specialists', especially in industrial relations and recruitment and selection. In the health service region, the contrast, whilst not so dramatic, was 'still very marked'.

Similarly, in the manufacturing organization the generalists did an average of 42 personnel tasks compared with 32 for the specialists, whilst in the RHA the comparable figures were 39 tasks for the generalists and 28 for the subordinates. In short, 'the contrast between generalist and specialist appears to be well founded'.[86]

Torrington and Hall, in contrast, in examining the 'personnel management process', which 'can lead to the effective management of human resources, as well as providing an effective management service to resourceful humans',[87] provide a useful classification of contemporary personnel work. They identify five areas of personnel management expertise which are required by personnel specialists. These areas are: personnel management and organization; employee resourcing; training and development; employee relations; and pay. They then divide each of these areas into sets of sub-activities which are summarized in Table 12.3.

## Roles

There is no generally agreed prescription for the work of personnel managers; the extent of their duties varies 'in practice from one employer to another and depends on several factors'. For analytical purposes it is useful to categorize personnel work into its executive, advisory and administrative roles. But the simplified view of the personnel manager as merely an adviser or as someone doing line management's work for them is 'misleading and inaccurate'.[88] In their executive roles personnel managers take full responsibility for particular aspects of personnel work such as in leading management negotiating teams in collective bargaining or in taking employment decisions. In their advisory roles personnel managers provide guidance to line managers on personnel policy and its implementation, as well as giving practical day-to-day help to line management in its dealings with subordinate employees. The administrative role of personnel managers includes maintaining personnel procedures and systems and monitoring their effectiveness.

Most personnel activities contain elements of the executive, advisory and administrative roles, particularly in human resource planning and control, recruitment and selection, industrial relations and collective bargaining, training and development, and health, safety and welfare. In human resource planning and control, for example, personnel managers sometimes have the executive authority to make human resource forecasts based on information provided by line management. They also play an advisory role aimed at controlling human resource levels and an administrative one of maintaining human resource records. In the area of recruitment and selection the executive role of the personnel manager is to determine selection methods, advertise jobs and to interview, with advice being provided to line management in making selection decisions. The administrative role includes organizing selection programmes, taking up references and making offers of employment.

In industrial relations and collective bargaining, personnel staff are involved in a number of tasks. These include acting as negotiators, attending management–union meetings and participating in disciplinary, grievance and disputes procedures, all of which include executive and advisory tasks. They also advise line managers on the provisions and implications of employment law. Further, personnel departments are usually responsible for applying and administering the collective agreements covering the terms and conditions of employment of particular bargaining units. Personnel has to ensure too that collective bargaining procedures are properly and consistently applied 'and that they are audited and reviewed regularly'.[89]

The role of the personnel function in training and development is primarily advisory, though personnel staff have executive responsibility when instructing or teaching in particular training programmes. In helping line managers to define staff training needs, for example, or in designing training schemes to satisfy these needs, the personnel function has essentially an advisory role. However, in maintaining and co-ordinating training programmes, personnel provides an administrative service. By contrast, the executive role of the personnel department in the field of health, safety and welfare is exemplified in employee counselling and welfare, with advice being given on pensions and health and safety at work. It is normally personnel's responsibility to provide the administrative link between employers and external medical and social services.

In the remaining major personnel activities, personnel managers and their subordinates are involved in a variety of roles. In pay and benefits determination, for example, the personnel role is often advisory but with executive elements. Pay administration, by definition, is largely administrative including organizing employee payments and dealing with individual pay complaints. In employee communications personnel staff provide advice in planning communications and in administering and maintaining communication procedures. Lastly, in collecting personnel information and maintaining personnel records and statistics, the personnel role is largely an administrative one.

## Organization

So far we have concentrated on the 'horizontal' activities and tasks of personnel staff, that is on the jobs which they do across personnel departments whether as generalist personnel managers or specialist personnel subordinates. In larger organizations personnel work is also differentiated 'vertically' between personnel managers and their subordinates, with jobs being delimited by levels of responsibility and degrees of discretion in doing them. One early classification of personnel activity based on a survey by the IPM suggests that there are four vertical levels at which personnel managers operate. These are:

1. Operational personnel officer, including those who are primarily concerned with the day to day personnel function carrying out policies determined by others.
2. Senior personnel officer, including those who not only carry out an operational role but also advise others on the implementation of broad policy outlines, and possibly contribute to the evolution of policy.
3. Personnel manager, including those whose role is primarily advisory and carries responsibility for subordinate personnel officers.
4. Senior personnel manager, including those who are primarily responsible for the creation of company personnel policy for approval by the board of directors and for the direction/coordination of personnel activities throughout the organization.[90]

In their study of the manufacturing organization and the RHA, Guest and Horwood suggest that 'the conventional model of organisation structure for large organisations contains four types of personnel role', similar to those of the IPM survey. These are: personnel directors or generalists dealing with all types of personnel issues and policy development; corporate specialists involved with personnel planning and co-ordination; personnel managers responsible for day-to-day personnel activities; and personnel assistants undertaking a narrow range of specialist duties. Yet neither of the organizations

studied conformed to this model structure, though the 'manufacturing company came close to it'.

As well as classifying the 85 horizontal personnel tasks into 12 types of activity, these authors provide a vertical classification based on an analysis of personnel work 'according to the degree of "autonomy" implicit in the nature of each task'. This was done to examine the division of labour between different personnel jobs and levels of organizational authority. Five 'autonomy classifications' were identified. These are:

| | | |
|---|---|---|
| (1) | 'Strategic' | Tasks involving overall direction and leadership of the function. |
| (2) | 'Analytical/ Conceptual' | Tasks involving research into and development of concepts and policy necessary to support performance of "strategic" tasks. |
| (3) | 'Advisory/ Responsive' | Tasks involving provision of specialist expertise or professional services in support of line management. |
| (4) | 'Instrumental–Active' | Tasks involving implementation of policy within broadly prescribed limits but with scope and need for creative input and judgment. |
| (5) | 'Instrumental–Passive' | Tasks involving implementation of administration systems providing little scope for independent judgment.[91] |

In the two organizations studied, the contrast between vertical personnel activities was considerable. In the manufacturing organization, for example, only corporate staff were engaged in strategic personnel activities, with none of this group involved in advisory or instrumental activities. By contrast, in the RHA, involvement in strategic personnel activities was just as heavy below regional level as at regional level. Similarly, personnel staff below corporate level in the manufacturing organization tended to be involved in a fairly wide range of non-strategic personnel activities. These included advisory services and routine implementation of personnel procedures. There also appeared to be a wider range of activities amongst personnel staff in the health region and its lower tiers, compared with their counterparts in the manufacturing company. In summary, in examining the vertical structure of the personnel function in the two organizations, the authors were able to identify 'a link between location in the organization and types of activity for the manufacturing organization but not for the Health Service Region'.[92]

## 12.5    Line Management and the Personnel Function

As already indicated, the nature of the personnel role is the subject of long-standing debate, especially in the managing of industrial relations. In some organizations personnel managers are essentially advisers to line managers, with the latter responsible for executive action affecting industrial relations within their own areas of responsibility. In other organizations full executive authority is given to a senior personnel or industrial relations generalist who has the executive authority to instruct line managers in courses of action either directly or through personnel subordinates. Nevertheless, 'a simple distinction between executive and advisory functions, while useful for analytical purposes, obviously needs to be qualified and is likely to become blurred in practice'.[93] From a managerial viewpoint all managers, line or personnel, need to have a clear understanding of their respective roles and responsibilities in industrial relations.

### Relations between line and personnel managers

Line management's job is to ensure that corporate policy is executed in their spheres of responsibility and that output targets and job tasks are achieved. Industrial relations and personnel activities form part of these responsibilities and the line manager's operational effectiveness is diminished where basic personnel and industrial relations decisions are referred to others. Workgroup and industrial relations problems are so interconnected that they cannot be properly separated. There are clear advantages for management in ensuring that decisions on everyday problems such as the handling of employee grievances or disciplinary matters are seen to come from the line manager concerned. Most day-to-day issues are best settled promptly by the people directly involved, when they occur. Line managers are also in the best position to communicate and consult with employees on matters bearing on industrial relations, thus demonstrating their awareness of industrial relations as an integral part of their job.

Since line managers are so immersed in target dates, operational schedules and budgetary control, they sometimes fail to give full weight to personnel issues and take hasty decisions harmful to industrial relations. 'In this context the personnel manager offers such help and advice as may be necessary to ensure equity and consistency in the application of policy.'[94] The role of first line management or workgroup supervisors in communicating policies and plans to subordinate employees is particularly crucial, since they form management's immediate face to face contact with employees with responsibility for workgroup performance. Given their job tasks, it is good practice to define the responsibilities and authority of supervisors in relation to their subordinates, senior managers, personnel staff and employee representatives. Supervisors can also usefully contribute to developing personnel policy, devising new work methods, handling change and participating in managerial preparations for negotiation. Properly utilized, workgroup supervisors can promote the orderly conduct of industrial relations.

Personnel managers make an important contribution to the conduct of industrial relations by taking an overall view of the function and by using their specialist knowledge and skills. Such skills include planning, negotiating and problem solving. Personnel managers also provide basic personnel services including: maintaining personnel records; administering recruitment procedures; inducting employees; co-ordinating industrial relations; and monitoring the consistent application of personnel policy. They also support line management by providing advice: to top management on formulating policy and corporate plans; to top and middle management on implementing policy and plans; and to line management on the everyday conduct of industrial relations. Another aspect of the personnel manager's job is the educative role: helping line management to understand the concepts and techniques of professional personnel management as they bear on industrial relations. In practice, however, line managers mostly judge personnel managers 'on the extent to which their advice is found to be constructive and helpful in solving problems or preventing their occurrence'. In effect, the task of the personnel manager 'is to make line managers more effective without diminishing their authority'.[95]

In collective bargaining, management has to prepare for negotiations, decide the composition and authority of its negotiating team, agree to the conduct of negotiations and ensure that concluded agreements are implemented. Preparatory work is complex and time consuming. Whilst personnel managers provide specialist knowledge and skills, it is also necessary to involve representative cross-sections of line managers at this stage. When bargaining, a wide variety of practice is found in the leadership, composition and authority of the management negotiating team. In some cases the lead is taken by a senior personnel manager, with line managers providing advice and support. In other cases a line manager leads with advice obtained from the personnel manager. Alternatively negotiations may be conducted by the personnel manager or line managers exclusively. In general, managerial objectives are most likely to be achieved where 'both personnel and line managers at appropriate levels are represented in negotiating teams'.[96]

Whatever its composition, everyone in the management negotiating team has to be clear about its authority to make and settle agreements over all sorts of issues. Although there is advantage in delegating the maximum authority to settle to the negotiators, some matters are always likely to require reference to or discussion with a higher authority as, for example, where policy affecting other bargaining units is affected. One arrangement is for the board or governing body to define the limits within which negotiators can decide, with consultations taking place between them as necessary. Final authority remains with the negotiators who have the knowledge of relevant circumstances and whose commitment to the final settlement is required.

In implementing collective agreements, management negotiators need to ensure that managers, supervisors and employees are fully informed and prepared for the changes being introduced. This can be a large-scale activity, with trade union and employee representatives requiring facilities and assistance to carry out their part in the exercise. This necessitates co-ordinating and monitoring agreements to ensure consistency. This can usefully be done by personnel managers, with line managers implementing the agreements affecting their immediate employees.

Communications and consultation require continual oversight from management. Overall responsibility for communications is sometimes delegated to the personnel department which identifies the methods of communication and decides what shall be communicated and when. This enables employees to be properly informed of all written policies and procedures affecting their jobs, including relevant legal requirements, whilst everyday responsibility for

communications normally rests with line managers. It is by face to face communication with their workgroups, however, that line managers provide the opportunity to avoid problem areas and to promote mutual understanding among the employees they manage.

Collaboration between personnel and line managers is also required in establishing and operating formal systems of consultation. For example, matters of common concern need to be identified; ways of injecting new ideas into consultative committees have to be considered; means of extending the range of subjects discussed require to be found; and methods of assessing the effectiveness of consultative committees have to be explored. In enterprises with well-established arrangements, these tasks are often the responsibility of the senior personnel manager. Line managers normally participate in committee proceedings, following up action in their own departments subsequently. The authority of such committees is enhanced considerably where senior line management participates as an active member.

In drafting and negotiating procedural agreements and in monitoring their operation, both personnel managers and line managers have roles to play. Personnel managers have the responsibility of drafting management's initial proposals, with line and personnel managers conducting negotiations subsequently. Personnel managers can provide advice and guidance by ensuring that procedures are observed, but line managers are normally responsible for ensuring that procedures are properly used in their areas of responsibility. This includes explaining procedures, rules and standards of conduct to their employees. It is particularly important that first line managers or supervisory managers do this, since it is at this level that breaches of rules and procedures most commonly occur. This happens when supervisors are bypassed and senior line management or the personnel department are directly approached. Where this happens too often, agreed procedures fall into disrepute and lose their authority.

When planning pay policies, management aims to control labour costs, prevent pay anomalies and avoid dissatisfactions which can harm industrial relations. This requires earnings surveys being carried out, pay comparisons being examined and suitable payment systems being devised. Many of these activities are handled by the personnel department but there must be close collaboration with line managers. In designing and operating a payment system, for example, line management can help determine what the objectives of the system are, making the selection from alternatives provided by the personnel specialist. From that point on, it is the line management's task to supervise the application of the payment system within their areas of responsibility, particularly ensuring that employees understand the system and how their pay is made up. The amount of discretion allowed to line managers to determine or make adjustments to an individual's pay varies. It is the personnel manager, though, who is in the best position to advise how 'to maintain a balanced wage structure that does not upset collective agreements and remains equitable as between groups and individuals'.[97]

## New model line managers?

There is some evidence, with the emergence of HRM policies and HRM practices in certain 'leading edge' organizations, that 'new' style and 'new' types of line managers are being appointed and developed within companies, with implications for their roles in the managing of people. In the case studies conducted by Storey, for example, it was noted that 'most of the major change programmes in this set of cases had originated outside personnel'. His research findings indicate that personnel specialists in the mainstream companies investigated by him had not been the main drivers of change and the new HRM. In most cases, 'personnel had found it "safer" and more attractive to remain in the proceduralist symbolic realm'. As a result, there was an expanded and changing role for line managers in the handling of human resources policies, personnel management practices and the managing of people, who were crucial in the achievement of organizational and cultural change.

At senior levels, 'the change seemed to involve a more active role for line and general managers in setting the direction for HR policy'. This spilled over into the areas of selection, communication, training and development and in attitudes and behaviour. These changes derived from organizational responses to environmental uncertainty and market turbulence during the 1980s. Managerial initiatives for organizational survival included structural change, decentralization and new styles of management, embracing renewed emphasis on customer service, product innovation and corporate competitiveness. All these factors have implications for the ways in which people are managed. According to Storey, 'steerage with regard to these matters has increasingly been taken up by operational managers of the organization rather than personnel specialists'.

Consequently, adjustments appear to have been made in the recruitment, selection and training of senior and middle line managers. Their roles are more demanding, the knowledge and skills required of them are more extensive and their enthusiasm and commitment are more essential than ever for organizational success and efficiency. 'There was very considerable evidence of transformation with *line managers as the objects of change*'. However, there was much less evidence that there were similar behavioural and attitudinal changes at shopfloor level.

'New' first line managers, in turn, were being expected to embrace the new management styles and philosophies. 'They were the key channels in the open two-way communications; they were to be monitored for "involving" employees and for "developing" them.' These 'new model' supervisors had wider responsibilities, more authority, higher pay and status, better training and competences than the 'old' type, traditional supervisors. They were also younger, nonunionized and expected promotion, on merit, to higher management positions during their careers. They clearly saw themselves as part of management and were confident about their capabilities and functions. In short:

> Through selection, deselection, training, revised reward packages, revised job remits, appraisal and other devices, there was a drive to shift from the 'traditional supervisor' model to the new 'head of section' or 'assistant manager' model. These line managers were likewise expected to take on an expanded set of responsibilities and to handle people management to a far greater degree than had been the case under the 'traditional supervisor' system.[98]

A longitudinal study of managers' attitudes and behaviour in industrial relations between 1980 and 1990 shows, despite the political and economic turmoils of the 'Thatcher' years, that these 'have altered more circumspectly, and in ways that cannot be "read off" directly from the far-reaching environmental changes of the period'. For example, managers retained a preference for unitary rather than pluralist models of industrial relations, a situation reinforced by changing patterns of power relations over the 1980s. Yet, on the other hand, because power relations had changed so dramatically, the unitarist preferences of managers were buttressed. But these new circumstances also enabled them to formulate coherent and innovative personnel and employee

*Table 12.4* Information for employees.

| Types of information | Examples |
| --- | --- |
| Job information | Job descriptions, job training, terms and conditions, contractual details, physical environment, relationships with others, promotion prospects, grievance and disciplinary procedures |
| General information | Management and organizational structures, products, customers, numbers employed, appointments, resignations, promotions, long-service awards, labour turnover, job security |
| Marketing information | Sales, market shares, exports, competition, trading position, order book |
| Policies and plans | Manpower, health and safety, training, industrial relations, pay, job evaluation, sickness, savings schemes, investment, new products |
| Financial information | Income, distribution of income, tax paid, unit costs, profit and loss account, balance sheet, sources and application of funds, added value, productivity |

relations strategies consistent with the emergence of HRM strategies in many companies. The findings also suggest that a more integrative approach to employee involvement has been occurring, 'with an increase in the experience of managerial committees, where there are employee or union representatives but a decline in the practice of regular meetings between supervisors and workgroups'.

There also appeared to be an increased level of endorsement by managers of 'market' rather than 'corporatist' approaches to labour markets and a rejection of an interventionist role by government in labour market regulation. Managers also tended to support the ideas of 'free enterprise' and the 'enterprise culture'. But 'the greatest changes appear to have been in the managers' assessments of trade union power and the consequences of this for the managerial role in industrial relations'.[99]

## 12.6 Employee Communication and Information

Effective communication between management and employees, and the dissemination of relevant information from management to employees, are now recognized as necessary conditions in any employer strategy aimed at positively involving employees in the enterprises in which they work. This requires appropriate communication structures and a managerial policy on what information is to be provided to employees either directly or through their representatives. The starting point is a positive commitment from top management which defines in broad terms the objectives being sought, how they are to be achieved and what needs to be communicated. A main aim is to encourage all employees to identify with the enterprise as a whole. In establishing and implementing its policy, management has to take account not only of employee needs but also any constraints placed on the employer. These include protecting confidentiality, balancing openness with secrecy and safeguarding organizational interests.

Communication channels within enterprises are vertical or horizontal. Vertical channels are those from senior management to employees, or from union members to their negotiators. Horizontal channels are those between management and union representatives at various levels of organizational decision making. To be successful, both vertical and horizontal channels need to facilitate two-way exchanges of information between those involved. This enables management to communicate to employees through their supervisors and to receive feedback, enables union members to communicate to their union negotiators through shop stewards and to receive feedback, and enables managerial and union representatives to communicate with each other.

If trade unions are recognized, it is essential from a managerial standpoint that where information is provided to employees, it should be done not only through their shop stewards but also their supervisors, though some managements communicate directly with their workforce. Trade union representatives cannot be expected to communicate management's point of view, since they are elected to represent employee interests not managerial ones. Rather, they are the focal point of upward communication or feedback from employees to management. Stewards have a prime duty to their members and provision needs to be made for them to have opportunities to communicate to and with their constituents. It is essential for management to ensure that shop stewards do not receive information before workgroup supervisors. 'Nothing more effectively destroys the morale of junior management than this.'[100]

As indicated in Table 12.4, there is a wide variety of information which employers can provide and communicate to employees or their representatives. The most basic information relates to the employee's immediate job. A number of surveys show that information about the individual employee's job and job tasks is what many employees consider to be their most important priority. A comprehensive and integrated employee communication and information strategy requires other corporate information to be made available to all employees, including supervisory and managerial staff. This encompasses general information about the enterprise such as: its structure, products, customers and personnel; marketing information about sales, competitive situation and trading position; corporate policies and plans, especially those covering manpower, investment and new products; and financial information in its widest sense. This assumes that management is able to collect and disseminate such information and is prepared to bear the economic costs of providing and distributing it.

In structuring effective communication and information channels, management has to take account of what is to be communicated, who is to be responsible for communicating it, to whom the information is directed, and the most appropriate form in which to present it. As already indicated, employee communication takes place between managers and individual employees or through representatives. Similarly communication can be oral, visual or written. A major factor influencing the choice of means is the number of employees to whom the information is directed. In general, where the number of employees to be given information is relatively small, verbal methods such as briefing groups or departmental meetings are preferable. But, as the number of employees requiring the information increases, either written or visual methods or both become more appropriate. These include: memoranda; minutes; videos; mass meetings; conferences; enterprise newsletters; and annual reports from top management to all employees. Personal letters to each employee from senior management are also used.

Where management and independent unions negotiate, it is a statutory duty of employers under the Employment Protection Act 1975 to disclose information to union negotiators 'which it would be in accordance with good industrial relations to disclose'.

> To determine what information will be relevant negotiators should take account of the subject-matter of the negotiations and the issues raised during them; the level at which negotiations take place (department, plant, division, or company level); the size of the company; and the type of business the company is engaged in.[101]

The sort of information which the code of practice says could be relevant includes: pay and benefits; conditions of service; manpower; performance; and financial details. It also recommends that employers and unions jointly should decide how disclosure can be most effectively implemented. 'They should consider what information is likely to be required, what is available, and what could reasonably be made available.'[102]

## 12.7    Summary Points

- The personnel function of management is concerned with the managing of people at work and with their relationships within the enterprise.
- The nature of the personnel function is, however, problematic and the subject of longstanding debate. There is no general agreement about what personnel activities and tasks should be allocated to line managers and personnel specialists respectively.
- The specialist personnel role is long-established and can be traced back in its welfare form to the early years of this century. While the number of personnel specialists employed in enterprises has increased in recent years, their power and status vary and no single model of the personnel function is universally accepted.
- Professional personnel management activity tends to be associated with foreign-owned companies, those recognizing trade unions, large concentrations of white collar employees and organizations having large numbers of employees.
- A number of roles for personnel management have been identified. These include: the welfare role, aimed at improving employee well-being; the management control role, aimed at human resource efficiency; the independent role, aimed at professional autonomy for the personnel specialist; the professional role, aimed at developing relevant occupational skills and values among

personnel practitioners; and, most recently, the human resource management (HRM) model, aimed at integrating personnel decisions with business decisions at corporate level.

- Given the contrasting operational interpretations of their function, it is not surprising that personnel specialists sometimes fail to gain the power, authority and status to influence personnel policy and to persuade line managers to adopt professional personnel practices. Functional success in the specialist personnel role is more likely where personnel practitioners adopt an employer frame of reference and contribute, through their professional skills and knowledge, to the effective managing of the contractual relationship between employers and employees.

- Three strategies are suggested by which personnel managers can achieve functional authority in organizations. Conformist innovators accept the dominant utilitarian values of their organizations and attempt to demonstrate the financial benefits of personnel management in achieving corporate efficiency and effectiveness. Deviant innovators, in contrast, seek a more independent role for the personnel specialist by challenging dominant organizational values and by defining the personnel management needs of line managers and providing the means to satisfy them. Diagnostic problem solving requires a contingent approach to personnel management, using conformist innovation or deviant innovation strategies as appropriate.

- Strategic HRM is largely concerned with how personnel management is able to contribute to business effectiveness and business strategy change. It focuses on the HRM cycle, which seeks to link performance with selection, appraisal, rewards and training and development.

- Espoused personnel and industrial relations policies provide written guidelines for promoting consistent action amongst line managers, while enabling employees and their representatives to know where they stand on personnel issues. They are an integral element in senior management's aim of achieving its corporate goals and objectives. In formulating and applying personnel policies, top management initiative is necessary, but it also requires involvement by line management, personnel, the unions and employees if these policies are to be legitimized.

- The LSE classification of personnel work provides 12 'activity' classifications, containing 85 separate tasks, and five 'autonomy' classifications. It also distinguishes between the activities and tasks of personnel managers and those of personnel subordinates. General personnel managers in charge of the personnel function normally engage in a wider variety of tasks than do specialist personnel subordinates.

- Torrington and Hall's classification of personnel work divides it into five major areas: personnel management and organization; employee resourcing; training and development; employee relations; and pay.

- Personnel work can be divided into executive, advisory and administrative roles, though in practice most activities incorporate elements of each. Vertically, personnel work falls into five 'autonomy' groupings: strategic; analytical/conceptual; advisory/responsive; instrumental/active; and instrumental/passive.

- Line and personnel managers play complementary but supportive roles in personnel management and industrial relations. Normally, line managers are responsible for the application of personnel policies and procedures in their areas of responsibility, with personnel managers providing advice, guidance and services to line managers on particular issues.

- The special contribution which personnel managers make in industrial relations derives from their ability to take an overview of the function and their professional knowledge and skills in negotiating. In pay issues, personnel normally provides the policy framework and line management supervises the operational details. But, ultimately, management's responsibility in industrial relations is collective.

- There is some evidence that, with the emergence of HRM policies and practices in some leading companies, new style first line managers are being appointed. They tend to be younger and more management oriented than their traditional counterparts. They are key levers in the development of integrated and business-centred personnel policies in organizations and act as primary agents of change.

- Research shows that most British managers prefer a unitary frame of reference in industrial relations and, underpinned by the economic and political changes of the 1980s, they largely endorse market rather than corporatist approaches to labour market and industrial relations issues.

# 12.8   References

1. D. Barber, *The Practice of Personnel Management*, Institute of Personnel Management, London, 1982, p. 8.
2. B. Ream, *Personnel Administration: A Guide to the Effective Management of Human Resources*, ICSA, Cambridge, 1984, p. 7.
3. A. Fowler, *Personnel Management in Local Government*, Institute of Personnel Management, London, 1980, p. 18.
4. M. Niven, *Personnel Management 1913–63*, Institute of Personnel Management, London, 1967, p. 152 and H. A. Clegg, *The Changing System of Industrial Relations in Britain*, Blackwell, Oxford, 1979, p. 218.
5. J. Hunt, The shifting focus of the personnel function, *Personnel Management*, February 1984, p. 15.
6. N. Millward, M. Stevens, D. Smart and W. Hawes, *Workplace Industrial Relations in Transition*, Dartmouth, Aldershot, 1992, p. 35.
7. K. Manning, The rise and fall of personnel, *Management Today*, March 1983, p. 74.
8. K. Legge, *Power, Innovation and Problem Solving in Personnel Management*, McGraw-Hill, Maidenhead, 1978, p. 37.
9. J. Harvey-Jones, How I see the personnel function, *Personnel Management*, September 1982, p. 26.
10. P. Parker, How I see the personnel function, *Personnel Management*, January 1983, p. 17.
11. *Ibid.*, p. 19.
12. A. Jarrett, How I see the personnel function, *Personnel Management*, June 1982, pp. 32–5.
13. G. Thomason, *A Textbook of Personnel Management*, Institute of Personnel Management, London, 1975, p. 26.
14. Quoted in Niven, *op. cit.*, p. 23.
15. D. Guest and R. Horwood, *The Role and Effectiveness of Personnel Managers: A Preliminary Report*, London School of Economics, London, 1982, p. 11.
16. *Ibid.*, p. 10.
17. *Ibid.*, p. 11.
18. S. Tyson, Personnel management in its organizational context, in K. Thurley and S. Wood (eds), *Industrial Relations and Management Strategy*, Cambridge University Press, Cambridge, 1983, p. 156.
19. D. Torrington and L. Hall, *Personnel Management*, London, Prentice-Hall, pp. 4–12.
20. Personnel Standards Lead Body, *A Perspective on Personnel*, PSLB, London, 1993, pp. 4, 5 and 18.
21. K. Legge and M. Exley, Authority, ambiguity and adaptation: the personnel specialist's dilemma, *Industrial Relations Journal*, Autumn 1976, p. 54.
22. *Ibid.*
23. D. Farnham, *Personnel in Context*, Institute of Personnel Management, London, 1990, p. 107.
24. T. P. Lyons, *The Personnel Function in a Changing Environment*, Pitman, London, 1971, p. 37.
25. Legge and Exley, *op. cit.*, p. 57.
26. G. Thomason, *A Textbook of Personnel Management*, 4th edn, Institute of Personnel Management, London, 1981, p. 55.
27. Farnham, *op. cit.*, p. 145.
28. T. J. Watson, *The Personnel Managers*, Routledge and Kegan Paul, London, 1977, p. 50.
29. Watson, *op. cit.*, p. 198.
30. C. Thomas, Personnel managers in a crisis of confidence, *Croner Employment Digest*, 354, 1993, p. 2.
31. D. Guest, Personnel management: the end of orthodoxy? *British Journal of Industrial Relations*, 29(2), 1991, p. 150.
32. Torrington and Hall, *op. cit.*, p. 16.
33. D. Torrington and L. Mackay, *The Changing Nature of Personnel Management*, Institute of Personnel Management, London, 1986, p. 177.
34. T. Watson, *Towards a General Theory of Personnel Management and Industrial Relations Management*, Trent Business School, Nottingham, 1985, p. 34.
35. Torrington and Mackay, *op. cit.*, p. 178.
36. S. Tyson, The management of the personnel function, *Journal of Management Studies*, 24(5), 1987, p. 525.
37. *Ibid.*, p. 526.
38. S. Tyson and A. Fell, *Evaluating the Personnel Function*, Hutchinson, London, 1986, p. 135.
39. A. Fowler, When chief executives discover HRM, *Personnel Management*, January 1987, p. 3.
40. *Ibid.*
41. M. Armstrong, HRM: a case of the emperor's new clothes? *Personnel Management*, August 1987, p. 31.
42. Manning, *op. cit.*, p. 73.
43. K. Thurley, Personnel management in the UK: a case for urgent treatment? *Personnel Management*, August 1981, pp. 24–9.
44. N. Cowan, Personnel management in the eighties: will we waste another decade? *Personnel Management*, January 1980, p. 23.
45. N. Cowan, Change and the personnel profession, *Personnel Management*, January 1988, p. 36.
46. P. Armstrong, The personnel profession in the age of management accountancy, Working paper, Industrial Relations Research Unit, University of Warwick, 1987, pp. 2 and 16.
47. K. Legge and M. Exley, Authority, ambiguity and adaptation: the personnel specialist's dilemma, *Industrial Relations Journal*, 6(3), 1975, p. 59.
48. P. Armstrong, *op. cit.*, p. 18.
49. D. Guest, Human resource management and industrial relations, *Journal of Management Studies*, 24(5), 1987, p. 504.
50. *Ibid.*, pp. 506, 511 and 509.
51. *Ibid.*, pp. 511, 513, 515 and 518.
52. P. Beaumont, Trade unions and HRM, *Industrial Relations Journal*, 2, 1991, p. 3.

53. A. Pettigrew, P. Sparrow and C. Hendry, Competitiveness, strategic change and human resource management, *Personnel Management*, November 1988.
54. G. Armstrong, Commitment through employee relations, Paper presented to IPM National Conference, 22 October 1987, Harrogate, pp. 1 and 4.
55. *Ibid.*, pp. 5, 6–9.
56. J. Storey, The people-management dimension in current programmes of organizational change, *Employee Relations*, 10(6), 1988, p. 17.
57. J. Storey, *Developments in the Management of Human Resources*, Blackwell, Oxford, 1992, pp. 23–5.
58. *Ibid.*, pp. 27, 116, 266, 269 and 278.
59. D. Torrington, L. Mackay and L. Hall, The changing nature of personnel management, *Employee Relations*, 7(5), 1985, p. 15.
60. D. Gowler and K. Legge, Personnel and paradigms: four perspectives on the future, *Industrial Relations Journal*, September 1986, p. 212f.
61. D. Torrington, Human resource management and the personnel function, in J. Storey (ed.), *New Perspectives on Human Resource Management*, Routledge, London, 1989, p. 66.
62. J. Storey and K. Sisson, Limitations to transformation: human resource management in the British context, *Industrial Relations Journal*, 3, 1992, pp. 60–3.
63. T. Keenoy, Human resource management: rhetoric, reality and contradiction, *International Journal of Human Resource Management*, 1(3), 1990, pp. 370 and 375.
64. *Ibid.*, p. 378.
65. *Ibid.*, p. 380.
66. Millward *et al.*, *op. cit.*, p. 25.
67. Fowler and Legge, *op. cit.*, p. 233.
68. Farnham, *op. cit.*, p. 320.
69. Legge and Exley, *op. cit.*, p. 59.
70. *Ibid.*, pp. 60 and 61.
71. *Ibid.*, p. 62.
72. Legge, *op. cit.*, p. 115.
73. T. Kochan and P. Capelli, The transformation of the industrial relations/human resources functions, in P. Osterman, *Internal Labour Markets*, MIT Press, Cambridge, Massachusetts, 1983, p. 13.
74. P. Miller, Strategic industrial relations and human resource management, *Journal of Management Studies*, 24(4), 1987, p. 352.
75. C. Hendy and A. Pettigrew, Human resource management: an agenda for the 1990s, *International Journal of Human Resource Management*, 1(1), 1990, pp. 21, 22 and 36.
76. Storey, *op. cit.*, p. 160.
77. Commission on Industrial Relations, *Report No. 34, The Role of Management in Industrial Relations*, HMSO, London, 1973, p. 6.
78. *Ibid.*
79. *Ibid.*, p. 15.
80. Department of Employment, *Industrial Relations Code of Practice*, HMSO, London, 1972, p. 2.
81. *Ibid.*, p. 9.
82. *Ibid.*, p. 11.
83. *Ibid.*, pp. 16, 19, 22, 24, 25 and 26.
84. G. R. Moxon, *Functions of a Personnel Department*, Institute of Personnel Management, London, 1951, p. 3.
85. D. Guest and R. Horwood, *The Role and Effectiveness of Personnel Managers*, LSE, London, 1980, pp. 24, 27 and 28.
86. *Ibid.*, pp. 31–3 and 37.
87. Torrington and Hall, *op. cit.*, p. xvii.
88. Fowler, *op. cit.*, p. 25.
89. Farnham, *op. cit.*, p. 123.
90. Barber, *op. cit.*, p. 10.
91. Guest and Horwood, *op. cit.*, pp. 37 and 20.
92. *Ibid.*, p. 41.
93. CIR, *op. cit.*, p. 16.
94. *Ibid.*, p. 18.
95. *Ibid.*, p. 20.
96. *Ibid.*, p. 21.
97. *Ibid.*, p. 25.
98. Storey, *op. cit.*, pp. 116, 187, 202, 214, 215 and 267.
99. M. Poole and R. Mansfield, Patterns of continuity and change in managerial attitudes and behaviour in industrial relations, 1980–1990, *British Journal of Industrial Relations*, 31(1), 1992, pp. 30–3.
100. Confederation of British Industry, *Communication with People at Work*, CBI, London, 1977, p. 18.
101. Advisory Conciliation and Arbitration Service, *Code of Practice 2. Disclosure of Information to Trade Unions for Collective Bargaining Purposes*, ACAS, London.
102. *Ibid.*, p. 5.

# 13

## Workplace Trade Union Organization and Representation

The position of workplace trade union representatives in British industrial relations has grown in importance since the end of the Second World War. They are present throughout public and private industry. Wherever trade unions are recognized by employers, trade union representatives usually emerge at workplace level to represent their members and the workgroups electing them. They are not a phenomenon of manual trade unionism alone, since white collar 'office' or 'departmental' representatives are also commonplace. In the postwar period workplace representatives, or shop stewards as they are generally known, moved 'from a somewhat obscure and relatively minor position in industrial relations to one of great prominence and widely acknowledged importance'.[1] This advance in the numbers, power and influence of workplace representatives was checked in the early 1980s. Since then their numerical decline has been substantial, and their representational and negotiating roles have become more constrained. Whether these changes are temporary or more long-lasting remains to be seen.

### 13.1 Trade Unions at the Workplace

The term 'shop steward' or 'steward' is the title usually given to the unpaid representatives of trade unions at the workplace. Stewards exist in most places of work where trade unions are recognized. In this chapter and elsewhere we use the term steward to describe those lay representatives of manual and non-manual unions whose duties centre on the workplace. Whatever their title, they represent their union at the workplace and those union members electing them to protect them in dealings with management.

> The general view of the shop steward . . . sees him as essentially a shop floor bargainer using every opportunity available to him to try to satisfy members' demands. . . . His activities, from the Management viewpoint, appear to involve a constant challenge of their prerogatives and authority.[2]

## Stewards and workplace representation

Trade unionism arose to protect employees and further their interests at the workplace. Although trade unions are established and durable organizations, the original need for workplace representation is as necessary as ever. Stewards not only represent unions, which often appear to be remote and impersonal bureaucracies in the eyes of many of their members, but also fulfil the ever-present need of the workgroup for familiar and tangible leadership which not only articulates their values and expectations within the workplace, but also is subject to their continuous influence and control. However, the role and behaviour of stewards vary enormously. Some of the factors influencing them include: the union and the industry to which they belong; the type of workgroups which they represent; and the traditions and attitudes of workers and management. They are also influenced by the type of product or service the industry supplies, its technology, whether collective bargaining is centralized or devolved, and the economic circumstances of the employers. Figure 13.1 gives some indication of the wide range of internal, external, institutional, personal, economic and social factors which influence the steward in his or her relationships with management, trade union, constituents and fellow stewards.

Irrespective of these factors, stewards seek the best pay and working conditions they can gain for their members. The universality of stewards, their influence and importance in the determination of pay and conditions at work, and their ability in many work situations to pursue courses of action independent of both management and full-time trade union officers, ensure them a major place in British industrial relations. But it has not always been so. In terms of the long history of trade unionism and of collective bargaining, the emergence of stewards is a comparatively recent phenomenon.

Before 1945, stewards with representative negotiat-

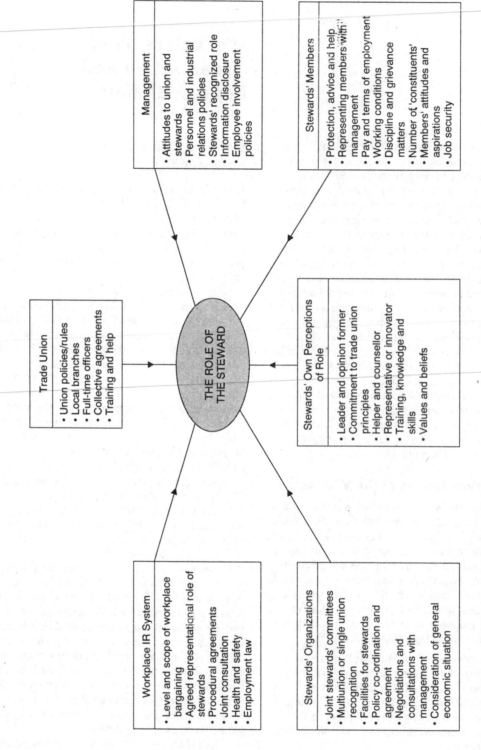

*Figure 13.1* Factors shaping the role of the steward.

ing functions were few in number and were limited to a handful of industries, such as engineering, shipbuilding and printing. Most union representatives at the workplace were 'collectors' whose main duty was to obtain maximum union membership and to collect weekly membership subscriptions or union dues. They rarely if ever represented members' interests to their employers but called in full-time officers when the need arose. An independent estimate of the number of stewards in 1960 put their figures at 90 000, with the Trades Union Congress (TUC) estimating that there were 200 000 of them at that time. The Royal Commission on Trade Unions and Employers' Associations in 1968 put the total at about 175 000. Still later, in 1971, a survey by the Commission on Industrial Relations indicated that there were between 250 000 and 300 000 stewards plus some 45 000 non-union workplace representatives. The TUC claimed in the early 1980s that the trade unions had about 300 000 stewards, 200 000 safety representatives and 100 000 pension trustees. This suggests that there were as many as 500 000 union workplace representatives, with an estimated annual turnover of 120 000 at that time. An extensive survey of workplace industrial relations in 1984 revealed, somewhat surprisingly, that despite a fall in union density during the 1980s, and high unemployment, 'there had been a slight increase in the number of lay [union] representatives'.[3] A further workplace survey in 1990, however, reported somewhat differently that:

> while changes in the number of [workplace] representatives are difficult to quantify precisely ... there is little doubt that there was a decline across the 1984 to 1990 period and that it was substantial.[4]

These figures must be compared with the approximately 3 000 full-time union officers whose numbers are likely to grow or decline in proportion to total union membership. It would appear, therefore, that a very large amount of trade union work and activities is carried out by stewards and other workplace representatives.

After 1945, then, the number of stewards in Britain steadily increased. This was accompanied in the early years by a growth in their bargaining strength and in their ability to represent members' grievances to management at the workplace. Their authority in relation to the formal structure of trade unionism and to the power of full-time officers was also substantially strengthened. There are several factors which gave rise to this power base in British industrial

relations. These included: the impact of relatively full employment between 1945 and 1979 on workplace discipline and on authority relations between managers and employees; the use of payment by results systems; the growth of overtime working; and the decentralization of collective bargaining in favour of company and workplace negotiations, including, in many cases, productivity and efficiency bargaining. Other factors which influenced the growth in power of stewards were: the reluctance of trade unions to appoint more full-time officers; the spread of the closed shop; the development of procedural agreements involving stewards; and a change of attitude within the trade unions favouring the appointment of workplace representatives. In more recent years, the passing of a considerable volume of employment protection law has also increased the functions of the steward at the workplace. The impact, after 1979, of economic recession, high unemployment, large-scale redundancies and a resurgence of managerial confidence on steward bargaining power and activities is discussed in section 13.5 below.

## Workplace representatives: their unions and members

Despite the important role which stewards have played in the development of trade unionism, and the large numbers that now daily represent their union and its members at the workplace, little mention is made of stewards in some union rule books. As the Donovan Report observed in 1968:

> Where union rule books mention shop stewards, and many of them do not, they generally say something about method of appointment, and the body to whom the stewards is [sic] nominally responsible. They may mention the duties of recruiting and retaining members, and collecting subscriptions. If the business of representing members is touched on, little is said about it.[5]

The Royal Commission went on to recommend that union rules concerning stewards in relation to such matters as elections, terms of office, the filling of casual vacancies, 'the bounds of the shop steward's jurisdiction, his relations with other union officials and his place in the union's organisation'[6] should be written into trade union rule books.

Similar conclusions were reached by an independent survey of over 30 union rule books. It concluded that:

their provisions are sparsely and vaguely worded, though a primary source of reference for all union officers. The failure of some rule books to define realistically a steward's function and responsibilities may reflect the attitude of a union to workplace representatives. Some unions appear to want to play down their significance, others deliberately leave their role relatively undefined to allow enlargement as dictated by local circumstances.[7]

As one of the members of the Royal Commission writing some years after the publication of its recommendations observed: 'most unions have not altered their rules on shop stewards, and rights to representation remain much as they were'.[8] In practice, however, many trade unions issue handbooks and other guidance for stewards containing information about union policy and instructions on what the unions believe to be their main duties and responsibilities on behalf of their unions and their members.

It is difficult not to conclude that the majority of unions, whilst accepting the essential role of stewards as official representatives of the trade unions, leave them very much alone to get on with their jobs with a minimum of formal regulation. It is reasonable to assume that the situation suits both unions and stewards alike. On the other hand, a detailed study of workplace industrial relations and the activities of stewards in a single plant stressed that 'the divorce between larger union and domestic organization has often been grossly exaggerated', and that 'stewards often place great emphasis upon the importance of the larger union as the embodiment of union principles and as a basis for their self-identity'.[9] A comprehensive survey of workplace industrial relations carried out after the Donovan inquiry came to broadly similar conclusions in 1980. It found that in all types of branches, but especially geographically based ones, 'shop stewards were much more frequent in their attendance than were other branch members. Stewards also commonly held positions on their branch committee'.[10] These findings suggest that too much emphasis is generally placed on the formal structure of trade union power as indicated by the union rule book, and too little attention is paid to the real incidence and distribution of power within trade unions at the workplace.

One of the difficulties unions face in formally recognizing stewards in union rule books is that of elevating individual union members to a special status bestowing powers and privileges upon them which ordinary members do not possess. One way out of this difficulty is establishing workplace union branches. Such branches are now more common, largely in the public sector, but are still substantially outnumbered by geographical multiemployer union branches. The formal status of stewards within many unions, therefore, remains uncertain. Where workplace branches are established, however, stewards are more likely to occupy formal office as branch officers than is the case with geographically based branches.

The steward has traditionally been seen as the representative of the trade union at the workplace whose first loyalty is to the union and to its policies. Some writers have pointed out, however, that the study of workgroups and of their values and expectations provides an equally important explanation of steward behaviour. This view is reinforced by the evidence that non-unionized workgroups often evolve their own leaders or representatives who put their views to management. One researcher has suggested:

> One of the central features of work is that it is usually done in groups, groups of individuals cooperating under the direction of a leader or leaders ... The working group is one of the main types of social group, and social interaction at work is one of the main forms of social interaction. Working groups differ from other groups ... in that they are brought together in order to collaborate over work and the pattern of relationships in the group is primarily determined by the task to be done.[11]

It seems apparent, therefore, that leaders can emerge within any workgroup. These workgroup leaders then express the views and anxieties of the group to management. The steward is just such a workgroup leader as well as being a trade union representative.

Much controversy surrounds the question as to what the dominant influences on the steward's role are and whether it is the workgroup or the union which commands the steward's first loyalty. There is considerable evidence to suggest, for example, that where there are divided loyalties or a conflict of interests between their members' aspirations and formal union policy, stewards generally side with their workgroups. Similarly, whilst full-time union officers oppose workgroups when they want to take action which is counter to official union policy, they usually do so with relative impunity. A steward adopting a similar approach will more often than not be quickly removed from leadership by the work-group. As an early study of industrial relations in a car plant noted:

> the unrest was on the shop floor. The stewards attempted to act constitutionally ... When this failed and their members took strike action, they attempted to obtain a return to work. They were under pressure from their members, and their leadership appeared reluctant.[12]

It is very important that comment, analysis and speculation concerning the numbers and activities of union stewards at the workplace is grounded in the best empirical evidence available. The latest available extensive research is to be found in the 1990 Workplace Industrial Relations Survey, jointly sponsored by the Employment Department, the Economic and Social Research Council, the Policy Studies Institute and ACAS. Its principal findings concerning workplace union representatives in 1990 included:

- there had been a clear and substantial decline in the number of union stewards between 1984 and 1990;
- the number of workplaces with one or more stewards showed a decline in all the main sectors of employment, with the greatest falls being in private sector services and the public sector;
- stewards remain strong in large workplaces, but the number of large workplaces has declined sharply during the 1980s;
- the presence of stewards in small workplaces is far less common;
- the incidence of stewards who spent all or most of their time on union or industrial relations duties, somewhat surprisingly, remained largely unchanged between 1984 and 1990;
- stewards who represent both manual and non-manual members are now more common than those who exclusively represent either manual or non-manual members.

## Elections and activities

Some union rule books contain rules broadly regulating the election of stewards and the length of time they serve before re-election. Some merely state that stewards will 'be appointed' and in a few cases the district officer or the union executive appoints stewards. A small number of rule books fail to mention stewards at all. Most unions are aware of the difficulties in enforcing detailed rules for electing stewards at the place of work and prefer a flexible approach which helps to ensure that somebody suitable is found to do the job. Some union rule books do not stipulate the precise method of electing stewards or the composition of the electorate. Similarly, the qualifications of those eligible to stand for office are often omitted, although some unions stipulate both a minimum period of union membership and a minimum age for those seeking to become stewards. Rule books generally have little to say about the removal of stewards if they fail in their duties or break union rules but union executive bodies sometimes have the power to remove stewards if necessary.

The reality of workplace representation is that stewards only retain their position and authority as long as they have the confidence and support of their members and of the workgroups they represent. It is because steward constituencies are relatively small, and because stewards are usually well known to their fellow workers, rather than because of the existence of carefully worded rule books, that they are likely to conduct themselves as democratic representatives. Comparatively few trade unionists are aware of these rules and few would be willing to enforce them if they had to.

> The members who elect him will regard him essentially as their representative in dealings with the management. Yet 'potentially, stewards face conflicting claims on their loyalty, and many encounter problems in reconciling the expectations of constituents with those of the union'.[13]

Surveys suggest that in general the job of the steward is not eagerly sought after. Neither are elections – usually by show of hand – fiercely contested. A survey conducted for the Donovan Commission in 1967, for example, indicated that 71 per cent of the stewards questioned were elected unopposed, 36 per cent, whilst wanting the job, had had to be asked to do it and 40 per cent had had to be persuaded to take on the task. Further surveys of workplace industrial relations in 1972 and 1973 confirmed these findings. In 1973, for example, 75 per cent of the stewards who were surveyed replied that they had been unopposed in their elections, compared with 78 per cent in 1972; 38 per cent had wanted the job but had had to be asked to take it on; whilst 37 per cent had had to be persuaded to become stewards. 'The remaining quarter wanted the job and did not have to be persuaded'.[14] Somewhat surprisingly, the situation had changed little by 1990, when the Workplace Industrial Relations Survey found that trade union representatives were generally appointed by informal methods. A show of hands at a meeting of members was by far the single most common method, followed by the appointment of a steward reflecting the general feeling of a meeting without a vote. Only a small proportion of stewards were elected by secret ballot or any other form of ballot.

> Allowing that union members have always been reluctant to take on the steward role, the use of non-elective appointment methods at a large number of workplaces in 1990 suggests that this reluctance may have increased and may partly explain the decline in the number of stewards as a whole.[15]

The size of a steward's constituency varies widely according to the trade union and the industry, the size of the employing establishment and the functions of stewards. Where large numbers of workers are concentrated in comparatively small working areas, stewards tend to represent more people than in scattered work situations with relatively small workgroups. There is also a tendency for stewards of skilled workgroups to represent fewer members than stewards from general unions whose membership is largely unskilled. The 1990 survey evidence suggests that the average number of members represented by stewards is about 20 but this figure hides very considerable variations between unions and sectors of employment. Senior stewards with more clearly defined collective bargaining functions represent much larger consituencies. During the 1970s there was a remarkable growth in the number of full-time stewards or conveners, who spent all or nearly all their work time on trade union duties connected with their workplace. Before the early 1970s full-time stewards were a rarity; by the late 1970s, there were many more of them, especially in large establishments. But by 1990, this situation had not changed significantly.

> Full-time conveners or representatives were as commonly reported in all three broad sectors of employment [private manufacturing, private services and the public sector] in 1990. So despite the overall decline in the incidence of lay representatives, full-time representatives ... appeared to be as common in 1990 as six years earlier.[16]

These senior stewards or conveners are invariably paid by their employers as full-time employees. An earlier survey revealed that the average steward spent approximately six hours a week on trade union duties and senior stewards about 10 hours. Nowadays, only a very small proportion of stewards lose pay from their employer as a result of their union activities, since the TULRC Act 1992 provides a statutory right for trade unionists to have time off work, with pay, to undertake their trade union duties and activities.

In most large establishments where trade union organization is strong and many stewards are appointed or elected, a structure of senior stewards and conveners emerges to form a heirarchy of representative authority. A survey in the 1960s showed that even in moderately sized workplaces, a small number of senior stewards and a convener were elected so that

> the senior shop steward system – in the sense that some stewards have more influence and facilities that others – is extremely widespread in ... British industry ... and may be regarded as the norm rather than the exception.[17]

A convener of stewards, as the name suggests, originally existed to call or to convene meetings of stewards. Today, the title implies a leadership role normally acquired through election from among a group of stewards.

In some multiunion establishments, a convener is elected to represent each union; in other cases one steward emerges as the convener because of his or her personal qualities rather than through being the representative of the largest union. The convener, or one of the conveners in some multiunion situations, acts as the chairperson of stewards when they form a joint committee.

> Management often acknowledge that conveners in particular hold influential positions, and they are often given much wider freedom of movement within the factory and special access to senior managers. The work's convener is often an experienced trade unionist, and ... many of them appear to hold office for long periods. ... [Their] knowledge of precedents, previous arrangements and unwritten understandings often give them added influence over individual stewards.[18]

Research also suggests that most managers find it easier to develop better working relationships with senior stewards and conveners than with less accessible full-time union officers, since the latter are usually less readily available for contact and do not possess the conveners' intimate knowledge of domestic working arrangements. Stewards often form joint stewards' committees or 'combine' committees. These consist either of stewards working at the workplace of a single employer or, in the case of joint stewards' committees, of stewards drawn from a number of establishments of the same employer. A multiestablishment manufacturing company, for example, often has stewards' committees at each establishment and a single stewards' committee covering all the establishments. Somewhat surprisingly given the clear evidence of the decline in overall steward numbers, the fall in trade union membership and density, and the decline in collective bargaining, the 1990 Workplace Industrial Relations Survey revealed that the incidence of joint shop stewards' committees had remained largely unchanged between 1984 and 1990. Even more paradoxically, management had in many cases supported their existence and activities. It is hard not to draw the conclusion that managements must have found these organizations useful in achieving their own objectives.

During the 1960s and early 1970s multiemployer bargaining, modified and restricted by successive incomes policies, determined the basic pay, hours of work and holidays for the majority of manual employees and to a lesser extent for non-manual employees. Stewards rarely took part in these national negotiations. A national survey of workplace industrial relations carried out in 1978, however, concluded that in manufacturing industry single employer collective agreements had largely replaced multiemployer agreements as the major influence upon the pay of manual workers. This conclusion was supported by the 1980 Workplace Industrial Relations Survey, which reported that it 'was true for manufacturing industry, and pay determination in manufacturing industry is of major importance'.[19] As stewards play an important part in negotiating pay agreements with single employers in manufacturing industry their influence is obvious. The 1984 workplace survey found, however, that for pay negotiations:

There had been a considerable change within the main sectors of the economy. ... In overall terms, the proportion of workplaces in which the pay of at least some workers was determined by negotiation with trade unions increased between 1980 and 1984, but this was largely the result of the increased proportion of workplaces in the public sector where trade union recognition is almost universal. In private manufacturing the decline in the proportion of plants with recognised manual unions implied that more manual workers in this sector were having their pay determined unilaterally by management.[20]

The 1990 workplace survey showed, however, that multiemployer bargaining over pay had experienced widespread decline, yet still remained the single most important collective bargaining method of pay determination. Pay increases determined by single employer and establishment bargaining did not, in volume terms, show any significant change. Importantly, however, the 1990 survey showed clearly that the method of determining pay which became more and more important during the 1980s was not collective bargaining – at any level – but the often unilateral decisions of managers at establishment level. This would suggest that the influence exercised by stewards over pay levels in all sectors of employment declined during the 1980s, and most probably this trend continued into the early 1990s.

There was a widespread decline in the extent to which basic rates [of pay] were set by multi-employer negotiations with trade unions. ... Where basic rates of pay were not subject to collective bargaining, it was increasingly the case that local management, rather than head offices, took the decisions.[21]

Stewards normally negotiate on pay matters at plant or company level, sometimes within the constraints of national agreements. They tend to concentrate on piecework prices and other forms of payment by results. They also influence items such as special payments for adverse working conditions, allowance or 'special' payments, 'inconvenience' money, travelling time and other marginal forms of pay. They seek to upgrade jobs through job evaluation and to determine the level and distribution of overtime. Stewards also obtain payments in exchange for new working methods or for relinquishing custom and practice and demarcation rules within the workplace. Finally, stewards negotiate on other conditions of employment, such as: the distribution and pace of work; shift premiums; quality control; manning levels; labour flexibility; physical conditions; the introduction of new technology; and the reorganization of work and working methods.

Stewards have traditionally dealt with safety problems. But the passing of the Health and Safety at Work etc. Act 1974, and the legal obligation laid upon employers to permit the appointment of employee safety representatives on workplace safety committees, has to some extent relieved stewards of this vital responsibility. Stewards also negotiate the distribution of working hours with managements, including starting and finishing times and meal and rest breaks. They are nearly always involved in questions of discipline, suspensions and possible dismissal of their members.

Another of their cardinal duties is representing their constituents, either individually or collectively, when they have a disagreement with an immediate supervisor or other members of management. Such disagreements arise out of disputes over pay, hours of work, working conditions, the pace or volume of work, lateness, absenteeism and the distribution of overtime. Conflict can also occur between employees and management over supervisory orders or instructions, arguments between fellow workers and personal conduct at work. Other procedural matters which stewards negotiate include: the quality and quantity of work; demarcation arrangements; and infringements by management of established custom and practice. When differences of opinion arise between their members and first line management, stewards normally take the complaint through the established grievance procedure.

Most stewards take their basic union duty of recruiting new members very seriously. Union rules sometimes specifically state that it is the principal job of the workplace representative to recruit new starters, inspect union cards, collect membership subscriptions and seek 100 per cent union membership at the place of work, or the closed shop as it is commonly known. It was estimated that in 1980 some 25 per cent of the workforce were covered by closed-shop arrangements, compared with about 16 per cent in the 1960s, including 9 per cent of all white collar workers. Of these, about 82 per cent were in post-entry closed shops and the remainder in pre-entry shops. Since 1980 the closed shop has declined considerably under the impact of legislation and changing employer and employee attitudes. The 1984 Workplace Industrial Relations Survey found a marked decline in the number of employees working in closed shops. 'We estimate closed shop membership to be between 3.5 and 3.7 million in mid 1984. This represented a fall of about 1.2 million from mid 1980.'[22] The Employment Act 1988 (now TULRC Act 1992) virtually outlawed the closed shop, making it unlawful to initiate or maintain a closed shop by threatening or taking industrial action for these pur-

poses. It also made dismissal on the grounds of non-membership of a trade union automatically unfair in all circumstances.

The 1990 workplace survey revealed that between 1984 and 1990 the number of employees covered by closed shop arrangements had fallen even more sharply.

> The closed shop – perhaps the clearest symbol of union strength at workplace level, and the object of successive legal restrictions over the course of the 1980s – showed the sharpest fall of any of our measures of trade union representation. Arrangements reported by managers covered nearly five million employees in 1980 and only half a million in 1990.[23]

## Attitudes and beliefs

One of the most difficult tasks for those studying industrial relations is to assess the attitudes, aims and values which the different participants to industrial relations bring to the bargaining table. Such behavioural qualities are important because they can influence the approach of the participants to negotiation, the decisions they make, the actions which follow, and the ideologies they propagate. The popular image of the steward, for example, tends to be that of a noisy, aggressive, left-wing, male manual worker who has little education, judgement, sophistication or concern for people other than those whom he represents. Yet this image bears as little resemblance to reality as the view that all managers are rapacious 'capitalists' obsessed with the pursuit of company profits or enterprise efficiency, without concern for or interest in their subordinate employees, whom they treat merely as 'hired hands' and as impersonal parts of the productive system.

Although both these stereotypes contain some elements of truth, surveys and case study research have shown that stewards' attitudes and values are diverse and wide ranging. The Royal Commission's report of 1968, in drawing heavily upon the first in-depth research on stewards to be undertaken, argued:

> it is often wide of the mark to describe shop stewards as 'trouble makers'. Trouble is thrust upon them. In circumstances of this kind they may be striving to bring some order into a chaotic situation, and management may rely heavily on their efforts to do so. ... Thus shop stewards are rarely agitators pushing workers

toward unconstitutional action. In some instances, they may be the mere mouthpieces of their work groups. But quite commonly they are supporters of order exercising a restraining influence on their members in conditions which promote disorder. . . . 'For the most part the steward is viewed by others, and views himself, as an accepted, and even moderating influence; more of a lubricant than an irritant'.[24]

Most of the attitudes, norms and views which people hold are the result of their background, education, experiences and social conditioning. Stewards are not exempt from these social processes. Their attitudes and behaviour are not only influenced by their personal values, social aims and political beliefs, but are also the result of the pressures brought to bear upon them by a range of external factors (Figure 13.1). These include their workgroups, management, other stewards, their union, the conditions prevailing at the workplace and the state of the local labour market. One survey concluded:

> Though most shop stewards seek and achieve amicable relations with management, motives are mixed. Stewards may not invariably be acting as they would like, but are responding to various pressures. The steward has a difficult political position between the conflicting interests of management and men – answerable to a union outside the immediate conflict and subject to the pressures of the nature and traditions of the workplace.[25]

Other research has emphasized the ideological awareness of stewards. It is argued, for instance, that the view of the steward as being at the centre of the web of conflicting pressures seeking only to balance them and to conciliate among them is a one-sided view. In the words of one steward:

> Basically, industry with the work force on one side and the management on the other, is a conflict of interest. Where you have a conflict of interest the work people are going to say, 'Look, what you've got we want; either some of it or all of it'. There's going to be a resistance to this and it's accepted that we go through the haggling process to sort out who's going to have what.[26]

In yet another study, the authors of a detailed and exhaustive single plant analysis of shop steward behaviour in Britain drew an interesting distinction between the attitudes of manual and of white collar stewards:

On the shop floor, stewards more consistently adopt a conflict image of industry and, along with this, express a stronger and more consistent commitment to union principles. On the staff side, there is a greater degree of ambivalence over the nature of relationships in industry, and a less certain commitment to union principles. Staff stewards, as a group, more readily espouse a belief in industrial harmony and individualism.[27]

It is evident that the forces and influences shaping the attitudes, beliefs and actions of stewards are extremely complicated. However, care should be taken not to assume that stewards merely respond to the multiplicity of pressures surrounding them. Some of them at least are influenced by political and trade union principles and social beliefs which rarely, if ever, are shared by management. It would be a mistake, nevertheless, to believe that such ideological differences between the participants in industrial relations need necessarily on their own lead to industrial conflict or even to bad industrial relations.

## 13.2 Workplace Representatives and Workplace Committees

### Background

In those workplaces where there are a number of stewards representing several trade unions, and where informal relationships cannot adequately deal with the problem of representative decision making, stewards create their own formal committees where all the stewards sit to determine policy and to make majority decisions. Such committees are rarely referred to in trade union rule books and they often act quite independently of the formal union structure and outside of its control. These committees which are an important expression of shop steward organization and power are usually referred to as 'joint stewards' committees' or JSCs. They only exist in a minority of workplaces, where stewards are well organized. They are more common in larger establishments than in smaller ones. It is in such committees that union workplace policy is largely determined and a number of representative stewards are chosen to negotiate with management, usually through a works committee on which both parties are represented.

The structure of stewards' committees is immensely varied and they depend for their form upon such factors as the needs of stewards, the organization of the workplace, its physical layout, and whether or not there is a single establishment or multi-establishment location. Where there is more than one establishment the structures created by stewards are sometimes called stewards 'combine committees'. Conversely, in very large workplaces with thousands of employees and many stewards, there are separate stewards committees for different departments or work areas. Each of these sends representatives to a central stewards committee largely dominated by experienced senior stewards and conveners. Since such large workplaces are usually multiunion establishments, stewards from many different unions are represented on these bodies.

These committees are usually under the democratic control of all the stewards within the workplace and they are ultimately accountable, in theory at least, to rank-and-file trade union members. JSCs make policy and take negotiating decisions often with little external influence by local trade union officers or their formal union hierarchies. Research indicates that JSCs are often controlled by small groups of senior stewards and conveners, some of whom work closely with their union full-time officers, whilst others are quite independent of theirs. In general, where the workplace is very large, and where bargaining is not closely regulated by national agreements, negotiations are mainly conditioned by relations between a small number of stewards and senior managers. In these circumstances, industrial relations is largely the autonomous product of bargains struck between stewards and management. Where such conditions exist, the quality of the stewards' representative committee structure is vital.

Normally, the JSC has as its chairperson the workplace convener or, where several union conveners exist, the one elected to do the job. A secretary and other officers are also elected and, except in very large establishments, all stewards attend JSC meetings. Where the employing establishment is so large that only a representative group of stewards sit on the JSC, meetings of all the stewards are held at regular intervals. It is then that the JSC defends its policies and subjects them to the majority approval of the stewards present. Care is taken to ensure that stewards on the JSC, and the negotiating team which bargains with management, are representative of the different elements within the unionized workforce. This means that representation has to be distributed according to union membership, to different work areas and departments and to skill, sex, job status and occupational groupings.

If a well-balanced JSC is to be achieved in an establishment, say, with only a few large departments and a large number of small workgroups, and where a large number of unskilled female employees and a small number of highly skilled craftworkers are employed, it is essential that the composition of the JSC takes these factors into account. Unless this is attempted, common policies commanding support amongst the unions are unlikely to emerge. In many workplaces, it is not possible to establish a JSC because of the fears of minority sections, such as maintenance workers or other skilled groups, that their interests and negotiating strength are subordinated to the wishes of the larger, less skilled groups. In consequence, two or more separate bargaining units emerge with which management has to deal separately and amongst whom considerable distrust and antagonism can develop.

Joint stewards' organizations, operating on a fairly formal basis and observing the usual rules and firm chairing necessary for effective working, are now widespread in the British workplace, though they are only found in a minority of establishments. They have emerged largely in response to the growth in the numbers of stewards and to their expanding representative and workplace bargaining functions. They are usually multiunion bodies which have to take account of all the representational complexities of the workplace. The extent to which they operate independently of the formal trade union structure depends upon a variety of factors. These include: the size of the establishment; the structures of the unions; the availability of full-time union officers; the degree of local bargaining; and the attitudes and industrial relations policies of management.

It is the prime function of stewards' committees from all parts of the establishment, and from other establishments in the case of multiplant enterprises, to raise those matters most concerning them and their members. JSCs are also used by small groups of senior stewards and conveners to determine a variety of industrial relations policy initiatives. These include, for example, the content of pay claims to be presented to management, but issues other than pay are obviously of great importance to JSCs. In the first workplace industrial relations survey in 1980:

> Joint shop stewards' meetings were reported in only a minority of establishments with two or more manual or two or more non-manual unions. They were more likely where the unions negotiated on pay on a joint basis in larger

establishments and where there was a full-time convener. However, the weak association with establishment level pay bargaining suggests that the meetings were involved with other issues besides pay.[28]

Four years later it was reported that:

Meetings between manual shop stewards and other stewards of their union at their workplace were less common in 1984 than in 1980, another indicator of the weakening of manual trade union organisations. There was no similar change for non-manual representatives. In multi-union workplaces joint union committees remained a minority occurrence, declining noticeably in manufacturing industry for both manual and non-manual unions.[29]

The 1990 Workplace Industrial Relations Survey, despite the overall decline in trade union membership and density, reported that:

the proportion of manual stewards reporting meetings with other representatives of the same union at the workplace increased slightly from 36 per cent in 1984 to 43 per cent in 1990. . . . Thus it seems that the overall decline in the reporting of these meetings in the early 1980s seems to have been reversed by the end of the decade. [Moreover,] the incidence of joint shop steward committees involving non-manual representatives increased by half between 1984 and 1990.[30]

While there is little empirical research evidence to support it, the conclusion may be drawn that during a decade of almost unprecedented change in employment practices and industrial relations, both stewards and management found joint stewards' committees useful as problem handling bodies.

## Workplace union branches

It is sometimes contended that the piecemeal development of workplace bargaining, and the emergence of JSCs and of works committees largely outside of union control, is the result of outdated and inadequate union structures. Union rule books, it is said, have failed to formalize shopfloor developments or to meet the needs of local stewards. Yet the common trade union practice of using the branch meeting as the basic unit of trade union organization and democracy is a product of nineteenth-century conditions. At that time the locality, area and occupation of trade

unionists meant far more than did the workplace, which was often small and where steward representation was largely unknown. As part of its proposals for reforming collective bargaining through company and plant agreements, the Donovan Commission advocated the establishment of workplace union branches which would, it believed, help to integrate stewards and workplace bargaining more firmly into the unions' formal structures. In the 1980 Workplace Industrial Relations Survey important differences were found:

between trade union branches whose members were drawn from a single workplace and branches encompassing members from several workplaces or employers. Branches based at the workplace were smaller, and meetings were attended by a higher proportion of members. In all types of branch, but especially geographical based ones, shop stewards were much more frequent in their attendance than were other branch members. Stewards also commonly held positions in their branch committee.[31]

Ten years later the 1990 workplace survey was unable to detect any substantial trend during the 1980s towards workplace trade union branches: 'there was no change in the incidence of workplace-based branches among any of the main unions in our sample, manual or non-manual'.[32] How much the development of workplace branches has contributed towards the resolution of the problems caused by multiunionism at the workplace is very difficult to assess. Workplace branches have probably had little more than a marginal impact upon workplace bargaining where JSCs and works committees are strongly established.

## Full-time union officers

The Royal Commission recommended the appointment of many more full-time trade union officers to cope with the additional burdens which extensive company and workplace bargaining cause for union negotiators. A higher proportion of full-time officers, it was argued, would encourage more efficient bargaining and would help to bring stewards and their unions into closer working relationships. To date, the trade unions have not significantly improved their officer-to-membership ratios. It is clear, however, that in the larger establishments, the appointment of full-time senior stewards or conveners has become commonplace. This trend has undoubtedly led to the independence of many JSCs and works committees from formal union accountability. Many unions and the TUC, however, have extended resources for the training of stewards. In courses, trade union principles are stressed along with the need for stewards to see themselves as an essential part of the union and not as isolated representatives of their members and their workgroups at the workplace. The 1980 Workplace Industrial Relations Survey concluded:

> In cases where stewards had received training, the very large majority of managers felt that the training was valuable. Eighty-four per cent judged that training did help stewards in their work as representatives. ... It is clear that the large majority of stewards gave the highest rating to training and nearly all felt it was useful.[33]

The 1990 workplace survey found that the provision for training for stewards remained high, and that while management support was less obvious it was, generally speaking, not obstructive. The TUC and individual unions still determined the content of most of the training, which reflected the need for stewards to be kept informed of legal changes which affected the workplace, and the need to sustain workplace union organization. By 1990, it would appear that steward training had become largely defensive and consolidatory.

A detailed survey of 14 local union branches found that a continuum of relationships exists between stewards' organizations at the workplace and the local union structure. The continuum ranges from full dependence through various degrees of co-operation to complete independence. But, it pointed out, the rapid development or workplace and company bargaining, and of workplace pay structures and procedural agreements, has in general been carried out by stewards with little real contact and support from their local unions. The study suggested that the position of stewards' organizations, and the degrees to which they were dependent on or independent of local union officers, could be explained in terms of the following major influences: the size of the establishment; the degree to which collective agreements were centralized or devolved; and the availability of full-time officers. Other factors affecting workplace–union relationships were steward experience, organization at establishment level, the scope of workplace bargaining and the attitudes to bargaining by both managers and full-time officers.

Shifts along the continuum of the steward and full-time officer relationship take place where changes occur in one or more of these major determining factors.

> The most general influence on dependence is the size of workplace organisation. The larger the workplace organisation the greater the resources at its disposal, and the more independent its behaviour. But size is not the only influence at work. The greater the unity within a workplace organisation, the trade union experience of its members and their status as employees, the larger will be the resources at its disposal, and the more it will tend to act on its own.

This study concluded that unions can encourage or discourage workplace independence 'by promoting or hindering organisation, unity and experience. Managers can also encourage workplace independence'. However, the availability of the full-time officer is for the union to determine, and, within limits:

> the lack of a full-time officer to whom its representatives can turn may push a workplace organisation towards independence, whereas the ready availability of a full-time officer may hold it back.[34]

The 1990 survey found that, in general, stewards were making greater demands on union full-time officials and union head offices for help and assistance than in 1984. Stewards also appear to have requested meetings between full-time officials and management more frequently in 1990 than in previous years. It would appear that under the pressures created by recession, redundancy and unemployment, stewards turned to their formal union structure for support.

> It appears, then, that trade unions in 1990 were much more heavily involved in workplace-level matters than they were in 1984. All levels of the union were affected, it seems, from the local paid official ... up to union national officers being much more commonly consulted directly by establishment-based representatives.[35]

## 13.3 Union Facilities at the Workplace

Stewards only emerged in significant numbers during the 1960s and 1970s, with relative economic prosperity and a fundamental shift in the balance of bargaining power in favour of trade unions in certain industries and workplaces. Other factors influencing steward autonomy included the growth of workplace bargaining in some sectors, and the restrictions imposed by trade unions and the law on the ability of employers to hire, use and dispose of labour unilaterally and at will. In many industries, stewards faced considerable employer opposition to their emergence, while encountering a marked reluctance by some full-time officers to allow them to negotiate with their employers. Consequently, left to their own devices and with little support from the employers or the formal union organizations, these early stewards had little recourse to facilities and formal communications necessary to perform their tasks effectively. These included secretarial assistance, research for collective bargaining and training and educational opportunities.

## Support facilities

The report of the Royal Commission on Trade Unions and Employers' Associations recognized that the reform of company and workplace bargaining would involve stewards in extensive and important negotiations. They would require improved facilities, better communications and relevant training to undertake their duties successfully. The Commission on Industrial Relations (CIR) was asked to consider these matters and to make recommendations. Its report on the facilities afforded to stewards, which is still relevant, points out that 'the need for facilities arises from the functions performed by stewards' and these 'functions and hence facilities must be considered within the context of varying industrial relations systems at industry, company and establishment level'. The CIR considered that management and stewards should carefully analyse the functions of stewards before deciding the range and types of facilities which they require. The report emphasized the importance of adequate steward facilities as a necessary condition for the establishment of 'good' industrial relations at workplace level, although these were not regarded as a sufficient condition. It also recommended that industry level agreements 'should cover as far as possible the main functions of the steward together with the broad principles which relate to the provision of facilities'.[36]

The CIR report also recommended that union rule books should define the duties and responsibilities of stewards more closely and that the right of stewards to leave their jobs to conduct union

business without loss of earnings should be conceded. It also felt that greater clarity and precision in the manner of steward elections were required. It saw the need, too, for: a more orderly approach to the issuing of steward credentials; the provision of facilities for trade unions to collect membership dues during works time and where possible by the deduction of dues from the payroll; and the supplying of office accommodation for meetings with other stewards and full-time union officers. The CIR also argued in favour of access to telephones, notice boards, and typing and duplicating facilities for stewards. This would require training opportunities for stewards appropriate to their needs. Finally, the report stressed, 'once white-collar trade unionism is established its representatives require the same joint agreements on functions and facilities as their counterparts in the manual unions'.[37]

In the same year as the publication of the CIR report, the TUC issued its own guide to trade unionists undertaking negotiating duties. It recommended, *inter alia*, that stewards needed the following facilities if they were to play their full part in collective bargaining and the improvement of industrial relations:

(a) the provision of a list of new entrants to the appropriate trade union representatives;

(b) facilities on the premises for shop stewards to explain to each new worker the advantages of trade union membership together with the terms of the collective agreements covering the establishment;

(c) facilities to collect union contributions or to inspect members' cards or the operation of a check-off system where this is desired by unions;

(d) a room, or at least a desk, in the workplace (in the case of a senior shop steward a separate office would be desirable) together with adequate facilities for storing correspondence and papers. Ready access to telephone and to typing and duplicating facilities;

(e) the provision of a notice board and the use of an internal post system;

(f) the use of a suitable room for the purpose of consulting and reporting to members when necessary during working hours and for meetings of shop stewards committees; and

(g) sufficient time off, with pay at average earnings, during working hours, for a representative to perform all his union duties which relate to the workplace; to attend training courses related to his duties as a union officer and to attend conferences called by his union. A representative should not have to use his holiday entitlement for this purpose.[38]

With the publication of these reports and guides many trade unions, stewards and employers became increasingly conscious of the need to provide stewards with adequate and relevant facilities if they were to fulfil their duties and responsibilities effectively. Although some managements realized that such facilities were essential for the effective conduct of workplace bargaining, it is reasonable to assume that other managements only reluctantly accepted stewards, and the range of issues which they sought to negotiate. Other employers continued to resist such claims, on the grounds of cost, especially in terms of pay for time off work and of lost production. Furthermore, these employers feared that in providing a wide range of facilities they would raise the status of stewards in the eyes of the manual workforce, white-collar employees and supervisory staff. It is extremely difficult to assess whether the provision of such facilities led to improved industrial relations or whether their absence resulted in contrary tendencies. By 1980 however:

> Substantial majorities of senior stewards for manual workers had access to some office services. Ninety-five per cent had access to a telephone. Nearly three-quarters had secretarial assistance or access to a photo-copier or a typewriter. Seventy-one per cent had at least the use of an office. It appeared that there had been a marked tendency for facilities of all types to be introduced in the previous five years.[39]

The 1990 Workplace Survey showed that the position regarding workplace facilities for stewards remained largely unchanged between 1984 and 1990.

## Communications

It is a conventional wisdom of industrial relations that effective channels of communication between the employer and its managers, on the one hand, and employees and their representatives, on the other, are essential for the avoidance of misunderstandings, suspicion, mistrust, unfounded rumours and, ultimately, industrial conflict. Communications between employers and employees, however, mean very different things to different people. They are seen by some managers, for example, as a method of increasing employee involvement and employee commitment to the principal objectives and policies of the organization. These are aimed at getting employees to share the views of managers on such things as capital investment, operational efficiency, work reorganization, new technologies, product development and human resources policy. This neo-unitary approach to the running of organizations is intended to obtain from all employees in the enterprise, regardless of their status, commitment to, and even enthusiasm for, the corporate goals and market objectives of the firm.

Other methods which are used to try to secure the agreement and commitment of employees and their representatives to employer policies include: joint consultative committees; quality control circles; employee participation schemes; career progression; profit sharing; share ownership; and staff appraisal. In return for employee acceptance of these approaches to conflict-free employee relations, management commits itself to provide job security, good pay and conditions, career opportunities and advancement, more interesting work, and harmonization of conditions of employment for all employees, irrespective of their job status. These aspects of personnel and human resources policy are dealt with in other chapters. Here we focus on how effective communications can be developed between managements and employees at the workplace and what information needs to be communicated between them.

Inadequate systems of communication on industrial relations policies, changes in working practices and the introduction of new policies affecting the working lives of employees, whilst perhaps not a direct cause of disputes, can certainly contribute to feelings of insecurity, confusion and resentment among employees. Lack of information from higher level management within the workplace, for example, can lead to the circulation of rumours which are invariably exaggerated. Once established, such rumours become difficult to reject or to rebut. The TUC has therefore argued that:

> Managements should ensure that workers are kept well-informed about issues which affect their interests; in particular the payments system, the procedure for resolving grievances and disputes, safety matters and opportunities for training and promotion. In order to prevent duplication of instructions they should also ensure that all managers are fully aware of their area of responsibility.[40]

Whilst the TUC appears to believe with some justification that good communications are the responsibility of management, the industrial relations code of practice suggested that it is a shared responsibility and that 'Management, employees' representatives and trade unions should co-operate in ensuring that effective communication and consultation take place.'[41] The nature of industrial organizations, however, indicates that the prime but not the exclusive responsibility for ensuring good communications rests with management. It is management which possesses most of the facts about its business and takes the basic decisions affecting the working lives of its labour force. But the supportive role of the trade unions and stewards is undoubtedly important, since they can do much to allay the distrust and suspicion of the employer's motives in many workplace situations.

By associating themselves with the communication of basic information and of industrial relations policies to all employees, stewards can often raise the threshold of trust and respect between management and employees. It is often overlooked, however, that people in subordinate positions fail either to 'hear' such information or to heed it. This arises because to 'hear' it from a greater power than themselves implies that they will be influenced by it.

> Talking about improving communications therefore involves losing our fear and suspicion about the use of power. . . . Full communication requires an equalization of power [whilst] a major barrier to communication in organizations and in classrooms . . . is that information comes *down* from superior to subordinate or from high status to low.[42]

The practical steps which can be taken to improve communications in industrial relations include the following. First, it is necessary to acknowledge that communication is a two-way process with management giving information to employees and stewards, and then receiving information back from them. This reverse flow of information from employees to management can be transmitted by stewards where they are recognized. It follows that stewards have to be fully aware of their responsibility for discussing industrial relations matters on the shopfloor and accurately reporting back the majority response of their members to management. But as many stewards regard themselves as opinion formers and opinion leaders, rather than as mere representatives, this is sometimes difficult.

Second, it is commonly believed that the most effective means of communication within the workplace is by word of mouth. This form of personal contact can be extremely time consuming yet is often very effective. In fact the most important method of communication is by word of mouth 'through personal contact between each manager and his immediate work group or individual employees, and between managers and employee representatives'.[43] But oral communications need to be supplemented by written information including circulars, notice board memoranda, handbooks and minutes of meetings. New employees can be given induction training which makes them aware of the principal policies of the employer and the unions. This ensures that they are aware of the main aspects of their contracts of employment and working conditions. Employee or company handbooks, containing information about the organization and its industrial relations and personnel management policies and practices, can be issued to all employees and provide the basis for successful induction training.

Third, management and unions can decide jointly what information on the enterprise and its policies should be disclosed to all employees. Headings in such a list include: information on future employment and manpower policies; the organization of work; product types and ranges; investment strategies; and the firm's personnel and industrial relations policies. Finally, management and unions need to regard the maintenance of good communications as a professional duty on both their parts. This means, in practice, drawing up a written communication plan and training their representatives in the art of effective and accurate communications with those with whom they come into contact. Figure 13.2 illustrates some of the needs and objectives which management and stewards seek through communications systems and procedures.

During the 1980s, some organizations and personnel departments came to the view that it was more effective to communicate directly with their employees on certain matters by writing to them at their home addresses. They did this rather than rely on stewards to convey managerial proposals indirectly to the workers they represented. These direct written communications, from top management to individual employees, were probably most successful where organizations sought to explain that they had no alternative but to make radical changes in manning levels and working practices, in the face of fierce market competition.

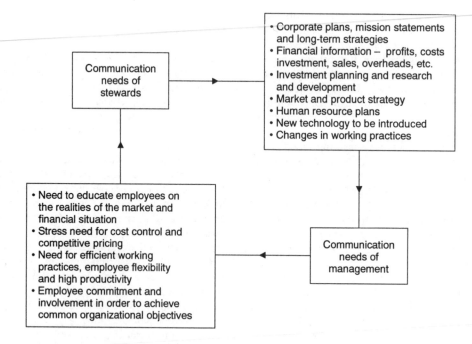

*Figure 13.2* Communication needs of management and stewards.

The advantages to management of approaching their employees directly hardly needs rehearsing. It not only minimizes the likelihood of employees hearing the 'wrong' message, it also reinforces the role of line management. . . . This development, commonplace for most of Britain's more successful companies, is increasingly marked in both public and private sector organizations.[44]

## Training

As the duties of stewards have become more complex and more demands are made upon their knowledge and abilities, and since stewards have moved more into the centre of the industrial relations stage in many instances, the greater becomes the need for specific education and training for the role. Whilst it is probably true that able and effective stewards are largely the product of selection processes among their fellow employees, and of the hard world of experience, there is little doubt that the growing complexity of the tasks which they face calls for carefully designed training courses.

A small number of training courses for stewards was provided in the 1950s. But they catered for only a handful of stewards who were usually from large companies in the industrial conurbations. These courses were normally provided by the Workers Educational Association, the extra-mural departments of universities, the technical colleges or by the trade unions themselves. Where courses were provided by public educational institutions they had first to be approved by either individual unions or the Education Department of the TUC. The Donovan Commission emphasized the need for more and better training in industrial relations and the CIR produced a report on future training needs and provision. The CIR revealed the paucity of steward and management training in industrial relations in a report which concluded:

> that training can play an important part in the achievement and maintenance of effective industrial relations . . . [and that] . . . employers and unions have a joint interest in training to improve the conduct of industrial relations.[45]

The TUC rejected this recommendation for joint responsibility arguing that 'the nature and function of union representatives is in any case a matter solely for the unions to decide as are their training and education needs'.[46]

The TUC in maintaining the sole right of the trade union movement to control the aims, content and nature of steward training in consultation with the public education service has pointed to the considerable use of public resources devoted to management education. These, it maintains, are very extensive compared with the much smaller public provision for trade union education and training. The TUC claims that, because of the ever increasing volume of legislation affecting trade unions and industrial relations, plus the need to modernize and improve collective bargaining and employee relations at the workplace, the training needs of workplace representatives have grown in importance. The EPC Act 1978 first gave trade union representatives, recognized by the employer, the right to time off work with pay to undertake appropriate training related to trade union duties and activities. The legislation, now incorporated in the TULRC Act 1992, lists the duties and activities which qualify for time off work for training. An ACAS Code of Practice on Time Off for Trade Union Duties and Activities gives practical guidance for trade unions, workplace representatives and employers. In particular, the Code states that time off for training might be necessary where substantial changes in the organization of work are being considered, where new legislation will affect workplace relations, or where significant changes are being proposed in the structure and organization of collective bargaining.

## 13.4  Collective Bargaining at the Workplace

Enterprise and workplace bargaining is conducted between union stewards and managers. Whilst it is sometimes the practice for full-time trade union officers and for employer associations' representatives to be informed of the content of such local agreements for their formal approval, their active participation in such negotiations is the exception rather than the rule. Local bargaining is therefore a largely autonomous process shaped by the traditions, constraints and circumstances peculiar to each of the varied enterprise and workplace conditions existing in Britain.

### *Bargaining principles*

Four of the underlying principles involved if effective negotiation by stewards is to take place include the following:

An understanding of *trade union principles* is

required to give trade union bargaining effort a sense of direction; *bargaining awareness* is the ability to identify issues for bargaining; a knowledge of the realities of industrial *power* is necessary, as is also an awareness of the nature of *bargaining relationships* between unions and management. But clearly, in practice, knowledge and understanding are not sufficient conditions for effective bargaining. A favourable balance of power and favourable bargaining relations are necessary.[47]

An understanding of '*trade union principles*' in bargaining is necessary if stewards are to mobilize their members' support and gain formal union approval for their bargaining objectives. Not all stewards have had sufficient trade union or bargaining experience to be consciously aware of these principles, though it is unusual for senior stewards and conveners not to have them. Furthermore, most experienced stewards see it as their duty to educate their members in union bargaining principles. Where bargaining takes place without reference to trade union principles, it may become ineffective and concerned with trivia. Alternatively, it may become 'unprincipled' in the sense that it concedes unfair advantages to certain workgroups and not to others, thus destroying trade union solidarity. The most important principle in bargaining is the creation and presentation of unity among stewards, their members and their unions. This unity of purpose is pursued not only as a union principle, but also because it is commonly agreed that 'unity is strength' and that disunity only benefits management at the bargaining table.

In its broadest idealistic sense, trade union unity involves all the unionized workers in Britain. But in the context of local bargaining, it usually involves only those union members forming the bargaining unit. 'The idea of unity also implies a concern with justice, fairness, equality and the protection of the less fortunate. Trade unionism is not, or should not be, solely about helping the relatively well-off become even better off.'[48]

Adherence to trade union principles is seen as largely a matter of moral purpose, but it also has a practical function in creating an agreed union ethic. This helps to generate solidarity amongst trade unionists and discourages the pursuit of sectional interests which can make the unions at workplace level the subject of damaging cynicism among their members. It would be unrealistic, however, not to recognize that in many circumstances sectional self-interest overrides principles of solidarity and equity. This is often the case where one group of workers can exploit a labour market advantage not open to other groups. In overtime working, for instance, ethical solidarity can be achieved by referring to the trade union principles of maximum hours of work, equity of treatment for all members and the wider fact that unemployment and overtime working can be viewed as ethically incompatible. But this view will not prevail if the workgroup concerned really wants the additional earnings and can see no advantage to the unemployed by refusing overtime.

The second condition for effective steward bargaining is *bargaining awareness*. Experienced and energetic shop stewards are not content with merely ensuring that management honours and observes collective agreements. Nor are they satisfied with just taking up the routine grievances of their members. They actively seek to expand the areas and the depth of bargaining by taking negotiating initiatives and by extending bargaining into areas traditionally controlled solely by management. Such stewards show a highly developed sense of awareness of the ultimate potentiality of enterprise and workplace bargaining.

> In principle, therefore, if workers are powerful enough they can increase the range of issues over which they bargain. In practice, the problem the steward faces is whether he and his members are powerful enough and whether he can afford to take the risk of finding out.[49]

Bargaining awareness is, therefore, a matter of perceiving bargaining opportunities and the balance of negotiating power between shop stewards and management.

A vital aspect of bargaining awareness is the recognition by stewards that they require adequate knowledge of their members' job content, pay and working conditions, and of conditions in other similar organizations. Stewards also need a continuous flow of information from management on a range of matters including manpower requirements, product design, sales policies, investment proposals, research programmes and so on. Awareness of changes in job allocation, variations in overtime and shiftworking, changes in management structures, and the rates of absenteeism and sickness with their possible causes are also relevant. Armed with such knowledge, stewards determined to expand the boundaries of bargaining develop bargaining initiatives which of necessity impinge upon areas previously under the unilateral control of management. Similarly,

stewards can use the findings of research departments or the services of specialized research organizations to advance their bargaining goals.

An understanding by shop stewards of the *balance of power* between themselves and management is the third essential element for effective enterprise and workplace bargaining. Historically, the employer has nearly always possessed greater market and economic power than either individual employees or even collective groups of workers. This has been reflected in the bargaining context. No employers have readily abandoned a position which allows them to determine pay and conditions of work unilaterally unless obliged to do so by the collective strength of trade unions. Even with the undeniable shift in the balance of bargaining power towards trade unions and their members and away from employers which took place, for example, between 1945 and 1979, the balance of negotiating power, generally speaking, remained with the employers. The focus of interest from the enterprise and workplace viewpoint is the relative shifts in the balance of power affecting the bargaining positions of management and unions. If both sides move towards a strike situation unsure of their relative strengths, for example, they might decide on caution and arrive at a compromise solution. If they do not and a strike ensues, then one side is bound to lose more than the other from the outcome. When work is resumed the balance of power will have changed and that fact will be reflected in future negotiations and relationships between the parties.

The balance of power can change, however, without conflict arising. For example, demand in the labour market may become slack with unemployment giving a bargaining advantage to the employer. Similarly, stewards might increase union membership to the point where management will privately acknowledge that the balance of power has shifted in the union's favour. Little change results, however, if the side which benefits from a shift in the balance of power neither recognizes that this is happening nor seizes the bargaining advantages offered by it. In short, movements in the balance of power must be followed or accompanied by a new bargaining awareness on the part of stewards and of management. Brief or short-term shifts in the balance of bargaining power offer less in the way of fundamental changes in the bargaining opportunities to either side than any long-term power shift, such as those brought about by heavy and prolonged unemployment accompanied by a diminishing social security threshold.

The factor which above all others appears to reduce the advantages for either side if the balance of power shifts is the quality of the 'bargaining relationships' between them. Its basis is the acceptance by management that trade unions and stewards are here to stay and that they cannot be eliminated by conflict and unremitting struggle, even in conditions of high unemployment. Equally, there is the recognition by trade unions that the abolition of private enterprises and of managerial control within them is not a political reality except, possibly, in the very long term. Besides, as many unions in the public sector recognize, the elimination of the private ownership of productive capital does not mean the removal of management with whom they are obliged to negotiate. With the acceptance of these economic and political realities, experienced managers and stewards appreciate the importance of developing and sustaining 'good' bargaining relationships between themselves:

> Both steward and manager, therefore, are in a way dependent upon the other for the general achievement of their goals. If each sees the other as powerful and important, they tend to develop a relationship of trust which helps each to achieve his respective goals. It should be emphasized that this does not necessarily mean that one or the other sells out, although clearly there is a danger. The trust relationship is one of dependence, and rests upon the existence of conflict combined with a recognition that some sort of accommodation is inevitable and that power, over a period, is more or less evenly balanced.[50]

If the power of either side or its representativeness changes dramatically, it is likely that established relationships will deteriorate. For example, if a management sees its sphere of control curtailed by growing union power and it seeks to handle this sensitively by fostering good relationships with its stewards, it might benefit from radical changes in the labour market or in internal divisions amongst the stewards. In such situations, it could well decide that the bargaining relationship no longer reflects the realities of the distribution of power. Accordingly, management might decide to take a harsher stance in its relationships with the stewards. Again, much depends upon whether the shift in power is slight and short term, or substantial and long term.

## Negotiating skills

Experienced stewards with proven bargaining abilities stress, not surprisingly, that negotiating skills are the result of inherent personal qualities rather than of training or instruction. Inherent qualities, they argue, are only marginally enhanced by training compared with actual experience of negotiations.

> In the workplace negotiators come up through the shop stewards' committee. Not every steward turns into a good negotiator, but it's the experience of being on a committee itself that does the real training of negotiators . . . we've gained a great deal from . . . role playing . . . they can give you confidence, but there's no substitute for the experience of the real thing.[51]

Stewards often point out that they have first to prove their ability at presenting a case on the joint stewards committee before their peers have sufficient confidence in their ability to negotiate with management. Less experienced stewards are allowed to attend negotiations with management as observers of the way in which senior stewards and conveners negotiate. In large enterprises or workplaces, stewards are encouraged to specialize so that their skill and detailed knowledge of, say, payment systems or job evaluation can be used on appropriate occasions. Both managers and stewards have much to gain by developing as much mutual respect and trust for each other as can be realistically achieved given the conflict-ridden nature of collective bargaining.

> If you know a particular manager always lies to you well obviously you react differently to him, but if you have a manager who always keeps agreements that he's made and signed, there's a mutual respect . . . I respect some managers even though I know full well we both have different roles to fulfil.[52]

When the joint stewards committee meets to prepare a package of claims to be presented to management, it needs to have a clear strategy if it is to be successful. First, it has to establish realizable targets for negotiation and to decide whether or not to demand the impossible or the unrealistic, knowing full well that it will soon move back to a more reasonable position. Alternatively, it has to decide whether it should make a realistic claim and stick to it. Both schools of thought have their devotees but it is essential that the committee decides what its sticking positions are. Having determined its bargaining objectives and tactics, the JSC then has to prepare a detailed and researched case. In the words of one steward:

> If there is a major problem or if it is the kind that's going to become a major issue I'll have to prepare myself very carefully right from the beginning. I've got to work for the long-term principle and I want to be consistent all the way.[53]

Once a case is prepared, and it has been influenced by trade union principles and a realistic assessment of the balance of bargaining power, the next step is to prepare the workforce by informing it of the content of the claim and winning its support and solidarity. 'The most important thing for improvements in conditions is membership pressure. But that pressure is affected by many factors including the lead given by shop stewards.' During negotiations most stewards stress the need for unity of approach and teamwork. If during bargaining with management representatives one or more stewards feel that negotiations are going adrift, they rarely say so openly, but request an adjournment to settle the matter. It is a cardinal rule in bargaining that the two sides do not disagree among themselves in public but sort out their differences in private. Adjournments are also used to ensure the accuracy of what is being negotiated.

> When you're negotiating big deals it becomes very important you get everything right because it's going to set your conditions for a year or so . . . We often have short adjournments, the very important five or ten minutes to make sure that things are right.[54]

Most negotiators on both sides of the bargaining table agree that 'face saving' is essential if either side is to continue effectively after making mistakes, revealing lack of knowledge or inexperience, or demonstrating that it is out of touch with those whom it represents. If a manager or a steward, for example, makes a statement or takes up a position which evidence or experience clearly invalidates, his or her position becomes untenable if the other side relentlessly exposes it. But if the negotiators quietly drop the matter and show that they accept, without ridicule or rancour, explanations, rationalizations, or excuses, no matter how thin they may appear to be, the issue can be forgotten and the individual and the negotiations can be saved. Similarly, flexibility on both sides is essential if they are to reach an agreement. Experienced negotiators do not often get trapped into making statements and taking up positions which prevent them exerting some degree of flexibility and having room for manoeuvre.

It is obviously important for stewards to keep their members constantly informed of the progress being made in negotiations but it is not possible to present a final agreement for their approval until the negotiations have been concluded. Experienced stewards usually have a shrewd idea of what their members will accept or reject, and the leadership ability to persuade their members that they should concur. The final agreement can be put to their members orally by the stewards, either department by department or at a mass meeting, where the communicative and verbal skills of the stewards are paramount. Alternatively, as is increasingly the case, the decision whether or not to accept management's final offer can be made by secret ballot. If their members accept the stewards' recommendations, there are no real problems. If they reject them, the stewards must be prepared either to go back and re-open negotiations or resign. As most stewards do not finally conclude agreements with management before getting majority membership support, they cannot reasonably be denied the right to re-negotiate. But they usually lose considerable respect and standing in the eyes of management and their members if the agreement which they recommend is rejected.

It is generally agreed that the threat of sanctions by either side harms the process of negotiation and the bargaining relationship, if it is used unwisely or as an empty gesture. Experienced negotiators on both sides are fully aware of the sanctions at their disposal and the realities of their use. To threaten the use of sanctions as a means of forcing the other side to concede more than it is able to is often seen as an empty bluff. This renders the chances of reaching a satisfactory compromise more remote. As one trade union negotiator has suggested:

> there are circumstances where the members have demonstrated their power before we ever get round the negotiating table. Then, it is very much in the mind of the management. If the lads come out on strike and I've persuaded them to go back to work on the basis of negotiations, that puts me in a very strong position.[55]

## Disclosure of information

It is now generally recognized that for effective bargaining to take place, it is good practice for management to disclose appropriate information about company activities, resources and policies to shop stewards. Trade unions have argued for a long time that management should 'open the books' so that the facts relating to collective bargaining can be more accurately judged. It is the belief of most trade unionists that if the main financial information concerning the enterprise is available for their close inspection, they are in a better position to judge what is a reasonable claim to make to management. Until the 1980s, very few employers were willing to disclose detailed information for bargaining purposes to stewards or trade unions. In this respect, the TUC argued that employers should disclose information on:

> General ownership and organisation structure; manpower and personnel information; financial information covering sales, costs, incomes, 'performance indicators' and the value of the company's assets; prospects and plans including information on investment, sales and manpower.[56]

The Confederation of British Industry has also advised its members that in order to avoid 'the risk of deterioration in industrial relations', companies need to respond to the pressure for 'more information from the top on what is happening and why', adding that 'satisfactory working relationships will not be achieved if employees feel insecure or suspicious'.[57] It has suggested possible areas of disclosure. These include: details of company organization; financial information including turnover, profits, dividends and directors' remuneration; and a summary of the company's competitive situation and productivity levels. Other items of possible disclosure are future plans, staffing information and policies on pay and conditions of employment.

It is extremely difficult to assess the impact of the various recommendations on disclosure of information and the appropriate clauses (181 to 185) of the Trade Union and Labour Relations (Consolidation) Act 1992. This Act provides a procedure enabling independent trade unions to obtain certain information from employers for the purposes of collective bargaining. At the same time, the Advisory Conciliation and Arbitration Service (ACAS) has a code of practice on disclosure of information to trade unions for collective bargaining purposes. This gives practical guidance to both employers and trade unions on disclosure of information which 'it would be in accordance with good industrial relations to disclose' and 'without which a trade union

representative would be impeded to a material extent in bargaining'.[58]

As a general guide, the ACAS code recommends the disclosure of information on pay and benefits, conditions of service, staffing, company performance and finance. It appears likely that the impact of the ACAS code, and the use made by the trade unions of the disclosure clauses in the TULRC Act 1992, has enabled stewards to obtain more information in the bargaining situation than hitherto. The 1990 Workplace Industrial Relations Survey found that little change had taken place since 1984 regarding requests by union representatives for the disclosure of information under the TULRC Act provisions, but pressure is likely to come as a result of the EU's works council directive.

> The figures show little change in the proportion of manual stewards who made such a request for information – a fifth did so in both surveys. Manual stewards in private manufacturing were about twice as likely to report such requests as those in private services or the public sector. The proportion of non-manual representatives making use of the disclosure provisions also remained about the same over the period.[59]

## 13.5 Workplace Industrial Relations in the 1990s

What employees do at work and how they do it is largely determined by managers and trade union representatives negotiating and discussing working arrangements at the many thousands of enterprises and workplaces in Britain. It is here that the core activities of industrial relations are to be found. Despite the fact that hundreds of thousands of managers and union representatives are involved daily in conducting localized industrial relations, far less is known about this aspect than about national collective bargaining, which is largely carried out in public view and is subject to considerable media attention.

The Donovan Commission in 1966 conducted the first substantial survey of workplace industrial relations in Britain, so that analysis could be based on empirical evidence rather than union speculation supplemented by useful but unrepresentative case studies. Further workplace surveys were carried out in 1973 and 1978, which, whilst being extremely useful, could not be described as comprehensive in their coverage. The first extensive and detailed survey of workplace industrial relations was carried out in 1980 by the Department of Employment working with the Policy Studies Institute and the Economic and Social Research Council. Its findings were published in 1983. A second survey, closely modelled on the 1980 survey, was conducted in 1984 and its findings were published in 1986. A third and more detailed survey took place in 1990 with its findings being published in 1992. These three major surveys provide invaluable empirical evidence of the changes which have taken place since 1979. Taken together the three surveys indicate several deep-seated trends which, it can be reasonably deduced, have continued into the 1990s.

It is a commonly held view that since 1979 trade union power, membership, influence and bargaining strength have declined dramatically at all levels from national collective bargaining to steward relationships with managers. The decline in trade union membership, in both absolute and density terms, can be clearly demonstrated statistically, as can the much reduced national influence of the trade unions upon the government and the legislation it has enacted. The changes at workplace level, however, are far more problematic, as the workplace survey evidence indicates. The accepted view is that employers and their workplace managers regained in the 1980s the confidence and power which they had lost in the 1960s and 1970s. Their regained power and confidence enabled them to secure changes in, for instance, the vital areas of contracts of employment, work restructuring, manning levels, discipline and flexible working patterns, with minimum resistance from employees or their representatives. In some workplaces, it was even contended that a new breed of aggressive 'macho' managers had emerged, with attitudes not dissimilar from those of the nineteenth-century 'ironmasters'. There is, however, little evidence that macho management is a reality in more than a very small number of workplaces. Its usefulness as a confidence-building myth for many managers could well have exceeded its reality in practice.

Workers and stewards, according to the popular interpretation of workplace behaviour since 1979, have acknowledged the realities of comparatively high unemployment, substantial redundancies, the importance of new technology and the need for the organizations employing them to improve their competitiveness. This has been done because of harsh market conditions, so that organizations may survive and the jobs of employees be secured for the future. Various measures have been taken by managers

to improve competitiveness, to reduce labour costs and to improve productivity. These have included reduced manning levels and the use of more peripheral labour, such as part-time female workers, those on short-term contracts, agency labour, homeworkers and the self-employed. An ACAS survey, published in 1987, of the extent to which employers had introduced policies designed to achieve flexibility in adjusting the size of their labour forces to fluctuating product or service market demand – numerical flexibility – found that:

> Overall two-thirds . . . said they employed some part-time employees. . . . Larger firms, those in the service and public sectors, and those in the South East, were especially heavy users of part-time labour. Particularly interestingly we found substantial use of part-timers in manufacturing industry, where until recently they were a relatively small part of the workforce, suggesting that here, too, the practice is spreading.
> We also found extensive and growing use of temporary workers and sub-contractors. Two-thirds of our respondents said they employed temporary workers and no fewer than one in seven reported some employees on fixed term contracts lasting less than twelve months. As many as three quarters also said that they used sub-contractors to perform tasks which might otherwise have been undertaken internally.[60]

Clearly this marked growth in the use of peripheral labour which, unlike core employees, can be dispensed with fairly rapidly should market conditions require a reduction in labour costs, has occurred in many more workplaces since 1987. This has been either with the agreement of stewards or with their reluctant acquiescence.

Similarly, managers have been able to secure changes in working practices which have enabled them to use labour more effectively by requiring a greater flexibility from employees. This has led to the emergence of multiskilled workers and to job descriptions requiring employees to perform a range of duties at management's discretion. Flexibility has also been extended to cover: spatial working requirements; flexible working hours; a greater degree of shiftworking; making production workers responsible for certain aspects of maintenance; pay flexibility linking pay to performance; and the accepted acquisition of a range of new skills.

We found that a quarter of our respondents reported that they had *succeeded* in introducing [skill] flexibility . . . during the previous three years. The most common forms involved the relaxation of traditional craft demarcations to allow skilled employees to do work previously undertaken by other craftsmen . . . In addition there was considerable – and growing – interest in many organisations in relaxing earlier divisions between manual, technical and clerical skills . . . Considerable change was also evident in hours of work, especially where shift working was undertaken. Over a quarter of our respondents had introduced shift working over the previous three years.[61]

The findings of the ACAS survey were supported by the 1990 workplace survey, which found that:

Overall, managers in over a third (36 per cent) of all workplaces in our sample reported that changes in working practices had been made. This was reflected across the three broad sectors of employment [manufacturing, services and construction].[62]

The 1990 workplace survey found, however, that important linkages existed between changes in working practices and the freedom which managers had to organize work as they wished.

In 1990 limits to managements' freedom to organise work were reported in a third of workplaces. Constraints of various kinds were more common in union than non-union workplaces.[63]

During the 1980s a number of comparatively new management practices were introduced which have undoubtedly required both employees and stewards to change their attitudes to the ways in which workplace industrial relations are conducted. These practices include: performance appraisal systems; total quality management; single status employment; harmonized working practices; employee involvement; corporate culture programmes; customer satisfaction training; induction training; equal opportunities programmes; team briefing and team working; and autonomous workgroups. Whilst some of these practices – employee appraisal, for example – have become widespread, others, such as corporate culture programmes, appear to be of limited application and validity. However, the net effect has been to require stewards to adjust to a whole range of unfamiliar

management practices which have cut across traditional trade union thinking and practices. Added to this rapidly changing industrial relations scene at the workplace have been the effects of new trade union legislation. This has restricted the scope for lawful industrial action and picketing and has effectively ended the ability of the unions to enforce closed shop agreements.

The 1990 workplace survey, which at the time of writing provides almost the only substantial body of empirical evidence on the changes which are taking place in workplace industrial relations, involved 2 000 workplaces and the in-depth interviewing of 4 000 managers and employee representatives in both public and private sectors of the economy. It was designed to follow closely the 1980 and 1984 surveys so that valid comparisons could be made between the periods. The most important finding of the 1984 survey was that the structure of workplace bargaining, and the procedural and institutional arrangements which support it, had survived the early 1980s almost unchanged. Where changes were clearly detected in the 1984 survey, they were largely the result of major changes in the pattern of employment, brought about by the decline in manufacturing industry, the growth in service sector employment and the decline in large industrial workplaces employing large numbers of full-time male manual workers. The survey provides little evidence that substantial changes in workplace industrial relations were the result of deliberate policy decisions by managements to eliminate or drastically curtail the trade union role at the workplace. 'The structural arrangements made by management for the organization and conduct of industrial relations at workplace level appeared to have changed little between our two surveys [1980 and 1984].'[64]

If increases in the numbers of stewards at workplaces can be seen as an indicator of growing trade union powers, as in the past, then it would be perhaps logical to look for a decline in shop steward numbers after 1979. Somewhat surprisingly the evidence from the 1984 workplace survey found that:

Taking all representatives, both manual and non-manual, in the economy as a whole, our estimates indicate a slight rise in the total number from about 310 000 to around 335 000, a rise of some 6 per cent.[65]

This increase in union workplace representatives, during four years of severe recession and rising unemployment, did not suggest a picture of macho management seeking to end the joint regulation of workplace practices and employment conditions.

The 1990 workplace survey, however, revealed a very different situation.

> In overall terms the proportion of establishments with recognised unions where at least one representative of a recognised union was reported dropped from 82 per cent in 1984 to 71 per cent in 1990, representing a fall from 54 per cent of all establishments to 38 per cent over the period.[66]

While, after 1984 at least, the incidence and numbers of workplace union representatives fell, there is little evidence that employers or managers sought, in any substantial way, to cease to negotiate with stewards or to derecognize unions at the workplace. There is, however, strong evidence from the 1990 survey that:

> where we were able to compare the scope of bargaining between one survey and another the indications were that its scope had declined within the unionised sector. Broadly speaking, fewer issues were subject to joint regulation in 1990 than in 1980. . . . Given the concentration of the unionised sector, the reduction in bargaining activity, overall, has been substantial.[67]

The closed shop, which has long been seen as a potent symbol by both managers and union representatives of workplace bargaining power, declined markedly between 1980 and 1984 and even more substantially after that:

> Our results confirmed that over the 1980s there was a dramatic decline of the closed shop as an institution. [Yet many] of the characteristics of these workplaces and their employees that had engendered high membership under a closed shop arrangement continued to do so without that institutional support.[68]

One of the most interesting characteristics detected by both the 1984 and 1990 workplace surveys was the continuing existence of joint consultation between managers and employees. There was also a greater concern for good communications and for methods of increasing employee involvement in the problems and policies of management. The overall objective was to create a sense of realism in employees concerning the competitive position of the organizations in which they worked and to seek co-operation in achieving higher levels of productivity. This was to be

achieved by a combination of new technologies, capital investment, product or service innovation, changes in working practices and an improved attitude to work. It is likely that workplace representatives and employees accepted the need for greater consultation, communication and involvement, as a means of improving their job security.

> Management initiatives aimed at increasing employees' involvement at work were made with rising frequency throughout the 1980s. The types of initiative continued to show considerable variety, ranging from new consultative meetings or committees to quality circles, briefing groups and increasing the flow of information to and from employees.[69]

The move towards formal workplace procedures for dealing with discipline, grievances, disputes, redundancies and changes in working practices, which were a central feature of the Donovan report on industrial relations, continued throughout the 1980s:

> another important and . . . widespread trade union activity is to take part in the resolution of grievances and disputes about disciplinary matters. Here there was no sign of any diminution of the role of the unions. In 1990 more establishments with recognised unions had formal grievance procedures and more had formal disciplinary and dismissal procedures than had done so a decade earlier.[70]

The 1990 survey also found that while the bargaining power of workplace union representatives had declined and the scope of workplace collective bargaining had contracted, stewards still retained substantial influence over the level of pay of their members.

> Our analysis of the data on pay levels in the 1990 survey . . . strongly suggested that trade unions continued to have a significant impact on pay levels, particularly on the pay of the lower paid and in workplaces where collective bargaining covered all or nearly all workers. But, of course, the number of such workplaces had declined.[71]

The salient findings revealed by the 1990 Workplace Industrial Relations Survey can be broadly summarized as follows.

- Despite the many claims made during the 1980s that workplace industrial relations had survived that decade largely intact, the 1990 survey revealed fundamental structural and attitudinal changes.

- Where the formal structure of workplace industrial relations had survived largely intact, albeit in a restricted form, its substance and functions had changed with the balance of power being clearly possessed by employers and managers.
- There had been a sharp decline in multiemployer, national industry-wide collective bargaining without a corresponding shift to single employer or company bargaining.
- No new pattern of workplace industrial relations had emerged to replace the traditional pattern of trade union representation and joint regulation.
- Far fewer workplaces had recognized trade unions and workplace collective bargaining had declined markedly: 'The fall was stark, substantial and incontrovertible'.[72]
- Where workplace collective bargaining survived, its scope, extent and depth had largely diminished, with negotiations or discussions concerning 'manning' levels often being removed from the agenda by management.
- Surprisingly, however, the unions at workplace level retained considerable influence over basic matters such as pay and fundamental terms of employment. Collective bargaining retained its clear premium advantage for employees over non-union, non-collective-bargaining workplaces.
- Despite a noticeable decline between 1984 and 1990, joint consultation remained important, as did other forms of employer–employee communications and methods aimed to encourage employee involvement and commitment.
- Union involvement in formal workplace procedures, particularly those concerned with grievances, discipline and dismissal, remained high.
- The closed shop, largely owing to legal enactment, had by 1990 almost disappeared.
- The level and incidence of workplace strikes and other forms of industrial action had, again largely owing to legal changes, fallen dramatically.
- Evidence obtained by the 1990 survey suggests a strong trend towards 'union-free' or 'employee relations' workplaces where management dominate, among other things, pay levels, staffing arrangements, working practices and labour flexibility. But this trend has not, as yet, developed into an alternative 'system' of workplace industrial relations.

It is essential to acknowledge that workplace industrial relations can only be understood if sufficient valid empirical evidence is available. Without it, analysis is hardly possible and statements are at best based on shrewd experience and at worst on wishful speculation. It must also be accepted that even carefully planned and executed surveys have their limitations and that sample representativeness is never perfect. Moreover, even if the survey evidence is accepted as generally valid, there arises the very difficult problem of how to interpret the evidence, what to place in a cause-and-effect relationship and what evidence indicates significant and lasting changes.

The findings of the 1990 Workplace Industrial Relations Survey permit, however hazardous, a number of tentative predictions to be advanced about the future form and structure of British workplace industrial relations.

First, it would appear that in the future a clear majority of British employees will work in non-union workplaces, where their pay and terms of employment will be largely determined by their employer, and that the proportion of employees working for employers where the 'traditional' system of union membership and representation, collective bargaining and joint regulation is followed will decline. The pace and extent of the decline, however, remain problematic.

Second, the growth and development of non-union workplaces will be characterized by an emphasis upon 'employee relations', joint consultation, an employer–employee relationship based on individualism, not collectivism, and growth in a range of management policies and practices designed to increase employee commitment, motivation and involvement.

Third, where union representation and collective bargaining are retained, many employers will seek, probably successfully, to limit their activity, scope and importance. Many employers will also undoubtedly seek to steer their workplace relations towards the non-union, employee relations model.

Fourth, should the unionized sector continue to demonstrate the clear wage and conditions of employment premium which, at present, results from collective bargaining and union representation, employees could well become disillusioned with the 'new' employee relations model. Furthermore, labour market movements might well, paradoxically, favour the 'old' unionized workplace industrial relations system.

Fifth, the 1990 workplace survey clearly demonstrates the important role played by structural changes in the British economy and the labour laws enacted since 1979, in dramatically reducing the dominance of workplace union representation and collective bargaining. It is not unreasonable to anticipate that these fundamental trends will continue largely unchecked.

Sixth, there are two largely unpredictable factors which could change the future of workplace industrial relations and divert the present clearly detectable trends. First, as the result of Britain's acceptance of the Maastricht Treaty, and despite Britain's opt out from the Social Chapter, EU policies might well restore trade union influence and legal interventions in the labour market which would favour the 'old' unionized industrial relations model. Second, the appeal and popularity of trade unionism might well return, as the Thatcher era retreats into history and disillusionment with free markets, economic individualism and enterprise culture grows.

## 13.6.   Summary Points

- After 1945 the importance of workplace trade union representation, workplace union representatives and workplace collective bargaining grew, and the importance of full-time union officials and national industry-wide collective bargaining declined.
- After the Donovan Commission's report in 1968, attempts to regulate and institutionalize the largely informal, fragmented and unregulated system of workplace industrial relations were only partially successful. The incidence of industrial conflict and wage/salary increases, which consistently outstripped productivity and the cost-of-living index, probably made political and legal intervention inevitable by the 1980s.
- Public policy during the 1980s, mainly based on tight financial and economic policies and on legal control, plus the restructuring forces at work in the economy, led to a sharp decline by the early 1990s of workplace trade union membership and activity, workplace collective bargaining and joint regulation. The level of industrial conflict, wage/salary increases and inflation fell sharply.
- The role of the workplace union representative

for almost forty years after 1945 was highly influential and enjoyed the support and approval of trade union members. Managements, until the 1980s, sought to contain and regulate stewards' activities rather than curtail or restrict them.
- The basis of the union steward's power and influence up to the 1980s rested on trade union solidarity at the workplace, the scope and depth of collective bargaining, involvement in procedural processes, the existence of full employment, the absence of legal regulation and the declining self-confidence and power of management. During the 1980s this structure and system were first challenged and then largely reversed.
- Union workplace representatives place considerable importance on the development of joint stewards' committees where common policies can be determined, internal union problems resolved, and collective bargaining and joint consultative responses to management planned.
- In order to operate effectively, trade unions acknowledge that stewards need time off work for their industrial relations duties, training and education, and the disclosure of information by management for collective bargaining purposes. These things were ensured by legislation during the 1970s, but withdrawn or restricted during the 1980s.
- A number of factors influence or determine the union steward's role: the attitudes and policies of management, the expectations and beliefs of the steward's members and supporters, the policies and practices of the steward's trade union, legal regulations, current economic circumstances, the joint stewards' committee, the workplace industrial relations system as it has evolved and the steward's own perception of his or her role, powers and responsibilities.
- In order to bargain collectively on behalf of their members at the workplace, stewards need an understanding of trade union principles and beliefs, a realistic assessment of their bargaining power, an appreciation of the employer's financial and competitive position, an awareness of bargaining opportunities and scope, and the possession of negotiating skills, experience and expertise.
- The latest Workplace Industrial Relations Survey (1990) has produced convincing evidence that workplace union membership, representation, collective bargaining, joint regulation and the closed shop have all declined in relative importance.

## 13.7 References

1. J. Goodman, The role of the shop steward, in S. Kessler and B. Weekes (eds), *Conflict at Work*, BBC, London, 1971, p. 53.
2. W. E. J. McCarthy, *Royal Commission on Trade Unions and Employers' Associations Research Papers. 1. The Role of the Shop Stewards in British Industrial Relations*, HMSO, London, 1967, p. 4.
3. N. Millward and M. Stevens, *British Workplace Industrial Relations 1980–84*, Gower, Aldershot, 1986, p. 304.
4. Neil Millward *et al.*, *Workplace Industrial Relations in Transition*, Dartmouth, Aldershot, 1992, p. 116.
5. Royal Commission on Trade Unions and Employers' Associations, *Report*, HMSO, London, 1968, p. 26.
6. *Ibid.*, p. 272.
7. J. Goodman and T. G. Whittingham, *Shop Stewards in British Industry*, McGraw-Hill, London, 1969, p. 40.
8. I. Boraston, H. Clegg, and M. Rimmer, *Workplace and Union*, Heinemann, London, 1975, p. 191.
9. E. Batstone, I. Boraston, and S. Frenkel, *Shop Stewards in Action*, Blackwell, Oxford, 1977, pp. 179 and 185.
10. W. W. Daniel and N. Millward, *Workplace Industrial Relations*, Heinemann, London, 1983, p. 284.
11. M. Argyle, *The Social Psychology of Work*, Penguin, Harmondsworth, 1974, p. 104.
12. G. Clack, *Industrial Relations in a British Car Factory*, Cambridge University Press, Cambridge, 1966, p. 61.
13. Goodman in Kessler and Weekes, *op. cit.*, p. 55.
14. S. Parker, *Workplace Industrial Relations*, HMSO, London, 1975, p. 18.
15. Millward *et al.*, *op. cit.*, pp. 138–9.
16. *Ibid.*, p. 113.
17. W. E. J. McCarthy and S. R. Parker, *Royal Commission on Trade Unions and Employers' Associations Research Papers. 10. Shop Stewards and Workshop Relations*, HMSO, London, 1968, p. 27.
18. Goodman in Kessler and Weekes, *op. cit.*, p. 55.
19. Daniel and Millward, *op. cit.*, p. 291.
20. Millward and Stevens, *op. cit.*, p. 312.
21. Millward *et al.*, *op. cit.*, p. 269.
22. Millward and Stevens, *op. cit.*, p. 305.
23. Millward *et al.*, *op. cit.*, p. 102.
24. Royal Commission, *op. cit.*, p. 28
25. Goodman and Whittingham, *op. cit.*, p. 99.
26. E. Coker and G. Stuttard (eds), *Industrial Studies 2: The Bargaining Context*, Arrow Books, London, 1976, p. 44.
27. Batstone *et al.*, *op. cit.*, p. 29.
28. Daniel and Millward, *op. cit.*, p. 285.
29. Millward and Stevens, *op. cit.*, p. 307.
30. Millward *et al.*, *op. cit.*, pp. 131–3.
31. Daniel and Millward, *op. cit.*, p. 284.
32. Millward *et al.*, *op. cit.*, p. 139.
33. Daniel and Millward, *op. cit.*, pp. 39–41.
34. Boraston *et al.*, *op. cit.*, pp. 187–8.
35. Millward *et al.*, *op. cit.*, p. 130.
36. Commission on Industrial Relations, *Report No. 17. Facilities Afforded to Shop Stewards*, HMSO, London, 1971, pp. 44 and 45.
37. *Ibid.*, p. 49.
38. Trades Union Congress, *Good Industrial Relations*, TUC, London, 1971, p. 17.
39. Daniel and Millward, *op. cit.*, pp. 42 and 43.
40. TUC, *op. cit.*, p. 27.
41. Department of Employment, *Industrial Relations Code of Practice*, HMSO, London, 1972, p. 14.
42. M. Pedler, Learning to negotiate, in E. Coker and G. Stuttard (eds), *Industrial Studies 2: The Bargaining Context*, Arrow Books, London, 1976, p. 105f.
43. Department of Employment, *op. cit.*, p. 14.
44. C. Brewster and S. Connock, *Industrial Relations: Cost-Effective Strategies*, Hutchinson, London, 1972, p. 52.
46. Trades Union Congress, *Report of the 107th Annual Trade Unions Congress*, TUC, London, 1976, p. 201.
47. E. Batstone, I. Boraston and E. Frenkel, Principles in workplace bargaining, in Coker and Stuttard, *op. cit.*, p. 20.
48. *Ibid.*, p. 23.
49. *Ibid.*, p. 26.
50. *Ibid.*, p. 36.
51. Trade union negotiators, *ibid.*, p. 44.
52. *Ibid.*, p. 46.
53. *Ibid.*, p. 48.
54. *Ibid.*, pp. 50 and 57.
55. *Ibid.*, p. 63.
56. Commission on Industrial Relations, *Report No. 31. Disclosure of Information*, HMSO, London, 1972, p. 12.
57. Confederation of British Industry, *The Provision of Information to Employees*, CBI, London, 1975, p. 3.
58. Advisory Conciliation and Arbitration Service, *Code of Practice 2. Disclosure of Information for Collective Bargaining Purposes*, HMSO, London, 1977, p. 2.
59. Millward *et al.*, *op. cit.*, p. 123.
60. ACAS, *Occasional Paper 41: Labour Flexibility in Britain*, ACAS, London, 1987, p. 37f.
61. *Ibid.*, p. 36.
62. Millward *et al.*, *op. cit.*, p. 334.
63. *Ibid.*, p. 342.
64. Millward and Stevens, *op. cit.*, pp. 299–300.
65. *Ibid.*, p. 301.
66. Millward *et al.*, *op. cit.*, p. 110.
67. *Ibid.*, p. 353.
68. *Ibid.*, p. 358.
69. *Ibid.*, p. 362.
70. *Ibid.*, p. 355.
71. *Ibid.*, p. 354.
72. *Ibid.*, p. 352.

# 14

# Negotiation, Consultation and Involvement

Negotiation in industrial relations is a power relationship between managerial and trade union representatives. It is an activity by which the two sides make joint agreements regulating the pay or market relations and managerial or authority relations between them. Consultation, by contrast, is the process whereby managerial representatives discuss matters of common interest with employee representatives, normally but not always trade unionists, prior to negotiating or taking a decision. Involvement is an employer-led process which attempts to find participative ways in which to manage staff, on a direct as opposed to a representative basis. In this chapter, we concentrate on the content and methods of negotiation as a process of joint job control, rather than its structural features which we describe in Chapter 6. We also examine the nature of joint consultation, its relationship to collective bargaining and developments in employee involvement.

## 14.1  Trade Union Recognition

Once a group of employees have decided that they wish to be represented by a trade union to engage in collective bargaining with their employer, the vital and crucial stage is to seek a recognition and negotiating procedure with management. There can be no collective bargaining unless employers are willing to recognize trade unions for negotiating purposes. Historically, trade union recognition has normally only been reluctantly conceded by most employers, and in some instances not until after bitter industrial conflict. In practice it has been government encouragement and favourable economic circumstances which have been significant factors in influencing private sector employers to recognize trade unions. In the public sector, with some notable exceptions, it is generally accepted policy that employers negotiate and consult with representative trade unions. The major exceptions are the armed services, the police service, doctors and dentists, nurses and midwives and professions allied to

medicine, and so-called 'top people' such as judges, Members of Parliament and senior civil servants. Unions were derecognized in one public sector group, however, the Government Communications Headquarters (GCHQ) at Cheltenham in January 1984, on the grounds of national security. Under the new arrangements, civil servants at GCHQ are 'permitted in future to belong only to a Departmental Staff Association approved by their Director',[1] not to trade unions. By 1989, all remaining trade unionists at GCHQ had been transferred, retired or dismissed.

Until the 1960s, little positive action was taken by government, with the major exceptions of the Whitley reports, either to encourage employees to join trade unions or to protect them from retaliatory action by their employers for so doing. Although governments encouraged their own employees to belong to trade unions, and public contractors were required to recognize the freedom of their employees to be trade union members through the Fair Wages Resolutions, employers were still legally able to discriminate against employees who were trade unionists. There were no legal obligations on employers requiring them to recognize trade unions when this was fairly and legitimately demanded by employee representatives.

The Donovan Commission recommended that any stipulation in a contract of employment requiring an employee not to belong to a trade union should be void and of no effect in law. It also proposed that an Industrial Relations Commission should be set up to investigate union recognition disputes, with authority to make recommendations for recognition where this was considered to be appropriate. Although the Commission on Industrial Relations was established in 1969 to undertake this task, the Industrial Relations Act 1971 subsequently introduced new rules for recognition, aimed at reducing the disruptive effects of multiunion recognition claims. It provided, for example, that if recognition issues could not be resolved voluntarily between the parties, then trade unions registered under the Act could seek the assistance of the National Industrial Relations Court (NIRC) and the Commission on Industrial Relations (CIR).

The problem of trade union recognition was further exacerbated by the requirement that recognition arrangements should observe one of the basic principles embodied in the Act, namely the right of individual employees to join or not to join a registered trade union. However, in attempting to focus trade union recognition decisions on the importance of determining appropriate bargaining units and effective negotiating agents in each case, the 1971 Act provided a departure from the traditional *ad hoc* methods of conceding recognition. Nevertheless throughout its duration, the legislation and its monitoring agencies, the NIRC and the CIR, were consistently opposed by the TUC and its affiliated organizations.

With the repeal of the Industrial Relations Act by the Trade Union and Labour Relations Act in 1974, the effect broadly was to return to the pre-1971 situation. It now became legally unfair, however, to dismiss an employee by virtue of his or her membership of an independent trade union, whilst the Employment Protection Act 1975 subsequently provided a set of procedures by which independent trade unions might refer recognition disputes with employers to the Advisory Conciliation and Arbitration Service (ACAS) for possible resolution.

Despite this legislation, the general issue of trade union recognition was not definitively resolved. The statutory procedures enabling unrecognized unions to obtain the help of ACAS in conciliating with uncooperative employers were repealed in the Employment Act 1980. Recognition issues were once again largely settled by the power that employers or unions were prepared to apply. It has been estimated, for example, that although there are no major recognition problems in the public sector except GCHQ and among some managerial grades, or among manual workers in most large manufacturing firms, problems continue to emerge in the private sector services, white-collar employment in private manufacturing, among manual workers in smaller firms, and among managers in the private sector. Agriculture also has a recognition problem with no effective collective bargaining having been established in this sector. The situation, however, has been affected by two factors. These are: first, the early work of the CIR and of ACAS in the trade union recognition field; and second, the development of managerial policies on union recognition and on derecognition.

## Recognition criteria

One purpose of the Employment Protection Act 1975 was to regularize the procedures by which recognition disputes between employers and independent trade unions could be constitutionally resolved. In that Act 'recognition' referred to 'recognition of the union by an employer, or two or more associated employers to any extent, for the purpose of collective bargaining', whilst a 'recognition issue' arose 'from a request by a trade union for recognition by an employer, or two or more employers, including . . . a request for further recognition'.[2] These definitions extended the scope of recognition from those cases where a union was pressing a claim for representative, consultative or negotiating rights in the first instance, to those where a claim was being pressed for the subject matter of negotiation to be extended.

The work of the CIR also provides a substantial body of experience on trade union recognition and it clearly influenced the ways in which ACAS operated in the field. A basic criterion which the CIR took into account in determining its recommendations on recognition, for example, was whether the employees concerned wanted to have their pay and conditions of employment determined by collective bargaining. One way in which this was done was through balloting the employees. In more complex cases, attitude surveys were used. A second criterion was the extent of union membership and potential membership if collective bargaining arrangements were to be established. It was in determining the bargaining unit, or the degree of common interest between employees, and in determining the negotiating agent or the appropriateness of the union, which the CIR considered to be of fundamental importance in making its recommendations. Any lack of clarity in defining a bargaining unit in recognition cases can easily lead to interunion conflicts, competitive union recruitment and subsequent breakdown of new or existing collective bargaining machinery. The CIR considered that the first issue to be decided in establishing a bargaining unit was the scope of the 'core' negotiating group. There are three possibilities in deciding how far a core group can be expanded: by vertical extension through including employees above or below the core group; by horizontal extension through including employee groups of equal status across the organization; or by incorporation of employees with similar job content and status from different work locations.

In determining the negotiating agent, the CIR established three principal standards to be met by a trade union to be recommended for bargaining purposes. These were: its support as a potential bargaining agent, including its actual membership and the number of employees who would be prepared to join if the union were recognized; its independence from employer influence; and its likely bargaining effectiveness. The CIR viewed organizational independence and negotiating effectiveness as being of high initial priority. If employee organizations fail to achieve these standards, employees can subsequently be left without adequate representation. Lack of independence, for example, can lead to further competitive membership recruitment and to unstable collective bargaining arrangements. Under Section 5 of the Trade Union and Labour Relations (Consolidation) Act 1992, an independent trade union is defined as an organization of workers which is neither under the domination or control of an employer or an employers' association, nor liable to interference in its internal affairs tending towards such control. It is the 1992 Act which lays the duty of determining trade union independence, and of issuing certificates of independence, upon the Certification Officer. Union 'independence', however, is no guarantee of employer recognition.

In assessing support for collective bargaining among employee groups, ACAS was influenced by the CIR's experience. Although it avoided using any single criterion in determining whether or not to recommend recognition after sounding out employee opinion, ACAS applied a number of criteria when it considered individual decisions. These included: current union membership; the employees' wishes for collective bargaining; the employees' wishes for representation by the referring union; potential union membership in the event of recognition; and the history of support for the union among the employees. None of these factors was necessarily decisive in itself. It was also necessary to consider other factors, such as the relevance of existing bargaining arrangements to which the applicant union was not a party and whether, in such circumstances, a recommendation would be conducive to good industrial relations.

## Managerial policy

According to the Institute of Personnel Management, employer recognition of a trade union's demand to represent employees for consultative or bargaining purposes represents a fundamental and irreversible change in the employment relationship. It is not therefore 'a step which should be taken without full consideration of its implications or as an immediate or *ad hoc* response to pressure from employees'.[3] Some employers in the private sector are increasingly formulating policies on trade union recognition. These aim not only at ensuring an ordered transition to formalized bargaining relationships with trade unions, but also at mitigating the worst possible problems associated with the proliferation of new unions competing for membership in the same job area or occupational group within their firms. It is not in the employer's interest to recognize too many unions or competing unions. This is one reason why some green field site employers were attracted to single-union deals in the 1980s.

For employers, recognition policies emerge and develop in four main stages: issues to be taken into account by management prior to a recognition claim being made; considerations in deciding whether or not management should recognize unions for bargaining purposes; factors in determining the nature of the initial agreement providing for formal recognition between the parties; and influences affecting the subsequent development of the relationship between the company and the trade union or unions. Prior to a recognition claim being received, some companies are increasingly aware of the need to establish a decision making framework for dealing with such claims. It is at this stage that employers consider the advisability of providing opportunities for a union to recruit members within their companies.

In responding to recognition claims, employers take a number of factors into account: whether the employees constitute an appropriate bargaining unit; the level of union membership in the group; the capacity of the union to adequately represent the employees concerned; the extent to which the union demands recognition; the current policy for recognition in the industry; the impact of recognition on existing collective bargaining arrangements, and so on. In doing this, management takes account of the fact that if a union considers that the company appears to be delaying its request for recognition unduly, either it has recourse to ACAS on a voluntary basis, or it might decide to pursue a policy of direct industrial action against the employer.

Once a decision has been made to recognize trade unions, the initial recognition agreement is of vital concern to both parties. First-time recognition takes three main forms; first, the right to representation, that is the right of the union to represent employees usually through union representatives on individual grievances at work; second, the right to consultation, that is the right of the union to be consulted on non-negotiable matters; and third, the right to negotiation, that is the right to represent members fully both in procedural and in substantive matters such as pay and conditions. In most cases, the initial agreement between a company and a trade union usually represents the first stage in a developing relationship and is more usually exploratory rather than comprehensive. However, once full trade union recognition is conceded by employers, and given a buoyant labour market, the boundaries of collective bargaining can become increasingly wide ranging.

## Derecognition

There is some indication that certain employers are more willing to derecognize trade unions than was the case in the past. The trend must not be exaggerated and while derecognition has occurred largely in the private sector, there are even some signs of declining employer commitment to union recognition, and to collective bargaining, in parts of the public sector, such as amongst certain managerial and professional grades of employee. Although union derecognition is not synonymous with absolute deunionization, whatever form it takes marks an important development in employer–employee relations.

A study by Claydon of union derecognition in Britain during the late 1980s analyses it in terms of two factors: the proportion of the workforce affected ('breadth' of derecognition) and the degree of rejection of unions by management ('depth' of derecognition). Claydon identifies three categories of breadth of derecognition:

- General derecognition. Collective bargaining rights are withdrawn from all employees throughout an organization or its operating division.
- Grade-specific derecognition. Withdrawal of collective bargaining rights is restricted to particular grades or sections of the workforce across the organization or its operating division.
- Plant-specific or site-specific derecognition. Bargaining rights are withdrawn from all unions at a particular plant or plants in a multiplant organization, but remain in others.

There are, in turn, five levels of depth of derecogni-

tion, demonstrating the extent to which trade unions retain elements of a relationship with the employer. These are:

- Partial derecognition. The union retains vestigial bargaining rights over non-pay issues and possibly some element of consultation on pay.
- Derecognition as a bargaining agent. The union retains rights to consultation on collective issues and to represent individual members' grievances.
- Collective derecognition. The union retains only the right to represent individual members' grievances.
- Complete derecognition. The union retains only the minimum legal right to provide legal services to members.
- Deunionization. The union retains no rights or facilities and union membership is discouraged.[4]

According to Claydon, 'collective grade-specific' and 'complete grade-specific' are the most common forms of derecognition. These have generally taken place in organizations following changes in ownership, management or corporate structure and have been concentrated amongst managerial, technical and professional staff. General derecognition appears to take place where union membership is low, where union organization is weak and in organizations involved in bitter industrial disputes. Plant-specific derecognition is relatively rare and appears to be affected by particular workforce characteristics. 'The factor which links all three categories is quality of membership support and the degree of attachment to the wider union which enables organisational resources to be mobilised in defence of collective bargaining'.[5]

## 14.2  Negotiating Scope

Industrial relations procedures and 'supporting agreements provide the framework within which industrial relations business is conducted' between employer and union representatives.[6] In addition to union recognition procedures, steward credential procedures and negotiating procedures, industrial relations procedures cover three major types of issue: discipline and dismissal; individual grievances; and disputes over pay and conditions. In public industry and the public services, procedures tend to be negotiated nationally, though they operate locally. In the private sector, the pattern is variable, with much more scope for local autonomy and for negotiating agreements at employer or establishment level.

There are other procedures which employers and unions use to 'do business' together. Some, for example, establish recruitment guidelines, defining the experience and qualifications needed to do the jobs to be filled. They ensure that no arbitrary conditions are imposed on an applicant's suitability for employment and that no one is discriminated against because of their age, sex, race or their trade union activities. In attempting to protect the jobs of their members, trade unions also negotiate procedures for dealing with redundancies as part of a joint approach to long-term human resource planning. As we outline below, management and unions consider how to minimize or avoid employee redundancies by reducing overtime, restricting recruitment, allowing natural wastage or by introducing short-time working when jobs are threatened. Where redundancies are unavoidable, it is normal practice to agree arrangements for retraining, redeploying, resettling, or retiring workers early. Voluntary rather than compulsory redundancy is commonly preferred, with compensatory payments for the loss of jobs involved. Most importantly, the order in which employees are to be made redundant and the criteria for selection have to be agreed. Provision is also made for informing local job centres about the numbers, skills, occupations, and date of availability of redundant workers to assist them to find new jobs.

Negotiation also determines union membership agreements, where union membership is nominally a condition of employment, although such situations are now relatively rare and effectively unlawful. Research shows that major changes in the nature of the closed shop have taken place since the late 1970s. Because of the legal restrictions on them, negotiations on closed shops, where they continue to operate, have resulted in increasingly informal agreements. With the law as it now stands, the future of the closed shop is increasingly problematic.

## Pay, hours and conditions

Substantive collective agreements determine the payments for particular jobs, the methods of calculating such payments, and the relationship of differential salary or wage payments within the job structure. The intervals at which payments are to be made, whether they are weekly, fortnightly or monthly for the hourly paid, or monthly in the case of salaried employees, are also subject to collective agreement. The method of paying employees, such as by cash, credit transfer, or cheque, is normally jointly agreed

too, providing that it complies with current wages legislation.

Payment systems vary according to the nature and organization of work, local conditions, technology employed and other factors. They are usually jointly negotiated where trade unions are recognized. There are various payment systems for the parties to choose from. These range from time rate systems, including salaries, to payment by results schemes, which relate the earnings of employees to an assessment of their job performance. Basic time rates, piecework prices, incentive bonus schemes, and 'lieu' bonuses for those not paid directly by results are usually negotiated between employer and union representatives or between individual employees and piecework rate fixers. Guaranteed weekly earnings for the hourly paid are also commonly negotiated to ensure minimum pay for employees, often for the standard work week, if they are subject to short-time working or to lay-off. They also specify the rates payable to suspended workers and the conditions under which these payment guarantees can be applied or withdrawn.

Pay is also negotiated for work performed in special circumstances. This includes 'London allowances', and 'plus payments' for work undertaken in difficult, dangerous, or unpleasant conditions such as dirt money, danger money, call-out payments and standby duty payments. Holiday pay and maternity pay for an agreed number of days per year are also negotiable, with sick pay increasingly coming within the ambit of joint negotiation too. In this case, agreement has to be reached on what entitlements employees have when sick, the period for which sickness payments – usually based on a sliding time scale – are to be made, the amount of payment in relation to normal earnings, and any arrangements concerning the provision of medical certificates.

Negotiations also cover job evaluation schemes, productivity payments, and merit money for particular groups of workers. Sometimes promotions are jointly regulated by management and unions. In some sectors this is done informally. Others have established more formal procedures for joint regulation, which provide for joint selection panels and give workers who consider they have been overlooked the right to have their case heard by a joint appeals board. Another item which is negotiable is retirement pensions. Here the parties need to establish whether the scheme is to be contributory or not. Where it is contributory, the relative amounts of the employer's and the employees' contributions have to be determined, as do the age of retirement, the entitlement of dependants if the retired employee dies, arrangements for transferability between schemes, and methods of safeguarding pensions against inflation.

It is common practice to negotiate the standard work week or the number of hours per week which employees are normally expected to work at their place of employment in national-level bargaining. Negotiable locally are stopping and starting times, breaks in working hours for meals and for rest periods, holiday entitlements, flexible working hours and holiday periods. Before 1940 holidays with pay were not general, especially among manual workers. One paid week came in at the end of the Second World War, two weeks in the early 1950s, three weeks in the 1960s, and four weeks' paid holiday during the 1970s. By the late 1980s it was estimated that about 88 per cent of adult men and 85 per cent of adult women in full-time employment had holiday entitlements of four weeks or more. Nearly a quarter had a minimum entitlement of five weeks or more.[7]

Special rates of pay, or pay premiums, for overtime working are normally subject to joint negotiation. Overtime premiums, for instance, can be at a time and a quarter, time and a third, time and two-fifths, time and a half, or double the standard hourly rate. For non-manual employees there is no substantial gap between normal hours and actual hours, with non-manuals enjoying relatively short actual hours of work judged by the standards of manual workers. In the case of manual employees, however, and despite the gradual diminution of the standard number of hours per work-week during the postwar period, there has been very little reduction in the actual numbers of hours worked by some adult male manual workers. Prior to World War One, for example, normal working hours were generally around 54 per week in manual employment in a six-day working week. Hours were reduced to 48 per week by joint negotiation in 1918, and during the interwar years normal weekly working hours for most manual employees were around 48 hours including Saturday mornings. Soon after the Second World War, the unions succeeded in negotiating reductions in normal working hours to 44 per week and to a five-day working week. Since then, the standard working week has been steadily reduced through negotiation, by stages, to 42½, 40, 39 and – for some groups of white-collar employees – 37½ hours by the late 1980s, though for a few groups it is 35 hours. By the beginning of 1987 the move away from the basic 40-hour week for

manual employees was virtually complete, with average basic hours at just under 39 hours compared with 40 hours in 1978.

The 1991 Labour Force Survey (LFS) identified some major changes in the hours worked and the structure of the labour force in the UK between 1984 and 1991. First, between 1984 and 1991, there was a fall from 22 to 15 per cent in the proportion of employees with basic usual hours of 40 per week. The average total usual hours of full-time employees were 43.6 per week, compared with 16.9 for part-time employees, with the hours for full-time men and women being 45.3 and 40.3 per week respectively. Second, between 1984 and 1991, there were increases in the proportion of employees working part-time – that is, with total hours of up to 30 per week – from 22 to 23 per cent and the proportion working total usual hours above 48 hours per week from 12 to 16 per cent. There was a corresponding fall from 41 to 36 per cent in the proportion of employees usually working a 'standard' week of between 35 and 40 total hours. Third, 9.7 per cent of employees in the UK worked fewer than 16 hours per week in their main job, compared with a European Community average of 5 per cent. Further, 16 per cent of UK employees usually worked over 48 hours, compared with an EC average of 6.8 per cent. As the 1991 LFS states:

it is possible to see that the UK with its [now] highly deregulated labour market has a greater diversity of working time than elsewhere in the EC. In other countries where the majority of employees work within a small range of hours it is quite feasible to talk of a 'standard' employee. However in the UK the idea of a standard amount of working time [sic] is less appropriate and even potentially misleading.[8]

Despite continual reductions in the length of the normal work-week, and rising unemployment, the average levels of overtime for male and manual employees, though not for female workers, continue to be relatively high. Such averages conceal wide variations within particular industries, among different sectors of employment, within companies, and by particular groups of workers. Some groups work much higher levels of overtime than the average, whilst others do much less or even none at all. It is characteristic of a lot of overtime working that it is not used to meet the short-term production exigencies of management but is a regular and expected item by employers and employees alike. Although other factors are involved:

the main reason why workers are willing to work high levels of overtime is clearly to raise their earnings, which would otherwise be much lower; and on the whole workers with lower hourly earnings are readier to work substantial overtime than those whose hourly earnings are higher.[9]

In many cases, there are considerable workgroup pressures not to allow overtime hours to be reduced to levels below those which have become customarily accepted by workers and by line management as being necessary to maintain individual and workgroup earnings. The demand for high levels of overtime paid at premium rates, in short, seems to be primarily influenced by relative pay factors and by the potential earnings expected by workers. To what extent levels of overtime among manual workers are affected by rising unemployment and the demand for more leisure has yet to be demonstrated. Significantly, perhaps, rising unemployment has not generally resulted in less overtime being worked.

In 1991, it was estimated that some 6 million employees usually worked some paid overtime in the UK and some 4.5 million worked some unpaid overtime, each week. Of those employees usually working paid overtime, the average was 7.1 hours per week, whilst for those working unpaid overtime the weekly average was 7.3 hours – though the two groups overlap and are not mutually exclusive. Overtime is clearly more common among certain groups of employees, with the highest level being found among full-time male employees who, on average, work five hours' overtime per week. This consists of three hours' paid and two hours' unpaid overtime. Although full-time female employees work fewer overtime hours than their male counterparts (2.9 hours in total), the proportion of female overtime which is made up of unpaid hours is considerably higher than that of men's at 59 per cent, compared with 40 per cent. 'This probably reflects the different occupational distribution of full-time men and women's employment, with full-time women being more likely to work in jobs where paid overtime is less a feature, e.g. white collar occupations including clerical and secretarial jobs.'[10]

A range of other working conditions is also negotiable between management and unions. These include the allocation, pace and quality of work. In manual employment staffing levels, job transfers, demarcation arrangements, general conditions in the workplace, and the introduction of new machinery or new jobs are all subject to negotiation where management and union representatives agree to it, although in recent years these are more likely to be unilaterally determined by management.

Trade unions are also vitally concerned to see that safe and healthy working conditions are established and maintained for their members. Although both management and unions have a common interest in advancing safety within the workplace, effective joint procedures are established for dealing with disputes on safety matters and for maintaining good industrial relations within the workplace. While final responsibility for safety rests with management, management cannot discharge its responsibility without a proper system of safety organization. Joint safety committees and workers' safety representatives are now an integral part of safety organization in many workplaces, as well as being a statutory requirement under the Health and Safety at Work etc. Act 1974. Their function is to promote co-operation between management and employees in achieving high standards of health and safety at work, and to inspect working conditions in the interests of all those employed in factories, shops, offices or elsewhere.

Other employment issues which are negotiated include: the recruitment of new labour; agreements on the number of apprentices to be employed; short-time working; redundancy questions; and union membership arrangements. Agreements are also negotiated for additional allowances like travelling expenses, special clothing and tool allowances, or for disturbance payments for employees required to move their homes when changing their jobs, though again these are often managerially rather than jointly regulated today.

## Shiftwork

It has long been recognized that shiftwork can make for the better use of costly fixed capital equipment. It provides output or services on a continuous basis, such as in public transport, hospitals and electricity generating, for those using them. In continuous process industries, like chemicals and steel making, shiftwork is unavoidable. From the employees' point of view, shiftwork entails working unsocial hours and can include considerable amounts of overtime. For these reasons, it is usual for them to demand not only that working arrangements involving unsocial hours of work carry additional payments, but also that shiftwork systems should be regulated jointly between managerial and union representatives.

Shift premia are paid either proportionally to pay

rates or as fixed amounts in addition to basic earnings. Which method is used mainly depends on the shiftwork system in operation. Permanent night shifts, for example, are mostly paid by the proportionate method. Double day shifts, on the other hand, are more frequently expressed as fixed additions. In practice, shift premia may understate the actual premium paid, since the basic rate for some occupational categories is increased for those on shiftwork. Some idea of the importance of shiftworking in Britain can be noted from the fact that if we include non-manual workers, it is probable that over 30 per cent of employees are now engaged on some kind of shiftworking arrangement.

It is the hours a week which a plant or establishment must be operated or a service provided that give a broad indication of the shift system required. The most common method is the 'continuous three shift' system. In this case, four crews are necessary to cover three eight-hour shifts over a seven-day period. Three crews, however, can provide continuous coverage from Monday to Friday through a 'discontinuous three shift' system, thus leaving weekends free. Where two crews operate a morning and night shift of eight hours each, they can give coverage for about 80 hours a week on a 'double day' basis. Two crews operating an alternating 'day and night shift' can cover the same number of hours. 'Permanent nights' are also possible, while another arrangement is to employ female workers part-time on a 'twilight' shift for about four hours at the end of the normal working day. In some service industries, such as in catering or hospital work, 'split' shifts are used. These alternate work and rest periods.

Most shift systems rotate: this can be anything between a four-day and eight-day cycle. In this way, the popular and unpopular shifts can be shared amongst employees. Furthermore, although eight-hour shifts are the most common, the length of individual shifts varies. This is sometimes because overtime is regularly worked. Employees on an alternating day and night system, for example, may work up to 12 hours on each shift. Whatever the method used, however, employees usually demand a say in the manner in which their shifts are operated and arranged.

## Redeployment and redundancy

Corporate growth and market changes require constant review of a company's products and methods of working. Similarly, in the public sector, fresh political and legislative initiatives continually affect the ways in which employers deal with their employees and manage organizational change. An employer's ability to maintain competitiveness in both international and localized markets, or to react effectively to government policy changes in the non-market sector, depends on the effective managerial handling of change. In these circumstances, it is inevitable that redeployment and reductions of labour and human resources are sometimes necessary in organizations, in the interests of corporate survival and future growth.

It is management which is responsible for deciding the size and most efficient use of its workforce. By carefully developing a planned strategy for managing its human resources, an employer can minimize disruption to its business plans, avoid job losses, mitigate employee resentment and ease the process of change. Effective human resource planning assists in determining existing and future staff needs. This, in turn, can improve job security and avoid short-term solutions to staffing matters which are not consistent with an organization's long-term needs. It is generally accepted as good management practice to consult with recognized trade union representatives on the staffing implications of any measures designed to improve organizational efficiency, and any resultant loss of employment. Employers normally deal with potential redundancies in one of three ways: an *ad hoc* approach; a formal policy; or a formal agreement. *Ad hoc* approaches are where there are no formally established arrangements for redeployment or redundancies. The practice varies according to the circumstances of each case. Formal policies set out the approach to be adopted unilaterally by management, when faced with carrying out redundancies. In these cases, union involvement with the contents of such policies is not normally part of the process. Formal agreements setting out the procedures to be followed when redundancies have to be considered are the result of negotiation and agreement between management and union representatives.

According to ACAS, 'full and effective consultation is recommended when drawing up a redundancy procedure. This will do much to allay unjustified fears and suspicions'.[11] Additionally, such consultation enables trade unions and their representatives to contribute their ideas and views on the matter. The advantage to management of a properly constituted redeployment and redundancy procedure is that it provides a joint agreement for avoiding or minimizing redundancies, and for carrying them out in a fair and reasonable way, when they are necessary. For employees and their unions, the main advantage of an agreed procedure is that it helps ensure fair treatment to all those affected. Where retraining, transfers and redeployment are incorporated in the agreement, it demonstrates the employer's commitment to continued employment opportunities and concern for the welfare of employees. It also provides the union with the opportunity to influence management policy and to minimize redundancy where possible.

The contents of a formal redeployment and redundancy procedure depend on the size of the employer, its personnel and industrial relations policy, and the location of its plants or establishments. A typical procedure contains some or all of the following elements: a statement of intent towards the maintenance of job security; details of consultative arrangements with the trade unions; the measures for minimizing or avoiding compulsory redundancies; guidance on the selection criteria to be used where redundancy is unavoidable; details of severance terms and relocation expenses; the appeals procedure; and help for those seeking training or alternative work.

The aim of consultation in redeployment and redundancy procedures is to provide, as soon as is practicably possible, the opportunity for all concerned to share the problem and to explore the available options. It helps create better co-operation between management and employees, reduce uncertainty in the establishment and facilitate better decision making. When faced with a redundancy situation, union representatives or individual employees are able to suggest acceptable alternative ways of tackling the problem or, if the redundancies are inevitable, ways of minimizing hardship. In carrying out redundancy programmes, employers are required to consult with union representatives in accordance with the statutory rules and those established within the European Union. These are minimum periods only, however, and it is good practice for the consultation process to precede any public announcement of the proposed redundancies, and the issuing of notices of termination.

Employers also have a statutory duty to disclose in writing, to recognized trade unions, information on the proposals for any intended redundancies, so that they can play a constructive role in the consultative process. In addition to the statutory requirements on the reasons for the proposals, the numbers involved and methods of selection for redundancy, it is good practice for employers to consult and negotiate on other matters. These include: how selection of those for redundancy is to be applied; arrangements for

travel and related expenses; retention of employee benefits where employees are made compulsorily redundant; and extensions of the length of the statutory trial period.

There are a number of measures which can be used to minimize or avoid compulsory redundancies. These include: natural wastage; restrictions on recruitment; retraining and redeployment of existing staff to other parts of the organization; reduction or elimination of overtime; short-time working or temporary lay-offs; retirement of those above normal retirement age; early retirement; and termination of the employment of temporary or contract staff. In the interests of good industrial relations, it is normally preferable to use one or more of these approaches rather than to impose job losses, when difficulties arise.

ACAS recommends that, as far as possible, objective criteria, precisely defined and capable of being applied in an independent way, 'should be used when determining which employees are to be selected for redundancy'. The purpose of having objective criteria is to ensure that employees are not unfairly selected for redundancy. 'The chosen criteria must be consistently applied by all employers, irrespective of size.' There are non-compulsory selection criteria and compulsory selection criteria. Non-compulsory criteria include voluntary redundancy and early retirement. Voluntary redundancy, for example, avoids the need for compulsory severance and has a less demoralizing and disruptive effect on the workforce. It is generally more expensive, since longer-serving employees tend to volunteer, thus attracting higher redundancy payments. It is also not uncommon for employers to offer enhanced payments as an incentive to attract people to leave. Early retirement can also be expensive, since it normally involves a long-term financial commitment to those taking redundancy in the form of a pension. Yet it is an acceptable alternative to compulsory redundancy for many employees, thus having a less detrimental effect on workforce morale.

Where these voluntary approaches do not produce sufficient volunteers, employer and union representatives have to consider the criteria to be used for enforcing redundancies. 'Where any agreed list of criteria is not exhaustive, this should be stated.' These criteria include: skills or qualifications; 'last in, first out'; standard of work performance or aptitude for work; and attendance or disciplinary records. In seeking to agree selection criteria, the parties normally have regard to the future viability of the employer and its need to maintain a balanced workforce after the redundancy programme. 'The drawing up of criteria, however, is not enough to guarantee fair and reasonable selection.' The criteria must be reasonably applied to the circumstances of each individual. Moreover, management is advised to consider establishing 'a redundancy appeals procedure to deal with complaints from employees who feel that selection criteria have been unfairly applied in their case'.[12]

## 14.3   The Pay–Work Bargain

Pay determination is central to the negotiating process. But pay is only one side of the bargaining equation: the other is the amount of work which employees agree to perform for a given payment. In practice, every employment contract consists of two elements: an agreement on the rate of pay (either per unit of time or per unit of output) or a pay rate bargain, and an agreement on the work to be done or an effort bargain. A collective agreement then – or an individual agreement between an employer and an employee – is a pay-work bargain which fixes the terms of exchange of work done for money payable between the parties. It attempts to define the relationship between the monetary rewards for working and the amount of work expected by employers for the job to be done. Basically, the pay–work bargain takes one of three forms: standard bargaining; effort bargaining; and productivity and efficiency bargaining – although these are not mutually exclusive categories of negotiation.

### Standard bargaining

The most typical type of pay-work bargain is standard bargaining. In standard collective bargaining, a specified rate of payment such as an hourly rate or a yearly salary is negotiated between employers and trade unions. This is paid to all employees, provided that a minimum standard of work is achieved over the agreed work period. In other words, for the given rate of payment, different employees may produce different amounts and quantities of output or contribute various levels and quantities of effort. In standard bargaining, therefore, there is no direct relationship between pay rewards and work done or between the pay rate and the effort bargain. This does not preclude standard bargaining providing a base rate of pay upon which an effort bargain can subsequently be struck.

Standard bargaining is typical in salaried employment where it is difficult to measure the work being performed or to determine the time required for carrying it out at a defined standard of performance by a qualified worker. Although clerical work measurement techniques may be applied to some categories of clerical employment, it is much more difficult in practice – although not impossible – to measure the effort, output or efficiency of professional groups of employees like teachers, nurses, research workers, or even managers, whose work can often only be qualitatively rather than quantitatively assessed.

Certain manual occupations cannot be objectively work measured either. In retail selling, in bar keeping and in restaurants, for example, although payment by results is sometimes used, it is extremely difficult in practice to relate job payment to job performance in any precise or equitable way. Standard bargaining tends to be used, therefore, where it is difficult to measure the work being done or where machine technology is the prime determinant of work effort: it merely attempts to establish standard payments for minimum levels of job performance. In these circumstances, the most that can be done to relate pay to performance is to attempt to establish a fair and agreed relationship between payment offered, on the one hand, and the skills, responsibilities, effort and working conditions for the job on the other. The technique sometimes used to achieve this objective is job evaluation. As a management technique, job evaluation seeks to bring about a systematic and rational relationship between jobs and rates of pay. It does not replace normal collective bargaining. 'A job evaluation exercise should never be regarded as a permanent fixing of differentials.'[13]

### Effort bargaining

It is unrealistic to suggest that standard bargaining is a satisfactory method of relating payment to work done in all instances. Indeed, much attention has been devoted towards devising satisfactory means whereby payment can be more closely linked to the output or productivity of workers, especially in manual employment where productivity can be measured and where wage payment systems are used. 'The commonest alternative has been to use the payment system as a means of functionally relating the output of the workers or work-group and the pay received.'[14] The use of payment by results (PBR), whether piecework, incentive bonuses or measured daywork, rests on three assumptions only the first of which can be taken as factually established: that work effort varies in its intensity; that the financial motive at work is the most important one; and that the best way of harnessing this motive to increase work effort by employees is to use PBR. By this view, effort intensity is determined independently of earnings with standard bargaining, so that an increased pay bargain does not on its own change the effort bargain. However:

> If one postulates that more output means more effort, then it is possible to conclude an effort bargain, and this is essentially what a successful financial incentive scheme does. The worker agrees to raise his output in exchange for the guarantee of higher earnings.[15]

What is being purchased by employers under effort bargaining is a supply of labour input for performing varying job tasks. Effort, however, is not easily quantifiable. It is only output or the application of effort which can be effectively measured since effort is purely subjective. It is clear that 'in the absence of an agreement on the effort intensity per unit of time that is being purchased, effort intensity can vary between certain limits'. Under these conditions, employees have an upper limit to the exertion which they are prepared to expend in their job tasks, whilst employers have a lower limit to the exertion which they expect from their subordinates. The purpose of effort bargaining is to determine those levels of output which relate to specific levels of payment, and to ensure equal pay for those employees contributing equal effort. The successful application of PBR requires, therefore, that employees as well as the employer share the same perceptions of what constitutes the right standard of effort for a given job, as well as the correct rate for doing it.

The belief that there is a 'correct' rate for a job is held by both management and employees alike. Where piecework payments are operative, for example, managerial and worker views as to what piecework price represents the correct rate inevitably differ and have to be reconciled by effort bargaining. 'A rate is "correct" if it matches notions of the "right" earnings with notions of the "right" standard of effort, and it is "loose" or "tight" if it does not do so.'[16] What happens in practice is that negotiators argue first about the right earnings for the job – the pay rate bargain – and, second, about the right effort and the right production standards in doing it – the effort bargain.

It seems likely that PBR works reasonably well where management and trade union representatives believe in the fairness of the bargain struck and where they behave accordingly. This happens when the bargain represents 'a fair day's work for a fair day's pay' for both sides, with successful operation of PBR depending on mutual skill in effort bargaining. Under effort bargaining, however, wages cannot be explained by labour market competition alone; they are also power phenomena to be understood through political analysis of the processes of collective bargaining, with the product market rather than the labour market having the major impact on piecework pay determination.

## Productivity and efficiency bargaining

In one respect, productivity bargaining is like effort bargaining; it is concerned with the problem of relating payment received to work done. Instead of operating through the payment system, however, it seeks to improve productive performance by employees in the pay bargaining process itself. As such:

> It involves the parties to the bargaining process in negotiating a package of changes in working method or organisation, agreeing on the precise contents of the package, their worth to the parties and the distribution of the cost savings between the reward to labour and other alternative destinations such as return to capital and the reduction or stabilisation of the product price.[17]

The term 'productivity bargaining' lacks precision but it may broadly be described as an agreement in which advantages of one kind or another, such as higher wages or increased leisure, 'are given to workers in return for agreement on their part to accept changes in working practice or in methods or in organisation of work which will lead to more efficient working'.[18] It is probably best conducted at company or workplace level. Although a productivity bargain is a one-off exercise relating pay increases to productivity increases, it does not preclude a series of bargains being struck over time. Further, the pay-work agreement determined through productivity bargaining contrasts with that negotiated through normal effort bargaining in an important respect. With PBR, the pay rewards allocated to wage earners can fluctuate from week to week as output or productivity varies. Under productivity bargaining, they are usually predetermined with fluctuating payments kept to a minimum as far as is possible.

The significance of productivity bargaining is threefold. First, compared with other approaches to the pay–work bargain, productivity bargaining seems to be more successful in tightening up the pay–productivity link within organizations. This has potential benefits for management, unions, employees, consumers and the national economy. It has been argued from the managerial viewpoint, for example, that productivity bargaining induces greater cost consciousness in management and that it brings management into closer contact with trade union negotiators. For the trade unions, it is suggested, productivity agreements extend the range of subject matter in collective bargaining, whilst employees, it is said, also gain because they can obtain more stable earnings and greater leisure opportunities from productivity package deals.

Second, it is argued, productivity bargaining opens up new sources of untapped productivity potential within an enterprise. This can be done, for instance, by grouping minor changes in working practices into a total productivity deal which then becomes worthy of consideration by both management and unions as a source of higher productivity and of improved wage payments respectively. Alternatively, a joint attack can be made in the negotiating process on problems in the wage payment system, in the working environment, or in both. These are unlikely to be dealt with in standard or effort bargaining, inhibited as they are by custom and practice and traditionally hostile negotiating stances.

The third significance of productivity bargaining is the opportunity provided for improving the climate of industrial relations between management and trade unions at company or establishment level, since effective productivity bargaining necessitates openness and trust between the parties in the negotiation process. Management, for example, has to take a more predictive and proactive approach to negotiation than it does in standard or effort bargaining. This requires abandoning defensive or reactive bargaining postures in favour of greater initiative in industrial relations planning and labour utilization, as well as being 'open' in the approach to union representatives. Trade union negotiators, on the other hand, also need to modify their traditional bargaining stances if productivity bargaining is to succeed. They have to accept, for example, greater involvement in those areas of decision making which are traditionally regarded as being within managerial discretion alone. Compared with other types of collective bargaining, union negotiators have to be

prepared to accept more participation by rank-and-file workers in formulating and applying the pay–work rules regulating employee behaviour.

In short, a joint problem-solving approach is required in genuine productivity negotiations, since it involves the better use of labour and the more effective use of capital equipment within the workplace. The sorts of issues bargained about include: removal of excessive overtime; increased flexibility in the use of labour among skilled trades and between skilled and less skilled workers; changes in staffing levels; and reductions in the labour force. Negotiations also focus on greater flexibility in the movement of labour within the enterprise; flexible working hours; the cutting out of time-wasting practices and non-working time; introducing new technology and so on. In return for concessions on matters of these sorts, and for contributions by their members towards cost savings, trade union negotiators correspondingly demand a wide range of benefits for their members. These include:

> higher earnings, greater stability of earnings, and increases in holiday and sick pay; shorter hours of work; better fringe benefits; better promotion prospects; security against redundancy; and other tangible benefits, e.g. increased interest in the job.[19]

Since there are many employees who are not directly engaged in productive output, the term 'productivity bargaining' is inapplicable to those non-manual workers for whom it is inappropriate to specify quantitative changes in working practices in exchange for higher payments. Productivity bargaining is also a dubious description for those pay–work bargains negotiated for manual workers who have previously conducted agreements specifying changes in working practices but for whom such agreements are no longer appropriate. It was the National Board for Prices and Incomes which first coined the phrase 'efficiency agreements' for those negotiations having the underlying aim of constantly raising efficiency 'on the basis of close and continuing co-operation between managements and workers so as to achieve and maintain the highest standards in the use of both equipment and manpower'.[20] Productivity bargaining can be used in those situations in which specific changes in working practices are agreed in return for direct improvements in pay and conditions. Efficiency bargaining, on the other hand, covers those circumstances in which improvements in pay and non-pay benefits are linked to forecasted and costed gains within the enterprise, resulting from co-operation between management and the workforce in organizational change and technological innovation.

The classical phase of productivity bargaining was the 1960s. Indeed, it was a deliberate government policy to support productivity agreements within the framework of successive incomes policies in that period. However, in deteriorating economic circumstances and with rising unemployment during the 1970s since then productivity bargaining has become a less acceptable means of conducting pay negotiations for most trade union negotiators, since it involves redundancies and job losses. Standard bargaining with its emphasis on the pay–rate bargain rather than on the effort bargain or the productivity bargain is the dominant trade union approach to negotiation. Less emphasis is now placed on the pay-productivity link in employer–union negotiations, with managements enforcing changes in working methods unilaterally. For the unions, more attention is focused on cost-of-living arguments by negotiators or claims to restore eroded pay differentials. As unemployment has risen, and management has sought productivity improvements, these have tended to be imposed unilaterally, sometimes by consultation but normally without negotiation.

It would be wrong to consider productivity bargaining as a new concept. Productivity agreements have been much more widespread and are of much longer standing than is sometimes assumed. Even the so-called pathfinding Fawley Productivity Agreements at the Esso Petroleum Company's oil refinery near Southampton in the early 1960s were by no means as pioneering as some commentators have implied. Their novelty lay in the range and depth of their coverage rather than in the concept of productivity bargaining as such. However, large numbers of organizations, both large and small, in the private sector and in the public sector, practised productivity bargaining in the 1960s. These included Alcan Industries, Dunlop Rubber, the Central Electricity Generating Board, Imperial Chemical Industries and the London Transport Executive. Four main types of productivity bargaining were conducted during this period: national negotiations into which a productivity element was injected; national negotiations aimed at establishing a framework for company bargaining; small-scale bargaining at plant level or below; and full-scale and comprehensive productivity package deals.

Productivity bargaining has not always received the full support of either union or managerial nego-

tiators. In the first place, productivity bargaining can have severe disadvantages for the workers and trade unions concerned. For example, it may threaten redundancy, affect some workers' earnings adversely, result in inconvenient hours of work, and generally cause a sense of anxiety and disturbance among employees. Similarly, difficulties are sometimes encountered by employers from those other employees, normally white-collar workers, who are outside the scope of productivity bargaining. These employees often feel that they are being treated unfairly because their productivity cannot be measured, or because they are already co-operating fully with management in their methods of working. More importantly, there are those trade unionists and their supporters who, because of their ideological perceptions, believe productivity bargaining to be 'part of a major offensive by the employing class of this country to shift the balance of forces in industry permanently in their direction'.[21] On these grounds, it is argued, productivity bargaining must be resisted and opposed by rank-and-file trade unionists in their own interests.

## 14.4    The Negotiation Process

Negotiation is defined as 'a process for resolving conflict between two ... parties whereby both modify their demands to achieve a mutually acceptable compromise'.[22] Industrial relations negotiation is the interactive activity by which representatives of management and unions make decisions on matters of joint concern to them and those whom they represent. Both parties are then jointly responsible for the mutually agreed decisions. Substantive bargaining normally seeks to resolve conflicts of interest between the parties, grievance bargaining concerns conflicts of right. There are at least three basic elements in the negotiation process. The first is that negotiation involves social relations between those individuals and groups which are party to collective bargaining; the second is the representative and communicative functions of negotiation; and the third is that differences in power exist between those represented in the negotiation process: employers and employees.

### The social contexts

Each management–union negotiation or set of negotiations is unique. Whilst situations repeat themselves in different negotiations, they never repeat themselves exactly. Nevertheless, three sets of factors seem to be of major influence in determining the climate of any particular negotiation: the institutional background; the behavioural contexts; and the ideologies and values of the negotiators. The institutional factors which have an impact on negotiation include the level of procedure within which negotiations take place, the type of claim under discussion, the balance of bargaining power between management and unions, and the degree of formality or informality in the negotiations. The ways in which a shop-floor grievance over shiftwork allowances might be resolved between the production manager and the senior workplace representative within a low-technology food canning factory, for example, would be quite different from negotiating a company-wide productivity agreement and package deal for process workers in a highly profitable multiplant chemical company.

The behavioural contexts of negotiation are also important in determining the climate of bargaining between the parties. These include, for example, the size of the negotiating groups, the interests which they represent, the personalities involved and their negotiating skills. At one extreme, negotiation takes place at the interpersonal level, between two people: a single managerial representative and one union negotiator. Most collective bargaining, however, involves inter-party negotiations. These range from fairly small groups on each side of the bargaining table to 20 or more representatives from management and a similar number of trade unionists representing different trade unions. Negotiations in the latter case are likely to be far more formal, protracted and difficult to resolve than when only two individuals are directly involved in, say, a relatively small-scale workplace issue. With larger groups there is a greater need for an ordered format to channel individual effort and synchronize the efforts of group members. 'This discourages a free and informal sort of individual participation and minimises the prospects of developing meaningful relationships within the group.'[23]

Bargaining is also likely to be affected by the ideologies and skills of the respective negotiators. As one full-time trade union officer in the Midlands is reported to have remarked:

If a manager is so anti-union it hurts him to sit and talk with the union official, and it shows in his actions, I don't show him any mercy. I'll do my best to grind him into the ground as quickly as I can. Every deal will be an expensive one and

then if someone more senior comes along to me and says 'What's with you and this bloke?' 'Well, I'm afraid we just don't get on. He hates us, and as long as he's in that position there'll be trouble in the firm.'

Similar but contrary views may well be felt by some management negotiators. It would also appear that negotiations are influenced by the relative experience and skills of the negotiators. In practice, there is probably no substitute for the experience of the give and take of real-life negotiation. 'We can learn a lot from education and training courses', it has been said, 'but there's no substitute for the experience of the real thing.'[24]

### Distributive and integrative bargaining

Another significant influence on the bargaining climate is the type of negotiation between the parties. The two pure types which exist are described as 'distributive' or 'competitive' bargaining and 'integrative' or 'co-operative' bargaining. Distributive bargaining occurs where management and unions are in a situation of basic conflict over the ways in which something might be divided or decided between them. There is, for instance, an inevitable conflict between management and unions when pay and profits have to be distributed between them. More pay for employees usually means less profit for the company, whilst more profit for the company normally means less pay for the employees. Similarly, in the public sector, conflicts emerge between employer representatives seeking more efficient working methods from their employees, such as a rise in productivity or by less recruitment, and employees opposing these moves. Distributive bargaining, in other words, is essentially a conflict-resolving process and a zero-sum game – a gain for one side must mean equal loss for the other. It typically aims to enable the parties to reach a compromise over how either fixed or limited resources may be allocated between them.

In integrative bargaining, by contrast, both sets of negotiators recognize that they may have one or more common problems which require mutual resolution between them. Compared with distributive bargaining, integrative bargaining is more a problem-solving process and a positive-sum game with benefits for both parties. It takes place, for example, in the development and negotiation of productivity agreements. Unlike distributive bargaining, genuine integrative bargaining aims to increase the size of the

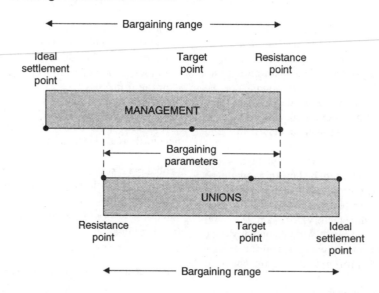

Figure 14.1 The negotiating continuum.

resources for distribution between the two sides rather than just dividing them between them. Integrative bargaining occurs, for instance, when a company is faced with a marked downturn in business. Either management or unions can use an integrative bargaining approach by identifying common goals for determining methods of dealing with possible reductions in hours, potential lay-offs, likely redundancies and so on. If they fail to do this, bargaining becomes purely distributive because of its win–lose implications for each party. This heightens conflict between them and a mutual sense of distrust emerges in the negotiation process.

It is quite clear that both the content and the styles of distributive and integrative bargaining differ. In the former, the parties are directly competing with each other and are in overt conflict over the distribution of fixed, limited resources. In distributive negotiations one side's gain is the other side's loss. Similarly, the attitudes of the respective parties to the negotiating process in distributive bargaining are likely to be hostile, suspicious and lacking in openness towards each other. In purely integrative bargaining, on the other hand, however rare it might be in practice, the parties need to co-operate to achieve their perceived common ends. There has to be considerable mutual trust and openness of communication between them for co-operative bargaining to take place. As a process, integrative bargaining is a much more tentative and exploratory method of negotiation than is distributive bargaining. More time

is required to carry it out, whilst the pace of negotiations may be slower than in distributive bargaining. Similarly, the negotiators have to be willing to talk about the goals at which they are really aiming.

Distributive and integrative bargaining, in short, have different objectives, their contents differ, and the negotiators involved in the two processes perceive themselves and their opponents in different ways. The real-life problems facing negotiators, however, are complicated by the fact that much bargaining in which they are involved is 'mixed' bargaining, being partly distributive and partly integrative. To shift from one type of negotiation to the other is a difficult task. What negotiators reveal to assist in joint problem-solving situations, for example, can weaken their bargaining position when it comes to distributing the resource gains which have been made.

## The negotiating continuum

Negotiation aims at reaching 'accommodations, often of a temporary nature, between different interests and expectations'. In industrial relations, it involves regulating the parties' different interests and pursuing their complementary objectives, although it is also part of a wider relationship of employment which is essentially collaborative. Negotiators, therefore, normally want to reach agreement. In every negotiation, there is a 'negotiating continuum', as shown in Figure 14.1, incorporating the 'bargaining range' of each side. An effective negotiation enables each party to identify the 'bargaining parameters' between them and to reach an agreed settlement within these parameters. 'Having discovered the possibility of a settlement, it is about securing that settlement at least cost and agreeing to its implementation.'[25]

As can be seen in Figure 14.1, management's bargaining range in a given negotiation runs from its ideal settlement point to its resistance point, with a target point of favourable and realistic expectation in an intermediate position between the two. The unions also have a bargaining range, but running in the opposite direction. The bargaining parameters lie between the resistance points of each side. A negotiated settlement is normally achieved within these parameters. In distributive bargaining it is the skill of the negotiators to probe each other's divergent target and resistance points in order to move towards a mutually acceptable compromise. The more skilled the negotiators, and the more equal the balance of bargaining power between them, the more likely it is that the final agreement and settlement will lie somewhere between each side's target points. Where bargaining power is unequal the stronger side is likely to achieve its bargaining objectives with little resistance from the other side. Where there is no overlap between the resistance points of either party, a bargaining 'gap' exists between them and negotiations between them are likely to break down.

## Negotiation phases

Negotiations proceed through a number of phases before managerial and union representatives can reach a mutually acceptable compromise and agreement together. Unless agreement is reached in the negotiating process, there is the likelihood that either party will force the other one to accept its demands by some form of industrial action or coercion. Effective industrial relations negotiations are aimed at preventing disputes arising between the parties and at reaching mutually acceptable agreements benefiting both sides represented at the negotiating table. This does not mean that each side 'wins' the negotiation. It means that each side achieves something in the negotiation which enables it to keep face with those whom it represents. An effective negotiation is therefore where both sides consider that the agreement on balance is fair, with both sides making concessions from their original positions.

In practice, a negotiating cycle proceeds through three main phases: preparation, negotiation and implementation. Preparation involves, for example,

'objective setting' and 'strategy determination'. Deciding bargaining objectives is not an easy task, since conflicts often develop within each side before negotiations between them commence. It is not unusual before negotiations commence, and even during them, for intra-group disagreements to emerge within the negotiating groups. The important thing is for neither party to weaken its bargaining position by showing less than a united front to its opponents. Each side's negotiating goals are determined by a process of 'intra-organizational' bargaining. This takes place among the bargaining teams prior to the commencement of negotiations. This enables them to show a common front to the opposing negotiating team. In this respect:

> intra-organizational bargaining within the union is particularly interesting. While it is true that for both parties to labor negotiations many individuals not present in negotiations are vitally concerned about what transpires at the bargaining table, the union negotiator is probably subject to more organizational constraints than his company counterpart.[26]

Having assessed their relative bargaining power, and decided their respective bargaining objectives and bargaining range, management and unions are then able to prepare their cases prior to presenting them. In examining their strategy determination before negotiating, each side is seeking for ways to adjust the outlook and expectations of their opponents in the negotiating process. This is a vital step in the negotiating cycle. It includes assessing the strengths and weaknesses of their case, the likely counter arguments to it, what might be conceded but what must be achieved, and its order of presentation. Strategy determination also involves making judgments about the likelihood of having to threaten or to resist sanctions in order to achieve one's bargaining objectives. Unions, for examples, have to consider the possibilities of working to rule, restricting output, banning overtime, working without enthusiasm, or even striking. Management, on the other hand, has to consider the possibilities of imposing more supervision, withholding overtime, laying off workers, or ultimately locking out employees.

When the parties start negotiating, it is sometimes customary for the trade unions to present their case first whether it is a substantive or a procedural claim, and for management to respond to it, though the process is generally reversed in productivity bargaining. The union's case in a pay claim having been made, for example, management often requests an adjournment to consider its reply. When this is ready, management responds with its counter arguments to the unions. The unions then sometimes request a further adjournment prior to making a revised and counter claim. After the parties come together again, they attempt to determine a final agreement which usually takes several meetings to achieve unless negotiations break down.

The negotiation phase normally proceeds through four subsidiary stages. They are not necessarily clearly delineated, and often the parties move backwards and forwards amongst the stages rather than proceeding smoothly towards final agreement. These negotiating stages are variously described as the 'initial' or 'arguing' stage, the 'exploratory' or 'proposing' stage, the 'consolidating' or 'bargaining' stage, and the 'decision' or 'agreeing' stage. The initial or arguing stage comprises opening statements from either side of their initial bargaining positions and their reasons for pursuing them as well as rejecting each other's claim or demands. This stage is in effect a 'safety valve' for each negotiating team. It enables each set of negotiators to 'let off steam' and establish the broad parameters within which it is prepared to negotiate with its opponents. It is characterized by listening, questioning and testing the commitment of each side to its opening and seemingly inflexible initial bargaining position. It is not actually negotiation since arguments cannot be negotiated: they merely reflect the initial tactical positions of both parties.

After the initial bargaining positions of the two sides have been established, negotiations proper begin, with an exploratory or proposing stage. At this point each party tries to find out where the other group really stands. External clues in pay bargaining, for example, come from knowledge of recent settlements elsewhere, the willingness and ability of the union to call and finance possible strike action, the state of the order book of the company, market conditions, shopfloor attitudes and traditions, likely support from other unions or other employers and so on. There are also a series of internal clues which can be discerned from around the negotiating table itself. Negotiators, for example, have to draw their own conclusions about the bargaining positions of their opponents by their behaviour across the bargaining table. Are they sincere, trustworthy, determined, flexible, receptive to pressure and so on? To do this, they ask direct questions, try out proposals, make demands and offers, 'they threaten and sometimes

abuse, they bring in time pressures and show impatience, all in the hope that their opponent might reveal and possibly move his target and resistance points'.[27] This is often a time-consuming and frustrating process. The proposals each side makes are highly conditional: 'if you do this, we could do that'. They provide, however, the basis for moving into the next negotiation stage.

This is the consolidating or bargaining stage. The parties now concentrate on convergent rather than divergent issues, thus minimizing conflict between them. Negotiators seek to avoid contentious matters and act on the understanding that everyone around the bargaining table wishes to move towards a final agreement. This stage of the negotiating cycle is about exchange, the central core of the bargaining process. Each side aims to gain something from the other for a concession on their part: 'if you do this, we will do that'. It is here that tactical adjustments are made by both parties in their aim to motivate the other side away from an unacceptable position to a mutually agreeable 'contract zone'.

Negotiation then moves rapidly into the decision or agreeing stage. It becomes increasingly apparent to the negotiators at this point that only a compromise settlement is attainable. Final concessions and trade-offs are made between the parties and a detailed summary of each item in the package must be read and agreed between the negotiators. The details are normally put in writing and a final settlement which on balance is adequate for both sides rather than ideal for either is the prime objective. With the negotiation phase of the negotiating cycle completed, it is the joint responsibility of both parties to implement and monitor their agreement. Each side then normally evaluates its bargaining outcomes with its objectives, its negotiating performance and its future plans. Whatever the negotiation outcome, however, it has been said:

> You learn negotiating skills by experience and observation. You know how far they will go, they know how far you will go and there are certain steps which both sides can take to resolve the problem. But the two sides can misjudge each other. You can't be 100 per cent sure that you've judged your case rightly or you've judged their reactions rightly.[28]

## 14.5  Joint Consultation

Joint consultation has a chequered history in British industrial relations. It seems to have enjoyed three periods of popularity during the last 50 years: throughout the Second World War, in the late 1940s and since the late 1970s. In the intervening period, the 1950s and 1960s, a decline in joint consultation set in in most sectors, though as the 1960s drew to an end it seems that joint consultative machinery had continued to exist in some sectors 'but that it generally did little which caught the imagination of the parties'.[29] A survey by ACAS of larger private manufacturing and service organizations in 1990 concluded: 'managers consult their employees on a wider range of issues than in the past and in a wide variety of ways'.[30] But, on a wider sample basis, the WIRS 1990 suggests that, since its 1984 survey, 'the overall proportion of workplaces with [joint consultative] committees fell between 1984 and 1990, from 34 per cent to 29 per cent'.[31]

## Types of consultation

One of the problems of examining joint consultation is that there is no generally agreed definition of the term. In practice joint consultation normally takes place at employer or enterprise level and there seem to be three approaches to it. These may be described as pseudo-consultation, classical consultation and integrative consultation. Pseudo-consultation exists where management takes a decision and informs employees of that decision through employee representatives. It is a system of consultation through which management merely communicates predetermined decisions with employee representatives. In this case management either passes information to employees or receives information from them. Employees have no power to influence managerial decisions and their representatives are not normally union members. Indeed, it is arguable that the express intention of such an approach is to prevent the emergence of employee-based power centres in non-union firms. There are still sections of private industry, where trade unionism is weak, which use this bland form of consultation or, more accurately, 'information-giving' by the employer to employee representatives. As a method of industrial relations, it merely seeks to maintain management's right to manage, neither to challenge it nor to legitimize managerial authority.

Classical consultation, as defined by the Institute of Personnel Management, is a method of:

involving employees through their representatives in discussion and consideration of relevant

matters which affect or concern those they represent, thereby allowing employees to influence the proposals before the final management decision is taken.[32]

For ACAS, joint consultation is defined as: 'management asking about things and listening before making decisions'.[33] Classical consultation of this type has four main characteristics. First, it focuses on matters of common interest to employers and employees, specifically excluding areas of potential conflict between them such as terms and conditions of work. Second, joint consultative machinery is normally kept separate from negotiating machinery. Third, it remains management's responsibility to take and implement the final decisions arising from the consultative process. Fourth, it involves all employees, including non-union employees such as supervisors and managerial staff. Classical consultation therefore involves a paradox, it is assumed 'that management should only agree to share responsibility on controversial and conflicting subjects like wages', as in collective bargaining, 'on common interest issues it cannot do more than consult'.[34]

Integrative consultation, by contrast, is not an instrument of management so much as a means of advancing employee participation within enterprises by 'settling democratically the purposes of industrial undertakings, purposes which managers themselves serve'.[35] Under these conditions the artificial distinctions between the subject matter of negotiation and consultation are blurred. Integrative consultation in other words enlarges the area of joint decision making between managerial and employee representatives. Management and unions discuss and explore matters which are of common concern to them such as increasing productivity or changing working methods. Often this is approached in a problem-solving manner with a view to coming to a joint decision. It is a process more akin to integrative bargaining than to classical consultation or distributive bargaining. Indeed, if joint consultation is to mean anything 'it must give employees a genuine influence on important decisions – it must have teeth'.[36]

Drawing on research he has conducted in the private sector over a number of years, Marchington provides a refined and persuasive classification of joint consultative committees (JCCs) and the joint consultative process. He argues that 'it is possible to put forward several different models of consultation, each of which displays markedly different characteristics'. He claims that the variation amongst them 'can be seen along at least five separate dimensions: purpose, subject matter, representation, process, and levels (or layers)' of employee involvement. He describes the 'four faces of consultation' as: the non-union model; the competitive model; the adjunct model; and the marginal model. The non-union model, for example, is similar to the pseudo-consultation approach outlined above. Its purpose is to prevent union organization in the workplace, 'by providing a mechanism for formal two-way communication and for tapping employee opinion'. The subject matter comprises business-centred or 'hard' information, as well as welfare or 'soft' information. Management is typically represented by senior line managers or personnel managers, who chair the meetings, with the employee representatives chosen from the workforce. The process is educative, that is 'to inform employee representatives and persuade them to go along with management thinking' and to defend established managerial prerogatives. Non-union JCCs are normally at establishment level only, with little likelihood of there being any multi-establishment coordination. However, given that the objective is to obstruct unionization, 'what goes on at the JCC is rather less important than what the committee manages to prevent'.[37]

Marchington's competitive model of joint consultation bears some relation to the classical consultation described earlier. Its purpose is to upgrade or revitalize JCCs to render collective bargaining less meaningful, thereby reducing union influence in the workplace. Its subject matter is high-level, hard, corporate information. Much emphasis is placed by management on the company's market position and 'part of the strategy will be to assist members to understand the problems which confront the company, and hence the logic and inescapability of management's solutions to these'. The management team is led by senior line managers and the workforce by shop stewards and other employee representatives. The process is educative and provides workers with advanced information of managerial plans in the company. Like the non-union model, it is likely that JCCs of the competitive type only operate at establishment level, or even at departmental level. In addition, 'combined with the upgrading of consultation there would also probably be the development of direct forms of employee involvement'. These include 'quality circles, team briefing, videos and so on'.

The adjunct model of consultation, like the integrative approach above, is where negotiation deals with matters of a distributive character, with JCCs 'dealing with issues of a more integrative nature which are reliant on high trust and open interactions' between management and union representatives. Additionally, this sort of consultation can also be a preliminary to negotiation. Problem solving 'characterises consultation within this model, and it is the one to which prescriptions for the successful JCC are usually addressed'. The subject matter of this model is therefore hard, high-level information and concerns 'trade prospects, business plans, orders, quality and customer relations'. Managerial representation is provided by senior line management and members from the personnel team, with the workforce represented by shop stewards. The process is one of mutual influence between the management and union representatives. Within it, advance information is provided to the members and management allows the union representatives to meet before the JCC takes place. This is to make the formal meetings more effective. In multiplant companies, there are multi-tiered JCCs clearly linked with one another. According to Marchington:

> Underlying these committees is the assumption that management and union representatives want the JCC to succeed, to play a part in company issues and to help lubricate relations in a more informal and less highly charged atmosphere than that of annual negotiations or dispute resolution. Prescriptions for success based upon pluralist notions are likely to be appropriate in these circumstances. . . .[38]

The marginal model of joint consultation is symbolic and without real substance. It is aimed at keeping employee representatives busy and at a low level of involvement. It normally covers soft welfare information and trivial matters of little interest to its participants. Management is often represented by the personnel department and the workforce by both union and non-union representatives. The process is essentially a firefighting one, where 'a good deal of the time is taken up with issues which have re-arisen from the previous meeting or may have dragged on for quite a number'. It normally takes place at establishment level with no links to other joint consultative machinery.[39]

Clearly there is some debate about the aims of consultation and its relationship with negotiation. Some view them as separate but related processes. Others contend that 'there is no absolute dividing line that constitutes a universal separation between them'.[40] This means that in practice managerial and employee

*Table 14.1* Proportion of establishments with JCCs 1984 and 1990 (per cent).

| | All establishments | | Manufacturing | | Private services | | Public sector | |
|---|---|---|---|---|---|---|---|---|
| | 1984 | 1990 | 1984 | 1990 | 1984 | 1990 | 1984 | 1990 |
| JCC exists | 34 | 29 | 30 | 23 | 24 | 19 | 48 | 49 |
| Workplace or higher level JCC, with local representatives | 41 | 35 | 33 | 25 | 28 | 25 | 62 | 59 |

*Source*: WIRS 1992

representatives need to consider carefully how to link the two. It may often be advantageous for the same committee to cover both. Where there are separate bodies, systematic communication between those in the two processes is essential.

In developing appropriate consultative machinery, management and employee representatives also have to consider the levels at which representative systems are most likely to be effective and how they can be linked horizontally and vertically. Problems can arise in multiunion situations, for example, or in integrating non-union and managerial staff into a consultative system where there is strong union organization amongst other employee groups. As Marchington concludes: 'joint consultation can vary widely in nature between different establishments and ... consequently prescriptions for success need to take this into account'.[41]

## The extent of consultation

Table 14.1 shows the extent of JCCs in Britain in 1984 and 1990. The first WIRS (1980) showed that workplace JCCs had become a common feature of British industry between 1975 and 1980. By 1984, it appeared that there was little or no change in the overall extent of workplace JCCs in the period since 1980, with just over a third having them. This came about from movements in different directions. There was a decrease in the reporting of JCCs in private manufacturing and an increase in the public sector. The decline in the incidence of JCCs in manufacturing continued in 1990 but there was little or no change in private services or the public sector. About a quarter of establishments in manufacturing had JCCs in 1990, representing a fall from 30 per cent in 1984 and 36 per cent in 1980. By contrast, about half of public

sector workplaces had JCCs in 1990 and a fifth of private services.

A broader measure of the incidence of joint consultative machinery available to employees at an individual workplace is whether it has either a workplace-level JCC or a higher-level committee with representatives from that workplace. Table 14.1 shows that there was also a decline in this broader measure of joint consultation, from 41 per cent of all establishments in 1984 to 35 per cent in 1990. 'In terms of the overall proportion of employees in such workplaces, the fall was more significant – from 62 per cent of employees in 1984 to half of employees in 1990.'[42] The decline was concentrated in manufacturing and the difference between the private and public sectors, identified in 1984, persisted. Three-fifths of public sector workplaces had JCCs on this broader definition, compared with a quarter of workplaces in manufacturing and private services.

It needs to be recognized that JCCs are not the only form of joint consultation practised between management and workforce representatives. A consultative technique being used in some organizations is 'joint working parties' (JWPs) or 'joint problem solving groups'. Their representatives are drawn from management and employee representatives but, unlike JCCs, they deal with one particular issue, or a set of closely related issues, and are sometimes used in unionized establishments to explore issues prior to negotiations between the parties. According to ACAS, two-fifths of the firms covered in its survey on consultation and communication in 1990 had convened a JWP in the previous years. The factors influencing the creation of JWPs appear to be: large organizations, undergoing complex changes, and unionized and foreign owned firms.

*Table 14.2* Subjects discussed in local JCCs (per cent).

| Topic | The most time consuming | Matters receiving discussion |
|---|---|---|
| Working conditions | 32 | 89 |
| Quality | 31 | 87 |
| Pay | 27 | 57 |
| Output | 26 | 82 |
| Welfare | 26 | 75 |
| Safety | 20 | 72 |
| Working methods | 18 | 78 |
| Financial results | 15 | 66 |
| Changes in staffing | 10 | 67 |
| New equipment | 10 | 83 |
| Training | 8 | 78 |

*Source*: ACAS 1990

*Table 14.3* Subjects discussed in JWPs.

| Item | Per cent of JWPs |
|---|---|
| Production issues | 52 |
| Pay and job evaluation | 35 |
| Training | 28 |
| Absence | 26 |
| Grievance and disciplinary matters/procedures | 25 |

*Source*: ACAS 1990

## Subject matter and the determinants of consultation

It can be seen from Table 14.2 that a wide range of topics are discussed in JCCs between management and employee representatives. The core of the discussions covers matters related to terms and conditions of employment and the physical output of goods and services. It is particularly interesting to note that almost one-third of managers reported that quality improvement has become an important issue for joint consultation. Analysis of the ACAS survey of 1990 also shows that some firms claim to consult their employees on a wider range of issues than others. In fact, two distinct patterns emerged. 'First, managers in workplaces where trade unions are recognised for collective bargaining are likely to consult on more issues than their counterparts in non-union establishments.' The second finding was that workplaces 'owned outside the UK tend to consult on a wider range of issues than British-owned firms'.[43]

JWPs also tackle a wide range of important issues. Around half of them discuss issues concerned with production costs, output and quality, with a further third discussing job evaluation, training and pay. As outlined in Table 14.3, some employers are using them to revise their approaches to discipline.

A number of explanations have been advanced to account for the incidence and extent of consultation in enterprises. One study, for example, suggests that the larger the size of a plant, 'the greater the likelihood of its having a [joint consultative] committee'. Multiunionism also appears to be associated

with the creation of JCCs, as are plants where there is single employer bargaining. The conclusions of these researchers are that JCCs 'are becoming increasingly heterogeneous in nature, both in terms of the characteristics of the plants where they are established and in terms of their performance as viewed by management'.[44]

Another study claims that there are three theses explaining fluctuations in the extent of joint consultation, over time. Its authors describe them respectively as the 'McCarthy thesis', the 'accommodation thesis' and the 'external threat thesis'. The McCarthy thesis suggests that there is an inverse relationship between trade union power and joint consultation. When union power is strong, joint consultation is weakened; and when union power is weak, joint consultation is strengthened. The accommodation thesis, in contrast, characterizes joint consultation as a 'management strategy to maintain its authority when challenged by rising trade union power'. Finally, the external threat thesis 'argues that an acute development of external pressure is required for the two sides to co-operate in joint consultation', since normally neither side to employment relations wishes to collaborate openly with the other. Whilst inclining to the external threat thesis, these authors believe that the time 'is long overdue for a greater refinement in our theories of joint consultation, especially in respect of the variation in its extent over time'.[45]

## 14.6    Employee Involvement and Communication

Employee involvement has a variety of definitions. The CBI, for example, in its statement of principles on employee involvement, believes that it:

- is a range of processes designed to engage the support, understanding and optimum contribution of all employees in an organization and their commitment to its objectives;

- assists an organization to give the best possible service to customers and clients in the most cost-effective way;
- entails providing employees with the opportunity to influence and where appropriate, take part in decision making on matters which affect them;
- is an intrinsic part of good management practice and is therefore not confined to relationships with employee representatives;
- can only be developed voluntarily and in ways suited to the activities, structure and history of an organization.

The CBI also believes that employee involvement promotes 'business success' by fostering shared commitment to organizational goals, demonstrating 'respect for individual employees' and enabling employees to achieve maximum job satisfaction. For the CBI, the sorts of employee involvement systems and techniques available to management include communication, consultation, 'decision making at the lowest practicable level', training, financial participation, harmonization and 'seeking individual contributions aimed at achieving continuous improvement in the organisation'.[46]

Recent Conservative governments are also 'wholly committed' to the promotion and encouragement of employee involvement. Norman Fowler, former Secretary of State for Employment, claims that 'employee involvement is one of the major success stories of British industry in recent years'. He believes that employee involvement is best developed voluntarily and that it depends 'on a spirit of co-operation, not on a legal basis'. That is 'why the government has consistently opposed pressure for legislation which would impose rigid requirements in place of flexibility and diversity'. In the government's view:

- Employee involvement is important for Britain as a whole as it is part of the government's drive to improve the flexibility and efficiency of the labour market. That drive has already had dramatic effects on the British economy.
- Employee involvement is important for companies because it increases their prosperity and productivity. Employees are increasingly demanding more say in their work.
- The government has a particular part to play in promoting financial participation, greater flexibility in pension provision and training.

The government has also argued that European Union proposals for 'compulsory legislation on worker participation would not be worthwhile for workers or their employers . . . and could destroy what they were designed for'.[47] It is government policy, therefore, to encourage the voluntary development of employee involvement and participation.

Perhaps the most useful short definition of employee involvement, however, is provided by Marchington and Goodman and their colleagues. They use the term 'employee involvement' to indicate that range of employment-related initiatives, largely designed and introduced by management, which 'are intended to improve communications with employees, to generate greater commitment, and enhance employee contributions to the organisation'.[48]

## Types and extent of employee involvement

A survey of employee involvement practices in 377 British companies by the Employment Department in 1991 found an increase in such arrangements since an earlier survey in 1988. Under Section 1 of the Employment Act 1982, companies with over 250 employees are required to state in their annual reports what action they have taken to promote employee involvement. The first finding of this survey was that virtually all companies to which the legislation applies now mention at least one employee involvement practice in their annual reports. Second, employee involvement increases with company size, with the largest relative increase between 1988 and 1991 taking place in smaller companies. Third, financial participation schemes have risen in importance from 53 per cent in 1988 to 77 per cent in 1991, and 'over half of all survey companies have a share scheme which all employees can join'. Fourth, the types of involvement practices reported to the Employment Department showed a shift towards more informal structures, away from formal, committee-based arrangements. Fifth, there is more emphasis on involving employees in improving quality and business performance than previously. Overall, then, employee involvement arrangements appear to have become consolidated in recent years, to suit individual companies, and 'they are now, even more than previously, an established part of working life'.[49]

Table 14.4 indicates the types of employee involvement arrangements typically found in the corporate sector. The Employment Department classified them

*Table 14.4* Employee involvement practices (by company size), percentage of companies.

| | 251–1 000 employees | | 1 001–5 000 employees | | Over 5 000 employees | | Total | |
|---|---|---|---|---|---|---|---|---|
| | 1991 $n=267$ | 1988 $n=200$ | 1991 $n=88$ | 1988 $n=66$ | 1991 $n=22$ | 1988 $n=16$ | 1991 $n=377$ | 1988 $n=282$ |
| **Information passing** | | | | | | | | |
| Publications | 37.8 | 25.0 | 45.5 | 51.0 | 59.1 | 68.0 | 40.8 | 33.5 |
| Employee report/accounts | 16.9 | 15.9 | 17.0 | 42.9 | 31.8 | 38.1 | 17.8 | 23.5 |
| Presentations/seminars | 10.9 | 5.7 | 23.9 | 11.2 | 36.4 | 30.9 | 15.4 | 8.4 |
| Noticeboards | 4.9 | 3.4 | 9.1 | 14.3 | 4.5 | 4.1 | 5.8 | 6.0 |
| Total (information passing) | 47.9 | 38.6 | 55.7 | 66.3 | 68.2 | 76.3 | 50.9 | 47.2 |
| **Interactive practices** | | | | | | | | |
| Meetings/management line communications | 50.6 | 55.7 | 59.1 | 69.4 | 54.5 | 84.5 | 52.8 | 60.5 |
| Briefing or discussion groups | 22.5 | 13.6 | 29.5 | 27.6 | 27.3 | 46.4 | 24.2 | 18.7 |
| Access to senior management | 13.1 | 10.2 | 25.0 | 9.2 | 22.7 | 17.5 | 16.4 | 10.4 |
| Consultative councils/groups (incl local) | 43.1 | 55.7 | 43.2 | 68.4 | 50.0 | 80.4 | 43.5 | 60.0 |
| TU and staff association channels | 30.3 | 31.8 | 28.4 | 35.7 | 36.4 | 49.5 | 30.2 | 33.7 |
| Quality circles and suggestion schemes | 14.6 | 8.0 | 21.6 | 12.2 | 9.1 | 12.4 | 15.9 | 9.2 |
| Training | 35.6 | 22.7 | 45.5 | 21.4 | 63.6 | 43.3 | 39.5 | 23.6 |
| Health and Safety committees/ Welfare committees | 29.6 | 13.6 | 35.2 | 23.5 | 40.9 | 26.8 | 31.6 | 16.7 |
| Pension scheme involvement | 8.2 | 10.2 | 12.5 | 15.3 | 13.6 | 22.7 | 9.5 | 12.1 |
| Total (interactive practices) | 77.9 | 69.3 | 83.0 | 82.7 | 95.5 | 89.7 | 80.1 | 73.6 |
| **Financial participation** | | | | | | | | |
| Employee share schemes | 71.2 | 44.3 | 76.1 | 62.2 | 81.8 | 78.4 | 72.9 | 50.4 |
| Incentive and bonus payments | 24.7 | 15.9 | 30.7 | 23.5 | 27.3 | 27.8 | 26.3 | 18.3 |
| Total (financial participation) | 75.7 | 47.7 | 79.5 | 63.3 | 81.8 | 81.4 | 76.9 | 53.2 |
| **Other** | | | | | | | | |
| Career development, TQM, Attitude surveys, Monthly management accounts, Board level participation, Study groups | 15.7 | 13.6 | 20.5 | 19.4 | 18.2 | 47.4 | 17.0 | 16.8 |
| Total companies reporting any practice (per cent) | 92.9 | 85.2 | 97.7 | 93.9 | 100.0 | 97.9 | 94.4 | 88.0 |

*Source*: Employment Department (1991)

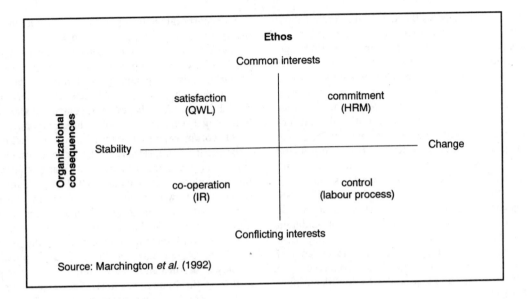

*Figure 14.2* Paradigms of participation.

into four main categories: information passing; interactive practices; financial participation; and other practices, such as total quality management (TQM), attitude surveys and study groups. Larger companies are more likely to report a wider range of employee involvement techniques than smaller ones. Further, whilst there have been increases in training, TQM and HRM initiatives since 1988, consultative committees appear to have reduced in importance. This view is confirmed by the WIRS 1990, which concludes not only that the late 1980s saw 'a fall in the proportion of workplaces with joint consultative committees' but also that 'managements were using a wide range of channels to communicate with their employees'. There was a substantial growth 'since the mid-1980s in the overall reporting of a wide range of initiatives for employee involvement' and this was combined with, 'more than before, an emphasis on involving workers in the improvement of quality and the success of the business'.[50]

## Explaining employee involvement

A study of developments in employee involvement conducted by researchers at the University of Manchester Institute of Science and Technology (UMIST) between June 1989 and May 1991, funded by the Employment Department, identifies four main 'paradigms' of employee participation. These are outlined in Figure 14.2 and are the control, satisfac-

tion, co-operation and commitment paradigms. The control paradigm is wholly management driven and largely suppresses employee participation, by strictly limiting any transfer of job control from management to employees. Indeed, labour process theory regards such initiatives as cosmetic and meaningless, since they merely give workers 'the illusion of making decisions by choosing among fixed and limited alternatives designed by management which deliberately leaves insignificant matters open to choice'.[51] The satisfaction paradigm, which is related to quality of working life (QWL) experiments, is rooted in the belief that 'involvement and satisfaction are related to each other, and that higher degrees of Employee Involvement will lead to higher levels of employee satisfaction'. The paradigm linking involvement and participation with co-operation focuses on the use of collective bargaining and joint consultation as conflict avoidance and conflict resolving mechanisms in managing industrial relations. Finally, the commitment paradigm, which is central to much of the literature on HRM, assumes that involvement and participation lead to an increase in the commitment of employees to their organization and, in turn, 'that commitment leads to more positive behaviour at work, including higher levels of performance'.[52]

The shift by some employers away from control, satisfaction and even co-operation strategies towards an 'employee commitment' one is the result of a variety of factors. These include both internal and external influences but the driving force behind all of them is the pressure upon management to adapt to organizational and environmental change. The traditional or control-oriented approach to workforce management took shape earlier this century with large-scale manufacturing production, a less educated workforce and well organized trade unions. At the heart of this traditional model of industrial relations management was the wish of managers to establish order, exercise control and achieve efficiency at work. Drawing on North American experience, one writer argues that under the commitment strategy, in contrast, jobs are designed to be broader than before and include efforts to upgrade operations, not just maintain them. Moreover, with relatively flat management hierarchies and minimal differences in status, 'control and lateral coordination depend on shared goals, and expertise rather than formal position determines influence'.

In the commitment strategy, the importance of accepting the challenge of giving employees, where possible, some security of employment is also argued. This can be done by offering them training and retraining, as old jobs are eliminated and new ones are created. Further:

> Under the commitment strategy, performance expectations are high and serve not to define minimum standards but to provide 'stretching objectives', emphasize continuous improvement, and reflect the requirements of the marketplace. Accordingly, compensation policies reflect less the old formulas of job evaluation than the heightened importance of group achievement, the expanded scope of individual contribution, and the growing concern for such questions of 'equity' as gain sharing, stock ownership, and profit sharing.[53]

Several sets of factors are claimed to influence management in introducing employee involvement techniques and methods into organizations, in both the private and public sectors. These include: providing information and education about the employer's business position; gaining employee commitment to organizational goals and objectives; securing enhanced employee contributions to the business; facilitating the recruitment and retention of key staff; containing industrial conflict and providing stability in the employment relationship; and having to apply company, governmental and legal directives in the workplace. In some organizations, however, employee involvement is primarily adopted as part of a broader corporate philosophy and 'becomes a kind of metaphor for [being] a good employer'.[54]

Another study, in illustrating the diversity of employee involvement practices in the UK, posits five scenarios illustrating management thinking behind the various schemes. The first scenario, 'incorporation and control', is the 'cycle of control' model and is most likely where there is strong union organization at the workplace, a tight external labour market and a competitive product market. Its aims are to achieve stable and harmonious industrial relations within the workplace. The second, 'HRM participation', scenario has two versions: the union by-passing model – with management seeking direct communications with workers and more flexible working practices – and the union avoidance model where employee participation is directed at improving employee performance and commitment, through nurturing the human resource. The research team 'came across few examples of full-blown "Strategic Human Resource Management"'. The third scenario, 'market participation', where union power at the workplace is weak and unproblematic, also has two versions. Either product market pressures impact on human resources issues and the focus is on customer service or quality, with employee involvement and effective communications being functional means towards these ends, or, where companies have problems in recruiting and retaining suitable staff, employers may seek to improve the quality of working life by providing employee involvement measures or additional fringe benefits to complement pay. 'The anticipated impact is to increase employee loyalty and reduce the labour market problems.'

The fourth scenario is 'philosophical participation', whose origins lie in employer, state or supra-state ideologies. Examples include participation schemes originating among Quaker firms, German-style works councils or, most recently, the European Union Charter of Fundamental Social Rights of Workers. The fifth scenario is 'faddish participation', where the likely cause is fashion, which requires management to be 'seen to do something and keep up with the competition, and sometimes a bright idea at the top, or requirement from a major customer'.[55] Here the impact of employee involvement and participation is likely to be fairly superficial and ephemeral, with little lasting influence on employer or employee behaviour.

Finally, research on employee involvement practices suggests that they develop in 'waves of interest', in terms of specific participatory techniques. These 'waves' appear to come in different shapes and sizes

*Table 14.5* Information for employees.

| Types of information | Examples |
| --- | --- |
| Job information | Job descriptions, job training, terms and conditions, contractual details, physical environment, relationships with others, promotion prospects, grievance and disciplinary procedures |
| General information | Management and organizational structures, products, customers, numbers employed, appointments, resignations, promotions, long-service awards, labour turnover, job security |
| Marketing information | Sales, market shares, exports, competition, trading position, order book |
| Policies and plans | Manpower, health and safety, training, industrial relations, pay, job evaluation, sickness, savings schemes, investment, new products |
| Financial information | Income, distribution of income, tax paid, unit costs, profit and loss account, balance sheet, sources and application of funds, added value, productivity |

and to last for different lengths of time, in different organizations. Typically, employee involvement (EI) is claimed to develop in line with the following pattern:

> one form of EI is introduced and operates within an organisation being followed ... by a separate and quite different EI programme. The first technique may or may not endure ... [but] it may become less prominent ... as attention is focused on the new idea and resources committed to it. Then, perhaps ... a third set of techniques or methods is introduced, and these operate alongside the previous two. Then a fourth scheme may be introduced, and so on. New forms of EI are not always introduced in a stepwise or phased manner ... and it is quite possible for two separate schemes to be initiated at the same time and achieve different degrees of centrality.

Older schemes may be revived, whilst others fail to take root or fade away altogether. But depending upon when the snapshot is taken, 'it is possible to assess the relative importance of each form against the others'.[56]

## Information giving

Information giving by employers to staff is, by definition, a one-way process of communication in organizations. It incorporates a number of methods of what is basically downward communication. The methods used include corporate publications – such as company newspapers, house journals or newsletters, potentially covering a wide range of information and data – the provision of annual reports and company accounts to employees and presentations

and seminars, by senior management, during working time. Noticeboards are also a relatively cheap way of communicating with employees but they can get cluttered and do not always present information in an attractive and efficient way.

In structuring effective communication and information channels, management has to take account of what is to be communicated, who is responsible for communicating it, to whom the information is directed and the most appropriate form in which to present it. The starting point is a positive commitment from top management which defines in broad terms the objectives being sought, how they are to be achieved and when the information is to be communicated. As indicated in Table 14.5, there is a wide variety of information which can be provided to employees – or to their representatives. Surveys show that information about jobs and job tasks rate high on employee priorities but more general information about the enterprise should not be neglected. This information includes: the structure, products and personnel of the organization; information about sales, competition and trading; outlines of corporate policies and plans; and financial information.

## Interactive practices

The most common form of interactive employee involvement is through departmental meetings or larger meetings between managers and their staff. These represent the bottom end of the communication system within an organization and are the basic means for enabling managers to pass on operational information to their staff and to get feedback from them. Another common method of facilitating employee communication is through team briefing, which is often based on models provided by the

Industrial Society. These tend to consist of between four and 20 members of a workgroup who meet for up to half an hour monthly, or bi-monthly, under the leadership of their supervisor or first line manager, to discuss matters of common interest.

Quality circles are groups meeting together on a regular basis to identify, analyse and solve problems of quality, productivity or other aspects of daily working life, using problem solving techniques. Membership of quality circles is normally voluntary and members are often from the same work area or do similar job tasks and activities. Having met together, quality circles then present their solutions to management and are usually involved in implementing and monitoring their outcomes. Where quality circles are used effectively, it has been shown that they positively develop individuals, provide personal progression for circle members, improve managerial leadership, promote teamwork and contribute to quality improvements.

Suggestion schemes are used to encourage employees to put forward ideas about improving working methods, productivity or the working environment in which people work. Rewards are normally provided for 'successful' suggestions and special suggestion boxes are used to collect ideas and filter them, prior to deciding their merits and utility to the organization. In some cases, attitude surveys are used by management to obtain structured feedback from staff on particular matters of concern to the employer. These issues include: diagnosing organizational problems; assessing the effects of change on employees; and getting feedback on specific management policies, actions and plans.

Training has become an increasingly important method of bilateral internal communication. It is seen by management as helping employees to understand the information given to them and as encouraging them to play fuller parts in the ways an employer conducts its affairs. Training is sometimes needed because information about corporate performance or management activities involves specialist terms and the application of data which are difficult to interpret. Training events are also useful means for giving employees information about their employment, telling them about future working arrangements and, most importantly, preparing them for organizational change. Training enables managers to become more aware of the importance of effective communications and to improve their ability to communicate.

Interactive communication, between management and employee or union representatives, also takes place through health and safety committees, consultative committees and pension scheme involvement. If unions or staff associations are recognized for these purposes, it is essential that the information provided to them is passed on to supervisory staff. Nothing more effectively destroys the morale of supervisors than being told by staff representatives what they should already know as first line managers.

## Financial involvement

There are a number of different forms of financial involvement. These include profit sharing, profit-related pay, employee share ownership and gain sharing. Each of them aims to integrate workers into the organizations employing them and to get them to identify more closely with the employers' goals and objectives. This approach to employee involvement has been encouraged by legislation since the late 1970s and has been actively supported by successive governments in the hope that financial involvement breaks down 'them and us' attitudes between management and workers in the workplace.

'Basic' profit sharing is a voluntary periodic bonus paid by an employer out of corporate profits, at its discretion, which is added to an employee's pay, after the company's legal obligations to its shareholders have been met. Some of the other main forms of financial involvement are now formally embodied in the law. These include: profit-related pay or bonuses, including those covered by the Finance Act 1987; deferred profit-sharing schemes; save-as-you-earn (SAYE) schemes; and other share ownership arrangements. Direct profit-related pay is the most common type of financial participation and was reported by the WIRS 1990 'in 40 per cent of establishments in the trading sector of the economy'. These schemes were concentrated among larger organizations, those with a high proportion of non-manual employees and those enterprises whose recent financial performance was above the average for their industry. Moreover, 'establishments with recognized unions were slightly less likely to have them than establishments without recognized unions'.

Deferred profit-sharing schemes, where profits are put in a trust fund which acquires shares in the employing company, accounted for 9 per cent of establishments with employee share ownership schemes in the WIRS 1990. Twenty-four per cent of the establishments had SAYE schemes, where employees can buy their employer's shares from the proceeds of a 'savings contract' agreed with the employer. Seventeen per cent of establishments had discretionary or executive share option schemes, where selected employees have the option to buy shares at a previous market price, and 7 per cent had other types of share ownership scheme. Taking 'employee share-ownership and profit-sharing arrangements together, 55 per cent of trading sector workplaces had one of the five types of employee financial participation scheme'.

From the evidence provided by the WIRS, there is little doubt that there was a substantial growth in profit-sharing and employee share ownership schemes between 1984 and 1990. The proportion of the industrial and commercial sectors having either cash-based or share-based profit sharing rose from 18 to 23 per cent during these years. Similarly, the proportion of trading sector establishments having share ownership schemes rose from 23 per cent in 1984 to 32 per cent in 1990. Moreover, the proportion of the workforce participating in share ownership schemes, where they were available, 'rose from 22 per cent in 1984 to 34 per cent in 1990'.[57]

Gain sharing, which is more widely practised in the USA than in Britain, is where a group incentive payment, linked to group performance, is paid to employees. Gain sharing schemes, such as the Rucker and Scanlon plans, are also more likely to involve trade unions in the ways in which they are operated. Gain sharing is particularly attractive to employers where labour costs are a high proportion of total costs and where it can be geared to improvements in quality, delivery and the cost of waste. On the other hand, gain sharing can inhibit change, specific formulae may be difficult for employees to understand and the schemes which are available often require a lot of monitoring and communication on the part of management and supervisors.

## Quality at work

Since the early 1980s, increasing interest has been shown by organizations, in both the private and public sectors, in the managing of quality at work. At its most basic, 'quality is about making products and delivering services that people want at prices they can afford'.[58] For ACAS, quality is 'defined as conformance to specification and fitness for purpose',[59] whilst the IPM claims that quality management is concerned with two areas of activity which aim to maximize customer satisfaction:

the development and implementation of processes designed to improve the efficiency of production, to eliminate waste and to maximise

resources; and the development of positive attitudes amongst employees responsible for operating and delivering the quality processes.[60]

Any focus on quality management has obvious implications for the managing of human resources, employee involvement and industrial relations, especially in terms of employee motivation, employee development, management style, organizational structure and, where they are recognized, trade union interests.

The factors leading to increasing management concern with quality at work are complex and diverse. They include: increased business competition, on a global scale; ever increasing quality standards expected by customers; the effects of new technology; the need to be flexible, especially in ever changing markets; and the need to address employee expectations for job fulfilment and satisfaction at work. In the public sector, in turn, the pressures have derived from a combination of factors, including market testing, compulsory competitive tendering, 'citizens' charters' initiatives and customer/client expectations.

Many of the early attempts at quality improvement took the form of quality circles. These are small groups of employees who meet regularly on a voluntary basis to identify, analyse and solve quality or other operational problems relevant to the organization. More recently, the importance of quality circles as means for improving quality at work has diminished and, 'both in the UK and in America, [they] have now almost disappeared as such from the quality company'. The emphasis is now being placed more on total quality management (TQM), which appears to be consistent with a move away from personnel management towards HRM, 'in that it puts the emphasis on employee commitment rather than compliance and it identifies line management as having key responsibility for the management of people'.[61] The essential differences between quality circles and TQM are illustrated in Table 14.6.

The concept of TQM cannot be easily defined and there is no single way in which organizations can develop the process and implement it. But in essence:

The aim is that everyone in the organisation should be dedicated to the never-ending improvement of their activities with the objective of satisfying their customers. Teamwork is an essential aspect of the improvement process, and the organisation is committed to improving the

*Table 14.6* The difference between quality circles and TQM.

|  | Quality circles | TQM |
|---|---|---|
| Aims | Employee relations improvements | Quality improvements |
| Choice | Voluntary | Compulsory |
| Structure | Bolt-on | Integrated quality system |
| Direction | Bottom-up | Top-down |
| Scope | Departments/units | Company-wide |

*Source*: Wilkinson *et al.* (1992)

quality of working life of their people and to their development through participation at all levels. External customers and suppliers are also integrated into the quality improvement process.[62]

TQM, then, is a strategy for improving corporate performance through the commitment and involvement of all employees in order to satisfy customer needs or client requirements. It seeks to do this at the optimum cost, through the continuous improvement of the organization's products or services, its management processes and the people involved.

Since TQM is a management-driven process, management has to involve the whole workforce in any TQM initiative. Ideally, management sets out to establish an educative process within the organization to gain the commitment and enthusiasm of the whole workforce to the TQM approach, since TQM relies on teamwork and co-operation among all employees. It follows that if employees are to be responsible for what they do, authority for this must be delegated downwards. This can challenge the role of first line managers, as well as placing greater emphasis on employee 'self-control, autonomy and creativity, [and] expecting active cooperation rather than mere compliance with the employment contract'. The TQM concept, therefore, comprises both production-oriented and employee-relations-oriented elements 'and this highlights the tensions between, on the one hand, following clearly laid-down instructions whilst, on the other, encouraging employee influence over the management process'.[63]

It is not surprising, where trade unions are recognized in organizations undergoing TQM initiatives, that concerns are often expressed by union representatives about proposed changes. Their concerns normally relate to employment security, the additional job responsibilities required of their

members, levels of payments and the future role of unions in the enterprise. Some managements incorporate union representatives in quality steering groups, whilst others assuage the unions' fears from the outset by carrying the unions with them in the change process, especially in the public sector. Research shows, however, that 'generally quality managers and managing directors do not see it as important to establish union agreement prior to a quality management programme'. Moreover, the senior management in at least one organization saw the aim of quality management 'as a diminution of union roles, and others recognised that this happened in practice although it was not an expressed aim'.[64]

## 14.7   Summary Points

- Negotiation is a voluntary activity providing employers and unions with autonomy in making industrial relations decisions. The willingness of employers to recognize trade unions for representational purposes is the crucial first step in establishing negotiating machinery.
- Section 11 of the Employment Protection Act 1975 provided a mechanism for independent trade unions to seek ACAS's assistance in obtaining recognition agreements from employers unwilling to grant recognition rights to well organized unions. It was later repealed by the Employment Act 1980.
- More recently, employers have been not only tougher in accepting new recognition claims but also willing to derecognize certain unions, to varying degrees, especially among white collar, professional and managerial staff.
- The range and scope of negotiation can be extensive. Rates of pay, hours, holiday pay, sick pay and pensions figure in the negotiation process.

The standard work week, shiftwork allowances, staffing levels, grievances, discipline and redundancy issues are also potentially open to negotiation.

- The pay–work bargain is central to negotiation. It consists of two elements: the pay-rate bargain and the effort bargain. In standard bargaining, there is no direct relationship between pay received and work done. In effort bargaining, attempts are made to relate employee or workgroup output to the wage payment system. Productivity and efficiency bargaining seek to improve employee performance within the negotiation process itself. To be successful, both productivity and effort bargaining require a favourable bargaining climate between negotiators.

- Negotiation is basically a power relationship. There are a variety of institutional, behavioural and negotiating factors determining the bargaining climate of any negotiation. One factor is whether the issues are distributive or integrative. Distributive bargaining is a competitive and conflict resolving process, whilst integrative bargaining is a co-operative and problem-solving process.

- Negotiations normally proceed through the following stages: arguing, proposing and bargaining. These are followed by implementation and monitoring of the joint agreement by both parties.

- Joint consultation has a fluctuating history and may be 'pseudo', classical or integrative. Another classification identifies the non-union, competitive, adjunct and marginal models. Its subject matter is wide ranging, including safety, conditions, training, welfare and quality. Joint consultation tends to be associated with unionized firms, foreign ownership and large plant size.

- Employee involvement is a relatively new set of industrial relations processes, aimed at promoting organizational success by fostering shared commitment to enterprise goals between management and the workforce.

- There are various types of employee involvement, including information passing, interactive practices, financial participation and TQM. The emergence of such activities, and their variants, appears to have coincided with the relative decline in importance of formal consultative committees in some organizations. Employee involvement practices tend to be associated with large organizations.

- Employee involvement, compared with control, satisfaction and co-operation strategies, seeks employee commitment in organizations and is management driven. It links with HRM – and TQM – and is assumed to lead to improved employee behaviour and high levels of corporate performance.

- The driving force behind employee involvement is pressure on management to adapt to organizational and environmental change. Five scenarios of employee participation are suggested: union incorporation and labour control; union by-passing and union avoidance HRM; product-driven and labour-driven market participation; philosophical participation; and faddish participation, with 'waves of interest' creating distinctive patterns of employee involvement at different times within an organization.

- Quality at work is becoming an increasingly widespread form of employee involvement, with significant impacts on employee, union and management behaviour in the workplace.

## 14.8   References

1. Society of Civil Servants, *GCHQ: The Campaign So Far*, CSU and SCPS, London, 1985, p. 3.
2. Employment Protection Act 1975, c. 71, ss 11(2) and 11(3).
3. Institute of Personnel Management, *Trade Union Recognition*, IPM, London, 1977, p. 24.
4. T. Claydon, Union deregulation in Britain in the 1980s, *British Journal of Industrial Relations*, 27(2), 1989, pp. 215–16.
5. *Ibid.*, p. 221.
6. J. Muir, *Industrial Relations Procedures and Agreements*, Gower, Aldershot, 1981, p. 177.
7. Recent changes in hours and holiday entitlements – manual employees, *Employment Gazette*, March 1987, p. 133.
8. G. Watson, Hours of work in Great Britain and Europe, *Employment Gazette*, November 1992, p. 555.
9. National Board of Prices and Incomes, *Report No. 161, Hours of Work, Overtime and Shiftworking*, HMSO, London, 1970, p. 51.
10. Watson, *op. cit.*, p. 550.
11. Advisory Conciliation and Arbitration Service, *Redundancy Handling*, ACAS, London, 1989, p. 6.
12. *Ibid.*, pp. 9 and 18.
13. J. Powell, *Work Study*, Arrow Books, London, 1976, p. 70.
14. R. B. McKersie and L. C. Hunter, *Pay, Productivity and Collective Bargaining*, Macmillan, London, 1973, p. 4.
15. H. Behrend, The effort bargain, *Industrial and Labor Relations Review*, July 1957, p. 506.

16. *Ibid.*, pp. 505 and 508.
17. McKersie and Hunter, *op. cit.*, p. 4.
18. Royal Commission on Trade Unions and Employers' Associations, *Research Papers 4. 1 Productivity Bargaining, 2 Restrictive Labour Practices*, HMSO, London, 1967, p. 1.
19. *Ibid.*, p. 27.
20. National Board for Prices and Incomes, *Report No. 123, Productivity Agreements*, HMSO, London, 1968, p. 38.
21. T. Cliff, *The Employers' Offensive*, Pluto Press, London, 1970, p. 3.
22. G. Kennedy, J. Benson and J. McMillan, *Managing Negotiations*, 2nd edn, Business Books, London, 1984, p. 12.
23. B. Kniveton and B. Towers, *Training for Negotiating*, Business Books, London, 1978, p. 63.
24. Quoted in E. Coker and G. Stuttard (eds), *Industrial Studies 2: The Bargaining Context*, Arrow Books, London, 1976, pp. 46 and 44.
25. Kennedy *et al.*, *op. cit.*, p. 20.
26. R. E. Walton and R. B. McKersie, *A Behavioral Theory of Labor Negotiations*, McGraw-Hill, New York, 1965, p. 6.
27. P. Warr, *Psychology and Collective Bargaining*, Hutchinson, London, 1973, p. 24.
28. Quoted in Coker and Stuttard, *op. cit.*, p. 58.
29. W. R. Hawes and C. C. P. Brookes, Change and renewal: joint consultation in industry, *Employment Gazette*, 88(4), April 1980, p. 356.
30. A. Scott, Consultation and consultation, *Employment Gazette*, September 1991, p. 511.
31. N. Millward, M. Stevens, D. Smart and W. Hawes, *Workplace Industrial Relations in Transition*, Dartmouth, Aldershot, 1992, p. 153.
32. Institute of Personnel Management, *Practical Participation and Involvement, 2 Representative Structures*, IPM, London, 1981, p. 8.
33. Scott, *op. cit.*, p. 508.
34. W. E. J. McCarthy, *Royal Commission on Trade Unions and Employers' Associations Research Papers 1: The Role of Shop Stewards in British Industrial Relations*, HMSO, London, 1968, p. 36.
35. H. A. Clegg and T. E. Chester, Joint consultation, in A. Flanders and H. A. Clegg (eds), *The System of Industrial Relations in Great Britain*, Blackwell, Oxford, 1967, p. 324.
36. J. Henderson, *The Case for Joint Consultation*, Industrial Society, London, 1970, p. 18.
37. M. Marchington, The four faces of employee consultation, *Personnel Management*, May 1988, pp. 44 and 45.
38. *Ibid.*, p. 46.
39. *Ibid.*, p. 47.
40. IPM (1981), *op. cit.*, p. 105.
41. Marchington, *op. cit.*, p. 47.
42. Millward *et al.*, *op. cit.*, p. 153.
43. Scott, *op. cit.*, p. 508.
44. P. B. Beaumont and D. R. Deaton, Joint consultative arrangements in Britain, *Journal of Management Studies*, 18(1), 1981, pp. 62 and 68.
45. P. Joyce and A. Woods, Joint consultation in Britain: results of a recent study during recession, *Employee Relations*, 6(3), 1984, pp. 2 and 6.
46. Peat Marwick Management Consultants, *Employee Involvement: Shaping the Future for Business*, London, 1990, p. 7.
47. Employment Department, *People and Companies*, HMSO, London, 1989, p. 2.
48. M. Marchington, J. Goodman, A. Wilkinson and P. Ackers, *New Developments in Employee Involvement*, London, 1992, p. ix.
49. A. Hibbert, Employee involvement: a recent survey, *Employment Gazette*, December 1991, p. 664.
50. *Ibid.* and Millward *et al.*, *op. cit.*, p. 180.
51. H. Braverman, *Labor and Monopoly Capital*, Monthly Review Press, New York, 1974, p. 35.
52. Marchington *et al.*, *op. cit.*, p. 9.
53. R. E. Walton, From control to commitment, *Harvard Business Review*, March–April 1985, p. 79.
54. Marchington *et al.*, *op. cit.*, p. 23.
55. P. Ackers, M. Marchington, A. Wilkinson and J. Goodman, The use of cycles? Explaining employee involvement in the 1990s, *Industrial Relations Journal*, 23(4), 1992, pp. 277–80.
56. Marchington *et al.*, *op. cit.*, p. 27.
57. Millward *et al.*, *op. cit.*, p. 264.
58. A. Hodgson, *Quality at Work*, Work Research Unit, London, 1988, p. 1.
59. Advisory Conciliation and Arbitration Service, *Total Quality Management*, ACAS, London, 1991, p. 2.
60. Institute of Personnel Management, *Quality: People Management Matters*, IPM, London, 1993, p. 1.
61. *Ibid.*, pp. 8 and 9.
62. S. Russell and B. Dale, *Quality Circles: A Broader Perspective*, Work Research Unit, ACAS, London, 1989, p. 2.
63. A. Wilkinson, M. Marchington, J. Goodman and P. Ackers, Total quality management and employee involvement, *Human Resource Management Journal*, 2(4), 1992, pp. 5 and 6.
64. IPM, *op. cit.*, pp. 10 and 25.

# 15

## Industrial Relations in Transition

From 1945 until the late 1970s, there was an industrial relations consensus in Britain, which was challenged only briefly in the period 1971–74 by the Industrial Relations Act 1971. This consensus was broadly accepted by most large employers, the vast majority of employees in both the private and public sectors, and successive governments. Britain's industrial relations consensus for the 35 years after the end of the Second World War was linked to its political and economic consensus, or postwar settlement, and had four main characteristics. First, there was the centrality and legitimacy of collective bargaining, and hence of trade unionism, as a method of conducting industrial relations between employer and employee representatives. Given the alternatives, collective bargaining was seen by its supporters as being the best method of determining the terms and conditions of employment of most of Britain's workforce. It was also seen as the most appropriate means of constraining unregulated managerial power and authority in the workplace. In this sense, properly instituted and conducted, collective bargaining was perceived as a process not only of determining wage and non-wage issues between employers and employees but also of extending democracy – industrial democracy – into factories, offices, public enterprises and other work establishments.

The second feature of the industrial relations consensus was the support given to collective bargaining by all governments, both Conservative and Labour, throughout the period. This included: encouraging and engaging in collective bargaining with public sector unions; providing legal props to collective bargaining through fair wage resolutions, wages councils and means for resolving industrial conflict between employers and organized workers; and facilitating union organization and union recognition generally. The latter was done by providing workers with the legal right to join a union and to take part in its activities, and by the union recognition procedures provided under Section 11 of the Employment Protection Act 1975. The law also provided other statutory rights for individual trade unionists, such as the right to time off work for trade union duties and activities and for approved training for trade union purposes.

The third feature of the industrial relations consensus was in relation to collective bargaining and trade disputes. The principle had been established, at the turn of the century, that the law should play only a residual or broadly abstentionist role in the regulation of relations between employers and organized labour, rather than an interventionist one. It was a central tenet of industrial relations voluntarism that collective bargaining was best conducted between autonomous employers and independent trade unions, largely unregulated by the law and by judicial interpretation of industrial relations behaviour. This was offset, however, in the period after the Second World War, by the continual search for an effective prices and incomes policy, initiated by successive governments. Such policies were aimed at keeping wage and price rises broadly in line with productivity increases in the economy generally. After the mid 1960s, there was also a gradual extension of statutory rights for individuals at work, the so-called 'statutory floor' of employment protection rights. But these did not preclude superior conditions being provided for employees by collective bargaining.

The fourth feature of the industrial relations consensus was government commitment to full employment. For most of the postwar period, successive governments saw the maintenance of full employment, largely through the application of demand management economic techniques, as a political priority. This clearly strengthened the collective bargaining power of trade unions, which were able to force up wage rates against both private and public sector employers. This was especially the case where either there were specific labour shortages, as in the private sector, or there was union monopoly bargaining power, as in parts of the public sector. Despite continuous attempts at trying to get union collaboration in moderating their wage demands through variants of incomes policy, no government was successful for any length of time in managing wage inflation effectively.

By 1979, the industrial relations consensus had reached its apogee. Collective bargaining arrangements determined the pay of over 70 per cent of the British workforce, even though total union density was only around the 55 per cent level. Also, trade union power appeared to be at a peak. This was reflected in union membership growth, the extension of closed-shop arrangements, the growth in numbers and influence of shop stewards, the willingness of union members to take industrial action against employers, and the wide scope of collective agreements and understandings negotiated between employers and union representatives. The new-found power and confidence of the unions and their leaders involved them bargaining with employers at industry, company and enterprise level on a range of employment issues. It also resulted in their being consulted by government nationally on a variety of economic and social issues affecting their members as citizens and workers.

Although the combined effect of changes in the balance of industrial and political power between employers and unions in the period 1945–79 must not be exaggerated, the trade union position at the bargaining table had been greatly enhanced in relative terms by favourable labour market factors and by government economic policy. Nevertheless, government and employers still possessed a clear dominance of economic and social power over organized labour, if they chose to use it. They did not do so probably because of the prevailing social ethos and the political and industrial relations consensus of the time. These reflected the general view that the trade union movement was approaching the peak of its power and that it would use this power both wisely and unselfishly in the national interest. By the end of the 1970s, however, many doubted if this was actually taking place. Furthermore, some commentators were expressing the view that the involvement of government, powerfully supported by national organizations of employers and trade unions, in almost every aspect of the national economy would lead eventually to a corporate State or one controlled by government in association with the powerful interests of society. This, it was argued, could create a situation giving individual citizens very little control over their daily lives and personal life chances. Added to this, there was growing concern that the interventionist

endeavours of successive governments to improve the performance, productivity and competitiveness of British industry and the economy had achieved very little. The standard of living enjoyed by the inhabitants of our major competitive trading nations continuously outstripped that of Britain's, for example, whilst governmental intervention, Keynesian economic policy, and union power, it was claimed, had apparently not led to sustained economic prosperity and growth. These themes were successfully exploited by the Conservative Party, led by Margaret Thatcher, at the 1979 general election. This was to be followed by a set of events which would not only effectively terminate the political and economic consensus of the postwar period but also impact on the industrial relations consensus too.

In the period after 1979, industrial relations in Britain have been epitomized by more assertive management, union realism and government hawkishness. This has been accompanied, paradoxically, by a depoliticizing of industrial relations. The economic market place has replaced the political market place as the primary arbiter of industrial relations decision making. Union bargaining power has become substantially weakened, industrial relations initiatives have swung significantly towards management, and successive governments have excluded the unions from governmental policy making. In the 1980s and 1990s, the unions and their members, and hence collective bargaining, were challenged, first, by economic recessions in the early 1980s and early 1990s and, second, by continuous industrial and economic change. The Conservative governments elected to office in 1979, 1983, 1987 and 1992 expounded totally different sets of economic and social policies, and ideologies, from those of earlier postwar administrations. The Conservatism of the New Right challenged the concept of the welfare state, the operation of Keynesian economic measures and rising real levels of public expenditure. The impact of these fundamental political and economic changes on industrial relations, trade unions and the employer-employee relationship has been considerable.

The economic policies of the new Conservatism were based on the theory that inflation and industrial decline in Britain were largely the result of the old economics of the postwar period. Supply side economic theorists claimed that Britain's economic ills resulted from a number of factors. These included: Keynesian mismanagement of the economy; inadequate control of the money supply; excessive levels of public spending; union restrictive practices; 'overmanning'; overpriced wages; low productivity per worker; poor-quality work and products; too much reliance on government subsidies; and too much government intervention in the economy. The Conservative governments of the 1980s and 1990s believed that only radical economic policies and new employment legislation, such as the Employment Acts 1980, 1982, 1988, 1989 and 1990, the Trade Union Act 1984 and the Trade Union Reform and Employment Rights Act 1993, could revive the British economy, control inflation and enable management to manage business enterprises efficiently.

The social consequences of these new policies have been as follows: unemployment rose to unprecedented postwar levels, with young people, black people and women disproportionately affected; bankruptcies increased in number; manufacturing capacity fell; interest rates reached previously unknown very high levels; and growth of public expenditure were drastically reduced. Although the economy went into sustained growth and rapid expansion in the late 1980s, this was accompanied by rising inflation, shortages of skilled labour, very high interest rates and imported balance of payments difficulties. Much of the landscape and topography of British industry had changed during the intervening period and Britain's manufacturing capacity has been drastically reduced. Some key public industries have been privatized and contracting out and competitive tendering introduced in the public sector.

Over the past 15 years there have been clear signs of: widening pay differentials between those with market forces working in their favour and those without market power; continuing high levels of unemployment amongst segments of the workforce; a substantial fall in union membership and density; and evidence that the new employment laws are influencing industrial relations behaviour between employers and employees, and between unions and their members. There have also been continuous managerial initiatives in industrial relations and personnel practices. These include: performance-related pay; employee commitment and employee involvement programmes; harmonization of conditions of employment; 'human resources' styles of personnel management; increased labour flexibility; and more sophisticated personnel policies. Compared with earlier periods, managerial power has been strengthened, union power weakened and government intervention in pay bargaining diluted.

Clearly, these economic and industrial relations developments could be of a temporary nature and

a return to the pattern of economic and industrial relations contexts more characteristic of the 1960s and 1970s could follow a change of economic and legal policy, or change of government. On the other hand, Britain could well have entered a period of economic, industrial and social change, incorporating a ratchet effect, from which there is no turning back. If this is so, then it is likely to have a distinctive impact on Britain's future patterns of industrial relations.

If the political and economic consensus of postwar Britain was effectively ended in the 1980s and 1990s, to be replaced by the conviction politics of successive Conservative administrations during this period, then what has happened to the industrial relations consensus? This is a difficult question to answer with precision, since there are contrary tendencies to account for. On the one side, there is the government's public policy stance. This emphasizes the importance of labour market flexibility and human resources efficiency, of depoliticizing industrial relations, and of individualizing relations between employers and their employees, and between unions and their members, wherever possible. In this scenario, collective bargaining seems to have a relegated role in regulating industrial relations decision making. Yet schoolteachers, nurses and midwives, the intelligence services and the police services apart, collective bargaining remains the main means by which terms and conditions of employment are determined for the majority of public sector workers, at most job levels, and for some parts of the private sector too. What is symbolically significant, however, is that under the TURERA 1992, ACAS no longer has the statutory duty to promote the development and extension of collective bargaining in Britain.

On the other side, however, there is substantial empirical evidence from the workplace surveys that the collective bargaining process has become modified and changed in the period since 1979. With trade unionism weakened, first by recession and latterly by changes in the industrial and occupational structures, there has been a general power shift at the collective bargaining table towards the employers in both the private and public sectors. Items formerly negotiated with union and workplace representatives, such as staffing levels and working practices, have in many instances been reclaimed as managerial rights. There are also instances of employers withdrawing negotiating rights from recognized unions, especially among white-collar staff, and replacing collective bargaining with employer regulation. In other cases, employers have imposed 'take back' bargaining, giving nothing in return for union concessions on their members' conditions of employment and job controls. The changes in employment and labour law which have been enacted during the past 15 years have also had their impact on the industrial relations consensus. One consequence is the fragmentation of worker and union solidarity in trade disputes. Another is the apparent willingness of some employers and trade unions to resort to using the law to pursue their industrial relations objectives, where they believe it to be in their interests to do so.

It would appear then that though the industrial relations consensus has been challenged, it has not been effectively replaced by a single dominant model of industrial relations in Britain. Significant aspects of the traditional consensus remain but adaptations, both within it and outside it, seem to be taking place. For different reasons, both government and some employers are introducing new behavioural norms into relations between employers and unions, between employers and employees, and between unions and their members. Controlling the bargaining agenda, for example, is a powerful managerial device for limiting union demands at the bargaining table, with the relative decline in union bargaining power. Whilst not a new negotiating technique in itself, it has gained some currency among certain managerial negotiators to facilitate employer-centred and management-led bargaining. Single-union recognition deals are one manifestation of this, as is the demand made by other employers for TUC unions to sit around the negotiating table with non-TUC unions. This is sometimes used by employers as a condition of continued union recognition. The practice of communicating directly with their workforces, to complement or even replace the role of union representatives in the process, is another example of managerial initiatives in industrial relations and the creating of new employee relations norms. Similarly, the adoption of human resources management techniques, sometimes to forestall union recognition claims from their employees, provides a further example of moves away from the old industrial relations consensus.

New norms are also developing between the trade unions and their members. This is in response to the statutory balloting requirements of employment legislation. With the legal right to be balloted on official industrial action, union elections and political fund reviews, union members are acquiring fresh expectations about their roles and responsibilities in internal union affairs. At the same time, union leaderships, whilst using these constitutional devices to their bargaining and members' advantage, cannot ignore the impact of these forms of direct democracy on internal union decision making and on their own legitimacy as organizational spokespersons and opinion formers.

The net result of these contextual, procedural, substantive, normative and legislative changes on British employer–union and management–employee relations is a weakening of the industrial relations consensus. Whilst it was always contentious to refer to the British industrial relations 'system', with the implication that it was a single coherent set of institutions and practices, it is even more doubtful whether such a 'system' exists today. What appears to be emerging is a more fragmented and fractionated set of employment relationships and practices. In effect, there seem to be four main models or patterns of industrial relations taking root in Britain, as the country moves towards the twenty-first century. These are: the non-union traditional model; the unionized traditional model; the non-union sophisticated model; and the unionized sophisticated model. These are summarized in Table 15.1.

The non-union traditional model is typically found in the small corporate sector. There is nothing new about this model. It is individualist and is rooted in unitary, non-union firms where managerial prerogative and unilateral managerial regulation are the main methods of taking industrial relations decisions. Such personnel policies which are operational within them are normally reactive and implied and the personnel management role, where it exists, is an administrative and welfare one. Typically, employees are likely to be compliant and deferential to managerial authority, often lacking loyalty to the employer and its products or services.

The unionized traditional model is also not a new one and is based on the old industrial relations consensus. This model is still the dominant one in much of the large corporate and public sectors. It is a collectivist approach, based on the hard variant of pluralism, where collective bargaining, or joint management–union regulation, is the preferred method of conducting industrial relations. The personnel management role provides the professional management of employment contracts, with pragmatic personnel policies. The trade unions, frequently organized in multiunion groupings, play an adversarial role in their dealings with employers and managers, with employee behaviour often instrumental and calculative in its orientation.

*Table 15.1* Models of industrial relations.

|  | Non-union, traditional model | Unionized, traditional model | Non-union, sophisticated model | Unionized sophisticated model |
|---|---|---|---|---|
| Managerial philosophy | Unitary | Hard pluralist | Neo-unitary | Soft pluralist |
| Preferred method of conducting industrial relations | Managerial prerogative | Collective bargaining | HRM techniques | Joint problem solving |
| Personnel policies | Reactive implied | Sectionalized pragmatic | Proactive explicit | Integrative comprehensive |
| Personnel role | 'Clerk of works' | 'Contracts manager' | 'Architect' | 'Architect' |
| Union role | Excluded | Adversarial multiunion | Excluded (non-union) | Collaborative single union |
| Typical employee behaviour | Compliant | Instrumental | Committed | Co-operative |
| Where applicable | Small corporate sector | Large corporate and public sector | Large corporate sector | Large corporate sector |

The non-union sophisticated model is a relatively new approach to managing industrial relations, or more correctly, 'employee relations'. It is based on an individualist neo-unitary managerial philosophy but is more sophisticated than traditional unitarism. It is practised in a minority of successful companies in the large corporate sector, some of which are foreign owned. It aims to incorporate employees into their employing organizations and to get their commitment to corporate goals and objectives. This is facilitated by progressive and enlightened personnel policies and practices, with the personnel department playing a proactive role in the managing of human resources. The emphasis is on effective human resources management (HRM), where line management plays a key role in applying HRM techniques and practices in their areas of responsibility.

The unionized sophisticated model is also a new approach to the managing of employee relations. Although collectivist in its philosophy, this model emphasizes a soft variant of pluralism. To date, it is not widespread and is found predominantly in large foreign-owned companies in the corporate sector. It uses a joint problem-solving or consultative approach as the preferred method of conducting industrial relations, emphasizing co-operation between employers and employees rather than conflict between them.

The union role is normally based on single union recognition, with 'no-strike' arrangements, which are aimed at sustaining the collaborative relationship established with the employer. Like the non-union sophisticated model, this model is developed within the framework of a proactive mode of personnel management or HRM and progressive personnel policies.

In summary, then, it appears that there are wider variations in British industrial relations practices, after the economic, technological and political changes of the 1980s and 1990s, compared with the period in which the former industrial relations consensus prevailed. Whilst elements of the old consensus remain, competing models of industrial relations seem to be emerging. These patterns of employee relations are managerially led, and government supported, not union led. They reflect, in part at least, increasingly sophisticated approaches to managing human resources at work and the changed balance of power between employers and organized labour. At the time of writing, it seems unlikely that the old consensus will re-emerge in the future. Whether any new consensus model of industrial relations is going to emerge, and what impact a change of government and European models will have on this is unclear.

# Select Bibliography

Adnett, J. (1989), *Labour Market Policy*, Longman, London.

Advisory Conciliation and Arbitration Service (Annual), *Annual Reports*, ACAS, London.

Advisory Conciliation and Arbitration Service (1977), *Code of Practice 2. Disclosure of Information for Collective Bargaining Purposes*, HMSO, London.

Advisory Conciliation and Arbitration Service (1977), *Code of Practice 3. Time Off for Trade Union Duties and Activities*, HMSO, London.

Advisory Conciliation and Arbitration Service (1983), *Collective Bargaining in Britain: Its Extent and Scope*, ACAS, London.

Advisory Conciliation and Arbitration Service (1987), *Discipline at Work*, HMSO, London.

Anderman, S. (1992), *Labour Law*, Butterworths, London.

Anthony, P. D. (1977), *The Conduct of Industrial Relations*, Institute of Personnel Management, London.

Armstrong, M. and Murlis, H. (1988), *Reward Management*, Kogan Page, London.

Armstrong, P. J., Goodman, J. F. B. and Hyman, J. D. (1981), *Ideology and Shopfloor Industrial Relations*, Croom Helm, London.

Ashdown, R. T. and Baker, K. H. (1973), *Department of Employment Manpower Papers Number 6. In Working Order: A Study of Industrial Discipline*, HMSO, London.

Atkinson, J. and Meager, N. (1986), *Changing Patterns of Work: How Companies Introduce Flexibility to Meet New Needs*, OECD, Paris.

Bain, G. S. (1970), *The Growth of White-Collar Unionism*, Oxford University Press, Oxford.

Bain, G. S. (ed.) (1983), *Industrial Relations in Britain*, Blackwell, Oxford.

Bain, G. S. and Price, R. (1980), *Profiles of Union Growth: A Comparative Statistical Portrait of Eight Countries*, Blackwell, Oxford.

Barnes, D. and Reid, E. (1980), *Governments and Trade Unions*, Heinemann, London.

Barrett, B., Rhodes, E. and Beishon, J. (ed.) (1975), *Industrial Relations and the Wider Society*, Collier Macmillan, London.

Bassett, P. (1986), *Strike Free: New Industrial Relations*, Macmillan, London.

Batstone, E. (1988), *The Reform of Workplace Industrial Relations*, Clarendon, Oxford.

Batstone, E., Boraston, I. and Frenkel, S. (1977), *Shop Stewards in Action*, Blackwell, Oxford.

Batstone, E., Boraston, I. and Frenkel, S. (1978), *The Social Organization of Strikes*, Blackwell, Oxford.

Batstone, E., Ferner, A. and Terry, M. (1984), *Consent and Efficiency*, Blackwell, Oxford.

Batstone, E. and Gourlay, S. (1986), *Unions, Unemployment and Innovation*, Blackwell, Oxford.

Batstone, E., Gourlay, S. and Levie, H. (1987), *New Technology and the Process of Labour Regulation*, Clarendon, Oxford.

Beaumont, P. (1981), *Government as an Employer: Setting an Example*, Royal Institute of Public Administration, London.

Beaumont, P. B. (1990), *Change in Industrial Relations*, Routledge, London.

Beaumont, P. (1992), *Public Sector Industrial Relations*, Routledge, London.

Beaumont, P. (1993), *Human Resource Management*, Sage, London.

Blackaby, F. (ed.) (1980), *The Future of Pay Bargaining*, Heinemann, London.

Blanchflower, D. and Oswald, A. (1986), *Profit Related Pay: Prose Rediscovered?*, New Bridge Street Consultants, London.

Boraston, I., Clegg, H. A. and Rimmer, M. (1975), *Workplace and Union*, Heinemann, London.

Bradley, K. and Gelb, A. (1983), *Worker Capitalism: The New Industrial Relations*, Heinemann, London.

Brewster, C. and Connock, S. (1985), *Industrial Relations: Cost Effective Strategies*, Hutchinson, London.

Brown, H. P. (1983), *The Origins of Trade Union Power*, Oxford University Press, Oxford.

Burrows, G. (1986), *No Strike Agreements and Pendulum Arbitration*, Institute of Personnel Management, London.

Casey, B., Lakey, J. and White, M. (1992), *Payment Systems: A Look at Current Practice*, Employment Department, London.

Central Arbitration Committee (Annual), *Annual Report*, HMSO, London.

Certification Office for Trade Unions and Employers' Associations (Annual), *Annual Report of the Certification Officer*, HMSO, London.

Child, J. (1984), *Organization: A Guide to Problems and Practice*, Harper and Row, London.

Clegg, H. A. (1971), *How to Run an Incomes Policy*, Heinemann, London.

Clegg, H. A. (1979), *The Changing System of Industrial Relations in Britain*, Blackwell, Oxford.

Clegg, H. A., Fox, A. and Thompson, A. F. (1964), *A History of British Trade Unions since 1889*, Oxford University Press, Oxford.

Clegg, H. A. (1985), *A History of British Trade Unions since 1889*. Vol. II, *1911–1933*, Clarendon, Oxford.

Coates, D. (1989), *The Crisis of Labour*, Philip Allan, Oxford.

Coates, K. and Topham, T. (1988), *Trade Unions in Britain*, Fontana, London.

Commission on Industrial Relations (1972), *CIR Study I. Employers' Organisations and Industrial Relations*, HMSO, London.

Commission on Industrial Relations (1973), *Report No. 34. The Role of Management in Industrial Relations*, HMSO, London.

Commission on Industrial Relations (1974), *Report No. 85. Industrial Relations in Multi-plant Undertakings*, HMSO, London.

Confederation of British Industry (1977), *The Future of Pay Determination*, CBI, London.

Confederation of British Industry (1979), *Pay: The Choice Ahead*, CBI, London.

Confederation of British Industry (1980), *Trade Unions in a Changing World*, CBI, London.

Confederation of British Industry (1985), *Incentive Payments*, CBI, London.

Confederation of British Industry (1987), *Manufacturing Industry Pay Negotiations and Industrial Action in the 1980s*, CBI, London.

Confederation of British Industry (1990), *Employee Involvement*, CBI, London.

Crouch, C. (1979), *The Politics of Industrial Relations*, Fontana, London.

Crouch, C. (1982), *Trade Unions: The Logic of Collective Action*, Fontana, London.

Currie, R. (1979), *Industrial Politics*, Clarendon, Oxford.

Curson, C. (ed.) (1986), *Flexible Patterns of Work*, Institute of Personnel Management, London.

Dale, B. and Plunkett, J. (1990), *Managing Quality*, Allen, London.

Daniel, W. W. (1987), *Workplace Industrial Relations and Technical Change*, Pinter, London.

Daniel, W. W. and Millward, N. (1983), *Workplace Industrial Relations in Britain*, Heinemann, London.

Department of Employment (1981), *Trade Union Immunities*, HMSO, London.

Department of Employment (1983), *Democracy in Trade Unions*, HMSO, London.

Department of Employment (1987), *Trade Unions and Their Members*, HMSO, London.

Department of Trade (1977), *Report of the Committee of Inquiry on Industrial Democracy*, HMSO, London.

Dickens, L. *et al.* (1958), *Dismissal: A Study of Unfair Dismissal and the Industrial Tribunal System*, Blackwell, Oxford.

Dunlop, J. T. (1958), *Industrial Relations Systems*, Southern Illinois University Press, Carbondale.

Dunn, S. and Gennard, J. (1984), *The Closed Shop in British Industry*, Macmillan, London.

Durcan, J. *et al.* (1983), *Strikes in Post-war Britain*, Allen and Unwin, London.

Edwards, P. K. (1986), *Conflict at Work*, Blackwell, Oxford.

Edwards, P. K. (1987), *Managing the Factory*, Blackwell, Oxford.

Ellis, V. (1981), *The Role of Trade Unions in the Promotion of Equal Opportunities*, Equal Opportunities Commission, London.

Fallick, J. and Elliott, R. F. (1981), *Incomes Policies, Inflation and Relative Pay*, Allen and Unwin, London.

Farnham, D. (1993), *Employee Relations*, Institute of Personnel Management, London.

Farnham, D. and Horton, S. (eds) (1993), *Managing the New Public Service*, Macmillan, London.

Fatchett, D. (1987), *Trade Unions and Politics in the 1980s*, Croom Helm, London.

Ferner, A. and Hyman, R. (1992), *Industrial Relations in the New Europe*, Blackwell, Oxford.

Flanders, A. D. (1970), *Management and Unions: The Theory and Reform of Industrial Relations*, Faber, London.

Fogarty, M. and Brooks, D. (1986), *Trade Unions and British Industrial Development*, Policy Studies Institute, London.

Fox, A. (1971), *A Sociology of Work in Industry*, Collier Macmillan, London.

Fox, A. (1974), *Man Mismanagement*, Hutchinson, London.

Fox, A. (1985), *History and Heritage*, Allen and Unwin, London.

Friedrichs, G. and Schaff, A. (eds) (1982), *Microelectronics and Society*, Pergamon, Oxford.

Gallie, D. (ed.) (1989), *Employment in Britain*, Blackwell, Oxford.

Gennard, J. (1977), *Financing Strikers*, Macmillan, London.

Geary, R. (1985), *Policing Industrial Disputes*, Cambridge University Press, Cambridge.

Goodman, J. F. B. and Whittingham, T. G. (1969), *Shop Stewards In British Industry*, McGraw-Hill, London.

Grant, W. and Marsh, D. (1977), *The Confederation of British Industry*, Hodder and Stoughton, London.

Guest, D. and Fatchett, D. (1974), *Worker Participation:*

*Individual Control and Performance*, Institute of Personnel Management, London.

Guest, D. and Horwood, R. (1980), *The Role and Effectiveness of Personnel Managers*, London School of Economics, London.

Guest, D. and Horwood, R. (1982), *Success and Satisfaction in Personnel Management*, London School of Economics, London.

Harper, S. (ed.) (1987), *Personnel Management Handbook*, Gower, London.

Hawkins, K. (1976), *British Industrial Relations 1945–1975*, Barrie and Jenkins, London.

Hawkins, K. (1981), *Trade Unions*, Hutchinson, London.

Hepple, B. and O'Higgins, P. (1981), *Employment Law*, 4th edn, Sweet and Maxwell, London.

Hunter, L. C. and Mulvey, C. (1981), *Economics of Wages and Labour*, Macmillan, London.

Hyman, R. (1975), *Industrial Relations: A Marxist Introduction*, Longmans, London.

Hyman, R. (1989), *The Political Economy of Industrial Relations*, Macmillan, Basingstoke.

Hyman, R. (1989), *Strikes*, Fontana, London.

Hyman, R. and Brough, I. (1975), *Social Values and Industrial Relations*, Blackwell, Oxford.

Industrial Relations Services (1988), *Industrial Relations in Britain*, Eclipse, London.

Institute of Personnel Management (1993), *Quality: People Management Matters*, IPM, London.

Kahn-Freund, O. (1979), *Labour Relations: Heritage and Adjustment*, Oxford University Press, Oxford.

Kahn-Freund, O. (1983), *Labour and the Law* (edited and translated by P. Davis and M. Freedland), Stevens, London.

Keenoy, T. (1984), *Invitation to Industrial Relations*, Blackwell, Oxford.

Kelly, J. (1988), *Trade Unions and Socialist Politics*, Verso, London.

Kennedy, G., Benson, J. and McMillan, J. (1984), *Managing Negotiations*, Business Books, London.

Legge, K. (1978), *Power, Innovation and Problem Solving in Personnel Management*, McGraw-Hill, London.

Lewis, D. (1990), *Essentials of Employment Law*, Institute of Personnel Management, London.

Lewis, R. (ed.) (1986), *Labour Law in Britain*, Blackwell, Oxford.

Lewis, R., Davies, P. and Wedderburn, K. W. (1979), *Industrial Relations Law and the Conservative Government*, Fabian Society, London.

Lewis, R. and Simpson, B. (1981), *Striking a Balance? Employment Law after the 1980 Act*, Martin Robertson, Oxford.

Lockyear, J. (1979), *Industrial Arbitration in Great Britain*, Institute of Personnel Management, London.

Lovell, J. and Roberts, B. C. (1968), *A Short History of the TUC*, Macmillan, London.

McCarthy, W. E. J. (ed.) (1985), *Trade Unions: Selected Readings*, Penguin, Harmondsworth.

McCarthy, W. E. J. and Ellis, N. D. (1973), *Management by Agreement*, Hutchinson, London.

MacInnes, J. (1987), *Thatcherism at Work*, Open University Press, Milton Keynes.

Marchington, M. and Parker, P. (1990), *Changing Patterns of Employee Relations*, Harvester, London.

Marchington, M., Goodman, J., Wilkinson, A. and Ackers, P. (1992), *New Developments in Employee Involvement*, Department of Employment, London.

Marginson, P. *et al.* (1988), *Beyond the Workplace*, Blackwell, Oxford.

Marsh, A. I. (1966), *Royal Commission on Trade Unions and Employers' Associations Research Papers 2 (Part 1) Disputes Procedures in British Industry*, HMSO, London.

Marsh, A. I. (1979), *Concise Encyclopaedia of Industrial Relations*, Gower, London.

Marsh, A. I. (1982), *Employee Relations Policy and Decision Making*, Gower, Aldershot.

Martin, R. (1980), *TUC: The Growth of a Pressure Group 1868–1976*, Clarendon, Oxford.

Martin, R. (1992), *Bargaining Power*, Clarendon, Oxford.

Millward, N. and Stevens, M. (1986), *British Workplace Industrial Relations 1980–84*, Gower, Aldershot.

Millward, N., Stevens, M., Smart, D. and Hawes, W. (1992), *Workplace Industrial Relations in Transition*, Dartmouth, Aldershot.

Moran, M. (1977), *The Politics of Industrial Relations*, Macmillan, London.

Morland, I. (1987), *Quality Circles*, ISP, London.

Mullard, M. (1992), *Understanding Economic Policy*, Routledge, London.

Musson, A. E. (1972), *British Trade Unions 1800–1875*, Macmillan, London.

Muir, J. (1981), *Industrial Relations Procedures and Agreements*, Gower, London.

Parker, P. A. L., Hawes, W. R. and Lumb, A. L. (1971), *Department of Employment Manpower Papers No. 3: The Reform of Collective Bargaining at Plant and Company Level*, HMSO, London.

Poole, M. and Mansfield, R. (eds) (1980), *Managerial Roles in Industrial Relations*, Gower, Farnborough.

Poole, M. *et al.* (1984), *Industrial Relations in the Future: Trends and Possibilities in Britain over the Next Decade*, Routledge and Kegan Paul, London.

Purcell, J. (1981), *Good Industrial Relations: Theory and Practice*, Macmillan, London.

Rajan, A. and Pearson, R. (1986), *UK Occupation and Employment Trends*, Butterworths, London.

Ramsey, J. C. and Hill, J. M. (1974), *Collective Agreements*, Institute of Personnel Management, London.

Richter, I. (1973), *Political Purpose in Trade Unions*, Allen and Unwin, London.

Rideout, R. (1989), *Principles of Labour Law*, Sweet and Maxwell, London.

Roomkin, M. (ed.) (1988), *The Changing Character of Managerial Employment*, Oxford University Press, Oxford.

Royal Commission on Trade Unions and Employers' Associations, (1968), *Report*, HMSO, London.

Saran, R. and Sheldrake, J. (1988), *Public Sector Bargaining in the 1980s*, Gower, Farnborough.

Singleton, N. (1975), *Industrial Relations Procedures*, HMSO, London.

Sisson, K. (ed.) (1989), *Personnel Management in Britain*, Blackwell, Oxford.

Smith, C. T. B., Clifton, R., Makeham, P. and Burn, R. V. (1978), *Department of Employment Manpower Paper No. 15: Strikes in Britain*, HMSO, London.

Smith, I. T. and Wood, J. C. (1980), *Industrial Law*, Butterworths, London.

Stephenson, G. M. and Brotherton, C. J. (eds) (1979), *Industrial Relations: A Social Psychological Approach*, Wiley, Chichester.

Storey, J. (1980), *The Challenge to Management Control*, Business Books, London.

Storey, J. (1983), *Managerial Prerogative and the Question of Control*, Routledge and Kegan Paul, London.

Storey, J. (ed.) (1989), *New Perspectives on Human Resource Management*, Routledge, London.

Storey, J. (1992), *Developments in the Management of Human Resources*, Blackwell, Oxford.

Taylor, A. J. (1987), *The Trade Unions and the Labour Party*, Croom Helm, London.

Taylor, R. (1980), *The Fifth Estate: Britain's Unions in the Modern World*, Pan, London.

Thomason, G. (1988), *A Textbook of Human Resource Management*, 5th edn, Institute of Personnel Management, London.

Thurley, K. and Wood, S. (eds) (1982), *Industrial Relations and Management Strategy*, Cambridge University Press, Cambridge.

Torrington, D. and Hall, L. (1991), *Personnel Management*, Prentice-Hall, London.

Towers, B. (ed.) (1992), *The Handbook of Human Resource Management*, Blackwell, Oxford.

Towers, B. (1992), *Issues in People Management 2: Choosing Bargaining Levels*, IPM, London.

Trades Union Congress (Annual), *TUC Reports*, TUC, London.

Trades Union Congress (1966), *Trade Unionism*, TUC, London.

Trades Union Congress (1991), *Collective Bargaining Strategy for the 1990s*, TUC, London.

Trades Union Congress (1991), *Unions and Europe in the 1990s*, TUC, London.

Turner, H. A. (1962), *Trade Union Growth, Structure and Policy*, Allen and Unwin, London.

Tyson, S. and Fell, A. (1986), *Evaluating the Personnel Function*, Hutchinson, London.

Tyson, S. *et al.* (1987), *Appraising and Exploring Organizations*, Croom Helm, London.

Undy, R. and Martin, R. (1984), *Ballots and Trade Union Democracy*, Blackwell, Oxford.

Undy, R., Ellis, V., McCarthy, W. E. J. and Halmos, A. M. (1981), *Change in Trade Unions*, Hutchinson, London.

Walton, R. and McKersie, R. (1965), *A Behavioral Theory of Labor Negotiations*, McGraw-Hill, New York.

Watson, D. (1988), *Managers of Discontent: Trade Union Officials and Industrial Relations Managers*, Associated Book Publishers, London.

Webb, S. and B. (1920), *Industrial Democracy*, Longmans, London.

Wedderburn, Lord (1986), *The Worker and the Law*, Penguin, Harmondsworth.

Wedderburn, K. W., Lewis, R. and Clarke, J. (eds) (1983), *Labour Law and Industrial Relations: Building on Kahn-Freund*, Oxford University Press, Oxford.

White, M. (1987), *Survey of Employers Workforce Policies and Practices*, Economic and Social Research Council, London.

Wigham, E. (1973), *The Power to Manage*, Macmillan, London.

# Index